GENEALOGICAL SOURCES

Reprinted From The Genealogy Section
INDIANA MAGAZINE OF HISTORY

Compiled by Dorothy L. Riker

Family History & Genealogy Section
Indiana Historical Society

1979

© Copyright 1979 by Indiana Historical Society

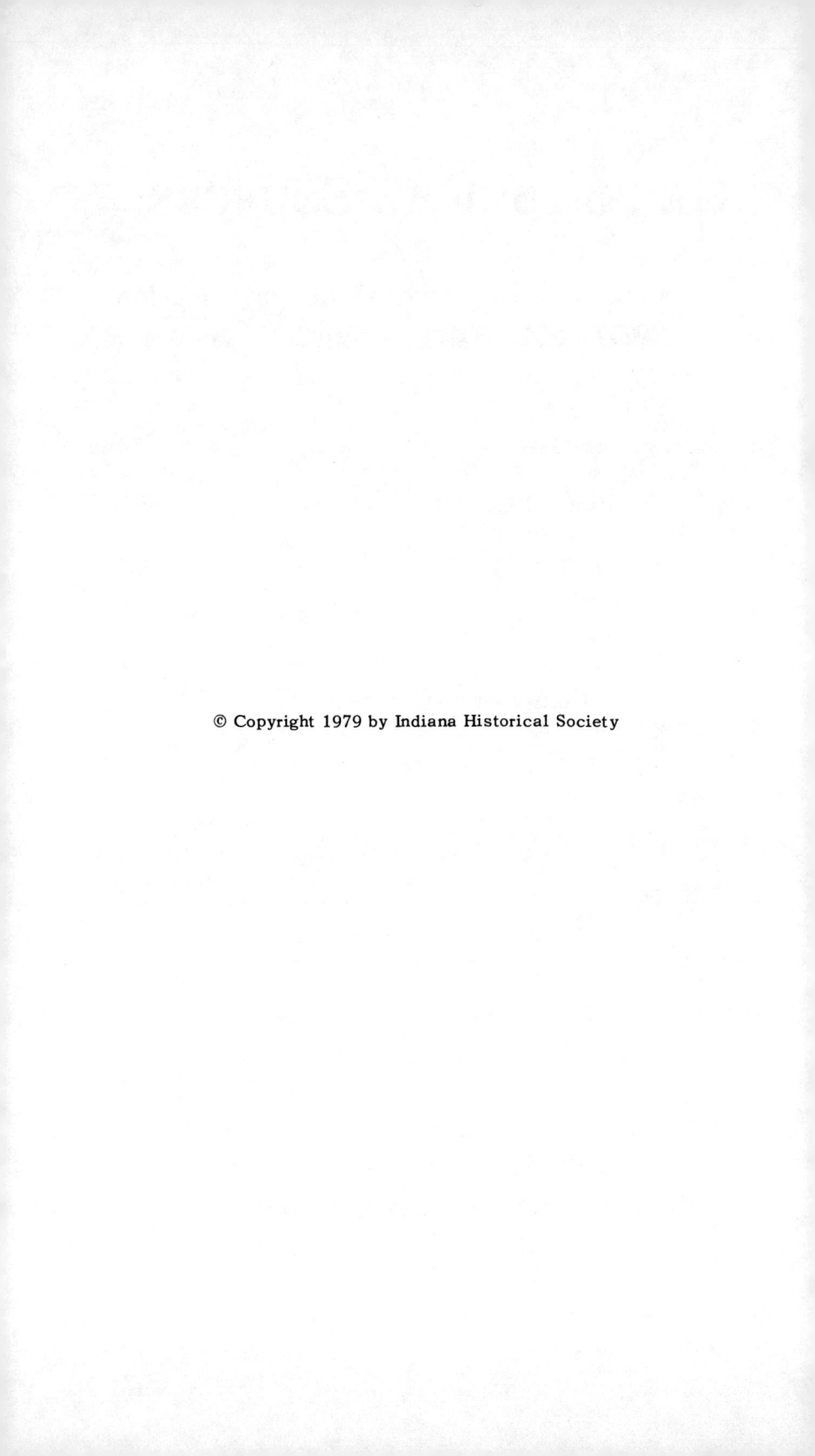

FOREWORD

Beginning with the September, 1936 issue of the Indiana Magazine of History (Vol. XXXII, No. 3) a new section was added entitled "Indiana Genealogy," edited by Martha Tucker (Mrs. Harvey) Morris of Salem, Indiana. The new section was sponsored by the Indiana Historical Society in response to the growing interest in family history; the Society of Indiana Pioneers aided for a brief time. Mrs. Morris continued as editor for five years after which the section had no separate editor but contributions were sent by various individuals directly to the editor of the Magazine. Though the content varied from issue to issue under this arrangement, the Genealogy Section continued to be carried as a part of the Magazine down to 1961 at which time the Indiana Historical Society began to issue a separate genealogical periodical, The Hoosier Genealogist.

A great deal of valuable genealogical material was published in the Indiana Magazine of History; some of it, such as Clark County Marriages and Executors Records have been reprinted in pamphlet form by the Historical Society; a few items have been reprinted in The Hoosier Genealogist. The greater part of the material is only available in the back issues of the Indiana Magazine of History and is unknown and not readily available to researchers today.

For the present publication, the material has been divided into (1) Marriage and Will Records; (2) Church and Cemetery Records; (3) Miscellaneous Records; (4) Bible Records; and (5) Family Genealogies. Footnotes that appeared in the original publication have been kept but in the rearrangement of the material they sometimes do not run consecutively; i.e., there may be a note 6 without notes 1-5; but the notes always match the text references regardless of the numbering. Because of the large body of records it has been necessary to omit the reprinting of the Queries. Likewise, in a few instances material has been included in this reprint which did not appear in the Genealogy Section of the Magazine, e.g., "The First Families of White Oak Springs."

We wish to express our appreciation to the present Editor of the Indiana Magazine of History for permission to reprint the material that appeared in the Genealogy Section of that periodical from 1936 through 1960.

CONTENTS

Marriage Records

	Page
Fayette County, 1819-1830	1-14
From IMH 52 (1956): 75-79, 187-90, 289-93	
Tippecanoe County, 1826-1830	14-20
From IMH 32 (1936): 316-18, 440-43	
Union County, 1821-1830	20-31
From IMH 50 (1954): 87-91, 192-99	

Note:
Marriage records for Clark, Monroe, Orange, and Wayne counties which were printed in IMH have already been reprinted by IHS; Clark in pamphlet form, the others in THG.

Will Records

Jackson County, 1817-1829	33
From IMH 34 (1938): 257-58	
Orange County, 1816-1835	34-46
From IMH 34 (1938): 384-87, 500-504; 35 (1939): 121-26	
Warrick County, 1814-1839	46-49
From IMH 44 (1948): 323-26	
Wayne County, 1811-1819	50, 51
From IMH 46 (1950): 217-19	

Note:
Will records for Clark and Harrison counties which were printed in IMH have already been reprinted by IHS, the first in pamphlet form, the last in THG.

Miscellaneous County Records

Early Schools of Clark County	53-66
From IMH 38 (1942): 321-24	
Heads of Families in Clay County, 1830	66-69
From IMH 56 (1960): 239-42	
Marriage Affidavits, Clay County, to 1852	69-72
From IMH 56 (1960): 243-48	
Record of Stock Marks, Jackson County, 1817-1838 . . .	73-78
From IMH 38 (1942): 217-22	
A Story of the Scotch Settlement, Jefferson County . . .	79-85
From IMH 42 (1946): 191-97	

The First Families of White Oak Springs, Pike County,
    1810 to 1817 86-126
    From IMH 36 (1940): 230-70

<u>Note:</u>
The 1850 Census of Harmony Township, Posey County. .
    IMH 42 (1946): 364-94 not reprinted

CEMETERY AND CHURCH RECORDS

Brown County
    Bean Blossom or Georgetown Cemetery. 127-135
        IMH 48 (1952): 205-13
    Coon or Fleener Cemetery 136-139
        IMH 48: 327-30
    Georgetown Presbyterian Church 140-143
        IMH 48: 431-34
    Oak Ridge Church and Cemetery 144-147
        IMH 46 (1950): 438-41

Harrison County
    Old Conrad Cemetery 147-150
        IMH 35 (1939): 446-48
    Silver Lake & Wilcoxin 150
        IMH 35: 449
    Old Goshen Church and Cemetery 151-155
        IMH 39 (1943): 315-19
    George Charley Burying Ground and Charley Family
        Cemetery 155,156
        IMH 36: 173-74

Hendricks County
    Vieley Cemetery 157-163
        IMH 36 (1940): 75-79, 171-73
    Cundiff, Bailey Farm, Griffith, Groover, Pritchett,
        Leach, and Montgomery Chapel Cemeteries 163-165
        IMH 36 (1940): 420-22

Henry County
    East Lebanon Cemetery 166
        IMH 36 (1940): 419

Jackson County
    Grassy Fork Township Cemetery 167-169
        IMH 40 (1944): 313-315

Jefferson County
  Carmel Presbyterian Church 170-174
    IMH 36 (1940): 410-414
  Caledonia Church and Cemetery 174,175
    IMH 41 (1945): 407-408

Lawrence County
  Elijah Allen Cemetery 176,177
    IMH 35 (1939): 117-118
  Granny White 178-180
    IMH 35: 222-24

Monroe County
  Chambers Cemetery 180,181
    IMH 33 (1937): 377-78
  Mt. Salem Church 182,183
    IMH 33: 257-58

Sullivan County
  Christian Church on Busseron Creek 184-200
    IMH 47 (1951): 111-27
  Little Flock Baptist Church 201-215
    IMH 49 (1953): 437-51
  Shelburn Baptist Church 215-228
    IMH 49: 235-48

Switzerland County
  Vevay Cemetery 229,230
    IMH 46 (1950): 118-19

Vigo County
  Honey Creek Monthly Meeting of Friends 231-242
    IMH 34 (1938): 281-92

Washington County
  Hardin Family Cemetery 243,244
    IMH 35 (1939): 119-20
  Providence Methodist Church Cemetery 245,246
    IMH 32 (1936): 438-39

FAMILY BIBLE RECORDS

Beard, James Dodd, Gage IMH 36 (1940): 319-20 247,248
Valentine Boruff IMH 34 (1938): 500 249
Easom Hannan, Powers IMH 34 (1938): 255-56 250,251

Stephen Harvey, Robertson, Elisha B. Lee IMH 33 (1937): 520-23	252-255
Hudelson and Bradley, Hawkins and West IMH 33 (1937): 373-76	255-258
Arthur Barrett, William Hunt, Samuel Holly, Ephraim Tucker IMH 34 (1938): 139-42	258-261
Roberts, Benjamin King IMH 32 (1936): 311-12, 313-15	262-265
Shipman, Kendrick IMH 32 (1936): 436-37	265,266
Tannehill, Rish, Adam Wible IMH 33 (1937): 253-56	267-270
Mathew Symons IMH 36 (1940): 79	270
Taylor IMH 33 (1937): 368-69	271,272

FAMILY GENEALOGIES

Atkinson IMH 39 (1943): 103-106	273-276
Bond IMH 32 (1936): 427-30	276-280
Christian Bowman IMH 34 (1938): 123-27	280-285
Daniel Bowman IMH 34 (1938): 242-44	285-288
Henry and John Bryan IMH 29 (1933): 344-46	289-292
Bundy IMH 42 (1946): 289-302	292-306
Dumont IMH 34 (1938): 409-16	306-313
Engle IMH 50 (1954): 317-20	314-317
Fauntleroy IMH 35 (1939): 210-17	317-324
Gilman IMH 37 (1941): 405-407	325-327
Graham IMH 39 (1943): 206-20	327-342
Simon Hadley IMH 41 (1945): 317-21	342-347
Anthony Halberstadt IMH 34 (1938): 489-92	347-351
J. Frank Hanly IMH 36 (1940): 81	351,352
Hardy IMH 34 (1938): 237-41	352-356
Harshbarger, Benjamin Van Cleave, Boone-Mayfield IMH 33 (1937): 505-15	357-366
Isaac Harvey and Enoch Smith IMH 33 (1937): 243-48	367-371
Hensel, Bickel, Rupp, Seitz IMH 45 (1949): 435-41	371-378
Hickman IMH 36 (1940): 313-15	378-380
John Hampden Holliday IMH 36 (1940): 66-70	380-385
Hallowell IMH 35 (1939): 106-12	385-391
Jacob Hoover IMH 34 (1938): 372-76	392-396
Jonas Hoover IMH 34 (1938): 245-50	397-402

Hughes-O'Neill IMH 35 (1939): 372-76 402-406
Kennerly IMH 36 (1940): 306-10 406-411
Light, Lucas, Moore IMH 34 (1938): 367-71 411-416
Ross-Welles IMH 34 (1938): 128-34 416-423
Shipman IMH 43 (1947): 198-202 423-427
Steele IMH 36 (1940): 311-12 427,428
Stewart IMH 32 (1936): 431-32 428,429
Surber IMH 33 (1937): 240-42 429-431
Thiebaud IMH 44 (1948) 326-34 431-439
John Van Cleave IMH 34 (1938): 493-95 439-442
Vandeveer IMH 55 (1959): 55-70 442-448
Woodburn and Van Cleave of Orange County 448-452
  IMH 33 (1937): 363-67
Philburd Wright IMH 36 (1940): 160-63 453-456

Note:

Genealogies omitted —

Rogers, Ward-Shipman and Allied Families
  IMH 44 (1948): 434-44; 45 (1949): 97-101, 209-18, 315-26.

Mouser-Schmidlapp Genealogy
  IMH 41 (1945): 307-16, 408-23

Both compiled by Mrs. Sylvan L. Mouser

FAYETTE COUNTY MARRIAGES, 1819-1830

Compiled from the first three volumes of Marriage Records in the Fayette County Courthouse, Connersville. The first volume has no number and is unpaged; the second and third volumes are labeled "A" and "B."

Marriages, 1819-1822

Alexander, William & Rebecca Lions, 1-7-1822
Alison, Timothy & Nancy Walker, 7-4-1819
Applegate, Bartholomew & Elizabeth Drake, 8-10-1821
Arnold, Ephraim & Ellen McLaughlin, 5-4-1820
Asher, Isaac & Martha Greer, 4-26-1822
Askew—see Eskum
Baird, James & Mary Youse, 1-6-1820
Ball, Stephen R. & Rachel Stebbins, 5-31-1821
Banster, James & Nancy Hallett, 9-5-1821
Barfell, James & Letty Warnock, 1-27-1820
Barner, John & Judith Ladd, 9-23-1820
Bates, John & Elizabeth Noble, 4-18-1822
Beach, Thomas & Nancy Moore, 2-4-1821
Beard, William & Rebecca Burtin, lic. 11-1-1821
Beck, Asa & Ann Percel, 5-2-1822
Bell, Joseph & Jane Endsley, 5-3-1821
Bishop, Austin & Ann Berry, June 1819 (lic. June 16)
Blair, Alexander & Sarah Huffman, 9-13-1821
Booe, Jacob & Nancy Hardenon, 9-19-1822
Booe, Phillip & Jemimah Clinton, 9-23-1821
Bradburn, John & Elizabeth Hamilton, 5-30-1822
Brown, James Washington & Margaret Vanmeter, 12-7-1820
Buckhannon, John & Mariah Smith, lic. 10-9-1820
Caldwell, Train & Sarah Dehaven, 8-17-1819
Caldwell, William & Elizabeth Alexander, 4-12-1821
Carpenter, Lyman & Dortha Perrin, 12-27-1821
Casady, Francis & Sally McCray, 7-26-1821
Catterlin, William & Rachel Harlan, 1-3-1822
Chinn, Chichester & Sally Jackson, 10-21-1821
Conn, William & Elizabeth Thomas, 2-22-1821
Conner, William & Eliza Chapman, 11-30-1820
Copsey, George Alexander & Sally Gran (?), 8-5-1821
Cornwall, Levy, & Polly Miller, 12-14-1820
Craft, Abraham & Margaret Allhounce, 9-25-1821
Craft, Francis & Polly Hougham, 2-14-1822
Crawford, Thomas & Margaret Sheepler, 11-6-1821
Crouch, John C. & Patience Worley, 7-13-1821
Crume, Marks & Cinthia Harlon, 3-24-1819
Dallas, Jesse & Mary Chambers, lic. 3-30-1819
Danner, Joseph & Mary Greeor, 1-10-1822
Davis, Jesse & Elizabeth Chase, 8-28-1822
Davis, Robert & Susan Manly, 7-27-1820
Davis, Wilbern & Nancy Dale, 2-22-1821
Dawson, Thomas & Rebecca Michel, 2-18-1820
Dawson, William & Cynthia Wandle (?), 2-19-1821
Dehaven, Samuel & Malinda Tyner, 12-6-1820
Denison, John W. & Margaret Swafford, 11-21-1820

Dickerson, Amos & Arilla Perkins, lic. 11-17-1820
Dickey, William & Jane Miller, 4-11-1821
Douthit, John & Nancy Conaway, 11-16-1820
Dungan, Benjamin & Betsey Delabar, 1-31-1822
Dungan, Joseph R. & Martha Anderson, 12-21-1820
Dungan, William & Elizabeth Dawson, 12-2-1819
Dunham, Nathaniel & Mary McCray, 10-23-1821
Elston, Josiah & Emelia Mayberry, 6-4-1821
Ennis, John & Catherine Messersmith, 6-18-1821
Eskum (Askew in return), Amos & Margaret Boston, 10-16-1822
Ewing, Henry & Margaret Phillis, 8-15-1820
Ferree, David & Tirzah Bell, 12-5-1820
Filpoat, Stephen & Rebecca Hawkins, 2-11-1819
Finch, Hiram & Abigail Miller, 4-6-1820
Fouch, Abraham & Elizabeth Vansicken, 11-19-1820
Fouch, Thomas & Sarah Wherett, 12-21-1820
Freeman, Elam S. & Sarah Grewell, 4-26-1821
Fryberger, George & Mary O'Neal, 12-16-1821
Fuel, Bennoni & Hannah Fisher, 10-21-1821
Fuller, Charles & Sally Lamson, 10-19-1819
Gard, William & Jane Fuel, 5-17-1819
Garwood, John L. & Mary Wilson, 9-23-1821
Gates, Uriah & Patsey Chinn, 1-22-1822
Gentry, Joseph & Mary Vanmeter, 5-18-1820
Goff, John & Lucy Johnson, 11-4-1819
Gorman, Daniel & Hannah Corbin (?), 9-30-1821
Grace, William & Mary Swift, 9-18-1820
Gray, John & Mary Ronald, 9-19-1821
Green, Samuel & Elizabeth Hittle, 12-27-1821
Grimel (?), Adam & Sally Littrel, 10-12-1820
Hager, John & Mary Ward, 1-6-1822
Hale, John & Nancy Kennel, 2-4-1822
Hamilton, Nathaniel & Lucinda Tyner, 11-7-1821
Hamilton, Robert & Rebecca Horrell, 9-12-1822
Hammond, Nathaniel & Hannah Vanmeter, 8-29-1822
Harding, Nel & Rebecca Wilson, 4-2-1820
Harlan, Jacob & Polly Simmonds, 2-8-1821
Harlan, Stephen & Dolly Sparks, 12-20-1821
Harter, William & Sally Williams, lic. 1-21-1822
Hays, John & Nancy Perkins, 6-2-1820
Heizer, Edward & Elizabeth Buckhannan, 11-4-1819
Helm, Samuel & Patience Wherrell (Wherrett?), 9-10-1820
Henderson, Eli & Sally Hamilton, lic. 9-5-1822
Henderson, Jonathan & Anna Loudenback, 9-11-1821
Hendricks, David & Elizabeth McCormack, 12-25-1821
Hendrix, Jesse & Polly Knott, 10-12-1820
Houghham, Aaron & Mary Parkhurst, lic. 11-30-1820
Houghton, John & Rachel Logan, 1-10-1822
Hubbell, Samuel & Mary Ann Rumley, 12-21-1820
Hulbert, Herry & Margaret Walker, 1-8-1822
Jacobs, Joseph & Cassander Rench, 4-23-1822
Jones, George & Sarah Williams, 2-10-1820
Jones, Martial & Elizabeth Miller, lic. 6-16-1821
Julian, George & Sarah Stafford, lic. 3-28-1820
Julin (Jacin?), Nathan & Rachel Baker, 4-7-1819
Kippers, James & Sally Thompson, 9-28-1819
Knight, David & Nancy Gillam, 8-8-1820
Larimore, Miles & Susannah Eskew, 3-23-1820
Lewis, Nathaniel & Elizabeth Peirson (?), 9-11-1820
Lyons, Abraham & Permelia Veatch, 2-24-1820
Lyons, Reuben & Fanny Sailor, 2-11-1821
McCarty, Thomas & Margaret Hale, 6-19-1821
McClary, Bartholomew & Susan Miller, 1-20-1820

McCrane, Jacob & Martha Dille, lic. 7-10-1822
McKinney, Mathew & Rhoda Parkhurst, 12-7-1820
McLaughlin, William & Elizabeth Taylor, 9-4-1820
McManus, George & Elizabeth Tedford, 6-10-1820
Martin, Isaac & Elizabeth Orr, 5-18-1820
Mason, Horatio & Amelice (Amelia?) Perin, 7-25-1819
Meeker, Minor & Rachael Thomas, 1-9-1820
Melone, Charles & Keziah Abbott, 9-1-1820
Miller, Abel & Anne Morris, 3-24-1822
Miller, Solomon & Susannah Corder, lic. 4-19-1821
Mills, Benjamin & Sally Thompson, 3-3-1822
Mills, Ephraim & Mary Wooster, lic. 10-24-1821
Mires, Henry & Nancy Albers (?), 10-12-1820
Morris, Perry & Edah Palmer, 12-31-1820
Muston (?), Smith & Mary Burton, lic. 2-16-1820
Myers, Joseph & Jane Kirckman, 4-7-1822
Nash, John & Dorcas Pearson, 8-9-1821
Newhouse, Isaac & Winiferd Sandefer, 9-12-1820
Newhouse, Samuel & Polly Kitchen, 12-20-1821
Newland, Harrod L. & Lucindy Rise Carlin (Caslin?), 2-26-1819
Norris, Robert S. & Martha Nicholas, 11-11-1819

Norton, David & Elizabeth Benefiel, 2-10-1820
Orwin, Martin B. & Nancy Julian, lic. 7-24-1820
Oscom (?), Jonathan & Nancy Bragg, 1-20-1820
Parkhurst, Isaac & Elizabeth Hornsted, 8-15-1820
Patten, John & Jane Elliott, lic. 11-15-1820
Penwell, John N. & Hetty H. Stockdale, 5-1-1821
Philpott—see Filpoat
Pogue, William & Anna Sailors, 12-23-1821
Pool, William & Margaret Kelso, 8-5-1819
Powel, Exsom & Elizabeth Loudenback, 8-22-1822
Redding, John & Dyantha Halbert, 7-1-1819
Reed, Eliphalet & Sarah Crouch, 6-29-1820
Reed, Enos & Patsey McCarty, 10-23-1821
Reed, John & Elizabeth Callan, 6-23-1820
Rementon, Martillow & Ann Lyons, 4-22-1821
Rench, Levi & Rebeckah Mills, 1-10-1822
Reu (?), Benjamin & Betsey Blood, 9-17-1820
Reynolds, David & Sarah Pernund (Penwell?), 3-16-1820
Rhoads, Palsor & Lenna Chambers, 6-3-1819
Richards, John & Nancy Brock, 3-25-1821
Right, Joseph & Patsey Grisham Barnes, 1-13-1822
Rumbley, James & Ginsey Lakey (Dakey?), lic. 11-1-1819
Rutter, Thomas G. & Hester Lefforce, 12-25-1821
Sandeford, Noah & Polly Withams, 9-13-1821
Sands, Daniel & Martha Turner, 3-30-1820
Selsur (?), Henry & Nancy Scott, 7-27-1820
Selvey, Travis & Elizabeth Powers, lic. 5-7-1822
Selvey, William & Nancy Mosely, 5-30-1822
Sheplor, Phillip & Elizabeth Thirston, 6-4-1819
Shirley, Analease & Philice Perrin, 6-24-1819
Shirts, George & Rebecca Finch, 11-8-1822
Smith, Isaac & Phebe Klinack (?), 5-25-1820
Smith, Jacob & Eliza Elliott, 10-4-1821
Smith, Jacob & Margaret Ronald, 12-13-1821
Smith, Jesse & Eadey Harper, 3-2-1820
Smith, Moses & Sally Harris, 10-16-1821
Smith, Samuel & Bethena Rainland, 9-12-1822
Smith, Tobias & Margarette Foster, 5-20-1819
Sutton, David & Elizabeth Shields, 11-14-1821
Sutton, Jonathan & Hannah Hubble, 9-5-1822
Swayze, John & Rachael Morgan, lic. 8-7-1822

Taylor, William & Elizabeth Scott, 1-30-1820
Thomas, Joseph & Elizabeth Picksley, 7-24-1822
Thomas, Richard & Marian Risk, 8-8-1822
Thomas, William F. & Naomi McCay, 10-5-1820
Thompson, John & Sarah Vansickle, 9-23-1822
Tiffany, William & Amy Magby, 10-12-1820
Tyler, John B. & Anna Jinks, lic. 4-5-1820
Tyner, Drewry & Isabella Dickey, 11-23-1820
Tyner, William & Prudence Caldwell, 11-4-1819
Vance, John & Nancy Martin, 8-24-1819
Vance, Samuel & Hannah White, lic. 7-21-1821
Vance, Samuel & Nancy H. Sutton, 10-27-1822
Vandegrift, Abraham & Patty Stevenson, 12-16-1821
Vangilder, Samuel & Nancy Stephenson, 5-21-1821
Vanmatre, Joseph B. & Nancy Love, 10-27-1821
Vanmeter, Joseph & Nancy Dils, 6-28-1821
Vanmeter, William & Elizabeth Bell, 6-1-1820
Walker, George B. & Margaret Gorman, 5-1-1821
Ward, Thompson & Nancy Sutton, 10-3-1822
Wardeman, George & Mary Elliott, 8-22-1821
Warren, William & Cortney Ellison, 11-9-1820
Webb, James & Tansy Hayes, 8-15-1820
Webster, Henry & Rebecca Reed, 5-13-1819
Welsh (?), John & Frances Conner, 11-18-1819
Westover, Hirum & Minerva Campbell, 2-17-1822
White, James & Nancy Morris, 5-30-1822
White, John & Ellenor Greer, 6-20-1820
White, William & Analiza Farel, 1-27-1820
Wick, William W. & Laura Finch, 8-20-1820
Williams, John & Eliz. McCormack, 10-14-1819
Williams, Mulbern & Nancy Newkin, 8-10-1819
Williams, Thomas & Rachel Hardy (Hardesty in return) 10-10-1822
Willis, Robert & Bethena B. Barnes, 11-28-1821
Wilson, Gideon & Catherine Wilson, 10-3-1819
Wilson, John & Dorcas Jones Orr, 12-21-1820
Wilson, John & Elizabeth Wilson, 2-8-1821
Witham, John & Nancy Bridges, 1-25-1821
Woodyard, Alexander & Deborah Ougham (Hougham?), 1-13-1822
Worster, Thomas & Elizabeth Howell, 7-2-1822
Wright—see Right

Marriages, 1823-1826

Adams, John & Margaret Savage, 2-20-1823
Alexander, William & Permelia Cunningham, 1-2-1824
Allen, John & Sarah Stuart, 10-13-1825
Alward, Ira & Jerusha Orr, 7-15-1825
Anderson, David & Rebecca Shipley, 5-12-1825
Anderson, George & Eliza Shipley, 7-29-1824
Ayres, Fleming & Elizabeth Scofield, 12-24-1822
Baker, John & Susanna Williams, 10-16-1823
Barnhart, George & Hannah L. Morris, 1-27-1824
Beauchamp, Noah & Lucinda McCormack, 5-23-1823
Beck, David & Lydia Sloan, alias Lydia Stout, 7-25-1824
Bell, John & Sally Barnes, 2-24-1825
Bell, Samuel & Kiziah Austin, 4-21-1825
Berry, Richard & Elizabeth Benton, 1-6-1825
Bird—See Byrd
Bishop, Robert & Rebecca Hamilton, lic. 8-14-1826
Booe, John & Jane Moffitt, 6-17-1826
Bradburn, Henry & Anne Hackleman, 4-28-1823
Brag, Henderson & Rosanna Eystone, lic. 9-16-1823

Brag, Wilson & Nancy Woods, 3-6-1823
Buck, Homer & Mary Jeffry, 2-27-1823
Bulkley, Nathan & Rebecca Reed, 12-15 (14?)-1825; lic. 12-12
Byrd (Byrt?), William & Harriett Henderson, 1-14-1824
Caldwell, Timothy & Elizabeth Rich, 6-10-1824
Campbell, Daniel & Mary Hawkins, 8-28-1823
Cassal (?), John & Susannah Richards, lic. 7-23-1823
Clifford, Ephraim & Catherine Barnhart, 10-26-1825
Cook, Joash & Nancy Tynes (Tyner?), 12-11-1823
Cooley, James M. & Eliza Peoples, 4-16-1824
Coshaw, John & Hannah Perin, 7-8-1824
Cunningham, John H. & Margaret Jack, 1-19-1826
Cutlar (?), Leonard & Eleanor Blair, 2-21-1825
Dailey, Jesse & Margaret Henry, lic. 1-29-1825

Dale, Samuel & Artimacy (?) Sample, 12-30-1824
Daniel, Payton & Nancy Embree, 3-24-1825
Danner, Joseph & Mary Greor, lic. 1-5-1823; m. 1-10-1822(23?)
Dawson, Asa & Betsy Smith, 1-5-1826
Dawson, John & Betsy Holland, 9-20-1824
Dawson, Matthias & Margaret Durbin, 3-10-1825
Degraaf, Aaron & Margaret Hill, 8-1-1826

Derry, Jeremiah & Lavina Street, 8-19-1824
Derry, Jeremiah & Malinda White, 5-11-1826
Dickey, Hugh, Jr. & Elmira Martin, 11-10-1824
Dickey, James & Jane Dickey (sic), 2-12-1824
Dickey, Samuel & Hannah McColley, 11-24-1825
Dungan, James & Sarah Hiers, 3-10-1825
Eacret (?), Samuel K. & Rachel Duffy, 2-17-1824

Eagan, John & Phebe Limpuss, 9-15-1823
Evans, William Henry & Hannah Rice Worster (?), 8-13-1823
Ferree, Thomas & Elizabeth Miller, lic. 3-28-1825
Fish, Charles & Eliza Hathaway, 5-19-1824
Fountain, Maser & Mary Clinton, 12-31-1822
Francis, Lathrop & Jane Woodyard, 9-28-1823
Garrett, Reuben & Sarah Dartes, 12-12-1822
Garrison, Robert & Mary Savage, 11-17-1825

Gifford, Solomon W. & Malinda Manlove, 10-8-1826
Gillam (?), Isaac & Polly Dale, 2-10-1823
Gilliland, James & Annis Kirkwood, 8-12-1824
Gilliland, John & Mary Kirkwood, 6-7-1826
Gleason, Harte & Sarah McGlothlin, 11-27-1825
Goodwin, Jonathan & Margaret Smith, 6-10-1824
Gray, Hugh & Susannah Ronnalds (?), 11-27-1822
Grewell, Haddock & Lucinda Burton, 1-23-1825
Griffis, Robert & Sarah Swift, 12-1-1825

Griffith, Elijah & Sarah Goe, 12-30-1824
Grossclop, Andrew & Fanny Messersmith, 5-30-1823
Hackleman, Jacob & Mary Ann Williams, 10-14-1824
Hamilton, Erastus & Eunice Russell, 2-6-1825
Hamilton, James & Mary Eyestone, lic. 7-12-1826
Hamilton, Nathan & Sally Johnson, 7-18-1824
Hammer, Joseph & Gemima Fullen (Fuller?), 12-5-1822
Harden, John & Malinda Caterlin, 6-12-1823
Hardesty, Daniel & Elizabeth Price, 3-19-1826
Harding, Isaac & Lydia Wilson, 2-28-1824
Harlan, James & Nancy Harlan (sic), 2-26-1824
Harrell (?), Moses & Frances Stott (?), 6-15-1823
Harrold, Jonathan & Elizabeth Barnhart, 10-14-1824
Hart, William & Eliza Cary, 10-3-1822
Havens, Joel & Polly Pearson, 12-13-1824
Hawk, Hanry & Mary Jane Foster, 11-10-1824 (lic.)

Hawkins, Litle & Clarissa Cunningham, 12-1-1825
Hayward, Joseph H. & Nancy Crandle, 6-22-1826
Heirs, Jacob & Ruiemma Goodwin, lic. 6-18-1823
Henry, David & Lydia Adams, 10-26-1823
Hiers, James & Rebecca Dungan, 4-14-1825
Hinton, Peter & Elizabeth Hamilton, 2-6-1825
Hobbs, William & Nancy Harrison (Harris?) of Wayne Co., 3-22-1824
Holland, Joshua & Rebeckah Williams, 11-30-1822
Hougham, Jonathan & Rebeckah Dungan, 10-23-1823
Huston, John & Mary Miller, 1-25-1826
Imel, Peter & Lavina Tirey (both of Wayne Co.), 3-8-1824
Irvin, John F. & Rebecca Beard, 1-22-1826
Jinks, John & Jane Ayers, 2-18-1824
Jones, Martial & Elizabeth Srawyer (Shroyer?) 2-26-1824
Kendal, John & Marian Early (Easly?), 1-29-1824
Kidd, Edmund J. & Christiana Decamp, 11-13-1823
Kirkpatrick, David & Jane Oldham, 3-3-1825
Kirkpatrick, John & Nancy Oldham, 5-27-1824
Kirkwood, James & —— McCormack, lic. 6-20-1826
Kirkwood, Thomas & Jane McCormack, 3-4-1824
Klum, John & Betsy Allison, 11-20-1823
Knott, Stephen & Hannah Payton, 12-29-1825
Kolb, Silas & Christina Penwell, 11-24-1824
Kolb, William & Syrena Tyner, 7-28-1824
Ladd, Noble H. & Mary Ann Wile, lic. 6-28-1826
Lain, William & Emely Bell, 1-20-1824
Lakin, Samuel & Rhoda Houghland, 11-11-1824
Lambert, Elie & Elizabeth Conner, 11-27-1825
Lane—see Lain
Larimore, Allen V. & Sarah Plummer, 10-12-1826
Law, Ephraim & Susannah Brannum, 2-6-1823
Law, Ephraim & Pricillia Monroe, 9-24-1824
Layton, Arthur & Dilila Aldridge, 7-10-1823
Leonard, Abner & Lucretia Armstrong, 9-2-1824
Leonard, Isaac & Christena Messersmith, 7-4-1824
Linder, John & Barbary Martin, 5-21-1826
Lize (Size?), Henry & Sarah Goodwin, 3-23-1825
Lodenback, Daniel & Alisey Powel, 1-30-1823
Lowe, Charles S. (?) & Elizabeth Dickey, 11-10-1825
Lucas, Eber (?) & Mary Nichols, 2-27-1823
McCleary, William & Margaret O'Neal, 10-14-1823
McConkey (Mayconkey), James & Prudence Manlove, 4-15-1824
McCormack, John (of Louisiana) & Catherine Sanders, 2-24-1824
McCormack, Levi & Hester Beauchamp, 4-25-1823
McCrory (?), Robert & Celina M. Saxon, 1-26-1823
Maple, Elijah H. & Sarah Coon, 7-18-1826
Martin, Charles & Nancy Smelling, 12-28-1824
Masters, John & Polly Silvey, lic. 11-29-1824
Mead, Stephen & July Weathers (Ibby Woothers in lic.), 4-25-1824
Merrifield, Richard & Paulina Coy, 8-4-1826
Messersmith, Andrew & Ruth Smith, lic. 6-21-1826 (return entered but not dated)
Messersmith, Hiram & Frances Simpson, 6-1-1826
Messersmith, Jacob & Barbary Ford, 1-9-1823
Messersmith, John & Sarah Grossclose, 5-25-1826
Miller, Isaac & Masey Richards, 10-24-1822
Miller, Richard & Eliza Higby, 11-11-1824
Montgomery, James & Catherine Groendyke, 12-4-1823
Montgomery, William & Rebecca Dawson, 6-16-1825
Moore, James & Sarah Craig, 4-1-1824
Moore, William & Rebecca Craig, 12-23-1824
Mowery, William & Catherine Vandalsem, 4-27-1826

Newhouse, Isaac & Elizabeth Kitchen, 1-6-1825
Newhouse, William & Sarah C. N. H. Conner, lic. 7-29-1826
Nicholas, William & Sarah Nicholas (sic), 8-3-1824
O'Banion, William & Malissa Porter, 11-11-1824
Oldham, John & Sarah Baldwin, 5-29-1825
Patten, David & Elizabeth Daniel, lic. 7-5-1825
Patterson, Joseph & Ruah Morris, 11-27-1823
Patterson, William & Climena Coy, 7-16-1825
Pell, Williams John & Ann Miller, 11-27-1823
Pence, Adam & Nancy Darter, 2-26-1824
Penwell, Reuben R. & Jemima Henderson, 8-26-1824
Perrin, Aaron & Betsey Simpson, 3-3-1825
Perrin, Hiram & Catherine Cain, 1-22-1823
Perrin, Moses & Mary Walling, 11-29-1825
Perverse, Samuel & Nancy Rutherford, lic. 7-11-1826
Petty, William & Elizabeth Johns, 10-24-1824
Philpott, John, Jr. & Nicy Hawkins, 2-11-1823
Plummer, Hiram & Lydia Vickrey, 11-10-1825
Plummer, Levi & Sarah Richards, 1-30-1824
Poak, John & Sarah Hemsted, 9-4-1823
Price, John & Mary Coovert, 7-17-1824
Pumphrey, Lot & Sophia Robinson, 1-23-1823
Putman, Joseph & Polly Hackleman, 2-10-1823
Ray, Martin M. & Rachel Catterlin, 1-18-1824
Rea, James C. & Mary Stockdale, 4-20-1823
Reed, Hardin & Mary Smith, 7-15-1826
Reese, Stephen & Polly, alias Mary, Tilyer, 5-15-1823
Rinearson, Richard & Nancy Scott, 2-5-1824
Risk, John & Keron Stubbs, 11-27-1825
Risk, William & Frances Eskew, lic. 5-21-1825
Robinson, Joel & Elizabeth Morris, 4-10-1823
Rollf, Joseph & Elizabeth Harrell, 4-18-1826
Rossell (Russell?), Nehemiah & Nancy Wherrett, 2-12-1824
Rumbley, James & Jane Lakey, 3-1-1825
Rutherford, John (of Union Co.) & Sarah Hudson, 6-25-1826
Ryckman, Bethuel & Christena Klum, 11-15-1823
Sample, Thomas Jefferson & Juliet Watton (Walton?), 8-31-1826
Shipley, Peter & Mariah Legg, 4-16-1826
Shnatterly, Joseph & Sarah Covert, lic. 8-30-1826
Silvey, Hiram & Anna Gunn, 8-8-1824
Silvey, Presley L. (S.?) & Fanny Steratt, 11-26-1823
Simpson, William & Sarah Sutton, 4-10-1823
Size—see Lize
Sleeth, Caleb & Sarah Frazure (Frazier), 5-9-1826
Smith, Thomas Simpson & Joana White, 8-3-1826
Sparks, Hugh & Rebecca Perverse, lic. 8-12-1826
Sparks, Isaac & Elenor Eagan, 9-2-1824
Stark, Benjamin & Fanny C. Phelps, 4-27-1826
Stephens (Stevens), King & Susana Scott, 10-?-1825 (lic. 10-21)
Stevens, Charles P. & Latetia Tharp, 4-27-1824
Stone, Silas & Martha S. (L.?) Dicken, 12-18-1823
Sutton, Platt & Sarah Simpson, 6-12-1823
Tharp, Joseph & Phebe Harris, 11-10-1825
Thomas, Alanson & Kitsey Orr, 12-2-1824
Thomas, Hewit & Charlotte Helm, 3-1-1826
Thomas, John & Clarissa Foreman, 1-1-1823
Thompson, Lewis & Pheby Dixon (Dickson), 2-27-1825
Trail, William & Sarah McCoun, 4-28-1825
Tweedy, Daniel Blakely & Mary Armstrong Biggs, 1-26-1826
Updegraft, Harmon & Louisa Hendricks, lic. 5-6-1826
Utter, Milton & Sarah Allen, 4-20-1823
Van Buskirk, Joseph & Abigal Vickrey, 12-15-1825

Vanmater, David & Mariah Vanmater (*sic*), 7-31-1823
Vanmeter, William & Elizabeth McNeal, lic. 9-13(14?)-1826
Van Vleer, John & Mary Stitt, 9-22-1825
Van Vleet, Abraham & Elizabeth Harrison, 1-28-1824
Veasey, Thomas & Nancy Witham, 12-22-1825
Veatch, James & Barbary Hammer, 12-15-1825
Veatch, Jonathan & Elizabeth Lyons, 11-21-1822
Vickrey, Martin & Margaret Galbreth, 2-5-1824
Wadsworth, Cornelius G. & Cassey Legg, 3-13-1823
Ward, Greenberry & Lovisa Edmonds, 9-15-1824
Wardle, Stephen & Elizabeth Roysdon, 11-2-1824
Waymire, Jacob & Rachel Brown, 9-23-1825
Webb, Calvin & Mary Prine (Perrine?), 12-31-1822
Webb, Forest & Clarissa H. Briant, 2-27-1823
Webster, Isaac & Nancy Simpson, 1-1-1823
White, Jacob & Minerva Allen, 11-25-1824
Whitelock, Abraham & Marget Risk, lic. 12-17(7?)-1823
Wilcox, Ira & Sally Wilson, 1-18-1825
Willey, John & Mary Thomas, 2-2-1826
Williams, Charles & Phebe R. Harris, lic. 2-28-1824 (Note opposite lic. says "No marriage seems to have taken place." Minister may have failed to send in return.)
Williams, Elisha & Martha, alias Patsey, Baker, 10-16-1823
Williams, John & Edah N. Reid, 11-16-1823
Williams, Jonas & Sarah Curtis, 7-15-1824
Williams, Thomas & Susan Hankins, 2-13-1823
Wilson, Nathan & Elizabeth Patterson, 1-1-1824
Winchel, Robert & Mary Williams, 7-3-1823
Woods, Jeremiah & Rachel Morris, 3-11-1824
Woolverton, Thomas & Eseneth Greene, 11-2-1825
Wyatt, David T. & Polly Coleman, 4-13-1823
Youse, Joshua & Phebe Stagg, lic. 12-29-1825

Marriages, 1825-1830

Aldridge, William & Mary Ann Moore, 10-8-1829 (p. 131)
Alexander, John & Prudence Ball, 12-16-1830 (p. 219)
Alexander, Simpson & Kitty Lane, 11-14-1830 (p. 212)
Allen, Joseph & Jemima Van Vleet, 10-27-1830 (p. 206)
Alward, Henry & Mariah Decamp, 7-27-1826 (p. 24)
Anderson, Jesse & Polly Smith, lic. 8-24-1827 (p. 44)
Baker, Abraham & Margaret Stephens, 4-10-1828 (p. 71)
Baker, Harrison & Elizabeth Isgrigg, lic. 3-16-1827 (p. 23)
Ball, Davis & Rhoda Woodcock, 1-12-1830 (p. 149)
Ballenger, James & Leah Wood, 10-1-1829 (p. 130)
Banks, Adam & Susanna Kolb, 8-13-1830 (p. 183)
Banks, John P. (Wayne Co.) & Alletha Durman, 12-13-1827 (p. 59)
Banks, William (Wayne Co.) & Mary Wilson, 7-31-1828 (p. 79)
Bates, James & Nancy Huston, 3-1-1827 (p. 26)
Bates, Robert (Rush Co.) & Rosilla Switcher, 10-5-1830 (p. 200)
Bates, Samuel & Peggy Knott, 8-21-1828 (p. 81)
Beeks, Lewis & Rebecca Van Matre, 7-26-1827 (p. 40)
Beel, Josiah & Mary Ann Stevens, 12-16-1830 (p. 218)
Bell, John (Union Co.) & Margaret Kenady, 7-3-1827 (p. 37)
Berry, Wilson & Maria Harrison, 2-3-1828 (p. 65)
Bilby, Joseph & Hannah Martin, 6-30-1830 (p. 172)
Billings, William & Elizabeth Harlen, 6-15-1829 (p. 122)
Bolin, John & Jane Peoples, 12-22-1829 (p. 144)
Bonwill, Henry (Franklin Co.) & Sally Smith, 4-16-1829 (p. 117)
Booe, Joseph & Mary Jack, 1-24-1828 (p. 63)
Boyd, Robert C. & Margaret Jane Taylor, 6-24-1830 (p. 171)
Bragg, Anderson & Sarah Lakin, 4-11-1828 (p. 72)
Bragg, William & Frances Parter (Patten?), 2-15-1827 (p. 19)

Briggs, Stephen & Elizabeth Reed, 11-27-1828 (p. 97)
Brown, Matthew & Julia Brummage, 2-10-1828 (p. 66)
Brownlee, Vincent & Betsey Thompson, 1-29-1829 (p. 103)
Buck, Harmon C. & Senia King, 1-22-1830 (p. 150)
Bulkley, Anson & Jane Harrel, 10-15-1829 (p. 132)
Bulkley, Jonathan & Christene Williams, 4-19-1827 (p. 33)
Burr, Joseph S. & Nancy Van Mater, 4-3-1827 (p. 31)
Burrows, Thomas & Delila Hendricks, 11-15-1827 (p. 53)
Burton, Calvin & Nancy Stuart, 1-6-1828 (p. 61)
Bussey, John & Mary Ashby (or Ashley?), 12-20-1829 (p. 141)
Butler, Sidney S. & Mary Lucas, 12-6-1827 (p. 58)
Byram, William & Dorothy Messersmith, 11-13-1827 (p. 52)
Caldwell, Benjamin & Charity Powell, 10-22-1829 (p. 135)
Caldwell, Moses & Dulcena Davis, lic. 10-25-1826 (p. 12)
Campbell, Charles & Jane Gilleland, 9-25-1828 (p. 87)
Carroll, Henry (Henry Co.) & Martha Paton, 1-3-1830 (p. 147)
Carver, Jonathan & Melinda Nelson, 8-17-1830 (p. 186)
Chambers, Thomas & Sarah Johnson, 12-27-1830 (p. 221)
Churchman, John & Dorcus Smith, 3-1-1827 (p. 22)
Coalscott, Ralph & Eliza Corbin, 11-29-1827 (p. 55)
Cole, Andrew M. B. & Mahala Gard, 2-14-1828 (p. 66)
Cole, Jacob L. & Mary Ann Miller, 2-22-1828 (p. 67)
Coleman, Alfred & Mary Murphey, 10-4-1827 (p. 50)
Coleman, Jonathan & Rachel Roisden (Risden?), 2-12-1827 (p. 21)
Conaway, Zechariah (Union Co.) & Susanna Williams, 3-25-1830 (p. 155)
Conkling, Josiah & Sarah Putman, 10-23-1828 (p. 92)
Connaway, Charles (Union Co.) & Maria White, 12-17-1829 (p. 140)
Conner, Carvener & Polly Newhouse, 9-10-1829 (p. 129)
Conner, James & Ruhama Darter, 10-28-1830 (p. 207)
Conner, James (Franklin Co.) & Eliza Risk, 9-25-1828 (p. 87)
Conner, James M. & Juliann Crislor (Crisler?), 2-26-1829 (p. 108)
Conner, Philomen & Ann Royster, 11-2-1829 (p. 137)
Cook, Jesse (Rush Co.) & Nancy Parten, 3-26-1829 (p. 113)
Cook, Richard (Wayne Co.) & Nancy Jackson, 11-19-1826 (p. 12)
Cook, William & Barbery Hinds, 8-11-1825 (p. 2)
Corbin, John & Mary Larimore, 6-18-1829 (p. 123)
Coshaw, Robert & Julia Perrin, 1-29-1829 (p. 102)
Crull, Daniel & Elizabeth Goodlander, 11-29-1827 (p. 54)
Custer, John T. & Eliza Berry, 12-26-1830 (p. 220)
Custer, William & Judith Kendall, 7-29-1830 (p. 179)
Dailey, John H. & Juliana Hardy, 11-11-1830 (p. 208)
Dance, John & Abigail Burrows, 10-12-1828 (p. 90)
Daniel, John & Mary Ayres, 8-11-1825 (p. 3)
Danner, John (Rush Co.) & Elizabeth Arnold, 3-5-1829 (p. 110)
Darnell, James & Elizabeth Olinger, 8-28-1827 (p. 43)
Darter, David & Mary Price, 10-15-1829 (p. 131)
Darter, Joseph & Polly Gossett (Garrett?), 1-4-1827 (p. 18)
Davis, John & Elizabeth Dehaven, 2-26-1829 (p. 109)
Davis, Paul & Jane Gordon, 8-23-1827 (p. 42)
Davis, Robert & Bethshaba Sparks, 1-7-1830 (p. 148)
Dawson, George & Polly Roysdon, 11-29-1827 (p. 55)
Dawson, Richard H. & Eliza Rathburn, 6-10-1827 (p. 36)
Dehaven, Richard & Margaret Isgrigg, 8-13-1829 (p. 127)
Deniston, James & Eleanor Williams, 1-19-1828 (p. 63)
Dickey, John & Susannah Parrish, 6-5-1828 (p. 76)
Dickson, William & Sarah Freeman, 10-5-1828 (p. 89)
Doan, Nathan (Wayne Co.) & Phoebe Gillison, 7-13-1830 (p. 175)
Draper, Joshua & Anna King, 10-22-1829 (p. 136)
Dunham, Quinton & Priscilla Arnold, 12-27-1829 (p. 145)
Dunn, Samuel & Lucinda Allison, 5-9-1830 (p. 165)
Easther, William & Judith Barner, 12-2-1827 (p. 57)
Eddy, Jonathan & Jane Hall, 9-13-1827 (p. 47)
Ellis, George S. (Wayne Co.) & Eleanor Williams, 8-14-1828 (p. 80)

Ellis, Jonathan & Charlotte Jeffery, 3-3-1829 (p. 111)
Ervin, Abner C. & Melinda Stephens, 4-17-1828 (p. 72)
Eskew, Daniel & Anna Lewis, 10-19-1826 (p. 7)
Eskew, William & Amelia Williams, 3-13-1828 (p. 68)
Ewing, George M. & Jemima Wood, 10-21-1830 (p. 202)
Fearis, George L. & Catharine Dickson, 7-29-1830 (p. 178)
Feliden, Jesse & Ruth Klink, 8-25-1829 (p. 127)
Ferguson, Francis & Mary Ann Monroe, 9-12-1830 (p. 193)
Finney, Stephen H. & Anny Cook, 2-25-1829 (p. 107)
Flowers, Samuel S. & Lucinda White, 8-4-25 (p. 2)
Frazee, James & Hannah Isgrigg, 10-26-1826 (p. 11)
Freeman, Tunis & Ruany Stockdale, 10-18-1829 (p. 134)
Freeman, William & Nancy Shields, 11-12-1826 (p. 9)
Furguson, Leham (Union Co.) & Hannah Knott, lic. 10-14-1828; m. 10-12-1828 (p. 91)
Gard. Sutherland & Mary Ellis, 9-20-1830 (p. 196)
Garrison, Elihu (Rush Co.) & Disey Stephens, 10-21-1828 (p. 94)
Gates, Samuel H. & Elmira Smith, 11-8-1828 (p. 95)
Gilmore, Thomas & Anna Ayres, 10-9-1828 (p. 89)
Gooding, David & Martha Beard, 1-15-1829 (p. 101)
Gooding, Samuel & Susannah Benge, 5-20-1830 (p. 168)
Goodlander, Philip & Claressa Webb, 12-18-1828 (p. 98)
Goodwin, Noah & Elizabeth Sury (?), 6-4-1828 (p. 77)
Gorden, Isaac & Polly Tharp, 10-15-1829 (p. 133)
Gorden, Jonathan & Matilda Tyner, 10-9-1828 (p. 90)
Gorden, William (St. of Ohio) & Elizabeth Kolb, 12-28-1829 (p. 142)
Gordon, David & Emily Tyner, lic. 5-30-1827 (p. 36)
Green, Daniel & Margaret (Peggy) Lair, 9-21-1826 (p. 23)
Green, Newel W. & Rebecca Miller, 5-1-1827 (p. 34)
Greer, George (Rush Co.) & Susan Porter, 1-27-1827 (p. 27)
Griffin, George (Rush Co.) & Margaret Reed, 2-26-1829 (p. 106)
Groenendyke, Thomas & Nancy Moffett, 11-29-1827 (p. 54)
Grose, Joseph & Mary Skinner, 12-17-1829 (p. 140)
Groves, Donavan (Rush Co.) & Eleanor Baker, 4-27-1830 (p. 163)
Groves, Joseph W. & Nancy Baker, 8-30-1828 (p. 81)
Grunendike, John & Elizabeth Smelser, 12-4-1826 (p. 17)
Guard, Lowry & Sarah Sutton, 10-30-1828 (p. 94)
Gunn, Robert & Sally Scott, 11-19-1829 (p. 138)
Hamel, William & Dorcas Mead, 12-26-1829 (p. 144)
Hamer, William H. & Harriet Curtis, 10-5-1830 (p. 199)
Hamilton, Samuel & Sarah Jones, 7-6-1828 (p. 77)
Hamilton, William & Margaret Burgess, 8-27-1826 (p. 20)
Hankins, Reuben & Mary Peoples, 9-16-1827 (p. 47)
Hanna, Joseph M. & Hannah Aldridge, 12-6-1829 (p. 139)
Hardy, John & Polly Bulkley, 5-22-1828 (p. 74)
Harlan, George & Sarah Martin, 8-25-1825 (p. 4)
Harlan, Matthew & Jemima Milner, 10-26-1826 (p. 9)
Harlen, Samuel & Narcissa How (Union Co.), 12-2-1830 (p. 215)
Hawkins, Joseph & Matilda Summers, 7-13-1827 (p. 39)
Hayward, Jacob & Rebecca Crandle, lic. 2-24-1829 (p. 109)
Heaton, Joseph & Edy (Ede?) Peppers, 8-16-1827 (p. 41)
Henderson, Nathan & Eleanor Jacobs, 1-12-1830 (p. 149)
Hendrix, George & Betsey Bailey, 4-2-1829 (p. 113)
Henning, Jacob & Catharine Runicks, 5-22-1829 (p. 121)
Hibbs, Thomas & Lavisa Norris, 11-21-1830 (p. 213)
Highley, James & Mary Webster, 2-10-1829 (p. 104)
Hill, James & Sarah Maskale, 9-7-1826 (p. 24)
Hillis, William (Putnam Co.) & Sarah Boyd, 3-8-1827 (p. 19)
Houston, John & Eliza Ross, 11-11-1830 (p. 209)
Howard, Samuel (Wayne Co.) & Katharine Coleman, 1-15-1827 (p. 18)
Hubble, William & Charity Harris, 10-4-1827 (p. 50)
Iles, Samuel & Nancy Smiley, 8-6-1830 (p. 181)
Irwine, William & Elizabeth Sutton, 7-28-1830 (p. 177)

Jackson, Jesse & Mary Edwards, 5-26-1830 (p. 169)
John, Benjamin & Hetty Neely, 3-29-1827 (p. 30)
John, Morgan & Matilda Harrison, 8-30-1829 (p. 128)
Johnson, Lawrence & Polly Pearce (Parce?), 10-26-1826 (p. 10)
Johnson, William & Mary Ann Cooper, 8-26-1830 (p. 188)
Jones, John & Mary Lawderback, 3-5-1829 (p. 110)
Jones, Jonathan & Maria Lathers (Lathors?), 1-27-1829 (p. 102)
Jones, Simpson (Franklin Co.) & Rebecca Mount, 3-11-1829 (p. 112)
Jones, Stephen & Ann Bolin, 9-1-1827 (p. 44)
Jones, Wesley (Wayne Co.) & Jane Dungan, 2-12-1829 (p. 105)
Justice, James & Malinda Porter, 10-22-1829 (p. 135)
Kelsey, Jonathan & Sarah Hatfield, 10-29-1829 (p. 136)
Kendal, Vachael & Celia Cook, 2-7-1827 (p. 27)
Kirkpatrick, William (Union Co.) & Susannah Corbin, 4-9-1829 (p. 115)
Klum, George & Mary Harell, 9-10-1829 (p. 129)
Klum, Henry & Ann Dicken, 11-16-1826 (p. 28)
Kolb, William & Kiziah Rich, 5-5-1828 (p. 74)
Lake, John & Lydia Harper, 9-9-1830 (p. 191)
Larimore, James W. & Mary Williams, 9-3-1828 (p. 83)
Lawson, Thomas & Jane Richardson, lic. 11-1-1826 (p. 10)
Lee, Stephen & Mary Budd, 2-12-1829 (p. 104)
Leforce, Abraham P. & Zilpah Mills, 1-1-1830 (p. 146)
Legg, William & Catharine Malinda Munger, 10-20-1830 (p. 203)
Leonard, Abner & Rachel Stibbens, 6-18-1829 (p. 124)
Lewark, Thomas J. & Elizabeth Stevens, 12-31-1829 (p. 145)
Lewis, John A. & Levice Baxter, 10-19-1828 (p. 92)
Ligthfoot (Lightfoot?), John B. (Rush Co.) & Rachel Kindle, 2-11-1829 (p. 105)
Linwell, James M. (St. of Kentucky) & Sarah Miskill, 2-5-1828 (p. 67)
Long, John & Sarah Terisa Deniston, 9-26-1827 (p. 45)
Lower, William & Rebecca Gooding, 5-14-1829 (p. 120)
Luark, John, Jr. & Sarah Martin, 2-12-1827 (p. 21)
Lyons, George P. & Sarah Atchison, 9-27-1827 (p. 49)
McCann (McCaun?), Jacob & Juliann Willey, 11-27-1828 (p. 97)
McConkey, John & Elizabeth Riley, 2-29-1830 (p. 152)
McCormick, Charles & Mary Hamilton, 12-31-1829 (p. 143)
McCoy, John & Nancy Berry, 6-12-1827 (p. 37)
McCray, James & Mary Harlan, 1-1-1829 (p. 100)
McCrurey, Samuel & Elsey Parrish, 9-11-1828 (p. 85)
McLoney, Alexander & Jemima Arnet, 10-15-1826 (p. 6)
Macy, William & Susanna Coffin, 3-14-1828 (p. 69)
Mansfield, Thomas W. (St. of Ohio) & Nancy Bayman, 9-9-1827 (p. 46)
Maple, Mentilla H. (Franklin Co.) & Elizabeth Coon, 8-13-1829 (p. 126)
Maple, William (Franklin Co.) & Sarah Vandolson (Vandalsem?), 3-26-1828 (p. 71)
Margeson, James & Sally Hamilton alias Sally Johnson, 12-11-1830 (p. 217)
Mark, Aaron & Rachel Garrett, 4-4-1827 (p. 32)
Mason, Horatio & Selina Gates, 10-20-1827 (p. 48)
Mathews, T. G. & Jane Morgan, 12-25-1828 (p. 99)
Mears, William & Cinthia Spergen (Spurgin?), 10-30-1827 (p. 51)
Medcalf, Joseph & Sarah Heck, 1-3-1828 (p. 60)
Melton, William & Sally Hackleman, 12-2-1830 (p. 216)
Messersmith, Elias & Polly McCormick, 10-15-1829 (p. 133)
Messersmith, Peter & Mary Smith, 11-14-1830 (p. 210)
Messersmith, Samuel & Charity Freeman, 1-6-1828 (p. 61)
Miller, Arthur & Rebecca Wherett, 1-31-1828 (p. 64)
Miller, John & Ann Orr, 11-22-1827 (p. 53)
Miller, John & Cynthia Manlove, 9-6-1828, (p. 82)
Miller, Robert & Rebecca Wilson alias Rebecca Cox, 7-22-1828 (p. 78)
Miller, Samuel & Eliza Jane Callen, 11-11-1830 (p. 211)
Milner, Amos & Rosanna Boyd, 10-2-1828 (p. 88)
Milner, Amos & Caty Larimore, 9-23-1830 (p. 198)

Montgomery, William & Mahala Johns, 9-19-1830 (p. 194)
Moore, Stephen & Eliza Sutton, 9-16-1828 (p. 84)
Moore, Thomas & Mildred Scott, 1-7-1830 (p. 148)
Morrow, Leonard P. & Sarah Williams, 8-10-1828 (p. 79)
Morrow, Richard F. & Levica Lewis, 2-25-1829 (p. 108)
Myers, Oliver & Hetty Bailey, 6-15-1829 (p. 123)
Nelson, Andrew & Elizabeth Carney, 9-4-1828 (p. 82)
Nelson, Simon & Mary Powell, 8-13-1830 (p. 184)
Newhouse, John & Sarah Williams, 11-6-1828 (p. 95)
Norris, Stephen & Ellenor Noble, lic. 8-28-1827 (p. 43)
Oldham, John (Rush Co.) & Margaret Dillon, 7-27-1830 (p. 176)
Orr, John & Partheria Smith, 9-8-1825 (p. 5)
Page, John & Nancy Smith, 2-7-1828 (p. 65)
Parker, Archibald & Anna Adkerson, 7-12-1827 (p. 38)
Patterson, Elijah (Rush Co.) & Mary Bragg, 9-20-1828 (p. 83)
Patterson, William & Nancy Helm, 8-11-1825 (p. 1)
Payton, Abram & Elizabeth McFerrin, 5-7-1829 (p. 118)
Payton, Lewis D. & Sarah McFerrin, 3-25-1830 (p. 155)
Payton, Samuel & Catharine Snyder, 12-9-1829 (p. 139)
Peoples, John & Harriet Tucker, 4-21-1827 (p. 33)
Peppers, John & Rebecca Dungan, 2-27-1828 (p. 68)
Personnett, John & Jane Burbridge, 9-23-1830 (p. 195)
Petty, William & Mary Ann Elizabeth Conner, 8-14-1828 (p. 80)
Pinkerton, Robert (St. of Ohio) & Nancy G. Orr, 5-17-1827 (p. 35)
Plummer, Henry (Rush Co.) & Perlina Ring, 8-16-1827 (p. 41)
Pollard, Richard & Sally Kulberson, 10-28-1828 (p. 93)
Pond, Eli & Emeline Johnson, 5-27-1830 (p. 170)
Porter, Patrick & Birtha Smith, 11-5-1829 (p. 137)
Porter, Samuel & Jerusha Crowfoot, 5-21-1829 (p. 120)
Powell, Isaac & Elizabeth Dale, 2-9-1830 (p. 151)
Pumphrey, Amos G. & Nancy Disher, lic. 8-14-1827 (p. 40)
Purdom, John & Nancy Huls, 2-5-1829 (p. 103)
Reece, Hiram & Edith Dungan, 10-23-1828 (p. 93)
Reed, James (St. of Ohio) & Jane Johns, 9-18-1827 (p. 48)
Reed, John & Margaret Culbertson, 4-9-1829 (p. 115)
Retherford, John (Union Co.) & Sarah Hudson, 6-26-1826 (p. 25)
Retherford, Joseph & Elizabeth Louderback, 5-6-1830 (p. 164)
Rich, Davis & Margaret Kolb, 12-28-1829 (p. 142)
Rich, John & Rebecca McCarty, 4-5-1827 (p. 31)
Rinerson, Cornelius & Elizabeth Coleman, 5-10-1829 (p. 119)
Rinerson, John & Sarah Ladley, 12-14-1826 (p. 15)
Robinson, Leonard & Electa Williams, 2-8-1830 (p. 151)
Ross, James C. & Leah Oldham, 7-16-1829 (p. 125)
Rowland, Calvin & Sarah Rinerson, 3-15-1829 (p. 114)
Royster, Stanhope & Betsey Martin, 8-28-1825 (p. 6)
Rumbley, James & Sarah Hulbert, 10-3-1827 (p. 51)
Sample, John & Frances C. Reid, 4-30-1829 (p. 117)
Saxon, Alexander G. & Margaret McCrory, 9-27-1827 (p. 49)
Saxon, Robert & Eliza Porter, 9-8-1829 (p. 128)
Scott, Noble Felix & Elizabeth Gunn (Grenn?), 3-5-1829 (p. 111)
Seely, Jesse & Zilpha Newland, 12-31-1829 (p. 146)
Seely, Samuel P. & Elizabeth S. Silvey, 11-14-1828 (p. 96)
Seward, Samuel P. & Eliza Martin Smith, 8-9-1829 (p. 126)
Shauls, Asa S. & Emela (Emely?) Chancy, 1-11-1828 (p. 62)
Shawhan, John (Rush Co.) & Sarah Parrish, 6-5-1828 (p. 76)
Shearly, Philomen, (Marion Co.) & Mary Callen, 9-18-1828 (p. 101)
Shelby, Evin & Phebe Van Vlair, 8-11-1825 (p. 4)
Shinkle, George & Melvina Bartlow, lic. 9-16-1826 (p. 7)
Shortridge. Harrison (Wayne Co.) & Mary Jane Loder, 9-2-1830 (p. 189)
Sibbit, Cornelius & Mary Higgins (Wayne Co.), lic. 7-27-1825 (p. 1)
Silvey, Thomas P. & Hannah Milner, 1-6-1830 (p. 147)
Simms, Christopher C. & Sarah Lake, 9-10-1829 (p. 130)
Smiley, Thomas & Mary Ball, 4-1-1829 (p. 114)

Smith, Abner & Maria Demoss, 11-20-1828 (p. 96)
Smith, Allen & Elizabeth Henderson, 7-27-1826 (p. 25)
Smith, Caleb B. & Elizabeth Watton, 7-8-1830 (p. 174)
Smith, Eppenetus & Lucinda Carroll, 11-16-1826 (p. 14)
Smith, Fielding & Susannah Smith, 8-11-1825 (p. 3)
Smith, George & Sally Roberts, 12-21-1826 (p. 17)
Smith, George M. & Mary Stauffer, 4-22-1828 (p. 73)
Smith, Isaac & Polly Butler, 11-28-1827 (p. 56)
Smith, Isaac M. & Catharine Crum, 10-22-1829 (p. 132)
Smith, James & Nancy Webb, 12-12-1826 (p. 16)
Smith, James & Mary Belk, 4-26-1827 (p. 34)
Smith, James & Elizabeth Long, 12-2-1830 (p. 214)
Smith, Joseph (Franklin Co.) & Susanna Carrel, lic. 2-11-1829 (p. 106)
Smith, Lewis & Elizabeth Porter, 12-25-1828 (p. 98)
Smith, Perry & Mary Lewis, 11-1-1827 (p. 52)
Smith, Roads & Christiana Conner, 9-8-1825 (p. 5)
Smith, Septimus & Nancy Oneill, 11-27-1828 (p. 99)
Smith, Thomas & Anna Baldwin, 3-22-1827 (p. 29)
Smith, Wiley G. & Maria G. Richer (?), 8-8-1827 (p. 38)
Smith, William & Elizabeth Grosclose, 9-9-1827 (p. 45)
Somers, Matthew & Tabitha Williams, 6-5-1828 (p. 75)
Sparks, John & Elizabeth Harlan, 11-2-1826 (p. 13)
Sparks, Stephen & Asenith Woolverton, 7-10-1828 (p. 78). (Return gives name as Stephen Harlan but Harlan was name of man making the return, so that he probably inserted his own name by accident.)
Sparks, William & Jane Swift, 3-4-1830 (p. 153)
Spencer, Joseph, Sr. & Mary Gooding, Sr., 4-21-1828 (p. 73)
Springer, Josiah & Julia Limpus, 2-7-1828 (p. 64)
Steel, Hans & Mary Smith, 5-14-1829 (p. 118)
Steel, James (Franklin Co.) & Jemima Smith, 4-19-1827 (p. 32)
Stephens, William & Hannah Hill, 2-27-1827 (p. 28)
Stevens, Samuel (Rush Co.) & Mary Johnson, 7-14-1830 (p. 167)
Stoddard, Joel & Ann Henry, 10-28-1830 (p. 205)
Stoddard, Thomas & Amelia Williams, 4-15-1829 (p. 116)
Street, Joseph & Rebecca Abrams, 9-2-1830 (p. 190)
Sutton, Josiah & Laury Ellis, 3-11-1828 (p. 69)
Swift, John & Elizabeth Tharp alias Elizabeth Lockwood, 3-30-1830 (p. 156)
Tate, William & Louisy Cunningham, 5-7-1829 (p. 119)
Tharp, William & Eleanor Bolin, 5-15-1830 (p. 166)
Thomas, Benjamin & Eliza Savage, 6-20-1829 (p. 124)
Thomas, James (Wayne Co.) & Lear (Leah?) Wilkerson, 7-18-1829 (p. 125)
Thomas, Jessee & Hannah Savage, 12-23-1829 (p. 143)
Thomas, Levi S. & Susan Maple, 4-4-1830 (p. 159)
Thomas, William & Polly Trowbridge, 9-15-1827 (p. 42)
Thompson, Jesse W. (St. of Ohio) & Mary Saunders, 5-17-1827 (p. 35)
Thompson, Thomas M. & Mary N. Gornell, 3-8-1827 (p. 29)
Travis, James & Betsey Patterson, 9-25-1828 (p. 84)
Turner, John & Polly Shepler, lic. 2-20-1827 (p. 26)
Tweedy, William B. & Lavina Williams, 3-19-1829 (p. 112)
Tyner, James & Lucinda Caldwell, 10-31-1829 (p. 134)
Tyner, John & Melissey Orr, 12-15-1826 (p. 15)
Updegraft, Harman & Louisa Hendricks, 5-7-1826 (p. 20)
Van Matre, Nehemiah & Elizabeth Royster, 11-29-1827 (p. 56)
Van Vleet, Abram & Jane Miers, 10-18-1826 (p. 8)
Vardaman, Morgan & Lucinda Walker, 8-12-1830 (p. 182)
Veysey, John & Catharine Carrack, 2-19-1829 (p. 107)
Wales, Julius & Elizabeth Johnson, lic. 12-25-1827 (p. 59). (A note appended by the Fayette County clerk states that the couple was never married.)
Walker, Henry & Sarah Conner, 11-16-1826 (p. 14)
Walker, William (Rush Co.) & Sarah Kinaston, 7-1-1830 (p. 173)

Walker, William Jr. & Hannah Stoddard, 9-23-1830 (p. 197)
Ward, Isaac & Sarah Dickey, 6-18-1829 (p. 122)
Ward, James & Osee Bell, 4-15-1830 (p. 161)
Webb, Calvin & Eliza Tolbert, 9-12-1830 (p. 192)
Webb, Newton & Eliza Hackleman, 4-4-1830 (p. 157)
Wells, James & Martha Bryant, 4-1-1830 (p. 158)
Wells, John & Susan Waters, lic. 6-6-1829 (p. 121)
Wherritt, Nicholas & Mary Scofield, lic. 11-15-1826 (p. 13)
Wherritt, William & Sarepta Thomas, 3-16-1830 (p. 154)
Whitaker (Whitacor?), John & Frances Webb, 4-9-1829 (p. 116)
White, Daniel H. & Elizabeth D. Boyd, 3-29-1827 (p. 30)
Whitelock, Joseph & Abigail Gorrell, 8-8-1830 (p. 180)
Whiteman, Joshua & Abigail Ellis, 12-2-1827 (p. 57)
Willey, Alfred & Amelia Waterman, 4-17-1830 (p. 162)
Williams, Isaac & Rebecca Thompson, 10-2-1828 (p. 88)
Williams, James & Polly Cooley, 10-28-1830 (p. 204)
Williams, Nathan P. & Patsey Eskew, 7-26-1827 (p. 39)
Williams, Robert & Elizabeth Hart, 3-4-1827 (p. 22)
Willis, Mark (Union Co.) & Margaret Strong, 8-17-1830 (p. 185)
Wilson, Andrew & Nancy Wilson, 12-5-1827 (p. 58)
Wilson, Charles & Anna Kinder, 8-20-1830 (p. 187)
Wilson, James & Clarissa Fountain, 11-15-1829 (p. 138)
Wilson, John & Nancy Swope (Henry Co.), 3-20-1828 (p. 70)
Wilson, John M. & Casander Steel, 11-27-1827 (p. 62)
Winshel (Winchell?), Richard & Drusila Herrel (Harrell?), 10-16-1828 (p. 91)
Wise, Samuel & Susanna White, lic. 10-4-1826 (p. 16)
Woods, James & Nancy Williams, 5-21-1828 (p. 75)
Woods, Robert & Hannah Heaton, 1-3-1828 (p. 60)
Woorster, Amos M. & Eliza Ann Tribbey (Trisbey?), 4-15-1830 (p. 160)
Worth, Joseph (Union Co.) & Sarah Hubble, 10-20-1830 (p. 201)
Wright, Justus & Mary Dailey, 4-17-1828 (p. 70)
Wright, Silas & Margaret Hamilton, 12-24-1829 (p. 141)

Marriage Records
TIPPECANOE COUNTY, INDIANA
From Book I, 1826-1830
Copied by MYRA ESAREY, Indianapolis, Ind.

Abbreviations: LA—Lawful Age AJ—Associate Judge
TC—Tippecanoe Co. DD—Doctor of Divinity
JP—Justice of Peace ECC—Elder Christian Church
MG—Minister of Gospel VDM—Visiting Deacon of Ministry

Treuary, William, to Rebecca Franklin, LA., TC., license Nov. 1, 1826; married by Levi Thornton, JP., Nov. 2, 1826, page 1.

Baum, George S., to Jane Menary, TC, Nov. 6, 1826; by Levi Thornton, JP., Nov. 9, 1826, p. 1.

McFarland, Moses, to Elisabeth Cuppy, TC, Jan. 31, 1827; by Abel Janney, JP, Feb. 4, 1827, p. 1.

Fautharp, Henry, to Eliza Black (dau. of Samuel Black) Feb. 13, 1827; TC; by Levi Thornton, JP, Feb. 14, 1827, p. 2.

Roberts, William, to Miranda Corbin, TC, LA, Feb. 22, 1827; by Wm. Bush, JP, Feb. 26, 1827, p. 3.

Jones, Henry F., to Keziah Talbert, TC, LA, Mar. 12, 1827, by John Provolt, AJ, March 15, 1827, p. 3.

Hicks, Aron, to Ruth Price, TC, Affidavit by Aron Merriman, Mar. 3, 1827 by Reuben Kelsey, JP, Mar. 29, 1827, p. 4.

Jamison, Charles, to Nancy Hickman, TC, LA, Mar. 21, 1827; by Reuben Kelsey, JP, Mar. 29, 1827, p. 4.
Ives, Asa O., to Polly Sargent, TC, LA (James Suit, bondsman), Apr. 2, 1827 by Reuben Kelsey, JP, Apr. 2, 1827, p. 5.
Wylie, Augustus (son of James), to Rebecca Farmer (dau. of Jesse), TC, June 7, 1827; by Stephen Kennedy, JP, June 11, 1827, p. 5.
Ely, Henry, to Mary Isley (dau. of Daniel), TC, June 7, 1828; by Levi Thornton JP, June 10, 1827, p. 6.
Tucker, Mason, to Luann Hoff, TC, LA, June 13, 1827; by Abel Janney, JP, June 14, 1827, p. 6.
Stansberry, Levi, to Delila Millicye, TC (Jesse Fouse, bondsman), by Reuben Kelsey, June 21, 1827, p. 7.
Bengaman, Henry, to Elizabeth McCombs, TC, LA, June 21, 1827; by Levi Thornton, JP, June 26, 1827, p. 7.
West, Jesse, to Margaret Provolt, TC, LA, July 7, 1827; by Stephen Kennedy, JP, July 19, 1827, p. 8.
Wade, James, to Katharine Bailey, TC, LA, July 31, 1827; by Levi Thornton, JP, Aug. 2, 1827, p. 8.
Clark, Hiram, to Harriot W. Smith, LA, TC, Aug. 16, 1827; by Abel Janney, JP, Aug. 19, 1827, p. 9.
Jones, Michael, to Polly Kinser, TC, LA, Sept. 5, 1827; by Abel Janney, JP, Sept. 6, 1827, p. 9.
Mikesel, John, to Sally Lucus, TC, LA, Sept. 15, 1827; by Levi Thornton, JP, Sept. 23, 1827, p. 10.
Key, Martin, to Sarah Logan, TC, LA, Oct. 8, 1827; by Aaron Payne, MG, Oct. 9, 1827, p. 10.
Waymire, Frederick (son of Andrew), to Frances C. Cochran (dau. of David H.), TC, Oct. 8, 1827; by Stephen Kennedy, JP, Oct. 11, 1827, p. 11.
Franklin, Preston, to Hannah Foust, TC, LA, Oct. 13, 1827, by Stephen Kennedy, JP, Oct. . . 1827, p. 11.
Shevalia, John B., to Susana Isaacs, TC (Reuben Kelsey, bondsman), Oct. 13, 1827; by Abel Janney, JP, Nov. 4, 1827, p. 12.
Marsh, Lemuel G., to Unice Dagett, TC (Reuben Kelsey, bondsman), Oct. 24, 1827; Reuben Kelsey, JP, Nov. 1, 1827, p. 12.
Freel, Elisha, to Elizabeth Tolover (dau. of John), TC, Dec. 15, 1827; by Reuben Kelsey, JP, Dec. 18, 1827, p. 13.
Bowen, Jesse, to Mary Poor, TC, LA, Dec. 29, 1827; by Reuben Kelsey, JP, Dec. 30, 1827, p. 13.
Freel, Amos, to Elizabeth Reynolds (dau. of Philip), TC, Jan. 23, 1828; by Reuben Kelsey, Jan. 27, 1828, p. 14.
Thornton, Isaac, to Patsy R. Reynolds, TC, LA, Jan. 23, 1828; by Reuben Kelsey, Jan. 27, 1828, p. 14.
Gray, John, to Sarah Blackburn, TC, LA, Feb. 2, 1828; by Solomon Crose, MG, Feb. 5, 1828, p. 15.
Sargent, James, to Susana Johnston, TC, LA, Feb. 5, 1828; by Levi Thornton, JP, Feb. 5, 1828, p. 15.
Bales, Solomon, to Sarah Haynes, TC, LA, Feb. 17, 1828; by Solomon Crose, MG, Feb. 21, 1828, p. 16.

Richey, Robert, to Elizabeth Guinn (James F. Brown, bondsman), TC, Feb. 20, 1828; by John Provolt, AJ, Feb. 21, 1828, p. 16.

Harram, Lyman, to Ellenor (Elenor) Baker (dau. of Daniel), TC, Mar. 15, 1828; by Wm. Bush, JP, Mar. 16, 1828, p. 17.

Schoonover, Nathaniel, L. A., to Margaret Schoonover (dau. of Abraham Schoonover), TC, Mar. 15, 1828; by Abel Janney, JP, Mar. 20, 1828, p. 17.

Russell, Thomas, to Jane Larey (dau. of Margaret Martin), TC, Mar. 24, 1828; by Solomon Crose, MG, Mar. 27, 1828, p. 18.

Dixon, Samuel A., to Elenor Richards, TC, LA, Mar. 31, 1828; by Levi Thornton, JP, April 3, 1828, p. 18.

Wright, Thomas Jefferson (son of Runnel), to Elizabeth Andrews, LA, TC, Apr. 2, 1828; by Levi Thornton, Apr. 3, 1828, p. 19.

Holloway, John, to Emily M. McGeorge, TC, LA, Apr. 8, 1828; by Reuben Kelsey, JP, Apr. 10, 1828, p. 19.

Ellis, Mordacai, LA, to Sarah Broccas (Brockus) (dau. of John), TC, Apr. 9, 1828; by Abel Janney, Apr. 17, 1828, p. 20.

Trekel, Stephen, to Jemima Kenser (dau. of Adam), TC, LA, Apr. 10, 1828; by Abel Janney, Apr. 15, 1828, p. 20.

Green, James, to Mary Parks, TC, LA, Apr. 26, 1828; by Abel Janney, May 1, 1828, p. 21.

Shepherd, Adam, to Nancy Galbreath, TC, LA, May 5, 1828; by Reuben Kelsey, May 8, 1828, p. 21.

Goldsberry, Silas, to Sarah Holladay, TC, LA, May 14, 1828; by Levi Thornton, May 15, 1828, p. 22.

McGuire, William, to Mary Ingersull (dau. of Benjamin), TC, LA, May 16, 1828; by Eli P. Farmer, MG, MEC, May 17, 1828, p. 22.

Ellis, Mordecai, to Cinderella Huff, TC, LA, May 31, 1828; by Abel Janney, JP, June 8, 1828, p. 23.

McDeed (son of James) to Carinda Davis Wylie, (dau. of James), TC, June 2, 1828; by Stephen Kennedy, JP, June 6, 1828, p. 23.

Morris, Henry, M.D., to Polly Reynolds (dau. of Philip), TC, LA, June 12, 1828; by Reuben Kelsey, June 15, 1828, p. 24.

Holladay, Thomas W., to Ann Kerr (dau. of James), TC, LA, June 23, 1828; by Levi Thornton, JP, June 26, 1828, p. 24.

Shortridge, Morgan, to Clarissa Burk, TC, LA, June 23, 1828; by Levi Thornton, JP, June 24, 1828, p. 25.

Holladay, John (son of Sam), to Rebecca Bailey, TC, LA, July 12, 1828; by Levi Thornton, JP, July 13, 1828, p. 25.

Kendall, Enion, to Polly Gates, TC, LA, July 15, 1828; by Reuben Kelsey, JP, July 17, 1828, p. 26.

Allen, John, to Elizazeth Langloy, TC, LA, July 16, 1828; by Reuben Kelsey, JP, July 17, 1828, p. 26.

Hilt, William, to Catherine Iseley (dau. of Daniel), TC, LA, July 26, 1828; by Andrew Simon, MG, Ger. Lutheran Church, July 27, 1828, p. 27.

Arman, Thomas, to Nancy Reynolds (dau. of Philip), TC, LA, July 28, 1828; by Reuben Kelsey, JP, July 31, 1828, p. 27.

Storm, David, to Rebecca Wright, TC, LA, Aug. 13, 1828; by L. Thornton, JP, Aug. 11, 1828, p. 28.
Bildeback, Thomas, to Rachel Bringham (dau. of Samuel), TC, LA, Aug. 18, 1828; by Philip McCormick, JP, Aug. 21, 1828, p. 28.
Cox, Alexander, to Anne Yount, TC, LA, Aug. 23, 1828; by Levi Thornton, JP, Aug. 24, 1828, p. 29.
Denny, William, to Beulah Ellis, TC, LA, Aug. 25, 1828; by Abel Janney, JP, Aug. 28, 1828, p. 29.
Ellis, James F. (son of Isaac), to Sarah Suit (dau. of James), TC, Sept. 8, 1828; by Philip McCormick, JP, Sept. 11, 1828, p. 30.
Patty, Eli, to Catharine Guinn, TC, LA, Sept. 18, 1828; by John Provolt, AJ, Sept. 18, 1828, p. 30.
Moffitt, James, to Mary Molder, TC, LA, Oct. 6, 1828; by Levi Thornton, JP, Oct. 6, 1828, p. 31.
Talbert, Joseph, to Elizabeth Sheriden, TC, LA, Oct. 13, 1828; by John Provolt, AJ, Oct. 16, 1828, p. 31.
Rau, Moses, to Elizabeth Roberts (usually residents within jurisdiction of TC), LA on affidavit of Reuben Kelsey, Nov. 2, 1828; by Reuben Kelsey, JP, Nov. 2, 1828, p. 32.
Newman, William, to Vermilla Wheeler, LA, TC, Nov. 11, 1828; by Abel Janney, JP, Nov. 13, 1828, p. 32.
Butcher, John, to Abagail Monohan, TC, LA, Nov. 17, 1828; by Solomon Crose, MG, Nov. 20, 1828, p. 33.
Vametre, Jacob B. (Vanmetre), to Sarah Taylor, TC, LA, Dec. 3, 1828; by Solomon Crose, MG, Dec. 8, 1828; p. 33.
Potter, Albin, to Nancy Anderson, TC, LA, Dec. 10, 1828; by Abel Janney, JP, Dec. 11, 1828, p. 34.
Huston, Robert, to Nancy Rock (one of the parties of Tippecanoe Co.), both LA, Dec. 15, 1828; by John Bishop, JP, Dec. 15, 1828, p. 34.
Davis, Levi, to Martha McCurdy, TC, LA, Dec. 27, 1828; by Levi Thornton, JP, Dec. 28, 1828, p. 35.
Mahan, Thomas, to Francis Underhill, TC, LA, Jan. 24, 1829; by Wm. Bush, JP, Jan. 29, 1829, p. 35.
Clark, Samuel O., to Mary Miller, TC, LA, Feb. 4, 1829; by Solomon Crose, MG, Feb. 5, 1829, p. 36.
Paige, James Sullivan, to Hannah Rarrick, both LA (affidavit of James Duncan), TC, Feb. 4, 1829; by Wm. Bush, JP, Feb. 4, 1829, p. 36.
Schoonover, Abraham, LA (affidavit of Nathaniel Schoonover), to Jane James, TC, LA, Feb. 4, 1829; by Abel Janney, JP, Feb. 5, 1829, p. 37.
Chamberlain, Benjamin Franklin, LA, to Phoeba Campbell, LA (by the consent of her mother), TC, Feb. 10, 1829; by Wm. Bush, JP, Feb. 12, 1829, p. 37.
Miller, James, to Precilla Travace, TC, LA, Feb. 11, 1829; by John Bishop, JP, Feb. 11, 1829, p. 38.
Weaver, Patrick Henry, to Ailsey Demmett, TC, LA, Feb. 23, 1829; by Abel Janney, JP, Feb. 26, 1829, p. 38.
Basye, John T., LA (by consent of Lismund Basye his father), to Delana Brown, TC, Feb. 24, 1829; by Wm. Bush, JP, Feb. 24, 1829, p. 39.

Ayres, Simeon S., to Sarah Amanda Claspill, TC, LA, Feb. 28, 1829; by James Crawford, MG, Mar. 1, 1829, p. 39.
McGuire, Nathaniel, to Jemima Mercer, TC, LA, Mar. 2, 1829; by Reuben Kelsey, JP, Mar. 4, 1829, p. 40.
Tullis, Moses, to Susana Murdock, TC, LA, Mar. 7, 1829; by Abel Janney, JP, Mar. 8, 1829, p. 40.
Roberts, Joseph, LA, to Sarah H. Burgess (dau. of Joseph), Mar. 14, 1829, TC (no return), p. 41.
Forgey, John S. to Mary Mott, TC, LA, Mar. 24, 1829 (no return), p. 41.
Farnsworth, David, to Indiana Cain (Affidavit of John M. Cain, brother of Indiana and James Cain, her uncle, for consent of her father, Cornelius Cain), TC, Mar. 24, 1829; by Wm. Clark, DD, Mar. 26, 1829, p. 42.
Cockran, William Kerr, to Margaret Stockton, TC, LA, Apr. 2, 1829; by James Crawford, MG, Apr. 2, 1829, p. 42.
Murphy, Thomas W. (consent of John Murphy, his guardian), to Mary Jorden (consent of Wm. Jorden her father), TC, Apr. 16, 1829; by John Bishop, JP, Apr. 21, 1829, p. 43.
Staley, Aron, to Catharine Persons, TC, LA, Apr. 28, 1829; by Stephen Kennedy, JP, Apr. 30, 1829, p. 43.
Rarrick, Henry, to Indiana Lamb, TC, LA, May 12, 1829; by Wm. Bush, JP, May 14, 1829, p. 44.
Carmean, Garrison, to Rachel Clark, TC, LA, May 14, 1829; by Stephen Kennedy, JP, May 14, 1829, p. 44.
Mickle, Joseph M. (consent of Elizabeth Mickle, his mother), to Elizabeth Hodgin, LA, both TC, May 20, 1829; by Philip McCormick, JP, May 20, 1829, p. 45.
Hunter, Daniel, to Amanda Jones, TC, LA, May 23, 1829; by L. Thornton, JP, May 28, 1829, p. 45.
Kinworthy, Joshua (consent of Robert Kinworthy, his father), to Rebecca Heston (dau. of Phineas), TC, May 27, 1829; by Abel Janney, JP, June 2, 1829, p. 46.
Anderson, William, to Rachel Goodden (dau. of Daniel), TC. LA, May 27, 1829; by Abel Janney, JP, June 4, 1829, p. 46.
Ivers, William, to Hannah Patty, TC, LA, June 17, 1829; by John Provolt, AJ, June 16, 1829, p. 47.
Provolt, Ezekiel, to Eliza Ann Ireland, TC, LA, June 24, 1829; by Stephen Kennedy, JP, June 25, 1829, p. 47.
Large, Jesse, to Polly Dawhitt (consent of Banet Dawhitt, her father), TC, LA, June 24, 1829; by John Bishop, JP, June 25, 1829, p. 48.
Johnson, Henry, to Mary White, TC, LA, June 24, 1829; by John Bishop, JP, July 1, 1829, p. 48.
Foust, Jesse, to Esther Schuck, LA, TC, July 1, 1829; by John Bishop, JP, July 2, 1829, p. 49.
Phebus, William, to Sophia Corwin (consent of Daniel Corwin, her father), July 7, 1829, TC, LA; by John Bishop, JP, July 12, 1829, p. 49.

Houghland, Eliza, to Sarah Adair (affidavit of Horace Stibbins on behalf of Sarah), TC, LA, July 8, 1829; by Levi Thornton, JP, July 8, 1829, p. 50.
Thomas, William, to Eliza Goddard (consent of Ashbea Goddard), TC, LA, July 11, 1829; by John Bishop, JP, July 12, 1829, p. 50.
Stanley, Joseph, to Lidia Bilderback (consent of Gabriel Bilderback, her father), TC, LA, July 14, 1829; by Abel Janney, JP, July 16, 1829, p. 51.
Timmons (Simmons), James, of Washington Tp., to Ellyn Nichols, Washington Tp., TC, LA (affidavit of Wm. Nichols), July 14, 1829; by Zabina Babcock, JP, July 10, 1829, p. 51.
Patton, David, to Lucinda Bush (consent of Michael Bush, her father), July 14, 1829, TC; by Levi Thornton, JP, July 14, 1829, p. 52.
Crouch, Joseph, to Jerutia Dehart (consent of Jacob Dehart, her father). TC, LA, July 27, 1829; by Solomon Crose, MG, July 30, 1829, p. 52.
Parcut, David, to Emily Parker, TC, LA, Aug. 3, 1829 (by affidavit of John Underhall); by William Bush, JP, Aug. 9, 1829, p. 53.
Wright, Parson, to Melinda Wiley, TC, LA, Aug. 3, 1829; by Levi Thornton, JP, Aug. 6, 1829, p. 53.
Wilson, Dudley W., to Mahala Wilson (consent of Arthur Wilson, father of Mahala and affidavit of Abraham Boltinhouse), TC, LA, Aug. 22, 1829; by Wm. Bush, JP, Aug. 23, 1829, p. 54.
Williams, David, to Nancy Ward, TC, LA, Sept. 2, 1829; by John Bishop, JP, Sept. 3, 1829, p. 54.
Bush, Abraham (Fountain Co.), to Mary B. Tullis, TC, LA (consent of Richard Bush, his father), Sept. 10, 1829; by John Bishop, JP, Sept. 10, 1829, p. 55.
Mead (Wead), John, to Charlotte Miller, TC, LA (affidavit of Samuel M. Holmes), Sept. 18, 1829; by Stephen Kennedy, JP, Sept. 19, 1829, p. 55.
Ellis, Nehemiah, to Elleanor Heath, TC, LA, Sept. 23, 1829; by John Bishop, JP, Sept. 24, 1829, p. 56.
Southard, Aron H., to Rebecca A. Hood, TC, LA, Sept. 29, 1829; by James Thompson, VDM, Jefferson, Wabash Co., Oct. 1, 1829, p. 56.
Franklin, William (Warren Co.), to Lidia Shelby, TC, LA, Oct. 12, 1829; by Philip McCormick, JP, Oct. 15, 1829, p. 57.
Kennedy, John, to Merena S. Wylie, TC, LA (consent of James Wylie, her father), Oct. 26, 1829; by John Provolt, AJ, Oct. 29, 1829, p. 57.
Moots, Samuel, to Mary Oxford, TC, LA, Oct. 30, 1829; by William Woods, JP, Nov. 1, 1829, p. 58.
Franklin, John, to Christina Conner, TC, LA, Nov. 12, 1829; by John Bishop, JP, Nov. 12, p. 58.
Murray, Michael, to Moranda Roberts, TC, LA, Nov. 23, 1829; by Wm. Bush, JP (no date given), p. 59.
Thornton, James, to Margaret Knapper, LA, TC, Dec. 1, 1829; by James H. Martin, MG, Dec. 4, 1829, p. 59.
Barton, Thomas, to Nancy Asher, TC, LA (consent of Charles Asher, her father), Dec. 1, 1829; by Zabina Babcock, JP, Dec. 3, 1829, p. 60.

Benny, Samuel, to Nancy Kerr, TC, LA, Dec. 9, 1829; by Solomon Crose, MG, Dec. 10, 1829, p. 60.
Denman, William, to Margaret Corbin, TC, LA, Dec. 9, 1829; by John Bishop, JP, Dec. 9, 1829, p. 61.
Irwin, Arthur, to Phoba West, TC, LA, Dec. 14, 1829; by John Provolt, AJ, Dec. 16, 1829, p. 61.
Replogle, Joseph, to Susan Mikesell, Dec. 16, 1829, TC, LA; by Samuel Arthur, MG, Dec. 17, 1829, p. 62.
Storm, Joseph, to Maria Johnson, TC, LA, Dec. 19, 1829; by Wm. Bush, JP, Dec. 20, 1829, p. 62.
Sanders, Jesse, to Catharine Arthur, TC, LA,, Dec. 21, 1829; by Samuel Arthur, MG, Dec. 21, 1829, p. 63.
Michael, Aron, to Rebecca Elliott, TC, LA (consent of John Elliott, her father), Dec. 22, 1829; by Zabina Babcock, JP, Dec. 31, 1829, p. 63.
Stockton, Daniel, to Emily Scott, TC, LA, Dec. 23, 1829; by Samuel Arthur, MG, Dec. 24, 1829, p. 64.
Brewer, William, to Anne Fuller, TC, LA, Dec. 26, 1829; by Robert Cochrane, ECC, Dec. 27, 1829, p. 64.
Scott, William, to Jane Sherry, TC, LA, Dec. 29, 1829; by Cyrus Ball, JP, Dec. 31, 1829, p. 65.
Owens, Isaac, to Tabitha Tolliver, TC, LA (consent of John Tolliver, her father), Dec. 29, 1829; by Philip McCormick, JP, Jan. 1, 1830, p. 65.

UNION COUNTY MARRIAGES, 1821-1830

Compiled by the Genealogy Division, Indiana State Library, from microfilm of Union County Marriage Records in the Union County Courthouse, Liberty. Book 1 covers the years 1821-1826; Book 2, 1826-1830. The beginning of each new page of the original record is noted.

Marriages, 1821-1826

Martin Wright to Polly Cartwright, Mar. 4, 1821, p. 1.
Anthony Nelson to Sophia Summey, Mar. 15, 1821.
George Talhunter [Talkington?] to Matilda Fisher, Mar. 29, 1821.
Charley Mansfield to Hannah Shafer, Apr. 8, 1821.
Hiram Price to Patricia McCallan [?], Apr. 8, 1821.
Joseph B. Wheeler to Christina Lassley, Apr. 7, 1821.
John Fosdick to Luisa Mead, Apr. 12, 1821.
Joseph Minor to Fanny Odle, Apr. 19, 1821, p. 2.
David North to Esther Minor, May 3, 1821.
Thomas Powers to Catherine Creek, May 6, 1821.
Abner McCarty to Jane Templeton, May 17, 1821.
Abraham Miller to Mary Thompson, May 31, 1821.
William Bradway to Elizabeth Hunter, June 7, 1821.
Jacob Newkirk to Mary Dickison, June 7, 1821.
Adam Miller to Sydney Johnston, June 28, 1821, p. 3.

Isaac Betts to Anne Creek, Mar. 8, 1821.
George Druck to Damascus Rambo, June 9, 1821.
David Stevenson to Lydia Gaby, June 14, 1821.
Uzziel Church to Mary Ann Bennett, July 5, 1821.
William Cosby to Elizabeth Crum, July 5, 1821, p. 4.
Nathan Thornton to Charity Cook, July 11, 1821.
Valentine Harlan to Elizabeth Harlan, July 29, 1821.
James Hopper to Harriett Burress [?], Aug. 30, 1821.
Pleasant Holloway to Samaria Stantz, Sep. 12, 1821, p. 5.
Joseph McMahan to Delilah Dunbar, Sep. 11, 1821 (date of license).
Martin Kingry to Phebe Lebrook [Lybrook?], Sep. 24, 1821 (date of license).
James Arnold to Nancy Styles, Oct. 24, 1821.
James Mansfield to May Andrews, Oct. 25, 1821.
John Burk to Peggy Yergar, Nov. 15, 1821, p. 6.
Benjamin Coffin to Hannah Stanton, Nov. 25, 1821.
Uriah Thornton to Charity Cook, Nov. 25, 1821.
George Key to Rebecca Rardin, Dec. 2, 1821, p. 7.
Isaac Darter to Sally Ewing, Dec. 6, 1821.
John Cunningham to Emelia Walker, Dec. 13, 1821, p. 8.
Joseph Stretch to Sally Dewey, Dec. 25, 1821.
Jonathan Hunt to Nancy Abrams, Jan. 13, 1822, p. 9.
Enoch Abraham to Catherine Lilley, alias Catherine Moffett, Jan. 19, 1822.
George Carr to Margot Orr, Jan. 19, 1822 (date of license).
Robert White to Jane Kirkpatrick, Feb. 14, 1822.
Daniel Burt to Elizabeth Ward, Feb. 21, 1822, p. 10.
Jonathan Hayworth to Elizabeth Wright, Mar. 20, 1822.
John Seward to Elizabeth Smith, Mar. 12, 1822.
Caleb Bates to Sarah Serring, Apr. 7, 1822, p. 11.
Joseph Camblin to Sarah Crouch, Apr. 10, 1822.
Jesse Hollingsworth to Sarah Lewis, May 19, 1822.
Isaac Ramsay to Rachel Cook, June 13, 1822, p. 12.
William Oldham to Naomi Morphew, July 7, 1822.
Daniel Morphew to Amy Grimes, July 18, 1822, p. 13.
John Shannon to Margaret Carmichael, July 21, 1822.
Nathan Crouch to Sarah Seaton, July 30, 1822.
Edward Railsback to Fransina Hunt, Aug. 8, 1822, p. 14.
Jeremiah Nugent to Sarah Langston, Aug. 15, 1822.
Samuel Ely to Caty Whisman, Aug. 22, 1822.
Ira Foster to Sarah McRay, Aug. 24, 1822, p. 15.
Levin Willis to Assenath Hazelton, Aug. 28, 1822.
George Whisman to Hannah Osson, Sept. 5, 1822, p. 16.
Thomas A. Thorn to Susanna Huff, Sep. 5, 1822.
James Hogan to Eliza Crouch, Sep. 3, 1822, p. 17.
Ebenezer Hayward to Sarah Shannon, Sep. 15, 1822.
Samuel Mager to Susanna Kingry, Sep. 17, 1822, p. 18.
Samuel Littrell to Nancy Steward, Sep. 18, 1822.
James Jay to Lydia Hollingsworth, Sep. 26, 1822, p. 19.

Robert Carr to Agness Huston, Sep. 28, 1822 (date of license).
John H. Newland to Mary Huff, Sep. 30, 1822, p. 20.
Lewis Walker to Hannah Ferguson, Nov. 21, 1822.
William Huston to Polly Cottrell, Dec. 5, 1822, p. 21.
Uzal Ward to Lydia Lafuze, Dec. 12, 1822.
William Macy to Rhoda Stanton, Dec. 25, 1822, p. 22.
Justice Fale to Rebecca Serring, Dec. 15, 1822.
Joseph Kingry to Elizabeth Mayer, Dec. 17, 1822, p. 23.
John Mailen to Sarah B. Ward, Oct. 31, 1823 [1822?].
Samuel Jennings to Sally Ann Springer, Jan. 9, 1823, p. 24.
Clemons Pritchet to Matilda Hayden, Feb. 11, 1823.
Simon Cassaday to Delia McCauly, Feb. 23, 1823, p. 25.
James W. Crist to Mary Lafuze, Feb. 28, 1823.
William W. Lafuze to Hannah Ward, Mar. 4, 1823, p. 26.
John Williams to Mary McCoy, Mar. 8, 1823.
James Presley to Elizabeth Hamilton, Jan. 23, 1823, p. 27.
Joseph Dawson to Priscilla Van Blair, Apr. 1, 1823.
William Campbell to Nancy Leviston, Mar. 20, 1823, p. 28.
Samuel Vaneton to Rebecca Knutt [Knott?], Apr. 17, 1823.
James Thomas to Nancy Ann Williams, Apr. 30, 1823, p. 29.
John S. Hunt to Tempy Estep, May 8, 1823.
Hugh Davis to Elizabeth Woods, June 5, 1823 (date of license), p. 30.
Adam Conn to May Clary, July 10, 1823.
Seth Summers to May McDowel, Aug. 4, 1823, p. 31.
Samuel Andrews to Rachael Kyger, July 17, 1823, p. 32.
David Berry, Jr. to Sarah Nutter, July 18, 1823, p. 33.
Daniel Smith to Elizabeth Lassly, Aug. 8, 1823, p. 34.
Noah Cartwright to Anna Minor, Aug. 12, 1823, p. 35.
John Shelby to Sarah McCauly, Aug. 21, 1823, p. 36.
Samuel Cunningham to Polly Walker, Aug. 26, 1823, p. 37.
Henry Hunter to Mary Hughes, Sep. 4, 1823, p. 38.
David Wilson to Peggy Conaway, Oct. 2, 1823, p. 39.
Richard Risher to Patsy Ring, Oct. 9, 1823, p. 40.
Gabriel Fender to Sarah McMahan, Oct. 23, 1823, p. 41.
Arthur F. Norris to Catharine Snowden, Oct. 30, 1823, p. 42.
Tilman Emmons to Nancy Wright, Oct. 30, 1823 (date of license), p. 43.
Joseph Harlan to Elizabeth Leviston, Oct. 30, 1823, p. 44.
Adam Snider to Elizabeth Whisman, Nov. 2, 1823, p. 45.
Samuel Larkin to Hannah Chenault, Nov. 11, 1823, p. 46.
Samuel Miller to Hannah Coddington, Nov. 21, 1823, p. 47.
Charles Wright to Charity Wright, Nov. 12, 1823, p. 48.
Pleasant Stanly to Mary Burroughs, Dec. 4, 1823, p. 49.
Josiah Heavenridge to Mary Burt, Dec. 11, 1823, p. 50.
Jacob Skillman to Rosana Hickman, Dec. 11, 1823, p. 51.
William Youse to Mary Ann Frazier, Dec. 30, 1823, p. 52.
James Scott to Hanna Conn, Dec. 23, 1823 (date of license), p. 53.
Moses Snider to Elizabeth Miller, Dec. 25, 1823, p. 54.

John W. Swann to Rosanna McGeer, Dec. 30, 1823 (date of license), p. 55.
Daniel Dwiggins to Sarah Knott, Jan. 8, 1824, p. 56.
Archibald Hill to Sarah Ferguson, Jan. 8, 1824, p. 57.
Christian Deardorf to Matilda Landes, Jan. 22, 1824, p. 58.
Isaac Miller to Jane Smith, Jan. 23, 1824, p. 59.
James G. Davis to Jane Chenault, Feb. 3, 1824, p. 60.
Hugh McGreer to Sally Leonard, Feb. 5, 1824, p. 61.
Asa Toler to Isabella Bridget, Feb. 15, 1824, p. 62.
Martha [?] Davenport to Nancy Witt, Feb. 12, 1824, p. 63.
Thomas Cason to Amelia Elston, Feb. 10, 1824, p. 64.
William Hand to Deborah Harris, Feb. 19, 1824, p. 65.
Joshua Cully to Mary Hanna, Feb. 6, 1824, p. 66.
Willis Kelly to Charity Hollingsworth, Feb. 29, 1824, p. 67.
Robert Paxton to Mary Ann McDill, Mar. 10, 1824, p. 68.
James Perry to Betsy Snowden, Mar. 14, 1824, p. 69.
Henry T. Williams to Polly Stiles, Mar. 18, 1824, p. 70.
Noah Miner to Susannah Hardman, Mar. 25, 1824, p. 71.
John Hardy to Polly Dwiggins, Mar. 23, 1824, p. 72.
Elisha Pelm to Sarah Hutchinson, Mar. 24, 1824, p. 73.
Elam Kelly to Sarah Holland, Apr. 1, 1824, p. 74.
Robert Hanna to Mary Scott, Apr. 1, 1824, p. 75.
Adam Mason to Sarah Youse, Apr. 8, 1824 (date of license), p. 76.
Henry Miller to Caty Seek, Apr. 15, 1824, p. 77.
William Duncan to Elizabeth Emmert, Apr. 27, 1824, p. 78.
John Brown to Mary M. Bowlsby, May 6, 1824, p. 79.
George C. Starbuck to Lydia Gardner, May 18, 1824, p. 80.
David Graham to Margaret Denniston, Aug. 17, 1824, pp. 80, 92.
David Denniston to Eleanor Williams, Aug. 19, 1824, pp. 80, 93.
Asa Mills to Elizabeth Hill alias Elizabeth Peterson, June 6, 1824, p. 81.
Nathaniel Cook to Susannah Madden, June 6, 1824, p. 82.
John Kyle to Nancy Orr, June 15, 1824, p. 83.
David Maquiston to Jane McDill, June 18, 1824 (date of license), p. 84.
Isaac Leviston to Polly Ratherford, June 25, 1824, p. 85.
Henry Waddle to Sally Sullivant, July 4, 1824, p. 86.
James Wales to Jane Haynes, July 27, 1824, p. 87.
John Berry to Eleanor Pattern, Aug. 7, 1824, p. 88.
John Huston to Sally Kingry, Aug. 10, 1824, p. 89.
Smith Dubois to Rachel Krom, Aug. 14, 1824, p. 90.
George R. Hanna to Polly Bridges, Aug. 15, 1824, p. 91.
Simon Emmert to Mary Canaday, Aug. 31, 1824, p. 94.
Robert Gilleland to Nancy Helmick, Sep. 7, 1824, p. 95.
Aaron Harlan to Lucetta Conaway, Sep. 2, 1824, p. 96.
Thomas Willis to Sally Nelson, Sep. 9, 1824, p. 97.
Abraham Cottrel to Susanna Hilderbrand, Oct. 12, 1824, p. 98.
David Alexander to Sarah Gott, Oct. 17, 1824, p. 99.
James Pentecost to Nancy Debolt, Oct. 28, 1824, p. 100.
Garrison Miner to Rebeckah Pritchard, Oct. 21, 1824, p. 101.

Josiah Bradway to Ailsey Austin, Oct. 20, 1824, p. 102.
Newton Wright to Elizabeth Summey, Nov. 11, 1824, p. 103.
Moses Robins to Elizabeth Long, Nov. 18, 1824, p. 104.
Elisha Watts to Mariam Miner, Dec. 26, 1824, p. 105.
Lewis R. Perdue to Elizabeth Springer, Dec. 26, 1824, p. 106.
Jacob Snowden to Eliza Ann Langston, Dec. 22, 1824, p. 107.
Ephraim Thomas, Jr. to Mahala Conn, Jan. 2, 1825, p. 108.
Josiah Garrison to Aby Bowlsby, Jan. 2, 1825, p. 109.
Isaac Williams to Polly Burk, Jan. 4, 1825, p. 110.
David Heckman to Mary Myer, Jan. 6, 1825, p. 111.
Squire Bell to Susanna Walker, Jan. 10, 1825, p. 112.
Isaac Ridenour to Anne Cottrell, Feb. 12, 1825, p. 113.
Josiah White to Elizabeth Flack, Feb. 17, 1825, p. 114.
William Aldridge to Jane Gilliland, Feb. 19, 1825 (date of license), p. 115.
Obed Davis to Sarah Woods, Feb. 24, 1825, p. 116.
Joseph Brown to Mary Creek, Mar. 10, 1825, p. 117.
Daniel McIntosh to Henrietta Crouch, Mar. 29, 1825, p. 118.
Jacob Rickenbaugh to Lacy Freeland, Mar. 13, 1825, p. 119.
Joshua Vaneton to Rebecka Lewis, Mar. 17, 1825, p. 120.
John Knott to Polly Chenault, Mar. 27, 1825, p. 121.
Jacob Alexander to Issabella Kingry, Apr. 3, 1825, p. 122.
Abel Abernathey to Jane McCullough, Apr. 7, 1825, p. 123.
Isaac Rentfro to Judy Deboy, May 14, 1825, p. 124.
George Fruits to Sally McKever, Apr. 13, 1825, p. 125.
Aaron D. Bowers to Matilda Shields, May 1, 1825, p. 126.
Joseph Jones to Mary Ann Skilman, May 21, 1825, p. 127.
Ross Smiley to Mary Abernathey, June 9, 1825, p. 128.
Daniel McCain to Mary Ann Wright, June 11, 1825, p. 129.
Robert Bennett to Sarah Weldon, June 30, 1825, p. 130.
John Keeney to Mary Crusan, July 12, 1825, p. 131.
James B. Elliott to Hetty McCoy, July 21, 1825, p. 132.
David Brown to Anne Billings, July 31, 1825, p. 133.
Washington Rinker to Polly Hazleton, July 28, 1825, p. 134.
Thomas I. Ferguson to Elizabeth Ferguson, Aug. 19, 1825, p. 135.
John Dunham to Sarah Willis, Sep. 8, 1825, p. 136.
Richard Strong to Susanny Gaby, Sep. 25, 1825, p. 137.
John McAter to Sarah Starr, Sep. 29, 1825, p. 138.
Isaac White to Rachel Sutton, Oct. 9, 1825, p. 139.
Elisha Burbage to Elizabeth McNemar, Oct. 10, 1825, p. 140.
Samuel Keffer to Elizabeth Lennen, Oct. 13, 1825, p. 141.
Otho H. Bennett to Nancy Ferguson, Oct. 13, 1825, p. 142.
Ebenezer McLean to Henrietta Weaver, Oct. 24, 1825, p. 143.
Jonathan McCarn to Hannah Owens, Oct. 27, 1825, p. 144.
Robert Walker to Mary Emmert, Nov. 7, 1825, p. 145.
William F. Stanton to Ann Fosher, Nov. 10, 1825, p. 146.
Moses Stinson to Rebecka Williams, Nov. 17, 1825, p. 147.
John Gray to Nancy Brown Hamilton, Dec. 15, 1825, p. 148.
Joshua Youse to Phebe Stagg, Dec. 29, 1825, p. 149.

Milton Knott to Catherine McNemar, Jan. 18, 1826, p. 150.
Isaac Snider to Catherine Miller, Jan. 18, 1826, p. 151.
George Newland to Catharine Templeton, Jan. 12, 1826, p. 152.
Henderson Harvey to Sally Rinker, Jan. 19, 1826, p. 153.
Andrew Dunbar to Sarah Stover, Jan. 26, 1826, p. 154.
John Dwiggins to Rebecca Knott, Feb. 13, 1826, p. 155.
George Miller to Nelly Smith, Feb. 9, 1826, p. 156.
Joel Stanly to Polly Owens, Feb. 14, 1826, p. 157.
Stephen Holoway to Phebe Hodson, Feb. 23, 1826, p. 158.
Benjamin Dubois to Elizabeth Wright, Mar. 7, 1826, p. 159.
James Hasty to Sarah Sprigg, Mar. 6, 1826, p. 160.
Samuel Witter to Caty Landes, Mar. 14, 1826, p. 161.
Charles Keeney to Mary Beck, Mar. 23, 1826, p. 162.
Martin Harroll to Nancy Ewing, Mar. 28, 1826, p. 163.
Isaac Bates to Jane Shields, Mar. 30, 1826, p. 164.
William Helmick to Jane Gilleland, Apr. 5, 1826, p. 165.
John Moyer to Sally Hardman, Apr. 18, 1826, p. 166.
Timothy C. Everts to Maria Holland, May 14, 1826, p. 167.
Samuel Miller to Margaretta Scott, June 1, 1826, p. 168.

Marriages, 1826-1830

Moses Strong to Sarah Baden, June 21, 1826, p. 1.
Henry Powell to Lydia Cook, June 20, 1826, p. 2.
Isaac Shelly to Catharine Foutz, June 28, p. 3.
Joseph W. Ruby to Ann Harlan, July 9, 1826, p. 4.
John Griffith to Lydia Babcock, July 14, 1826, p. 5.
William Aldridge to Sarah Mixell, July 14, 1826, p. 6.
Simon Mead to Polly Crane, July 20, 1826, p. 7.
Moses Freeman to Jemima Bowers, July 30, 1826.
Daniel Stephenson to Polly Osbon, Aug. 15, 1826, p. 8.
Ray Moss to Nancy Hopper, Sep. 4, 1826 (date of return).
Jesse Robb to Elizabeth Kline, Aug. 15, 1826, p. 9.
Henry Williams to Nancy Biggs, Aug. 13, 1826.
Asa Hogue to Nancy McCullough, Aug. 31, 1826, p. 10.
Elias Hall to Abigail Gentry, Aug. 31, 1826.
Brewer Ball to Jemima Loney, Sep. 3, 1826, p. 11.
Alexander Gilleland to Sally Scott, Sep. 14, 1826.
William Moffit to Sally Dwiggins, Oct 26, 1826, p. 12.
Robert Reeds to Eunice S. Chase, Oct. 31, 1826.
Edwin L. Carwile to Sally Satre, Nov. 2, 1826, p. 13.
Samuel Cason to Polly Burckhalter, Nov. 14, 1826.
Samuel Rich to Charity Gard, Nov. 23, 1826, p. 14.
James Stanly to Esther Thompson, Nov. 23, 1826.
Lewis Glidewell to Nancy Talbert, Nov. 23, 1826, p. 15.
Alexander White to Rachel Creek, Nov. 30, 1826.
Isum Summey to Nancy Burt, Dec. 7, 1826, p. 16.
William Runyon to Lucy S. Burgess, Dec. 14, 1826.
David Ward to Eleanor Lafuse, Dec. 14, 1826, p. 17.
Eli Thornton to Sarah Madden, Dec. 24, 1826.

Simeon Beck to Elizabeth Williams, Jan. 4, 1827, p. 18.
John Gary to Sally Powell, Jan. 30, 1827.
William Simpson to Elizabeth Riggs, Jan. 18, 1827, p. 19.
James Wasson to Elizabeth Reddick, Jan. 15, 1827 (date of license).
Reuben Dare to Charlotte Dubois, Feb. 1, 1827, p. 20.
Abraham Shelly to Cynthia Wortman, Feb. 2, 1827.
Samuel Harvey to Sophronia Hazelton, Feb. 8, 1827, p. 21.
David Fosher to Elizabeth Kernodle, Jan. 11, 1827.
Larkin Osbon to Mary Howel, Feb. 15, 1827, p. 22.
Micajah Elston to Alsey Tanner, Feb. 15, 1827.
Hugh Bowlan to Sally G. Swann, Feb. 22, 1827, p. 23.
Thomas Wolverton to Rebecca Crawford, Mar. 1, 1827.
Ross Murphy to Ann Shoemaker, Feb. 22, 1827, p. 24.
Samuel Mow to Rebecca Armstrong, Feb. 25, 1827.
Benjamin Melser to Betsey Ann Willis, Mar. 15, 1827, p. 25.
George Smith to Eupheme Wilson, Mar. 4, 1827.
Joseph Shields to Matilda Kirkpatrick, Mar. 8, 1827, p. 26.
Jacob Kingry to Sally Moyer, Mar. 14, 1827.
William McQuoid to Nancy Copeland, Mar. 15, 1827, p. 27.
William Wilson to Katharine Spitznogle, Mar. 17, 1827.
Samuel Paxton to Hannah Paxton, Mar. 22, 1827, p. 28.
Jeremiah Oliver to Lucinda Hesler, Mar. 22, 1827.
Levi Osbon to Rebecca West, Mar. 22, 1827, p. 29.
James McMillen to Cassy Essley, Apr. 1, 1827.
Abraham Peyton to Elizabeth Farmer, Mar. 26, 1827, p. 30.
Jeremiah Pritchard to Rebecca Cartwright, Apr. 5, 1827.
William H. Sample to Nelly Abernathey, Apr. 12, 1827, p. 31.
Willis Wright to Mary Stanton, Apr. 18, 1827.
William Robinson to Elizabeth Shelly, Apr. 19, 1827, p. 32.
Josiah B. Gentry to Elizabeth Shoemaker, Apr. 19, 1827.
Robert Scott to Mary Gilleland, Apr. 19, 1827, p. 33.
Amos Ward to Mary Shepherd, Apr. 26, 1827.
Wilson Bragg to Elizabeth Henry, May 10, 1827, p. 34.
George Witt to Esther Snider, May 2, 1827.
Clements Pritchard to Mary Hayden, May 6, 1827, p. 35.
William Probus to Aseneth Swift, May 6, 1827 (Aseneth Tuttle on marriage return).
James Wright to Sarah Summey, May 8, 1827 (date of license), p. 36.
Jesse Williams to Elizabeth Aldridge, May 13, 1827.
Henry Langston to Keziah Snowden, May 20, 1827, p. 37.
George Pinkerton to Elizabeth McDill, June 27, 1827.
Ellis Harlan to Louisa Shortridge, June 14, 1827, p. 38.
William Clugston to Margaret Davey, June 11, 1827 (date of license).
Ai Veach to Elizabeth W. Wright, July 15, 1827, p. 39.
John Stover to Sally Walker, Oct. 1, 1827.
James Alexander to Catherine Hartzel, July 26, 1827, p. 40.
Caleb W. Witt to Elizabeth Mench, Aug. 12, 1827.
George Heavenridge to Marie Morgan, Aug. 12, 1827, p. 41.
Martin Capper to Nancy Nutt, Aug. 16, 1827.

Turner Cartwright to Mary Hancock, Sep. 27, 1827, p. 42.
Thomas Ward to Rachel McHaffie, Sep. 5, 1827 (date of license).
Alfred Haynes to Mary Leeper, Oct. 4, 1827, p. 43.
John Ray to Phebe Goble, Oct. 4, 1827.
Abraham Huffman to Phebe Lister, Oct. 11, 1827, p. 44.
Martin Miller to Casandina Yaman, Nov. 1, 1827.
Dudley Willits to Polly Ruby, Nov. 15, p. 45.
Joel Stanley to Christina McCarn, Nov. 18, 1827.
Henry Miller to Elizabeth Neicely, Nov. 22, 1827, p. 46.
Charles Dubois to Margaret Cooms, Jan. 18, 1828.
John Helmick to Margaret Gilleland, Dec. 11, 1827, p. 47.
James Cason to Margaret Rutherford, Dec. 13, 1827.
Isaac Miller to Elizabeth Coddington, Jan. 2, 1828, p. 48.
William Hughs to Sarah Ogden, Dec. 27, 1827.
David Stanton to Nancy Sullivan, Jan. 2, 1828, p. 49.
John Yaryan to Clarissa Ward, Jan. 1, 1828.
Joseph Wells to Mary Bishop, Jan. 5, 1828 (date of license), p. 50.
Joseph McVey to Sarah A. Bromhall, Jan. 24, 1828.
John Patterson to Mary Williams, Jan. 26, 1828 (date of license), p. 51.
William B. Crist to Margaret Lafuse, Feb. 7, 1828.
William Biddle to Jane Campbell, Feb. 12, 1828, p. 52.
Samuel Farlow to Elizabeth Heavenridge, Feb. 10, 1828.
Enoch Hollingsworth to Margaret Mills, Feb. 14, 1828, p. 53.
Samuel Goudy to Mary Shoemaker, Feb. 21, 1828.
Simon Snider to Sarah Witt, Feb. 28, 1828, p. 54.
William Beck to Effy Norris, Feb. 28, 1828.
Jabez Casto to Esther Ewing, Mar. 2, 1828, p. 55.
Brison Armstrong to Margaret Mow, Mar. 4, 1828.
Samuel Carson (of Franklin Co.) to Elizabeth Thomson, Mar. 6, 1828, p. 56.
William Swann to Peggy Fise (?), Mar. 13, 1828.
William Sankey to Ann Lindsey, Mar. 20, 1828, p. 57.
John Whitneck to Lucy Kingery, Mar. 23, 1828.
Joseph Hollingsworth to Mary Bates, Apr. 10, 1828, p. 58.
Richard Hollis to Alithay Davis, Apr. 13, 1828.
Caleb Canaday to Martha Dwiggins, Apr. 19, 1828, p. 59.
Charles Nutter to Elizabeth Sullivan, May 15, 1828.
Enoch Coddington to Martha Yaryan, May 29, 1828, p. 60.
John Ferguson to Bethena Deacons, May 26, 1828.
Levi Squires to Nancy Jones, June 1, 1828, p. 61.
Thomas Smith to Polly Miller, June 5, 1828.
Daniel Witt to Katharine Messamore, June 19, 1828, p. 62.
John Sankey to Elizabeth Sumpter, June 19, 1828.
James Broomhall to Levisa Davis, July 13, 1828, p. 63.
Joshua Dye to Mary Nickels, July 19, 1828 (date of license).
Paul M. Barnard to Lurana Ogburn, July 24, 1828, p. 64.
John L. Smith to Eliza Hill, July 31, 1828.
Philip McNamer to Mary Ann Harper, Sep. 11, 1828, p. 65.
William McGreer to Eliza Brandenburgh, July 31, 1828.
Levin Dwiggins to Polly Stover, Aug. 10, 1828, p. 66.

Leonard Coffman to Susana Cassner, Aug. 23, 1828.
George Yaryan to Rebecca Baily, Aug. 31, 1828, p. 67.
Jacob Black to Mary Messamore, Sep. 2, 1828.
Elijah McMahan to Charity Beck, Sep. 4, 1828, p. 68.
Nathan Harper to Elizabeth Grigs, Sep. 5, 1828.
Thomas Starr to Rachel Job, Sep. 14, 1828, p. 69.
Daniel Petre to Polly Hanes, Sep. 12, 1828 (date of license).
Joseph Hayden to Margaret McComas, June 22, 1828, p. 70.
Lewis Mead to Fanny Kingery, June 21, 1828.
Thomas Shields to Hannah Kirkpatrick, June 29, 1828, p. 71.
John Olvy to Lydia Martin, July 4, 1828.
John Tucker to Sally Brown, Sep. 20, 1828, p. 72.
Zachariah Clevinger to Eliza McDowel, Sep. 21, 1828.
John M. Hendricks to Elizabeth Welden, Oct. 25, 1828, p. 73.
Jonathan Crandel to Ruth Mitchel, Sep. 25, 1828.
Samuel Parkhurst to Sally Wright, Sep. 25, 1828, p. 74.
John F. Bennett to Nancy Burroughs, Sep. 25, 1828 (date of license).
Joseph Vannoy to Margaret Starns, Oct. 2, 1828, p. 75.
Benjamin Thomas to Loretta Morgan, Oct. 2, 1828.
James Herron to Eliza Smith, Nov. 8, 1828, p. 76.
John Wickersham to Eliza Starbuck, Oct. 9, 1828.
John Sprout to Charlotte Wilson, Oct. 9, 1828, p. 77.
John Hickman to Sally Cartwright, Oct. 16, 1828.
Alston Wyatt to Elizabeth Moss, Oct. 23, 1828, p. 78.
Robert Burbage to Mary Rader, Oct. 23, 1828.
Thomas Patterson to Jane Wetsel, Oct. 23, 1828, p. 79.
Philip Moss to Barbary Moyer, Nov. 27, 1828.
David Lynch to Hannah Thomas, Nov. 27, 1828, p. 80.
John C. Reddish to Anna Rose, Nov. 30, 1828.
John Leeper to Telitha Ray, Dec. 10, 1828, p. 81.
Joseph Walker to Sarah Martin, Dec. 11, 1828.
Jacob Shewmon to Elizabeth Capper, Dec. 18, 1828, p. 82.
William Gray to Mary Hamilton, Dec. 24, 1828.
Hugh Abernathy to Mary Ann McCullough, Dec. 25, 1828, p. 83.
James Paxton to Polly Paxton, Dec. 31, 1828.
John Powell to Polly Johnson, Dec. 29, 1828, p. 84.
Jefferson Colvin to Rebecca F. Bennett, Jan. 1, 1829.
Thomas Cromwell to Catherine Norris, Jan. 1, 1829, p. 85.
John Miller to Emily Yaman, Jan. 1, 1829.
Jefferson Russel to Sarah Griggs, Jan. 1, 1829, p. 86.
Samuel Paxton to Margaret S. Whiteman, Jan. 15, 1829.
Isaac Cooms to Elmira Starbuck, Jan. 15, 1829, p. 87.
Ephraim Goble to Mary Griggs, Jan. 29, 1829.
John Herron to Rebecca Farmer, Feb. 4, 1829, p. 88.
David Creek to Margaret Meek, Feb. 21, 1829.
Joel Coleson to Elizabeth Young, Feb. 5, 1829, p. 89.
Ezekiel Rose to Harriet Coleson, Feb. 5, 1829.
Calvin Sullivan to Elizabeth Witter, Feb. 12, 1829, p. 90.
William McNabb to Anna Young, Feb. 19, 1829.

John Boyers to Margaret Lewis, Feb. 19, 1829, p. 91.
Jefferson Ward to Mary McHaffie, Feb. 19, 1829.
Ashbill McCollam to Elizabeth Soliday, Feb. 26, 1829, p. 92.
Daniel Poland to Elizabeth Goudy, Mar. 1, 1829.
Edmond Peters to Sarah Sanders, Mar. 3, 1829, p. 93.
Smith Staten to Nancy Goble, Mar. 12, 1829.
Josiah Grover to Sophia Everts, Mar. 10, 1829, p. 94.
Jacob Moyer to Sarah Landes, Mar. 15, 1829.
Stephen Cuzick to Elizabeth Fisher, Mar. 12, 1829, p. 95.
Joseph Billings to Mary Davis, Mar. 15, 1829.
John Morrison to Harriet Johnson, Mar. 17, 1829, p, 96.
John Smith to Barbary Barnhart, Mar. 26, 1829.
James H. Johnston to Eliza Ann McCord, Mar. 26, 1829, p. 97.
Benjamin Brown to Catharine Miller, Apr. 9, 1829.
Isaac M. Serring to Naomi Dunbar, Apr. 12, 1829, p. 98.
Samuel Scott to Elizabeth Herrick, Apr. 16, 1829.
William Harris to Sally Ann McLean, Apr. 30, 1829, p. 99.
Isaac Whiteman to Sally Rinker, May 14, 1829.
John Quick to Nancy Clary, May 27, 1829, p. 100.
Hezekiah Miner to Ruth Evans, June 9, 1829.
James Johnson to Ailsey Davis, June 18, 1829, p. 101.
William S. Clark to Elizabeth Huston, June 26, 1829.
Philip Veach to Polly Majors, June 27, 1829, p. 102.
John Ridenour to Sarah Cottrall, July 5, 1829.
William Meek to Sarah Foutz, July 16, 1829, p. 103.
Andrew Ray to Jane Allen, July 16, 1829.
Joseph Willis to Jane Waddle, July 19, 1829, p. 104.
Levi Mills to Janet Starns, July 23, 1829.
Isaac G. Crawford to Mary Ann Shroyer, July 26, 1829, p. 105.
Jacob Keltner to Hannah Melser, Aug. 9, 1829.
Isaiah Langston to Esther Miller, Aug. 20, 1829, p. 106.
William Yaman to Fanny Ann Ogden, Aug. 20, 1829.
Robert Cook to Elizabeth Kingery, Aug. 27, 1829, p. 107.
Vincent Rose to Sarah Bradway, Sep. 3, 1829.
John Wright to Nancy Wright, Sep. 9, 1829, p. 108.
Joseph Stover to Lydia Rinker, Sep. 17, 1829.
Daniel Stanton, to Mary Bratten, Sep. 17, 1829, p. 109.
Samuel Rupe to Rachel Whitinger, Sep. 22, 1829.
William Becket to Katharine Lynch, Oct. 1, 1829, p. 110.
William Young to Nancy Ring, Oct. 4, 1829.
William Newnum to Deborah Degrauft, Oct. 3, 1829, p. 111.
Jeremiah Aldridge to Mary Harden, Oct. 11, 1829.
Henry Hubbard to Rachel Gaby, Oct. 15, 1829, p. 112.
William Stanton to Ann Lewis, Oct. 13, 1829.
Daniel Trimbley to Cintha Rubey, Oct. 15, 1829, p. 113.
Robert Deever to Jane Drury, Oct. 29, 1829.
Jacob Gary to Hannah Johnson, Nov. 5, 1829, p. 114.
William Messmore to Mary Kernodle, Nov. 8, 1829.
James Morrison to Nancy Kingery, Dec. 3, 1829, p. 115.

Jacob Blew to Mary Stout, Dec. 26, 1829.
Jacob Baker to Mary Ann Chesney, Dec. 11, 1829, p. 116.
Christian Routszong to Katharine Cline, Dec. 10, 1829.
John McNamer to Peggy Wright, Dec. 10, 1829, p. 117.
James Wright to Nancy Cason, Dec. 15, 1829.
John C. Heavenridge to Hannah Vanvacter, Dec. 17, 1829, p. 118.
Philemon Jenkins to Martha Carpenter, Dec. 24, 1829.
Isaac B. Day to Deborah Brown, Dec. 31, 1829, p. 119.
Solomon Bratten to Anna Lennon (?), Dec. 31, 1829.
George Williams to Brittania Gambril, Jan. 7, 1830, p. 120.
William Ward to Elizabeth McIntosh, Jan. 14, 1830.
Henry Simpson to Malinda Lemmons, Feb. 2, 1830, p. 121.
George W. Cottral to Ruth Macy, Jan. 16, 1830.
Jacob Hetzler to Sarah Freeman, Jan. 21, 1830, p. 122.
Joseph Noble to Eleanor Lemmons, Jan. 21, 1830.
David Jefferson to Sarah Williams, Jan. 28, 1830, p. 123.
Hiram S. Norris to Elizabeth Elwell, Jan. 28, 1830.
William Dennington to Margaret C. McCaffie, Jan. 28, 1830, p. 124.
John Sample to Theodotia Ann Cory, Jan. 28, 1830.
Joseph Arnet to Christina Moyer, Feb. 4, 1830, p. 125.
John W. Holland to Sally Waddle, Feb. 11, 1830.
Levi Davis to Harriet Woods, Feb. 11, 1830, p. 126.
Hugh Cuzick to Nancy Lynch, Feb. 16, 1830.
Benjamin Jones to Sarah Merchant, Feb. 15, 1830 (date of license), p. 127.
Isaac Dewey to Rebecca Cunningham, Feb. 25, 1830.
Wiley Etchison to Jane Scott, Mar. 4, 1830, p. 128.
Samuel Stanley to Rebecca Richey, Feb. 28, 1830.
George Winchel to Jane Ewing, Mar. 4, 1830, p. 129.
John Huddleston to Susannah Moyer, Mar. 4, 1830.
Sampson Cully to Elizabeth Johnson, Mar. 4, 1830, p. 130.
Levi Nugent to Elizabeth Witt, Mar. 18, 1830.
Jonathan Barnard to Mary Moyer, Mar. 25, 1830, p. 131.
Thomas K. Harding to Rachel Knott, Mar. 28, 1830.
Bird Toler to Elizabeth Bridget, Apr. 4, 1830, p. 132.
Adam Nees to Mary Nees, Apr. 4, 1830.
John Cook to Sarah Willis, Apr. 17, 1830, p. 133.
John Cunningham to Mary Crissman, Apr. 22, 1830.
Robert Flack to Anna Weeks, Apr. 20, 1830, p. 134.
Samuel Hamilton to Jane McClurken, Apr. 22, 1830.
John Stith to Sarah Childers, Apr. 26, 1830, p. 135.
John Throyer to Amanda Mead, May 6, 1830.
Abraham Miller to Susanna Lybrook, May 6, 1830, p. 136.
Abraham Bland to Emily Snowden, May 4, 1830.
Aaron Rice to Nancy Shroyer, May 6, 1830, p. 137.
Simeon P. Gage to Anna Davis, May 12, 1830.
John Clear to Elizabeth Allen, May 16, 1830, p. 138.
Samuel Bigger to Ellen Williamson, May 25, 1830.
Benjamin E. Harriman to Malinda Preston, June 17, 1830, p. 139.

William Hawes to Esther Crane, June 20, 1830.
Richard Ring to Sarah Cully, June 24, 1830, p. 140.
George McVey to Polly Kingery, June 27, 1830.
William Patten to Lydia Essly, July 16, 1830, p. 141.
Joseph Ellis to Fanny Moss, July 22, 1830.
James Imel to Drucilla Good, July 29, 1830, p. 142.
Elam Howren to Sarah Agee, Aug. 14, 1830.
John Skinner to Isabel Ewing, Aug. 27, 1830, p. 143.
Elias Cruzan to Sally Paten, Aug. 26, 1830.
William Starr to Elizabeth Beck, Sep. 2, 1830, p. 144.
Andrew Jones to Anna Ragan, Sep. 2, 1830.
Thomas Burrows to Sarah Stanley, Sep. 9, 1830, p. 145.
Chauncey H. Burr to Jane Williams, Sep. 14, 1830.
Nathan Hamilton to Abi Bowlsby, Sep. 16, 1830, p. 146.
John Ferguson to Elizabeth Knott, Sep. 30, 1830.
Hill Hamilton to Nancy Kingery, Sep. 30, 1830, p. 147.
Lorenzo Gard to Melinda Perkins, Oct. 7, 1830.
Caleb Serring to Mary Moor, Oct. 7, 1830, p. 148.
Archibald McGuiston to Mary Bones, Oct. 13, 1830 (date of license).
John A. Boyd to Rebecca Maze, Oct. 28, 1830, p. 149.
William Sprout to Hannah Nelson, Oct. 21, 1830.
John Stutsman to Anna Walker, Oct. 28, 1830, p. 150.
William Poland to Elizabeth Mills, Oct. 31, 1830.
Henry H. Cuppy to Elizabeth Foutz, Nov. 4, 1830, p. 151.
Abraham F. Whiteman to Mary Rinker, Nov. 7, 1830.
John Gilbert to Anna Long, Nov. 1, 1830, p. 152.
David McGuiston to Sarah McDill, Nov. 4, 1830 (date of license).
Jacob Landes to Mary Kingery, Nov. 13, 1830, p. 153.
John Keever to Sarah Brooks, Nov. 22, 1830.
David Vanvacter to Harriet Ward, Nov. 25, 1830, p. 154.
Silas H. Cory to Katherine Cromwell, Dec. 13, 1830.
David Pagin to Mary Miller, Dec. 23, 1830, p. 155.
Nathan Robinson to Margaret Shelly, Dec. 23, 1830.
Israel Hamilton (of Preble Co., Ohio) to Julian Mitchel, Dec. 28, 1830 (date of license), p. 156.
Andrew B. Price to Abagail Mann, Dec. 28, 1830 (date of license).
Levi Taylor to Elizabeth Grimes, Jan. 6, 1831, p. 157.
William Bailey to Matilda Johnson, Dec. 30, 1830.

Abstracts of Early Wills of Jackson County, Indiana

Sullivan, Patrick—June 29, 1817; probated Feb. 27 1818; names wife Jane, son Patrick, son Henry, son William, daughters Jane, Catherine, Elizabeth, Margaret, Sarah, and Susannah; children not of age, son John, Catherine, Elizabeth, Margaret, Sarah, and Susannah. Will Book, No. 1, Jackson County, Indiana, 1.

Jessop, Thomas—Dec. 9, 1819; probated March 15, 1820; wife, Mary; children, Thomas, Isaac, Nathan, Jessop, Ruth Perisho, Ester Newby, Patience Mills, Sarah Gray; witnesses, Thomas Storm, George Jones, Jesse Dixon; executors, Isaac, Jessop, Enoch. *Ibid.*, 4.

Draper, Nathan—Apr. 6, 1822; probated June 5, 1822; wife, Mary; son Jonathan, son Robert, son Nathan, son Peter, daughter Mary; mentions brother-in-law, Thomas Jessop. *Ibid.*, 6.

Alsup, John—Aug. 30, 1824; probated Nov. 8, 1824; wife and William Newland executors; no children mentioned. *Ibid.*, 12.

Rephart, George—August 15, 1824; probated Aug. 21, 1824; witnesses, Jesse B. Durham, Henry Boas, Sr., and Henry Boas, Jr. (No wife or children mentioned); devises to George Iseninge $40; "for which I hold notes"; all money due to him from Government mentioned; Henry Boas, Sr., Executor. *Ibid.*, 14.

Marshall, William—Jan. 1, 1825; probated Oct. 1, 1825; wife Elizabeth, sons Claver and Malen, Simon, Jehu (?), John, William, daughters, Rebecca, Leah, and Rachel. Witnesses: Samuel Stamfield-Solomon Ruddick-William Cox. *Ibid.*, 15.

Keith, Daniel—April 2, 1824, probated Oct. 23, 1824; wife, Rosy; daughters, Rosanah, Polly, Prudence Jones, Elizabeth Reddick; one-third of estate divided; Constance Ione, ten dollars she has in her own hands; witnesses, Elisha Ruddick, James Denny and William Payne. *Ibid.*, 18.

Green, William C.—May 30, 1829; probated Aug. 10, 1829; wife, Elizabeth; sons, Robert, Clark, and McCallan; daughters, Henrietta, Emily, Camila; brother-in-law, Jarry Coots; a sum to be given to him, equal to sum given to him, by each of "my brothers separately," and if he likes to remain with the family, and work with the sons of the farm; beloved wife, Elizabeth, and my brother Nathaniel Green, Executors; witnesses, Seth K. Kenckley—Charles Bakelshymer and David McIntire. *Ibid.*, 20.

Early Wills of Orange County, Indiana
(Abstracts and Notes)
By Mrs. N. B. Mavity

Baker, James.[1] Will executed June 1, 1816—probated June 20, 1816—wife, Polly. Children: John, James, Jinny—executors: Hugh Holmes of Orange County, Indiana and Larkin Davis of Jessamine County, Kentucky—witnesses: Richard L. Kirby, John Scott and Nancy Kirby.

Holliday, Robert.[2] Will—February 13, 1816—probated November 20, 1816—wife, Hannah—children: Abigail, Mary, Jacob, Henry, Robert, Deborah, Hannah, Rebecca, John—executors: sons Henry and Robert.

Gawdy (Goudy), William. Will—September 2, 1816—probate not given—to Catherine Hamilton of Pittsburgh, Pennsylvania, $15.00—rest of estate to Sarah Gawdy of Chambersburg, a minor, in care of Samuel Cooper of Chambersburg, Pennsylvania—witnesses: Eleanor Chambers, John McVey, Thomas Lindley, gentleman Thomas Fulton, executor.

Wells, William.[3] Will—October 16, 1814—probated, April 16, 1817 —wife, Esther—children: Joseph, Nathan, John, Esther, Sarah, Charity, Stephen, Susannah Ray, Elizabeth Cameron, William.

Burgar, Michael. Will—January 24, 1818—probated (date not given—wife, Elizabeth—children: John, James, Elizabeth, Mary, Hannah, Daniel—executors: wife Elizabeth and son John—witnesses: Evan Jones, Thomas Atkinson.

Johnson, David. Will—June 21, 1817—probated February 18, 1818— wife, Peggy—children: Joseph, Jesse, Sarah, David, Lydia, Ephriam Wesley, Ruthey, Eli Burket, Matilda, Thomas—executor (not given)— witnesses: James Gregory, Joseph Anderson, Beverly Gregory.

Morris, Benjamin. Will—October 28, 1818—probated November 23,

---

[1] The son John, mentioned in the will of James Baker, was born in Woodford County, Kentucky, near Versailles, October 12, 1812. His parents brought him to Indiana in 1815. He became a prominent lawyer and lived in Bedford, Indiana, many years; moved to Vincennes in 1859, and later to Washington, Indiana. His father, James Baker, was born in Orange County, Virginia, in 1785, moved to Kentucky in 1805 and came to Orange County, Indiana, in 1815, as stated above, where he died in 1816. John Baker married Sarah Delard, daughter of John Delard, who was born in Mercer County, Kentucky, in 1798. His father, Ettienne Delard, of South Carolina, born in 1767, was a Revolutionary soldier and of Huguenot descent as stated in Goodspeed's *History of Knox and Davies Counties, Indiana* (1886, pp. 192, 310). Polly Baker, wife of James, is said to have been a Davis, sister of Larkin Davis, who entered land in the north part of Paoli Township, and is buried there. They were children of Thomas Davis, a Revolutionary soldier. Mrs. Alleyna Brown McNabb, of the John Wallace Chapter, D.A.R., of Bedford, Indiana, is a member on the record of Thomas Davis. James Baker, Jr., the second son, mentioned in the will, was born in Woodford County, Kentucky, March 29, 1814; married Sarah Burgess in 1834 according to the account in Goodspeed's *History of Lawrence, Orange and Washington Counties, Indiana* (1884, p. 662). Jane (Jinny) Baker, born in 1816, married Dr. James Dillard.

[2] Hinshaw's *Encyclopedia of American Quaker Genealogy* (1936, I, p. 436) gives the record of the Holliday family, with dates, including the name and dates of another son, William. Robert Holliday was the son of Henry and Mary Holliday (p. 399 of last reference in note 1). Robert and Hannah Holliday were born in Chester County, Pennsylvania. Hannah was the daughter of John and Mary Newlin Holliday.

[3] Miss Mabel Claxton, of French Lick, Indiana, has the Revolutionary record of Nathan Wells. He is said to be buried at Lick Creek Quaker Cemetery, in Orange County, but the grave is not marked. Miss Claxton has, also, the Revolutionary record of Joseph Wells, from North Carolina.

1818—wife, Jane—children: William, Nancy and infants—executor and witnesses (not given).

Brouen (Braven), David. Will—July 4, 1818—probated January 26, 1819—wife, Abigail—children: David, James, Mary, Wilson, Janie, Betsy—executor and witnesses (not given).

Burtner, John. Will—April 20, 1820—probated September 6, 1820 —wife, Elizabeth and her mother, Juliann Burtner—these to be executors—witnesses: John Haynes, Joshua Carter, Martin Outsinger.

Riley, Edward. Will—August 9, 1819—probated April 14, 1820— wife, Elizabeth and son, Edward—other legatees, Mary Hogg, Elener Wilson, Abraham Riley, John Riley, James Riley, Thomas Riley, William Riley, Isaac Riley, Jacob Riley, Elizabeth Roads, Sally Hart—witnesses: Isaac and James Riley—executors (not given).

Raymond, David. Will—August 20, 1818, at Huntsville, Alabama— probated April 16, 1820. (This is a lengthy will, evidently by a man of some wealth. Wife, deceased. Father-in-law living, name given, Timothy Leonard. Brother, Daniel Raymond, mentioned. In accordance with wishes of his deceased wife $100 to be presented to her friend, Mary W. G. Howe of Bennington, Vermont. Books to be presented to the following, as was the wish of deceased wife: to his brother, Daniel and James; to her brothers, Frederick and Edward; to Thomas Perkins, to Emily Hodges, to Hester Lancing, to Sarah Hull. Testator's sister Sarah and his wife's sister Mary to be models, in education of his daughter. Sister Abigail and her children mentioned).

Freeman, Daniel. Will—October 6, 1822—probated October 22, 1822 —wife, Jane—sons, Joshua, Daniel—daughters, Rebecca McVey, Fanny Bradford—witnesses—Joshua Hadley and Aaron Maris—executor (not given).

Jones, Evan. Will—September 29, 1821—probated October 22, 1822 —wife, Sarah—children: John, David, Samuel, Mary, Sarah, Evan, Lucinda, Isaac B., William—executor and witnesses (not given).

Doak, Joseph W.[4] Will—July 5, 1820—probated October 29, 1822— wife, Polly—children (referred to but not named)—executor and witnesses (not given).

Copelin, Ann. Will—August 10, 1821—probated November 30, 1822 —Ann, widow of Jacob, bequeaths to son Thomas, etc.—witnesses: J. Moser, James Clements.

Lockhart, William. Will—November 15, 1822—probated December 10, 1822—wife, Hannah—daughter, Peggy—and heir of Rachel Underwood—executor and witnesses (not given).

Hollowell, Jesse. Will—December 6, 1820—probated, December 17, 1822—wife, Elizabeth—children: James, John, Mary, Sally, Jesse Woodard—executors: John Hollowell and his son Henry (brother and nephew of deceased).

Briner, Peter. Will—January 23, 1823—probated April 21, 1823—

---

[4] Joseph W. Doak was the great grandfather of N. B. Navity, of French Lick, Indiana. His wife was Mary (Polly) Irvin, daughter of Samuel Irvin, Revolutionary soldier. Robert Doak was a son. A daughter, Jane Doak, married Samuel Lynd, and another daughter, Martha, married Isaac Potter. There is a Doak family history, but we do not have this volume.

wife, Catherine—children: Elizabeth Robbins, Catherine Walker, Mary Cook, John, Andrew, George, Peter.

Hoemler (Hemler), John. Will—March 10, 1823 (?)—probated, April 21, 1823—wife, Catherine—children (referred to but not named) —"Land in Illinois, a tract appropriated for Military bounties"— latter's tools mentioned—executors: Ephriam Doan and his wife—witnesses: Joseph Athon, William Rhodes, Ebenezer Doan. (Hoemler must have been a soldier, since he had the land mentioned. Ephriam Doan was a hatter, who lived at Paoli).

Clark, Robert. Will—July 1, 1823—probated, August 23, 1823—wife, Alley Clark—One dollar to be paid to the following: Presley Allgood, Jesse Hutchins, Benjamin Melone, Elizabeth Allgood, Lydia Hutchins —grandchildren mentioned (Presley Allgood's children and the children of Jesse Hutchins)—witnesses: James Curry, Thomas Copelin.

Rayburn, Cornelius (known as Neely Rayburn). Will—September 26, 1823—probated, October 11, 1823—wife, Bethilda—children: Andrew, James, Sarah—witnesses: Lewis Byram, Henry B. Prentiss.

Wells, Joseph. Will—September 11, 1823—probated October 20, 1823 —children: Isaac, Zachariah, Charity Freeman, Nathan, Levi, Peter, Jonathan, Jesse—executors: Ephriam Doan and Joseph Farlow.

Dixon, John. Will—September 9, 1823—probated January 30, 1824 —wife, Ruth—children: Elizabeth Marshall, Rebecca Towell, Simon Dixon, Rachel Hobson, Ruth Doan, Amy Hiatt, John, Solomon, Zacharias, Thomas Elwood, Levina Dixon.

Warden, William. Will—May 4, 1824—probated June 19, 1824— wife, Katherine—children (referred to)—mention of lands in Kentucky—witnesses: Joel Vandeveer, Mary Crutchfield.

Allen, Peleg R. Will—April 16, 1825—probated May 25, 1825— wife, Ann B. Allen—("My dear sister Hannah Spooner". In case of my wife's death before my own, I appoint as executors, my friends, Dr. Burr Bradley, of Salem, Indiana, and Dr. William Scribner of Paoli, Frederick B. Leonard, student of medicine of Lansingburg, N.Y., John B. Chipman, merchant, of Lansingburg, N.Y., and Dr. Elisah Sheldon and Gershom Clark, druggist of Troy, N.Y., and Philander Chase, Bishop of the diocese of Ohio, to have full and complete power to make disposal of my property. To the 3 sons of my deceased brother John Allen, and the 5 sons of my sister Hannah Spooner, the title to my lands on White River, in the Pride Settlement. To all that may fall to me by will from my wife, from the estate of Timothy Leonard, deceased, to the American Tract Society, the Ohio Protestant Episcopal Society, for Missionary purposes, the Theological Seminary of the Protestant Episcopal Church, in the diocese of Ohio, the Missionary Society of Indiana, to be expended in this state, to be divided equally, each alike. Frederick B. Leonard mentioned as a brother-in-law. (Dr. Allen was one of Paoli's early physicians. See will of David Raymond, in this list, whose wife was a sister of Dr. Allen's wife).

Smith, Jacob. Will—August 13, 1824—probated June 10, 1825— wife, Susannah—son, Ambrose—daughters: Polly, Eliza, Dilla, Lucy, Frances (the daughters were under 18 years)—witnesses: John Chenoweth, Aaron Vandeveer.

Nichols, Nathan. Will—December 16, 1823—probated July 7, 1825 —wife, Nancy—children: Simeon, George, Silas, Nathan, Thomas, John, Jennie, Sally, Nancy, William J., Cyrus E., Hugh H., Martin M.— executors: wife (Nancy) and Thomas Copeland.

Davis, Mary. Will—September 2, 1823—probated August 5, 1825 —to grandchildren: Jonathan, Joseph, Mary, Martha Woodard, Margaret Bouge (?)—to his daughter, Elizabeth Hollowell—witnesses: Alexander Morris, Washington Morris, James Hollowell.

Darroch, Daniel. Will—November 29, 1825—probated December 22, 1825—wife, Nancy—brother, Duncan—witnesses: John Maris, Abraham Holliday.

Wilson, Joseph. Will—February 4, 1824—probated April 13, 1826— wife, Mary—sons: Joseph, Andrew, Nathaniel—daughters: Margaret Fields and Rachel Fields. (Joseph Wilson was a Revolutionary soldier. On June 5, 1938, a Government marker was dedicated by the D.A.R. Chapter in Orangeville Township, Orange County, Indiana).

Thomas, Lewis. Will—February 4, 1824—probated April 13, 1826 —beloved wife (name not given)—children: Ruth, Tilden, Lewis, Joseph, Stephen—one dollar each to be given to Charles Bouchman, John Bouchman, Burrell Graham, Eli Morris, James Atkinson, William Trueblood, Daniel Lambdin—executors: his son Tilden and his beloved friend Shadrach Ditto.

Carr, Michael. Will—December 23, 1826—probated February 19, 1872—daughter, Betsy Carr, to be executor—bequests to Michael Lindsay, Thomas G. Carr, Polly Lindsay, James Carr, Samuel Campbell, Margaret Mitchell, heirs of William Carr: Amanda, Polly, Emily. (Miss Josephine Lindsay of Mitchell, Indiana, has records of this family).

Wood, Francis. Will executed September 11, 1827—probated October 6, 1827—to Sarah Ann Perrott, daughter of Samuel Perrott, certain lands, etc.—should Sarah Ann not live to have an heir, the property to be divided among Peter Ragle, John Ragle, Margaret Ragle, Susan Ragle, and Samuel Perrott's three children—property in Orleans mentioned—proved by two subscribing witnesses: G. Berry and James Perrott.

Freeman, Jane. Will—April 26, 1827—probated August 23, 1827— mentions daughters Fanny Bradford and Rebecca McVey, granddaughter Sarilda Freeman, grandson Zeno Blanchard Freeman, sons John, Daniel, and Joshua—to my granddaughter Jane Doan, one picture, a dish, the chaise, and Richard Davidson's Journal.[2]

Glover, Stephen. Will—October 27, 1826—probated November 22, 1827—mentions wife Sally, children Mariah, William, Robert, James, Huldah, Jane, Sarah, Nathan.[3]

Lindley, Jonathan. Will—September 22, 1824—probated April 22, 1828—mentions wife Martha, daughter Gulielma and other children: Jonathan, Catherine McVey, Thomas, William, Sarah Hadley, Deborah Jones, Hannah Braxton, Mary Dixon, Queen Esther Lindley, Elenor Chambers, Rebecca Henley, Zacharias, Jonathan Dix, and sister, De-

[2] See Will of Daniel Freeman, husband of Jane Freeman, *ibid.*, 385.
[3] Stephen Glover was the son of Uriah Glover, said to have been a Revolutionary soldier. See *Indiana Magazine of History* (March, 1938), XXXIV, 135.

borah Newlin—books to be divided among the children—"My big Bible is bequeathed to Martha, then to go to Gulielma."[4] (The will is very lengthy and disposes of large amounts of property. The pages in the will record are quite soiled; probably no will in the book has been more widely read and copied.)

Lindley, Thomas.[5] Will—May 3, 1828—probated May 22, 1828—mentions wife, Amy, and children: William, Samuel, John, Mary, Thomas Elwood.

Elrod, Robert. Will—July 6, 1828—probated September 9, 1828—mentions wife Elizabeth, and children: Noah, Sarah, Stephen, Benjamin, John, Robert, Elizabeth Evans.

Blackburn, Joseph. Will—July 22, 1828—probated September 25, 1828—Joseph Blackburn of Paoli, late from Bedford County, Pennsylvania—brother-in-law, Joseph Potts of Paoli, to hold all of estate for infant daughter, Jane Eliza Blackburn. In case of death of daughter before reaching maturity, the estate to go to testator's brother Lewis, of Ohio, and brothers Samuel, John, Josiah, sister Esther, brother-in-law John Potts, sister-in-law Elizabeth Fou, formerly Potts, Mary Belek, formerly Potts, nephew Josiah Penrose, infant son of William Penrose, all of Bedford County, Pennsylvania, said Joseph Potts, sister-in-law Sarah, now of Paoli, and sister Margaret Blackburn of Bedford County, Pennsylvania. Witnesses: Daniel Dayhuff, Z. Lindley, Ephraim Doan, C. F. Spooner.

Lindley, Owen. Date of execution of will missing—probated July 21, 1828—mentions wife Grace and children: James, Thomas, Aaron, Sarah McVey, Martha Thompson, Polly Hollowell, Queen Amy, Elizabeth, Elener, Grace, David, Owen, Chambers.—witnesses: Thomas Newlin, Aaron Andrew, Silas Dixon.

Ribble, John. Will—June 2, 1828—probated January 17, 1829—mentions wife Margaret and children: John Strite, Lorran, Barbary, Catherine, Susan, Sarah Ruth.

Gwinn, Isom. Will—October 26, 1830—probated January 6, 1831—wife Mary, children mentioned but names not given.

Cox, Joseph. Will—November 17, 1818—probated February 18, 1831—wife Mary, children mentioned but names not given.

Clifton, William. Will—March 30, 1831—probated May 31, 1831—wife Jenny, children mentioned but names not given—executors: wife and Calramdor Reubison.

Jones, Samuel. Will—March 29, 1831—probated July 7, 1831—mentions wife Amelia, sons: Moses, David, Samuel; presumably daughters: Elizabeth Woodward and Nancy Busick—Littleton Woodward and wife are mentioned as "living in my house."—executor, Thomas Vandeveer.

Pearce, Philip Crafford. Will—Octover 9, 1829—probated August 10, 1831—wife Catherine—to Berilla Elliot, one bed and bedding—Absolem McCabe to take part of real estate when wife's interest shall cease.[6]

[4] This Bible is in the possession of Miss Mary Cammack, Plainfield, Indiana, a granddaughter of Gulielma (Lindley) Woody.
[5] Thomas Lindley, son of Jonathan Lindley, whose will appears above.
[6] This family is of Southeast Township, Orange County, Indiana.

Freeman, Benjamin. Will—September 17, 1831—probated April 2, 1832—mentions wife Polly[7] and sons: Hilliman, Benjamin, George, John, William—other legatees: heirs of daughter Sidney; sons of Gabriel Freeman, deceased: Benjamin and Edmund; heirs of daughter Sally, deceased, first wife of Levi Johnson.

Cutsinger, Martin. Will—December 12, 1831—probated May 21, 1832—no wife mentioned—children: Jacob, Catherine Freit, Elizabeth Freit, Michael, Polly Sparling, Margaret Gammon, William, Sally Cutsinger, Martin.

Webb, Martin. Will—November 24, 1828—date probated omitted on record—mentions wife Martha and children: Andrew, John, William, Nancy, Caty, and "one she is like for."

Gifford, Levi. Will—August 5, 1832—probated September 15, 1832 mentions wife Mararet and sons: Peleg, Jesse, Levi; surviving children of Abagail and Daniel Ellis.

White, Joseph. Will—February 8, 1833—probated May 13, 1833—mentions wife Jane and eldest son; other legatees: Sarah Williams, the heirs to Elizabeth Williams, the heirs of Polly Hinton, Hannah Standeford, Ephriam Linn, Jane White, Amelia White—Hannah Standeford to have a certain tract of land during her life, and same then to go to her children: William, Wesley, John Robison, and Joseph Wright.—witnesses: William Case, Jane Hutchison.

Towell, Jesse, Jr. Will—July 21, 1833—probated December 9, 1833 —mentions wife (name not given), infant daughters Parthena and Mary Ann; wife's sister Margaret White, son John W. Towell.—executor, John Towell, Sr., his father.

wife Elizabeth—witnesses: John Prosses, Hiram Kirk, Alfred Bruner.

Byram, Lewis. Will—April 25, 1834—probated August 11, 1834— wife Elizabeth—witnesses: John Prosses, Hiram Kirk, Alfred Bruner.

Bond, Reuben. Will—June 25, 1834—Probated August 4, 1834— mentions wife Penelope, children: Martha, Jane, John, Martha Anelya, Mary Ann, Henrietta—executor, Ezer Cleveland. A will made in South Carolina is revoked.[8]

McCracken, Robert. Will—September 20, 1834—probated November 11, 1834—mentions son Thomas, Eleanor McCracken and other children: John, Peter, Robert, Lucy, Shade, Elizabeth Street, Polly.

Towell, Jesse, Sr. Will—May 4, 1834—probated June 2, 1834— mentions wife of son John and her many kindnesses, and his daughters: Rebecca Hadley, Mary Piggott, Margaret Hadley; children of Sarah Harvey, deceased.—son Daniel mentioned in an added note—executor, son John—witnesses: Thomas Newlin, Solomon Cox.

Lindley, Thomas. Will—November 23, 1835—probated December 14, 1835—mentions sons Reuben and Thomas, and daughters: Jane Green, Sarah Andrew, Mary Newlin, Hannah Cloud, Eleanor Love— executor, John Cloud—witnesses: David Lindley, Samuel Lindley.[9]

---

[7] The first wife of Benjamin Freeman was Margaret Divine. They were married in Mercer County, Kentucky, in 1786. Polly Watts, mentioned as his wife in the will, was a second wife.

[8] Reuben Bond is said to have been a well-respected colored man of Northwest Township, Orange County, Indiana.

[9] Jane Andrew Maris, my grandmother, was the daughter of Sarah Andrew, daughter of Thomas Lindley.

Evans, Caleb. Will—Orleans, Indiana, August 20, 1835—probated October 22, 1835—"I, Caleb Evans a citizen of Chester County, Pennsylvania . . . . "—effects in tse hands of John B. Moyer, innkeeper at Orleans, Indiana, horse, saddle, bridle, clothing, saddlebags, valise, $495.00 cash—mentions sisters: Mary Gibbs, wife of William Gibbs, Ann Merrydith, wife of Richard Merrydith, of West Caln Township, Chester County, Pennsylvania, Leah Patton, wife of T. H. Patton of Salisbury Township, Lancaster County, Pennsylvania—mentions also Caleb Evans, Jr., son of Joseph and Zilpha Evans of Huntington County, Pennsylvania.

Holliday, Hannah. Will—April 12, 1829—probated October 17, 1835—mentions son Henry, housekeeper, Jane Hadley—residue of estate to be sold and divided agreeable to the will of her deceased husband—witnesses: John McDaniel, Aaron Andrew.

Erton, Peter. Will—September 21, 1835—probated November 28, 1835—to son-in-law, Thomas Bedster and his wife Matilda, real estate and personal property—to Zachariah Green and his wife, one dollar—to son Henry Erton, one dollar—to son-in-law John Teter and his wife Nancy, one dollar—witnesses: James Wilson, Azor Wilson. (The testator was a Revolutionary War pensioner.)

Johnson, Lancelot. Will—September 3, 1836—probated September 25, 1836—wife Nancy R. Johnson; children mentioned, but names not given.

Millis, Enoch. Will—February 29, 1836—probated May 14, 1836—mentions wife **Susannah,** brother **Nichosan** and sons: Edward and Jacob, under 21 years of age—daughters: Polly, Lydia Ann, Sarah Jane, Hester Ellen. This is a very lengthy will, much land is described.

Willson, Absolem. Will—April 10, 1835—proved May 5, 1835—mentions daughters Priscilla and Elizabeth; children of daughter Fanny, deceased—witnesses: Isaac Bridgewater, David T. Wilson, Jno. Prosser.

Lindsay, Mary. Will—January 18, 1836—probated March 5, 1836—mentions Polly Case, who had already received some personal property; children: James, Michael, Fulton; the children of his deceased daughter Eliza Vontress, to wit: Susan Lindsay Vontress, Samuel Tyler Vontress, Eliza Lindasy Vontress. Elizabeth Carr estate is mentioned, as is the estate of the testator's father, Michael Carr.

Seybold, Jno. Will—June 10, 1830—probated August 1, 1836—wife Sarah—witnesses: John Moore, Thomas Moore, William Leonard, Reuben Moore.

Carter, Shadrach Blunt Anderson. Will—March 5, 1835—probated April 7, 1835—mentions wife Margaret and children: Elizabeth Kene Vontress (later Conder), Catherine Carpenter, Maria Jane, B. A. Shadrach, Ann Eliza, Margaret, Theophilus, John Conder Carpenter, Harriet Frances, and Henry Carpenter Carter. (This is a very long will.)

Carr, Elizabeth. Will—September 2, 1835—probated September 22, 1835—mentions sister Margaret Mitchell and nieces: Emily Carr, Mary Carr, Susan Mitchell, and Elizabeth Campbell; nephews: Elzey Mitchell,

David Campbell, son of Samuel Campbell, and Michael Lindsay; brothers: Thomas G. and James Carr; sisters Polly Lindsay and Sina Campbell—executors: Samuel Campbell and John Hostutter.

Lynch, Clayton. Will—January 10, 1837—probated February 6, 1837—mentions wife Ann and children: John, William, Pennelajane, James, Mary Elmira, Thomas H., Henry M., George Lynch—executor, Samuel Stalcup.

Lindley, William. Will—December 22, 1835—probated March 7, 1837—mentions wife Annie, and children: Thomas Samuel, James, Owen, William, David, Jonathan, Sally Lee, Mary Lee, Annie Harned, and Grace Wilkins Lindley; the sons of Grace Wilkins: John and William, under 21—executors: sons Owen and William and grandson Thomas.

Ellexson, Jeremiah. Will—executed December 26, 1937—probated February 12, 1838—mentions wife, Winifred—daughters: Mary [Ellexson] Nail of Washington County, Indiana, Zilpha [Ellexson] Rogers, Elizabeth and Winifred—references to other children who are not mentioned by name.

Chandler, William. Will—April 23, 1837—probated May 8, 1837—mentions children: Elizabeth (eldest daughter), Robin, Catherine, Sarah, Isaac, Rachel, William—wife, Mary—Ambors Goff and rest of wife's children—executors: wife (Mary) and Joel Vandeveer.

Duncan, George. Will—December 9, 1838—probated February 21, 1839—mentions wife, Patsy D. Duncan—lawful heirs of daughter Emily B. Riley—"my body to be buried at the discretion of Alexander Wallace and Patsy D. Duncan."[2]

Reed, Joshua.[3] Will—December 24, 1823—probated November term of court, 1838—mentions daughters: Rachel Phillipps, Martha Marts, Mary Mahan—"my body to be buried at discretion of Thomas Phillips, Jacob Marts, and Peter Mahan"—witnesses: Alexander Wallace, Asa Burt, Edward Kearby.

Duncan, George, Sr.[4] Will—June 26, 1832—probated March 23, 1839—mentions wife, Elizabeth—children: Luvina Vest, Sarah Kearby, Jane Boon, Polly Holmes, Fleming A. Duncan, George Duncan—witnesses: Alexander Wallace, Linzey Duncan.

Smith, Humphrey. Will—August 25, 1831—probated August 19, 1839—mentions wife, Abigail—sons of wife, Caleb and Jarvis—son of testator, Allen Smith, Caleb and Jarvis—testator's daughter, Malissa Smith.

Cunningham, William. Will—July 14, 1833—probated October 6, 1839—mentions wife, Deborah—daughters: Elizabeth Buckhanan, Anna Cunningham—son-in-law, John Buckhanan, and his son William.

Trimble, Jane. Will—June 21, 1839—probated October 11, 1839—mentions daughters: Mary, Margaret and Elizabeth Trimble, Sarah Martin, wife of Nathan—sons: Thomas and George—"My late husband, George Trimble."

---

[2] George Duncan was buried at Stamper Creek Cemetery, Orange County, Indiana.
[3] Revolutionary soldier. See Mrs. Roscoe C. O'Bryne, ed., *Roster of Soldiers and Patriots of the American Revolution Buried in Indiana* (Brookville, Indiana, 1938).
[4] Revolutionary soldier. *Ibid.*, 130. He is buried in Stamper Creek Cemetery, Orange County, Indiana.

Boswell, Ichabod. Will—August 21, 1840—probated September 11, 1840—mentions wife, and heirs (none by name)—"My worthy son Samuel Holaday to be executor of my will."

Noblitt, Abraham. Will—August 26, 1840—probated September 21, 1840—mentions wife, Amelia; sons: Vandeveer, William, and John T.; daughters: Nancy Lynch and Cynthia Noblitt.

Hill, Joseph. Will—June 21, 1840—probated October 3, 1840—mentions legal heirs of daughter Elizabeth (late Elizabeth Dixon)—son-in-law, James Huston and Nancy his wife—son-in-law Busick Sanford and wife Jane—son Josiah Hill (daughter, Mary Ann Hill and wife, Nancy Hill)—second wife's children: Franklin, Margaret Jane, William, Joseph, Abigail.

Harmon, Edwin F.[5] Will—October 5, 1839—probated November 11, 1840—mentions mother and father—sisters: Polina and Lavisa Merilla—brother, William Watson—Miss Betsey Brewer.

Sears, John, Sr. Will—April, 1840—probated June 19, 1841—mentions wife, Polly—children: Francis Asbury, Daniel Fletcher, Eliza Ann, Mary Jane, John, William, Franklin, Martha Talbott, Thomas Morris—children of a former marriage: James B. Sears and Elizabeth Gunton.

Featherkile, George. Will—January 1, 1835—probated March 19, 1842—mentions wife, Polly—children: Anna Johnson, Polly Tyler, George Featherkile, Adam Featherkile.

Osborn, Abraham. Will—May 23, 1842—probated July 18, 1842—mentions wife, Martha—sons: Abraham K., William C., Jesse—daughters: Abagail Holaday, Mary Wilson, Rebecca Phipher, Hannah Moorman, Elizabeth Hill, Achsah Osborn, and Sarah Ann Osborn—witnesses: Joseph Henley, Andrew Wilson.

Denny, Simon. Will—September 23, 1837—probated July 19, 1842—mentions sons, Samuel and Davis.

Cloud, John. Will—August 5, 1842—probated September 26, 1842—mentions wife, Hannah—after Hannah's death, property to be sold and funds to go to Lick Creek Monthly Meeting of Friends to be used in the promotion of useful education—witnesses, Aaron Andrew, Thomas Newlin.—executors, Silas Dixon, Levi Woody.

Cornwell, Peter. Will—September 26, 1842—probated October 19, 1842—mentions wife, Elizabeth—children: Simon A., Nancy, William, Elizabeth.

Self, John. Will—August 15, 1843—probated September 12, 1843—mentions wife and children (not by name).

Atkinson, Thomas. Will—November 2, 1840—probated April 20, 1844—mentions children: Thomas, Robert, Arthur, Henry, Ann, Margaret, Ruth, Mary—sons, John and Arthur to be executors.

[5] Edwin Harmon was a brother to William Watson Harmon who was given the contract for the carpenter work for the Orange County Courthouse. He also built the old Presbyterian church and the Simpson home on North Gospel Street at Paoli. The Harmon family came from Massachusetts. They are buried in the Paoli Cemetery.

Busick, Benjamin. Will—April 18, 1944—probated September 2, 1844—mentions wife, Eliza, her heirs and assigns forever.

Ross—William. Will—August 28, 1844—probated December 11, 1844—property bequeathed to Polly, wife of John W. Sears.

Campbell, Robert. Will—February 19, 1845—probated May 27, 1845—certain tract of land where there is a family graveyard to be kept for that purpose—mentions sons: Robert A. M. Campbell (a minor), John H., Samuel, David M.—daughter, Nan Taylor—heirs of "my daughters who are dead.[6]

Farlow, Joseph.[7] Will—July 5, 1845—probated August 9, 1845—mentions wife, Ruth—daughter, Deborah Jones—sons, Jonathan and Nathan—son-in-law, Archibald Moulder and wife Hannah—daughter Mary's children: Mary Ann, Thomas, and Mary.

Moulder, Jacob. Will—October 18, 1845—probated March 20, 1846—mentions wife, Elizabeth—daughter, Susannah Lindley—sons: John, William, Lewis, Archibald, Oliver—daughters: Sally, Lydia, Mary Ann—Betsy Jane and Archibald O. Moulder—children of Alexander Moulder—witnesses, Thomas Braxton and Thomas Newlin.

Throop, John.[8] Will—December 28, 1846—probated February 8, 1847—mentions John S. Moore and Rebecca Jane Moore ("the children of my daughter Jane Moore")—Jane Lefler (my adopted granddaughter)—children: Oliver M. Throop, Jane Moore, Sophia Throop, John T. Throop.

Scott, William. Will—December 14, 1841—probated May 28, 1847—mentions wife, Nancy S. Scott—grandsons, William A. D. Scott and Samuel T. Scott—Martha Jane McPheeters and her heirs—"I reserve one-fourth acre of land, where the graveyard now is, for a family burying place, never to be transferred out of the family."—witnesses: Simeon Frost and Mary Frost.

Leonard, Thomas. Will—January 4, 1843—probated August 18, 1847—mentions wife (not by name)—Jonathan Leonard, Isaac Leonard, Jemima Harvey, James Leonard, Jane Seybold, Rachel Taylor, Nancy Seybold, Mary Compton, Baily Leonard, Jeruel Leonard, Jabez Leonard, and Martha Cox.

Meriam, Eliza.[9] Will—July 8, 1847—probated September 25, 1847—mentions daughter, Helen M. Lewis and her children—mentions desire to be buried in the "burying ground" at Paoli, adjoining the grave of her husband (John Meriam)—executor, John Wise—witnesses: G. W. Wise and A. J. Simpson.

---

[6] See sketch of W. C. Campbell, *History of Lawrence, Orange, and Washington Counties, Indiana* (Chicago, 1884), 605.

[7] Joseph Farlow was a large landowner south of Paoli in the vicinity of the Beech Grove Friends Church.

[8] The Throop family settled at an early date in Orange County, having migrated from Stafford County, Virginia. Miss Sophia Throop is said to have been the first woman teacher of Orange County. Miss Jennie Throop, a granddaughter of John Throop, was a well-known teacher for many years.

[9] Eliza Meriam, wife of John Meriam, died on July 15, 1847, at the age of sixty-one. She was a Prentiss (Prentice) of Vermont. John Meriam was one of the men who founded the town of Hindostan of Martin County, Indiana, one of the famous Hoosier "ghost towns." He came later to Orange County, established a tavern known as "Mansion House," on the public square in Paoli. Mrs. Meriam continued the tavern after her husband's death.

Cook, Jacob. Will—August 11, 1847—probated September 30, 1847—mentions wife, Catharine—sons: Absolem, Abraham, Valentine—daughters: Elizabeth Smith and Polly Underwood—minor heirs of Absolem McCabe (deceased)—grandson David R. Bledsoe.

Moorman, Zachariah. Will—August 9, 1847—probated August 25, 1847—mentions wife, Nancy—children (not by name)—lot No. 84 in Paoli to be sold.[10]

Chastain, William. Will—undated—probated December 11, 1847—mentions wife (not by name)—sons: James M., William, Isaac.

Shirley, Henry. Will—December 22, 1847—probated January 4, 1848—mentions wife, Catherine—children: George, Garrett, John, Westly, Susannah, Harriet, Margaret Hertsel (formerly Shirley), Henry Brassie, heir of Ann Brassie (formerly Ann Shirley), "my scholarship in Indiana Asbury University"—executors: Andrew Wilson and George Shirley.

Porter, James. Will—February 6, 1847—probated February 28, 1848—mentions two eldest sons, Thomas B. and James S.—daughter Mary Hix—youngest son David—executor, James P. Campbell.

Gillum, John. Will—December 3, 1847—probated April 15, 1848—mentions wife, Susannah—children: Mahala, Areana, Cameliza, Leer [Leah?], Seth, Thomas, James, Osburn, William, John Westly—witnesses, Thomas Newlin and Michael Mavity.

Piggott, Jacob Jackson. Will—December 7, 1848—probated December 1848—mentions wife, Nancy—four sons—three daughters (not by name)—brother-in-law, Elijah Frazier, to be executor.

Williams, Francis. Will—July 6, 1846—probated February 29, 1848—mentions daughter, Catherine Boyden—son William—children of deceased daughter Anna Gherkin—executor, William Boyden.

Finley, David. Will—March 25, 1834—probated September 26, 1848—mentions wife, Elizabeth—heirs of son Jefferson Finley: Josephine, Samuel, Elizabeth.

Thornton, Thomas Volney.[11] Will—December 4, 1848—probated May 29, 1849—mentions wife, Clarinda C. Thornton—brothers: Joseph, George, Jefferson C.—sisters: Elizabeth M. Thornton, Caroline T. Woolfolk, Harriet M. Norris—half-brother Henry P. Thornton—Joseph, son of sister Caroline—nephew and namesake, Thomas V. Thornton, son of George.

William, John. Will—May 26, 1849—probated July 19, 1849—mentions wife, Rachel—sons: Isaac, Robert, John—grandson, William Bloomer Carter.

Towell, Jesse H. Will—May 18, 1849—probated August 7, 1849—mentions wife, Elizabeth—witnesses: Thomas Newlin and John Dixon, son of Simon.

[10] The date of death given on Zachariah Moorman's tombstone in the Paoli Cemetery (August 10, 1843) is incorrect.

[11] Thomas Volney Thornton was a prominent lawyer of Paoli. His wife, Clarinda Thornton, "married against discipline," as shown by the minutes of the Lick Creek monthly meeting, held in Orange County, February 19, 1835. The Simpson home on North Gospel Street, Paoli, was built for them and the site for the Presbyterian church of Paoli was given by Mr. Thornton.

Cosgrove, Patrick.[12]—Will—March 15, 1849—probated August 14, 1849—mentions wife, Charity—two sons, John and James.

Self, Thomas. Will—August 19, 1849—probated January 12, 1850 —mentions son, Thomas A. Self—Hannah Stout, an heir—the heirs of Elizabeth Ferguson, to wit: Joseph S. Ferguson, John M. Ferguson —other children: William A., Thomas, John, Phillip, George, James Alexander—executors: son, James Alexander Self, and "my esteemed friend William Holoday"—witnesses: William Pierson, John B. Cartwright.

Pound, Joseph. Will—November 20, 1849—probated April 16, 1850 —mentions son-in-law to be executor—wife Hannah—children and their heirs (not by name)—witnesses: Alfred Elliot and Abraham Tegarden.

Trimble, Moses. Will—January 31, 1848—probated June 15, 1850— mentions James Jackson Trimble, John Dixon Trimble—Jane Belcher's children—Isabell Wolfington to have $30, and her living from the farm while she remains single—Lucinda Leonard and William Trimble to have money—executors: William Marley and William Leonard.

Irvine, William.[13] Will—September, 1846—probated October 18, 1850—mentions sons: William W. and Jesse A.—daughters: Sarah Jeter, Anna Baker, Eliza Spear, Martha McLane—children of deceased daughter—Lucinda Tegarden—"my unfortunate daughter, Jane Irvine."

McCracken, John. Will—September 14, 1850—probated May 29, 1851—mentions wife, Margaret—sons Ansil and Daniel—Azra Cobb's heirs—witnesses: James Clark and John P. Davis.

McDonald, William. Will—April 11, 1851—probated June 18, 1851 —mentions grandchildren: William M. Hobson, Rachel Hobson, Hiram Hobson—executors: Eli Allen and Clement McDonald—witnesses: Jonathan Palmer and Harmon Hobson.

Roberts, Andrew. Will—June 16, 1851—probated August 25, 1851 —mentions wife, Nancy—sons (not by name)—witnesses: Arthur J. Simpson and James C. Holmes.

Hardman, Daniel. Will—July 17, 1851—probated September 29, 1851—mentions six oldest children: Washington, Mary, Lumenious, Leonard, Abraham, John—other sons: David and Marion—wife Elizabeth—house and lots in town of Salem (the property of Margaret Hardman, deceased)—executors: Lumenious Hardman and son-in-law— give youngest children named: David, Marion, Margaret, Peter and Mary Evaline.

Lindley, Martha.[14] Will—November 30, 1830—probated November 27, 1851—to my daughter Gulielma, "the watch which was left to me by her father"—mentions six children: Hezekiah Henley, John Henley, Joseph Henley, Henry Henley, Mary [Henley] Braxton, Rebecca Henley —executors: sons Joseph and Henry Henley—witnesses: Thomas Newlin and Owen Thompson.

---

[12] A soldier of the Mexican War. His wife was Charity Underwood, widow of Benjamin Underwood.

[13] See *Roster of Soldiers and Patriots of the American Revolution Buried in Indiana*, 203.

[14] Martha Henley Lindley was the second wife of Jonathan Lindley. She was a widow whose maiden name was Saunders. Gulielma Lindley was the only child of this marriage.

Reed, Jesse. Will—October 1, 1851—probated January 7, 1852—mentions wife, Elizabeth—children: Henry, Jeremiah, George, William, Margaret.

Scott, Eliza. Will—February 6, 1852—probated March 8, 1852—mentions mother-in-law, Nancy Scott—children: Emily, Martha Ann, William D., Samuel C., Margaret, Hannah C. Hill—executor, Samuel R. McClain [McClane].

McClane, William. Will—January 28, 1852—probated March 8, 1852—mentions wife, Caroline—daughters: Marthy Ann, Mary Elizabeth, Rachel Catherine—brother Samuel R. McClane to be executor—witnesses: Levi Gifford, Sr., and Abraham Wells.

Lewis, John M. Will—April 20, 1837—probated April 30, 1852—mentions wife, Elizabeth—son, David S. Lewis, to be executor together with wife. Codicil dated January 18, 1843, names Joshua Lewis co-executor with David Lewis—codicil dated March 22, 1852—to son Abraham J. Lewis and his heirs, the share of my real estate which would have descended to son George W. Lewis and his heirs.

Magner, Elizabeth Jane. Will—June 18, 1852—probated September 6, 1852—mentions sisters, Mary Ann Magner and Martha Sarah Magner—two brothers who are at home with "my mother," James H. and Orin M. Magner—"brother John, having left home, is not to receive any portion"—witnesses: John Baker and Sarah Magner.

Abstracts of Warrick County, Indiana, Wills, 1814-1839

Thomas J. Dillingham

James, Ellenor. Will dated Feb. 17, 1816; no record of probate. Heirs: sons, Samuel, Lewis, Henry; daughters, Ruth, Ellenor Hay; granddaughter, Ellenor James. Executors: Lewis James, George W. Tevault. Witnesses: Benjamin W. Knox, Britain West. Warrick County, Indiana, Deed Records, 1813-1817, p. 128.

Arnold, Joseph. Will dated June 23, 1814; probated Nov. 11, 1814. Heirs: wife, Hannah; children, John, Rachel, William, Sarah. Executor not given. Witnesses: James Cross, Thomas Lee. Owned land in Muhlenberg County, Kentucky. *Ibid.*, 1817-1819, p. 2.

Winkler, David, Sr. Will dated Dec. 21, 1821; probated Mar. 5, 1822. Heirs: wife, Sarah; sons, Edmond F., Young U., Thomas, John P.; other heirs, Polly Jones, Vashti Wallis, Elizabeth Allison, Joseph, Henry, David and Andrew Winkler. Executors: Joseph and Henry Winkler. Witnesses: John and Thomas Jones, William Smith. *Ibid.*, 9.

Rhodes, Daniel. Will dated Nov. 22, 1818; probated Mar. 1819. Heirs: wife, Mary; children, Daniel, Andrew, Isaac, Sally, William (son by a former marriage). Executors: Joseph Arnold, Mary Rhodes. Witnesses: Henry Rhodes, Jacob Matthews, William G. Buckler. *Ibid.*, 9-10.

Lawrence, David. Will dated Jan. 25, 1818; probated May 31, 1819. Heirs: wife, Sally, and children (names not given). Executor: wife. Witnesses: G. W. Tevault, William Hancock, James Lenn. Wished wife to remove to Tennessee as it would be more convenient to give children schooling. *Ibid.*, 11-12.

Thomas, Westly. Will dated June 28, 1815; recorded Apr. 19, 1823. Heirs: wife, Sarah; daughters, Polly and Cloey Thomas, and an unborn child. Executors: Thomas Downs, David Cazebier, Sarah Thomas. Witnesses: Robert Simmons, Jonathan Chinoweth, Frederick Cazebier. *Ibid.*, 79.

Penrod, John. Will dated Jan. 14, 1823; probated Mar. 12, 1823. Heirs: wife, Sarah; son-in-law, George Mease; children, Elijah, Sarah, Peely (?), Polly, Anny, Lydia, Jacob; other heirs, James Bell and wife Massa, Jonathan Penrod, Hannah Lout. Executor: Isaac Husband, of Pennsylvania, and in case of his death, Alexander Ogle. Witnesses: Thomas Fitzgerald, Alva Parker, Mary D. Tarlton. *Ibid.*, 88-90. An earlier will, dated July 11, 1822, is recorded in *ibid.*, 49.

Stone, Calvin. Will dated Aug. 13, 1823; probated Nov. 19, 1823. Heirs: wife, Polly; four sons (names not given); daughter, Sally. Executors: Polly Stone, Chester Elliott. Witnesses: R. S. Ellis, Rowland Ellis. *Ibid.*, 92-93.

Pasko, Alva.[1] Will dated May 13, 1824; probated Aug. 5, 1824. Heirs: wife, Lucy; son, Otis Bramin. Executors: Chester Elliott, Lucy Pasko. Witnesses: Joseph Baldwin, Alfred Baldwin, Timothy Judd. *Ibid.*, 93-94.

Hargrove, Hezekiah, Sr. Will dated Oct. 14, 1827; probated Oct. 19, 1827. Heirs: sons, Seth, Eldred G. C., Miles B., Hezekiah Harvey, James, John, William; other heirs, William Gray, Isham Kelley. Executors: sons, James, John, and William. Witnesses: Tubby Bloyd, William Day. *Ibid.*, 123.

Karr, John. Will dated Aug. 27, 1827; probated Feb., 1846. Heirs: brothers-in-law, Solomon Vanada, William Briscoe. Executors: same as heirs. Witnesses: Joseph Arnold, Karr Briscoe. Owned land in Livingston County, Kentucky. *Ibid.*, 124; Warrick County, Indiana, Will Records, I (1831-1859), 50.

Lawrence, John. Will dated Jan. 30, 1828; date of probate not given. Heirs: sisters, Susan Alexander, Rebecca Cox, and Mary Loy; brother, David; others, George and Evaline Merret, Elizabeth Loony. No executor named. Witnesses: M. Leeright, Stephen Merret. Warrick County, Indiana, Deed Records, 1827-1829, p. 125.

Smith, Harvey. Will dated Nov. 20, 1828; probated Jan. 5, 1829. Heirs: wife, Anner. Executors: wife and Alpha Frisbie. Witnesses: Thomas Day, Robert McClary, James E. Lowell. *Ibid.*, 125.

Tevault, George W., of Ohio Twp. Will dated Jan. 11, 1829; probated Jan. 29, 1829. Heirs: daughter, Naomi Bullet; son, William G.

---

[1] Pasko, Boonville's first physician, died August 2, 1824, age 37. The sale bill of his estate, including medical equipment and supplies, is recorded in Warrick County, Indiana, Record Book, IIa, in the Recorder's Office, Boonville, Indiana.

H. Tevault. Executor: Moses P. Condict. Witnesses: James Phillips, Lyndon Hines, John Cox, Ross B. Duncan, Ira H. Bostwick. *Ibid.*, 126.

Van Kirk, Richard and Rhoda. Joint will dated July 10, 1829. Date of probate not given. Heir: son, Joseph. Witnesses: Morgan and Fielden G. Glenn. Owned property in Daviess County, Kentucky. *Ibid.*, 128.

Roberts, William H. Will dated Aug. 9, 1828; probated Mar. 6, 1831. Heirs: children, Leanna Young, William, Jane Clem, Elizabeth Miller, Solomon, Thomas; Anna Brant (relationship not given). Executors: William Roberts, Brittain Glenn. Witnesses: Samuel Horton, Nathaniel Woodruff. Warrick County, Indiana, Will Records, I, 1.

Adams, Joseph. Will dated Mar. 31, 1831; probated May 5, 1831. Heirs: wife, Nancy. Executor: wife. Witnesses: Thomas Hudspeth, Edward Baker, Jacob Harpole, Jacob Hargrove. *Ibid.*, I, 2.

Bostwick, Ira. Will dated Aug. 10, 1831; probated Aug. 13, 1831. Heirs: wife, Calista. Executor: Olney Hines. Witnesses: B. W. Love. William H. Tevault, L. Bostwick. *Ibid.*, I, 3.

Baldwin, Joseph. Will dated Jan. 11, 1832; probated Feb. 26, 1832. Heirs: wife, Sarah; children, Alanson, Alfred, Polly Fitzgerald, Eliza Smith, Mariah Graham, Lorinda Matthewson, Minerva Minor, Emeline Baldwin. Executor: wife. Witnesses: George Whitman, Joseph W. Camp. *Ibid.*, I, 3.

Scott, James C. Will dated June 30, 1832; probated July 11, 1832. Heirs: wife, Anna; sons, James and Joseph. Executor: wife. Witnesses: David Hall, Tubby Bloyd. *Ibid.*, I, 4.

Harned, Jonathan. Will dated Aug. 13, 1831; probated Oct. 17, 1831. Heirs: wife, Elizabeth. Executor: John A. Graham. Witnesses: John B. King, W. Barker, N. A. Hanks. *Ibid.*, I, 5.

Gentry, Shelton. Will dated Oct. 30, 1833; probated Nov. 10, 1833. Heirs: wife, Sarah; children, Jesse, David, Nancy, Jane, Susannah, Polly, Elizabeth. Executors: John Phillips, Thomas Stephenson. Witnesses: George Gentry, Z. Skelton. *Ibid.*, I, 6.

Drake, James. Will dated Mar. 30, 1834; probated Apr. 4, 1834. Heirs: father and mother, sister, Atis Drake, E. T. Coe. Executor: Elias T. Coe. Witnesses: Zabina Lovejoy, Edward Baker, James Arnold. *Ibid.*, I, 7.

Hudson, Isaac. Will dated Feb. 14, 1834; probated June 25, 1834. Heirs: wife, Nancy; grandson, William McMurtry; children, Isaac, Daniel, Enoch, Sally Hinman, Matilda Patterson, Polly Hinman, Betsey Wilder. Executors: Isaac Hudson, James Hinman. Witnesses: J. A. Brackenridge, Mark Taylor. *Ibid.*, I, 8.

Miller, Phillip Henry. Will dated Oct. 10, 1834; probated Nov. 8, 1834. Heirs: wife, Anna; sons, John, Benjamin H., Isaac, Hiram, William M.; Sally Sheets (relationship not given). Executors: William Luce, John G. Jukes. Witnesses: Larken Bristow, John G. Jukes. Property in Muhlenberg County, Kentucky. *Ibid.*, I, 10-12.

Johnson, Jacob. Will dated July 31, 1833; probated Nov. 22, 1834. Heirs: wife, Fariby; children, Warren, Jeremiah, Albert L., Nancy, Kelley, Jacob, Minas, Zachariah, Polly. Executors: Jacob and Kelley

Johnson. Witnesses: J. C. Graham, Abraham Hougland, J. A. Graham, James McCulla. *Ibid.*, I, 13-15.

Frame, Daniel. Will dated Aug. 29, 1835; probated Sep. 17, 1835. Heirs: wife, name not given. Executor: Edward Baker. Witnesses: G. H. Roberts, Thomas J. Williams. *Ibid.*, I, 16-17.

Frame, James H., of Ohio Township. Will dated Nov. 10, 1835; probated Dec. 7, 1835. Heirs: wife, Elizabeth; daughter, Martha Caroline Frame. Executors: John B. and William H. Frame. Witnesses: John B. and William H. Frame, Timothy Butler. *Ibid.*, I, 18.

Hargrave, Seth. Will dated Apr. 24, 1836; probated May 28, 1836. Heirs: 3 children, names not given. To be buried in burying ground at Bakers near his wife's grave. Executors: Francis M. Ashley and William Gray. Witnesses: H. H. Hargrave, Polly C. Day. *Ibid.*, I, 19.

Campbell, William. Will dated Jan. 30, 1837; probated May 6, 1837. Wife, Elizabeth; children, William Webb, William Hargrave, Cutbird Williams, Thomas Campbell; grandchildren, William C., Hugh, and Lettice Ward. Executors: William Webb and William Hargrave. Witnesses: J. A. Graham, James H. Condict. *Ibid.*, I, 20.

Taylor, George, of Taylorsville (now Selvin). Will dated Aug. 25, 1837; probated Oct. 27, 1837. Heirs: wife, Edney, and 5 youngest children; older children married and have received their share. Names of children not given. Executor: wife. Witnesses: William Jones, of Jonesboro, Spencer County; Norman Roberts, Warrick County. *Ibid.*, I, 21.

Bryant, William, of Ohio Township. Will dated Jan. 24, 1837; probated Feb. 20, 1838. Heirs: wife and children, names not given. Money owing to him from Horatio T. Bryant. Executor: William Perry. Witnesses: M. P. Condict, Moses Smith, James Foshee (?). *Ibid.*, I, 22.

Condict, Philip L. Will dated Apr. 11, 1839; probated Apr. 27, 1839. Heirs: brother, E. B. L. Condict, sister, Emeline Igleheart and her 2 children, Moses C. and John D. Igleheart, nephew, Philip M. Condict, other brothers and sisters, names not given. Executor: Moses P. Condict. Witnesses: E. B. L. Condict, Christopher Lockyear. *Ibid.*, I, 23, 50.

Ellis, Roland. Will dated Nov. 4, 1838; probated July 27, 1839. Heirs: wife; son, Roland S. Ellis; granddaughter, Malinda Ellis; daughters, Polly Stone, Abigail Elliott, Zelpha Fuquay. Executor: son, R. S. Ellis. Owned land in section 6, T 6 S, R 8 W. Witnesses: J. C. Graham, Elizabeth B. Smith, J. A. Graham. *Ibid.*, I, 24-25.

Dorsey, ———.[2] Unwritten will dated July 16, 1839; probated July 23, 1839. Heirs: wife and children, names not given. Sworn to by John McCord and Austin Kelley. *Ibid.*, I, 25.

Baker, John McCord. Will dated Sep. 15, 1839; probated Oct. 3, 1839. Heirs not named. Executors: Edward Baker and John D. Littlepage, to dispose of estate as they see fit after debts are paid. Witnesses: Simon Lewis, Stephen Ravenscraft, J. A. Lamb. *Ibid.*, I, 26.

Abstracts of Early Wayne County Wills

Symons, Jesse. Will dated January 8, 1812; proved April 22, 1812. Heirs: sons, Thomas, Nathan, Jesse; daughter, Lydia Bell; granddaughters, Sarah and Lydia Symons. Owned land in section 22, township 16 north, range 12 east. Executors: son Jesse and John Smith. Witnesses: William Pike, Daniel Trimble. Wayne County Will Records, 1812-30, pp. 1-2.

Little, Jacob, Sr. Will dated November 24, 1812; proved February 22, 1813. Heirs: wife, Hannah Little; children, Abraham, Lewis, Peter, Jacob, Charity Barfield, Mary March, Christina Jones; grandson, Laban Garner. Executor: George Hunt. Witnesses: Jacob Rupe, Henry Fender, William Durham. *Ibid.*, 2-4.

Sutherland, William. Will dated March 25, 1815; proved July 17, 1815. Heirs: wife, Lydia Sutherland; children, John, William, Betsy, David, Hannah, Anna, Forger, Nancy. Executors: Andrew Woods, son John. Witnesses: George Hunt, Joseph Davisson. *Ibid.*, 4-5.

Way, Henry. Will dated May 29, 1815; proved October Term 1815. Heirs: wife, Charloty; sons, Seth, Joseph, Paul, Nathan; daughters, Rachel Way, Lydia Frisbee (?), Mary Brock; younger children, Anne, Charloty, Henry, William. Executors: wife and son Seth. Witnesses: James Morrison, Benjamin Hutchens, Joseph Ladd. *Ibid.*, 5-7.

Fouts, Daniel. Will dated September 25, 1815; proved February 26, 1816. Heirs: wife, Sally; daughters, Polly, Sally; sons, Noah, Jesse. Owned northwest quarter of section 18, township 12 north, range 1 west. Executor: George Hunt. Witnesses: Andrew Fouts, Isaac Esteb. *Ibid.*, 7-8.

Whitehead, Lazarus. Will dated February 4, 1815; proved January 31, 1816. Heirs: wife, Martha; children, Lazarus, John, Martha Hunt, Polly Hunt. Owned land in North Carolina. Executors: sons John and Lazarus. Witnesses: John Ellis, Stephen Williams. *Ibid.*, 9-10.

Bonine, Daniel. Will dated September 25, 1815; proved August 5, 1816. Heirs: wife, Mary; children of deceased daughter, Mary John; daughters, Hannah Copeland, Elizabeth Burgher, Sarah Jones, Rachel Williams, Rebekah Hoover, Ann, Lydia; sons, David, Isaac, Thomas, and James. Member of Friends Church. Executors: sons David and Isaac. Witnesses: Jonathan Townsend, David Willis, Jonathan Brattain. *Ibid.*, 10-11.

Lewis, William. Will dated March 13, 1816; proved June 1, 1816. Heirs: wife, Hannah; children, Martha, Thomas, William, Elizabeth, James, Preston (?) Applebury, Cynthia Lewis. Member of Friends Church. Executors: wife, Nathan Farlow, Samuel Stover. Witnesses: Richard G. Paris, Lewis L. Canada, Garizon (?) Dawson. *Ibid.*, 12-13.

Hawkins, John. Will not dated; proved March 5, 1816. Heirs: wife (name not given); children, Nathan, James, Martha Comer, Mary Comer, Sarah Cook, Ann Hawkins, Rebecca Hawkins, Tamar (or Lamar) Smith, Lydia Wright, William. Owned land in South Carolina on a branch of Tyger River called Long Run and in section 27 & 28 on Whitewater River. Executors: sons Amos and John (not mentioned in list of heirs). Witnesses: Jacob Jessop, William McClain, Isaac Jessop. *Ibid.*, 13-14.

Price, William. Will dated April 26 (?), 1817; proved May 3, 1817. Heirs: wife, Sally, and children (names not given). Executors: Abijah Cain, Caleb Smith. Witnesses: George Smith, ——— Cox. *Ibid.*, 27.

Greene (or Grave?), Jacob. Will dated February 13, 1817; proved June 2, 1817. Heirs: granddaughters, Esther and Lydia, daughters of deceased son, John; daughter-in-law, Mary, widow of son John; sons, Enos, Jonathan, Jacob, Nathan. Executor: son Jacob. Witnesses: John Thomas, William Starbuck, Jeremiah Cox, Jr. *Ibid.*, 28-29.

Willis, Jesse. Will dated May 5, 1817; proved October 13, 1817. Heirs: wife, Sarah; children, Isaac, John, David, William, Jesse, Rachel, Mary. Executors: John Canaday, son Isaac. Witnesses: Elihu Swain, John Canaday. *Ibid.*, 29-31.

Higgins, William. Letters of administration in the estate of Higgins granted to Jehu Perkins, January 27, 1818. *Ibid.*, 32.

Hunt, Samuel. Letters of administration in the estate of Hunt granted to Beal Butler and Caleb Harvey, November 27, 1817. *Ibid.*, 32-33.

Porter, Jerry. Letters of administration in the estate of Porter granted to Thomas Brierly, February 24, 1818. *Ibid.*, 33-34.

Miller, Christian. Will dated March 27, 1818; proved May Term 1818. Heirs: wife, Catharina; sons, Adam, Samuel, Henry, Isaac, and Christian; daughters, Elizabeth, Catharina, Polly, and Aree (?). No executor named. No witnesses. *Ibid.*, 35-36.

Smithson, Josiah. Letters of administration in the estate of Smithson granted to Caleb Smith and Joseph Ratliff, July 13, 1818.

Hunt, Charles. Will dated June 17, 1814; proved November 19, 1818. Heirs: daughters, Polly, Rebecca, Sally, Nancy, Caty; sons, Jonathan, James, George, John, Timothy, Smith, William, Charles, Stephen G. Executors: sons Jonathan, James, and Timothy. Witnesses: John Ring, Nathan Roysden, Benjamin Brown. *Ibid.*, 37-38.

Hollett, Mark, of Waterloo, Wayne Co. Will dated October 15, 1818; recorded November 9, 1818. Heirs: wife, Ann Newsom, and children (names not given). Executors: Asahel Woodward, John McCombs. Witnesses: Charles H. Stanly, Eli Heaton, Catherine McCarty. *Ibid.*, 39.

Alderson, William. Letters of administration in estate of Alderson granted to John Gailbreath, November 24, 1818. *Ibid.*, 40.

Hollet, George. Letters of administration in estate of Hollett granted to Thomas Hollett, December 8, 1818. *Ibid.*, 40.

Young, Jesse. Letters of administration in estate of Young granted to William Young and Moses Martindale, January 16, 1819. *Ibid.*, 41.

Elliott, Israel. Will dated January 4, 1819; proved May 3, 1819. Heirs: wife, Wilmet (?); son, Jacob; daughters, Eve Shoemaker, Esther, Rose, Edith. Executors: Jacob Elliott, George Holman, John Maxwell. Witnesses: Jacob N. Booker, Samuel Booker. *Ibid.*, 42.

Bundy, Joseph. Will dated August 27, 1817; proved May 10, 1819. Heirs: sons, Nathan, George, Josiah; daughters, Sarah Bell, Mary Delon, Gulielma Morris, and Charity (?) Morris; granddaughters: Mary Morris, wife of Joshua Morris, Elizabeth Henley, wife of Jordan Henley. Executors: George and Josiah. Witnesses: Isaac Willits, Loring A. Waldo, Jehoshaphat Morris. *Ibid.*, 43-44.

TWO EARLY SCHOOLS OF CLARK COUNTY, INDIANA

Elizabeth Hayward

From letters and ledger pages preserved by the descendants of Isaac McCoy it is possible to gain a partial conception of what education in early Indiana was like, and of the conditions under which some of the early educators in the state worked.[1] Four of these teachers, who taught at two Clark County schools which have long since gone out of existence, the Clark County Seminary, in Charlestown, Indiana, and the Jeffersonville (Indiana) Primary and Classical School, were connected by blood or by marriage. They were Isaac McCoy, principal of the Clark County Seminary from 1836 to 1839, his bride, Celenda Alden (Converse) McCoy, his brother, William McCoy and Mrs. McCoy's half-brother, Josiah Holt. All were "on the south side of thirty." Mr. and Mrs. McCoy were twenty-nine at the time of their marriage, William McCoy was twenty-five and Holt probably less than twenty-seven.[2]

Isaac McCoy, who bore a name that was confusingly common in his day, was a son of John and Jane (Collins) M'Coy of Clark County, Indiana.[3] He was the nephew as well as a namesake of the Isaac McCoy who was a missionary to the Indians. His birthdate was February 12, 1809,[4] the very day on which Abraham Lincoln was born. The profession of teaching was his life work. He studied at Indiana University for three years, then transferred to Hanover College where he was graduated with the first class in 1834.[5]

---

[1] The author is indebted to Miss Ernestine Stanford of Washington, D. C., for permission to examine the collection of old family papers now in her keeping and to use them as the chief basis of this article. The papers have been kept for over a century in a sturdy wooden chest that served as Isaac McCoy's trunk when he went to college about 1830.

[2] Charles A. Converse, *Some of the Ancestors and Descendants of Samuel Converse, Jr., of Thompson Parish, Killingly, Connecticut* . . . (2 vols., Boston, 1905), II, 504; tombstone of William McCoy, Silver Creek Cemetery, Clark County, Indiana; Stanford MSS.

[3] William H. McCoy, *Notes on the McCoy Family* (ed. by Elizabeth Hayward, Rutland, Vermont, 1939), 9.

[4] Elizabeth Hayward, *Family Bible Records* (Ridgewood, New Jersey, 1941), 5.

[5] "Isaac has passed his examinations some time ago at Hanover College, has taken his degrees. . . . " John M'Coy, Charlestown, Indiana, September 10, 1834, to his brother Isaac McCoy, Westport (now Kansas City), Jackson County, Missouri. This letter is in the keeping of Mrs. W. E. Davis, Piqua, Ohio.

He received the degree of M.A. from Hanover in 1837.[6] It appears, therefore, that he was a man well prepared for his profession. His teaching career began in Indiana, where, in 1835, he taught at the seminary in Wilmington, Dearborn County.[7] From 1836 to 1839 he served as principal of the Clark County Seminary, taught the Jeffersonville Primary and Classical School from 1841 to 1842 and, although his father disapproved, taught in Connecticut, his wife's early home, from 1842 to 1844.[8] John M'Coy wrote in his diary during his son's absence: "Have to regret my Son's wasting his time in New England when he might be more useful to himself and others in the West."[9] On Isaac McCoy's return he spent a single year again teaching in Indiana, and then went to southern Illinois where for over thirty-one years he continued to teach.[10] It is a sad commentary on the low pay he received for his labors that a relation should say of him that he was the only one of the six sons of John M'Coy to live in poverty.[11]

In the 1830's schools in southern Indiana were by no means firmly established. The private support upon which they depended was often irregular. In the tuition accounts of the Clark County Seminary, given below, it is noted that nine parents gaves notes instead of cash when the time came to settle up, while the notation, "Ran Away," appearing after one man's name tersely tells the story of a bad debt. The figures given in the records below also show that the total return received was low—less than two hundred dollars a

---

[6] Henry W. Burger, Registrar, Hanover College, Hanover, Indiana, January 21, 1939, to Mrs. Sumner Hayward, Ridgewood, New Jersey.

[7] His brother William and sister Eliza were among his pupils at Wilmington. John M'Coy, Charlestown, Indiana, May 30, 1835, to his brother, Isaac McCoy, Westport, Missouri. McCoy MSS, XXII, in the Kansas Historical Society Library, Topeka, Kansas.

[8] Burger to Hayward, January 21, 1939.

[9] Diary of John M'Coy of Clark County, Indiana, January 1, 1842—December 31, 1844, entry for July 29, 1843. This diary is in the keeping of W. O. McCoy, Salem, Indiana.

[10] Burger to Hayward, January 21, 1939.

[11] Mrs. F. M. Sparks, Marion, Illinois, August 4, 1927, to Mrs. G. E. Stanford, Rock Island, Illinois. Stanford MSS. The sons of John M'Coy, other than the two mentioned in this account, were Lewis and Spencer Collins, farmers, Clark County, Indiana, George Rice, physician, Golconda, Illinois, and John C., first city attorney of Dallas, Texas. Martin M. Hester, *Descendants of John Lawrence Hester and Godfrey Stough* (n. p., 1905), 52-56; William H. McCoy. Franklin, Indiana, July 18, 1915, to Mary Elizabeth McCoy, Newark, New Jersey; Neander M. Woods, *Woods-McAfee Memorial* (Louisville, 1905), 297-99; Dallas, Texas, *Daily*, April 30, 1887, p. 1.

year at the Jeffersonville school, only four hundred eighty-five dollars in Charlestown, the latter amount to be divided among four teachers.

In spite of the poor financial standing of education it was an attractive field for some young people. William McCoy, one of the four teachers at Clark County Seminary, spoke of his own feelings as well as the general attitude towards education when, in writing his sister, Thirza (McCoy) McCormick, he said:

In comparing the pursuits of life I esteem an education preferable to any other. I have a full determination of acquiring an education if health and other circumstances permit. Education is a thing we cannot lose; it cannot be taken from us; it not only makes a person happy but qualifies him for usefulness; he can be useful to others. Yet education has a great many enemies in this country. The very name of college, seminary or grammar school is disgusting to some people. . . . No person possessed with reasonable principles who will examine the institutions can oppose them. No person does oppose them but those who are wound up in the garb of ignorance and will not listen to reason.[12]

When he wrote this, William McCoy was only nineteen years old. He backed his opinions with action, paying his father, John M'Coy, the considerable sum of one hundred dollars so that he might be released from obligation to him for the remaining years of his minority, and be free to devote his time and labor to acquiring an education.[13] Presumably his father approved his course, for he himself, as a founder of Franklin College,[14] had a keen interest in furthering the cause of higher education in Indiana.

A more detailed description of education in Indiana and her neighboring states was given by the Rev. Dr. Jonathan Going, corresponding secretary (1832-37) of the Baptist Home Mission Society,[15] to the Rev. Mr. S. S. Mallery of Norwich, Connecticut, in response to an inquiry on behalf of Celenda Alden Converse. In reporting his conversation with Dr. Going to Miss Converse, Mallery wrote:

---

[12] William McCoy, Washington County, Indiana, February 22, 1834, to John and Thirza McCormick, Monroe County, Indiana. This letter is in the keeping of Mrs. F. C. Hills, Mattoon, Illinois.

[13] William H. McCoy in an undated clipping, probably from *The Journal and Messenger*, 1891.

[14] John F. Cady, *The Centennial History of Franklin College* (n. p., 1934), 21-22, 29.

[15] William Cathcart, *The Baptist Encyclopedia* (2 vols., Philadelphia, 1881), I, 457.

In almost any of the western states a person can with but little trouble collect a school. They have no regular system like what prevails in New England. A teacher has to set up for herself and engage her scholars, which is easily done as soon as it is known that she wants a school. Dr. Going saw a Connecticut wooden nutmeg peddler who had sold out all his "concerns" and seemed disposed to tarry a little longer in the country. He happened to be where there were about half a dozen men together for some purpose or other when one of them in the hearing of Dr. G. asked the peddler if he wanted to get work. "No," he answered. "Well, what would you like to do?" "Why, I don't know but I would take a school if I could get one." And though he looked as though the thought of teaching school never entered his head till that moment in fifteen minutes he had twenty or more scholars pledged. . . . Female schools have not till recently been much known at the west but they are beginning to be quite popular in many portions of the country. . . . From having travelled extensively in the West he [Dr. Going] knows that there are abundant opportunities for teachers to sustain themselves and be useful.[16]

Before venturing to leave her home in Willington, Connecticut, Miss Converse also sought advice from a transplanted easterner, Mary A. Clapp, who by 1836 had had a year's experience teaching in Lawrenceburg, Dearborn County, Indiana. Miss Clapp's reply, with her impressions of Indiana as well as her advice to her correspondent, is worth quoting at length:

With joy I recognized your name and remembered that we were once classmates at Charlestown [Massachusetts] Female Seminary and tho' we were now separated there was a prospect we should still meet on earth. . . . I made what inquiries my prescribed limits would admit but learned of no situation to teach this winter. The Spring is the time to get schools, as they generally employ men in the winter when they can get them. This Spring there are many schools to be had in this State and even County. As soon as the River and Canals and Railroads are in operation you had best start. . . .

The field is truly interesting to a truly philosophic soul who is willing to suffer and toil with a small compensation. There are many prejudices to overcome. . . .

I think our Eastern friends have but a poor idea of the Western customs and wants. The information which has been communicated by Agents who have gathered what they could by travelling is very limited and often erronious, tho' well meant, I doubt not. It takes some time to become acquainted and form just ideas; more I think than a traveller can do with merely conversing with a few in a place.

As to the climate, it is milder in winter and far more change-

---

[16] S. S. Mallery, Norwich, Connecticut, June 18, 1835, to C. A. Converse, Wesleyan Academy, Wilbraham, Massachusetts. Stanford MSS.

able than at the East. We have had but one snow as yet. The Summers are pretty warm from what I am told, and what little experience I have had. . . . The morning may be delightful and warm, in two hours clouds may blow up and Cloaks may be necessary, so that great care is requisite to those who are not acclimated to this region. As to clothing, come well prepared with good durable things, but not finery. [Bring] good Shawls and many of them, for they are poor here, and come very high. This is a muddy region, being of clay soil. However town and country vary much. . . .

Our vegetable productions are much the same as at the East but the manner of cooking is widely different, but we Yankees must not be epicures in this country. The people of this state are called Hooshier or Hooshieroon. . . . As to the expense of coming— it will probably be about 90 dollars, you had better have 100. The middle route is much the best and most expeditious. Come to N. Y., thence to Phil., Pittsburg, then the Ohio River to Cincinnati, from thence to this place which is on the River. If you should come here please inquire on landing for Doct. Ferris. At his house you will be made welcome till you can obtain a school. If you can obtain one or two young ladies to come with you bring them and we will find them common schools for they have not many other. Tell them to expect many trials, many which they are unacquainted with, but let this not discourage them, for God will support them if they are actuated by right motives. . . .

Same qualifications as at the East relative to education,[17] with a facility to communicate what you do know. Manner easy and social but not too free. Their friendship is not so permanent as we have been accustomed to.

The art of painting by theory and needlework in some towns is very desirable. A superficial education is most pleasing to young ladies here. The ornamental branches . . . much thought of . . . Plain dress is very important as they will be more likely to copy the evil than the good.

There is much good society and some hearty Christians such as would feast the soul to converse with. . . . We have [word illegible] preaching half of the time, no meeting-house, no schoolhouse— keep in private rooms. Prayer meeting Friday evening, Bible class Thurs. eve., Sabbath School Sunday from three to four. The people here will not go to preaching Sunday afternoon any-hour. This at first will seem to you painful but custom will make it seem better after a while. . . .

As to baggage, pack it close as possible and take care not to lose it on the way. Have it labelled for this place; watch it close. I am told there is no danger in travelling alone without a gentleman;

---

[17] Celenda Converse's qualifications may be assumed from her certificate from the Wesleyan Academy, where in 1835-1836, "She attended . . . to the following branches of study: The Latin and Spanish Languages, Arithmetic & Algebra, Nat. Philosy., Chemistry, Botany, Mental Philosy. & Rhetoric & Composition, in all of which her recitations and exercises were creditable to herself and satisfactory to her Teachers." Stanford MSS.

take two or three ladies. I should not be afraid to travel from one part of the United States to the other—*no* danger. I came about 200 miles alone. I was a month coming (across the Lake I came, which is called the Northern Route, poor enough.)

. . . Come then, dear Sister, I bid you welcome to all the toils, privations and all the luxury of doing good.[18]

Undismayed by the picture drawn by Miss Clapp, Celenda Converse came to Indiana in the spring of 1836. She readily found a district school to teach, about four miles from Lawrenceburg. In a year or two she met Isaac McCoy, then teaching in Dearborn County, and became engaged to him. They were married April 30, 1838.[19] In making plans for their future it was evident that Isaac McCoy expected his bride to continue teaching but at the Clark County Seminary instead of the district school. He wrote her:

It is very essentially to be desired that we return in time to be here [Charlestown] during the greater part of the week next previous to beginning school. Mrs. Jennings leaves us tomorrow and I am extremely anxious to introduce you to the acquaintance of the citizens before the other school takes advantage of the abandoned state of our Seminary occasioned by Mrs. J.'s departure. If it suit you, I would be glad to return on Tuesday the 1st May.[20]

That she did teach at the Clark·County Seminary is plain from a letter written by Isaac McCoy's father a few weeks later, in which he said, "Isaac with his wife and William is engaged in the County Seminary."[21] Many other letters in the Stanford papers confirm the fact that Mrs. McCoy continued to teach after her marriage.

William McCoy, whose views on education have already been quoted, was the third teacher at the seminary of whose career we know something. He was the eighth child of John and Jane (Collins) M'Coy, born December 21, 1814.[22] His original intent, as shown previously, was to devote his life to education. He attended the county seminaries at Wilmington and Charlestown, then taught at Livonia, Salem,

---

[18] Mary S. Clapp, Lawrenceburg, Dearborn County, Indiana, February 21, 1836, to Celenda Converse, Willington, Connecticut. Stanford MSS.

[19] Converse, *Some of the Ancestors and Descendants of Samuel Converse, Jr.*, II, 504.

[20] Isaac McCoy, Charlestown, Indiana, April 18, 1838, to Celenda A. Converse, Lawrenceburg, Dearborn County, Indiana, Stanford MSS.

[21] John M'Coy, Charlestown, Indiana, May 16, 1838, to his brother Isaac McCoy, Washington, [D. C.]. McCoy MSS., XXV.

[22] Hayward, *Family Bible Records*, 5.

Jeffersonville and Aurora.[23] Influenced perhaps by a visit to his uncle, the Rev. Isaac McCoy, at the Baptist mission at Westport, Jackson County, Missouri, in 1834, as well as by his father's advice: "If you feel like you could devote your life and your all to the service of your Divine Master and the good of mankind, confer not with flesh and blood but go to work immediately,"[24] he left teaching to become a Baptist minister. He was not ordained until 1843, so that in the period we are considering he was still employed in teaching.

The fourth teacher at Clark County Seminary, Josiah Holt, was a newcomer to Indiana. He was the younger half-brother of Celenda (Converse) McCoy and like her had been educated in New England.[25] From Elizabethtown, New Jersey, where he was teaching in the spring of 1838, he wrote his half-sister: "If Mr. McCoy should need an assistant for a term or two and thinks there is a prospect of my soon procuring a good school I should like very much to come to Indiana."[26] Evidently he received an affirmative reply for when Isaac McCoy wrote his wife, then visiting in Lawrenceburg, in August of that year, he spoke of "Brother Josiah" teaching at the Seminary and sharing his bachelor quarters during her absence. "Never fear for us," he told her, "we know how to roast and stew equal to any old bachelors. We have just been taking a hearty repast tonight. O that you were here a moment or two at a time, you would laugh to see us."[27]

The household was soon darkened, however, by the serious illness of Josiah Holt. A series of letters in the Stanford collection tells of his failing health, the anxiety felt by the distant parents and the remedies unavailingly applied to check the progress of his disease. A rough draft of a

---

[23] Major William W. Harris, The McCoy Family. This manuscript contains a statement from John Milton McCoy (1835-1922).

[24] John M'Coy, Charlestown, Indiana, September 17, 1834, to his son William McCoy, Westport, Jackson County, Missouri; John M'Coy, September 10, 1834, to his brother Isaac McCoy, Westport, Jackson County, Missouri; John M'Coy, January 30, 1839, to his son William McCoy, Salem, Indiana. These letters are in the keeping of Mrs. W. E. Davis, Piqua, Ohio. See also Elizabeth Hayward, "Genealogical Notes of Some Indiana Pioneers," *Indiana Magazine of History*, XXXVII (1941), 296.

[25] Stanford MSS.

[26] Josiah Holt, Elizabethtown (now Elizabeth), New Jersey. May 1, 1838, to C. A. Converse, Lawrenceburg, Indiana. Stanford MSS.

[27] Isaac McCoy, Charlestown, Indiana, August 22, 1838, to Mrs. Isaac McCoy, Lawrenceburg, Indiana. Stanford MSS.

letter to his parents gives news of his death on June 12, 1839, at Isaac McCoy's home.[28] Since Josiah Holt was bedfast by March, 1839, it is probable that his teaching career in Clark County was brief, possibly not longer than six or eight months.

While Holt's life was short and William McCoy's talents later found another outlet than teaching, it is interesting to know that Isaac McCoy and his wife continued to the end of their active lives as educators. Their lives had a singular unity. Both were born in 1809, both died in 1882, and both, with singleness of purpose, devoted their lives to teaching.[29] In the face of hardship and privation, ignorance and prejudice, these early educators helped to blaze the trail which was eventually to lead to the present progressive, state-supported system of education in Indiana.

School Records[30]
CLARK COUNTY SEMINARY
Session 4th Continued
Commencing Nov. 7, 1837

[Parent or Guardian]	No. of students	Tuition
Ford, Lemuel	3	$15.25
Foulk, Aaron	2	14.50
Foresythe, Jas.	1	3.25
Foresythe, David	1	2.50
Griffith	1	8.25
Hammond, Rezin	3	12.06
Harris, Jonah	3	14.25
Hartley, H.	2	9.50
Hay, A. P.	2	16.50
Hinds, Jesse	1	4.56
Houston, L. B.	3	13.46
Huckleberry, William	1	6.25
Hughs, Mrs.	1	2.50
James, Beverly W.	1	3.96

---

[28] Celenda McCoy, June 16, 1839, (no place given), to her mother and stepfather, Mr. and Mrs. Leonard Holt, Willington, Connecticut. Stanford MSS.

[29] Converse, *Some of the ancestors and descendants of Samuel Converse, Jr.*, II, 504.

[30] The ledger pages which give the names of parents, pupils and other particulars are darkened, torn and stained. One corner appears to be scorched. In view of their fragile condition it seems advisable to preserve them by printing their contents here. For the convenience of those who may look for names on these lists the order has been made alphabetical. Genealogists may find it helpful to know how many children of seminary (high school) age there were in a given family in 1837-1838 as shown in the records of the fourth and fifth sessions of the Clark County Seminary. The register of the seminary gives names of parents; that of the Jeffersonville school those of pupils.

Johnson, T.	1	6.25
King, William F.	1	5.67
Laws, Robt.	3	13.82
Martin, Aaron	1	5.39
MCampbell, Samuel	2	4.50
McCormic, Thomas[31]	1	5.39
McCoy, Lewis[32]	1	4.10
McCune, J. L. P.	3	15.75
Miller, John	1	6.25
Morrow, William	2	11.00
Owens, James	1	7.25
Parker, John	2	9.50
Perdue, Mrs.	1	4.10
Price, Mrs.	1	4.25
Roe, John E.	1	6.25
Rowland, Mrs.	2	8.75
Rowland, Jno.	2	7.78
Russell, J.	2	10.21
Sharpe, Jas.	3	18.25
Sprowl, J. W.	1	5.00
Strutt, Mr.	1	3.89
Tunstall, Mr.	1	1.39
Walter, Mr.	1	4.75
Wilkes, Henry	1	5.43
Willhoyte, Richard	1	3.75
Willson, Jas.	2	9.50
Work, Wm.	1	7.25
Work, Samuel	1	7.25

CLARK CO. SEMINARY
Tuition fees of
Session 5th
Commencing May 7th 1838

[Parent or Guardian]	No. of Students	Tuition
Athon, Dr. Jas.	1	3.25
Barringer, J.[33]		
Boyer, Jas.	1	2.50
Boyer, Mrs.	2	8.75
Canfield, H.	1	4.82
Carr, John	1	4.25
Coble, A.	2	6.71
Cole, C.	2	8.00
Cole, M.	1	4.75

[31] Thomas McCormick (1804-1878) had no children of his own who were old enough, in 1837, to attend a seminary. Probably the child whose tuition he paid was his stepson. Basil Bowen Coombs, born August 5, 1824. died September 11, 1857. John Milton McCoy, McCoy Genealogy. This manuscript was compiled prior to 1921.

[32] Lewis McCoy (1806-1874) was a brother of Isaac McCoy. Hayward, *Family Bible Records*, 5. Hester, *Descendants of John Lawrence Hester and Godfrey Stough*, 52-56.

[33] A line is drawn through this name.

Collins, Jas.	1	2.53
Davis, Mrs.	1	2.50
Demar, Wm.	2	9.50
Denny, John	2	6.50
Dewey, Chas.	1	8.25
Dietz, G. W.	3	11.03
Downs, Mrs.	1	2.25
Duitt, Mrs.	1	4.75
Ellis, R.	1	3.25
Ferguson, B.	1	8.25
Ford, L.	2	7.25
Garner, Mrs.	4	11.00
Hammond, R.	2	9.50
Hartman, C.	1	4.75
Hess, Mrs.	2	9 50
Houston, L. B.	3	12.25
Howk, Mrs.	1	8.00
Laws, R.	1	3.89
Long, E.	1	4.75
Long, J. W.	1	1.25
MCune, J. L. P.	3	14.25
Parker, John	2	8.50
Parker, Wm.	1	6.25
Pearcy, A. J.	1	6.25
Perdue, Mrs.	1	5.10
Piersol, John	1	2.25
Price, Mrs.	3	6.75
Randall, Dr. J.	2	8.50
St. Clair, Mr.	2	5.00
Sharpe, James	3	7.50
Sprowl, Wm.	1	7.00
Suttle, T.	2	4.25
Walter, A.	2	5.50
Warfield, Dr. B. H.	1	3.25
Wilhoyte, R.	1	5.25
Wilson, James	2	9.50
Wise, Frederic	1	8.25
Work, Samuel	1	2.25

CLARK CO. SEMINARY
Tuition Fees of Session 6th[34]
Commencing Nov. 5th, 1838

[Parent or Guardian] Tuition
Abbott, J. C. 5.10

[34] The number of students is not given for this session.
The parents of Sarah Ann Osgood, who is known to have attended the Seminary during this time, are not listed as paying tuition. Probably as the protegée of the McCoys she did not pay anything. Her enrollment, too, was for only a brief period. Mrs. McCoy wrote of her, "Among the some hundreds of youths and children whom it was my privilege to instruct I think that none were more successful in their advancement. . . . In August 1838 while on a visit to my friends

Alpha, M.	1.10
Athon, Dr. Jas.	6.25
Barringer, John	5.00
Canfield, H.	7.25
Clark, Mr.	1.67
Collins, Jas.	5.11
Denny, Jno.	5.96
Dewey, Chas.	13.00
Dietz, G. W.	10.00
Duitt, Mrs.	4.53
Durham, S. W.	5.58
Ferguson, B.	18.11
Fleshman, Mr.	1.53
Foresythe, D.	3.25
Hammond, R.	1.67
Harper, J.	5.68
Hartman, C.	9.50
Hess, Mrs.	2.53
Hinds, J.	3.39
Houston, L. B.	4.75
Huckleberry, Wm.	6.34
Kirkpatrick, W.	5.67
Laughery, Mrs.	2.50
Laws, H.	3.85
Laws, R.	3.85
Parker, Wm.	6.25
Pearcy, A. J.	6.34
Price, Mrs.	6.45
Randall, Dr. J.	8.00
Rowland, Mrs.	1.75
Sellers, M. W.	5.91
Stuart, Al.	1.00
Sutton, (remitted)	.75
Walter, A.	4.75
Whitmarsh, Dr.	6.58
Wybrant, Mr.	4.75

in Lawrenceburg I invited her to return with me to Charlestown, which she did, and became a member of my family and attended the Clark Co. Seminary of which Mr. McCoy was then Principal. But in a few weeks she was again called from the pursuit of science to the business of imparting instruction. In a neighborhood West of Charlestown a school was much needed, and though it was her wish to pursue her studies for a while longer, yet aiming to be useful rather than to gratify herself . . . she undertook the school at the earnest solicitation of a friend in that place, Lydia McCormic." Celenda C. McCoy, Biography of Sarah Ann Osgood [1819-1852], fragmentary, Stanford MSS.

Sarah Ann Osgood became a close friend of Isaac McCoy's sister, Eliza McCoy, and like her, became a missionary to the Indians. Calvin McCormick, *The Memoir of Miss Eliza McCoy* (Dallas, 1892), 38, 43-44, 75-77.

JEFFERSONVILLE PRIMARY & CLASSICAL SCHOOL
1841, Sept. 20. Commenced 1st quarter—Isaac M'Coy—Teacher

	Students' Names	Tuition
1.	Richard Buck	.75
2.	Brice Curran	2.00
3.	William Curran	5.00
4.	Amanda Hall	3.00
5.	James A. Holt	4.00
6.	Henry C. Rease	2.50
7.	Georgia Ann Reed	1.00
8.	John Ryan	.75
9.	Cornelius B. Ruddle	2.33⅓
10.	Elizabeth S. Ruddle	2.16⅔
11.	Stephen R. Ruddle	2.33⅓
12.	Christiana P. Shryer	2.50
13.	Mary A. Waggener	3.00
14.	Susan E. Waggener	3.00
15.	Wm. Weathers	.43¾
		34.77

1841, Dec. 13th. Commences 2nd quarter—Isaac M'Coy—Teacher

	Students' Names	Tuition
1.	Richard Buck	2.50
2.	Robt. Chalfant	1.50
3.	Ruth E. Chalfant	1.50
4.	William Curran	6.00
5.	Margaret Fite	2.50
6.	Rebecca J. D. Hall, & Amanda	6.75
7.	William Hardman	3.00
8.	Enoch Howard	2.50
9.	William Howard	1.00
10.	James A. Holt	5.00
11.	Susan Jackson	2.50
12.	Thirza J. McCormick[35]	1.00
13.	Rice F. McGrew	4.00
14.	Jno. Warren Miller	2.00
15.	Georgia Ann Read	1.00
16.	Cornelius B. Ruddell	2.33
17.	Sarah E. Ruddell	1.75
18.	Stephen R. Ruddell	2.33
19.	John Ryan	2.50
20.	M. D. L. Tomlin	2.25
21.	William Vanpelt	1.00
22.	Henry Waggener	4.00
23.	James Wathen	2.00
24.	William Weathers	2.50

[35] Thirza Jane McCormick (1831-1924) was the daughter of John and Thirza (McCoy) McCormick. She married Frank Adams Christian of Grand View, Illinois, in 1854. Mrs. I. D. Hesler (granddaughter), Hillsboro, Illinois, August 8, 1939, to Mrs. Sumner Hayward, Ridgewood, New Jersey.

25.	A. J. Wolverton	2.50
26.	Matthew Wright	1.00

66.91

1842, Mar. 21st   Commenced 3rd quarter—Isaac M'Coy—Teacher

1.	Aaron Applegate	1.75
2.	Nelson Applegate	1.75
3.	Isabella Brown	1.00
4.	Susan Brown	1.00
5.	Richard Buck	1.50
6.	Ruth E. Chalfant	1.50
7.	V. D. Collins	3.33⅓
8.	Matilda A. Ferguson	2.50
9.	Nancy A. Ferguson	2.75
10.	Rebecca J. D. Hall	5.00
11.	Hester Ann Hart	2.50
12.	Enoch Howard	1.75
13.	William Howard	1.75
14.	Amelia Leach	.50
15.	John Leach	1.00
16.	Gates M'Garah	.37½
17.	Feilding [sic] R. M'Grew	.75
18.	James Mayberry	.37½
19.	Warren Miller	2.87½
20.	Georgia A. Read	2.00
21.	John Ryan	2.50
22.	Christiana P. Shryer	.50
23.	William S. Tomlin	4.00
24.	Lafayette M. Tomlin	3.00
25.	Elbert Vanpelt	2.25
26.	Andrew J. Wathen	6.00
27.	George W. Wathen	6.00
28.	James Wathen	3.00
29.	William Weathers	2.66⅔
30.	Matthew Wright	.75

66.62½

1842, June 27th   Commences 4th term—Isaac M'Coy—Teacher

1.	Aaron Applegate	1.00
2.	Nelson Applegate	1.00
3.	Isabella Brown	1.00
4.	Susan Brown	1.00
5.	Richard Buck	1.50
6.	Ruth E. Chalfant	1.50
7.	Lloyd Gates	.87½
8.	John Gill	.18¾
9.	Amelia Leach	1.50
10.	John Leach	1.50
11.	James Mabury	1.12½
12.	Gates M'Garah	2.00

13. F. R. M'Grew	1.87½
14. Warren Miller	1.25
15. Isaiah Prather	.75
16. John Ryan	1.87½
17. C. P. Shryer	1.87½
18. Lafayette Tomlin	.75
19. James Underwood	.50
20. William Vanpelt	.25
21. James Wathen	1.75
	$ 25.06¼
Amount of previous	168.30½
Do. of 4 terms	$193.36¾
Two dollars to be deducted from Mr. Fite's bill	2.00
	$191.36¾

Heads of Families in Clay County, Indiana, 1830

Since there is a lack of information available on early families in Clay County because of the destruction of the courthouse records by fire in 1851, the Genealogy Committee of the Indiana Historical Society feels that it would be helpful to make available the names of families residing in the county at the time the census was taken in 1830. Clay County was formed by act of February 12, 1825, effective April 1 of that year. The area comprising the new county had formerly been a part of Owen, Putnam, Vigo, and Sullivan counties. The names listed below are transcribed from a photostatic copy of the Fifth Census of the United States: 1830, which is in the Genealogy Division of the Indiana State Library, Indianapolis.

Acre [or Acres], John
Acre [or Acres], Luke
Alexander, Joseph
Allen, Robert
Anderson, Isaac
Anderson, Reuben
Archer, Abigail
Archer, Patrick
Archer, Simon
Archer, William R.

Ballard, William
Barnett, James
Barnett, Peter
Basye, Thomas
Beavers, William
Beavins, Elijah [S.?]
Benham, Peter
Biggs, Robert
Birch, Robert
Birchfield, Jane

Bleavins, Warren
Bowlin, Celey
Bowlin, Elisabeth
Bowlin, Noah
Bowlin, William
Bowls, Martin
Brady, Isaac
Breeden, Elijah
Breeden, Philip
Breedin, William
Briley, Absalem
Briley, James
Brown, Benjamin
Buchannan, David C.
Buckelow, William
Bundy, Nancy
Bundy, Simeon
Burnett, Elisha
Bybee, Lee
Carman, Benjamin
Carpenter, William
Carrell, Hickman
Carrell, James
Case, Joseph
Casiah, James
Casiah, Samuel
Chamberlin, Sarah
Chance, Daniel
Chance, John
Chance, Pernal
Chance, Randolph
Chance, Tilman
Christie, David
Christie, William
Christie, William M.
Church, Enoch
Church, Joel
Clark, Charles
Coale, William
Coffelt [or Coffett], George
Coffelt [or Coffett], James
Coffman, Sarah
Comer [or Comes], Matthew
Cooksey, William T.
Cooly, Samuel
Cooprider, John
Cooprider, Peter
Cowen, Riley
Cox, Eli
Cox, Matthew

Crafton, James
Crafton, William
Creech, William
Crist, William
Croake, Robert W.
Crossley, John
Crossley, Thomas C.
Crummel, Joshua
Crummel, Levi
Crummel, Nicholas G.
Crummel, Thomas
Curry, Henderson
Dalton, Jacob
Deal, Michael
Deal, William
Defore, James
Denny, Zachariah
Dickings, James
Downning, James H.
Downs, Isaac
Drake, William, Jr.
Drake, William, Senr.
Dutton, John
Dyar, Ezekial
Dyar, Luke, Jr.
Dyar, Luke, Senr.
Eckara, Moses
Ellis, Stephen
Ely, George
Flanagan, Isaac
Flick, Hiram
Fortener, Lewis
Frazure, James
Galaspy, Thomas L.
Gerrel, John
Godwin, Nathan
Godwin, Netheldre[dge?]
Goodrich, Jacob
Gowens, Canaan
Grabel, Jonathan
Graves, John
Graves, Sarah
Graves, William
Green, Henry
Green, James
Green, Lewis
Griffith, Joseph
Griffy, Bartly
Hackworth, Samuel
Hale, William

Hall, Joseph
Harpool, Nicholess
Heddy, James
Hix, Uriah
Holson, Nicholas
Holt, Francis
Hudson, James
Hufman, Jacob
Hufman, John
Hufman, Solomon
Jewell, John
Johnson, Benjamin
Johnson, Charnel C.
Johnson, Eliphalet
Johnson, Simon
Jones, Allen
Jones, Fletcher
Jones, Hiram
Jones, Joseph
Jones, Pearce
Jones, Wesley
Kelly, William
Killeon, Eli H.
Killion, Aaron L.
Killion, Gabriel C.
Killion, Mathias J.
Kindle, William
Kintzley, Christian
Kintzley, George
Landers, Zacharia
Lartham, John, Jr.
Lartham, John, Senr.
Lartham, Labern
Lawson, Charles
Leonard, Lawrence
Lite, Bird
Luther, Jacob
Luther, James
Luther, John
Luther, Joseph
Luther, Michael
Luther, Peter
Luther, Samuel
Luther, Sarah
Luther, Thomas
Luther, William
Luther, William, Jr.
McBride, William
McCollister, John
McIntire, Jesse

McIntire, Nancy
McKinley, George G.
Mace, Isaac
Maguire, James
Maguire, William
Mann, Hezek[i?]ah, Jr.
Mann, John
Maxwell, William
Melton, Eli
Melton, Jesse G.
Melton, John
Melton, Watson
Miers, Archibald
Miers, Joseph
Miers, Michael
Miers, West
Miers, William
Monroe, Abram
Moore, Samuel
Moore, Thomas
Moore, Thomas, Jr.
Moore, William [1]
Moore, William [2]
Morgan, Even
Mostiller, Elizabeth M.
Mostiller, Joseph
Murphy, [Sion?]
Music, Samuel
Nuckles, David
Ott, Isaac
Owen, David
Owen, Joel
Owen, Jonathan
Owen, Presly
Owen, William
Owens, Wilbern
[Pane?], Elizabeth
Parr, Moses
Peyton, Jared
Peyton, Wesly
Phips, Ambrose
Phips, Benjamin
Piner, Nathan
Pitts, Ezekiel
Prater, Archib[ald?]
Pritchet, James
Rawley, Elijah
Rawley, Ev[i?]n
Ray, Jesse
Reed, Jacob

Rice, William
Richerson, John
Ringo, William
Rizley, Hiram
Rizley, John
Rizley, Samuel
Roberts, Thomas
Roberts, Thomas [S.?]
Ross, William
Ruddle, James
Runalds, Richard
Runnels, James
Runnels, Sarah
Scamerhorn, John
Scarlet, Polly
Scrotchfield, James
Shull, Isaac
Slavin[s?], Samuel
Smith, John R.
Smith, Oliver
Snider, James
Snoddy, Josiah
Stallcup, Elias
Steed, Samuel
Stewart, William
Stockton, Daniel
Strader, Jesse
Sturdevant, John
Taylor, Abraham
Taylor, Richard S. [D.?]
Thomas, David
Thomas, James

Thomas, James, Jr.
Thompson, Lawrence
Tranum, Sheltun [J.?]
Vanmeter, Abraham
Vantrece, Jacob
Vest, Caleb
Vest, Thomas
Walker, Danial
Walker, Davis
Walker, Ephram
Walker, James
Walker, Levie
Walker, Mary
Walker, Richard
Walker, William
Weathers, Thomas
Webster, Daniel
Wheeler, Benjamin
Wheeler, Joshua
Wheeler, Thomas
White, James
White, Mathew
Widener, Jacob
Wiley, Alexander
Wilkes, Francis
Wilson, James
Wools, Danial [W.?]
Wright, Elijah
Zenor, George
Zenor, George, Jr.
Zenor, Joseph

Marriage Affidavits, Clay County, Indiana, to 1852

Compiled and edited by Carolynne Wendel

Published below is a list of affidavits attesting to Clay County marriages that took place before or during 1852. After the original marriage records were destroyed in the courthouse fire on November 30, 1851, Clay County marriages prior to that time were re-recorded by affidavit. Since a marriage could not be recorded unless the persons involved arranged for it, the list published here undoubtedly does not include all Clay County marriages that occurred by 1852. The original affidavits are recorded in a volume at the County

Clerk's Office, Brazil, Indiana. The list given here was compiled from a microfilm copy of the affidavits which is filed at the Genealogy Division, Indiana State Library, Indianapolis.

AFFIDAVITS

William [K?] Houston—Jane Miles	lic. April 30, 1849	p. 7[1]
Enos Miles—Caroline B. Osborn	lic. Aug. 11, 1851	7
Jesse Fuller—Susan Thorp	lic. Nov. 16, 1845†[2]	8
George Pinckly—Rebecca Williams	lic. Jan. 30, 1838†	9
Redman Jones—Elizabeth Smith	lic. Aug. 27, 1844†	10
Andrew H. Turner—Starlin Peyton	Nov. 2, 1852†	11
John Latham—Sophia D. Nees	1852	12
William B. Parker—Martha E. Linley	lic. Oct. 6, 1851†	13
Alvin B. Thorp—Sarah Tribble	Feb. 1, 1849†	14
Samuel Auston Edmondson—Elizabeth Freedly	Oct. or Nov., 1849	15
Michael McCullough—Eliza Jane Zenor	Sept. 1, 1842	16
Squire L. Case—Nancy Acrea	Nov. 24, 1842	17
William Blunk—Catharine Arnold	Jan. 2, 1844	18
Burley E. Tilley—Hetta Helton	Sept. 11, 1844	19
David T. Walker—Mary Ann Cromwell	Oct. 17, 1844	20
William L. Cromwell—Susan Rizley	Oct. 31, 1844	21
Absalom B. Wheeler—Jane Lowdermilk	Mar. 2, 1845	22
James Sparks—Elizabeth Walker	Sept. 25, 1845	23
Elisha B. Peyton—Mahalia Walker	Nov. 13, 1845	24
James Deal—Hannah Case	Feb. 2, 1846	25
David T. Sparkes—Susan E. Walker	Oct. [14?], 1846	26
George Drake—Eliza Ann Gildea	Apr. 23, 1846	27
Elias Helton—Susannah Tilley	Aug. 28, 1846	28
Linsey Stinson—Sally Ann Graves	Dec. 27, 1846	29
John Eades—Delila Ann Killion	Feb. 1, 1847	30
Oliver Cromwell, Jr.—Elizabeth Walker	May 9, 1847	31
David Parker—Nancy Payne	Feb. 18, 1847	32
John Mills—Sarah Cromwell	Mar. 25, 1847	33
Charles Welburn—Mary Long	Aug. 13, 1847	34
Daniel D. Walker—Elizabeth Ann Rizley	Oct. 14, 1847	35
William Walker—Mary Jane Phipps	Aug. 3, 1848	36
Robert McIntire—Alley Carter	Oct. 3, 1848	37
Samuel C. Blunk—Rachel Ann Hues	Oct. 21, 1848	38
George W. Reed—Elizabeth Eddy	Nov. 16, 1848	39

[1] Dates preceded by "lic." refer to the day the marriage license was issued. All other dates given are the day of marriage. Page numbers refer to the page on which the affidavit appears in the Clay County record book in which it is recorded.

[2] In some of the affidavits, the date of the marriage license or of the marriage is given as "on or about" a certain day. In the compilation printed here, each of these doubtful dates is marked by a dagger.

Benjamin [Gamere?]—Amanda Cromwell	July 29, 1849	40
James P. Hickman—Sally Ann Scamahorn	Aug. 19, 1849	41
Aaron Stark—Lydia Elen Wilson	Aug. 27, 1849	42
John D. Mace—Sally Ann Zenor	Dec. 2, 1849	43
Charles N. Mills—Sarah Roberts	Oct. 27, 1849	44
William McCullough—Elizabeth Mace	Nov. 7, 1850	45
Jared P. Peyton—Mariah H. Walker	Nov. 28, 1850	46
Laban Latham—Mary Ann Parker	Dec. 26, 1850	47
Edmond Butt [or Bull]—Jane Mace	Dec. 29, 1850	48
Hezekiah Wheeler—Effy Harp	July 20, 1851	49
William Anderson—Dorcas Hinote	Sept. 28, 1851	50
George Hantwerk—Susan Lints	Nov. 3, 1851	51
Ananias W. Lowdermilk—Frances Wheeler	Jan. 25, 1851	52
Dillon W. Bridges, Jr.—Lucinda Davis	Sept. 3, 1850	54
John Dalgarn—Harriet Phegley	[n.d.]	55
Jonathan M. Parker—Eliza Latham	Mar., 1851	56
Michael Myers—Charlotte Latham	Aug., 1846	57
Andrew H. Nees—Martha Slack	Nov., 1848	58
John Oswalt—Eupha Latham	Dec., 1845	59
William Zenor—Elizabeth Latham	Mar., 1839	60
West Myers—Cloah Cromwell	May, 1835	61
Henry Gilbrech—Martha Crafton	Sept. 24, 1850†	62
Shallum Thomas—Mary Stigler	Dec. 1, 1831†	63
William Thomas—Betsey Godwin	Nov. 1, 1830†	65
Hiram Rizley—Louisa Parish	Nov. 1, 1826†	66
Bird Light—Catharine Lake	Jan. 3, 1828†	67
Levi Walker—Drusilla Thomas	Mar. 2, 1838†	68
Luke Dyer—Olive Hicks	Oct. 17, 1826†	69
George W. Randall—Nancy J. Peyton	lic. Aug. 23, 1850†	70
Charles Rheile—Amelia Wittenberg	Apr., [1851?]	71
David S. Grimes—Caroline Pickard	Aug. 7, 1852	73
Samuel S. Baily—Eliza E. Ness	Dec., 1836	75
David Kimery—Sarah Ann Turner	Nov., 1845	76
William Slack—Margury Lowdermilk	Jan. 10, 1833	77
John T. Alexander—Esther Denny	Dec., 1832	78
James T. Alexander—Cyntha Ann Downing	Jan., 1839	79
Ransalaer Horton—Sarah Dalton	June 29, 1836	80
George H. Alexander—Sarah E. Buckallew	Aug., 1843	81
William L. Alexander—Ann Alexander	May, 1840	82
Owen D. Cromwell—Huldah Rizley	July, 1837	83
John Bybee[3]—Mary Drake	Sept., 1838	84
George M. Alexander—Sophiah Ann Vanmeter	Feb., 1847	85
James Dalgarn—Margaret Booth	Mar., 1842	86
Thomas Drake—Mariah Bybee	Jan., 1841	87
Wesley M. Peyton—Nancy Chance	Sept., 1829	88
James Anderson—Elizabeth Cagle	Nov., 1832	89
Robert Anderson—Lydia Cagle	Jan., 1836	90

[3] The heading of the affidavit gives Bybee's first name as "John." In the affidavit itself, however, his name appears as "Thomas John."

James A. Pickard—Sarah Luther	lic. May 23, 1850	93
William Anderson—Barbary Neese	Sept. 24, 1835	94
Washington Neese—Leah Anderson	Jan., 1836	95
William Nees—Martha Birchfield	Dec. 23, 1838†	96
David Coble—Mary Ann Margaret McIntire	Jan. 17, 1833†	98
William Drake—Elizabeth McIntire	June 22, 1831	99
Thompson Boothe—Huldah Thomas	June 7, 1831†	100
Isaac Mace—Delana Acre	Dec. 21, 1832†	101
William M. Acre—Pherabe Walker	Dec. 12, 1832†	102
Philip Nelson—Margaret Nees	1838	103
Luke Anderson—Nancy Hinote	June, 1839	105
Nathan D. Walker—Sarah Rizley	May 1, 1838	106
James P. Thomas—Barbary Barnett	Fall, 1828 or 1829	107
Isaac N. Morris—Naomi A. Witty	lic. Aug. 26, 1849†	108
Isaac N. Morris—Nancy A. Witty	lic. Oct. 26, 1852†	109
Milo Hoyt—Isabella Barrett	Apr., 1849	112
Henry Nees—Mary Ann Wright	Apr. 18, 1847	114
Baldwin H. Witty—Elizabeth Walker	Mar. 7, 1837	115
James B. Reed—Nancy Jane Miller	Feb. 29, 1844†	116
John Linn—Mary Alexander	1848 or 1849	120
Elias Cooprider—Polley Lankford	Oct. 13, 1832†	122
Oliver Cromwell—Nancy L. Bybee	Aug., 1831	125
Herod Rizley—Merom Ramsey	Sept., 1831	126
Samuel Long—Arra Carroll	1840	128
Morgan B. Ringo—Mary Ann McKinley	Fall, 1842	129
Edmund Phigley—Rebecca Lucas	Dec. 11, 1845	131
Isom D. Yocom—Mary Wilson	May, 1841†	132
Francis B. Yocom—Rhoda Webster	July 11, 1833†	133

RECORD OF STOCK MARKS, JACKSON COUNTY, 1817-1838
Contributed by Bernice Sallee Martin

During the summer of 1939, while searching for some genealogical material in the Museum of the Jackson County Historical Society, in the Jackson County State Forest, my attention was directed to an interesting old record book. It is entitled *Book No. 1, Record of Marks* and is the original record kept by the Recorder of Jackson County, Indiana, from 1817 to 1878 of the marks used by the pioneers on the ears of their hogs.

In early days there were few fences, and hogs roamed at will through the woods to fatten on beech mast and acorns. It was therefore necessary to have some system of marking as proof of ownership. To avoid duplication and to protect themselves in case a question arose concerning ownership, the settlers registered their marks with the County Recorder. Even in Territorial days, hog raising was important enough that laws were made providing punishment for theft of hogs, alteration of marks, and failure to report strays.

Mrs. Anna Borders, curator of the Jackson County Museum, graciously gave me permission to copy these old entries to assist me in my search for some pioneer ancestors. Recently it occurred to me that this list really serves as a rough directory of Jackson County in early days, and might be valuable to many persons seeking proof of residence of their ancestors. I copied only the names and the dates of recording with an occasional description to show the variety of styles in which hogs wore their ears in those days. The pages of this old book are loose, and since they are not numbered there is no way of telling if any are missing. Some entries seem to have been made in the spaces between earlier entries—possibly to save paper.

Book No. 1
Record of Marks

Demsey Moris' Mark
   A swallow fork in right ear and crop and half-crop in the left
                                        6th May 1817
Jacob Morris   6—June—1817
Lewis Rogers   7—June—1817

William Newland	7—June—1817
James Smith	24—June—1817
Wm. Kelley	5—July—1817
Michael Beem	8—July—1817
Solomon Cox	12—July—1817
Michael Beem, Sr.	16—July—1817
Millington Jackson	8—Aug.—1817
Abraham Huff	14—Aug.—1817
Jabez Crane orders his mark transferred to Jonas Crane	10—Sept.—1817
Asa Crane	10—Sept.—1817
Job Carter	28—Sept.—1817
John Parkes	27—Dec.—1817
James Tagert	7—April—1817
Isaac Williams	7—April—1817
William Wilson	25—April—1817
Jesse Butler	25—April—1817
Edward G. Jacobs	25—April—1817
John Ritter	12—May—1817
Edward Cooley	30—May—1817
Thomas Cooley	30—May—1817
Thomas Newby	8—March—1817
William Tabour	18—March—1817
John Craig	18—March—1817
Noah C. Willis	26—March—1817
Peter Herrington	6—April—1817
John Hover [Hoover?]	7—April—1817
Rebecca Bright	22—Jan.—1818
John Griffith	24—Jan.—1818
John Stephens	26—Jan.—1818
Thomas Cox	9—Mar.—1818
John Dopson	May—21—1818
John Arther	July 13—1818
Martin Douglass	Aug. 19—1818
George Jones	20—Oct.—1818
William Jones	20—Oct.—1818
George Iseminger	21—Oct.—1818
Jabes Crane	Nov. 2—1818
Peter Lyster	Nov. 16—1818
Stephen McCoy	Nov. 28—1818
Thomas Smith	7—Dec.—1818
William Russell	7—Dec.—1818

William Standerford	Dec. 19—1818
Thomas Whitson	Dec. 19—1818
Peter Johnson	Dec. 19—1818
Andrew Johnson	Dec. 28—1818
John Mapes	Jan. 14—1819
Levi Spring	Jan. 14—1819
Adam Miller	Jan. 22—1819
Joseph Goss	Jan. 28—1819
William Cockerham	Jan. 28—1819
Jesse Tabour	Jan. 28—1819
George C. Brightman	Feb. 9—1819
Obediah Walker	Feb. 15—1819
Jehu Mash	Feb. 17—1819
Jonathan L. Right [Wright?]	Feb. 26—1819
James Dudley	Feb. 27—1819
Smith Wright	March 11—1819
Gabriel Newby	April 10—1819
Elijah Olds	April 12—1819
John Robertson	17—April—1819
Joshua Moore	10—May—1819
Solomon Cox	10—May—1819
John Blair	10—May—1819
Jesse Tuel	22—May—1819
John Weathers	11—June—1819
William Flinn, Jr.'s Mark A smooth crop of the left ear	25—June—1819
Abraham Keller	13—July—1819
Caleb Elliott	30—July—1819
David Benton	23—Aug.—1819
John Standfield	24—Aug.—1819
James Hamilton	25—Sept.—1819
John Jacobs	30—Sept.—1819
John Kindred	2—Oct.—1819
John Whitkinnack [?]	2—Sept.—1819
Daniel Weddle's Mark A swallow fork in each ear and an under bit in each	2—Sept.—1819
Elias Day	13—Oct.—1819
Robert Holmes	20—Oct.—1819
Wm. H. Smith	26—Oct.—1819
Andrew B. Holland	Nov. 1—1819
Abel Findley	29—Nov.—1819

William Findley	29—Nov.—1819
William Summers	4—Dec.—1818
Caleb White	27—Dec.—1819
Maxilian [?] White	27—Dec.—1819
Thomas Wright	3—Jan.—1820
Basel Prathers	15—Jan.—1820
Edward Weddle's Mark	
A under stope in the right and crop and	
slit in the left	25—Jan.—1820
Henry Benton	26—Jan.—1820
Walter Benton	2—Feb.—1820
Isaiah Hornaday	2—Feb.—1820
James Slead [?]	22—Mar.—1820
James Copland	23—Mar.—1820
James Hanam	23—Mar.—1820
David Crane	5—Apr.—1820
William Robertson	Apr.—7—1820
Rufus Amans [?]	Aprile 27—1820
John Hubard	no date given
William H. Ewing	2—Nov.—1820
Joseph Hiett	2—Dec.—1820
David Kelley	18—Dec.—1820
David Kelley, Jr.	18—Dec.—1820
Jacob Hiatt	12—Apr.—1821
Alexander Howard	20—Sept.—1821
James Kelley	17—Nov.—1821
Jacob C. Baldwin	Dec. 12—1821
George Thompson	Dec. 12—1821
Jacob Scott	Jan. 1—1822
Nehemiah Whelen	Jan. 15—1822
John Newby	Jan. 15—1822
Asa Ketchell	Jan. 15—1822
Joel Williams	Jan. 21—1822
George Kress	Jan. 26—1822
John Ewalt	Jan. 29—1822
George Smallwood	Feb. 13—1822
Alexander Thompson	Feb. 13—1822
William Congleton [?]	Feb. 13—1822
John Chilcott	Mar. 19—1822
Samuel C. Tate	Apr. 3—1822
James Woodmansee	Apr. 7—1822
Joel Grantham	Apr. 27—1822

William Morgan	May 24—1822
Samuel Standfield	June 3—1822
Jonathan Crums	29—Sept.—1822
David Weddel's Mark A smooth crop of each ear and under bit in each	29—Sept.—1822
Solomon Watson	4—Nov.—1822
George Wagoner	28—Nov.—1822
William Marshall	28—Nov.—1822
Robert Gillaspie	5—Dec.—1822
John Marling	5—Dec.—1822
Absalom Parker	Jan. 17—1823
Luther Bedel	Mar. 18—1823
David Burr	Dec. 10—1823
Gabriel Woodmansee	Mar. 6—1824
Patrick Karnes	6—Mar.—1824
William Goforth	10—Mar.—1824
David Johnson	23—Mar.—1824
James Johnson	23—Mar.—1824
Elisha Sanderson	27—Mar.—1824
Ebenezer Henderson	8—Apr.—1824
John Reed	5—June—1824
James Brown	15—Oct.—1824
Hugh Brown	15—Dec.—1824
William Johnson	16—Dec.—1824
William Moore	Jan. 7—1825
James Wheeler	30—Jan.—1825
John Weathers	Feb. 5—1825
Moses Sewell	Mar. 25—1825
William Cardale	Apr. 26—1825
James Wilson	5—Oct.—1825
John C. Vermilya	10—Oct.—1825
Aaron Holman	24—Dec.—1825
John Hanners	12—Jan.—1826
John C. Barnes	22—Apr.—1826
John L. Jones	17—June—1826
Samuel Prather	17—June—1826
Stephen Cox	21—Aug.—1826
Hiram Noe	7—Aug.—1826
Isaac [?] Dixon	12—Aug.—1826
David Cordale	20—Oct.—1826
Uriah Hicks	31—Jan.—1827

Orange Monroe	17—Feb.—1827
Benjamin Draper	10—Nov.—1827
Solomon Ruddick	14—Mar.—1828
William Shields	15—July—1828
Thomas Collins	21—Jan.—1829
Matthew Tanner	21—Jan.—1830
George Keller	25—Jan.—1830
Joseph Goss	26—Jan.—1830
John A. Weddle	26—Mar.—1830
Willis Owens	20—Nov.—1830
John Owens	20—Nov.—1830
William Baldwin	6th—Dec.—1830
Jacob Watson	12th—Jan.—1831
Alexander Sweaney	Jan. 29th—1831
Willis Morgan	May 4—1831
Stephen Cockerham	24—Sept.—1831
Francis Elliott	Jan. 21—1833
George Standfield	Feb. 23—1833
John Powell	July 15—1833
Gabriel Chamlin [?]	Aug. 17—1833
George Kindle	Nov. 9—1833
Medy [?] W. Shields	Dec. 2—1833
Jacob Goutrey [Guthrie]	Apr. 22—1834
William Swine [Schwein?]	Jan. 30—1835
Nathan C. Rucker	Apr. 6—1835
Daniel Weddle	Feb. 28—1837
Josephus Crenshaw	Aug. 4—1837
Coleman Comstock	Dec. 30—1837
James Dudley	Dec. 30—1837
Henry Lyser [?]	Feb. 9—1838
Frederick Barkman	23rd April—1838
Dancil [or Daniel] Phifer [?]	9—Jan.—1838
Henry C. Dalton	Feb. 10, 1873

[These last two entries, 35 years later than the previous one, are both on the last page.]

Adam Heller	Mar. 15—1878

See Book No. 2—page 6

[Location of Book No. 2 not known]

A STORY OF THE SCOTCH SETTLEMENT JEFFERSON COUNTY, INDIANA

Edited by Mary Hill

Following the Napoleonic Wars conditions were deplorable in Scotland as well as in most countries of Europe. Times were hard, food was scarce and people were desperate. Many an adventurous soul wanted to learn about the New World and wished to bring up his family in the United States. So, we find, between 1815 and 1820, a goodly number of Scotchmen settled in the northeast part of Milton Township and the southeast part of Shelby Township of Jefferson County, Indiana, and the west part of Pleasant Township, Switzerland County, Indiana. They had come overland to Pittsburgh and then down the Ohio River to Vevay and Madison. It is said the first ones settled here because the land reminded them of their own beloved Scotland. They wrote home and persuaded others to come. Each farmer had a small place, hilly and rugged, heavily wooded, with small streams and springs. He erected a small cabin, later putting up a brick or stone house, started an orchard, raised sheep and cattle, and cleared enough land for his crops. His wife tended the garden, spun the flax or wool for their clothing, tended the bees, made cheese and soap, and gathered the wild herbs and roots for medicine. These settlers were a sturdy, thrifty, industrious, and God-fearing people. One of their first tasks was to build a church, their "kirk." Three Culbertson brothers, each gave an acre of land, which is still used for the church and graveyard. The church is now in Switzerland County, while the cemetery is across the road in Jefferson County. Many of the stones have the Scotch thistle and give the birthplace of the person. The church is called "Caledonia" and the neighborhood the "Scotch Settlement."

The following letter was written from Caledonia, Jefferson County, Indiana, January 22, 1837, by William Morton to Thomas Bishop in Scotland, urging him to come to this country. Bishop evidently took his friend's advice for we find him in this country. He and his wife, Elizabeth Ingalls, came to America on the steamer "New York." Bishop was twenty-six years of age and his wife twenty-two. His naturalization papers were taken out in Trimble County, Kentucky, and they state that he had been a resident of the United States for five years, three years in Indiana and two in Kentucky. His last years, however, were spent in the Scotch Settlement, for he and his wife were buried in the graveyard at Caledonia. The stones bear the inscription "Thomas Bishop, 1811-1880" and "Elizabeth, wife of Thomas Bishop, 1815-1872."

Jan. 22, 1837.

Dear Thomas;
Yours of the 15th October came to hand last week....you wish information from me about coming hear, with that I will most cherfuley comply as far as I am able in the first place you must lay in provisions for 8 weeks oatmeal and cakes baked thick and well fired potatos, butter tea, sugar a curran lof or two. if you intend to visit Cannada you must come by N. York and come on to bufalo, leave your luggage ther and take a steam bot for Cannada, on your return to come here come up the lake to Cleveland, then take the cannal to the ohio river, then to Madison but if you intend to come direct here come by Philadelphia and Pittsburg you can come that way a week sooner and fuley as cheap ther is canal and railroad to Pitts. then down the ohio river if you can get a ship to Phila. it would be better if not you can very easy get from N. York to Philadelphia there are some things you could bring out and have a good profit on if you can get past the custom hous sutch as womens dress handerchefs murine shawls blanket shawls and blankets particularly blankets would be as good as anything they sel for ten dollars a pair and all wearing apparel is exempt from duty you can pas them for your own some blew cots [coats] fashionably made would do well. Brother James wishes you to bring the works of a 8 day clock for him my sister wants two large blanket shawls black and red square checks. There is another way I would propose for you to com and I think the best and most profitable that is by New orleans and bring a large quantity of crockery I will give you some of its prices here; printed teas, 6 cups and saucers, 75 cents; printed plates 7 inch, 75 cents [?]; 12 inch, 1 dollar; teapot a dollar; common ware, 6 cups & saucers, 37 cents; plates, 7 inch, 37 cents; bowls of all sizes a good article there will be little or no expense on it to orleans from that to Madison is 50 cents per cwt. ther would be some duty on it at orleans but not mutch and your own passage to Madison if you come [illegible] brother Andrew would like to have a light iron plow if you come this way you would likely have to go to Liverpool for a ship and the best time would be in December or January You need not be afraid of the winter pasage for once you get off the British Coast the wether is often better in winter then in spring you must now take choice of the 3 different ways, but I think the Cannada will be the most expensive and orleans the most profitable way for you, tel your brother that I received his letter by Alex Graham with a new silver coin in it for whitch I esteam him verry

mutch I was about to writ to him when I received yours then I thought I would write you first Last summer Thos. Graham quit baking and bought a farm 5 miles from Madison and has been living on it since. Alex Graham and family had a passage of 9 weeks and 3 days owing to bad weather and an unscilful Captain about the first of September they all arrived at Madison in good health but it did not last long for in 2 days after their mother got sick and in two weeks she died that discouraged them all they are dissatisfied with the country but cant give no other reason for it only they like Scotland better. Thomas dont like to farm mutch he intends to bake again he offered his brothers the farm for 3 years rent free but they wont accept of it. W. Graham is working for W. Ween, has 12 dollars a month he says he will return to Scotland again the rest of them are on the farm with Thomas. I dont know what they intend to do. A few days after I wrote your brother last I received a letter from your friend in New York State whitch I was mutch pleased with I will give you a copy of it perhaps you may cal on him and take a good look of his daughter your brother talked of coming to see her but got discouraged at me not talking faverabule of the american ladies but he need not misunderstand me for I have very little scil and she is part Scotch and you know I am very parshal to them I dont know how far he is from New York but if you go there you can soon find out.

[The letter of John Bishop follows:]

Argyle, N.Y. 24 Feby, 1836

Dear Sir;

Yours of the 24th of October last never come to hand untill the 16th instant this was on account of having a wrong direction and it was nearly by accident I heard of it as the postoffice whitch it came to is ten miles from where I live the object of your adress is to obtain information respecting myself & relations in this country for the purpose of giving information concerning us to friends in Scotland. I shall most cheerfully comply with your requist and give you as distinct an account as I can. My father's name was WILLIAM BISHOP, he was a stone cutter to trade he left Scotland came to America in the year 1774 in company with two men of the name of Gowans they parted from eatch other as I have been informed in the city of New York and my father went northward into the interior of York State, the two Gowans into Pennsylvania, the certificate my father brought with him bears date from the Parish of West Calder in the county of Mid Lothian, North Britain. As the American revolutionary war comenced shortly after he arrived in this country he thought it best not to settle himself in the world till it was over accordingly he did not get married untill the year 1787 when he was married to my mother by whom he had three children, two sons, of whom I am the oldest, and one daughter. I was born in May 1788 my mother died when I was 12 years old my father never married again and died twenty one years ago from family afflictions and woraldly losses my father was kept always in low circumstances as to woraldly property my mother was for maney years previous to her death afflicted with a cancer in her breast whitch rendered her unable for business and cost a great deal for medical aid and attendance. my parents though poor in this world wer always respectable.

I am in the 48th year of my age have been married 23 years & have but one child a daughter who is now 21 years of age, my brother & sister are both married and has eatch of them large families, my brother lives in the state of ohio. my sister in the western part of york state. as to worldly circumstances I am neather poor or ritch I own 100 acres of land and by industry and economy can make a comfortable living and ought therfor to be contented and thankful. Last summer I received three letters from friends in Scotland people of whom I had no knowledge whatever for the correspondence my father & his people in Scotland was broken off before my remembrance & I never saw but one letter that came from them one of the above mentioned letters was from a John Bishop, from one of my uncles whose name was John Bishop of Foulsshilds, and from the information he gives me I think he is my 2d cousin he says his father & grandfather were both of the same name with himself that his grandfather died thirty years ago & his father about three years ago. I presume this is the same with your correspondence. another of these letters was from a William Hunter who says he is a full cousin of my own & he gives me a full account of my grandfathers descendants, he dates his letter from Raw Camps Hinknewton near Edinburgh, the third of said letters was from a William Bishop of West Calder and appears to be a very distant relation. I have written two letters to them but have not yet received any returns from them. when you write home to your correspondent you had better let them know what information you have got and especially where I live for their letters came with a wrong direction and it was not untill they were advertised in a newspaper that I heard of either them or you. I think from what I can learn the people of Scotland and [illegible] errors respecting America, the first is they appear to me to be in a great measure ignorant of the geography of this country they do not consider the vast distance people may be from one another here. had your correspondent known that you and me are eight or nine hundred miles apart he would hardly employed you to find me out. The William Bishop, West Calder, who has written me has a brother caled Peter Bishop, living in Upper Cannada, and he had been writting to him to call upon me, not considering that him and me are not less than three or four hundred miles from each other. The second error whitch I think they are labouring under is that because land is plenty here they think the people must all be wealthy. this is a great mistake. If you should ever have another occasion to write to me direct to John Bishop, Argyle, washington Co. New York. In case my letters whitch I sent to Scotland should have miscarried let friends there know how to direct them to me, I am sir with the greatest respect,
         Yours,
         JOHN BISHOP.

Since I commenced this letter to you there has been a number of people aplying to me for to get you to bring out things to them & call on their friends the following notes is from the Rev. Mr. Horn, when you write Mr. Bishop desire him if he be in Edinburgh to call on Mrs. Horn's sister, Mrs. David Lindsay, 65 Lawnston Place, and ask if she has any word to us, and also if he could send word to Miss Miekle, Cornwalk, Dr. Miekle's daughter that he designs to come here and that he will convey any word to us. Your attention to the above & obliged, your friend, W. Horn, (be patient not half done yet). Thomas Graham's wife wants a blanket shawl; brother George wants a german flut with some sets of music for it and som wants a sut of blue cloth what would you think of looking some of the Panbrokers shops for clothes I think you could fit some of our half yankeys there and have some profit. You might bring a good number of sacks they would do well & some moleskin trousers som trinkets and toe pieces for shoes. Dont bring any guns nor watches nor Crystal tumblers nor dram glasses they are all cheaper here than there. if you think [illegible] the Crockery perhaps Andrew Mungal could instruct you how & what to get & I know of nothing that would pay you better. if you sail for New York get a ship at Greenock or Leath if you go to Liverpool you would likely get into a ship ful of Irish passengers & they are the most disagreeable & most depraved wretches you ever was amongst. if you go by orleans you will shun that evil. there is yet another good article to bring that I have not mentioned that is Lots of Cash but it must be Gold or bills of exchange there is a great los on silver without it is dollars they are worth 6 [?] shillings & one penny; a souverin is worth 6 [?] dollars & 80 cents you need not bring any seeds the Climate dont sut them thos that I brought dun no good. Dont wish to put yourself to mutch trouble about all them requests that is made.

If you should not come out this spring & still want information about it let me know what it is & I will attend to it with the greatest of pleasure. I am mutch obliged to you for your kind offer to bring me one of my old sweethearts it would be very acceptable but I doubt it would be a harder task for you than all the other articles which I have mentioned. I wish to be remembered to your brother & sisters & old sweethearts & all other friends give my respects to Jannet Ingals & tel her I am obliged to for her respects to me in John's letter give my respects to my friends in Blackburn & tell Miss Prentace that I have forgot altogether about that half promise. If you should be troubled with sea sickness get a broad belt & put it around your body about the lower part of your stomack & lace it very tight perhaps it give you some relief. I think that is all now.

       I remain, Yours truley,
        W. MORTON.

If you dont come pleas write.
Dont bring the plow.

    W.M.

Addressed to Mr. Thomas Bishop

Whiteburn, Lincthgow County,
Scotland.

Mar. 19, 1837.

A letter written to
    Mr. Thomas Bishop
    Midseat
    Foulshield
    by Whitburn

15 Main St. Gorbals
Glasgow June 26, 1837

Sir
    I beg to acquaint you that a ship sails from Greenock on July 20th next An Advertisement appeared both in the Herald of Friday, and of today—I sent for a copy of the newspaper, but they were all sold, so I have written down a correct Copy of the Advertisement, which you will read on the other side of this letter
    I might have called on William Morrison here, but I did not see what I could enquire about, as you only can know what luggage you mean to take with you
    If you mean to go with this ship, you have little time to lose.
        Your mo obed servant
        J. S. Drummond

Drummond failed to write the advertisement on the back of the letter.

A letter written to
    Thomas Bishop, Farmer
    Midseat, Foulshield
    By Whitburn

15 Main St. Gorbals
Grasglow, July 14, 1837

Deer Thomas,
    In case I should be out of town on Monday first—I called at Wm. Morrisons office today—when a young man (I suppose a Clerk) told me that it is fixed—that the ship New York will be dispatched on Saturday the 22d instant—so that you would require to be in Glasgow on Friday afternoon to get matters arranged here—and you should send a cart with your luggage on Friday night to be in Glasgow about 4 or 5 o'clock in the morning, and you could then take it down to the Broomelaw & get the things put right yourselves— to be ready to leave the Broomelaw at 6 o'clock—you would require to go at the same time, or else you may be too late
    Or Another plan,—in case you should be detained, you might be more safe to be here and have your luggage here on Friday forenoon, and set off for Greenock with the whole, in the afternoon—you could easily manage this by send off the cart of Thursday night & set off yourselves also on Friday morning, so as to be in Glasgow rather before the cart comes—I think this last plan is the safest—you had better be in Greenock on Friday night than perhaps be too late on Saturday
    If the luggage & yourselves are here on Friday anytime before

12 o'clock you have plenty of time to go to Greenock in the afternoon—
If you were going to have much luggage, you could take the cart to Greenock by the toll road—but if you have only some chests & boxes & things of that kind, you will easily get them into the same boat with yourselves.

I am
Your Obed servant
J. S. Drummond

Friday night 9 o'clock
July 14, 1837

Thomas Bishop's Naturalization Papers

Commonwealth of Kentucky
Trimble County & Circuit Oct term 1842

Thomas Bishop personally appeared in open court and took the oath to support the Constitution of the United States; and also upon oath duly administered absolutely and entirely renounced and abjured all allegiance and fidelity to every foreign prince, potentate, state or sovereignty whatever and particularly to queen Victoria of Great Britain of whose realm he was late a subject and it appearing to the satisfaction of the court from record evidence that the said Thomas Bishop more than two years ago before the Jefferson circuit court for the state of Indiana declared his intention to renounce and abjure his allegiance &c And by the oath of Rufus King that the said Thomas Bishop has been a resident of the United States five years last past; and further by the oath of said King that he has resided in the state of Kentucky for two years past and that he has behaved as a man of good moral character attached to the principles of the Constitution of the United States and well disposed to the good order and happenings of the same And thereupon the said Thomas Bishop is admitted to all the privileges and immunities of an american citizen under the Constitution and laws of the United States

Commonwealth of Kentucky
Trimble County & Circuit

I William Samuel clerk of the circuit court for the County of Trimble in the state of Kentucky do certify that the above is a true copy from the records in my office
In Testimony whereof I have here unto set my name and affixed a scrall (there being no seal procured for said office) in the town of Bedford this 14th day of February 1843 And in the 51st Year of the Commonwealth

W. Samuel Clk

The First Families of White Oak Springs, 1810 to 1817

MARGARET STORY JEAN* AND ALINE JEAN TREANOR

For a brief span of years between 1807 and 1814, the most populous and the most important settlement on the Buffalo Trace in Indiana Territory from Clarksville to Vincennes was White Oak Springs.[1] The White Oak Springs Fort stood within a large stockade on high ground directly beside the Trace in White River Township of Knox County. It was about one mile west of the present Pike County courthouse at Petersburg, Indiana, and about one day's journey from Vincennes. Because of its accessible location and its safe and commodious arrangements, it served as a hostel for travellers to and from the territorial capital, and as an outpost and powder-base for the territorial militia.

The White Oaks Springs settlement had its beginnings between 1800 and 1807, when a little group of immigrant families clustered themselves about the Fort on adjacent quarter sections of land on both sides of the Trace, and it has had continuous existence from their day to this, as White Oak Springs until 1817, and as Petersburg thenceforward.[2] The families that comprised the community of White Oak Springs before 1810 were: the Tislow, Coonrod, Miley[3] and Coleman families, who were German and came more or less directly from Pennsylvania;[4] the Brenton and Arnold families, who came from Virginia, the first and probably the

---

* Mrs. Margaret Story Jean died on February 26, 1937, but much of the research for this paper was done by her, and its organization had been undertaken before her death.

[1] For personal confirmation of this statement the authors are indebted to Mr. George R. Wilson, author of the *History of Dubois County* (Jasper, 1910) and *Early Indiana Trails and Surveys* (Indianapolis, 1919). Ft. MacDonald (1801) at the Mudholes in the DuBois County area and Parker's Improvement (1805), later New Albany (1812), were the only other settlements, and neither was so populous or so favorably located for the use of travelers. Clarksville is today a town of about 2,500 population, located between Jeffersonville and New Albany.

[2] For a study of White Oak Spring before 1810, see Margaret Story Jean and Aline Jean Treanor, "The First Families of White Oak Springs," *Indiana Magazine of History* (December, 1935), XXXI, 290-316.

[3] The supposition that the Miley family was German is substantiated by a quotation from a letter written November 18, 1809, by S. R. Henderson to Emory Harrell, both of whom were grandsons of Moses and Mary Miley Harrell: "The (Miley) family was Pennsylvania Dutch . . . . They came from Pennsylvania and I have heard my Grandma say that up to the age of seven she couldn't speak a word of English."

[4] Recent information received indicates that William Coleman, petitioner for the Rock Ford Ferry (1809) was the father of Page, Henry, and Phillip Coleman. The latter settled in the neighborhood of the later town of Winslow, where his descendants still live. Page was the ancestor of the Petersburg family. To his first marriage with a Miss Bass were born James, Thad, Lee, and Albert B. (called "Hix"); to his second marriage with a Miss Evans were born Newton and Belle Coleman.

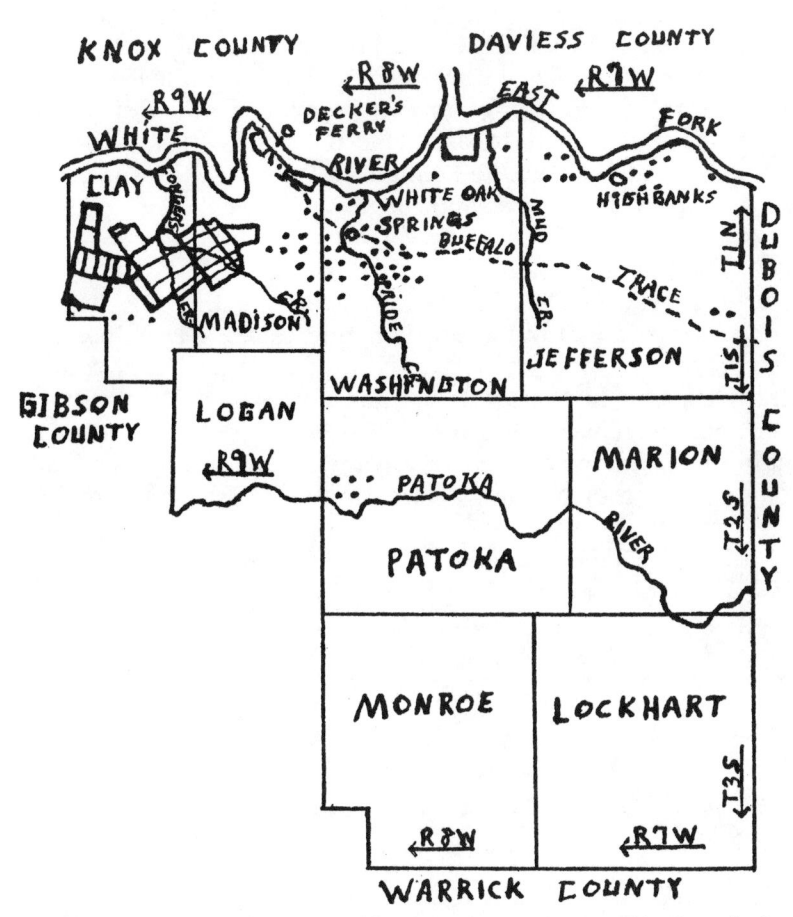

MAP I. Pike County, Indiana, county and township boundaries as of 1940. Settlements of 1816, when the area was a part of Gibson County. U. S. land claims (quarter-sections) are marked by dots, one dot for each quarter-section. Ancient grants are marked off in plots, which were lettered and numbered. Scale: 6 miles to 1 inch.

second of whom by way of a stopover of some years in Kentucky;[5] the Prides from Virginia, by way of North Carolina; the Risleys from New Jersey; and the Schearmahon and Walker families, of whom no previous findings were made.[6] Another member of this group whose name was omitted, but who has every right to be included, was Lemuel Baldwin.[7] In the present paper, the account of White Oak Springs and how it grew is continued through the period from 1810 to 1817.[8]

The ten families named above who settled at White Oak Springs previous to 1810 were bound together by ties of intermarriage and other common interests.[9] From the contemporary records, it seems clear that leadership among them reposed in Wolsey Pride and James and Henry Brenton: in the pioneer, Wolsey Pride, by virtue of his ownership of the fort and stockade; in the old veteran of the Revolution and Indian wars, James Brenton, because of the au-

---

[5] Josiah Arnold, a Revolutionary soldier from Virginia, who is buried in the Arnold graveyard a few miles northeast of Petersburg, was the original immigrant of this name, instead of his son Jeremiah, as was stated in the article cited in Note 2, above. Beulah B. Gray, "History of Jefferson Township", Petersburg *Press*, June, 1929; Mrs. Roscoe O'Byrne, *Soldiers and Patriots of the American Revolution Buried in Indiana* (Brookville, Ind., 1938).

[6] John and Jonathan Walker were land claimants in the DuBois County area (1814-1816), and Isaac and Jonathan were listed as residents of DuBois County in the census of 1820. The conclusion that some members of this family were domiciled around White Oak Springs is based upon numerous items of evidence such as: the signature of Thomas to the White Oak Springs-Rock Ford Ferry road petition, April, 1810; the marriages of Isaac to Susanna Risley, October, 1810, and of Jonathan to Polly Brenton, March, 1811, both girls of White Oak Springs; and the frequent later appearance of the name James Walker on the Pike County Commissioner's and Court records. From George R. Wilson's *History Of DuBois County*, we learn that Jonathan Walker did not confine his activities to any one location, as he was famous for his pugilistic prowess "from one end of the Buffalo Trace to the other".

[7] The name of Lemuel Baldwin appeared first in 1808 on a claim to NW ¼ Sec. 34, Tp.1.N, R8W, which cornered on the White Oak Springs quarter section. It appears on militia and marriage records within the next few years, and, in 1823, disappears completely from the deed records with the sale of the above mentioned quarter section to Franklin Sawyer. Nothing was learned of Lemuel Baldwin's subsequent whereabouts, or of his possible descendants. His only contemporary of the same name observed on the records was Daniel Baldwin.

[8] This paper does not conform to the pattern set in the preceding paper. The first dealt with ten families and presented some biography and genealogy relating to their members. The present one deals with more than a hundred families, and the presentation of biography and genealogy relating to all of them is impossible within the limits. All such materail has therefore been omitted. In compliance with the suggestion of Miss Esther U. McNitt, head of the Indiana History Division of the State Library, it will be complied later and made available for reference in bound manuscript form in the Indiana State Library and the Petersburg Public Library. For the collection of this body of Pike County biography and genealogy, which was made by means of personal interviews and correspondence, the authors are indebted to a greater number of descendants than there were original members of the First Families of White Oak Springs. Space forbids therefore any more than general acknowledgment of their aid to the authors in the preparation of this paper and the volume which will be its by-product. To Miss McNitt and to Miss Anna Poucher, head of the Genealogy Division of the State Library, and their assistants, we owe acknowledgment for never-failing attention and invaluable assistance.

[9] "White Oak Springs" was used to refer both to the Fort site, and to the community which grew up around it. The name is so used in this paper. The smaller unit was the NE ¼ Sec. 28, Tp.1.N, R8W, and the community unit was practically the entire congressional township, lying within the boundaries of the present civil townships of Washington and Madison in Pike County.

thority of his years, education and experience; and in Justice Henry Brenton as the appointed guardian of the peace and morals of White River Township.

The leadership of James Brenton continued to prevail in 1810, as witness the record of the Court of Common Pleas, Knox County, March term:

The petition of James Brenton and others, citizens of White River Township, praying for reasons stated therein that the township may be divided, and that all that part of said township which lies east of Conger's Creek may be erected into a new township. Ordered that the same be, and it is divided agreeable to the prayer of said petition to be known by the name of Madison Township, but the division of White River Township is not to affect the ensuing election.[10]

Changes of more importance, however, than that of township division were imminent at White Oak Springs. New life and new leadership were in prospect, for already on their way from North Carolina (April, 1810) were resourceful men of will and disposition to make "the Ohio country," and as it turned out, White Oak Springs, their sphere of future influence and action. Not even such worthies as Wolsey Pride, James Brenton or Henry Brenton could hope to maintain a monopoly of prestige in the presence of Hosea Smith, Moses Harrell, and Joab Chappell.[11]

For they it was, with families and friends to the number of twenty, who arrived at White Oak Springs in June, 1810, the vanguard of a migration which continued for over a decade[12] and literally transplanted a population from the piney groves and coastal swamps of the Albemarle shores to the hardwood forests and the productive virgin soils of the White River valley.

The company of Messrs. Smith, Harrell, Chappell *et al.* was from Perquimans County, and comprised a representa-

---

[10] This division failed also to take immediate effect for other than election purposes, as it was in a petition to the Knox County Court, April term, 1810, that the "undersigned householders of the township of White River" prayed for a road from "White Oak Springs to the Rock Ford Ferry", the "undersigned" being a fairly complete roster of the citizens of White Oak Springs. "The First Families of White Oak Springs", *loc. cit.*, 290-316.

[11] Twenty-three letters written by Hosea Smith at White Oak Springs to relatives in Perquimans County over the period 1810 to 1823 are in the possession of Mrs. Claud Uland, 616 No. Twelfth St., Vincennes, Indiana. Mrs. Uland is a descendant of Hosea Smith. For the use of a copy of these letters in preparation of this paper we are indebted to the kindness of Mr. and Mrs. Fred V. Chew of Bloomington, Ind.

[12] In addition to the immigrants named in the body of this paper, the following also come from Perquimans County to Pike County: 1820, Jessie Alexander (brother to Charles, Ashberry and Isaac) and wife, Maria; by 1821, William Chappell and Josiah Chappell (nephews of Jacob and Joab Chappell) and the latter's wife, Esther Perry Chappell; by 1823 Nixon Lamb, brother to Stanton.

tive group of its inter-related Quaker families.[13] A list of those who are known to have completed the journey to White Oak Springs follows:

> Hosea Smith (b. Pasquotank Co., N.C., 1773)
> Mrs. Hosea Smith (Huldah Harrell Wilson, widow of Jonathan Wilson, b. Nansemond Co., Vir., 1774)
> Theophila Smith (12 yrs. old, b. Perquimans Co., N.C.)
> Henry Smith (8 yrs. old, by Perquimans Co.)
> Onias Smith (5 yrs. old, b. Perquimans Co.)
> Stanton Lamb (8 yrs. old, son of Hosea Smith's widowed sister, Lovey Smith Lamb)
> Moses Harrell (unmarried; b. Nansemond Co., Vir., 1789)
> Jason Harrell (unmarried; brother of Mrs. Hosea Smith; d. at White Oak Springs, 1823)
> Joab Chappell (b. Perquimans Co., 1781)
> Mrs. Joab Chappell (Elizabeth Elliott; b. 1787)
> Peninah Chappell (1 yr. old)
> Gausby Elliott (did not remain at White Oak Springs)
> Jacob Price (d. at White Oak Springs, 1814)

Hosea Smith was an earnest believer in divine guidance, and his arrival at White Oak Springs must have confirmed his faith in the wisdom of the Almighty. He felt an affinity for the place from the moment he laid eyes on it. It evoked his pride and devotion as if endowed with personality. He reached his destination on June 5, 1810, and on June 14 he wrote to his brother John: "I can inform the [thee] now that I have got home. . . . I have purchased Land at this place caled [sic] the White Oak Springs . . . . I like the Land the best I ever saw . . . ."[14]

The uneasy anticipation of Indian hostilities which was being felt by settlers on all the Indiana frontiers was shared by those at White Oak Springs, and it is doubtful if any of the company of Hosea Smith took immediate steps toward independent settlement. There were cabins enough for a dozen families within the protection of the stockade. Joab Chappell shared the cultivation and the profits of the growing crops, and in October Moses Harrell opened a school. Hosea Smith urged his friends and relatives in North Carolina to come, saying that, "they might better themselves if they had not one Dollar after geting hear [sic]."

White Oak Springs was beginning to hear the buzz of

---
[13] For a picturesque description of this civilization, see Catherine Seyton Albertson, *In Ancient Albemarle* (Raleigh, N.C., 1914).
[14] Hosea Smith to John Smith, June 5, 1810. (Hosea Smith letters. See Note 11 above.)

the "westward swarming," to use Carl Sandburg's phrase, and to see and be a part of "what the moon saw" on the Buffalo Trace. "There hath abundance of people moved in this fall. Travellers from all parts seem to be a moveing daily," Hosea Smith wrote in November, 1810, "some to Plattoker [Patoka], some over the Wabash on the Donation, some on busroe settlement, an abundance to the new purchase, and a number over the Mississippi and some up the Misseory to St. Lewis and different parts."[15]

The abundance of people who moved into White Oak Springs in the fall of 1810 was followed by others in each succeeding year. Exact dates and details of their coming have not been preserved, however, as were those of Hosea Smith's, and it may be learned who they were only from a search of public and private records, and by inquiry into the various family traditions current among their descendants. From such sources a list has been compiled. In Township 1 North, Range 8 West, which was the White Oak Springs congressional township, United States land claimants up to 1817, with their former locations and racial orogins if known, were[16]:

1807	Wolsey Pride[17]	NW 27	Vir., N. C.
	Geo. Wallace Jr.	SW 27	
	Paul Tislow	NE 29	Pa., Ky. (German)
	Henry Brenton	SE 19	Vir., Mercer Co., Ky.
	James Brenton	NW 28	" " " "
1808	Silas Risley	NE 27	New Jersey
	Wosley Pride	NE 28	
	Lemuel Baldwin	NW 34	
1810	James Lindsay	SW 19	Warren Co., Ky. (Irish)

[15] "Plattoker" probably meant Patoka River. The "Donation" was evidently the Vincennes Donation Tract, which comprised more than 100,000 acres on both sides the Wabash set aside by Acts of Congress of August 29th, 1788, and March 3, 1791, for "granting of lands to the inhabitants and settlers at Vincennes and the Illinois country and for confirming them in their possessions". "Busroe" no doubt means Busseron Township, Knox County, which was laid out in 1810, and was already in process of settlement by Shakers' from Massachusetts and Ohio. The "new purchase" could not have been, of course, the Indian cession of 1818, which by custom has been granted the sole right to the title "The New Purchase"; it could have been the cession of 1809, made by the Delaware, Eel River, Pottawatomie and Miami tribes. This was called the Harrison Purchase and extended northeast of the Vincennes Tract to the "Ten O'clock Line."

[16] Former locations named are for the most part authenticated by family tradition and private records. A few however are inferred from the evidence of public records. Data, unless otherwise noted, is taken from the public records of Pike County. For kindly assistance in finding and collecting it, the authors are indebted to the Pike County officers contemporary with the research, and especially to Mrs. Esta Garland, deputy recorder.

[17] "The First Families of White Oak Spring", loc. cit., 290-316.

1812	Hosea Smith	SE 28	Perquimans Co., N.
	Aaron Decker[18]	S fr. 6 & 7, E fr. 7	
	James Brenton	SW 21	
1813	Henry Miley	NW 26	Pa. (German)
	Moses Harrell	SE 27	Nansemond Co., Vir. (English)
	John Coonrod	SE 22	Lancaster Co., Pa., a Jefferson Co., Ky. (German)
1814	John Coonrod	NW 22	
		SW 22	
	Bryant D. Savarns	NE 26	
	Henry Miley Jr.	SW 23	Pennsylvania (Germa
	Henry Brenton	E½ NE 30	
	Hosea Smith	NE 33	
	Paul Tislow	NW 35	
	Hosea Smith	SE 33	
	Paul Tislow	NE 34	
1815	Daniel Coonrod	NW 23	Pa. and Ky. (German
	David Hornaday	E½ SW 28	Chatham Co. N. C. (English)
	Breeding & Ewing[19]	NW 29	
	David Wease[20]	SW 29	Hampshire Co., Vir.
	Joshua Selby	SE 31	
	David Leonard	S fr. SE 15	
	Wm. Crayton	NW 33	
	John Cummings	NW 13	
	Breeding & Ewing	SW 20	Vir. or N. C., or both
	Thomas J. Withers[21]	SE 20	
	Campbell & Harrell	NE 21	
	Moses Harrell	SE 21	

---

[18] Aaron Decker was a member of the Virginia family of that name which came to Knox County about 1795. He was at this time operating the old ferry across White River on the Buffalo Trace which was started by Joshua Harbin in 1797. His land claim was to a few acres adjoining the French grant of Toussaint DuBois, which was allowed in 1806, and described as "opposite Harbin's Ferry". Did Aaron Decker move the Ferry landing from its old location on the DuBois claim to his own acres? It seems possible.

[19] Nathaniel Ewing was receiver of the public monies of the United States Land Office from 1807 to 1824. He made Vincennes his home until his death in 1846, and was an active politician and anti-slavery leader. Henry Cauthron, *History of the City of Vincennes*. Nathaniel Breeding was Ewing's nephew and the two did business in partnership until the latter's death in 1818, speculating in land in most of the southern Indiana counties. Neither ever lived at White Oak Springs.

[20] There is no tradition among David Wease's descendants as to his previous location. The name is found on public records in but one other location previous to the date of settlement at White Oaks Springs. Adam Wease, Sr., Adam Wease, Jr., Michael Wease, John Wease and Jacob Wease were listed as householders, census of 1790, in Hampshire County, Virginia (later West Virginia). Two of the above, or others of the same name, were Revolutionary soldiers, Adam Wease in the Romney Militia, and one Michael, whose name is recorded *Weese, Wease,* and *Wieste* in the Eighth Va. Reg., Continental Line. John H. Gwathmey, *Historical Register Virginians in the Revolution* (Richmond, Virginia, 1938).

[21] A large Withers family (also spelled *Weathers*) lived in several counties of both Virginia and North Carolina in Revolutionary times. Laban Mile Hoffman, *Our Kin* (Charlotte, N.C., 1915). The White Oak Springs immigrant may have been connected with this family but further research would be necessary to show it.

	John Coonrod	NW 22	
	David Kinman	SE 32	Greene Co. Georgia
1816	Paul Tislow	NE 35	
	Tarlton Boren	E½ SW 32	
	Thomas J. Withers	NE 32	Halifax Co., N. C. (Scotch-Irish)
	James Campbell	SW 26	

Traditions and records other than land entries attest the presence also at White Oak Springs of the following, all of whom remained and became citizens of Petersburg, or residents of nearby farms:

1811	Charles Alexander	Tyrell Co., N. C.
1812 or 1813	Henry Marrich and family Malachi Harrick (14 yrs. old)	Virginia
	Thomas C. and Rachel Wright Stewart	Virginia and Warren County, Ky.
	Elijah Lane	Jefferson Co., Ky.
1815	Archibald Campbell	Halifax Co., N.C. (Scotch-Irish)
	Henry K. Campbell	" " " " "
	David Parks	
	Thomas Milbourn	
1816	J. W. Loan	Breckenridge Co., Ky.
	Isabella Loan	Shelby Co., Ky.
	Thomas Meade and family	North Carolina

Until 1813, there were no land entries made in the Pike County area outside White Oak Springs. Mention must be made, however, before going further, of lands held by right of ancient grants—French, British, United States and United States Military. Thirty-two tracts of land from 50 to 400 acres each, about 6,000 acres in all, were so held, all except three lying in the valley of Conger's Creek and its forks within the area of the present Clay and Madison Townships of Pike County (Township 1 North, Range 9 West). In 1806 and 1807 the validity of these grants was confirmed by the United States upon recommendation of the land commissioners of Indiana Territory and their owners given legal title to their lands. The number of owners (25), plus the contiguous situations of their lands, combine to suggest the existence of a community contemporary with and comparable in size to that at White Oak Springs. Exhaustive inquiry has not been made into the history of the occupation of these tracts, but cursory investigation reveals that more than half of them were held by lifelong residents of Vincennes and the area comprising the present townships of Harrison, Johnson, and Decker of Knox County. Families of the names of Pea, Glass, Frederick, and Catt, which are undoubtedly descended from the holders of the ancient grants, have occupied the Conger's Creek vicinity for generations; but, except in the case of Jacob Pea and possibly the Fredericks, no evidence has been found that the original owners were occupying their grants in the period covered by this paper. It seems fair to conclude therefore that probably fewer than a dozen holders of ancient grants in the Pike County area could have been living on the 6,000 acres so held in the period of the flourishing of White Oak Springs.[22]

In 1813 and the following years up to 1817, more than

---

[22] Mr. Samuel E. Dillin, Attorney, of Petersburg kindly furnished the following complete list of ancient grant-holders in the Pike County area, having compiled the names from the abstract files of his legal firm. Additional information and spelling variants in parentheses are taken from the report of the land commissioners of Indiana Territory to the Secretary of the Treasury, dated January 3, 1807, on land climants in the District of Vincennes, *American State Papers, I, Public Lands.* All the grants except the last three listed lay within Tp.1,N, R9W.

Survey Number	Name of Claimant	No. of Acres	Within Secton Nos.
1	Sebastian Frederick	300	18 & 19
2	Heirs of John Glass	300	20
3	Busseron heirs (3, 4, and 5 allowed to	340.27	31 & 30
4	Busseron heirs Toussaint Du Bois)	300	31 & 30
5	Busseron heirs	204.18	31 & 30
6	Busseron heirs	50	27 & 32
7	Busseron heirs	50	27 & 32
8	Phillip Catt (Christian Hall, original claimant)	50	20
9	John Marshall (John Harbin, original claimant)	300	20, 21, 28 & 29
10	George Leech	100	21 & 28
11	Lewis Frederick	234.15	21, 28 & 29
12	Sebastian Frederick	300	21, 28 & 33
13	Phillip Catt	300	21 & 27
14	Phillip Catt	300	26 & 27
15	Wm. Reedy	50	22
16	John Pea (Jacob Pea, original claimant)	300	26 & 27
17	Isaac Wilson	100	26 & 35
18	Albert Wilson heirs	120	26
19	John Pea in the right of Berryain Brandoin)	100	23
24	Jacob Pea in the right of Antonia Catty (Antoine Caty)	50	26
25	Henry Pea in the right of Chas. Bonnette (Bonneau)	50	22 & 23
37	Jacob Pea in the right of Micnaek Boulelain (Bordeleau)	50	23
49	Jacob Pea		
52	James Fansby in the right of Wm. Fansby (Fernsley)	100 400	25 & 26 25
225	Jacob Howell	100	25, 26, 30 & 31
146	Joshua Harbin heirs	300	29 & 32
233	Wm. McIntosh (Louis Plouchon, original claimant)	136	33 & 34
Location no. 9	Frederick Lindy	200	30 & 31

The following three grants lay almost entirely within the later area of Washington Township, Pike County:
James Patton (Jonathan Conger, original claimant) 400 acres within Sections 6 & 7, Tp.1N, R7W, and within Sections 1 & 12, Tp.1N, R8W, and within Sections 6 & 7, Tp. 1N, R7W and Secs. 1 & 12, Tp.1N, R8W.
Thomas Barton (Amable Pearou, original claimant) 204 acres within Sections 7 & 18, Tp.1N, R8W.
Troussaint DuBois, 50 acres, within Section 7, Tp.1N, R9W and Secs. 1 & 21, Tp.1N, R8W.

a dozen land entries were made in the area of the later Jefferson Township, Pike County, and the settlement was named Highbanks. Its settlers were:

		(in Tp.1N, R7W)	
1813	Jeremiah Arnold	SW 9	from Virginia
	Levi Kinman	S fr. 11	Greene Co., Ga.
	" "	S fr. 14	
	Hiram Kinman	NW 24	" " "
1815	Geo. Rapp & Associates[23]	NW 8	Posey Co., Ind.
1816	James Kinman	W fr. 10	Greene Co., Ga.
	Randle Lett	" " 13	Georgia (French)
	" "	SEfr.14	
	Alexander McCain	SW 15	
	George Teverbaugh[24]	SW 27	Hampshire Co., Vir.
		(in Tp.1N, R6W)	
1814	Wosley Pride	NW 18	
	Thomas Pride	NE 17	
	Ebenezer Case	S fr. 7	
	John Case	SW 18	
1815	Paul Tislow	SE 18	
1816	James Brenton	SE 32	
	" "	SE 31	

Outside the neighborhoods of White Oak Springs and Highbanks, there were but seven scattered land claims in the Pike County area in the territorial period of Indiana. It is no wonder that so many of the old tales begin, "My folks moved to Pike County when it was nothing but a great big woods." These claimants and their lands were:

		(in Tp.1S R8W, later Littles)
1814	Robert Brenton	W½ SW 27
	Sally Jerrell	NE and NW 34
1815	James Hedges	SE 26
1816	John Wyatt	E½ SE 28 (in Tp.1S R9W, later Union)
1814	Phillip Defendoll	NE & NW 5
1815	Benjamin Reynolds	NE 4

Circumstances suggest, and, in several instances, tradi-

---

[23] "George Rapp and Associates" was the name under which the Harmonie Community of Posey County transacted business. J. S. Duss, *George Rapp and His Associates* (Indianapolis, 1914); George Browning Lockwood, *The New Harmony Communities* (Marion, Indiana, 1902).

[24] The presumption is that George Teverbough was a member of the family of that name which settled in the Harrison Township area, Knox County, about 1790. He married Patience Severns (1811), daughter of Bryant Savarns (Severns) of White Oak Springs. (Members of the latter family seldom spelled their name the same way twice. *Sovereigns* was another version.)

tion verifies, that there were others in addition to those named on the foregoing lists who came to White Oak Springs for temporary residence, the protection of the Fort, the transaction of business, or for the pleasure of visiting friends and relatives. A few had made permanent settlement on lands to which they entered claim later, others were only temporarily located. From around Highbanks, and the Conger's Creek vicinity, from situations isolated from neighborhoods, and from the far distant areas of the later DuBois and Gibson Counties, they converged upon White Oak Springs. Among them were:

Arrival in vicinity of White Oak Springs[25]	Former location	Permanent Settlement
1810 John Wease[26]	Hampshire Co., Vir.	Petersburg
Job Wease[26]	" " "	
Jacob Pancake[27]	⎰Hampshire Co., Vir.	Monroe Tp., Pike C
Joseph Pancake[27]	and	
Dorothy Pancake[27]	⎱Bulleit Co., Ky.	
1811 John Johnson[28]	Virginia	Petersburg
Ashberry Alexander	Tyrell Co., N.C.	Du Bois County
John Chambers[29]	Hampshire Co., Vir.	Petersburg
John Butler[30]		Du Bois Co.
James Butler	" " "	

[25] Almost all these dates are the first recorded dates referring to the families named. Traditional dates, many of which are undoubtedly correct, are met with earlier.

[26] These men were brothers of David Wease (See Note 20 above). John was a land claimant in 1817 to SW ¼ Section 23, Tp.IN, R8W. He was granted a Knox County license to marry Polly Jarrald on July 17, 1810. Job was granted a Pike County license to marry Rachel Harbison on September 6, 1817. Mary Ann Wease, their sister, married Zachariah Selby.

[27] Two ancient grants made to members of this family were confirmed in 1806 and 1807. Title to 225 acres of Knox County lands was given to Jacob, Joseph, and Dorothy, and title to 300 acres on Marie Creek to Joseph. The three named were brothers and sisters, members of a large family which included also Rachel (Montgomery), Margaret, a spinster, and William. One family tradition has it that they came from Bullitt County, Kentucky (another, Mercer County), but the authors believe that they came originally from Hampshire County, Virginia. The name, not found elsewhere, was common before 1800 in the area which forms the present West Virginia County of Hampshire (and which is only a fractional part of the original Virginia County of 1790). Revolutionary soldiers of Hampshire County included one John Pancake and two Joseph Pancakes, Sr. and Jr. A village of Pancake commemorates their former presence there to this day.

[28] There were at least three men of this name on territorial records, and it has not been possible to identify the references to the John Johnson who moved to White Oak Springs in 1810 or 1811, became agent for Pike County in 1817 and represented Pike County in the State Legislature for eight years after its organization. He is chiefly notable as the grandfather of John W. Foster, probably the most distinguished man ever born in Pike County, having served the American public as lawyer, soldier, diplomat, editor, Secretary of State, professor ,and author.

[29] John Chambers arrived in Knox County, according to tradition, in 1809. He was granted a Revolutionary pension as a citizen of Gibson County in 1818, and was recorded as a citizen of Pike County in 1820. He entered Revolutionary service in Hampshire County, Virginia, but a study of the name of Chambers on the census of 1790 suggests that Greenbrier County was the family's place of residence.

[30] John and James Butler were early settlers in the neighborhood of the later Hayesville, DuBois County. One or the other, or both, had a fortified cabin around

	John Butler Jr.		Petersburg
	Jacob Harbison[31]	South Carolina	Du Bois Co.
1812	Joshua Selby	Maryland & Ky.	Madison Tp., Pike Co.
	Isaiah Gladish[32]	Richmond Co., N.C.	
1813	David Kinman	Greene Co., Ga.	Petersburg
	Zephaniah Selby	Maryland & Ky.	Madison Tp., Pike Co.
	Zachariah Selby	" " "	" " " "
	Jeremiah Selby	" " "	" " " "
	James Crow	Georgia & Kentucky	Hazelton, Gibson Co.
	James Ashby[33]	Hampshire Co., Vir.	Patoka Tp., Pike Co.
	Benj. Ashby	" " "	" " " "
	Warner Ashby	" " "	" " " "
1814	Jeremiah Gladish	Richmond Co., N.C.	Madison Tp., Pike Co.
1815	Isaac Alexander & wife[34]	Tyrell Co., N.C.	Du Bois Co.
	Ashberry Alexander (3 yrs. old)	" " "	" " "
	James Dillin	Tyrell Co., N.C.	" " "
	Samuel Dillin	" " "	" " "
	Brittaina Dillin	" " "	" " "
	Jacob Chappell & wife[35]	Perquimans Co., N.C.	Monroe Tp., Pike Co.

1812 which was called Ft. Butler. They were not land owners, but were listed as householders in DuBois County in the census of 1820 and that of 1830. There was a John Butler, however, who was continuously on Pike County records until 1835. He may have been the same who married Peggy Harbison on November 7, 1809, and who signed himself John Butler, Jr., to various documents. He was perhaps a son of the other John Butler. For information in regard to the DuBois County residents, see Wilson, *DuBois County*.

[31] Jacob Harbison was the son of James Harbison, a Revolutionary soldier from South Carolina who settled in the Mudholes neighborhood. Jacob made land claims in the DuBois County area in 1816 and was a resident of that county in 1820. He married a daughter of James Brenton of White Oak Springs, and a study of his militia and jury service, and other activities, indicates that White Oak Springs was his second home, if not, for a period, his first.

[32] This Isaiah Gladish is believed to have been a brother of Jeremiah Gladish, which contradicts the family tradition that Jeremiah's brother Isaiah remained in North Carolina when his five brothers emigrated to Georgia, Kentucky, and Indiana. A search of early records in all states reveals no family or person of this name except that of Richard Gladish (Gladdis) of Richmond County, North Carolina, who was the father of Jeremiah of White Oak Springs, and probably of this Isaiah Gladish.

[33] The conclusion that the Ashbys came from Hampshire County, Virginia, is based upon a study of the name *Ashby* in the census lists of 1790. The coincidence of their names and those of others who came into the Pike and DuBois County area in the period 1800 to 1830, with the names on the list of Hampshire County residents, census of 1790 and other contemporary records, suggests that there was a large migration of trans-Alleghany Virginia pioneers into the area of Pike and DuBois Counties. Tradition and private records of the Davisson family of Pike County support this supposition, but, as most of these families settled outside White Oak Springs, or came into the area later than the period covered in this paper, no inquiry has been made and no other evidence can be cited than that of the names on public records common to both localities. They are: Wease, Chambers, Pancake, Davisson, Welton, Radcliffe, Teverbaugh, Butler, Milbourn, Miles, Shook, Tevault, Risley, Corn, Arnold, Leonard, and MacBride.

[34] Mrs. Alexander was Charlotte Hunnings Dillin before her marriage to Isaac Alexander. She was the widow of Benjamin Dillin, a Revolutionary soldier of Tyrell County, North Carolina, and the mother of his four minor children, named above.

[35] Mrs. Chappell was Rachel Lane Rogerson, a widow, before her marriage to Jacob Chappell. She is known to have had five children by her first marriage, but only the three named above are known to have come to Indiana. The names or presence of the other two sons have not been found registered on any record.

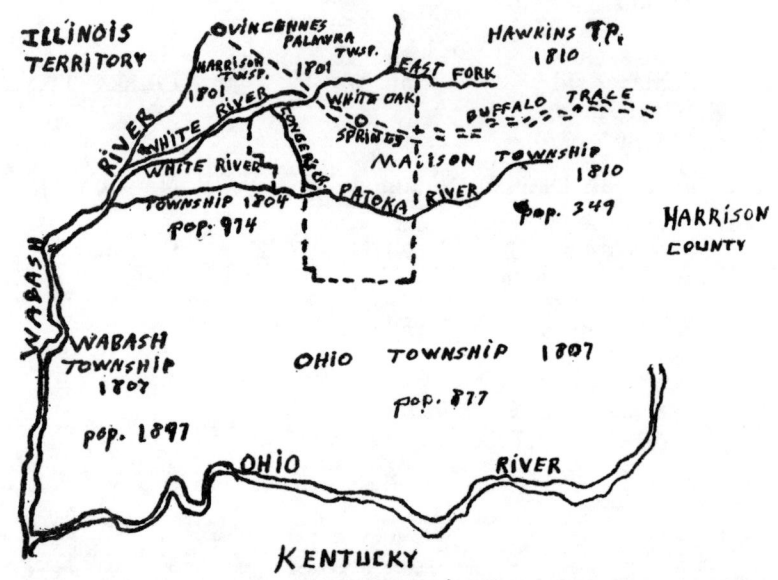

MAP II. Knox County area south of White River and the Buffalo Trace, designated White River Township in 1804; with subsequent subdivisions up to 1810. Population, U. S. census, 1810. Pike County boundaries as of 1940 indicated by dotted line. Scale 24 miles to 1 inch.

Job Chappell (2 yrs. old)	"	"	"	"	"	"	"
Ann Rogerson	"	"	"	"	"	"	"
Solomon Rogerson	"	"	"	"	"	"	"
Mary (Polly) Rogerson	"	"	"	"	"	"	"
Zachariah Dillin	Tyrell Co., N.C.			Du Bois Co.			
1816 Elijah Malott & family	Jefferson Co., Ky.			Madison Tp., Pike Co.			

The names cited above do not of course represent a census of the population of the Pike County area. In the first place, in the cases of land claimants and others, only family heads are named. Moreover, there are surely unavoidable omissions of unrecorded transients and of permanent settlers who failed to register their presence until a later period. An estimate may be made however of the total number of persons represented by the hundred and some single men and family heads on the lists. A study of such an estimate against the background of the official enumerations for White River and Madison Townships in 1810, and for Gibson County in 1815, reveals no glaring incongruities. There is fair reason to believe that a fairly good accounting has been made by family names of the population of the Pike County area in the territorial period. (See Maps II and III.)[36]

The compilation of the above names and dates was by no means the dull task that their bare statistical look suggests, for in the process of the research, the persons behind the names took on personality, dates connoted significant events, and life at White Oak Springs became focussed closely enough to take on a reality to the senses. For what the authors can impart and share of the satisfaction and delight they have had in this recreation, they submit the following summaries and samples of their research.

As a result of the unsettled questions between Governor Harrison and the Indian tribes, the year 1811 was about the most unfavorable year that immigrants could have chosen to come into Indiana Territory. Hardy souls came neverthe-

---

[36] Miss Dorothy Ryker, of the editorial staff of the Indiana Historical Bureau, furnished copies of court orders and territorial acts affecting township boundaries of Knox County, from which Map II was constructed. The records used included: *Executive Journal*, Indiana Territory, Feb. 3, 1801; Record of Court of General Quarter Sessions, Knox County, 1801-1805, February term, 1801, p. 4, and February term, 1804, 67; Record of Court of Common Pleas, Knox County, 1807-1810, November term, 1807, 64-65; Acts of Indiana Territory, 1808, 3; Record of Court of Common Pleas, Knox County, 1807-1810, March term, 1810, 233.

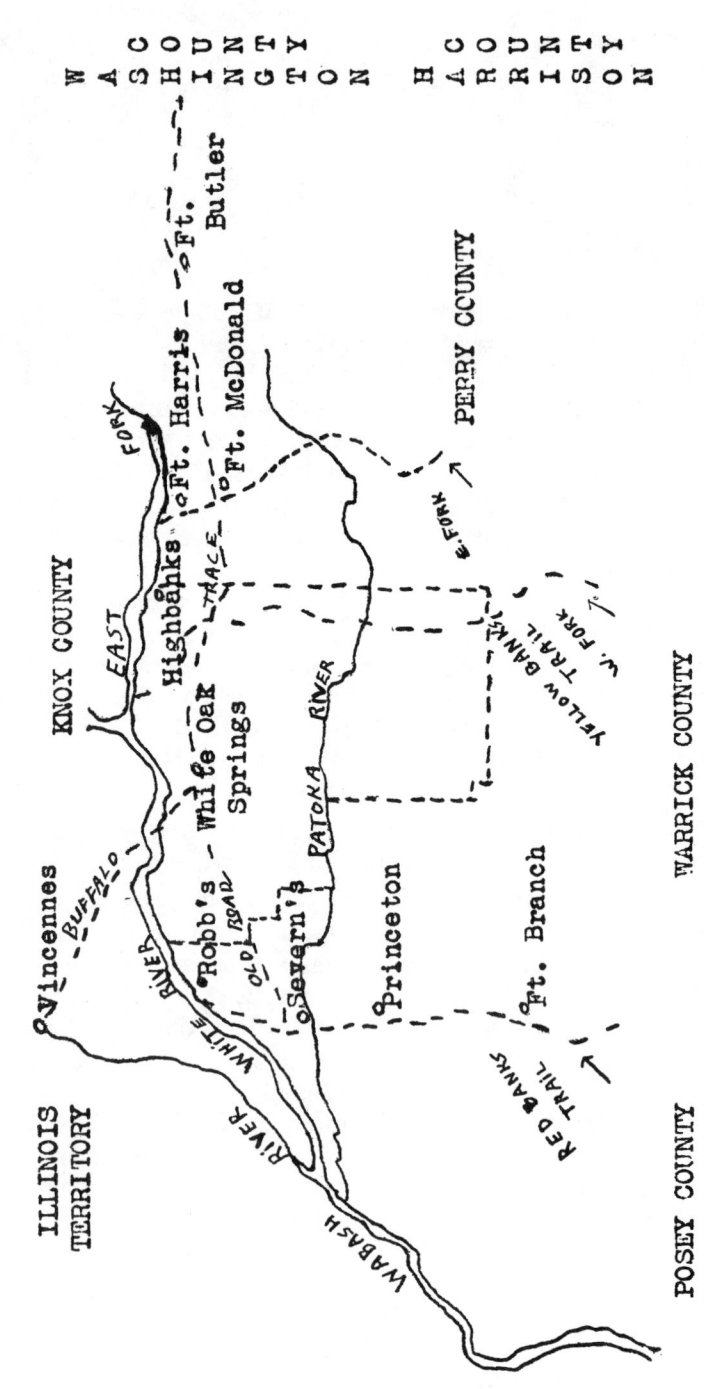

MAP III. Gibson County, settlements and roads, 1815. Population as of territorial census of 1815 was 5,330. Pike County boundaries as of 1940 indicated by dotted line. Scale 24 miles to 1 inch.

less, and a few stopped at White Oak Springs. William and Keziah Ball Gray arrived from Virginia and took up their residence at the Fort. Charles and Ashberry Alexander, neighbors of Hosea Smith's grandmother, arrived from Tyrell County, North Carolina. Joab Chappell took his family to his chosen location six miles east on the Trace (SEC31,Tp.1N R6W); but they became apprehensive of Indian attack, and shortly rejoined the group at the Fort.

When Governor Harrison mustered the militia for his fall campaign in September, 1811, the following members of the White Oak Springs neighborhood were assigned to service in Col. Luke Decker's[37] battalion under Captain Walter Wilson[38] of Vincennes and Lieutenant Benjamin Beckes[39] of Harrison Township, Knox County:[40]

> Daniel Risley, Corporal
> Peter Brenton, Corporal
> William Brenton
> Wolsey Pride
> Robert Brenton
> William Pride
> Joab Chappell
> John Risley
> Jonathan Walker
> Jacob Harbison
> James Walker
> Isaac Walker
> Abraham Pea

Members of the same company who moved to White Oak Springs after the battle of Tippecanoe were:

> Thomas J. Withers, Sergeant
> John Chambers
> Thomas Milbourn

The performance of Captain Wilson's company of militia at the battle of Tippecanoe was specifically commended by General Harrison in his official dispatch to the Secretary of

---

[37] Luke Decker was a member of the Vincennes family of that name (Note 18 above); Goodspeed's *History of Knox and Daviess Counties* (Chicago, 1886).

[38] Captain Wilson was General Harrison's confidential messenger in his negotiations with Tecumseh. He served in the militia of Knox County from 1802 on, in every grade of service. He was also a Justice of the Peace of Knox County.

[39] Benjamin Beckes was a well-to-do farmer who lived near Vincennes. He served conspicuously in the Indiana Militia over a long period of years. *History of Knox and Daviess Counties*; Cauthorne, *History of the City of Vincennes*.

[40] These names appear on the payroll of Captain Wilson's Company of Infantry, Fourth Regiment, Indiana Militia, September 18, 1811, to November 18, 1811. (Photostat copy in Indiana State Library.)

War written on November 18, 1811, less than two weeks after the battle. Following a tribute to the gallantry and bravery of the United States Regulars who took part, he wrote that "Wilson's and Scott's companies charged with the regular troops and proved themselves worthy of doing so."[41]

At this point it must be admitted that only about half the boys from White Oak Springs and thereabouts lasted the campaign through to share the Governor's praise for the fine showing of Captain Wilson's Company. The rolls reveal that Robert Brenton, Thomas Milbourn, Jacob Harbison, John Risley, and Jonathan Walker deserted on October 24, and that Peter and William Brenton were permitted to return home on account of illness on October 27. However, failure of these men to take part in the major engagement of the campaign seems to have done them no irreparable discredit. All the deserters were back in the militia service in 1812, except Thomas Milbourn, who returned in 1813.[42] In March, 1815, Peter Brenton was appointed Ensign in the First Battalion, Third Regiment, and Robert Brenton was commissioned Lieutenant of the Second Battalion, First Regiment. Evidence of the esteem in which Peter Brenton was held among his superior officers would be forthcoming in connection with an important later event. The only member of the White Oak Springs contingent in the Governor's army to receive any distinguishing mark was Wolsey Pride. He was credited with the assignment of "extra duty caring for the sick," which reveals the woodsman and bear hunter in a humane role not customarily accorded him.

Participants in the Battle of Tippecanoe from other parts who afterward settled at White Oak Springs were: Hugh Shaw, a member of Captain David Robb's[43] company, later the husband of Henry Brenton's daughter Sary (Sally); and Elijah Lane, who served in Captain Frederick Geiger's[44] com-

---

[41] *William Henry Harrison, Messages and Letters*, edited by Logan Esarey (Indianapolis, 1922) I, 627.

[42] The mild punishment for dessertion suggests that the offense may have been lightly considered. By the law of 1807, it consisted of a fine, "not exceeding fifty dollars," and the obligation "to march on the next tour of duty under the same penalties as the first." Laws of *Indiana Territory*, 1801-1809, edited by Francis S. Philbrick (Indianapolis, 1931), 419.

[43] David Robb was a native of Ireland who settled in 1800 near the site of the later town of Hazelton. *History of Gibson County* (Edwardsville, Ill., 1884).

[44] Captain Fredrick Geiger organized his company of Kentucky Volunteers at Louisville. He was wounded in action, but remained in command of his company. Alfred Pirtle, *Battle of Tippecanoe* (Louisville, 1900).

pany of Kentucky mounted riflemen and was wounded during the progress of the battle.

With the return of the Indian fighters, things around White Oak Springs began to pick up and hum. A new year was upon them. The Indians were subdued, they thought, and optimism was in the air. Wolsey Pride retired to the enjoyment of the elbow room on his choice quarter section near Highbanks and Hosea Smith completed the business of acquiring legal title to White Oak Springs, "my plantation," as he now called it. Jacob Chappell and his wife returned to their cabin up the Trace with their little daughter and a young son, Stephen, born at the Fort while his father was with General Harrison at the battle of Tippecanoe. William Gray and his wife hunted a location, and settled upon forty acres near Highbanks (NW¼ of NE¼, Sec. 21, Tp.1N., R6W), close to Wolsey Pride's new claim. Peter Brenton acquired the Silas Risley place, a quarter section which included what was probably the handsomest site in the White Oak Springs vicinity, and which he was to donate later for the county seat of Pike County.[45]

The early established group at White Oak Springs became now indeed the "old settlers." The new immigration provided a new infusion of life blood, which was felt immediately in the quickened course of events and the richer quality of life. There were numerous weddings "in our midst," Knox County marriage licenses showing:

July 17, 1810, John Wease to Polly Jerrald
October 24, 1810, Isaac Walker to Susanna Risley
December 8, 1810, Wm. T. Bass to Dorothy Pancake
March 23, 1811, Henry Miley to Nancy Pride
May 6, 1811, Jonathan Walker to Polly Brinton
September 5, 1811, George Tivebaugh to Patience Severns
December 16, 1811, Daniel Baldwin to Hannah Butler
April 7, 1812, David Wease to Elizabeth Harbison
May 22, 1812, Ashberry Alexander to Betsy Lindsey

John Johnson was appointed Justice of the Peace January 2, 1811, and the records show that he performed the Walker-Brinton and the Miley-Pride marriages listed above. There

---

[45] No deed is recorded in either the Pride-Smith transaction, or the Risley-Brenton, as the original owners had neved had legal title to their lands. Wolsey Pride and Silas Risley were the original claimants, but Hosea Smith and Peter Brenton were the first title-holders to their respective lands. This is the distinction as made by the General Land Office. The account of the Pride-Smith transaction in the Pike County deed book reads: "Title to 2 tracts (NW 28, TIN R8W and 60 acres off the west end of NE adjoining east side of above) entered by Woolsey Pride but cancelled before redeemed passed to Hosea Smith."

is no record of the officiating minister or justice for the other marriages, and we suspect that Johnson performed some of them also.

No less important than the literal enrichment of the life-stream of the community, was the stream of fresh ideas set flowing by the newcomers to White Oak Springs. They were people with a variety of cultural backgrounds, and religious and political beliefs.

If there was any unanimity of opinion among "new" and "old" settlers alike, it was no doubt centered in devotion to the young United States of America. The revolutionary soldiers, Josiah Arnold, James Brenton, Thomas Meade, John Coonrod and Henry Marrick[46] had themselves assisted in its struggle for birth, and they, with their children, and other children and grandchildren of veterans made up a considerable part of the population. Events of 1811 to 1813 were, moreover, such as to refresh and stimulate patriotic solicitude.

There may also have been considerable, though perhaps not unanimous, subscription among these natives of slave-owning states to anti-slavery sentiment. The Quakers were committed to it, and we infer that others were also, from the fact that they chose to come into a territory expected to be a free state, and that they brought no slaves with them.[47]

Territorial affairs were a close second in interest to national and affected life at White Oak Springs, even more intimately. Indian policies, compulsory militia service, county and township boundary changes, political parties and party politics, and changes in methods and personnel of territorial government, were vital issues. Upon these there were undoubtedly differences of opinion.

There is notable evidence that not all such differences, whether upon public or personal matters, were considered peacefully or settled amicably. Many of the cases in the first courts (Knox, Gibson, Pike) which involved citizens of White Oak Springs were cases of assault and battery and of trespass on the case. Not even the old Quaker neighbors of

---

[46] Henry Marrick swore to Revolutionary service with Virginia troops and applied for a pension in the March term of the Pike County Court, 1820; but his name is not on record either in the Pension Department of the Veteran's Administration or in the office of the Adjutant General of the War Department. Inasmuch as John H. Gwathmey, editor of the *Historical Register, Virginians in the Revolution* (Richmond, Virginia, 1938), states that at least 1/3 of the records of the Virginia militia privates who served in the Revolution have been lost forever, it seems safe to believe Mr. Merrick's oath, and to consider his service record among the lost.

[47] No slaves are known to have been brought to White Oak Springs in this period, although several were brought within the next few years by at least three families, and county records show that they were exchanged by sale, gift, and bequest.

North Carolina days escaped disagreement, one of the first cases tried in the Pike County court being that of Joab Chappell vs. Hosea Smith for trespass *vi et armis*.[48] It was a poor dispirited soul who could fail to have cause to sue or be sued at least once each term of court.

We suspect that there was some truth in the Augusta (Georgia) *Sentinel's* charge that, "a North Carolinian cannot salute you without putting his finger in your eye," as well as in the Raleigh (North Carolina) *Star's* denial, which explained that, "the practice of gouging had long since yielded to the advance of civilization and refinement, and had retired to Georgia and the wilds of Louisiana"[49] (May 31, 1810). Should the paper have added "and to Indiana"?

There were gentler sides, however, to community life around White Oak Springs than the above would suggest, and the forces of religion were strongly felt. All the members of the Perquimans County immigration came from old Quaker families which had resided for a century in the centers of southern Quakerism within the counties of Nansemond and Isle of Wight, Virginia, and Perquimans and Pasquotank, North Carolina. Jason Harrell and the little boy, Stanton Lamb, carried certificates of membership with requests for admission "to some monthly meeting in Ohio" and the others probably did the same. David Hornaday and Hannah Whitehead, who came in 1811, were from Chatham County, North Carolina, where members of their families belonged to the Cane Creek monthly meeting.[50] Viewed in the light of their later lives, all were righteous and godly people, and it seems that they should have been weighty Friends, with concern for the immediate organization of a meeting. Hosea Smith wrote to Gabriel Elliot of Perquimans County in November, 1810, saying: "I am in hopes in time if it is the Will of Providence that there may be a meeting of Friends near this place." Less expectantly, he wrote, in 1812, that, "the old man our father would be much delighted and satisfied to be here but the undertaking of such a journey would be hard and tiresome to come in a unsettled place where we

---

[48] The defendant pleaded not guilty: "thereupon came a jury" which found him guilty and assessed damages of $40. The defendant appealed and made a showing but his appeal was denied.

[49] Quoted from Guion Griffes Johnson, *Ante-Bellum North Carolina* (Raleigh, 1937).

[50] Sources of our information are: Minutes of the Perquimans County, N.C., monthly meeting; the Western Branch m.m. of Perquimans County; the Cane Creek m.m. of old Orange County, N.C.; and others. See Wm. Wade Hinshaw, *Encyc. of American Quaker Gen.*, I.

hant [sic] at this time meetings and other conveniences he might wish for."[51]

Hosea Smith's pious hope went unfulfilled and no meeting was ever organized at White Oak Springs. It is not for us to raise the whys and wherefores of the will of Providence in this matter, but from a strictly human point of view there were obvious obstacles to the observance of the Friends' discipline. Joab Chappell violated it immediately upon his arrival and Moses Harrell later by their engagements in militia service. Marriage within the society was foreclosed to them, as members of their own group were already closely related, and they were isolated from other groups. The plain language of Friends was ill-adapted to frontier situations which required rough dealing, and the stricture of plain dress lost pertinence in an economy which prescribed linsey-woolsey and leather. The difficulties of first-comers to a wilderness were hardly met by arbitrary rules of meticulous conduct.

Religious observance at White Oaks Springs was not, however, to depend wholly upon any one group of its settlers. Contemporary with the coming of the natives of the Albemarle from the ancient tide-water stronghold of American civilization, there was an assemblage of seasoned pioneers from the wide-spread outposts of its latest frontiers. Many were straight from the camps of the Great Revival which had rocked the South,[52] and from the headquarters of the Cumberland revolt against Calvinism.[53] Among them were evangels of the old and the new doctrines which had lately undergone the fire of volcanic phenomena and emerged in variety and temper suited to frontier needs. Certain of these doctrines gripped the people of White Oak Springs, including the Quakers, and shook them into action for the salvation of their souls. Only brief scenes of this drama have been preserved for us. From them and from its final outcome we may conceive something of its intensity and its importance to those taking part.

Archibald Campbell was an ardent believer in Methodism and promoted camp meetings for the propagation of his faith. His family and those of his two brothers (possibly three),

---

[51] Gabriel Elliot was the husband of Mrs. Hosea Smith's sister, Mary. Hosea Smith's reference to "the old man our father," may therefore be to Silas Harrell, Mrs. Smith's father, rather than to John Smith, Hosea Smith's father.

[52] See Catherine C. Cleveland. *Great Revival in the West*, 1797-1805 (Chicago, 1916).

[53] See Robert V. Foster, *A Sketch of the History of the Cumberland Presbyterian Church* (New York, 1911).

and the family of Henry Marrick were the original members of the "class," which was formally organized in 1828, and has had continuous existence from then until 1940 as the Methodist Episcopal Church of Petersburg. It is now, of course, just the Methodist Church.

David Hornaday fell under the influence of the Baptist Church of Christ and became an expounder of its principles and an exhorter before its congregations. This church grew out of the Elk and Duck River Association which was organized in 1808 by the Baptists of the Muscle Shoals neighborhood on the Tennessee River. It held generally to Calvanism and practiced closed communion and foot washing. Other practices are revealed by the contents of the following church document:

Pike Co., State of Indiana, May 8, 1825.
To those it may concern, etc.—
We the Presbretery being legily called by the Baptist Church of Christ to examine the qualifications of Br. David Hornida for the Gospile Minnistry and after exam'n-fasting, praying and the Imposition or laying on of hands, the said David Hornida is authorized to go forth in the full funktean [function] of a Gospile Minnester to preach the word of God, administer babtism, and the Lord's supper and perform minnester's dutys as directed in the Scriptures of truth etc. where God may cast his lot.
        Attested by   Alexander Devin[54]
                                    Jeremiah Cash[55]

David Hornaday's first lot was cast at Highbanks, and during his lifetime of service his "funktean" as "Minnester of the Gospile" was performed among congregations in the Pike County area. The Hornaday Baptist Church of Petersburg is a memorial to this pioneer preacher and has within its keeping the above "authorization."

The Cumberland Presbyterians were another Tennessee group of separatists. They subscribed to strong Arminian modifications of the Calvinistic doctrine, and their influence was felt at White Oak Springs fresh from its headwaters in the person of Nancy Lindsay Gladish. She was the wife of Jeremiah Gladish and the daughter of James Lindsay. Both her own family and that of her father arrived at White Oak

---

[54] Alexander Devin was a Regular Baptist minister who moved from Virginia to the neighborhood of Princeton in 1808. See Gil R. Stormont, *History of Gibson County* (Indianapolis, 1914).

[55] Jeremiah Cash was a Regular Baptist elder. He belonged to the church at Patoka (Gibson County) which was organized about 1810. He was its third pastor and served as such for a number of years. See Stormont, *op. cit.*

Springs in the very year of the Cumberlands' final break with the main Presbyterian body (1810). All, or most of the members of these families were, then or later, Cumberland Presbyterians, but tradition, doubtless for good and sufficient reason, singles out the young wife and mother (she was twentyone and had a one year old son, James) for the distinction of being "the first Cumberland Presbyterian ever to cross the Ohio River." Her faith spread swiftly to many families, including the Alexanders, Dillins, Johnsons, Meads, Weases, and Mileys. Their early congregation was organized as a church at Petersburg in 1821, and claim is made that it was the first of the denomination in the state.[56] It continued to be a well supported and flourishing church until, following the national movement of 1906, it united with the Petersburg Presbyterian church.[57]

David Parks signed himself "Minister of the Gospel" in 1817, being the first citizen of White Oak Springs to be so designated in any record, but of what denomination we have been unable to learn. He is probably but one of the many whose toil in the vineyards is long forgotten.

Many of the newcomers were men of gifts and skills and all joined in the common objective of creating a civilization. They were not content with life as Dennis Hanks described it in Spencer County, when he said: "We lived the same as the Indians, 'ceptin' we took an interest in politics and religion."

Hosea Smith was a surveyor, and the services of no profession were more acutely needed. Government surveys completed in 1805 were marked by mile posts and blazed bearing and line trees, into sections and quarter sections, but into no smaller tracts. Moreover, "county towns" were to be laid out in the near future, of which Hosea Smith was to lay out at least three—Portersville, Petersburg, and Jasper. Henry Marrick and Thomas Milbourn were carpenters and builders, the former also a cabinet and coffin maker. There is comfort in the thought of what the skill of these men contributed to the decencies of living and dying at White Oak Springs. J. W. Loan started a general store. David Miley was a wheelwright, his specialty being spinning wheels.

---

[56] Shiloh Church in DuBois County claims to have been the second. Ashberry Alexander was one of its founders. See George R. Wilson. *History of DuBois County.*

[57] The Presbyterian Church of Petersburg was not organized until 1848, and its founders were mainly members of lately arrived families from Ohio and Pennsylvania.

Archibald Campbell, James Lindsay and Elijah Lane were blacksmiths. Campbell, of stalwart frame and evangelistic fervor, became a sort of mythical hero in the folklore of White Oak Springs. There is evidence that the other two did their share of the blacksmithing business. James Lindsay owned a set of tools including bellows, an anvil, a vise, and two sledge hammers. This equipment sold for $143.95 following his death in 1817. The useful nature of Elijah Lane's services are suggested by the items of a bill which he submitted for collection (estate of Daniel Adamson, 1830). Some of them were:

>To make a spade .25
>To sharp a plow .12½
>To one clove's pinn; (clevis?) .25
>To irone a well bucket off 1.25

Moses Harrell had set up a horse mill by 1815, possibly as early as 1812. In the March term of the Gibson County Court of 1816, he applied for a writ of *ad quod damnum* for a water mill on Pride's Creek (NE 21), to which he and James Campbell had entered claim in 1815. Although water mills of the period were commonly used for both grinding and sawing, we think it likely that this was exclusively a grist mill, as Thomas Milbourn set up a sawmill on Pride's Creek in 1822.

The periodic journeys of menfolk to mill through the vicissitudes of winter weather and bad roads, and the distress of women left alone with their children in terror of Indians and wild animals, compose a classic chapter in the history of most pioneer communities, and that of White Oak Springs is no exception. Mrs. Zachariah Selby (Mary Ann Wease) whose husband and two brothers had moved from Kentucky in 1807 to a location "about six miles west of White Oak Springs" told her granddaughters, Mrs. Mary Ann Selby Colvin and Mrs. America Selby Pomernecke, that at the time she had her first baby the Indians "lived in the same yard" with them. When her husband went to mill at Wheeling (Knox County) or Vincennes, he feared to leave her alone among them and so she and her baby would ride behind him and the grain sacks as far as the White Oak Springs Fort, where she would wait the two or three days until his return. Later, when the Indians had proved themselves friendly, she remained at home. Just when Moses Harrell's mill went into operation we do not know, but let us hope it was promptly.

As a tribute to sentiment, attention is called to the fact that upon the same day that Moses Harrell got the writ issued for his mill site (March 12, 1816), he also acquired a license to marry Miss Mary Miley, and that Justice Hosea Smith subsequently made them man and wife.

Life and liberty were not yet secure in the new county of Gibson, township of Madison, and civic progress and the pursuit of happiness did not proceed without alarms and interruptions. The Indian tribes, heartened by British successes at Detroit and Fort Dearborn (Chicago) in the war that Congress had declared on Great Britain in June, 1812, and restocked with British food and ammunition, resumed their former assaults on the frontiers in August.

Militia service was compulsory for every free, able-bodied, white, male citizen of the territory between the ages of 18 and 45, with few provisions for exemption and refusal subject to fine by the courts.[58] Called for service on August 11, in the First Regiment commanded by Col. Ephraim Jordan[59] were:[60]

Jacob Pancake	Silas Risley	Thomas Pride
David Wease	Jacob Scamahorn	John Tislow
David Miley	John Risley	Joshua Selby
Isaiah Gladish	Jacob Harbison	Lemuel Baldwin
Henry Coleman	John Miley	Sebastian Frederick
Francis Coleman	John Butler	Peter Frederick
William Bass	John Cummins	

Serving from August 13 to November 19, were: James Lindsay, Sergeant, and William Coleman

In early September, Fort Wayne and Fort Harrison (Terre Haute) were surrounded and threatened, and a number of persons were shot from ambush. Nearer home, on the third of the month, twenty-three members of the unprotected Pigeon Roost settlement (within the present limits of Scott County) were cruelly murdered. Reserves were thereupon called out and White Oak Springs was stripped of men of the

---

[58] *Laws of Indiana Territory, 1601-1809*, edited by Francis S. Philbrick, 399.

[59] Col. Jordan was an early settler of Palmyra Township, Knox County. He engaged in public service throughout the territorial period, as a judge of the Courts of Quarter Sessions, and as an officer in the Knox County Militia in every rank from Lieutenant to Colonel.

[60] These names appear upon the Muster, Pay and Receipt Rolls of Indiana Territory, War of 1812. (Photostat copies, Indiana State Library).

specified qualifications for the militia. Serving from September 6 to November 9, in Captain Beckes' Company, were:

John Chambers, second corporal
Hugh Shaw Jr.
Thomas J. Withers

Serving September 10 to 21, in Captain John Johnson's Company of mounted riflemen, were:

George Teverbaugh, Lieutenant
Ashberry Alexander, Ensign
Joab Chappell
James Walker
John Butler
Robert Brenton
Jonathan Walker
Moses Harrell
John Tislow
Daniel Coleman
Henry Brenton
Jacob Harbison
John Risley
Francis Coleman
Isaiah Gladish
Joshua Selby
Henry Coonrod
Lemuel Baldwin
Henry Coleman
Peter Frederick

In 1813 there were fewer militia duties performed by the men of White Oak Springs. We are at loss to account for this, inasmuch as the need was as great as in 1812, and in fact, the territory-wide enlistment was larger. Moreover, the militia law remained as strict as in 1812. The few who were called saw some interesting service, however, for, by this time, the militia was on the offensive, scouring the Territory clean of Indians and their villages. From February to April, in Captain John Johnson's Company, were:

Jacob Pancake
Jeremiah Arnold
John Wease
Zachariah Selby
James Butler

From April to August, in Captain William Hargrove's[61] Company, were:

Jacob Pancake
John Risley
Hugh Shaw Jr.

From May to August, in Captain Craven Peyton's Company of mounted rangers, were:

Henry Miley
Thomas Pride
John Butler
James Butler

---

[61] William Hargrove was a South Carolinian who settled in the neighbrohood of the later town of Princeton about 1804. He had served three years in the Kentucky Militia, and proceeded to hold every rank from Captain to Colonel in the Indiana Militia. Letters exchanged between him and Governor Harrison are one of the few sources of knowledge concerning White Oak Springs in th period previous to 1810.

Jacob Harbison   William Gray
Thomas Milbourn   John Miley

It was the mounted rangers of Captain Peyton's Company with picked men from several other companies under Col. Joseph Bartholomew who made a tour of the Delaware towns on the upper west fork of White River, engaging in several skirmishes, destroying the grain of the Indians and burning what was left of their villages after their owners had deserted them.[62]

During the latter part of 1813 successes were all on the American side, an armistice was signed in October, and in 1814 the militia law was relaxed. On October 14, 1814, Ashberry Alexander was appointed captain in the First Regiment, Second Battalion; Robert Brenton lieutenant; and Thomas Pride ensign. There were also other short single periods of service; but the frontier was practically clear of Indians, the worst of their threat to the pioneer existence was ended and the need of the militia was about over. In 1816 the Gibson County Court (May term) recognized the existence of local companies when it formed the new Harbison Township from "all that portion of Madison lying east of the present line dividing Capt. Hope's and Capt. Harrell's companies."[63] The chief purpose of the militia service was now accomplished, and it subsequently declined in importance until membership required little more than muster day attendance.[64]

For the benefit of any curious person who may wonder what the pay was for militia service, we cite the following pay voucher items:

> David Miley, private, Aug. 11 to Sept. 20, 1812, $ 8.88
> David Wease, corporal, Aug. 11 to Sept. 20, 1812,   9.17
> Jacob Pancake, sergeant, Aug. 11 to Sept. 20, 1812, 10.66

Along with threat of violence from the Indians, White Oak Springs suffered violence from the forces of nature.[65]

---

[62] John B. Dillon, *History of Indiana* (Indianapolis, 1859), p. 524.

[63] The authors were unable to learn exactly who these captains were. Jason and Moses Harrell resided at White Oak Springs, and the Hope family in the area of Harbison Township, DuBois County. The latter family included James, Thomas, Richard and Adam, the last named the first sheriff of Pike County.

[64] See Logan Esarey, *History of Indiana* (I, p. 496).

[65] It seems pertinent to report that the authors found no recorded information and heard no tradition that could be construed to mean that White Oak Springs ever suffered from any hostile Indian attack. This was a great disillusionment for one of the authors of this article, who spent many exciting childhood hours re-enacting the bloody defense of the Fort from behind the portholes of the two story log house which remained of the buildings that had stood within the stockade. This has now been razed, and there is no reminder of White Oak Springs to appeal to the historic sense or the imagination of the present generation of children.

Earthquakes were felt in June and September of 1812, caused, according to Hosea Smith, "by the burning mountains of the Western ocean." Floods in April, 1813, sent the streams out of their banks, drowned stock, washed away homes, and prevented the passing of the mails for more than a month. "The greatest fresh in White River known since settled," Hosea Smith called it.

The untoward behaviour of Nature and natives was not, however, the worst that hindered the orderly and satisfactory progress of personal and community affairs at White Oak Springs. In March, 1813, Gibson County was formed from the Knox County townships of Madison and White River, plus some additional territory to the north and south (See map III). (Madison was still "all that portion east of Congo's Creek," and White River "the tract west of Madison lying between White River and Pattocco.") White Oak Springs seems to have had no hand or voice in the new county organization. Isaac Montgomery and Daniel Putnam of Princeton were named associate judges, James Crow of the David Robb settlement (later Hazelton) sheriff, and the out-of-the-way, new-begun village of Princeton was chosen for the county seat. The appointment of Hosea Smith Justice of the Peace was, moreover, an unpopular one. Most of the ensuing cases in the Gibson County Court which involved the gentlemen from White Oak Springs were actions of "contemp" for refusal to attend court at the new county seat, or appeals from the jurisdiction of Justice Hosea Smith. A few quotations from the docket indicate the trend of feeling:

October, 1814—Wm. McDonald[66] vs. Hosea Smith, case dismissed.

March, 1815—(Henry Miley and Peter Brenton on the jury)
An attachment ordered issued against Ashbury Alexander and Moses Harrell for contemp of this court by their nonattendance at the present term to give evidence.

March, 1815—Paul Tislow vs. James Brenton, an appeal from Hosea Smith's jurisdiction. Appeal denied, judgment of the justice affirmed.

October, 1815—Ordered that Henry Brenton, John Brenton, and James Brenton show cause why they should not be fined for not attending the present term of court as grand jurors.

---

[66] William McDonald was the head of the pioneer family of that name. The McDonalds were the first settlers of the DuBois County area (1801). See George R. Wilson, *History of DuBois County*.

June, 1816—Paul Tislow vs. Samuel Kinman, an appeal from judgment of Justice Smith. Appeal dismissed for want of proper security.

Inasmuch as frontier justice is commonly the laughing stock of sophisticated generations, it seems that an instance which commands respect today is worthy of report. In the case cited above Paul Tislow *vs.* James Brenton, the judge handed down an opinion which for sound reasoning, clear-cut language, and adherence to the point might well serve as a model for present day judges. The conclusions, moreover, are a statement of law which would stand in the higher courts of the state of Indiana, in 1940, as firmly as in the territorial courts of 1813.[67] From the GIBSON COUNTY CIVIL ORDER BOOK A:

March term, 1815—Paul Tislow vs. James Brenton
On certiorari on motion of G. W. Johnston council for defendant for a writ against Hosea Smith Esqr. Justice of the Peace for the County of Gobson to show cause by and upon the first day of ensuing term of court, if any he hath, why a mandamus should not issue against him to certify to this court records of his judgment in the above cause whereupon the same is granted and it is ordered that a copy of this order be served on the said Hosea Smith Esqr. by the sheriff.

In this cause the court delivered the following opinion:

This writ of certiorari has been brought by Paul Tislow to reverse a judgment obtained against him on James Brenton in a court for the trial of small causes before Justice Smith. It appears from the record that the deft. appeared and attended to the trial.

The reasons assigned in the reversal of the judgment are 1st, that the warrant is defective, 2nd., that the Justice refused to permit the deft. upon his own request to swear to the truth of his account.

As to the 1st. ground:—In the assignment it was suggested by this court and admitted by Tislow's council that the appearance of a defdt. and preceeding to trial cured any defect in the process. But it was contended that this doctrine does not apply in Justices' Courts because as was said they are not courts of record. They have authority to fine and imprison: besides, they are directed and obligated by express words in the statute to keep a docket in which must be entered all the proceedings in the cause—R. C. 220—and further the statute of 1811 authorizes the courts of common pleas to issue writs of certiorari and makes it the duty of the Justice to whom a certiorari is directed to send up a fair transcript of his record, which requisition of the law would be absurd if there were no records belonging to the court. As therefore it is admitted that appearances and proceeding to trial cures defect in process in court of record the same circumstances cure defects of process in Justices' Courts, which are to all intents and purposes,

---

[67] For comment on this opinion, we are indebted to the Hon. Walter E. Treanor, Judge of the United States Circuit Court of Appeals, Seventh Circuit, Chicago.

courts of record. With respect to the second ground urged for reversal has been argued that the Justice committed error in refusing to permit the defdt. at his own request, to swear to the truth of his account, the Justice giving as reason for such refusal that he was appraised it could be proved that defts. account had been paid.

This court consider it totally immaterial whether the reasons given by the Justice for the refusal are sound or not; the only question is —did he commit an error in not complying with defts. request? We are of the opinion he did not; the defdt. had no right nor had the Justice any Authority to permit him, to swear to the truth of his account, unless particularly requested so to do by the adverse party— Acts of 1813, page 115—but it does not appear from the record that any such request was made.

The judgment of the Justice is therefore affirmed with costs."

The author of the above was none other than Isaac Blackford, then President Judge of the Gibson County Court, later Justice of the Supreme court of the state of Indiana from 1817 to 1853[68]

An event occurred in 1813 (May 1) which was even more distressing than the change of a county seat. This was the removal of the territorial capital from Vincennes to Corydon by order of the territorial legislature. Whatever character and importance White Oak Springs had, or might have, it owed to its propinquity to the territorial capital and its situation on the main traveled road thereto. The effect of this act of the legislature was to reduce it to a condition of provincial isolation, and to remove from its reach the world of affairs. Hosea Smith could no longer write the news of public men and events in Indiana territory to the folks back in Carolina with the authoritative and familiar preface "I heard the Governor say. . . . " Corydon was almost as inaccessible as a foreign capital, and the trip there was too difficult and too expensive to make for any except necessary and urgent business. George Chambers made it in 1824 to settle the estate of his father, John Chambers, and among his expense items filed, "two trips to Cordden—$18."

In 1814, the post road was rerouted and White Oak Springs left off, the new route passing to the north by way of Washington Courthouse (Salem, 1814) and Lindley's Mills (Paoli, 1816).[69] In 1815, however, a post office was granted

---

[68] William W. Woolen, *Historical Sketches of Indiana* (Indianapolis, 1883) 344-352; Leander J. Monks, *Courts and Lawyers of Indiana* (Indianapolis, 1916), 187-195; *Southern Law Review*, n.s., VI, 907.

[69] George E. Amick, "Post Roads in Southern Indiana," *Indiana Magazine of History* (Dec., 1934), XXX, 331-334.

to White Oak Springs, but it cannot be reported that communication with the outside world was assured thereafter, for alas, not so. From the content of the following letter we infer that in its new status White Oak Springs merely suffered a new ignominy, that of having the post rider go by without stopping:[70]

Dec. 12, 1815

The Postmaster General to
Hosea Smith, Esqr. P.M. White Oak Springs, I. T.
Sir, I have received yours of the 16th Ult. I wish you to inform the mail carrier that it is his duty to call at your office with the mail—and you can show him this letter as your authority.

R. J. M. [Meigs]

Transportation and communication were beginning to take other roads and other directions and to pass by and around the little community south of White River, a trend which continued over a period of years and finally left it in the remote seclusion of the backwoods. Except for the alleviation furnished by the limited service of the Evansville and Terre Haute Railroad (1881), this condition was suffered for a century. Only since modern transportation and state highway building have penetrated its isolation has Petersburg had the easy rapport with affairs of state and nation that White Oak Springs enjoyed in the period 1807 to 1814; and the little city of Petersburg has never achieved the relative importance in the days of Indiana's statehood that distinguished White Oak Springs in the early territorial period.

Time crept on, and death and taxes took their toll. The tax rates as prescribed by the Gibson County Court for 1813 were:[71]

> For each 100 acres first rate land 25¢
> For each 100 acres second rate land 18¾¢
> For each 100 acres third rate land 6¼¢
> For each horse creature over 3 yrs. old 31¼¢

The first coroner's jury in Gibson County was impanelled on November 27, 1813, for the purpose of an inquest on the body of Walter Jerrel. It held that his death was occasioned by the accidental fire of his own gun. On the jury were:

---

[70] *Territorial Papers of the United States*, edited by Clarence Edwin Carter, (Washington, D.C., 1939), VIII.

[71] The odd and fractional sums chosen for the tax rates suggest that Spanish coins, the "fip," 6¼c, and the "bit," 12½c, were in common circulation.

James Lindsay, foreman
Henry Brenton
Henry Miley
David Miley Sr.
Wm. Craton
Jonathan Walker
Jacob Harbison
Peter Brenton
John Butler Jr.
David Weace
Thomas Milburn
Henry Miley Jr. [son of David Miley]

Among the Gibson County Court's appointments and orders for Madison Township were:

1813—Assessor   Hosea Smith
     Constable   Abraham Pea

1814—Road Supervisors   James Brenton and James Lindsay
     Election Superintendent John Johnson
     Election to be held at Hosea Smith's.

1815—Overseers of the poor   Jacob Pea and Henry Brenton
     Election Superintendent Henry Brenton
     Election to be held at Hosea Smith's.

"Hosea Smith's" was of course the Fort, still, as ever since its founding, the center of community affairs. Theophila Smith Alexander often told her granddaughter, Mrs. Anna Alexander Brenton, of the visits of Indians to the Fort. She said they would crouch in a ring around the walls of her mother's kitchen, each with his dog at his side. When her mother passed refreshments, all shared with their pets, while not one, to her amazement and indignation, ever asked for food to take to his wife and children, or carried away any of his portion for them.

The only available first-hand accounts of life at White Oak Springs are the brief comments of Hosea Smith in his letters. It was not the time nor the place for any effort approaching the literary. In fact, there was a high percentage of illiteracy, as may be noted from the many signatures on Pike County records followed by "his (x) mark." There were numerous and notable exceptions, however. John Coonrod signed his name in beautiful German script, "Johannes Coonrod," and the Miley family owned, and surely some could read, a small library of German books. James

Brenton acted as secretary for public meetings and was the author of petitions and resolutions. Hosea Smith kept accounts of his personal and official business, his big walnut desk being stuffed, as his grandchildren remembered, with correspondence and legal papers. Paul Tislow made scrupulous reports to the Court of an estate which he admistered. David Miley gave expert clerical service to Pike County for many years in every county office. Thomas J. Withers and Henry Brenton served as associate judges, their office elective and presupposing superior wisdom and common sense rather than knowledge of law. David Kinman was the only poet among them, as well as can be learned. Unfortunately in the one example of his work preserved, his "Journey Song," he did not describe life at White Oak Springs. He did, however, describe experiences and give utterance to emotions shared by all who joined him there, for which he may properly be called The Poet of White Oak Springs. All had suffered the same sadness and anxiety of leave-taking of which he wrote:

> Farewell my old neighbors, I bid you adieu
> I am going to travel the wilderness through
> I am going to travel the desert all through
> So farewell my old relation, I bid you adieu.

Almost all had travelled the same westward road and felt the rebirth of hope and the new vision which Cumberland, of which he wrote, symbolized:

> We crossed over Tennessee, we crossed over Clinch,
> Pursuing our journey, determined not to flinch
> We scaled the high mountain, on the summit did stand
> And traveled down the western side to sweet Cumberland.

Life was undoubtedly very real and very earnest at White Oak Springs, but it had its lighter moments and days. According to the stories prefaced by "my grandmother used to tell," or "my grandfather told us," phrases which may be quoted from interviews with a number of grandchildren of White Oak Springs, camp meetings and muster days were the most memorable occasions. Play-parties must have been a form of amusement for the young, as Skip-to-my-Lou and Weevily Wheat were still being played at parties in Petersburg in the first decade of the twentieth century. Infares also survived to the near-present, and prove that weddings were occasions for celebration. Opportunities were not lacking as the number of marriages which Justice Hosea Smith performed during his tenure of office show a far departure from the little series of Arnold to Coonrod, Coonrod to Miley, Miley to Pride, Pride to Brenton marriages which Squire Henry Brenton performed in the cozy old days of 1809. The new justice performed marriage ties for the following:[72]

> July 25, 1813, Lemuel Baldwin to Jane Lynn
> July 28, 1813, David Hornaday to Hannah Whitehead
> October 26, 1813, James Ashby to Charlotte Decker
> August 18, 1814, John Luster to Rachel Pea
> July 10, 1814, Robert McClure to Phoebe Jerald
> December 10, 1814, Henry Coleman to Sarah Jerrald
> April 27, 1815, Charles Alexander to Theophila Smith
> January 7, 1816, Jeremiah Kinman to Hannah Pride
> January 14, 1816, Daniel Coleman to Huldah Jerrel
> March 12, 1816, Moses Harrell to Mary Miley
> March 21, 1816, John Miley to Mary Ricks
> August 8, 1816, James Walker to Polly Martin
> November 27, 1816, John Tislow to Rebecka Miley

Licenses were also issued, but without record of the officiating justice or minister, to the following:

> March 12, 1816, Thomas Williams to Hannah Lindsey
> April 18, 1816, Henry Brenton to Mary Borders
> August 31, 1816, John Brenton to Degeneracy Caldwell

Perhaps next in interest to the occasions mentioned above was a public sale. A sort of side-wise glimpse of one is afforded by the estate papers of William C. Brenton (sometimes signed Willie) who died in 1815, leaving no heirs. Paul Tislow was appointed administrator of his estate, and as such itemized his transactions for the court to the last detail. The following are typical:

> Wm. Brenton Deceased to J. Kuykendall,[73] December 10, 1815,
> Sundrey Medicn $1.37½
> Received the above in full, J. A. Kuykendall.

> December 16, 1815, the Est. of Wm. Brenton, de.
> to Robert McCoy Dr.[74]
> For making his coffin and furnishing part of plank and nails $2.50.

Personally appeared before me, one of the justices assigned to keep

---

[72] Gibson County Marriage Licenses.
[73] Dr. Joseph Kuykendall was coroner of Knox County from 1802 to 1810. *Executive Journal of Indiana Territory*, July 9, 1802.
[74] Robert McCoy, a Revolutionary soldier, belonging to the Virginia family of that name which settled in Harrison Township, Knox County, between 1790 and 1800. *History of Knox and Daviess Counties*.

the peace for the county of Gibson, Indiana Territory, James Lindsey and Peter Brenton, and made oath that the appraisement of the estate of Wm. C. Brenton had been done by them according to law. Given under my bond and seal the 29th of December, 1815. Hosea Smith.

Inventory of the Sale of Estate of
William Brenton, late of Gibson Co.

James Brenton,	one cow	$12.62½
John Butler,	one loom	12.62½
Elizabeth Soverns,	one waist coat	1.62½
" "	one pair pantaloons	4.01
" "	one close body coat	11.13½
" "	one waistcoat	11.76
" "	one shirt	1.33
Daniel Coleman	one pair pantaloons	4.81
John Brenton	one waistcoat	1.06½
B. D. Soverns	one pot	2.00
" "	one trunk	5.12½
Silas Soverns	one mare	24.82½
John Cummin	one pr. saddle bags	2.84½
Thos. Milburn	one saddle	4.00
Henry Conrod	one great coat	10.75
Paul Tislow	one improvement	6.00
David Parks	one gun	24.37½
Paul Tislow	To cash rec'd	58.
		117.85
	Rec'd for ranging service	151.00
		263.85

Paul Tislow Administrator.

Received of Paul Tislow 75¢ for being clerk at the sail
Received of Paul Tislow 75¢ for being clerk at the sail of the goods of Wm. Brenton Deceist by me. David Parks

Received of poll tislo one dollar for criing the sail of William brenton's estate dezzeast 1815. Thomas Milburn

Received of Paul Tislow $1.25 for whisky applied to the use of sale of the property of Wm. Brenton, Deceased.
J. W. Loan.

A year after the administrator had made his supposedly final report to the court, he sent the following notice:

One reed came into my hands as the property of William Brenton sometime in the summer of 1817 not accounted for in the appraisement of said Brenton's property. The reed is now in my possession and subject to the order of the court.

Willie Brenton was, we should say, fairly well stocked with this world's goods, as measured by the standard of his time and place. He had the first two of what his contemporary, Daniel Boone, called the three necessities of a man's existence—a good rifle-gun, a good horse, and a good woman. Brenton's possession of a loom, a reed and an "improvement," suggests moreover, that his menage may have been at one time graced by the presence of the third of Boone's necessities.

There are a number of household inventories of the period on record, all of which emphasize the scarcity and high intrinsic value of personal property. Counterpanes and camphor bottles, chopping axes and razor cases were traded, mortgaged and disposed of by will as carefully as rifle-guns, horses, and quarter sections. By far the most pretentious of these inventories is that of Hosea Smith's chattels recorded in connection with a mortgage. In contrast to the one-man outfit of the "Lone Ranger," Willie Brenton, and to the property described in most such recorded lists, Smith's array of wealth seems grand indeed:

> All the cattle and hogs in my mark
> All the beds and bed clothing
> all the pot metal and kitchen furniture
> 3 axes
> 1 clock
> 1 walnut desk
> 2 tables
> 12 chairs
> 2 trunks
> 1 loom
> gears of harness
> all the flax and spinning wheels
> all my books
> all my delf ware and tin and pewter with knives
> and forks and grindstone and tools
> bacon and hog's lard and all the crop of corn
> and wheat now in the house and growing
> 2 head of horses one called Ball and the other Bonaparte
> all the plows and gears and all the hoes.

The foregoing picture of people and events in and about White Oak Springs has been drawn from every source known and available to the authors. Even so, it is indistinct and uncertain. One feature is clear, however, and that is the resemblance of the early community to that of today. No student of the community's past who is also an observer of its present could escape the conclusion that Petersburg is the heir of the flesh and spirit of White Oak Springs.

More than thirty of the family names of White Oak Springs (about 50 in all) survive in Petersburg today, as does the blood of some families whose names have disappeared. The authors, being neither native nor kin to natives, had no especially favorable opportunity to observe this phenomenon. Yet during the fraction of the author's lifetimes spent there, they knew personally the descendants of at least thirty of the original immigrants; and, as was learned while making this study, as many as thirty descendants of one immigrant. It is a statistical project to compute the descendants of ancestors such as Stanton Lamb, one of whose children is reported to have complained that "not one of my father's children ever got acquainted with all the others"; or such as the Kinman brothers, David, James, Levi, and Jeremiah, to members of whose families forty-nine marriage licenses were issued by the clerks of the Pike County Court between 1817 and 1847.

Perusal of the locals and personals in any past or current issue of the Petersburg *Press* or the *Pike County Democrat* discloses that the descendants of pioneers still make the news. They are the "substantial citizens" of the town and surrounding farms. They practice law, carry the mails, teach in the city and country schools, keep store, hold county and state offices, and engage in banking, farming and business. They send their sons and daugters to Indiana University,[75] lead a church choir or the city band, grow flowers and play bridge for amusement, and belong to Kiwanis and D.A.R. Yes, and if the whole truth be required, there are those who loaf upon the street corners, disagree with one another as did their forefathers of old, get themselves locked in the county jail, and help to fill the docket of the Circuit Court of Pike and DuBois Counties.

Petersburg has, of course, had other accreditions of population. The immigration that first populated White Oak Springs continued for another decade. The arrival from eastern states in the eighteen-forties of other pre-Revolutionary American families resulted in the founding of the Pres-

---

[75] A descendant of Moses and Mary Miley Harrell, and also of James Dillin, was elected to the Indiana University chapter of Phi Beta Kappa upon her graduation last year, and she is but one among many descendants of the First Families of White Oak Springs who have received similar academic honors.

byterian Church, and Blythewood Academy, a school for young ladies. A few German and Jewish families came after the Civil War, and enough German, Irish, and other Catholics to form a congregation, though not enough to the present date to support a resident priest. In late years, the accents of a few French and Italian newcomers fall strangely on ears so long accustomed only to English.

The town has had other extraneous influences also which should not be overlooked. Many of its educators, preachers, newspaper editors, and other cultural leaders have been outsiders. Development of natural resources and public improvements have depended largely upon imported capital and labor. The Wabash and Erie Canal, Maysville to Petersburg to Evansville section (1850), the Evansville and Terre Haute Railroad (1881), deep vein coal mining (1896), the telephone (1897), oil and gas production (1897), macadamized roads (1901), the glass factory (1903), modern highways (1930), and strip coal mining in the present decade have brought in executives and workers.[76] But a surprising majority of these people turned out to be transients performing their labors for a while and departing. The comparative few who have remained were chiefly those who fused their lives and fortunes with the never-failing main source of population that had its roots at White Oak Springs.

All things considered, it seems proper to state that Petersburg is the issue of White Oak Springs, and that its civic morals, culture levels and social standards are the accumulation of currents of thought and action which were set flowing between 1800 and 1817, and still flow in 1940—broadened some, but with little change in course and with few ripples and eddies to mark tributary influences.

This account may fittingly close with an account of the tragio-comic proceedings which wrought the change of the community's center and name from White Oak Springs to Petersburg. Hosea Smith had a prominent part in it, of course, although the outcome was exactly contrary to his calculations. Foreseeing the imminent formation of a new county, he prepared to meet the ensuing demand for a suitable county seat. On the White Oak Springs quarter section he laid out a town, named it Alexandria in honor of his son-

---

[76] Credit is due to Mr. Marmaduke MacClellan Stoops, editor from 1892 to 1925 of the *Pike County Democrat*, for checking the material and dates in this paragraph, and for other favors.

in-law, Charles Alexander, and advertised it in the *Western Sun* (Vincennes):

ALEXANDRIA

This town is laid out in a liberal plan and convenient form as it respects streets, alleys & with a spacious public square. It is most delightfully situated on elevated ground, (at the White-Oak Springs, Indiana State, Gibson County) on a sandy soil, which is pleasant and agreeable even in wet seasons—it is situated one and a half miles from White River, where is an elegant situation for a warehouse, and 5 below the forks of the river, from Princeton 23, from Vincennes 20, from the Mudholes 20, and 50 from the Ohio, near the mouth of Sinking or Clover Creek, from which place a good road may be had on high ground.

ALEXANDRIA is well watered with never failing springs, suitable for tanneries and distilleries, and situated in the centre of a populous settlement, surrounded by the most fertile soil, and on the main road leading from Princeton to Louisville—and by an experience of ten years is found to be as healthy as any place on the western waters—to men of enterprize and industry it offers as many advantages as any place in the state—the sale of lots will commence on Friday the sixth of September at 9 o'clock, A.M.—a credit of 18 months will be given to all purchasers of lots—due attendance will be given by
July 17, 1816   H. Smith, Proprietor

The lot sale was held as per the advertisement and the lots were purchased at prices ranging from $17.75 to $120. Alexandria's lamps were trimmed and burning. It awaited only the coming of the bridegroom in the person of the committee to be entrusted with choosing the site for the new county seat. This committee was named in section five of the acts of the legislature which created the new county of Pike (December 21, 1816). The members were instructed "to convene at the house of Hosea Smith in Alexandria on February 2nd next." It was further enacted that, "until suitable accommodations can be had, all the courts of justice shall be held at the house of Hosea Smith." Everything certainly looked favorable to Hosea Smith's well laid plans.

However, while Hosea Smith had gone much farther with his preparations than any other, he was not the only person with the conviction that his site was the ideal choice for the commissioners. Peter Brenton was possessed with the selfsame notion in regard to the quarter section he had acquired from Silas Risley in 1812. Moreover, he was willing to donate it. All that motivated Peter Brenton to this burst of generosity may never be known. It may have been solely public spirit, but a guess may be ventured that, unless he was more saintly than human, incentive must have been added to his original motive by the thought of beating Hosea Smith at his own game.

There were present in the situation all the components of a first rate factional line up and squabble, with Alexandria lot purchasers on the side of Hosea Smith and the unbiased friends of public economy and personal supporters of Peter Brenton opposing. No inkling of such survives, however, and only the bare factual conclusions of the conflict are known.

Came the commissioners—and who should they be but Benjamin V. Beckes of Vincennes, under whose lieutenancy Peter Brenton had served his brief term as corporal in the Tippecanoe campaign; Ephraim Jordan of Vincennes, the old militiaman with whom James Brenton had seen eye to eye since 1807,[77] a lieutenant-colonel in the same campaign; William Hargrove of Princeton, veteran of the ranger service, a familiar visitor at White Oak Springs since 1807, a captain at Tippecanoe; George Rogers Clark Sullivan, a former Kentuckian active in territorial affairs, at this time postmaster at Vincennes, also a veteran of Tippecanoe; and Geo. W. Boone of Harrison County. For a number of excellent reasons, according to their report, including, "its eligible and beautiful situation," "its natural advantages," and "with due regard to its present and future population," the commissioners favored Peter Brenton's site.

At that moment, white Oak Springs received its commitment to obscurity, and Alexandria to ghostly oblivion; but Hosea Smith was on hand with his indispensable services to plan and survey the new town to be named "Petersburgh" (modern spellers drop the h) for Peter Brenton. Though it may have been a heavy task, he did it handsomely, with Main Street a hundred feet wide running the picturesque ridge course of the Buffalo Trace northeast by southwest for a third of a mile, "from Henry Miley's ash tree to Peter Brenton's new building." In order to give the town this beautiful setting and at the same time plat it in symmetrical form, additional acres to those offered by Peter Brenton were required. Henry Miley responded to the public need with a grant of twenty-six acres and John Coonrod with two and a half acres, neither it appears asking recompense or recog-

---

[77] "The First Families of White Oak Springs," *loc. cit.*

Infant son of W. E. and Grazilda Brummet, March 31, 1902.
Harman Brummet, died Dec. 3, 1916, age 73 yrs, 3 mo., 29 da.
Lucy A. Brummet, died Aug. 22, 1904, age 49 yrs, 6 mo., 18 da.
Nettie, dau. of H. and A. Brummet, 1874-1875.
John Wesley, son of John G. and Elizabeth Cain [Kain], died April 10, 1852.
Nancy Campbell, died Dec. 31, 1874, age 64 yrs, 9 mo., 21 da.
Oatis, son of J. T. and M. L. Campbell, born Aug. 22, 1900, died at birth.
Robert, son of H. and R. Campbell, born June 2, 1861, died Oct. 14, 1876.
Robert Waltman Campbell, died Aug. 1, 1879, age 77 yrs, 1 mo., 4 da.
Hariet Campbell, died Jan. 9, 1903, age 67 yrs, 4 mo., 23 da.
James Dewitt Campbell, died Feb. 10, 1880, age 49 yrs.
Ruth Carter, born Nov. 10, 1862, died Sept. 6, 1884.
Jahiel M., son of E. and N. A. Carter, died Oct. 21, 1867, age 13 yrs, 4 mo.
Arthur E., son of W. D. and M. A. Clark, died Nov. 22, 1877, 4 yrs, 10 mo., 18 da.
Adeline Cornelius, died Jan. 23, 1860, 24 yrs, 8 mo., 21 da., wife of James Cornelius.
Abraham Cramer, born in Marion, Ohio, July 16, 1849, died April 4, 1924.
Nettie J., wife of David Crouch, born March 19, 1866, died Aug. 19, 1903.
Ruby L. Derringer, dau. of John W. Turner [Big John], died Aug. 31, 1949, 51 yrs, 4 mo., 24 da., wife of William Derringer.
Nancy Davis [Brummet stone] April 28, 1812, June 8, 1872.
Traecy Donelson, wife of John Donelson, born Dec. 17, 1816, died Oct. 10, 1848.
Ida L., dau. of H. and N. Dowden, died Aug. 24, 1873, 9 mo., 12 da.
Mary E., wife of Lemuel Glidden, died Sept. 19, 1912, age 64 yrs, 11 mo., 3 da.
Lemuel Glidden, died March 29, 1875, 30 yrs, 2 mo., 11 da., Co. K 145 Reg. Ind. Vol.
Russell P. Glidden, born Dec. 20, 1858, died Sept. 30, 1880.
Margaret E. Glidden, wife of Russell P., born June 15, 1826.
Francis O. Glidden, born Aug. 28, 1863, died March 15, 1883.
  [On same stone as Russell P. and Margaret Glidden.]

Lewis F., son of I. and M. G. Glidden, died March 18, 1871, 4 yrs, 6 mo., 21 da.

William E., son of S. and M. Gooden, died Oct. 28, 1864, age 11 da.

Jennie, dau. of J. T. and L. Hamblen, died June 18, 1872, age 1 yr, 3 mo., 2 da.

John Helms, March 19, 1852, May 26, 1916.

Lettie, wife of John Helms, born May 14, 1857.

Elizabeth, wife of T. Henry, died Jan. 8, 1865, age 59 yrs, 8 mo., 28 da.

Margaret, wife of Christopher Johnson, died Feb. 25, 1863, age 37 yrs, 9 mo., 20 da.

Rosalah S., dau. of C. and M. Johnson, died Sept. 29, 1863, 8 yrs, 11 mo., 5 da.

Martha E., dau. of C. and M. Johnson, died Oct. 1, 1863, age 12 yrs, 8 mo., 24 da.

Arthur J., son of C. and M. Johnson, died Oct. 12, 1863, age 6 yrs, 11 mo., 22 da.

Infant dau. of ———. 187—. [Since this is near the Johnson lot, it may be in the family.]

Lewis Jones, born Oct. 9, 1824, died June 22, 1912.

Margaret, wife of Lewis Jones, born June 22, 1826, died May 15, 1897.

John H., son of L. and M. A. Jones, died Oct. 22, 1866, age 15 yrs, 5 mo., 20 da.

Sarah A., dau. of L. and M. A. Jones, died Oct. 7, 1866, age 8 yrs, 1 mo., 7 da.

Hannah J., dau. of L. and M. Jones, died June 12, 1861, age 3 yrs, 1 mo., 7 da.

John G. Kain [Cain] born Oct. 29, 1816, died Feb. 2, 1875.

Jno. Kelley, Co. C 22nd Ind. Inf.

Joseph Kelly, born Jan. 17, 1789, died Nov. 7, 1853.

Ardelia Kelso, March 15, 1868, Dec. 12, 1880.

Sarah E., dau. of T. J. and S. F. Kelso, died Aug. 31, 1862, 2 yrs, 1 mo., 28 da.

Robert C., son of T. J. and S. F. Kelso, died Sept. 4, 1863, 1 yr, 10 mo., 29 da.

John D. Kennedy, died Nov. 19, 1864, age 63 yrs, 8 mo.

John D. Kennedy, died Oct. 29, 1864, 63 yrs.

John Livingston, Dec. 25, 1851, Sept. 26, 1917.

Minerva A. Livingston, April 19, 1848.

Samuel F. Long, 1866-1909.

M.A.P. [No other marking.]

Charles K. McDonald, 1878-1905.
John T. McDonald, 1846-1915.
Malvine M. McDonald [same stone as John T.] 1857-1921.
Robt. McIlhenny, born Nov. 12, 1804, died Feb. 8, 1856, 51 yrs, 2 mo., 26 da.
Curtis Maris, died March 26, 1857, 50 yrs, 4 mo., 26 da.
James D. Martin, died Aug. 27, 1853, age 35 yrs.
Emaline, dau. of James and Mary Martin, died June 26, 1851, 1 yr, 2 mo., 12 da.
Elmer C. Merida, March 8, 1903, April 4, 1913.
Benj. F. Milburn, 1853-1920.
Lizzie, wife of Benj. Milburn, 1853.
Benj. H. Miller, Ind. Bugler 166, Depot Brig. World War I, Oct. 28, 1888, Sept. 3, 1947.
John Miller, 1846-1924.
Mary Miller, 1853-1924.
John Thomas Miller, born Aug. 2, 1882, died about age of 2 years.
Maxie May, dau. of J. and M. Miller, wife of Albert Fritch, born Nov. 30, 1875, died Oct. 6, 1902.
William I. Moore, Aug. 26, 1866, Feb. 16, 1928.
Minerva, wife of William Moore, April 2, 1874, March 2, 1923.
Emma M. Monroe, died May 5, 1937, 33 yrs, 9 mo., 17 da.
James R. Morrison, 1865-1946.
Isaac P. Mosier, Sept. 14, 1851, June 19, 1914.
Jennie C., wife of Isaac Mosier, born Jan. 8, 1851.
Ona B. Mosier, wife of J. C. Mosier, 1878-1911.
Maurice, son of J. C. and Ona Mosier, 1906-1926.
Jacob M. Neely, died Sept. 2, 1841, 36 yrs, 5 mo.
Jerusha, dau. of Jacob and Nancy Neeley, died May 16, 1852, 9 yrs, 1 mo., 26 da.
Eva, dau. of R. and M. Neely, died Oct. 11, 1869, 23 da.
Alexander Obeny, died June 20, 1888, 61 yrs, 11 mo., 24 da., Co. H 82 Ind. Vol. Inf.
David Obeny, son of A. and Anna Obeny, died March 23, 1858, 1 mo., 29 da.
Mary M. Obeny, dau. of A. and Anna Obeny, died March 15, 1877, age 20 yrs, 6 mo., 24 da.
William A. Oliver, March 26, 1847, Jan. 24, 1913.
Mary, wife of William Oliver, Oct. 20, 1845, Dec. 23, 1902.
Anna May, dau. of William and Mary Oliver, Nov. 13, 1875, Jan. 10, 1876.
Rosa L. Oliver, 1883-1907.

Martha A. Oliver, 1858-1928.
Andrew Oliver, died June 21, 1882, 67 yrs, 2 mo., 27 da.
Elizabeth Ortto [?], died March 12, 1857, 77 yrs, 1 mo., 11 da.
James C. Parmerlee, died Aug. 10, 1872, 66 yrs, 1 mo., 23 da.
Amos Parmerlee, May 11, 1845, Oct. 20, 1895.
Ellen, wife of Amos Parmerlee, born Nov. 9, 1849, died Aug. 31, 1936.
Charlie, son of W. and A. M. Parmerlee, died Jan. 30, 1873, age 9 mo., 28 da.
Daniel Y., son of James and Nancy Parmerlee, died July 30, 1861, 7 yrs, 9 mo., 13 da.
David M., son of James and Nancy Parmerlee, died May 21, 1852, 1 yr, 15 da.
Columbus Parsley, March 11, 1830, Aug. 24, 1914.
Sara, wife of C. Parsley, July 2, 1843, Jan. 6, 1909.
John T., son of C. and S. Parsley, March 24, 1877, 4 mo. 8 da.
S. S. Parsley, 76 yrs, 8 mo., 6 da.
Susan, wife of S. S. Parsley, age 83 yrs.
Newton, son of S. S. and Susan Parsley, born in Hamblen Twp. Brown Co., Feb. 10, 1838, Aug. 16, 1876.
George W. Parsley, son of N. and M. E. Parsley, died Aug. 7, 1871.
Nettie, dau. of J. and S. J. Parsley, died July 19, 1873 [?], age 14 da. [?].
Elizabeth, wife of C. Parsley, died Dec. 16, 1871, 39 yrs, 7 mo., 17 da.
Daniel Parsley, Oct. 5, 1859, Aug. 29, 1928.
Ella Parsley, Dec. 23, 1869, Feb. 19, 1944.
Edward Parsley, July 31, 1867, March 3, 1943.
Eliza, wife of T. H. Patterson, born Oct. 5, 1848, died March 13, 1875, 27 yrs, 5 mo., 8 da.
Eliza G., dau. of T. H. and E. G. Patterson, born March 7, 1875, died March 21, 1875, 14 da.
Martha, wife of T. H. Patterson, died Feb. 6, 1869, 29 yrs, 4 mo., 14 da.
Abraham Prosser, died, Feb. 19, 1882, 76 yrs, 2 mo., 18 da.
Rebecca, wife of Abraham Prosser, died March 21, 1838, 31 yrs, 2 mo., 7 da.
Willard Prosser, 1857-1936.
America Prosser 1859-1931 [also known as "Sissie."]
Isaac P., son of W. M. and A. E. Prosser, Sept. 9, 1881, age 2 mo., 9 da.
James Prosser, died March 1, 1885, 64 yrs, 11 mo., 4 da.

Margaret J., wife of James Prosser, died Jan. 15, 1876, 55 yrs, 4 mo., 16 da.
Isaac N. Prosser, 1832-1866.
Isaac N. Prosser, born Dec. 18, 1832, died Dec. 25, 1865 [new stone]
Hannah, wife of Isaac Prosser, 1836-1914.
Manerva J., dau. of J. and M. Prosser, died March 20, 1841, 18 mo., 18 da.
Dr. John Prosser, died May 27, 1850, 31 yrs, 5 mo., 28 da.
Sarah E., wife of Dr. John Prosser, died Sept. 27, 1875, 61 yrs, 29 da.
John Prosser, 1872-1943.
Lewis Prosser, died June 17, 1863, 36 yrs, 9 mo., 29 da.
Daniel Prosser, died March 30, 1873, age 86 yrs, 2 mo., 16 da.
Martha, wife of A. Prosser, died Sept. 13, 1881, 65 yrs, 9 mo., 2 da.
Nancy, dau. of J. and M. Prosser, died Dec. 13, 1865, 3 yrs, 7 mo.
Clara E. Rooney, 1897-1938.
Francis A. Rund, Feb. 16, 1816, Aug. 19, 1896 [born in Germany].
Therisia, wife of F. A. Rund, died Sept. 1, 1869, 51 yrs, 5 mo. [born in Germany].
Children of H. S. and Jane Rund, Gaynell, 1892-1893, Grant, May 21-30, 1903.
Robert, son of A. and M. Rund, died March 14, 1876, 2 mo., 8 da.
Oriah, son of F. A. and R. Rund, died Nov. 24, 1877, age 3 mo., 7 da.
John W. Shaffer, died Dec. 17, 1897, 63 yrs, 17 da.
Elizabeth, wife of John S. Shaffer, died Aug. 12, 1878, 36 yrs, 3 mo., 17 da.
David, son of J. W. and E. Shaffer, died July 17, 1878, age 2 mo., 26 da.
David Shaffer, died Aug. 11, 1885, 82 yrs, 10 mo., 4 da.
Mary, wife of David Shaffer, died Oct. 10, 1865, 59 yrs, 5 mo., 24 da.
Margaret Shaffer, died Jan. 12, 1892, 63 yrs, 9 mo., 13 da.
Alfred Smith, died Feb. 20, 1879, 81 yrs, 4 mo., 12 da.
George W. Smith, died July 1, 1848, 68 yrs, 18 da.
Margaret A., dau. of G. W. and E. Smith, died June 15, 1864, 18 yrs, 7 mo., 1 da.
Infant dau. of G. W. and E. Smith, June 20, 1852, 1 yr, 14 da.

William Snider, Jan. 13, 1839, June 18, 1913.
Ellen, wife of William Snider, Jan. 13, 1853, June 8, 1903.
Virgil B., son of A. C. and A. E. Spencer, died Dec. 29, 1884 [?] age 2 yrs, 5 da.
George Staples, died April 18, 1877, 56 yrs.
Ann Staples, died July 17, 1865, 31 yrs. [Allie Staples known to be buried here may be the same as Ann Staples.]
Sarah F. Stevens, Feb. 16, 1867, Feb. 22, 1947.
Children of Mr. and Mrs. Leslie Stewart, Harold A. Stewart, born April 19, 1913, died July 23, 1915, Milan W. Stewart, born March 3, 1915, died Oct. 10, 1915.
Aramentia Stone, born Sept. 3, 1843, in Greenville, E. Tenn., and raised in Georgia, died Dec. 1, 1872.
Hannah L., wife of W. W. Stone, born Feb. 3, 1811, in Greenville, E. Tenn., died Jan. 1, 1892, 80 yrs, 10 mo., 28 da.
Sarah E., wife of John Stone, died March 11, 1869, 25 yrs, 11 da.
Washington W. Stone, died March 25, 1866, 58 [?] yrs, 13 [?] mo., 3 da.
[One marker near Stone family lot is broken and illegible.]
James R. Strode, born April 30, 1825, died Oct. 19, 1864.
Lizzie J., dau. of E. R. and Elizabeth Stuart, died July 1, 1869, age 4 yrs, 5 mo., 22 da.
[Many of the Turner stones only have initials. Being in possession of the Turner Bible records, have given dates, especially of John W. Turner family.]
Rebecca, wife of Elisha Daniel Turner, born Aug. 10, 1835, died Aug. 23, 1898.
John W. Turner [known as Big John], Nov. 14, 1852, Feb. 16, 1916.
Nancy, wife [1st] of J. W. Turner, died Feb. 25, 1884, 33 yrs, 5 mo., 21 da.
William Perry Turner, son of J. W. and Nancy Turner, born Nov. 17, 1874, died Nov. 14, 1893.
Bertha Jane, dau. of J. W. and Nancy Turner, born Sept. 9, 1876, died Nov. 21, 1896.
Lettie Francis, daughter of J. W. and Nancy Turner, born Aug. 19, 1878. Died.
Charlie D. Turner, son of J. W. and Nancy Turner, born Aug. 3, 1882, died Nov. 26, 1883.
Martha Belle (Waltman), wife (2nd) of J. W. Turner, born Jan. 1, 1862, died Jan. 5, 1895.

Zora J., dau. of J. W. and Martha Belle Turner, born June 5, 1886, died Jan. 1, 1905, age 19 yrs, 6 mo., 26 da.

Charles Turner, son of J. W. and Martha Belle Turner, born Sept. 30, 1887, died 1948.

Jessie Ruth, dau. of J. W. and Martha Belle Turner, born June 18, 1891, died March 22, 1892.

Ruth, dau. of Charles and Ershel Turner, born Sept. 28, 1912, died Jan. 13, 1922.

Irene, dau. of Charles and Ershel Turner, born Dec. 8, 1922, died Dec. 20, 1922.

Alvis E. Turner, 1928-1931.

Lewis A. Turner, 1859-1938.

Latonia Turner, 1861, died April 17, 1951.

John Daniel Turner, 1863-1940.

John Turner (born in Va.) July 28, 1798, died May 17, 1871, 72 yrs, 9 mo., 19 da.

Elizabeth T. (Potts) Turner, wife of John Turner, died Sept. 21, 1881, 82 yrs, 10 mo., 24 da.

John William Turner, son of John and Elizabeth T. (Potts) Turner, born July 28, 1833, died Oct. 17, 1867.

James R. Turner, son of John and Elizabeth T. Turner, born July 27, 1836, died —— [no stone].

Nettie, wife of J. R. Turner, March 13, 1841, Jan. 28, 1907.

Mary Alice Turner, died April 25, 1945, 72 yrs, 1 mo., 1 da.

Samuel I., son of Thomas and Martha Wallas, died Oct. 19, 1860, 6 mo., 21 da.

Mina M., dau. of Thomas and Martha Wallas, died Oct. 16, 1860, age 4 yrs, 8 da.

Infant son of Thomas and Martha Wallas, died Aug. 10, 1861.

Charles Wallace, born Oct. 11, 1877, died March 30, 1905.

Franklin Walker, died Nov. 15, 1890, age 82 yrs, 6 mo., 3 da.

John B., son of F. and F. Walker, died Nov. 12, 1871, 26 yrs, 1 mo., 17 da.

Charlie, son of D. R. Walker, died Sept. 9, 1880, age 10 mo., 25 da.

John W., son of D. R. Walker, died March 15, 1872, 4 yrs, 2 mo., 6 da.

Newton A. Walker, born Dec. 26, 1868, died May 29, 1924.

Mary V. Walker, wife of Newton A. Walker, born May 18, 1868, died Feb. 18, 1909.

Dudley Walker, born Jan. 21, 1841, died Sept. 19, 1925.

Elizabeth K. Walker, born Sept. 2, 1841, died Aug. 10, 1909 [on same stone as Dudley Walker].

Thomas Waltman, 1837-1907. Charter member of Bean Blossom Lodge F. and A.M. No. 527.
A. E. Waltman, 1846-1933.
William M. Waltman, Nov. 15, 1844, June 15, 1915.
Marry E., his wife [Waltman] April 19, 1845, Feb. 6, 1929.
Thomas Waltman, died May 28, 1881, 75 yrs, 3 mo., 26 da.
Catherine, wife of Thomas Waltman, died April 19, 1854, 44 yrs, 3 mo., 28 da.
Jacob Waltman, died March 24, 1873, 21 yrs, 1 mo., 22 da.
Charlie, son of R [?] and E [?] Waltman, died March 22, 1878, 10 yrs [?], 11 da.
John S. Waltman, March 9, 1868, Feb. 28, 1939.
Ina E. Waltman, Jan. 4, 1871, June 1, 1920.
Elizabeth A., dau. of H. and S. J. Waltman, born May 12, 1858, died Sept. 2, 1882.
Robert D., son of H. and S. J. Waltman, born Oct. 13, 1852, died June 12, 1853.
Michael Waltman, died Feb. 16, 1877, 63 yrs, 6 mo., 5 da.
Susan, wife of M. Waltman, died July 21, 1868, 50 yrs, 4 mo.
Hiram Waltman, born Oct. 15, 1830, Frederick Co. Md., died Sept. 20, 1901.
Elizabeth [Frownfelter] wife of Hiram Waltman, April 5, 1841, Feb. 22, 1905.
Seward Watson, July 28, 1868, April 3, 1942.
Sarah Watson, April 10, 1871, Feb. 18, 1943.
Laura Watson, Oct. 31, 1870, Feb. 22, 1930.
James H., son of W. G. and R. W. Watson, died Nov. 2, 1865, 1 yr, 11 mo., 2 da.
Catherine, Consort of James M. Yoder, Died April 25, 1872, 23 yrs, 10 mo., 24 da.
Aaron Zody, 1854-1937.
Emma J. Zody, 1867-1936.
Son of A. S. and E. J. Zody, died Sept. 9, 1887, 2 da.
Alexander G. Zook, born Feb. 5, 1825, died May 8, 1903.
Mary A., wife of A. G. Zook, born Nov. 14, 1829, died Aug. 30, 1864.
Anthony Zook, M.D., son of Alexander and Mary Zook, born around 1850.

Persons Thought to Be Buried at Bean Blossom Cemetery
Hannah E. (Turner) Prosser, wife of Lewis Prosser
Calvin Mosier
George Turner
Rebecca Prosser, wife of George Turner

Coon or Fleener Cemetery
Nova May Mertens

The Coon or Fleener Cemetery of Jackson Township, Brown County, Indiana, is about four miles southwest of Morgantown, Indiana, on the farm now owned by T. M. Butler. This plot was donated by Jacob Fleener, one of the first settlers of Jackson Township, who came to the county as early as 1823 or 1824 from Tennessee. The plot is located about a quarter of a mile from the road on which Fleener built the typical double log house. Since there was no church in the community at this early date, religious services were held in his home, which were attended by the families in the neighborhood. Later a family by the name of Coon purchased the farm and since that time the cemetery has been known as the Coon Cemetery. One of Fleener's daughters married William Riley Ritter whose farm joined the Fleener farm and the cemetery is sometimes called the Ritter Cemetery, but more frequently referred to as the Coon or Fleener Cemetery. Inscriptions from the stones are as follows:

Mary Hobbs Abbey, b. 1804, d. 1883. On same lot as Adella and Martin Neidigh.

Sarah Barns, d. 1875, wife of Noah Barns, age 64 yrs.

Wiley Burns, b Oct. 16, 1832, d. Jan. 4, 1913. Co. H 70 Ind. Vol.

Emily A. Burns, b. April 30, 1847, d. May 27, 1932.

Anna A. Davis, d. Sept. 18, 1872. Dau. of J. C. and A. R. Davis, 3 yrs., 3 mo. 17 da.

Jacob Fleener, d. June 25, 1865, 61 yrs. 9 mo. 15 da.

Sarah Fleener, d. Jan. 24, 1852, wife of Jacob Fleener, 24 yrs. 7 mo. 2 da.

Hannah H. Fleener, d. Feb. 11, 1866, 64 yrs. 11 mo. 2 da., wife of Jacob Fleener.

James Henry Fleener, b. Dec. 19, 1853, d. May 9, 1859, son of J. and H. Fleener.

Mary Frownfelter, d. May 29, 1895, 85 yrs. 1 mo. 10 da.

Aaron Frownfelter, d. Jan. 23, 1856, 63 yrs. 3 mo. 25 da.

Jacob Frownfelter, d. Feb. 11, 1892, 83 yrs, 4 mo. 1 da.

Marcus Harden, d. Mar. 29, 1866, son of J. B. and M. T. Harden, 9 mo. 9 da.

Margaret M. Kelso, d. Sept. 7, 1850, 5 yrs. 3 mo. 1 da.

Martha Catherine (Null) Long, b. June 1, 1852, d. June 28, 1902, wife of Alfred Long.

Alfred Long, b. April 9, 1848, d. Oct. 28, 1923, Civil War Vet.

Anna Viola Long, d. May 18, 1877, 2 yrs. 9 mo., dau. of A[lfred] and M[artha] Long.

Lucinda Long, d. Mar. 5, 1862, dau. of A[lfred] and M[artha] Long.

Mable Long, b. Aug. 4, 1890, d. Sept. 10, 1900, dau. of Samuel F. and Rosa Long.

C. D. Melton, Co. G 27 Ind. Inf.

Robert Melton, b. Jan. 26, 1840, G.A.R.

Eliz. A. Melton, b. June 3, 1849, d. May 10, 1900, wife of Robt. Melton.

Thomas A. Melton, b. July 7, 1868.

James W. Melton, b. June 28, 1879, d. May 9, 1886.

Walter C. Melton, b. June 22, 1886, d. April 5, 1896.

Wm. John Merriman, b. Feb. 11, 1833, d. July 12, 1906, [son of Wm. of Va. and Knox Co. Tenn., Morgan, and Brown cos. Ind.].

Rachel Catherine Merriman, Aug. 20, 1841, d. June 5, 1929, wife of Wm. John Merriman.

Lewis Merriman, [b. Oct. 18, 1860, d. Sept. 7, 1922], son of Wm. John and Rachel Merriman.

Ivy Francis Merriman, [b. Dec. 27, 1872, d. 1936], son of Wm. John and Rachel Merriman.

Cordelia Merriman, b. 1871, d. 1910, wife of William Merriman.

William Merriman, b. Sept. 7, 1863, d. May 13, 1944, son of Wm. John and Rachel Merriman.

David Miller, b. June 18, 1812, d. Aug. 20, 1896.

Sarah A. Miller, b. Aug. 21, 1819, d. Sept. 11, 1916.

Mary J. Murry, b. Mar. 13, 1870, d. Feb. 14, 1904. [On same lot as Thomas A. Melton]

Jesse Moore, d. Dec. 15, 1895, 75 yrs. 11 mo.

Mary J. Moore, b. May 17, 1829, d. July 4, 1904, 75 yrs. 1 mo. 17 da.

Thomas A. Moore, b. May 24, 1848, d. Jan. 14, 1914, only child of Jesse and Mary Moore.

S. Neidigh, b. Jan. 10, 1806, d. Sept. 1, 1883.

M. Neidigh, b. Feb. 1, 1811, d. Oct. 8, 1894, wife of S. Neidigh.

John Neidigh, b. May 15, 1817, d. May 21, 1905.

Nancy Neidigh, Feb. 4, 1827, d. Mar. 14, 1886, wife of John Neidigh.

Catherine Neidigh, d. Oct. 29, 1857, Consort of John Neidigh, 66 yrs. 10 mo. 26 da.

Alexander Neidigh, b. June 1, 1813, d. Oct. 20, 1863.
Eliz. McNeely Hill Neidigh, d. April 14, 1887, 60 yrs.
Roscoe Neidigh, b. 1888, d. 1891.
Adella Neidigh, b. 1832, d. 1914.
Martin A. Neidigh, b. 1858, d. 1932.
Henry Oliver, b. Dec. 2, 1862, d. Aug. 9, 1866.
Harriet E. Reed, d. Sept. 12, 1853, dau. of H. D. and S. A. Reed, 2 yrs. 4 mo. 9 da.
Oliver A. Read, b. Dec. 27, 1867, d. Mar. 12, 1868, son of C. W. and C.
Lydia Lucetta Read, b. Feb. 10, 1851, d. Sept. 16, 1867, 16 yrs. 7 mo. 6 da.
Sarah Ritter, b. Aug. 16, 1814, d. Aug. 25, 1852, wife of J[esse] Ritter.
Frances D. Ritter, d. July 20, 1877, wife of J[esse] Ritter.
Two infants—Ritter, children of J[esse] and S[arah] Ritter.
Jesse D. Ritter, d. Aug. 19, 1877, 18 yrs. 2 mo., son of J[esse] and E. P. Ritter.
Lucinda Ritter, b. Feb. 7, 1852, d. April 1 ,1864, dau. of J[esse] and S[arah] Ritter.
Wm. Riley Ritter,† b. May 13, 1837, d. Feb. 12, 1923, son of Jesse Ritter.
Hannah Margaret Ritter,† b. Mar. 17, 1840, d. Mar. 25, 1916, wife of Wm. Riley.
J[esse] Anderson Ritter,† b. Mar. 29, 1874, d. Dec. 3, 1927, son of Wm. Riley.
Angeline Ritter,† b. Sept. 28, 1879, d. Oct. 17, 1917, wife of Jesse Anderson Ritter.
Jesse Ritter,† b. Aug. 30, 1813, d. April 17, 1896.
William Rude, d. Jan. 3, 1869, 79 yrs. 9 mo. 29 da.
Sarah Rude, d. June 21, 1868, 66 yrs, 4 mo. 15 da.
James W. Scripter, d. Aug. 9, 1869, 24 yrs, 7 mo. 1 da, husband of H. E. Scripter.
Chas. W. Scripter, d. Mar. 29, 1874, 6 yrs. 10 mo. 17 da., son of J. W. and M. Scripter.
Andrew Sherman, b. Feb. 25, 1865, d. Aug. 10, 1866.
Henry Sherman, b. Dec. 2, 1862, d. Aug. 9, 1866.
Samuel Smith, b. Dec. 13, 1824, d. Jan. 21, 1902.
Barbara Smith, b. June 9, 1838, d. Feb. 21, 1904.
Mary M. Smith, b. July 24, 1880, d. Dec. 31, 1880, 4 mo. 7 da., dau. of Sam and B. E. Smith.

† Dates were provided by Mrs. Wiley Burns of Morgantown, Indiana, from Bible Records.

Lucretia Smith, d. June 25, 1875, wife of W. S. Smith, 72 yrs. 11 mo. 9 da.
Margaret Smith, d. Nov. 1, 1869, dau. of W. and L., 39 yrs. 10 mo. 19 da.
Mary Smith, d. July 31, 1871, 39 yrs. 23 da., dau. of W. and L.
Margaret J. Smith, d. Oct. 13, 1875, 11 yrs. 7 mo. 3 da., dau. of J. and S. Smith.
Cordelia Smith, b. 1855, d. 1940.
Smith—Stone broken and only the name of Smith appears.
Catherine Siler, b. 1855 [?]
Ottis D. Steele,‡ b. June 27, 1874, d. Sept. 14, 1881, son of John and Rebecca Steele.
Eliz. E. Stuart, b. Oct. 9, 1862, d. Nov. 18, 1893, 31 yrs. 29 da., wife of William.
Isaac Stump, d. July 27, 1877, 30 yrs. 3 mo. 10 da.
Eliz. Stump, b. 1850, d. 1926, dau. of Wm. and Araminta Stump.
Jessie Cloe Turner, b. Dec. 26, 1890, d. July 2, 1891, dau. of James and Laura Turner.
Clara Turner, wife of John Turner, b. Oct. 31, 1873, d. Sept., 1900.
Gracie Ethel Turner, b. Sept. 3, 1889, d. at age of 6, dau. of John and Clara Turner.
James H. Whitaker, b. Sept. 26, 1876.
Kate Whitaker, b. Dec. 23, 1879, d. Jan. 20, 1913.
Maurice Whitaker, b. Feb. 19, 1907, d. Dec. 21, 1909, son of James and Kate Whitaker.
Infant Whitaker, b. Feb. 19, 1907, d. Feb. 19, 1907, son of James and Kate Whitaker.
Joseph Wilkinson, d. Mar. 7, 1853, son of Merida and Nancy J. Wilkinson.

Persons Thought to Be Buried in This Cemetery

Lytle Clark, b. ca. 1834 Garrard Co. Ky., son of Abner and Adeline Clark.
William Clark, b. ca. 1822 Garrard Co. Ky., son of Abner and Adeline Clark.
Maud (Cornelius) Stump, b. ca. 1875, wife of Arwine Stump.
Abe Stump.
Nancy Nelvina (Merriman) Neidigh, b. Sept. 27, 1830, d. June 25, 1857, dau. of William and Catherine Merriman.

---

‡ Mrs. Effie Barns of Indianapolis, Indiana, furnished the date from Bible Records.

The Georgetown Presbyterian Church
Nova May Mertens

A committee of the Presbytery of Indianapolis consisting of D. V. Smock and B. F. Woods, ministers, and David Demaree, elder, organized the Georgetown Presbyterian Church on October 25, 1845. George Bergen, Margaret Eoff, Elizabeth McIlhenny, Robert McIlhenny, William Moreland, John Prosser, and Sarah Prosser were enrolled as members. The ruling elders chosen at that time were George Bergen, Robert McIlhenny, and John Prosser.

Before a house of worship was constructed, these Brown County citizens held services in their homes. Just when the first church was built is not known, but the land for this frame structure was a gift from the Waltman family, and the lumber was sawed at the Thomas Waltman Lumber Mill, east of Georgetown. Many of the logs from this building were used when the second church was built, which is still standing.

The minutes of the Indiana Synod of the Presbyterian church indicate that a minister served this congregation until 1920 when Frank C. Hood from Franklin was listed as the pastor-at-large. Three years later ministers no longer shepherded this flock, and on September 20, 1937, the Georgetown Presbyterian Church met its demise.[1] The Methodists endeavored to reorganize a church, but their venture proved unsuccessful. The building, however, was kept in repair by descendants of old Presbyterian members, mostly the Waltman family. Funerals and reunions made use of this house of worship until a few years ago when it was sold to the Mennonites.

Three books contain the transactions of the Georgetown Presbyterian Church. Book one, which has been lost, covered the period from October 25, 1845, to September 17, 1859; Book two, September 18, 1859, to May 15, 1897; and Book three,

---

[1] *Ninety-eighth Meeting of the Synod of Indiana of the Presbyterian Church in the U.S.A., Held in the First Presbyterian Church of Gary, Indiana, October 2-4, 1923* (n.p., n.d.), 68; *Minutes of the One Hundred Thirteenth Meeting of the Synod of Indiana of the Presbyterian Church in the U.S.A., Held in Crawfordsville, Indiana, June 6-9, 1938* (n.p., n.d.), 74.

May 16, 1897, to December 21, 1930. The "date of admission" to the church of the membership which follows in many instances was given in the original books.[2]

Adams, A. W.
Adams, Andrew
Adams, Mrs. Andrew
Adams, David B.
Adams, Desdimony
Adams, L. Kate
Adams, Mrs. Lorena
Adams, Mary L.
Adams, William A.
Alender, Mrs. L.
Alender, Mary Nettie
Alexander, Carry C.
Alexander, Eliza
Alexander, George
Alexander, Jane
Alexander, Mary
Alexander, Rebecca
Alexander, S. P.
Alexander, Stephen
Allen, Lafayett
Allen, Sarah
Allender,
  Mrs. Elizabeth
Allison, G. W.
Allison, John C.
Anderson, Josephine C.
Arwine, Enoch L.
Arwine, Mary J.
Arwine, S. Adelaide
Arwine, William

Banta, G—li
Banta, William
Baughman, Lillian
Baughman, Mary
Baughman,
  Mrs. Mary A.
Baughman, William
Baughman, Willis
Bay, James H.
Bay, Mrs. Nancy J.
Bell, Matilda
Bergen, Abraham
Bergen, Alonzo N.

Bergen, George
Bergen, Margaret J.
Bergen, Sarah A. E.
Branstetter, Rebecca
Brummit,
  Mrs. Grazilda
Cain, Dean (Turner)
Calvin, Collins M.
Calvin, Mary
Calvin, Sarah
Calvin, Timothy D.
Campbell, Eliza J.
Campbell, Elizabeth
Campbell, Hariette
Campbell, Jane Banta
Campbell, John A.
Campbell, Joshua
Campbell, Margaret A.
Campbell, Mary
Campbell, Nancy
Campbell, Nancy E.
Campbell, Oma
Campbell, Robert W.
Campbell, Sarah N.
Choran, Martha
Clipper, Harley
Clipper, Rosie
Clupper, Gladys
Cochran, Thomas
Coffey, Richard
Coffland, Eliza
Coffland, Ellen
Coffland, Lorena
Coffland, Ruth Ann
Coffland, Sarah R.
Coffland, Thomas
Crab, Elizabeth
Crab, William
Crane, Mrs. Hannah
Culley, Lorena M.
Culley, Mary E.

Dallas, Alexander

Dallas, Catherine
Davis, Ella M.
Davis, Enoch
Davis, Eva E.
Davis, Frank
Davis, George
Davis, Mrs. G.
Davis, Granville E.
Davis, John
Davis, Robert
Davis, Mrs. [Robert]
Davis, William
Deist, Mrs. Louisa
Deist, Mary J.
Demaree, David
Demaree, Elizabeth
Demaree, S. W.
Derringer, Verna
Diest, John
Dolsberry, Sarah
Douden, Harvy
Douden, Nancy
Dowden, Lizzie
Dowden, Vernie
Dowden, William
Dowden, Mrs. William
Duly, Gustie

Eoff, Margaret

Flint, Albert M.

Gerherd, Elizabeth A.
Gibson, Charles
Gibson, Sarah E.
Gordon, Williard
Gorman, Joseph H.
Gray, Andrew
Gray, Sarah J.
Gwinn, Rachel

Haggart, Mary
Hamblin, James T.
Harden, John

---

[2] Book two and three are in the Indiana Division, Indiana State Library, Indianapolis, Indiana.

Helms, Nettie
Henry, Sarah
Hiatt, Ethel
Hiatt, Norma
Hiatt, W. E.
Honeycut, Moses
Howers, Mrs.
Hulin, Ella
Hulin, Lida M.
Hulin, Nancy Jane
Hulin, Wilburn
Hunt, John
Hunt, Mary
Hurd, Ida
Hurdle, James
Hurdle, Minerva J.
Hurdle, Sarah
Hurdle, Tressia
Hutchison, Ann E.
Hutchison, Frances
Hutchison, Harriet
Hutchison, Janet

Jorden, H. C.

Kain, Evan
Kaper, Mary B.
Kasserman,
  Mrs. Margaret
Keller, John J.
Keller, Phoeba
Keller, Wilson
Kelley, Jane
Kelley, William J.
Kelly, Eliza Ann
Kelly, Hannah
Kennedy, Christianna
Kennedy, James
Kennedy, John
Kennedy, Margaretta
Kennedy, Moses
Kennedy, Patience
Kephart, John S.

Lamer, Tamer
Long, Jennie
Long, Marie
Long, Sam
Long, Mrs. Sam

McDonald, Edward M.

McDonald, Mrs. F.
McDonald, George
McDonald,
  Mrs. Minerva
McDonald, Opal
McDonald, Sarah
McGlashan, Martha A.
McGlashan, Thos. C.
McIlhenny, Elizabeth
McIlhenny, Robert
McIlhenny, Mrs. Ruth
McIlhenny, Samuel
McIlhenny, Sarah G.
  (married Hiram
  Waltman)

Mandeville, Mary
Milbourn, Mrs. F.
Milbourn, Frank
Miller, Sam A.
Mobley, Catherine
Mobley, Lewis
Mobley, Mary R.
Mobley, William H.
Monroe, Alex
Monroe, Boyd
Monroe, Mrs. Maggie
Moore, Charles
Moore, Mrs. Maggie
Moreland, William
Moser, Janie
Moser, Jennie
Moser, Mrs. Lizzie
Moser, Ona (Culver)
Mosier, John
Myers, Jane

Neff, Mrs. Lizzie
Neff, Oliver A.
Neidlinger,
  Christopher
Neidlinger,
  Mrs. Christopher
Neidlinger, Master
Neidlinger, Miss

Obney, Alexander
Obney, Ami
Oliver, Andrew J.
Oliver, James H.
Oliver, Mrs. Jane

Oliver, Maggie
Oliver, Mary Sheffer
Oliver, Mary
Oliver, Mrs. Minnie
Oliver, Nancy A.
Oliver, William

Palmer, Georgie
Palmer, Henry
Palmer, Mrs. Maggie
Palmer, Rose
Parmerlee, Amos
Parmerlee, Ann Eliza
Parmarlee, Mrs. Ella
Parmarlee, Marcus H.
Parmarlee, Rebecca
Parmerlee, Sarah
Parsley, Dan
Parsley, Ed
Parsley, Mrs. Ed.
Parsley, Edith
Parsley, Mrs. Ella
Parsley, Mary
Parsley, Millie
Parsley, Roma
Parsley, Solomon A.
Patterson, J. W.
Patterson, Martha
Patterson, Thomas H.
Phillips, James
Prosser, Abraham
Prosser, Elizabeth
Prosser, Anne E.
Prosser, Ella
Prosser, Isaac
Prosser, James
Prosser, James F.
Prosser, James J.
Prosser, John
Prosser, Joseph
Prosser, Margaret
Prosser, Margaret J.
Prosser, Mary J.
Prosser, Mary M.
Prosser, Robert N.
Prosser, Sadie
Prosser, Samantha A.
Prosser, Sarah
Prosser, Sarah A.
Prosser, Sarah E.
Prosser, Silas C.

Quail, Mary Ann
Quail, Thomas

Ralston, Alice
Ralston, Harrison
Reeves, Annie
Robins, Henry
Robins, Mary
Rund, Angus (August)
Rund, Anna M.
Rund, August
Rund, Flora
Rund, Lewis
Rund, Mary A.
Rund,
  Mrs. S. (Kephart)
Rund, Mrs. Sarah
Rund, Theresa

Schrock, Mrs.
Shafer, Arnold
Shafer David
Shafer, James
Shafer, John
Shafer, Mahlan
Shafer, Margaret
Shafer, Mrs. Martha
Shafer, Mary
Shaffer, Mrs. C.
Shaffer, David
Shaffer, Ida
Shelman, John
Smith, Della
Smith, Elizabeth
Smith, George
Smith, Leander
Smith, Nancy
Smith, Prairie
Snider, Bernice
Snider, Emma
Spencer, Allexander C.
Staples, Zachary T.
Stewart, Eliza
Stewart, Heyemiah
Stewart, William E.
Stinson, Elisabeth
Stinson, John

Stinson, Moses
Stuart, Emma
Stump, Abigail
Stump, Abraham
Swift, Alonzo

Thomas, Mrs. Spicy
Thomas, William
Tracy, India
Trayster, Robbert
Tumbeson, Manville
Turner, Chip
Turner, E. D.
Turner,
  Janie (Fleener)
Turner, John
Turner, Lena (Kain)
Turner, Mrs. Letha
Turner, Lewis
Turner,
  Mrs. Martha B.
Turner, Nancy
Turner, Rebekah
Tuttle, Pamelia

Vanausdall, Rebecca
Vanausdall, Silas

Wagner, Mrs. Nellie
Walker, Dud
Walker, Mrs. Dud
Walker, Dydley
Walker, Elizabeth
Walker, Frank
Walker, Mrs. Mary
Walker, Randolph
Wallace,
  Margaret Jane
Wallis, Joseph
Wallis,
  Julia A. (Gearhard)
Waltman, Bessie
Waltman,
  Mrs. Catherine
Waltman, Edward C.
Waltman, Ella
Waltman, Ambrose

Waltman,
  Mrs. Ambrose
Waltman, Emma J.
Waltman, H. McIntire
  (McIntyre)
Waltman, Hiram D.
Waltman, Hiram
Waltman, Mrs. Hiram
Waltman, Irene
Waltman, Julia Ann
Waltman, Margaret
Waltman, Margaret
  (Donovan)
Waltman, Mary
Waltman, Mellie
Waltman, Michel
Waltman, Minnie
Waltman, Minnie A.
Waltman, R. J.
Waltman, R. (Zody)
Waltman, Sarah J.
Waltman, Saraphine
Waltman, Mrs. Tamie
Waltman, Thomas
Waltman, Walter V.
Ward, Clementine
Ward, Hannah Jettie
Ward, James G.
Ward, Rufus
Ward, Mrs. Sarepta
Waugh, Elam H.
Waugh, Samuel N.
Waugh, William A.
Weddle, Maud
  (Milbourn)
Wright, Carey C.
Wright, Mary
Wright, Robert
Wright, William

Yoder, Catherine
Yoder, James

Zody, Mrs. Emma
Zody, Bertha
Zody, Nellie
Zook, John

The Oak Ridge Church and Cemetery
Nova May Mertens

Around 1875, the inhabitants of Jackson Township, Brown County, Indiana, living about two miles north of Helmsburg felt the need for a house of worship. Consequently plans were made to build, and the two sons of Jacob Frownfelter assumed the leadership for the construction of the first log church. The next problem which confronted the group was an appropriate name. Several meetings were held for this purpose but without success. Finally when another meeting took place Jacob Frownfelter was determined to settle the question and at the proper moment rose to his feet and remarked, "This is an oak ridge from one end to the other [referring to the timber] so why not call it Oak Ridge Church?"

By 1900, the size of the congregation necessitated larger quarters. Therefore, a few rods south of the log church on land donated by William Snider a new white frame building was constructed which is still used as a community church.

Approximately one hundred graves may be found in the cemetery adjoining the church on the south. At first there were few burials due to the poor condition of the roads, but as the highways were improved more families placed their loved ones to rest in this cemetery, which includes a few Civil and World War veterans. Among the oldest graves are members of the Snider family who originally had been laid to rest in the Myers Cemetery, and one grave for a member of the Frownfelter family moved from the Kuhn or Fleener Cemetery.

William Snider, b. Sept. 18, 1843; Co. D. 25th Reg. Ind. Vol.
Emaline, wife of William Snider, b. Nov. 9, 1843; d. Feb. 8, 1907.
James Edgar, son of William and Emaline Snider, d. March 31, 1872, at age of 3 mo.
Rosebelle, dau. of William and I. E. Snider, d. March 20, 1874, age 11 mo., 20 da.
Infant Snider, d. March 16, 1916.
Douglas Wade, b. 1860; d. 1941.
Mary Jane Wade, b. 1861, d. 1940.

Myrtle, wife of R. C. Snider, b. Feb. 17, 1881; d. Feb. 11, 1907.
Sadie Wade, b. 1869; d. March 17, 1950, age 81 yrs., 2 mo., 12 da.
Joseph M. Wade, b. 1832; d. 1906.
Phoebe A. Wade, b. 1833; d. 1923.
D. W. Miller, son of David and Sarah Miller, b. 1838; d. 1920; 55th Reg. Ind. Vol.
James Smith, b. July 1, 1830.
Joseph Tutterow, b. Oct. 15, 1848; d. Sept. 9, 1915.
Sarah A. Tutterow, b. Aug. 26, 1860; d. June 21, 1925.
Lucy Hughes, b. Oct. 23, 1845.
Walter Hughes, b. 1881; d. 1924.
Sarah Kephart, b. 1850; d. 1936.
Harold Lee Rund, b. Apr. 29, 1911; d. Jan. 4, 1913.
Lorna Dell Kaserman, b. Jan. 15; d. Jan. 17, 1920.
James David Kaserman, b. Oct. 29, 1876; d. Oct. 19, 1950.
Nora Luvena Kaserman, b. Sept. 18, 1883; d. Jan. 24, 1920.
James Gahn, b. July 16, 1857; d. July 2, 1920.
Laura Gahn, d. Dec. 11, 1867; d. May 9, 1945.
Margaret Snyder, b. 1858; d. 1908.
Lewis Prosser, b. 1866; d. 1941.
Ida Bell Prosser, b. 1878; d. 1949.
Katherine Murphy, b. 1839; d. 1925.
Jean E. Brown, b. 1930; d. 1932.
Mary A. Brown, b. 1928; d. 1932.
Ishmael L. Brown, b. 1913; d. 1938.
Thomas J. Kelso, b. Aug. 22, 1833; d. July 10, 1910; Co. K., Ind. Vol.
John Steele, b. 1836; d. 1915.
Rebecca Steele, b. 1853; d. June 12, 1935; 82 yrs., 2 mo., 6 da.
Perry Baker, b. 1855, d. 1933.
Mary Baker, b. 1853; d. 1931.
James Derringer, b. 1865; d. 1936.
Cordelia Derringer, b. 1870, d. 1920.
Archie Leroy Derringer, b. Oct. 14, 1899; d. Apr. 14, 1949.
Infant Sisson, Twin, d. Aug. 30, 1948.
Walter Ray Schrock, d. July 2, 1948; age 19 yrs., 2 mo., 25 da.
Albert Wampler, b. Oct. 31, 1891; d. May 20, 1947.
Freda May Neal, b. Sept. 3, 1923; d. June 18, 1925.
Alice Neal, b. 1880; d. 1947.
Mary S. Pitzer, b. 1867; d. 1945.
Henry D. Neidigh, b. 1862; d. 1945.
Florence J. Neidigh, b. 1869; d. 1934.
Sarah F. Kelso, wife of Thomas Kelso, b. May 3, 1835; d. July 10, 1910.
Lewis Kelso, b. 1880; d. 1934.
Carl Edgar, son of Lewis and Ida M. Kelso, b. Sept. 23, 1907; d. Jan. 15, 1915.
Daniel W. David, b. Feb. 25, 1858; d. Aug. 24, 1937.
Infant Shillingford, d. March 31, 1914.
Chelsie L. Shillingford, b. Feb. 23, 1883; d. April 17, 1939.
Susie Ellen Bush, b. 1893; d. 1923.
Wm. J. Long, b. 1843; d. 1925.

Mary A. Long, b. 1843; d. 1917.
Elijah Long, b. April 9, 1844; d. May 30, 1927; Enlisted June 10, 1862, Co. G., 55 Reg. Ind. Vol.
Robert E. Long, b. Aug. 7, 1880; d. Oct. 1933.
Ray Derringer, b 1896, d. 1928.
Ruth Derringer, b. 1893; d. 1929.
Charles M. Gill, b. 1871; d. 1949.
William G. Smith, b. 1860; d. 1929.
Clara G. Smith, b. 1859; d. 1929.
Martha J. Stephens, b. 1858; d. 1944.
Homer C. Stephens, b. 1860; d. 1927.
James Bailey, b. Aug. 8, 1860; d. 1948.
Mary J. Bailey, b. Sept. 27, 1864; d. May 12, 1941.
Martin L. Morrison, b. Aug. 31, 1854; d. Jan. 27, 1930.
Sarah C Morrison, b. Nov. 13, 1855; d. May 13, 1929.
Leah Katherine Morrison, b. Feb. 27, 1908; d. Nov. 30, 1940.
Harry B. Cope, b. 1875; d. 1924.
Harold Cope, b. 1900; d. 1923.
Charles William Stephens, d. Oct. 4, 1938; Indiana Fireman ICL, U.S. Navy.
Merrette I. Hessennauer Long, b. July 5, 1903; d. Aug. 9, 1941; Wife of Glenn Long.
Willard Long, b. 1861; d. 1941.
Marcena Long, b. 1865; d. 1938.
Jas. W. Steele, b. Jan. 8, 1941; d. Nov. 17, 1925; Co. I. 63 Ind. Inf.
Edgar D. Steele, d. Oct. 14, 1933; age 53 yrs., 6 mo., 8 da.; Ind. Pvt. 3 Arty.
Ruth Beaver, b. 1858; d. 1945.
Albert Long, b. 1858; d. 1932.
Esther L. Bond, b. 1924; d. 1932.
Lucille R. Raridon, b. 1900; d. 1946.
William Otto Tutterow, b. March 25, 1897; d. Dec. 24, 1944.
Marvin E. Tutterow, b. Aug. 5, 1925; d. Dec. 23, 1944; Died of wounds received in Belgium, and was buried in N. France.
Infant son of Mr. and Mrs. W. O. Tutterow, d. Feb. 15, 1936.
Ralph Ramsey, b. 1905; d. 1947.
Owen Richardson, b. 1850; d. 1919.
Elmer Richardson, b. 1882; d. 1934.
David Frownfelter, b. April 29, 1846; d. May 6, 1933.
Lucinda Frownfelter, b. Jan. 15, 1849; d. March 28, 1933.
Frances Harding, d. Aug. 18, 1937.
Lewis J. Snider, b. 1872; d. 1948.
Warren Snider, b. 1900; d. 1942.
Charles F. Leonard, d. Sept. 2, 1949; age 91 yrs., 7 mo., 14 da.
Josie Baughman, b. 1882; d. 1947.
Elizabeth A. Brown, d. May 28, 1948; 1 yr., 1 mo., 28 da.
George Christian Merriman, b. Sept. 14, 1875; d. Dec. 12, 1947.
Infant of James and Gladys Fritch, Violet Marie Fritch, b. Sept. 7, 1924; d. Dec. 4, 1926.

James Lloyd Merriman, son of George and Rebecca Merriman, b. Feb. 4, 1908; died at age of 16 months.
Mary Smith, d. July 194—.
Jacob W. Frownfelter, b. 1848; d. 1920.
Annie M. Frownfelter, b. 1867; d. 1936.
Samuel Frownfelter, b. 1850; d. 1933.
Clarence C. Beeler, b. 1861; d. 1920.
Mary H. Beeler, b. 1882; d. 1927.
Joseph Hughes, b. Aug. 3, 1844; d. Aug. 14, 1914; Co. I, 63 Reg. Ind. Vol.
Sarah Ann (Clark) Turner, b. March 11, 1840; d. March 2, 1910.
John Turner, b. Oct. 31, 1867; d. Nov. 1930.
James Lewis Turner, b. Feb. 5, 1864; d. June 20, 1947.
Laura Ellen Turner, b. July 14, 1865; d. April 9, 1939.
Infant son of Frederick and Nova Mertens, b. Feb. 23, 1927; died at birth.
Rufus (Jack Turner, b. Feb. 23, 1889; d. Nov. 5, 1932; [Date of birth on stone is 1890, but is incorrect.]

The Old Conrad Cemetery Records[1]

Copied by Maurice Griffin and Frederick P. Griffin

Jacob Conrad—d. Oct. 10, 1841; aged 80 yrs.
Mary—wife of Jacob Conrad; d. Jan. 17, 1841; aged 77 yrs., 4 mos.
Phebe Jane Conrad—dau. of J. and E. Conrad; b. Dec. 10, 1832; d. May 21, 1834.
Henry Conrad—b. 1800; d. March 12, 1858.
Polly—wife of Henry Conrad; b. Jan. 1806; d. July 23, 1884.
George Conrad—b. May 22, 1806; d. Nov. 4, 1883.
Nancy—wife of G. Conrad; b. Sept. 8, 1804; d. Dec. 25, 1862.
Philip Conrad—d. Feb. 16, 1881; aged 55 yrs., 9 mos, 11 days.
Eliza R.—wife of P. Conrad; d. July 28, 1869; aged 44 yrs., 3 mos., 24 days.
Peter Server—son of John and Elizabeth Server; b. July 18, 1815; d. Dec. 10, 1815; aged 4 mos., 22 days.
Jacob A. Server—son of Peter and Dorothy Server; d. Sept. 2, 1835; aged 34 yrs.

---

[1] Jacob Conrad, who immigrated to Corydon from Pennsylvania, built a hotel in 1807 about a mile and a half east of Corydon on the Corydon-New Albany Pike. During the time that Corydon was the capital of Indiana (1813-1825), Jacob Conrad's hotel was the principal one and also the most popular. The Conrad Cemetery is located a short distance east of the spot where the Old Capital Hotel once stood. The record is complete, every legible name being copied from the stones in the Cemetery. There are several scores of stones on which there are now no records. The records were copied on October 29, 1939.

Dorothy Server—wife of Peter Server; d. July 2, 1828; aged 68 yrs.

Samuel Wesley Row—d. June 20, 1849; aged 22 yrs., 10 days.

Daniel Hamilton Row—d. Jan. 29, 1845; aged 19 yrs., 9 mos., 19 days.

Jesse S. Rowe—b. Nov. 6, 1809; d. July 7, 1854.

Daniel Row—d. Sept. 18, 1864; aged 79 yrs.

Mary Rowe—d. April 13, 1875; aged 89 yrs., 2 mos., 22 days.

John H. Allburn—b. Jan. 21, 1809; d. July 28, 1838.

John J. Allburn—d. Oct. 24, 1839; aged 13 mos., 11 days.

Margaret Mugler—dau. of J. G. and M. Mugler; d. July 31, 1847; aged 15 yrs., 6 mos.

Infant daughter of P. and Anna Zenor—b. and d. May 16, 1855.

John H. Zenor—son of A. and A. M. Zenor; d. Aug. 16, 1862; aged 3 mos., 7 days.

Christopher Shuck—b. July 11, 1766; d. April 21, 1833.

Mary C.—wife of Christopher Shuck; b. July 11, 1773; d. Sept. 17, 1822.

Elizabeth Shuck—d. Feb. 13, 1863; aged 24 yrs., 4 mos., 8 d.

Mary A. Shuck—wife of H. Shuck; d. Sept. 8, 1864; aged 23 yrs., 3 mos., 13 days.

Cora A.—dau. of H. and M. A. Shuck; d. Sept. 2, 1864; aged 22 days.

Henry Shuck—b. 1835; d. 1922.

Eliza J.—wife of H. Shuck; b. March 8, 1844; d. Jan. 9, 1903.

George Shuck—b. June 21, 1800; d. Sept. 21, 1889.

Mahala Shuck—wife of George Shuck; b. Sept. 18, 1805; d. June 14, 1894.

Rebecca—dau. of J. S. and M. Gilham; b. Oct. 5, 1853; d. Oct. 10, 1853.

Diana E.—dau. of J. S. and M. Gilham; b. Jan. 14, 1855; d. March 1, 1856.

Eli Leo—son of J. A. and M. E. Lone; b. Dec. 23, 1870; d. Aug. 23, 1879.

Infant of J. A. and M. E. Lone—b. and d. Dec. 21, 1861.

Samuel—son of D. and M. Pfrimmer; d. July 18, 1860; aged 4 mos., 5 days.

John Dick—b. June 1, 1797; d. March 16, 1859.

Margaret—wife of John Dick; d. Sept. 7, 1858; aged 58 yrs.

John J.—son of H. and S. Dick; b. Feb. 16, 1863; d. April 22, 1863.
James A.—son of A. A. and M. C. Wright; d. June 26, 1865; aged 7 yrs., 11 mos., 22 days.
William H.—son of A. A. and M. C. Wright; d. March 7, 1866; aged 5 mos., 13 days.
Samuel Emily—Company K, 59th Indiana; d. May 1, 1884; aged 70 yrs.
Elizabeth E.—wife of Samuel Emily; b. March 20, 1824; d. May 4, 1902.
Clarence D., Flosie E., and Walter D.—children of D and L. Emily; d. 1890, 1891, 1893.
James Allen—d. March 23, 1885; aged 39 yrs.
Ella V.—dau. of J. and M. A. Allen; d. Sept. 9, 1875; aged 5 yrs., 5 mos., 13 days.
Johnie M.—son of J. and M. A. Allen; d. Jan. 18, 1875; aged 1 yr., 4 mos., 23 days.
John A. Kelly—d. Jan. 23, 1892; aged 80 yrs.
Eveline—wife of John A. Kelly; d. May 16, 1890; aged 76 yrs.
Read Crandall—b. Dec. 22, 1791; d. July 22, 1870.
Polly—wife of Read Crandall; d. Sept. 14, 1865; aged 80 yrs.
A. C. Crandall—b. 1860; d. 1895.
Nellie L.—dau. of A. C. Crandall; b. 1893; d. 1909.
Daniel F. Lemmon—b. July 18, 1844; d. April 18, 1914.
Lucinda Lemmon—wife of Daniel F. Lemmon; b. Oct. 31, 1844; d. April 21, 1914.
James W.—son of D. F. and Lucinda Lemmon; b. May 20, 1875; d. Nov. 18, 1877.
Infant daughter of D. F. and L. Lemmon—d. June 29, 1864.
Nancy Jane Venner—wife of John S. Venner; d. Feb. 4, 1866; aged 27 yrs., 1 mo., 27 days.
Mary B.—dau. of G. W. and M. E. Venner; d. Aug. 15, 1872; aged 2 mos., 27 days.
Lucinda C., dau. of S. and S. Gates; d. Aug. 22, 1864; aged 1 yr., 28 days.
Sampson Turley—aged 88 yrs., 8 mos., 16 days.
Lydia A. Turley—b. April 28, 1856; d. Aug. 19, 1898.
Infant—son of W. H. and E. Turley; b. and d. 1866.
Cordelia—dau. of W. H. and R. Turley; b. Oct. 19, 1863; d. July 18, 1864.
Rebecca—wife of W. H. Turley; b. July 1, 1826; d. April 7, 1864.

George Stonecipher—b. Jan. 10, 1789; d. Sept. 26, 1878; aged 89 yrs., 8 mos., 16 days.

Mary Ann—wife of Geo Stonecypher [sic] and dau. of Jacob Young; d. Nov. 9, 1868; aged 70 yrs, 7 mos.

George Lear—d. June 12, 1874; aged 69 yrs., 3 mos., 29 days.

Elizabeth—wife of Geo Lear; b. Feb. 22, 1822; d. Jan. 8, 1899; aged 76 yrs., 10 mos., 16 days.

Silver Lake Cemetery Records:[1]

Phebe—wife of Alexander McKinzie; d. July 29, 1849; aged 35 yrs., 9 mos., 35 days.

Summers Dean—d. Aug. 27, 1849; aged 42 yrs., 7 mos., 20 d.

Phebe—dau. of John and Mary McKinzy [sic]; b. March 28, 1831; d. Oct. 18, 1851; aged 17 yrs., 7 mos., 10 days.

Mary—wife of John McKinzie; b. July 1, 1801; d. 1853.

John McKinzie—consort of Susannah and wife Mary McKinzie[2]; d. March 27, 1859; aged 60 yrs., 9 mos., 11 days.

Rebecca—wife of Daniel Dean, and dau. of Benjamin Haines and Mary Haines; b. Feb. 14, 1813; d. June 27, 1852.

Julia A. Haines—b. Oct. 8, 1825; d. Aug. 14, 1827.

Elizabeth Haines—b. Feb. 24, 1812; d. Dec. 29, 1833.

Parents, Mary Haines—b. 1787; d. Jan. 1839; aged 52 yrs., 9 days.

Samuel Haines—d. June 1849; aged 60 yrs., 10 mos., 12 days.

Ruth Haines—d. June, 1849; aged 30 yrs., 4 mos., 144 days.

Wilcoxin Cemetery Records:[3]

Aaron Wilcoxson—b. June 11, 1764; d. July 11, 1830.

Wiliam T. Wilcoxson—b. June 12, 1810; d. Aug. 12, 1840.

Hannah Wilcoxson—b. Feb. 3, 1766; d. June 18, 1839.

Pleasant Wilcoxson—b. July 28, 1842; d. Aug. 7, 1842.

Nancy Wilcoxson—wife of William T. Wilcoxson; b. Nov. 2, 1817; d. Nov. 20, 1847.

Harvey Wilcoxson—b. Oct. 25, 1847; d. May 8, 1848.

Judah Black[4]—b. Jan. 14, 1763; d. Jan. 18, 1842.

---

[1] This cemetery is in the northern part of Harrison County, Indiana, near what was known as Silver Lake. This like, which was drained several years ago, covered twenty-six acres. The McKinzies were settlers on the lake farm, while the Haines family settled in Washington County, Indiana, about one and a half miles west of Silver Lake. There are several graves which are not marked.

[2] This item is copied as found on the stone. It does not make sense, but seems a clumsy attempt to say, that, after the death of his first wife (Mary) in 1858, John McKinzie married Susannah as his second wife.

[3] This cemetery is near Pekin, Washington County, Indiana, on the farm of Edgar S. Marshall.

[4] Judah Black was a colored woman, perhaps a servant in the Wilcoxson home.

OLD GOSHEN CHURCH AND CEMETERY

Contributed By

FREDERICK P. GRIFFIN

By an act of the 1943 General Assembly, the Conservation Commission was authorized to receive, accept, administer, and maintain the Old Goshen Baptist Church and Cemetery in Harrison County as a public memorial to the pioneer settlers of Indiana. Built of massive oak and poplar logs, the church building is still in comparatively good condition after standing one hundred and twenty years.

It was in the first decade of the nineteenth century that Squire Boone, brother of Daniel, crossed the Ohio River from his home in Kentucky and established a new home some six miles north of the river in what is now Harrison County. With him were his four sons, Moses, Isaiah, Enoch, and Jonathan, and five sons of his cousin. Under the strong arms of these sturdy men, the wilderness soon began to take on the aspects of a settled community. A mill was built for grinding the grain of the neighborhood. When Harrison County was organized in 1808, Moses Boone was appointed one of the judges.

Religious services were, no doubt, held in the various homes of the neighborhood at first, but it was not long before the building of a church was discussed. The building now to be preserved by the state is thought to have been completed in 1813.[1] It stands on State Highway 11, about two and one-half miles north of Laconia. Moses Boone, on whose land it was erected, deeded the land to the church trustees in 1821; he also took a leading part in its construction. The Reverend David A. Leonard who died in 1819 and was buried in the church cemetery may have been the first pastor.

After being used by the Baptists for sixty or seventy years, the building was leased for brief periods to Dunkard and United Brethren congregations. In the forties it served as a school house. The benches, made of hewn logs and

---

[1] Information about the church is difficult to find. The early church records were destroyed by fire. County histories, deed records, and a newspaper article by John M. Dannenfelser, Jr. (clipping in Corydon Public Library) were the principal sources used. Mrs. Kate Douglass Funk, of Corydon and Indianapolis, has been helpful in securing information.

without backs, are now in the Old Capitol in Corydon. Small holes chipped in the west wall indicate the location of the shelf upon which the pupils did their writing. The original floor was of wide rough boards placed on slab sills of beech. A balcony, built about seven feet above the lower section, extended two-thirds of the way across the building from north to south. The building was repaired in 1913, but little change was made in its outward appearance.

In the large cemetery adjoining the church, many of the early settlers of the neighborhood are buried. Many graves are marked only by a rough slab with no name. All the inscriptions which were legible were copied in 1940 by Samuel P. Hayes, of Corydon, and myself. The original inscriptions have been shortened and abbreviations used to save space in printing.

Joel Cotner, b. Jan. 13, 1809; d. June, 1890.
Belinda, w. of Joel Cotner, Aug., 1811.
John, s. of Henry and Mary E. Guest, b. Mar. 29, 1849; d. July 11, 1849.
Margaret C., dau. of Henry and Mary E. Guest, b. Mar. 14, 1873; d. July, 1873.
Magdalena, w. of A. M. Hunter; d. Aug. 24, 1854. Age 45 yrs.
Catharine, dau. of Abner M. and M. M. Hunter; d. Apr. 14, 1853. Age 18 yrs. 5 mos. 7 days.
Mary Ann, w. of Joel B. Rissler, b. 1829; d. 1850.
Elender, w. of W. Gaither; d. Oct. 10, 1855. Age 61 yrs. 7 mos. 21 days.
Rachel E., dau. of S. and M. E. Funk; d. Dec. 30, 1860. Age 2 yrs. 4 mos. 16 days.
Luther J. Wade; d. Aug. 15, 1931. Age 46 yrs. 5 mos. 9 days.
Anna Rebecca Jenkins; d. Mar. 12, 1938. Age 82 yrs. 11 mos. 24 days.
Mary, w. of James Jenkins, b. Sept. 16, 1832; d. May 13, 1882.
Calvin S., husband of L. Noon, b. Feb. 28, 1816; d. Aug. 14, 1885.
Lanta, w. of C. S. Noon, b. Dec. 11, 1810; d. June 18, 1896.
Solomon Harbaugh; d. Sept. 22, 1877. Age 75 yrs. 7 mos. 17 days.
Margaret, w. of Solomon Harbaugh; d. Apr. 3, 1875. Age 73 yrs. 10 mos.
Charles J. Harbaugh, s. of S. and M. Harbaugh; d. Oct. 21, 1837. Age 2 yrs. 1 mo. 29 days.
Alma F. Harbaugh, b. Jan. 19, 1878; d. Mar. 10, 1878.
Wm. H. Harbaugh, b. Nov. 14, 1832; d. Dec. 17, 1888.
Annie M., w. of W. H. Harbaugh, b. Nov. 26, 1842; d. Feb. 11, 1907.
Ada Luckett.
Benjamin D. Luckett.
Adam and Nancy Douglass.
Benjamin D., s. of Joel and Kate Bartley, b. May 15, 1850; d. Aug. 12, 1850.
Infant son of Joel and Kate Bartley, b. and d. Mar. 12, 1853.
Helen E., dau. of Joel and Kate Bartley, b. Jan. 15, 1849; d. Feb. 24, 1850.

Joel F. Bartley, b. Jan. 15, 1808; d. Sept. 27, 1883.
Catherine Bartley, b. Mar. 10, 1824; d. Aug. 6, 1905.
Sarah M. Douglass, b. May 13, 1822; d. Oct. 14, 1895.
Narcecy Gulpernia Gaither, age 17 mos. save 9 days; d. Oct. 3, 1834.
Nancy Emley Gaither, age 8 yrs. save 9 days; d. Sept. 14, 1834.
Jane, w. of R. G. Bartley, b. Mar. 15, 1815; d. Nov. 4, 1857.
Martha G. Groves, b. Dec. 22, 1840; d. Oct. 19, 1846.
Mary T., dau. of J. F. and A. J. Newman, b. July 22, 1834; d. Dec. 11, 1850 [stone broken].
Benjamin L., s. of J. F. and A. J. Newman, b. May 26, 1846; d. Feb. 5, 1848 [stone broken].
Mary L., dau. of J. F. and A. J. Newman, b. Dec. 10, 1850; d. May 22, 1851 [stone broken].
Susan C., w. of J. C. Lynn Esq. dec'd.; d. Jan. 18, 1852, age 27 yrs. 2 mos. 10 days.
Benjamin F., s. of J. W. and H. A. Miller, b. Feb. 19, 1853; d. Mar. 1, 1853.
Peter Miller who dept. this life 31st Dec. 1832 in 29th year of his age, a native of Washington Co., Pa.
Jacob Miller who dept. this life 9th Sept. 1840 in 37th year of his age, a native of Washington Co., Pa.
Peter Miller, Seigniour who dept. this life Oct. 10, 1842, age 67 yrs. 2 mos. 15 days. A native of Pennsylvania.
Isiah Inman, s. of Isiah and Charlotte Inman; d. Nov. 10, 1835. Age 9 yrs. 3 mos. 7 days.
Mary Ann Crosmon Inman, dau. of Isiah and Charlotte Inman; d. Oct. 20, 1832. Age 9 yrs. 10 mos. 6 days.
Chas. Inman; d. Oct. 30, 1832. Age 47 yrs. 1 mo. 27 days.
Our Baby, Claude Anderson; d. May 25, 1924.
Aaron Howe; d. Aug. 16, 1839. Age 21 yrs. 10 mos. 21 days.
Ann Pindell, w. of Jacob Pindell; d. July 5, 1838 in her 39th year.
Isaac Cotner; d. Aug. 1, 1844. Age 16 yrs. 11 mos. 13 days.
John Cotner [stone weathered away].
M. S. [nothing more on stone].
Anthony Cotner.
John C. Cotner; d. Sept. 23, 1848. Age 33 yrs. 3 mos. 27 days.
Lucinda, w. of Peter Frakes and dau. of John and Mary Cotner; d. July 9, 1849. Age 36 yrs. 17 days.
Mary H., infant dau. of Peter and Lucinda Frakes; d. July 14, 1849. Age 2 mos. 15 days.
Maria Boon; d. May 8, 1834 [creek slab; almost illegible].
Hannah Boon; d. Dec. 18, 1833. Age 64 yrs. [creek slab; almost illegible].
Mel. [creek slab; almost illegible].
Sarah, w. of Henry Lenau; d. May 10, 1887.
Henry L. Lenau; d. Apr. 29, 1881. About 78 yrs.
Martha M. Lenau; d. July 14, 1849. Age 2 yrs. [creek slab].
S. L. [nothing more on stone].
Catharine Houser.
Sarah Cable; d. Mar. 16, 1832. Age 17 yrs. 10 mos.

James R. Nantz, consort of Nancy Nantz; d. Feb. 18, 1849. Age 54 yrs. 1 mo. 13 days.
Nancy, consort of James R. Nantz; d. Sept. 8, 1849. Age 46 yrs. 11 mos. 3 days.
Venevia C., dau. of James R. and Nancy Nantz; d. Aug. 3, 1847. Age 17 yrs. 3 mos. 7 days.
Altha Ann Nantz; d. Oct. 15, 1844. Age 1 mo. 3 days.
Eunice Eliza, dau. of Chas. and Versalia C. Inman; d. Feb. 18, 1847. Age 6 mos. 6 days.
Mary Angeline, dau. of Orville and Sarah C. Nantz; d. Feb. 22, 1850. Age 6 yrs. 7 mos.
Wm. S. Nantz; d. June 9, 1842. Age 8 yrs. 4 mos. 19 days.
Hannah, w. of Hugh McIntire; d. Aug. 29, 1845. Age 66 yrs.
Lawson J., s. of Jeremiah and Sarah Woods; d. July 16, 1847. Age 34 yrs. 6 mos.
Sarah Woods; d. Aug. 9, 1852 [stone broken].
W. Thomas, Company G, 50th Indiana Infantry [government stone].
Thomas M., s. of James Pell and Elizabeth, his wife, d. June 23, 1830. Age 21 yrs. 11 mos. 7 days.
Jesse H., s. of Jas. and Elizabeth Pell; d. July 3, 1827. Age 8 yrs. 7 mos. 2 days.
Wm. T., s. of Jas. and Elizabeth Pell; d. Oct. 7, 1822. Age 5 yrs. 10 mos.
Ezekiel, s. of Jas. and Elizabeth Pell; d. Jan. 18, 1825. Age 2 yrs. 4 mos. 17 days.
Timothy Pell; d. Sept. 3, 1824. Age 23 yrs.
Margaret Pell, w. of Wm. Pell; d. Nov. 19, 1828. Age 58 yrs.
Isaac Cable, d. Sept. 22, 1824. Age 39 yrs.
Frederick Cotner—the faith doctor.
Rev. David A. Leonard; d. July 22, 1819. Age 45 yrs. [two stones].
Elizabeth, w. of John B. Keller; d. Oct. 16, 1824. Age 29 yrs. 4 mos. 3 days [large flat stone].
Hamilton, s. of Geo. W. and Lucy Boone; d. June 9, 1841. Age 32 yrs.
Geo. W. Boone; d. July 1, 1857. Age 74 yrs. 3 mos. 25 days.
Lucy, w. of G. W. Boone; d. of cholera, Sept. 18, 1833. Age 54 yrs. Also their daughter, Helen, w. of H. Luckett, died same day in her 27th year.
Milton Boone; d. Sept. 17, 1818. Age 7 yrs. Son of Geo. Boone.
Fielding, s. of E. B. and U. Boone, b. Sept. 11, 1838; d. June 13, 1862. Joined 50th Regiment, Indiana Militia, Company C.
Blanch, dau. of C. and M. C. May, b. Jan. 20, 1870; d. Mar. 27, 1872.
Lavina B., w. of C. M. Dawson; d. May 14, 1874. Age 42 yrs.
Hiram C., s. of Samuel and Mary P. Boone, b. Oct. 29, 1820; d. July 12, 1849.
Samuel, s. of Samuel Boone of Fredericktown, Md., b. Mar. 9, 1778; d. Jan. 8, 1856.
Elizabeth, dau. of Samuel and Mary P. Boone, and w. of Dr. John D. Weaver, b. Dec. 14, 1812; d. Dec. 31, 1857.
Fielding M., s. of Samuel and Mary Boone, b. Aug. 13, 1815; d. July 11, 1871.

Upton Boone, b. 1808; d. May 17, 1887.
Elizabeth Howser, w. of Upton Boone, b. Dec. 13, 1810; d. Oct. 9, 1890.
Wm. S. May, s. of Conrad and Mary C. May, b. Feb. 27, 1868; d. Aug. 6, 1893.
Conrad May; d. Sept. 7, 1902. Age about 60 yrs.
Mary C., w. of Conrad May, b. Feb. 20, 1836; d. May 11, 1914.
Mayme May, b. 1879; d. 1935.
Horace Boone, b. May 31, 1846; d. Jan. 30, 1915.
Harriet E., w. of Horace Boone, b. Dec. 26, 1845; d. Oct. 30, 1932.
Mary M. Hoby, b. 1850; d. 1926.
Craven Boone, b. May 3, 1807; d. June 21, 1886.
Sarah Newman, w. of Craven Boone, b. Oct. 20, 1811; d. Oct. 8, 1877.
Craven G. Boone, b. Apr. 23, 1873; d. Oct. 7, 1906.
Hadie L., w. of Craven Boone, b. Apr. 29, 1877; d. Mar. 19, 1922.
Carrie M., w. of Wm. F. Rasure, b. 1890; d. 1933.
Samuel Boone, b. Aug. 6, 1843; d. July 4, 1925.
Mary, w. of Samuel Boone, b. Dec. 24, 1855; d. July 26, 1922.
Upton, s. of Samuel and Mary Boone, b. Mar. 21, 1881; d. Aug. 9, 1896.
Ada B., w. of J. E. Byrum, b. Aug. 4, 1879; d. Nov. 12, 1897.
Lavina Boone, b. Nov. 10, 1809; d. Mar. 19, 1899.
Mary Boone; d. June 26, 1929. Age 66 yrs. 7 mos. 2 days.
Wm. Pennebaker, b. in Pennsylvania; d. in Indiana, 1822. Age 67 yrs.
Mary, dau. of Wm. and Mary C. Pennebaker and w. of Samuel Boone, b. May 8, 1790; d. June 24, 1844.
Landsdale Homer, s. of Samuel and Mary P. Boone, b. Sept. 4, 1828; d. Dec. 13, 1829.
Mary Jane, dau. of Samuel and Mary P. Boone, b. May 4, 1818; d. Sept. 1818.
Julia Ann, dau. of Samuel and Mary P. Boone, b. Apr. 8, 1822; d. Oct. 1823.
Thomas Mitchel, s. of Samuel and Mary P. Boone, b. 1831; d. 1832.
Jane Ann, dau. of Samuel and Mary P. Boone, b. Aug. 3, 1826; d. July 8, 1843.
Helen, dau. of Samuel and Mary P. Boone, b. Apr. 2, 1824; d. July 9, 1849.

George Charley, Jr., Burying Ground:[10]

George B. Charley—d. Feb. 18, 1863; aged 57 yrs., 11 mos., 12 days.
Sarah C.—dau. of G. B. and C. Charley; d. July 24, 1846; aged 9 mos.
Anastasie—dau. of G. B. and C. Charley; d. May 16, 1850; aged 2 yrs., 10 mos.
Charlotte—dau. of G. B. and C. Charley; d. May 11, 1856; aged 6 yrs., 11 mos., 15 days.
Emeline—dau. of G. B. and C. Charley; d. Feb. 20, 1864; aged 12 yrs., 2 mos., 22 days.
Pleasant Willard—son of P. G. and E. Charley; d. Jan. 13, 1866; aged 9 yrs., 3 mos., 11 days.
Analiza—dau. of P. G. and E. Charley; d. April 27, 1862; aged 10 mos., 3 days.

---

[10] Located one mile east of Nevin on State Road 135, Harrison Township, Harrison County, Indiana. George Charley, Jr., inherited this farm from his father.

THE CHARLEY FAMILY CEMETERY—HARRISON COUNTY[6]

Copied by SAMUEL P. HAYES and FREDERICK P. GRIFFIN

William L. Conrad—1866-1937.
Elsie H. Conrad—[b] 1876 [no death date].
David Grable—consort of Potiah P. Grable; b. Dec. 25, 1800; d. Jan. 10, 1865.
Fielding—son of J. and N. Fleshman; b. Feb. 8, 1816; d. in his second year and eight months. [sic]
Jacob—son of J. and M. Fleshman; b. June 26, 1829; d. in his third year and four months. [sic]
Jacob Fleshman—b. March 6, 1789; d. April 11, 1856.
Polly Fleshman—b. March 24, 1794; d. March 31, 1866.
Perry—son of Phillip and Lydia Brandenburg; d. March 20, 1854; aged 18 yrs., 1 mo., 11 days.
Infant daughter of Philip and Lydia Brandenburg—d. April 9, 1838; aged 2 days.
In memory of George Charley[7] who was born Oct. 5, 1763 and deceased Aug. 5, 1833 aged 70 yrs., 10 mos. [Another stone found over against the fence reads: "In memory of George Charley—was born Oct. 1763 died 33 Age 70 yrs. 10 mo."].
Infant child of J. L. and F. A. Miles—b. and d. July 25, 1848.
John H.—son of P. and C. J. Conrad—d. Feb. 2, 1864; aged 3 yrs., 2 mos., 3 days.
Christena—wife of John Hendricks; b. March 2, 1811; d. Oct. [—] 1845 [stone broken].
Tobias Hendricks—d. March 19, 1851; aged 96 yrs.
Felicia Ann Grable—b. Oct. 25, 1809; died [—] 14, 1837.
John Grable—b. Jan. 1803; d. Nov. 1834.
Matilda Charley—[no dates].[8]
Sara B.—wife of Joseph Charley and J. J. Mauck—b. July 3, 1826; d. July 23, 1907.
Joseph Charley[9]—d. Feb. 8, 1861; aged 45 yrs., 3 mos., 20 days.
Matilda—dau. of J. and S. B. Charley; d. March 26, 1854; aged 3 yrs., 6 mos., 1 day.
John J. Mauck—b. Jan. 1, 1826; d. May 27, 1902.
Otto L. Hottell—b. Nov. 11, 1868; d. Aug. 20, 1895.
David S. Charley—b. Feb. 15, 1846; d. Oct. 12, 1912.
Rilda R.—wife of D. S. Charley; b. July 10, 1849; d. May 4, 1888.
James Green, d. Dec. 5, 1933.

---

[6] This cemetery is located about three miles northeast of Corydon on Big Indian Creek and the Corydon-Crandall road, on land entered by George Charley. The records were copied on November 26, 1939.

[7] George Charley, Sr., served in the Revolutionary War as a private, for three years. He married Christina ——— in 1790. They had children: Peter b. 1791; Polly b. 1794; Elizabeth b. 1796; Sarah b. 1798; Anna b. 1801; Lydia b. 1803; m. Philip Brandenburg; George b. 1805; Jacob b. 1807; Christena b. 1811; Susannah b. 1813; Joseph b. 1815. *Roster of Soldiers and Patriots of the American Revolution Buried in Indiana* (Indiana Daughters of the American Revolution, 1938), 95.

[8] See *Matilda*, third name below.

[9] Son of George Charley, Sr.

Cemetery Records of Hendricks County

Copied by ROSCOE R. LEAK

The Vieley Cemetery:[1]

Sarah Fowler—1836-1876.
Stephen Fowler—1836-1900.
Sarah Wise—d. Oct. 1, 1875.
Enos Leach—d. Jan. 16, 1870; aged 69 yrs., 1 mo., 4 days.
Elizabeth G. Leach—wife of Enos Leach; d. Feb. 24, 1891; aged 66 yrs., 1 mo., 7 days (dau. of William and Sarah Montgomery).
John E.—Son of W. B. and R. A. Moon; d. Dec. 3, 1871; aged 14 yrs., 7 mos., 15 days.
Rebecca T.—wife of George F. Hall; d. April 6, 1870; aged 33 yrs., 7 mos., 9 days.
Marie Rachel—wife of Caleb F. Adams; d. Sept. 8, 1873; aged 23 yrs., 4 mos., 9 days.
Thomas T. Wilson—d. Dec. 19, 1872; aged 38 yrs., 2 mos., 1 day.
Lavina—wife of Fountain Hardwick; d. Aug. 27, 1875; aged 21 yrs., 3 mos., 3 days.
Dr. John Thomas Hall—b. in Boyle Co., Ky., Feb. 16, 1842; d. June 22, 1872.
Sarah—wife of G. W. Leak; d. Feb. 3, 1868; aged 38 yrs., 3 mos., 13 days.
George W. Leak—d. April 3, 1906; aged 77 yrs., 5 mos., 16 days.
William E. Leak—d. Feb. 14, 1868; aged 4 yrs., 9 mos., 14 days.
Mary E. Leak—d. April 23, 1870; aged 5 yrs., 14 days.
Elizabeth A. Leak—d. Feb. 17, 1868; aged 7 yrs., 9 mos., 16 days.
Matilda E. Leak—d. Feb. 15, 1868; aged, 16 yrs., 5 mos., 3 days.
Amanda Dowden—wife of William E.; b. Aug. 1, 1839; d. Oct. 12, 1899.
William Dowden—b. June 13, 1826; d. Jan. 11, 1888.
Emma Thompson—wife of H. H. Thompson; d. Jan. 9, 1889.
John McMains—d. March 6, 1877; aged 35 yrs., 12 days.
Lina Armstrong—wife of John F. Armstrong; b. Aug. 14, 1865; d. Feb. 18, 1890.
Abel Strickland.
Jane Strickland.[2]
William G. Eldre.
Oliver Cundiff—son of J. M. and H. A. Cundiff; b. July 30, 1857; d. Jan. 25, 1888.
James M. Cundiff—b. Aug. 22, 1825; d. Feb. 20, 1888.
Harriet A. Cundiff—wife of J. M. Cundiff; b. Jan. 11, 1835; d. Dec. 21, 1898.
Amanda Thompson Jeger—wife of Hother; d. Feb. 8, 1879; aged 25 yrs., 8 mos., 8 days.
James W. Thompson—1827-1900.

---

[1] This cemetery is located on State Road 34, one-fourth of a mile east of Lizton, (Sec. 28, Tp.17N., R1W). It is dedicated to the memory of Union Township, Hendricks County, Indiana, Pioneers. Several of the charter members of the Lizton Christian Church are buried in this cemetery, as well as many prominent pioneers.

[2] Abel and Jane Strickland, pioneers. It has come down in community tradition that Abel helped clear the trees in 1827, to make the right of way for the Indianapolis-Crawfordsville road, which runs by the cemetery where he now sleeps. It is now known as State Road 34.

Elizabeth Thompson—1827-1866.

Mary Reeves—wife of G. W. R.; d. March 7, 1879; aged 44 yrs., 8 mos., 28 days.

George W. Reeves—d. April 1, 1881; aged 50 yrs., 6 mos., 11 days.

William L. Leach—d. Oct. 23, 1889; aged 26 yrs., 2 mos., 29 days.

Abraham Leach—son of James M. and Elizabeth Leach; d. Oct. 24, 1878; aged 11 yrs., 3 mos., 11 days.

Herbert H. Leach, son of J. M. and E. Leach; d. Dec. 4, 1877, aged 7 mos., 10 days.

Isaac Rutledge—b. June 2, 1831; m. March 7, 1851; d. March 19, 1866.

Millie Bradley Rutledge—b. April 3, 1831; d. October 4, 1904.

William Baker Buzzard—d. Nov. 10, 1871; aged 47 yrs., 6 mos., 6 days.

Arthur Buzzard—son of W. B. and M.; d. Aug. 12, 1870; aged 5 mos.

David S. Buzzard—d. Feb. 8, 1870; aged 73 yrs., 9 mos., 22 days.

Louisa M. Buzzard—wife of D. S. Buzzard; d. March 9, 1869; aged 68 yrs., 3 mos., 7 days.

America A. (Leak) Nelson[3]—wife of Thomas J. Nelson; d. Sept. 25, 1879; aged 31 yrs., 9 mos., 14 days.

Franklin Blair Leak—d. July 12, 1866; aged 22 yrs., 8 mos., 27 days.

William O. Leak—d. Oct. 24, 1870; aged 9 yrs., 8 mos., 27 days.

Mary Lucy Leak—d. Nov. 2, 1870; aged 15 yrs., 3 mos., 9 days.

Charles E. Leak—d. Oct. 10, 1863; aged 2 yrs., 8 mos., 13 days.

James L. Leak—b. Bracken Co., Ky., July 14, 1816; d. Sept. 6, 1883.

Harriet A. Leak—wife of J. L. Leak; b. Frederick Co., Va., Sept. 21, 1822; d. March 23, 1889.

Margaret J. Leak—wife of J. M. Leak; d. Feb. 15, 1898.

Eva—dau. of J. M. and M. J. Leak.

Oertie Leak—child of M. J. Leak.

Mary F. Leak—wife of J. M. Leak, d. Nov. 9, 1872; aged 24 yrs., 9 mos., 8 days.

Daniel Dickey—d. Jan. 25, 1865; aged 63 yrs., 6 mos., 22 days.

Warren Leak—son of John A. and Nevada Leak.

John L. Kendall—son of J. H. and Margaret K.; b. May 14, 1867; d. May 22, 1901.

Oliver M. Kendall—son of J. H. and M. Kendall; d. Jan. 16, 1872; aged 4 yrs. [3 yrs.], 1 mo., 18 days.

Rachel Kendall—b. Feb. 12, 1873; d. Jan. 15, 1881.

Harvey B. Leak—son of E. A. and G.; b. Dec. 23, 1889; d. July 26, 1890.

Charles W. Davidson—d. Sept. 12, 1893; aged 24 yrs., 4 mos., 2 days.

John N. Davidson—d. Dec. 22, 1888; aged 47 yrs., 11 mos., 16 days.

Mary E. Buzzard—d. April 19, 1880.

Alsa Ann Davidson—wife of John N.; 1844-1911.

Morton N. Riggs—d. Oct. 17, 1868; aged 56 yrs., 5 mos., 28 days.

Richard F. Rainey.

Thomas Adams—d. Oct. 2, 1872; aged 69 yrs., 5 mos., 11 days.

Hanna Adams—wife of Thomas; b. Nov. 21, 1806; d. July 4, 1882.

---

[3] America A., Franklin Blair, William O., Mary Lucy and Charles E. Leak were the children of James Lawrence and Harriet Amanda (Buzzard) Leak.

Mary S. Bryant—wife of J. O.; d. Aug. 23, 1863; aged 35 yrs., 6 mos., 6 days.
Nannie Bronaugh—d. Jan. 1, 1867; aged 16 yrs.
Mary Bronaugh—b. June 18, 1819; d. Nov. 5, 1887.
Robert Bronaugh—b. Nov. 12, 1819; d. Aug. 16, 1894.
Margaret Woody—wife of Miller; d. March 27, 1879; aged 37 yrs., 9 mos., 8 days.
Charles Rainey.
Mary E. Rainey.
Nancy J. Richardson—dau. of W. H. and K.; d. Aug. 24, 1869; aged 17 yrs., 4 mos., 12 days.
Lucy Spry—d. Jan. 1, 1865; aged 70 yrs., 11 mos., 15 days.
W. H. Richardson—d. April 15, 1874; aged 48 yrs., 8 mos., 16 days.
Sarah M. Foxworthy—dau. of W. H. and M. J.; b. April 26, 1859; d. March 3, 1881.
William H. Foxworthy—b. Aug. 24, 1829; d. July 9, 1887.
Dayton Foxworthy—son of W. H. and M. J.; b. Feb. 14, 1865; d. Feb. 20, 1893.
Mary E. Foxworthy—dau. of W. H. and M. J.; b. April 8, 1867; d. May 4, 1876.
Lola M. Parsons—dau. of G. M. and N.; d. Oct. 11, 1874; aged 37 yrs., 6 mos., 12 days.
Martha Wilson—wife of George Wilson; d. March 3, 1859; aged 43 yrs., 6 mos., 11 days.
George W. Wilson, son of G. and M.
Synthia Fitzsimmons—dau. of M. F. and S.; d. Aug. 25, 1867; aged 14 yrs., 5 mos., 4 days.
Hugh F. Adams.
Levi Fay Adams—son of Hugh F.; d. July 22, 1889; aged 1 yr., 6 mos., 17 days.
Jesse Vieley (for whom this cemetery was named)—d. March 2, 1879; aged 59 yrs., 4 mos., 8 days.
Elizabeth Vieley (for whom Lizton was first called New Elizabeth)—wife of Jesse; 1826-1906.
Harriet Gardner—wife of William G.; dau. of Jesse and E. Vieley; d. May 1, 1887; aged 26 yrs., 11 mos., 28 days.
Jesse C. Leachman—1860-1886.
Robert Leachman—1868-1875.
Harvey Leachman—1883-1884.
Melvin M. Leachman—1836-1880.
Nancy Lewis.
Mary M. Runnels—dau. of T. M. and Lucinda; d. April 13, 1868; aged 10 mos., 18 days (Lucinda, second wife of Thomas M. R.)
Lewis Leak, no marker.
Elizabeth Leak—wife of Lewis; d. Jan. 31, 1859; aged 50 yrs., 5 mos., 10 days.
John R. Leak—son of L. and E. Leak; d. April 25, 1859; aged 20 yrs., 9 mos., 3 days.
Susan J. Runnels—first wife of T. M.; dau. of Lewis Leak; d. May 23, 1859; aged 23 yrs., 5 mos., 3 days.

Allen Hayden—no marker; son-in-law of Lewis Leak; Civil War soldier.
Marion Leak—no marker; son of Lewis; Civil War soldier.
Mary A. Miller—dau. of Henry and Hanna; d. Sept. 30, 1875; aged 30 yrs., 2 mos., 25 days.
Cora A. Sourwine—dau. of Isaiah and Rebecca; d. May 7, 1875; aged 4 yrs., 2 mos., 4 days.
Evaline Boswell—wife of Abednago; d. June 14, 1875; aged 66 yrs.
William Lewis—son of S. J. and H. A.; d. Feb. 11, 1865.
Stephen J. Lewis—d. July 27, 1870; aged 33 yrs., 3 mos., 20 days.
Ezekiel Davison—d. July 11, 1865; aged 56 yrs., 1 mo., 6 days.
Sarah Baker—wife of John Baker; d. Sept. 25, 1858; aged 30 yrs., 1 mo., 23 days.
Margaret Baker—dau. of John and Sarah; d. Dec. 9, 1874; aged 16 yrs., 4 mos., 29 days.
David C. Lane—b. Jan. 18, 1839; d. April 15, 1899.
Hannah Lane—wife of David; d. Aug. 18, 1868; aged 29 yrs., 5 mos., 29 days.
Sarah E. Lane—dau. of D. C. and H. J.; d. Feb. 9, 1867; aged 1 yr., 1 mo., 7 days.
Stephen T. Lewis—d. Oct. 13, 1855; aged 42 yrs., 1 mo., 12 days.
Nancy Thompson—wife of Joseph (wife first of Stephen T. Lewis); d. April 3, 1859; aged 41 yrs., 21 days.
Eliza Cundiff—wife of John Cundiff (wife first of William Leak); d. April 24, 1864; aged 55 yrs., 6 mos., 27 days.
Oliver L. Leachman, 1872-1873.
J. Alonzo Leachman, 1867-1868.
Urban Hale, son of J. R. and S. N.; d. March 26, 1883; aged 1 mo., 18 days.
Ettie Hale—dau. of J. R. and S. N.; d. July 11, 1876; aged 1 mo., 11 days.
Mollie E. Hale—d. Feb. 15, 1875; aged 7 yrs., 10 mos., 27 days.
Nettie S. Hale—d. Feb. 17, 1875; aged 9 yrs., 3 mos., 26 days.
Susan McClintic—wife of James R. Hale; b. Aug. 11, 1843; d. March 11, 1898.
Landrum F. Leak—d. Dec. 5, 1889; aged 71 yrs., 11 mos., 2 days.
Sarah Leak—wife of Landrum; [dates not legible.]
Abraham Hamilton—d. Aug. 6, 1891; aged 84 yrs., 5 mos., 23 days.
Fanny Hamilton—wife of A. H.; d. Jan. 18, 1879; aged 68 yrs., 1 mo., 5 days.
Joan Hamilton—dau. of A. and F. H.; d. Aug. 23, 1852; aged 7 yrs., 9 mos., 8 days.
Julia Hamilton—dau. of A. and F.; d. Sept. 30, 1854; aged 1 mo., 20 days.
Mary Hamilton—dau. of A. and F.; d. Dec. 12, 1863; aged 14 yrs., 7 mos., 14 days.
Catherine Hamilton—wife of John Hamilton who died in Tennessee about 1830, mother of Abraham and Edny Hamilton; d. Nov. 9, 1866; aged 92 yrs., 23 days.
Edny Hamilton—d. Aug. 14, 1887; aged 67 yrs., 4 mos., 12 days.
Joshua E. Dickerson—son of Henry and Catherine Dickerson; d. Sept. 1, 1871; aged 22 days.

Henry L. McCrosky—d. Sept. 17, 1859; aged 19 yrs., 9 mos., 13 days.
James W. McCrosky—d. Dec. 14, 1856; aged 20 yrs., 2 mos., 22 days.
Alexander McCrosky—d. March 5, 1846; aged 7 yrs., 10 mos.
Blair McCrosky—d. Oct. 11, 1849; aged 43 yrs., 3 mos., 15 days.
Elizabeth McCrosky—wife of Blair McCrosky; d. Feb. 3, 1845; aged 29 yrs., 2 mos. [dau. of Archibald and Sarah Alexander; charter member of the Lizton Christian Church].[2]
Sarah C. Alexander—wife of A. Alexander; d. Dec. 19, 1867; aged 74 yrs.
Archibald Alexander[3]—d. Jan. 3, 1855; aged 64 yrs., 8 days.
James P. Alexander—d. May 23, 1861; aged 36 yrs., 2 mos., 4 days.
William H. Leachman—son of D. and M.; d. Dec. 21, 1859; aged 7 mos.
Mary Leachman—wife of Dr. D. Leachman; d. June 18, 1869; aged 25 yrs., 10 mos., 20 days.
Dr. Darius Leachman—d. March 31, 1877; aged 47 yrs., 1 mo., 15 days.
Samuel Reynolds—d. March 27, 1868; aged 73 yrs., 6 mos., 11 days.
Elizabeth Reynolds—wife of Samuel; d. Apr. 27, 1896; aged 92 yrs., 10 mos., 26 days.
Lydia Baker—wife of James H. Baker; b. Sept. 24, 1829; d. July 22, 1900.
Eddie Herbster—son of M. M. and M. E.; d. Sept. 23, 1881; aged 2 yrs., 3 mos., 1 day.
Benjamin Hamilton—son of John W. and Nancy Hamilton; d. Jan. 9, 1887; aged 2 mos., 26 days.
Bessie Hamilton—dau. of J. W. and N. [no dates].
John L. Kendall—d. Feb. 19, 1876; aged 66 yrs., 5 mos., 5 days.
Roy Davis Leak—son of S. and E. Leak; d. Aug. 15, 1887; aged 1 mo.
Flora Eva Davis—dau. of J. H. and Eliza Davis; d. Jan. 27, 1862; aged 2 yrs., 9 mos., 21 days.
Angeline Davis—wife[4] of Job. H. Davis; d. Jan. 27, 1847; b. 1821 [dau. of James and Elizabeth Leak].
Olive H. Davis—son of J.H.andEliza; d. Sept. 1, 1853; aged 7 mos.
Martha J. McClintick—dau. of G. W. and H.; d. Oct. 26, 1855; aged 1 yr., 10 mos.
Mary E. McClintick—dau. of G. W. and H.; d. Sept. 26, 1855; aged 4 yrs., 1 day.
Samuel E. McClintick—son of H and M. McClintick; d. July 19, 1847; aged 19 yrs., 9 mos., 4 days.
Mary E.—dau. of H. and M. McClintick; d. Sept. 21, 1847; aged 4 yrs., 4 mos., 11 days.
Samuel H. McClintick—son of G. W. and H.; d. Dec. 19, 1855; aged 29 days.
Stephen P. Lewis—d. Feb. 4, 1847; aged 9 yrs., 5 mos., 14 days.
Louisa Lewis—wife[5] of Joseph P. Lewis; d. Sept. 9, 1856; aged 44 yrs., 7 mos., 8 days [dau. of James and Eliza Leak. Joseph P. Lewis and Louisa were charter members of the Lizton Christian Church].

[2] The grave of Mrs. Elizabeth (Alexander) McCrosky is the first marked grave in Vieley Cemetery.
[3] The Lizton Christian Church was organized at Archibald Alexander's home in 1837 and first called Alexander's Church.
[4] First wife.
[5] First wife.

Maria Davison—wife of Ezekiel; d. Sept. 18, 1848; aged 37 yrs., 11 mos., 18 days.
John Cunliff—d. Dec. 16, 1868; aged 80 yrs., 4 mos., 26 days.
Sarah—wife of John Cunliff; d. July 31, 1851, in the 60th year of her age.
Hezekiah McClintick—d. Dec. 17, 1876; aged 74 yrs., 4 mos., 23 days.
George McClintick—d. June 17, 1884; aged 53 yrs., 9 mos., 16 days.
Susan E. Reynolds—dau. of S. and E.; d. July 5, 1851; aged 2 yrs., 9 mos., 18 days.
John N. Murry—son of M. L. and N. E. Murry; d. July 15, 1888, aged 5 yrs., 5 mos., 28 days.
Tempa Brookshire—dau. of J. and A.; d. July 17, 1851; aged 1 yr., 4 mos., 4 days.
Sarah E. Hampton—dau. of A. and N.; d. July 26, 1851; aged 1 yr., 7 mos., 13 days.
Joseph F. Reynolds—son of G. and R.; d. Aug. 10, 1855; aged 8 yrs., 10 mos., 12 days.
Mary Jane Hampton—dau. of John and Nancy; d. March 27, 1859, aged 20 yrs., 3 mos., 7 days.
Isaac Burnett—1811-1878.
Mary S. Burnett—1851-1877.
Mary R. Burnett—1813-1862.
Eliza M. Burnett—1849-1852.
Nancy M. Burnett—1847-1856.
James Adams—d. Sept. 20, 1867; aged 42 yrs.
Martha Adams—dau. of J. and N.; d. March 31, 1861; aged 10 mos.
Nancy Adams—b. March 29, 1826; d. Sept. 23, 1892.
Mary E. Davidson—dau. of J. L. and L.; d. Apr. 29, 1864; aged 8 mos., 27 days.
Nona—dau. of William E. and Maggie Leak; d. Jan. 22, 1897; aged 7 yrs., 8 mos., 13 days.
Eliza Leak—wife of T. J. Leak; d. 1891 [birth date illegible].
Thomas J. Leak—b. June 6, 1831; d. Feb. 22, 1903 [bro. of George W. and son of William Leak].
J. L. Davidson—Co. C, 51 Reg. Ind. Vol.; d. Dec. 31, 1864; aged 32 yrs., 8 mos., 14 days.
Sarah S. Ledbetter—wife of Job L.; d. Nov. 11, 1865; aged 32 yrs., 11 mos., 17 days.
Sarah F. Wheat—dau. of G. W. and M. E. Wheat; d. Sept. 8, 1874; aged 24 yrs., 5 mos., 7 days.
Ally Brookshire—wife of J. Brookshire; d. Apr. 6, 1855; aged 42 yrs., 10 mos., 27 days.
Thomas Rainey—d. March 17, 1859; aged 76 yrs.
Edwin—son of William and M. Johnson; d. Sept. 13, 1855; aged 7 yrs., 2 mos., 3 days.
John F. Johnson—son of William and M.; b. May 14, 1859; d. March 2, 1867.
Mary Johnson—d. Jan. 1, 1871; aged 45 yrs., 10 mos., 2 days.
Robert W. Johnson—b. Nov. 8, 1857; d. July 7, 1897.

Martin Griggs—d. Aug. 25, 1873; aged 42 yrs., 7 mos., 24 days, of cholera.
Simon F. Lambert—son of J. and S. S.; d. Feb. 19, 1870; aged 7 yrs., 5 mos., 7 days.
Sarah S.—wife of John Lambert; d. Nov. 20, 1875; aged 32 yrs., 7 mos., 18 days.
Benjamin F. Hedges—[soldier in War of 1812. He and his children, Oscar and Laura, died of cholera; no markers].
Ida May Lipes—[dau. of B. F. Hedges; no marker].
Mary E. Adams—dau. of W. and S. M. Adams; d. Jan. 23, 1871; aged 11 yrs., 8 mos., 22 days.
Catherine Dooley—d. March 1, 1874; aged 68 yrs., 5 mos., 10 days.
[Elijah Copeland and mother, "Granny" Copeland; unmarked graves. Elijah a Civil War soldier].
Solomon Adams—d. June 9, 1863; aged 64 yrs., 4 mos., 20 days.
Nancy Adams—wife of Solomon; d. July 2, 1863; aged 52 yrs., 4 mos., 29 days.
Catherine Tony—wife of Elkin; d. Jan. 22, 1867; aged 38 yrs., 9 mos., 3 days.
Fannie E.—wife of William R. Davis; d. Aug. 22, 1873, aged 18 yrs., 7 mos., 21 days [first victim of cholera].
John W. Dickerson—son of H. and C.; d. Sept. 22, 1871; aged 1 yr., 2 mos., 29 days.
Ailsie Scott—dau. of James E. and E. J.
Ellen Jane Scott—wife of James E.; d. March 28, 1887; aged 33 yrs., 11 mos., 14 days.
Samuel O.—son of J. E. and E. J. Scott; d. Sept. 20, 1885; aged 4 mos., 20 days.
George W. Wheat—b. March 27, 1823; d. March 18, 1903.
Euphemia Wheat—wife of George W. Wheat; b. Nov. 18, 1836; d. July 26, 1894.

Cundiff Cemetery:[2]

Susan—wife of Elias Leach; d. Sept. 23, 1875; aged 56 yrs., 11 mos., 2 days.
Elias Leach—b. 1815, d. 1906 [b. May 10, 1815; d. Aug. 31, 1906].
Isaac Vieley—d. Feb. 8, 1849; aged 62 yrs., 2 mos., 18 days.
Nancy Duncan—d. May 10, 1835; aged 51 yrs. [This is the oldest grave in the township.]
Francis M.—son of D. S. and L. M. Buzzard; d. Aug. 23, 1838; aged 11 yrs., 9 mos., 13 days.
William Leak—d. Sept. 11, 1845; aged 43 yrs., 3 mos.
Virginia O.—wife of Charles M. Leak; d. Feb. 19, 1866; aged 25 yrs.

Bailey Farm:[3]

Elizabeth—wife of James Leak; b. Nov. 8, 1786; d. May 22, 1852.[4]
James Leak—b. Sept. 21, 1787; d. Nov. 14, 1865.[5]

---

[2] Located in sec. 2, tp. 17N, R1W, one-half mile north of Lizton.

[3] Located in tp. 17N, R1W, one mile north of Lizton.

[4] Elizabeth Vermillion Leak was born on the site of Washington, D.C.

[5] James Leak was born in Virginia, a son of Robert and Susan (Leak) Leak who died in Bracken County, New York.

Griffith Cemetery:[6]

Jackson Griffith—d. June 13, 1860; aged 53 yrs., 7 mos., 22 days.
William P.—son of J. and N. Griffith; d. Nov. 4, 1864; aged 18 yrs., 3 mos., 28 days; Co. H, Eleventh Indiana Cavalry.
James M.—son of Jackson and Nancy Griffith; d. Sept. 29, 1847; aged 15 yrs., 8 mos., 3 days.
Benjamin Griffith—d. Nov. 22, 1852; aged 70 yrs., 9 mos., 21 days.
Ruth—wife of Benjamin Griffith; d. June 24, 1855; aged 68 yrs.
Nancy—wife of John D. Hiatt; d. Jan. 17, 1853; aged 23 yrs., 6 mos.
Mary—dau. of Henry and Hannah Lewis; d. May 4, 1849; aged 19 yrs., 9 mos., 17 days.

Groover Cemetery:[7]

Ida—wife of A. Pigg; 1808-1859.
Claborn—husband of Bashaba Davidson; d. Aug. 29, 1861; aged 55 yrs., 5 mos., 29 days.
Martha—wife of Henry Hendricks; d. Sept. 11, 1855.
Henry Hendricks—d. May 19, 1855; aged 87 yrs., 6 mos., 3 days.
Ely Martin—d. Sept. 8, 1869; aged 30 yrs., 7 mos., 2 days.
James Martin—1797-1847.
Mary Martin—1800-1879.
Evaline—wife of Landrum Leak; d. Sept. 2, 1845; aged 25 yrs.
George Bishop—d. Nov. 30, 1854; aged 26 yrs., 8 mos.
Katherine—wife of Thomas J. Pigg; d. Oct. 24, 1855; aged 21 yrs., 2 mos.
David—son of M. and R. Bishop; d. Dec. 2, 1855; aged 24 yrs., 5 mos., 17 days.
Editha—dau. of Anderson and Ida Pigg; d. Dec. 14, 1855; aged 16 yrs., 2 mos., 8 days.
Martha—dau. of Miller and Rebecca Bishop; d. June 27, 1857.
Mary—wife of Jesse Hendrix; d. Jan. 8, 1859; aged 54 yrs., 7 mos., 10 days.
William Knott—d. June 9, 1852; aged 80 yrs., 5 mos., 4 days.
William S.—son of Jesse and Mary Hendrix; d. Oct. 25, 1845; aged 18 yrs.
Eli Hendrix—d. Oct. 2, 1869; aged 58 yrs., 10 mos., 23 days.
Mary E. Hendrix—wife of Eli; b. 1815; d. Apr. 12, 1882.
Thomas—son of J. R. and M. Jackson; d. Dec. 22, 1865; aged 21 yrs., 2 mos., 20 days; Co. K, 41st Regiment, 2d Cavalry, Indiana Volunteers.
John Patterson—d. Sept. 11, 1851; aged 60 yrs.
Mary—dau. of J. and A. Stutsman; d. Oct. 17, 1845; aged 14 yrs., 3 mos., 4 days.
James H. Groover—1819-1899; and his wife Nancy Hencricks, 1821-1909.

[6] Located in sec. 19, tp. 17, R1W, two miles northwest of Lizton.
[7] Located in sec. 19, tp. 17, R1W, two miles northwest of Lizton.

Pritchett Cemetery:[8]

John—son of T. G. and M. Pritchett; d. July 9, 1874; aged 21 yrs., 5 mos.
Mary—wife of John Pritchett; d. Dec. 10, 1856; aged 75 yrs., 6 mos., 7 days.
John Pritchett—d. Aug. 5, 1858; aged 75 yrs., 11 mos., 19 days.

Leach Cemetery:[9]

Meredith Leach—d. Oct. 19, 1859; aged 50 yrs., 6 mos., 23 days.
Eliza—wife of M. Leach; b. March 12, 1808; d. Oct. 9, 1888; aged 80 yrs., 6 mos., 27 days.
James V. Leach—d. Jan. 30, 1864; aged 15 yrs., 1 mo., 15 days.
Unmarked double grave under west slab. [John Leach—b. Feb. 19, 1777; d. Oct. 9, 1837. Mary Hall Leach—wife of John Leach, 1771-1850.][10]

Leach Cemetery:[11]

Anderson Leach—d. Sept. 14, 1863; aged 52 yrs., 1 mo., 22 days.
Matilda—wife of A. Leach; d. Aug. 25, 1873; aged 67 yrs., 8 mos., 5 days.
Susan—dau. of A. and M. Leach; d. Oct. 18, 1847; aged 12 yrs., 11 mos., 17 days.

Montgomery Chapel Cemetery:[12]

Warren E. Hedge—Civil War soldier.
Tranum Toney—d. Jan. 16, 1875; aged 63 yrs., 6 mos.
William Montgomery—d. Oct. 21, 1856; aged 76 yrs., 10 mos., 11 days.
Sarah—wife of William Montgomery; d. May 23, 1859; aged 78 yrs., 6 mos., 18 days.
William W. Kendall—d. Aug. 15, 1879; aged 33 yrs., 10 mos., 23 days; Co. F, 133rd Regiment, Indiana Volunteers, Civil War.
Francis A. Scott—b. Dec. 13, 1816; d. June 9, 1895.
Malinda Scott—wife of Francis Scott; b. May 6, 1822; d. Oct. 5, 1862.
A. W. Jones—d. Jan. 7, 1864; aged 24 yrs., 2 mos., 22 days; Co. C, 51st Regiment, Indiana Volunteers, Civil War.
Samuel Jones—b. Oct. 17, 1814; d. Sept. 9, 1893.
Mary M. Jones—b. June 14, 1815; d. Oct. 11, 1873.
Isom Scott—b. Jan. 5, 1822; d. Aug. 1, 1863.
Polly Scott—b. Dec. 8, 1821; d. April 8, 1908.
Sarah A.—wife of A. D. Rainey; d. July 11, 1873; aged 25 yrs., 8 mos., 28 days.
Margaret S. Scott—d. April 6, 1874; aged 17 yrs., 11 mos.
William G. Montgomery—d. June 5, 1875; aged 35 yrs., 29 days.

---

[8] Located in sec.6, tp.16N, R1W, two miles southwest of Lizton.
[9] Located in sec.6, tp.16N, R1W.
[10] John Leach was the father of Enos, Meredith, Anderson, Elias, and others. His was the second grave in Union Township.
[11] This is a second Leach Cemetery, located in tp.17N, R1W.
[12] Located in sec32, tp.17N, R1W, one-half mile south of Lizton. This Methodist Church was organized in 1832 at the home of William Montgomery.

EAST LEBANON CEMETERY—HENRY COUNTY

Copied by EUGENE STUDEBAKER WIERBACH

Joshua Hickman—Minister of the Gospel in the Regular Baptist Church; d. Aug. 19, 1842; aged 76 yrs., 4 mos., 9 days; "He lies in the affections of his friends."

Josinah—wife of Joshua Hickman; d. June 3, 1857; aged 89 yrs., 4 mos., 19 days.

James T. Hickman—1837-1921.

Judith A. Hickman—1842-1909.

Elcie Dodd—d. Jan. 10, 1865; aged 66 yrs., 7 mos., 24 days.

James Dodd—d. June 24, 1861; aged 81 yrs., 6 mos., 3 days.

Lewis Veach—d. Feb. 17, 1859; aged 68 yrs., 6 mos., 7 days.

Elenor—his [Lewis Veach's] wife; d. April 1, 1865; aged 76 yrs., 6 mos., 2 days.

Mary A.—wife of Henry H. Veach; d. Feb. 1, 1863; aged 28 yrs., 5 mos., 19 days.

Jesse Veach—d. March 4, 1843; aged 2 yrs.

William Veach—d. July 15, 1840; aged 1 yr., 2 mos., 26 days.

William Veach—b. Oct. 9, 1805; d. Jan. 8, 1870.

Elizabeth—first wife [of William Veach]; b. May 12, 1813; d. Aug. 8, 1854.

Mary Bales—second wife [of William Veach]; b. April 9, 1824; d. Sept. 3, 1915.

John Mellett—d. Sept. 13, 1859; aged 47 yrs., 6 mos., 20 days.

Sarah—his [John Mellet's] wife; d. Aug. 21, 1883; aged 74 yrs., 4 mos., 12 days.

Mary Ann—wife of John Mellett, Esq.; d. Feb. 8, 1853; aged 57 yrs., 10 mos., 1 day.

John Mellett—d. July, 1838; aged 60 yrs.

J. Arthur—son of J. and M. A. Mellett; d. Oct. 30, 1839; aged 1 yr., 9 mos.

William Mellett Sr.—d. March 31, 1855; aged 73 yrs.

William H. Mellett—d. Aug. 19, 1851; aged 18 yrs.

John C. Mellett—b. April 27, 1803; d. Dec. 25, 1853.

Arthur C. Mellett—son of J. C. and Cynthia Mellett; d. Aug. 20, 1833; aged 3 yrs., 11 mos., 8 days.

Rebecca A.—dau. of John C. and Cynthia Mellett; d. Sept. 5, 1864; aged 17 yrs., 7 mos., 12 days.

Abel Williams—1774-1847.

Rebecca Williams—1787-1866.

Joshua L. Williams—1806-1826.

Van Williams—b. 1817; d. April 1, 1842.

Rebecca—consort of Dr. Wm. R. Williams; d. July 16, 1857; aged 41 yrs., 11 mos., 9 days.

Sarah Ann—dau. of Wm. H. and Rebecca Williams; d. June 15, 1842; aged 6 yrs., 5 mos., 14 days.

Josinah—wife of Wm. Kinsey; d. Oct. 18, 1850.

THE PIONEER CEMETERY OF GRASSY FORK TOWNSHIP, JACKSON COUNTY

Roy H. Beldon

Situated one-half mile north of the Waskom Muscatatuck River bridge, no public road leads to the pioneer cemetery in southern Grassy Fork Township in Jackson County. In early days, it was reached by a winding road through the forest, and it was over this type of path that the early settlers bore their loved ones to their final resting place. At that time, the cemetery was a beautiful cleared knoll overlooking the winding Muscatatuck River and the primitive forest of its broad valley.

Although I knew it to be in a wilderness state, I came upon and was in the cemetery before I realized the fact, so badly has it been neglected. Wild cherry, hackberry, oak, and walnut trees that measure eighteen inches in diameter have grown near or on the graves. Briar patches are broad and dense and cover many graves. Underneath these briars were ridges of fresh turned earth, which reminded me of new graves; but this could not be true, because this cemetery has not been used for some fifty years. The fresh earth was that of recently dug woodchuck holes.

I found this pioneer cemetery divided by a line fence. Farmers have not curved their fencing around it for years. Constructed of barbed wire, supported by posts, its strands stapled to some of the trees, this fence now divides cow pastures on two separate farms, namely, the Waskom farm and the Henry Fogelding farm.

On the north side of the fence I found only one stone standing on which was carved this:
Sarah, Wife of A. O. Belding, Sr.
Born August 20, 1805. Died June 13, 1859
Flat on the ground are three other stones from which I dug away earth and grass and scraped moss in order to read the names and dates:

Aaron O. Belding, born November 22, 1796
Died April 15, 1867
James O., Son of N. B. & E. Fislar
Died August 7, 1864. Aged 1 yr. 11 Mo. 29 da.
James, Son of A. & A. L Woodmansee

Died January 4, 1816. Aged 9 yrs.
Thomas J., Son of A. & H. Perry
Died November 20, 1849. Aged 7 mo. 3 da.
In memory of Elizabeth, Wife of Joseph Brown
who departed this life September 8 [Dates weathered away]
Joseph Brown
[Dates weathered and crumbled off]
Mary E., Daughter of A. C. and S. H. Keach
Born February 21, 1851
Died July 3, 1857
William H. Fislar, born February 3, 1842
Died May 3, 1864
Sarah, Consort of Harden Hancock
[Dates crumbled away]
Albert, Son of H. & E. Hancock
Died April 12, 1855. Aged 4 yrs. 5 mo. 1 da.
Mary A., Daughter of H. & S. Hancock
Died August 12, 1842. Aged about 3 yrs.
Indiana, Daughter of P. S. and N. J. Ramey
Died December 21, 1853. Aged 2 mo. 27 da.

Indications of other graves were unmarked.

Then I climbed over the fence into the briars, weeds, thorns, and weeds of the south half of the cemetery. I found there an iron fence and a five-foot stone wall, each enclosing two graves.

Ruben Rucker, departed this life October 16,
18— [Date crumbled off]. Aged 38 yrs.
Ruben Rucker, Sr., Born September 15, 1781
Died December 27, 1846
Elizabeth Rucker, Consort of Ruben Rucker
Born September 11, 1784
Died October 22, 1842

On the arch of the stone enclosure was this:

Erected by J. B. Rucker
    Gone Home
Elizabeth, Wife of J. B. Rucker
Born February 13, 1825. Died August 30, 1846
Colby, Son of A. & E. Rucker
Died July 4, 1849. Aged 1 yr. 1 mo. 1 da.
Rhuben Rucker, born January 16, 1817
Died August 28, 1854
Elizabeth Roberts, born May 18, 1844
Died January 18, 1866
John Moore, born November 1, 1783
Died February 24, 1849
Anthony Moore, Born June 21, 1826
Died April 9, 1846

John Moore, Born January 26, 1834
Died January 3, 1854
Miles Moore, Born November 19, 1830
Died January 28, 1855

Although it stands four and one-half feet high and is still in good condition, this next stone was almost overlooked as it was completely covered by vegetation.

James R., Son of E. H. and J. A. Ponell
Born February 13, 18—[Date crumbled]
Died February 16, 1862
John Downing
Died January 17, 1862. Aged 57 yrs.
[Masonic emblem on this stone.]
Pernina Downing, Wife of John Downing, departed this life on the 8th day of January 1844. Aged 34.

Through the briars and near a freshly made woodchuck hole, I saw a stone which appears to have been more recently placed. It marks the grave of a Revolutionary War veteran.

Michel L. Downing
  Va. Mil.
  Rev. War.

A number of graves are unmarked and the names of the dead may never be learned. Perhaps I missed some marked graves due to the vegetation.

It is certain that a philanthropist or philanthropic organization is needed to save this neglected but very interesting cemetery to posterity.

Carmel Presbyterian Church

Mary Hill

A history of Carmel Congregation of the United Presbyterian Church, located near Hanover, Indiana, from its beginning in 1812 down to 1882, was read by the Reverend H. P. Jackson at the seventieth anniversary celebration of the church on August 23, 1882. This history, later printed and published in pamphlet form by the Madison *Courier*, is of interest to a genealogist because of the names, dates, and family records given in it. The account which follows is based on the Reverend Jackson's paper.

On August 8, 1797, the Reverend Andrew Fulton, in company with the Reverend Robert Armstrong, sailed from Scotland for America, and arrived in New York on October 13. They went first to Philadelphia where they hired a wagoner to haul their books and baggage to Pittsburgh. They themselves went by stage to Lancaster, then to Carlisle, and from there on foot to Pittsburgh. Here they stayed until February 21, 1798, when they embarked for Limestone, now Maysville, Kentucky. From Limestone they went overland to Lexington.

Fulton was born and educated in Scotland. He was licensed to preach at Kilmarnock on December 17, 1793. He served in Kentucky at Drennon's Creek in Henry County and at Bear Grass near Louisville, for seventeen years. When some of the members of the congregations seceded and moved to Jefferson County, Indiana, Fulton visited them there. He preached his first sermon in Jefferson County at the home of George Shannon, Sr., on the bank of the Ohio. Sometime in 1812, a congregation was formed, which took the name of Carmel, the first Associate, or United, Presbyterian congregation in Indiana. The names of its first members were George Shannon, Sr., Ann Shannon, John Anderson, James Anderson, Jane Anderson, Samuel Ledgerwood, ——— Ledgerwood, John Swann, Sr., Jennet Swann, Thomas Taylor William Hay, Jane Hay, Benjamin Miller, Sarah Miller, William Anderson, Sr., Catherine Anderson, and perhaps others. In October 1816, the Reverend Fulton removed to Jefferson County and was installed as the pastor of this church. He also preached frequently at Rykers Ridge at the home of Samuel Ledgerwood.

The first building for Carmel congregation was erected in 1816 on the farm of James Matthews. It was a wooden structure, thirty by forty feet. In 1839 an additional twenty feet was added, and in 1853 a brick church was built, forty-six by sixty feet, at a cost of $3000.

While in Kentucky Rev. Fulton had married Margaret Anderson, a sister of James and John Anderson. Of their children, Jane, the eldest daughter married the Reverend James Adams and had one son Thomas Leander Adams who removed to LaPorte. Mary, another daughter, married a Dr. Cowden. She died at Washington, Iowa. Andrew, their son, who was born just a few hours before his father's death, was graduated from Hanover College in 1836, studied medicine, and died in Kansas City, Missouri. Rev. Fulton died on September 10, 1818, aged sixty-three years. His widow married Colonel James Morrow of Xenia, Ohio, where they lived for a while, but returned to Hanover where Margaret died and was buried beside her first husband.

The Reverend Andrew Isaac, then came to Carmel, and, being a Scotsman, the congregation gave him a call in October, 1820. He was born in Carr's Croft near Perth in 1789, educated at Edinburgh and came to America in 1819. He served in Albany Presbytery until 1820. He preached at Carmel twenty-three Sabbaths, Madison thirteen, and Big Creek four. In 1827, he was installed as pastor at Londonderry, Ohio. He died on September 12, 1840. He was married to Jane Rintoul in Scotland. Their son, William Roseburg Isaac, was born in Pittsburgh in 1820 and died at Londonderry, Ohio, in 1845. One daughter, unmarried, lived near New Concord, Ohio. Mrs. Isaac died at Londonderry in 1872.

John Wallace was called to Carmel in 1830, and died on March 22, 1833, at Vicksburg, Mississippi. James M. Henderson was the next pastor. He was born on February 28, 1805, in Washington County, Pennsylvania, of Scottish-American ancestry. He was installed as pastor of Carmel, Madison and Big Creek on May 8, 1834, from which pastorate he resigned in 1835. His wife, whom he married on October 3, 1832, was Nancy McClenahan. They had seven children. One son served as pastor at Elmira, Illinois; another was buried in Carmel Cemetery.

The fifth pastor of Carmel Church was Moses Arnott, born on June 18, 1820, in Cambridge, Washington County,

Pennsylvania. He came to Carmel in November, 1846, and began his work there on the second Sabbath in July, 1847, preaching at Carmel and New Washington. While he was there, the Carmel and Bethel congregations were united as related below. He was married in 1848 to Mary H. Pollock, of Westmoreland County, Pennsylvania. They had nine children, four of whom were buried at Carmel. Rev. Arnott died at the home of Mary and Eliza Latta, at Carmel, and was buried on July 5, 1874. One daughter, Martha, married R. H. Swann, and a son John Arnott was a lawyer in Canby, Minnesota.

The sixth pastor was H. P. Jackson, born on April 18, 1836, near Cedarville, Ohio. He was married on February 14, 1866, to Maggie Frazier Dunlap of Cedarville. He came to Carmel on June 17, 1875.

Bethel Church was organized on May 28, 1828. It was first called Jefferson, then Bethel. The following were received as members: Ann Shannon, Margaret Shannon, a Mrs. Gray, John Swann, Sr., Jennet Swann, William McCasland and wife, Michael Kinnear and wife, James Patterson, George Shannon, Jr., and wife, Andrew Swann and wife, Thomas Baird and wife, John Shannon and wife, Thomas Shannon and wife, George Reed and his wife Jane, William Gordon, and James Swann. George Shannon, Sr., and Thomas Gray, Sr., were elders. Until the church was built in 1830, preaching was held at the home of George Shannon, Sr.

John McDill was installed as pastor at Bethel Church on June 22, 1835. He was born in Preble County, Ohio, in 1806, and graduated from Miami University in 1820. He married Mrs. Fannie W. Johnson, widowed daughter of the Reverend R. G. Wilson, president of Ohio University at Athens, Ohio. He died in Hanover on July 27, 1840, and was buried in Bethel Cemetery, leaving a widow, a stepdaughter, Agnes Johnson, a son, James Wilson McDill, a daughter, Mary, who was born in Hanover, and another daughter, Martha, who was born in Athens. Agnes Johnson was married at Hanover to the Reverend Robert Hopkins who was drowned in Minnesota. She later married the Reverend Samuel W. Pond, and lived at Shakopee, Minnesota. In 1852, the widow of John McDill was married to William Pinkerton of Bloomingburg, Fayette County, Ohio. Mary and Martha McDill both married Pinkertons.

John H. Bonner was installed at Bethel in April, 1845. He preached at Bethel, at Hopewell in Scott County, and at Grayfriar's, three and one-half miles west of New Washington in Clark County. The following are the names of preachers who also filled the pulpit: Campbell, Turner, Worth, Warner, R. E. Stewart, N. C. McDill, Joseph Steel, Reid, Robertson, J. R. Brown, McCague, Sturgeon, J. S. McCracken, and N. R. Kirkpatrick.

In 1854, the Bethel and Caledonia congregations were united as one charge with N. C. Kirkpatrick as pastor. In 1858, Bethel and Carmel were united with the Reverend Moses Arnott in charge as mentioned above.

The first Session of Carmel Church in 1812 was composed of James Anderson, George Shannon, and Samuel Ledgerwood. James Anderson was born near Brownsville, Fayette County, Pennsylvania, in 1780. He removed with his father's family to a site near Lexington, Kentucky, then to Ohio, and finally to Indiana in 1810. He was married by the Reverend Andrew Fulton on January 29, 1807, to Jennet Laing, of Henry County, Kentucky. They had six children. Mr. Anderson died at the home of his son-in-law, the Reverend James Brown, in Madison, on June 3, 1848, aged 68 years. His wife died about the same time.

George Shannon, Sr., was born March 4, 1759, in Lancaster County, Pennsylvania, and was married to Ann Reid on March 24, 1785, in Lancaster County. They came soon after to Scott County, Kentucky. Mr. Shannon served through Indian Wars, and was wounded in the battle known as "Crawford's Defeat." He removed to Greene County, Ohio, and, in 1810, to Jefferson County, Indiana, near where Bethel Church now stands. He died on December 5, 1840, aged eighty-one years, eleven months and one day. He was buried at Bethel Cemetery.

Ruling elders of Carmel Church included: Alexander Thompson, an elder in Pennsylvania, installed in August, 1817; died July 22, 1823, aged 62 years. William Watson, installed in August, 1817; died on April 15, 1852, aged 76 years. James Matthews, installed on February 23, 1825; died on October 23, 1851, aged 81 years. John Anderson, installed on May 8, 1825; moved west in 1837. George Currie, installed on May 8, 1835; died on March 10, 1868, aged 74 years. James Hamilton, installed May 8, 1835; died on October

26, 1874, aged 79 years. William Patterson, installed on May 8, 1835; died on October 19, 1869, aged 70 years. Robert Taylor, installed on October 5, 1849; died on October 11, 1872, aged 72 years. Thomas Clegg, installed on March 29, 1839; moved west in 1840. Alexander Hannah, installed on October 5, 1849; moved to Greene County, Indiana. John L. Anderson, installed on October 5, 1849; moved west and died on September 15, 1876. James A. Cochren, ordained in April, 1872. Robert Taylor, Jr., ordained in April, 1872. John P. Matthews, ordained on January 9, 1877. James Hanna, ordained on January 9, 1877. John McKee, ordained October, 1881; moved to Tipton County, Indiana.

Ruling elders of Bethel Church included: George Shannon, Sr., and Thomas Gray, Sr., 1828. James Patterson, installed on June 7, 1828; died on March 14, 1854, aged 77 years. William D. Thorn, ordained June 23, 1838; moved West. Thomas Shannon, ordained on November 12, 1842; died on August 16, 1868, aged 73 years. James McMillan, installed on November 4, 1843; died on October 1, 1855, aged 68 years. Robert Irvin, installed on October 2, 1847; removed in 1849. Henry J. Bonner, installed on October 2, 1847; removed in 1851. Andrew Mann, ordained on November 30, 1851; moved west in 1878. James L. Swann, ordained on October 7, 1854; died on December 31, 1878, aged 72 years. Charles L. Gordon, ordained on October 7, 1854; removed in 1860.

THE CALEDONIA CHURCH AND CEMETERY
Mrs. Effa M. Danner

In a grove beside a little glen on a ridge extending back from the Ohio River is the Caledonia Church. With its large auditorium, Sunday School rooms, study, basement, furnace, and electric lights, it would grace a city, but it is the center of a rural community, several miles from any village, on the boundary between Jefferson and Switzerland counties.

The Caledonia United Presbyterian Church, a Scotch organization, is an old institution dating back to early pioneer days. The first family from Scotland settled in this neighborhood in 1816: others rapidly followed until there were thirty families in all, directly from Scotland, composing the first congregation. They were: Welch, Morton, Weir, Culbertson, Witherspoon, Glen, Dalglish, Brown, Scott, Dow,

Sterritt, Tait, Anderson, Shaw, Ralston, Crawford, Gray, Jamison, Wilkie, Imire, Irvine, Bell, Storie, Stevenson, Spier, Thompson, Kirkwood, McKeand, Graham, Gunnion. The present congregation is composed principally of the descendants of these families.

In 1818 a praying society was organized and met in the cabin homes. A log church or "kirk" was built in 1819 or 1820. Across the road in Jefferson County, a stone church was built in 1827. A third church, made of brick molded and kilned on the premises, was built in 1872, a few feet northwest of the stone building. The present church was erected in 1920-1921, at a cost of twenty-five thousand dollars; it is back over the county line in Switzerland County. In the history of the congregation, there have been only twelve pastors in 118 years. Now in its 129th year as a congregation, its church building is recognized as one of the most beautiful country churches in the state, an ideal spot for quiet, restful contemplation of the things of the spirit.

A walk through the near-by cemetery reveals the names of some of the founders of the church:

Mary Culbertson, native of Argileshire, Scotland, died 1821, aged 74.
William Culbertson, native of Agileshire, Scotland, died 1836, aged 74.
Agnes Graham, consort of Alex Graham, native of Edinburgshire, Scotland, died Sep. 22, 1836, aged 58.
Alexander Graham, native of Scotland, born Mar. 17, 1776; died June 9, 1860, aged 84 yrs. 2 mos. 21 days.

On vine-covered sides of a rather imposing monument are these inscriptions: S. F. Morton died and was buried here July 27, 1856, aged 25. Ann Morton, consort of Andrew, died December 1843, aged 54 (what became of Andrew is left to the imagination). On another side, one reads: "Susan, and all her father's pride, lies buried here." Other inscriptions in the cemetery read:

Marrion Robertson, native of County Renfrew in Scotland, and wife of Robert Spiers, died 1839, age 39.
Jane, consort of Hugh Stevenson, native of Ayrshire, Scotland, died May 24, 1829, aged 42 yrs, 8 mos.
Agnes, wife of Thomas Thompson, native of West Galter, Scotland, died 1848, aged 43.
William Wilkie, native of Queen's Ferry, Scotland, died Nov. 28, 1831, aged 42.
Hellen Morris, native of Leith, Scotland, wife of William Wilkie, died Dec. 21, 1832, aged 46.

Lawrence County Cemetery Records
Copied by BERNICE S. MARTIN

The Elijah Allen Cemetery:[1]

Cooper, Brillia I., dau. G. L. and Ph. E. Cooper; b. Dec. 10, 1873; d. Feb. 4, 1874.
Cooper, Hannory—b. Jan. 17, 1873; d. Feb. 3, 1873.
Cooper, Ory Coline—b. Jan. 17, 1873; d. Feb. 14, 1873.
Darr, Elizabeth—b. Oct. 28, 1822; d. Sept. 11, 1896.
Darr, Elizabeth—b. Oct. 28, 1822; d. Sept. 11, 1896.
Darr, John P.—b. Dec. 22, 1815; d. May 15, 1893.
Darr, George W.—b. Jan. 1, 1856; d. Feb. 7, 1906.
Darr, Hannah—b. Jan. 17, 1858; d. Apr. 4, 1896.
Darr, Rachael—dau. of J. P. and E. Darr; d. July 21, 1843; age 1 yr., 6 mos., 2 days.
Darr, Sophie M.—*geb.* Dec. 11, 1794; *gest.* Nov. 21, 1854.
Flinn, Charley W.—Sept. 3, 1874; Dec. 28, 1918.
Flinn, George—b. Feb. 11, 1748; d. Jan. 6, 1828.
Flinn, Jno.—Co. H., 24th Ind. Inf. (no dates).
Flinn, Luther C.—b. Feb. 28, 1877; d. Nov. 18, 1900.
Flinn, Millie A.—wife of Thomas Flinn; June 16, 1844; Aug. 26, 1929.
Flinn, Thomas—May 16, 1844; Feb. 17, 1927.
Glaesline, Arminey—dau. of G. M. and P. Glaesline; b. Sept. 15, 1850; d. Aug. 13, 1851.
Glaesline, Ens A.—son of G. M. and P. Glaesline; b. Sept. 15, 1850; d. Aug. 18, 1851.
Glaesline, Eliza C.—1856 (no other data).
Glaesline, Mariah E.—1856-1920.
Glaesline, Generall—son of G. M. and P. Glaesline; d. May 22, 1855; age 6 mos., 21 days.
Glaesline, George M.—Jan. 4, 1816; d. Jan. 13, 1884.
Glaesline, Nancy Ann D.—dau. of G. M. and P. Glaesline; d. May 28, 1855; age 2 yrs., 11 mos., 19 days.
Glaesline, Patience—wife of G. M. Glaesline;—b. Jan. 6, 1818; d. May 14, 1898.
Gutherie, James A.—b.. Aug. 15, 1841; d. Jan. 25, 1862.
Gutherie, Rachel—b. May 2, 1811; d. Sept. 22, 1836.
Guthery, Eley A.—dau. of H. and N. Guthery; b. Mar. 25, 1815; d. Jan. 15, 1850.
Guthery, Hughey—b. 1774; d. Jan. 25, 1847 (new stone).
Guthery, Nancy, Wife of H. Guthery—b. Oct., 1780; d. Dec. 11, 1862.
Guthrie, Daniel—b. Feb. 14, 1737; d. Sept. 17, 1826.
Guthrie, Hugh—d. Jan. 25, 1847 (old stone).
Guthrie—infant son of Sam'l and S. Guthrie; b. and d. Nov. 14, 1832.
Guthrie, Jane—b. Feb., 1747; d. Aug. 18, 1826.
Guthrie, Louisa J.—dau. of Sam'l and S. Guthrie; b. July 3, 1852; d. Aug. 24, 1853.
Guthrie, William—b. Aug. 19, 1805; d. July 9, 1836.

---

[1] Mrs. Bernice S. Martin, who copied these records, is a resident of Bedford, Indiana. The Elijah Allen Cemetery is located at Leesville, Lawrence County, Indiana.

Henderson, Joseph—b. July 8, 1808, in Montgomery Co., Va.; d. Aug. 13, 1872.
Henderson, Pheba—b. May 3, 1820, in Penn.; dau. of L. and S. White; d. Feb. 2, 1858.
Hubard, Sarah L.[2]—b. Sept. 16, 1861; d. June 10, 1870.
Hubard, William H.—b. Apr. 15, 1866; d. Aug., 1870.
Kindred, Nancy P.—dau. of Wm. and R. Kindred; d. June 30, 1851; age 11 mos., 1 day.
Kindred, Rachel—wife of Wm. D. Kindred; d. June 29, 1851; age 43 [?] yrs., 3 mos., 8 days.
Kindred, William D.—b. Sept. 18, 1810; d. July 22, 1858.
Lemp, Karline, G.S.C.—*geb.* Dec. 15, 1849; *gest.* Apr. 10, 1855.
Mathews, Alfred A.—son of Matthew and Nancy Mathews; b. March 11, 1857; d. Nov. 27, 1858.
Mathews, Isaac—b. Mar. 16, 1805; d. Oct. 17, 1880.
Mathews, Mary—wife of Isaac Mathews; b. Oct. 5, 1801; d. March 3, 1870.
Mathews, Matthew—Jan. 9, 1835; April 19, 1919.
Mathews, Nancy E.—Dec. 16, 1833; May 8, 1911.
Mathews, Theodore Emery—son of F. I. and J. W. Mathews;—Dec. 7, 1888; Nov. 7, 1892.
Mathis, Jacob—b. Nov. 29, 1837; d. Jan. 24, 1879.
Mathis, William—Co. G, 140th Ind. Inf. (no dates).
McKimmey, Euretta—wife of L. McKimmey; b. Dec. 25, 1830; d. March 18, 1858; dau. of I. and M. Mathews.
McKimmey, Isaac C.—son of L. A. and Euretta McKimmey; b. July 28, 1855; d. Nov. 28, 1862.
McKimmey, Louis A.—b. Nov. 29, 1833; d. June 24, 1859.
Riley, Harvey—b. Oct. 10, 1878; d. July 2, 1880.
Rosenbaum, Sarah—wife of C. J. Rosenbaum; Apr. 12, 1846; age 22 yrs., 5 mos., 18 days.
Weddle, Florence—dau. of H. A. and M. S. Weddle; b. Aug. 17, 1873; d. Sept. 26, 1873.
Williams, Addie O.—b. Nov. 20, 1888; d. Aug. 23, 1890.
Williams, Charley M.—1874-1931.
Williams, Elizabeth J.—dau. of Jacob F. and Emily J. Williams; b. June 27, 1843; d. Sept. 21, 1905.
William, Emily P.—1876-19—.
Williams, Emily J.—wife of Jacob F. Williams; b. Dec. 25, 1821; d. Oct. 24, 1904.
Williams, Hattie P.—b. Aug. 10, 1881; d. Aug. 2 [?], 1881.
Williams, Isaac—b. Apr. 29, 1811; d. Feb. 5, 1872.
Williams, Jacob F.—b. June 19, 1815; d. Nov. 27, 1860.
Williams, J. L.—Co. D, 33rd. Ind. Inf. (no dates).
Williams, Ova O.—b. Mar. 20, 1900; d. Feb. 19, 1901[3]

---

[2] Sarah L. and William H. Hubbard were children of J. H. and M. A. Hubbard.
[3] There is an additional stone bearing no name and a single date, Nov. 27, 1832. There are also about one hundred ten graves that can be located by depressions in the earth or by rough sandstone slabs. This cemetery is the burial place of many of Lawrence County's first settlers.

Records from the Granny White Cemetery[1]

Allen, Daniel Boon—b. May 30, 1840 (no death date).
Allen, Hannah—b. Jan. 17, 1858; d. June 4, 1886.
Allen, William—b. May 31, 1825; d. Feb. 28, 1874.
Bagwell, Andrew J.—b. March 10, 1882; aged 63 yrs.
Boston, Charlott Belle—dau. W. L. and Sara Boston; d. Feb. 18, 1866; aged 9 yrs. 10 mos. 25 days.
Chess, Henry Howard—b. July 18, 1902; d. Nov. 7, 1902.
Clendenin, Hannah—b. March 9, 1838.
Clendenin, Myrah—b. Aug. 10, 1810 (or 1840).
Clendenin, Vilet—b. Jan. 9, 1836.
Clendennin, ——— (dates effaced by weathering).
Cumings, Elizabeth—b. Dec. 22, 1759; d. Apr. 21, 1847.
Elston, Sarah A.—b. Jan. 10, 1811; d. Feb. 6, 1886.
Elston, Thomas M.—b. Aug. 7, 1806; d. Oct. 14, 1870.
Flinn, Jane—b. May 27, 1810 (or 1840).
Fountain, Essie Z.—dau. of J. C. and R. Fountain; b. Sept. 20, 1888; d. Feb. 3, 1889.
Fountain, Homer H.—son of Rebecca and J. C. Fountain; b. Nov. 5, 1885; d. July 21, 1887.
Fountain, Rebecca—wife of J. C. Fountain; b. Jan. 31, 1863; d. May 2, 1900.
Gutherie, Leannah (Leannan)—b. May 8, 1817; d. Dec. 9, ——— (year effaced).
Guthery, Anjeline—b. Dec. 15, 1838.
Guthrey, Hiram—b. Nov. 16, 1832; d. July 27, 1833.
Guthrey, Irey—b. May 1, 1834.
Guthrey, Mary Ann—b. May 2, 1824; d. Dec. 29, ——— year effaced).
Guthrie, Elizabeth—b. Mar. 16, 1787; d. June 5, 1867.
Guthrie, Hugh—d. July 17, 1873; aged 54 yrs. 9 mos. 23 days.
Guthrie, Isabel—b. May 4, 1816; d. Mar. 19, 1845.
Guthrie, Jane Rogers—d. Jan., 1928; aged 101 yrs. 7 mos.
Guthrie, Hugh—1818-1873—Jane, 1827-1928.[2]
Guthrie, Jacob—son of Hugh and Jane Guthrie; d. Oct. 11, 1860; aged 10 yrs. 1 mo. 9 days.

---

[1] This is an abandoned cemetery located near Leesville, Lawrence County, Indiana. The records were copied from the gravestones by Miss Esther A. Darr and Mrs. Goldie M. Carr of Brownstown, Indiana, and Mrs. Bernice S. Martin of Bedford, Indiana.

[2] The Guthrie stone has been erected in recent years. It carries the names of Hugh Guthrie and Jane. The latter, Jane Rogers Guthrie, was the wife of Hugh. Both names are found on older stones, and both are listed twice.

Guthrie, John—b. Nov. 8, 1785; d. Nov. 6, 1851.
Guthrie, John C.—b. Nov. 12, 1843; d. Apr. 11, 1848.
Guthrie, Margaret—dau. of H. and J. Guthrie; b. Mar. 28, 1862; d. May 11, 1862.
Guthrie, Nancy—b. Oct. 1, 1838.
Guthrie, Pelina—b. Nov. 4, 1827; d. July 12, 1848.
Harrison, William—b. Jan. 26, 1785; d. Jan. 28, 1844 (or 1854).
Henderson, Edith—dau. of J. R. and A. Henderson—d. Mar. 12, 1885; aged 6 days.
Henderson, Frances G.—dau. of J. R. and Anna H.; b. June 19, 1886; d. Sept. 10, 1886.
Henderson, Ralph E.—son of J. R. and A. Henderson; b. July 29, 1887; d. Sept. 25, 1887.
Holland, Euretta—wife of J. Holland; b. Dec. 27, 1816; d. Mar. 13, 1908.
Holland, John—b. Dec. 30, 1814; d. Oct. 24, 1875.
Holland, John R.—b. July 25, 1852; d. Apr. 5, 1880.
Holland, Lula May—dau. of W. A. and Mary C. A. Holland; b. June 27, 1881; d. Aug. 25, 1881.
Holland, Mary Jane—wife of Wm. A. Holland; b. June 15, 1830; d. July 15, 1868.
Holland, Melinda—dau. of John and Euretta Holland; b. Oct. 15, 1840; d. Oct. 28, 1841.
Holland, Phetna—wife of Wm. Holland; b. Jan. 16, 1805; d. Dec. 20, 1863.
Holland, Phetnam—dau. of John and Euretta Holland; b. July 2, 1842; d. Dec. 18, 1849.
Holland, Samuel—infant son of W. A. and M. J. Holland; d. Feb. 1, 1857; aged 9 mos.
Holland, Thomas—son of John and Euretta Holland; b. Jan. 5, 1856; d. Sept. 28, 1863.
Holland, Wm. A.—b. Sept. 5, 1830; d. June 17, 1905.
Hughes, John L.—son of M. and L. Hughes; b. Oct. 17, 1852; d. Apr. 17, 1853.
Hughes, Lucy—wife of Martin Hughes; b. Sept. 14, 1823; d. Apr. 26, 1890.
Hughes, Martin—b. Jan. 27, 1817; d. Mar. 29, 1904.
Hughes, Mary E.—dau. of M. and L. Hughes; Sept. 20, 1850; June 25, 1859.
Hughes, Wm. H.—son of M. and L. Hughes; b. May 28, 1856; d. Sept. 1868.

May, George—b. Jan. 28, 1786; d. Sept. 29, 1870; Lincoln Co., Ky., Militia, War of 1812.
May, Hannah—b. Sept. 24, 1803; d. Mar. 26, 1895.
Newkirk, Benjamine—b. Jan. 29, 1812; d. Mar. 5, 1887.
Newkirk, Eupha—wife of Benjamine Newkirk; b. July 28, 1818; d. June 11, 1863.
Nixon, Nora D.—dau. of F. T. and A. E. Nixon; b. Sept. 29, 1880; d. Nov. 26, 1884.
Rogers, Lilly—dau. of A. D. and N. Rogers; d. June 20, 1861; aged 26 yrs. 4 mos. 9 days.
Smith, Holland—b. May 8, 1868; d. Jan. 28, 1878.
Smith, Oscar—(dates hidden by large tree).
Smith, Sally—b. June 29, 1838; d. Feb. 23, 1907.
Smith, Dr. W. H.—b. Sept. 5, 1830; d. Oct. 30, 1911.
Sutherland, Lockey—b. Mar. 28, 1814; d. July 23, 1839.
White, David—b. Feb. 25, 1774; d. Jan. 10, 1842.
White, Sally[3]—b. Oct. 27, 1785; d. Jan. 21, 1879.
Wray, Polly—b. Nov. 15, 1783; d. Feb. 28, 1843.

---

[3] Sally White is the "Granny White" whose log home has been restored in Spring Mill Park. David White was her second husband. Elizabeth Cumings (see above) was Granny White's mother. The Granny White Cemetery is overgrown with trees, bushes, and briers. Many graves are marked only with rough slabs. No doubt other stones are completely covered. The Granny White Cemetery and the Elijah Allen cemetery are the two oldest cemeteries in Lawrence County—B.S.M.

Monroe County Cemetery Records

PERSONS BURIED IN THE CHAMBERS CEMETERY*

Freddie, son of A. J. and I. Chambers—died Apr. 17, 1892, aged 6 years, 6 mos., 27 days.

Martha E., wife of J. G. Chambers—born June 2, 1844, died Dec. 25, 1870.

Minnie, daughter of A. J. Chambers—Oct. 13, 1884, Sept. 6, 1885.

Jane, wife of J. G. Chambers—died Sept. 2, 1865, aged 23 years, 8 mos., 18 days.

Anna, daughter of A. & O. Chambers—Dec. 7, 1862-May 10, 1865.

Olie Chambers—1825-1884.

Hezekiah Chambers—Apr. 7, 1812-May 10, 1888.

Ozias Chambers—died Aug. 10, 1872, aged 61 years, 4 mos., 7 days.

Noah Chambers—1865-1884.

Daisy E., daughter of John and Lillie B. Chambers—Sept. 25, 1876-Nov. 27, 1876.

William, son of O. & M. Chambers—Died Aug. 19, 1861, aged 11 yrs., 9 mos., 1 days.

Samantha A., daughter of O. & M. Chambers—died Feb. 6, 1864, aged 23 years, 9 mos., 3 days.

---

* The Chambers Cemetery is located near Harrodsburg, Monroe County, Indiana, about one-half mile east of State Highway 37. The records were copied by Mrs. Charles R. Emery, Bloomington, Indiana. Verses, scripture passages, and other like matter have been omitted.

Nancy, daughter of H. & M. Chambers—died Nov. 15, 1853, aged 17 mos., 17 days.

Julia A., daughter of O. & M. Chambers—died Nov. 15, 1858, aged 1 yr. & 2 mos.

Elizabeth, widow of Jesse Cole—died Sept. 20, 1856, aged 72 yrs.

Hiram H. Chambers—died Oct. 6, 1852, aged 24 yrs., 3 mos., 17 days.

William S. Chambers—died Jan. 16, 1855, aged 69 yrs.

Mary, wife of Wm. S. Chambers—died Feb. 16, 1849, aged 60 yrs.

Nancy, wife of Thos. Hously and daughter of Wm. S. and Mary Chambers—died Sept, 1840, aged [stone has sunk too far into the earth for the remainder of inscription to be read.]

Thomas, son of Wm. S. and Mary Chambers—died 1834, aged 1 yr.

Stouten, son of Wm. S. and Mary Chambers—died Sept. 1832, aged 2 yrs.

John, son of Wm. S. and Mary Chambers—died Sept. 15, 1833, aged 17 yrs.

Shelton Chambers—died Oct. 30, 1865, aged 28 yrs., 3 mos., 26 days.

Rebekah A., consort of Shelton Chambers and daughter of P. and B. A. Gaither—born June 16, 1839, died March 7, 1871.

Infant twin daughters of Shelton and Rebekah Chambers—born and died in 1860.

Martha, daughter of D. and S. Chambers—July 11, 1860-Aug. 1, 1860.

Infant daughter of D. and S. Chambers—died Mar. 21, 1858, aged 1 day.

Wm. P. Chambers—Sept. 27, 1850-Aug. 17, 1851.

Julia Ann Chambers—Sept. 11, 1843-July 18, 1847.

Margaret, daughter of H. and M. Chambers—died Oct. 3, 1853, aged 11 yrs., 2 mos., 3 days.

Anthony Chambers—died Apr. 25, 1848, aged 51 yrs.

Mary C., wife of Anthony Chambers—died Feb. 24, 1859, aged 54 yrs.

Malinda, wife of Hezekiah Chambers—died Oct. 4, 1871, aged 54 yrs., 7 mos., 2 days.

Silas, son of H. and M. Chambers—died Nov. 10, 1872, aged 24 yrs., 4 mos., 25 days.

Mary E. Chambers—died 1905, aged 69 yrs.

John A. Medcalf—July 1, 1827-Sept. 10, 1876.

Jacob Chambers—died Jan. 25, 1882, aged 47 years, 7 mos., 2 days.

Delitha, wife of J. Pennington—died April 17, 1868, aged 21 yrs., 6 mos., 13 days.

Infant daughter of H. and M. Chambers—Dec. 31, 1842, aged 19 days.

Mary S., daughter of H. and M. Chambers—July 16, 1846, aged 6 mos. and 7 days.

Alexander Chambers [died] Aug. 30, 1876, aged 49 yrs. and 9 mo.

Katie, daughter of A. and M. Chambers—died Apr. 23, 1875, aged 3 mos., 28 days.

Persons Buried in Mt. Salem Cemetery[1]

James Mitchell—Oct. 14, 1767—June 9, 1846.
Nancy Mitchell—June 25, 1771—Oct. 10, 1844.
Mary E., daughter of Joseph and E. F. Mitchell—July 31, 1830—Aug. 24, 1838.
Richard Perry—died Sept. 30, 1870, aged 48 year 6 months 15 days.
Barbary, wife of Richard Perry—born Jan. 2, 1824, married March 17, 1842, died June 18, 1847.
Rachel Buck, wife of J. Buck—died Oct. 5, 1866, aged 66 years.
David Perry—April 4, 1790—May 20, 1854, aged 64 years.
Lorinda, wife of David Perry—born about 1800, died April 15, 1840.
Moses H., son of Jacob and Sophia Trisler—Jan. 15, 1841—Aug. 25, 1841.
Joseph M. Buck—Oct. 11, 1852—Aug. 17, 1853.
Mary A. Bennett, wife of J. Bennett—March 15, 1818—Dec. 26, 1842.
Basil Hill—died Nov. 28, 1866, aged 64 years, 5 month, 3 days.
Isaac Hill, son of Basil and Charity Hill—Jan. 9, 1825—Sept. 26, 1851.
Sophia Hill—Jan. 19, 1814—Oct. 14, 1854.
Thomas Hill—March 6, 1777—May 5, 1850.
Millek Hill—Jan. 28, 1778—Oct. 14, 1854.
Florence, daughter of J. and Susan Woodward—1851-1857.
Joseph H., son of J. and Martha Dillman—Aug. 16, 1851—May 16, 1857.
Martin L., son of J. and Martha Dillman—Nov. 1, 1852—July 25, 1853.
Mary E., daughter of Louis and Lydia Litz—July 14, 1869—Aug. 24, 1870.
Sarah Jane, daughter of J. and P. Fox—died Jan. 22, 1854, aged 6 years, 9 months, 5 days.
Vitelle, daughter of L. and L. A. Litz—May 14, 1880—June 1, 1891.
William H. Fox—Oct. 4, 1844—March 12, 1864.
James T., son of J. and M. Fox—died March 23, 1872, aged 12 years, 9 months, 7 days.
James Fox—Aug. 14, 1817—March 16, 1877, aged 59 years, 7 months, 2 days.
Benjamin F. Helms—Oct. 19, 1841—Nov. 5, 1875.
Benj. F., son of Wm. and N. Taylor—died Dec. 6, 1861, aged 16 years, 9 months, 9 days. Co. G 31st Regt. Ind. Vol.
William Taylor—July 15, 1789—Nov. 11, 1849, aged 60 years, 3 months, 26 days.
Nancy, wife of William Taylor—April 26, 1800—March 1, 1845, aged 44 years, 10 months, 5 days.
Son of Jesse and Mary Fox—May 7, 1884—June 13, 1888.
Daisie, daughter of Jesse and Mary Fox—June 17, 1892—July 1, 1892.
John A. Fox—May 4, 1819—March 4, 1885.
Mary J. Fox—Oct. 22, 1829—Dec. 23, 1906.
Salmon, son of F. and S. M. Howard—died Oct. 17, 1847, aged 6 years, 11 months, 25 days.

---

[1] This cemetery is located on what is now State Highway No. 37, about six miles south of Bloomington, Indiana. The inscriptions were copied by Mrs. Charles R. Emery of Bloomington, Indiana.

Rebecca, daughter of F. and S. M. Howard—died July 11, 1849, aged 2 months, 1 day.
Eli Howard—died Feb. 21, 1870, aged 37 years, 8 months, 23 days. Co. J. 59th Regt. Ind. Vol.
Nelson Fox—died Sept. 2, 1932, aged 73 years, 11 months, 9 days.
John H. Hines—died Oct. 20, 1867, aged 27 years, 7 months, 18 days.
Jerusha Ann, daughter of S. B. and M. Perry—Jan. 12, 1854—Nov. 19, 1854.
Samuel B. Perry—died July 27, 1863, aged 37 years, 6 months, 8 days.
Mariah, daughter of G. and F. Finley—died May 6, 1869, aged 38 years, 6 days.
George Finley—Feb. 15, 1789—Nov. 3, 1851.
Fanny, wife of George Finley—Jan. 9, 1875, aged 79 years, 4 days.
George Iseminger—Sept. 23, 1766—Nov. 23, 1848.
Almira, wife of John Horton—died Dec. 25, 1848, aged 27 years, 20 days.
Elizabeth A., wife of C. G. Harrell—died April 25, 1857, aged 29 years, 5 months, 2 days.
Milton J., son of B. and A. Trisler—died March 8, 1858, aged 1 month, 29 days.
Daniel Trisler—died Feb. 2, 1867, aged 33 years, 11 days.
James W. Anderson, son of G. A. and K. Anderson—Nov. 19, 1805—March 15, 1841.
In memory of Katherine Anderson, consort of George Anderson,—March 22, 1782—Sept. 22, 1845, aged 63 years, 6 months.
William Ross—May 17, 1758—April 21, 1875, aged 116 years, 11 months, 4 days.
Elizabeth Ross—Oct. 21, 1791—Feb. 13, 1852.
Reuben Ross—Jan. 12, 1822—Sept. 23, 1840.
Sally Young—died Aug. 13, 1859, aged 44 years, 10 days.
Mary E. Young—died March 31, 1852, aged 1 month, 2 days.
Avis W. Ross—Feb. 12, 1887—May 27, 1892.
Eddie W. Ross—Sept. 12, 1871—Sept. 21, 1872.
Jennie E. Ross—Sept. 12, 1859—March 7, 1875.
Catherine Ross—Aug. 30, 1853—Sept. 30, 1876.
Walter W. Ross—May 12, 1883—Oct. 28, 1885.
Emma Ross—Sept. 28, 1861—Feb. 3, 1880.
Elizabeth, wife of W. W. Ross—Jan. 20, 1840—July 19, 1874.

(The following names and dates are from Bible records. They are known to be buried in Mt. Salem Cemetery, but lie in unmarked graves.)
William Wilson Ross—July 22, 1830—Dec. 30, 1912.
Eliza Ellen Ross, his wife—Aug. 8, 1847—Sept. 26, 1911.
Foris Sylvester—Feb. —, 1841—Oct. 27, 1921. Co. G, 31st Regt. Ind. Vol.
Rachel Emma Sylvester, his wife—Aug. 5, 1855—July 13, 1928.

A Minute Book for the Christian Church on Busseron Creek

Record of the Christian Church at Palmers Prairie Sullivan County, Indiana. 1827? 1831?

*Contributed by Chloe Siner Morgan**

Towards the close of the first third of the nineteenth century the teachings of Alexander Campbell and his father, Thomas, who had come over to Pennsylvania from Scotland some twenty years earlier, resulted in the organization of a distinct and separate church denomination, which Campbell's followers in 1830 chose to call The Christian Church. This was another evidence of the continuation of the Reformation, the search for the true original manner of worship. The story of this evolution, which has been most ably presented in various volumes by church historians, should be consulted for information too lengthy to be included in these pages. Let it be sufficient to say that this evidence of Campbell's teachings found immediately materialization in southern Indiana, among the pioneer settlers who were for the most part second to sixth generation Americans from Virginia, the Carolinas, and Georgia, as well as from eastern Pennsylvania and New Jersey.

The little groups of homeseekers who laboriously pushed their way into that part of Knox County which in 1816 and 1818 became respectively designated Sullivan and Vigo had come by way of Kentucky or Tennessee or from across the Miami bottoms in Ohio. Often families had divided along the way, older brothers or parents stopping and the younger ones traveling farther into the wilderness. Thus there continued through the first generation after the progression the tendency to keep in touch with the relatives left behind. And as for the county lines of Sullivan and Vigo, as well as Knox, they had no reality. There was much visiting back and

---

* Mrs. Chloe Siner Morgan, a resident of Bloomington, is the wife of the late Dr. William Thomas Morgan, professor of European history at Indiana University, 1919-1946, with whom she collaborated in the five volume *Bibliography of British History, 1700-1715; with Special Reference to the Reign of Queen Anne* (1934-1942). She was one time assistant professor of English in Iowa State Teachers College, and lecturer in English in the École Normale des Institutrices, Blois, France.

forth, and even much moving back and forth. Distinctly Vigo families had in many instances taken first root in Sullivan, and vice versa.

As to ancestral nativity the earliest settlers in both counties were generally English, Scots, or Scots Irish (Scots who had been living in Ireland for generations), Irish, and Pennsylvania Dutch first settlers in Germantown (1683-1710) who had intermarried with English families from New York, New Jersey, and New England, and a few whose names indicated German origin. There was a sprinkling of those with Anglicized French names dating from the invasion of the British Isles by William the Conqueror with his French barons. A few there were who could have traced their ancestry to the Mayflower or to a New England provincial governor, or even to the early nobility of Great Britain, had they possessed the time, the inclination, or the facilities to determine such connections. Some families handed down oral traditions of estates in "the Old Country" or of service in the recent American Revolution and its aftermath, the short flurry of 1812.

As for their religious heritage, there were those from Church of England families, Baptists, Presbyterians, and others who had come to America as Quakers but through intermarriage had changed to Presbyterians, then Baptists and Primitive Baptist. Here in the wilderness they wanted a church as soon as possible. The earliest church in the community of which Palmers Prairie in Sullivan County was a part was a Baptist (Missionary) instituted in 1821 on the neighboring prairie named for the William Curry family, the first to build a cabin there. When this little church (Little Flock, a mile southwest of Shelburn) celebrated its centennial, the claim was made that it was the oldest church in the county. Whether or not the original Palmers Prairie Church situated a few miles from Busseron Creek, was the first Christian church in the county can be determined only if other churches examine their records, and publish them. At any rate the early membership list includes persons from the region of Caledonia, Cass, and Shakers Prairie (between Oaktown and Carlisle), and the place where Sullivan was later established.

Indeed, this little record book of Palmers Prairie offers certain date problems in connection with that church's establishmen. An examination of the two title pages encourages speculation. An examination of the inside pages discloses conflicting dates. One can only arrive at an approximate date; for this is undoubtedly not the first record ever kept.

Below the carefully printed first page title appears in a less firm hand a date which might be 1837, 1857, or—more likely—1831. But it might be 1859, the date that is found near the top of the first membership list, after the names of Elders John Maxwell and Thomas Nesbit! Then, below that date at the right hand corner of the page are the words: "Organized Jan- 17 183 [MS torn]."

The second title page only adds to the confusion. Above the title, prominently placed in the middle of the space, is the unmistakable date, 1827. But across the top of the figures are two thin crossed curved lines. Can this be intended as a deletion or as a pen flourish by way of decoration?

On the seventh page from the back of the book, the puzzle becomes more intricate. Here one finds an attempt towards making a summary of the original church officers. This attempted date results in: "Church organized in 1831. (1827)-"

We are still in the dark; but considering the 1830 separation of the Christian church from the Baptist Association, we are inclined to favor the date, 1831. Perhaps the discovery of the deed for the land upon which the old church and its cemetery stands, or a time-yellowed letter in a family Bible may sometime disclose the truth. Whatever the true date may be, this little list of names which includes those of individuals remembered to be living there even before 1831, should offer considerable stimulus towards genealogical research.

There are certain features within the book which point towards a still earlier membership list, whether ever recorded or not. Among internal evidences is the absence of the names of several persons contemporaneous with the founding of the church. Indeed, comparatively few of the persons of mature years living in the community in 1830 seem to be listed in these pages. Among these few are the Elders John Maxwell and his wife, Thomas Nesbit, and Rebecca Benefield, who seems to be the mother of G. W., Willis, John, Sally McGrew, Susan Liston, and Mary. Possibly there are many more. One name which one might expect to find is that of Andrew McGarvey, who according to family tradition and that of William G. McClannahan, sexton for almost a generation during the middle period, was the first person buried in Palmers Prairie Cemetery. One fails to find either his name or that of his wife, Nancy Ellen, though she long survived him and is likely buried in the Old Shake Cemetery near Paxton, the community of her daughter, Nellie (Mrs. Whitaker Purcell). One son of this couple, Ezekiel (b. January 1, 1811; d. April 6, 1877), who with his second wife, Martha Lou Rainey (Borders McKinley) and his third wife, Mary Ann Raines, are recorded in this book, is buried in this churchyard.

This family is said to have come from Ireland about 1819 and settled first on Turkey Creek between Lexington and Louisville, Kentucky. The eldest son of Andrew, Samuel, lived there until the end of the Civil War, then moved to Honey Creek Hill, now known as Alandale, at the southern edge of Harrison Prairie and a few miles south of Terre Haute. Both he and his wife are buried in the Hull Cemetery. Two other sons, John and James, remained in Kentucky. Andrew and his wife and the two youngest children, after a few years in Kentucky came to Palmers Prairie before the church was built there. They assisted in operating a cooperative store and distillery on the ground where the church now stands, bearing their share of the flatboat building and operating to and from New Orleans in the store's interest. They owned several farms on Palmers Prairie where they manufactured brick and tile, and another a few miles southeast of Shelburn. Ezekiel once owned the land where Sullivan Courthouse now stands. Through Andrew's and Nancy Ellen's brothers and sisters Ezekiel was a first cousin to Russell McKinley of Sullivan, for whose daughter the hospital is named, and to the Beard brothers and sisters: Felix, John, Stephen, and their sister, Mrs. Edward Roll of Sullivan and Vigo counties, as well as to the Jane (Russell) Hill of this record, and her brother Spencer Russell, all of whom had come from Kentucky. Another cousin was the second wife of Joseph William Wolfe, early Christian preacher, and lawyer from 1860, and Circuit Court clerk of Sullivan.

We cannot be certain about the generation of the earliest Raines name on the record, since the use of senior and junior here makes for confusion. William I (d. June 7, 1873), a pensioner of the War of 1812, married "Peggy Damson," really Margaret Dampster, in 1817, according to the Mercer

County Marriage Records at Harrodsburg, Kentucky. They were living at Frankfort, Kentucky, shortly before their migration to Palmers Prairie when their fourth child, Mary Ann (b. February 14, 1826) was three months old. This William, whose middle name was Pendleton, had a son William, whose son William is still living in Sullivan County. All these William Raines's were members of Palmer Prairie Church. William Raines I had also a son Allen, an uncle Allen who moved to Illinois, and a brother Allen (b. March 20, 1797; m. Rosanna Parker, September 6, 1821, in Mercer County, Kentucky; d. April 20, 1873). The names of several of the children of this couple appear on the early pages of this record. The son William Mereday handed down to his grandson Bert M. of Terre Haute the almost unique name, Mereday. This son William Mereday and his sister, Elizabeth Ferree, were ever closely associated with the Prairie and its church. Other sons and daughters left the community. After the death of his wife, Rosanna, Allen moved in the early sixties to Sedalia, Missouri, with his son Cornelius. There were other Raines brothers: James, reputedly a Revolutionary soldier and never married, and Adam who had no children. A sister, Elizabeth, was the second wife of William Patton and had two daughters. Another, probably Mary, married a Hawkins. Still another, Sally, married George Plough, according to the Mercer County records, June 5, 1819. This George Plough was one of the old-fashioned "bleeding doctors" of the community. These were the parents of Dr. George Plough, a graduate of Rush Medical College, who practiced medicine at Hymera until he was ninety.

Possibly some of the Raines brothers and sisters remained in Kentucky or even in Tennessee or possibly Virginia, the colony to which this southern Raines line came from England at a very early period. Some light upon the origin and history of the first years of this Virginia line and its branch that went into Georgia is shed by a Georgia branch descendant, Stella Pickett Hardy, in her *Colonial Families of the Southern States of America* (New York, 1911). Much has been written about Captain John Raines who, under General James Robertson, assisted towards the end of the American Revolution in opening up Tennessee and Kentucky. No one, however, has attempted to discover the thread of relationship which likely existed between Captain John and the Mereday

Raines of this Tennessee expedition with the Harrodsburg Raines brothers and sisters who in 1826 and somewhat later moved into Palmers Prairie.

Similar digressions might be made in the discussion of others of the early settlers of Palmers Prairie, whose names, it seems, might be expected to appear on these minutes, if they are indeed the earliest minutes. We must make due consideration, of course, to our lack of knowledge of many of these families and to the known fact that the early families were divided within themselves as to denominational allegiance. We must take into consideration, also, the possibility that some of the earliest generation there were Presbyterian or Anglican and still held to these faiths, despite the absence of these church homes in the region.

The deciding evidence against these minutes as a first list of members lies not so much in the omissions as in the inclusions. Some of the names which appear on the first pages of this book are recognized as those who were in their infancy when the church was founded. Some were not then even living in that part of Indiana or in Indiana at all. Among these names should be pointed out those of Susan Ann (Benefield) Liston (b. February 5, 1824, in Lawrence County, Indiana, to William and Rebecca (Bailey) Benefield) and her husband, Edmund (b. December 7, 1814, to William and Nancy (Patton) Liston). Another such name is that of Susan Ann's sister-in-law, Elizabeth Jane (McGrew) Benefield (Mrs. G. W.) who was born in Sullivan County, August 14, 1837, to Felix G. McGrew and his wife, Julia Ann Pound.

Another factor which makes more intricate this maze is that caused by the repetitions of names in the several revisions of the record; yet all this seems to be sufficient data to place this record as one belonging to about 1859, the date which appears after the names of Elders John Maxwell and Thomas Nesbit. If any whose ancestors appear in this list will search their family Bible records and their old deeds and marriage certificates, much more light may be shed upon this early Christian church community of fertile meadows through which flows the creek which rises in the vicinity of Blackhawk and empties its waters into the Wabash in the vicinity of Oaktown, that creek which memorializes Major François R. Busseron who assisted Colonel George Rogers Clark in the taking of Vincennes (Fort Sackville).

Those who would seek out this little white church and its interesting cemetery, possibly a last resting place as early as 1822, will have little difficulty in finding it. Palmers Prairie is one of a series of small prairies which dot the Wabash Valley from Vincennes to Terre Haute. This particular prairie about which twines the once exuberant Busseron and its tributaries, Stonequarry and "Kittle" Creek, is situated at the near center of a triangle of which Shelburn (laid out in 1855), Sullivan (incorporated in 1853), and Caledonia are the points. The church is closer to Shelburn than to Sullivan, and the nearest group of houses is the little coal town, Glendora, which had its origin shortly after 1903 when the deep coal veins began to be exploited by outside interests.

1. John Maxwell
2. Mary M. Maxwell
3. Thomas Nesbit
4. Elisabeth Nesbit
5. Levi Maxwell
6. Lidia Maxwell
7. Jackson Rich
8. Sally A. Rich
9. Jane Hill
10. Edmund Liston
11. Susan A. Liston
12. Talton Hawkins
13. Mary M. Hawkins
14. Sarah Houston
15. Mary L. Brodie
16. Sarah L. Nesbit
17. Eliza A. Nesbit
18. Armina M. Moore
19. Solomon Ring and
20. Wife
21. Julia Marlow
22. George Marlow
23. Sarah Marlow
24. Elisabeth Walls
25. Sabra Rich
26. David Ferguson, Sen.
27. Lucy Ferguson
28. William Mitcheal
29. Sarah Carrithers
30. Russell Mitcheal
31. Sarah Mitcheal
32. Elisabeth Mitcheal
33. Averilla Grigsby
34. Nancy Malone
35. Mary Carter
36. Uriah F[er]ree
37. Elisabeth F[er]ree
38. Rosa Rain[e]s
39. Cornelius Rain[e]s
40. Naoma J. Rain[e]s
41. Sarilda Rain[e]s
42. William Rain[e]s, Sen.
43. David Ferguson, Jun.
44. Lucinda Fe[r]guson
45. William Walls
46. Malissa Walls
47. John Mitcheal
48. Rebecca Mitchell
49. Rebecca Skinner
50. Rebecca Benefield
51. Rebecca Osborn
52. David Plough
53. Nancy Plough
54. Joshua Stark

55. Lucinda Stark
56. Sarah A. Stark
57. Abraham Stark
58. Daniel A. Stark
59. Friend Lemons
60. Rebecca Lemons
61. John B. Wagoner
62. John Trublood
63. Netacris Trublood
64. Margaret Walls
65. Jane McKinl[e]y
66. Mary A. Hill
67. Reece M. Nesbit
68. Mary E. Nesbit
69. Benjamin Malone
70. William Rain[e]s, Jun.
71. Leanah McKimmy
72. Thomas T. Nesbit, Jun.
73. Sarah J. Mitcheal
74. Nancy D. Rain[e]s
75. Sarah Malone
76. Sarah Brock
77. Polly Brock
78. Harlen Walters
79. Samuel Patton
80. Mary Patton
81. Elisabeth Rusher
82. Miner Rusher
83. Polly Rusher
84. Luticia Ingle
85. William Wetherman and
86. Wife
87. William Rowe
88. Elisabeth A. Walls
89. James Rain[e]s
90. William Chowning
91. Nancy Bo[t]ts
92. Lucinda Bo[t]ts
93. Sarah Walls
94. Wesley Plough
95. Margaret Cochron
96. Mary J. Benefield
97. James McGarv[e]y
98. Micheal Borders
99. Nancy Borders
100. Sarah Boats [Botts]
101. John Bailey
102. Elisabeth Bailey
103. Walker Rusher
104. Sarah Plough
105. Nancy Plough
106. Plough
107. William Shaw
108. Martin Elliott
109. George Brock
110. Rebecka Brock
111. Wm. Rusher
112. Jamima Hart
113. Elizabeth Borders
114. Ezekiel McGarv[e]y
115. Martha McGarv[e]y
116. Wm. Breaheave [Breedlove]
117. Mary Jane Miller
118. Bonwell D. Miller
119. Samuel McClanihan [McClannahan]
120. Polly McClanihan [McClannahan]
121. Samuele Hopewell
122. Sarah Hopewell
123. Alford Caise
124. Abriham Stark
125. Daniel A. Stark
126. Sarah F[er]ree
127. Wm. Patton
128. Elizabeth Patton
129. Owens Nesbit
130. Daniel Case
131. Lusinda Case
132. Wm. C. McClanihan [McClannahan]
133. Elizabeth McKinley
134. Wm. R. Maxwell

135. Rebeca Maxwell
136. Rachel Wagoner
137. Naoma Wagoner
138. Eliza Ann Liston
139. Sarah Elizabeth Hawkins
140. Sabra Jane Rich
141. Perry Maxwell
142. Robert Skinner
143. Adam Hawkins
144. Stephen Lovelace
145. Martin Akim McClan[n]ahan
146. Wm. Skinner
147. Samuel Dudley
148. Mrs. Jane Dudley
Hillekiah Lovelace
John Bowles
Sarah Bowles
John T. Beard
Elden Davis
Elizabeth Raines
Anna Akers
Phebe A. Combs
Louisa Siner
Hester A. Botts
F. M. Botts
Mary Raines

Joseph D. McClan[n]ahan
Melinda Shaw
Letty Bailey
Leonard Borders
Jonathan Davis
Perlina Davis
Lydia Davis
Elizabeth Bennifield
Margaret J. Riley
Tarlton Hawkins
Permilia J. Ingle
Mrs. Draper
Synthia Melone
Polly Melone
Thomas B. Skinner
George W. Patton
Robt. A. Mitchel
Benjamin Stice
America Stice
Mary J. Boles
Mrs. Cahill
Jane Stanley
Mary Ferree
Mary J. Nesbit
Jackson Rich, Jun.
George B. Hawkins
Lewis Hale

Revision of the Church Book at Palmer's Prairie, Sullivan Co. Indiana.

John Bailey
John Maxwell
Thomas Nesbit
Elizabeth Nesbit
Jane Hill
Susan A. Liston
Tarlton Hawkins
Sarah Houston
Mary L. Brodie
Sarah J. Beard

Eliza A. Curry
Armina M. Moore
Solomon Ring and Wife
Elizabeth Wall
Sabra Mitchel
Russel Mitchel
Averilla Grigsby
Nancy Breedlove
Uriah Ferree
Elizabeth Ferree

Naoma J. Raines
Cerilda Raines
David Ferguson
Lucinda Ferguson
Wm. Wall
Melissa Wall
Rebeca Skinner
Rebecca Bennifield
Rebecca Osburn
John Trueblood
Netacris Trueblood
Mary A. Hill
Rees M. Nesbit
Mary E. Nesbit
Benjamin Melone
Wm. Raines, Jun.
Thomas T. Nesbit
Nancy D. Raines
Sarah Lovelace
Samuel Patton
Mary Wagoner
Elizabeth Botts
Minor Rusher
Polly Rusher
Elizabeth A. Walls
James Raines
John W. Plew
Margaret Cochran
Mary J. Bennifield
Michael Borders
Sarah Cunningham
Ezekial McGarv[e]y
Martha McGarv[e]y
Wm. Breedlove
Mary J. Miller
B. D. Miller
Samuel McClanahan
Mary or (Polly
        McClan[n]ahan
Samuel Hopewell
Sarah Hopewell
Wm. Patton

Elizabeth Patton
Campbell O. Nesbit
Daniel Case
Lucinda Case
Wm. C. McClan[n]ahan
Elizabeth McKinley
Wm R. Maxwell
Rebecca Maxwell
Rachel Wagoner
Naoma Wagoner
Eliza A. Liston
Sarah E. Hawkins
Sabra J. Rich
Wm. P. Maxwell
Robert Skinner
Adam Hawkins
Stephen Lovelace
Martin A. McClan[n]ahan
Jane Dudley
Hillekiah Lovelace
John Bowles
Sarah Bowles
John T. Beard
Eleanor Davis
Elizabeth Raines
Anna Akers
Phebe Combs
Louisa Siner
Hester A. Botts
Mary Rain[e]s McGarv[e]y
Joseph D. McClan[n]ahan
Melinda Shaw
Letty Bailey
Leonard Borders
Johnathan Davis
Permilia Davis
Lydia Davis
Elizabeth Bennifield
Margaret J. Riley
Permilia Ingle
Synthia Melone
Polly Melone

Thomas B. Skinner
George W. Patton
Benjamin Stice
America Stice
Mary J. Bowles
Mrs. Cahill
Mary Ferree Skinner
Mary J. Nesbit
Jackson Rich, Jun.
George R. Hawkins
Lewis Hale
John T. McClan[n]ahan
Elizabeth Bailey
Miss Nancy D. Plew
Francis Doty
Sarah Doty
Rebecca Wall
Anderson Ward
Elizabeth Ward
Wm. M. Raines
Alvire Raines, his Wife
James Smith
Nancy Smith
Wm. Hainey
Mary E. Hainey
Georg Hainey
Margaret J. Bailey
John Lovelace
Cornelius D. Raines
Catharine Raines

Nancy J. Stice
Sarah Perkizer
Nancy J. Smock
Stephen Ferguson
Leah Ferguson
Julia Ferree
Sarah Rusher
Elizabeth Gambol
John Mitchel
Elizabeth Mitchel
Thomas Hale
Thomas Hale
James S. Neal
Sarah A. Badders
Eliza Badders
G. W. Badders
Peter Houck
Sarah Houck
Elzee Rusher and wife
Tho. J. Robbins
Margaret M. Robbins
Eld. G. W. A. Luzader
Charlotte Luzader
Sarah Ward
Nancy Ward
Eld. Levi Woodward and wife
Eld. Thomas Wolfe and wife
Thomas Chambers and wife
Mary A[nn] Raines

Names Palmers Prairie Church

1. Lucinda Woodward
2. John Boles
3. Mary A. Boles, his wife
4. George H. Pirtle and
5. Wife
6. Tenyason Wagoner
7. Thomas Nesbit and
8. Wife
9. J. S. Park and
10. Wife
11. Thomas T. Nesbit, Jun.
12. Mary J. Nesbit
13. William Wall
14. Barthada Wall
15. Nancy Jane Wolfe
16. George W. Wolfe
17. and Wife
18. John Wall

19. J. D. McClan[n]ahan
20. James Bunch
21. and Wife
22. Eleck Davis
23. Elizabeth Hawkins
24. Simira Marlow
25. Stephen Moser
26. Maryann Engle
27. Sintha Cox
28. John Wolfe
29. Ellen Keen
30. John Houstain
31. and Wife
32. Oregon Marlow
33. Nathan Wells
34. Tidwell Bidle
35. James H. Hill
36. Ransom Hawkins
37. Samuel McGarv[e]y
38. John Cahhal
39. Sarah E. Osburn
40. Mary Bell Osburn

41. Hattie Bailey
42. Emerrine Bennett
43. Della Boles
44. Abraham Mahan
45. Albert Smith
46. Allice E. Smith
47. Jenette Hummel
48. Charles Smith
49. Joseph Hill
50. Jacob Pirtel
51. Elizabeth Ward
52. Mary Wall
53. Marcus Wolfe
54. Aaron E. Wolfe
55. William Tool
56. Henry Gambill and Wife
Elder William Holt and
Rhoda Holt, his Wife
Elizabeth Benifield
Josie Holt
Adam Raines and Wife
Aaron Sluder and Wife

November, 1879

1. Gertrude Hendricks
2. Minary Houston
3. Myrta A. Ford
4. Hannah Hummel
5. Catharine Ward
6. Jane Melone
7. Narcissus Hill
8. Hettie Botts
9. Mary Ann Keen
10. Albert Hill
11. James F. McClan[n]ahan
12. Joseph Wolfe
13. Gertrude Benefield
14. Jocy Nesbit
15. Flora Marlow
16. Aetna Shelburn[e]
17. Frank Hawkins

18. Leona Benefield
19. Lizzie Shelburn
20. James F. Raines
21. Thomas E. Ward
22. James Steele
23. Olla Smith
24. Armilda Keen
25. Ann Willis
26. Robert P. Raines
27. Alexander Davis and
   Wife
28. M. A. McClan[n]ahan
29. and Wife
30. Deella Boles
31. Lina Crawford
32. Charles Smith
33. Henderson Boles

34. Winny A. Plew
35. Margaret Marlow
36. Will McKinley
37. B. W. Fry
38. and Wife
39. Anna Hawkins
40. Thomas Nesbit, Jr. and Wife
41. John Roberts and his Wife
42. Pleasant Miller
43. Margaret Hoskins

November, 1882

1. Tacy Luzader
2. Josephine Chastain
3. Mellissa Chastain
4. Missouri Chastain
5. James Bilyew and Wife
6. Lyman Ford and Wife
7. Martha McClan[n]ahan
8. Sarah Arnett
9. Samuel Patton and Wife
10. John Hawkins and Wife
11. Jesse Powel and family
12. John W. Cooney
13. Kate Brodie
14. Parthada Hawkins
15. Mary Coulson
16. Jennie Raines

April 26, 1885

John Mosir
Manda Bylyew

Church organized in 1831. (1827)—the Church on Busseron Creek—300 members or more all together.

First two elders	{ John Maxwell { Thomas Nesbit
First two deacons	{ Levis Maxwell { Jackson Rich
Pres[ent] Eld[ers]	{ T. J. Wolfe { N. Ferree { J. N. Bilyew 1886 { Thomas Nesbit, Sr.
Pres[ent] Deacons	{ Wm. G. McClan[n]ahan { John B. Hawkins { Samuel Patton { Thomas T. Nesbit, Sr.
Pres[ent] Tr.	{ U. Ferree { J. N. Bilyew
Treasurer	Bilyew
Clerk	Wm. M. Raines

Revision of Palmer's Prairie Church Record, February 14, 1886

1. Mrs. Jane Hill
2. Mrs. Susan A. Liston
3. Uriah Ferree and Wife
5. Mrs. Sarah Houston
6. Mrs. Rebecca Benefield
7. Benjamin Melone, and Wife
8. Mrs. Polly Rusher
9. Miss Mary J. Benefield
10. Wm. H. Rusher and Wife
12. Mrs. Sabra Jane Marlow
13. Mrs. Ellen Raines
14. Marion Botts and Wife
16. Mrs. Mary McGarvey
17. J. D. McClan[n]ahan
18. Jonathan Davis and wife
20. Wm. G. McClan[n]ahan and wife
22. Mrs. G. W. Benefield (Eliz.)
23. Mrs. Willis Benefield (Eliz.)
24. Mrs. Elizabeth Botts
25. Mrs. Sarah Cunningham
26. Wm. M. Raines and Wife
28. Miss Nancy Ward
29. Eld. T. J. Wolfe and Wife
31. Mrs. Samira Crawford
32. Mrs. Mary Ann Houpt
33. Miss Cyntha Cox
34. Miss Elizabeth Ward
35. Mrs. Belle Cass
36. James Houston and Wife
Sarah Cox
William Marlow and Wife
Adam Raines and Wife
The "faithful" which came in under the preaching of Rev. Ingram, Nov., 1879.
38. Minary Houston
39. Mrs. Joseph Wolfe
40. Catherine Ward
41. Jane Melone
42. Mrs. Hettie Wyman
43. Mary Ann Keen
44. Josie Nesbit
45. Flora Marlow
46. James F. Raines and Wife
48. Thomas E. Ward
49. James Steele
50. Armilda Keen
51. Alex Davis and Wife
53. Martin A. McClan[n]ahan and Wife
55. Mrs. Winny A. Plew
56. Maggie Marlow
57. Thos. T. Nesbit (Jun.) and Wife
59. Mrs. Maggie Wilson

The "faithful" who came in under Rev. Ingram's preaching Nov. 1882.

60. Miss Tacy Luzader
61. Mrs. Josephine Raines
62. Mrs. Melissa Smith
63. Miss Missouri Chastain
64. James Bilyew and wife
66. Samuel Patton and wife
68. John B. Hawkins and wife
69. Miss Katie Brodie
70. Mrs. Parthada Hawkins
71. John Mosier
72. Mrs. Lena Maxwell
73. Aaron Sluder and wife

Those who came in under Rev. J. W. Perkins' Preaching, Feb., 1886.

1. Flora Raines
2. Jonathan Raines
3. Matilda Hill
4. Sylvester McGrew and wife
6. Marion Delapp
7. Anne Davis
8. Henry Smith
9. Mollie Wall
10. Stella McGarvey
11. Oliver Smith
12. Mary Raines
13. Mattie Ward
14. Lizzie Shelburn[e]
15. James Ferree
16. Geo. F. Botts
17. Thos Nesbit, (Sen.), and wife
19. Joe Hill and wife
21. Jeannette Hummel
22. Joseph Wolfe
23. Maggie Raines
24. Maggie Houston
25. Ella Davis
26. Geo. Ferree and wife
28. Hannah Cunningham
29. Laura Wall
30. John Ward
31. Willie Kirk
32. Joseph Wyman
33. Wm. Wall and wife
35. Achsah Benefield
36. John Hardy Siner
37. Etna Shelburn[e]
38. Ceph Shelburn[e]
39. Sintha Delapp
40. John A. Wilson

November, 1886

41. Mrs. Kate Ward
42. Nannie Skinner
43. Luie McClan[n]ahan
44. Rennie C. Wall
45. John E. Neal
46. Mary Neal, his wife
47. Robert Benefield
48. Tarlton Hawkins
49. Emma Park
50. Noah Bridwell
51. Reason Nesbit
52. Mary E. Nesbit
53. Mollie A. Nesbit
54. William Cunningham
55. Ranson Cunningham
56. Sue Ward
57. Perry Davis
58. Samuel Wolfe
59. James Carrithers
60. Dora Marlow

November, 1891

1. George Brow[n]ing
2. Lillie Pain
3. Stella Rich
4. Ida Botts
5. Dela Botts
6. Mrs. [William, Jr.] Shelburn[e]
7. Jackson Rich
8. Fanny A. Rusher
9. William Shelburn[e]. Jr.

1893

1. Mrs. Akers
2. Nervie Tipton
3. Sattie Davis
4. May Mosier

Those who came in under the Preaching of Jessie Wilson, 1894.

1. Inis Bailey
2. Duglas Rich
3. Mrs. Hendricks
4. Tressie Bailey
5. Maggie C. Ward
6. Lola Bailey
7. Flora Botts
8. Flora Pain
9. Harvy Tipton
10. Perry Davis
11. Fanny Marlow
12. Mrs. Mosier

Those who became members of Palmer's Prairie Church under the preaching of brother Jesse Wilson in the year, 1895.

J. H. McBride
Thomas Taylor
Ida Marcum
    Lovelace
Ira Wence
Gertrude Hendricks
Bertha Rich
Ora Hendricks

Those persons who became members of the Church of Christ at Palmer's Prairie under the preaching of Bro. Williams.

Dec. 26 Gertie Ward
Dec. 27 John Wence
Dec. 27 Mrs. John Wence

Members received during preaching of Bro. H. C. Shaw, Nov. 4, 1899.

David Hummel
Cordia Nesbit
Amanda Dodds
Eva Davis
Alice Davis
Bertha Hendricks
Elsie Hendricks
Ethel Hendricks
William Miller
E. McClellan Leach
William Raines [III]
Ida Raines [his wife]
Luella Gray
Claude Raines
Flavia Rusher
James F. Akers
Joseph Sommers
Ethel Case
Ed Engle
Maude Rich
Susie Tipton
Elmer Chastain

All the above came into the Body of Christ by Immersion.

Albert Wright Nora Wright
Mrs. Albert Wright

1903

Joel Rusher

December 1903

Glenn Mosier Dan Burroughs
Lucy Case

Little Flock Baptist Church (1821), Sullivan County

Chloe Siner Morgan*

With the exception of the Shakers "at West Union on Busseron Creek," the little church on Currys Prairie, so aptly named Little Flock by its eleven constituent members of June, 1821, was the first church in Sullivan County. And with the exception of First Prairie Creek (1818) in the southwest corner of Vigo County, there was probably no other Indiana Baptist church in the Wabash area north of Maria Creek (1809), fifteen miles northeast of Vincennes. This church was but slightly more than a score of years behind the first Baptist church which came to southern Indiana in Clark County. While the French had brought Roman Catholicism to the Vincennes district within the first half of the eighteenth century,[1] the Baptists, the forerunners of Protestantism in southern Indiana, did not build a church earlier than 1798. (See the Minute Book of this first church, styled progressively: The Fourteen Mile Church (1798), Owens Creek Baptist Church (1806-1837). The first entry is dated "February, 1799." In the back of the second book, which is in the Indiana State Library, an entry reads: "Minutes of Silver Creek Association, held at Sliver Creek, before the 4th Lords Day in July, 1812." On p. 114, a new membership list is entitled: "Names of Members of Silver

---

* Mrs. William Thomas Morgan is a faculty research fellow at Indiana University.

[1] For the difference of opinion concerning the date of the founding of Vincennes and the first Catholic church there, see Gilbert J. Garrahan, S.J., *Vincennes: A Chapter in the Ecclesiastical History of the West* (n.p., 1931); John D. Barnhart (ed.), *The French Period in Indiana, A Pamphlet of Readings* (Bloomington, n.d.); Herman Alerding, *A History of the Catholic Church in the Diocese of Vincennes*, (Indianapolis, 1883); Pierre-Georges Roy, "Sieur de Vincennes Identified," Indiana Historical Society *Publications* (Indianapolis, 1895-), VII (1923); Paul C. Phillips, "Vincennes in Its Relation to French Colonial Policy," *Indiana Magazine of History* (Bloomington, 1905-), XVII (1921), 311. According to these authorities, Francois Marie Bissot de Vincennes, the founder of the city of Vincennes and constructor of the fort around which the village grew, took up his work on the site about 1731-1733. The date of the founding of the church is based on the first church marriage record, dated April 21, 1749, and the record of the first baptism, June 25, 1749.

Creek, August 27, 1825." See also, William Warren Sweet, Editor, *Religion on the American Frontier: The Baptists 1783-1830* (New York, 1931), 30; A. H. Newman, *A History of the Baptist Churches in the United States* (New York, 1915), 340; David Benedict, *A General History of the Baptist Denomination in America* (New York, 1853), 870-871; and John F. Cady, *The Origin and Development of the Missionary Baptist Church in Indiana* (Berne, Indiana, 1942), 17-18, 105, 162, 168, 203, 227, 230, 240, 263.)

When Little Flock was constituted, the district in which it lay comprised the Wabash District Association, which had been organized in 1809 and remained during its first ten years in correspondence with the Baptist Board of Foreign Missions. Toward the end of the ten-year period a schism occurred in the association because of the teaching of Daniel Parker, who held some "Anti-ism" views which were opposed to the tenets of the Missionary Baptists. The Wabash District Association had included churches lying on both sides of the Wabash River in the old undivided pre-1816 Knox County, the Indiana churches being Bethel, Maria Creek, Patoka, Salem, and Wabash. The differences between the two Baptist factions necessitated the organization, in 1824, of the Union Association, in order to preserve Missionary principles. This new association, which included the counties of Daviess, Knox, Pike, and Sullivan, was carved out of "that part of the Wabash District Association that lies on the Indiana side of the Wabash River. It began with eight churches, six ordained ministers and 360 members. . . . The oldest church in Union Association was Wabash Baptist Church, organized some time prior to 1809. Maria Creek was the next, formed in 1809." [See William Taylor Stott, *Indiana Baptist History, 1798-1908* (n.p., 1908), 61-63, 129-131.] By 1812, according to Newman (341), "there were in the whole of Indiana [but] 29 churches and 1726 members."

Although Little Flock in Sullivan County had been constituted almost three years before the organization of Union Association, the church may not have become sufficiently established in time to enter the Wabash District Association before the split occurred. The first minutes of the little church on Currys Prairie, approximately two miles south of old Currysville, were not recorded until 1824, at the time the members called as their first minister "our beloved brother Willis Pierson," who, with his brother Moses, had come from Kentucky in 1820 and founded Pierson Township in the southeast corner of Vigo County, which had been divided from Sullivan in 1818.

Little Flock joined Union Association; and when in 1834 another association split off from Union, choosing the name Currys Prairie, Little Flock became a member of that body. This new association, according to Stott (129), embraced "the churches lying east of the Wabash river, and north between Vincennes and Terre Haute, including the latter." The First Baptist Church of Terre Haute, however, was not constituted until July 9, 1836.

Up to the summer of 1826 the small membership of Little Flock could meet comfortably in the log schoolhouse or in the homes, for their communicants were still far from numerous. They had started with eleven members, and by July 8, 1826, had received a total of forty-five, ten of whom were lost by letter. With approximately thirty-five members and their unbaptized families, they decided that it was time to build a meeting house. On July 8, 1826, they bought from Tyre Harris, one of the constituent members, a plot of ground as a building spot, obtaining it for the "consideration of $5.00." The deed was made to Richard Dodd, William T. Lloyd, and William B. Eldridge, "Trustees of the Baptist Church in the Township of Hamilton, called Little Flock Church." (Though the site was in Hamilton Township, it could not have been more than a stone's throw of Curry; and some old map may show that Curry was divided from Hamilton at some later date. The church *was* on Currys Prairie.) This deed was not recorded until August 15, 1904, for no suitable explanation, except that the man from whom the land had been secured had never recorded the deed to the original purchase.

The plot of ground which provided for a future Little Flock Meeting House and churchyard was a small portion of the 79.98-acre farm which Tyre Harris and his wife Susanah had purchased August 28, 1821, for "full payment," and which was not recorded until October 7, 1903. This is described as: "The east half of the northeast quarter of Section 4, Township 8 North, Range 9 west." Perhaps the trip to Merom, where the deeds were then made, was too difficult to take for the recordings and later the matter was forgotten. (U.S.A. Deed Record 86, p. 562, by James Monroe, President.)

Such were the preliminaries to the founding of this church, which, according to Stott (178), "For many years ... led in the number of members, but at length it was equalled and then surpassed by the First Terre Haute church, which in 1905 reported 855 members."

Little Flock, despite its comparatively prosperous early growth, remained true to its name. Throughout the years 1821 to 1862—the years included in the earliest minute book here under consideration—but 410 names are recorded. Eventually, in less than a score of years after this church had celebrated its centennial, its dwindling congregation razed their old meeting house—the third built on the spot—and transferred their membership to Shelburne Baptist Church within the town, founded in 1855 by Paschal Shelburne, a native of Virginia. (See "Shelburne Baptist Church: the Constituent Membership Record, May 7, 1870," *Indiana Magazine of History*, June, 1953.)

Only the old cemetery remains as a mute reminder of the early history of this little community of hopeful, earnest, Godfearing pioneers. Many of the family names recorded in the churchyard and on the minute book of the church have faded from Currys Prairie but their descendants are legion. Grandchildren, great-grandchildren, and great-great-grandchildren, *ad infinitim,* in the true pioneer spirit of their forefathers, have passed out into the wide open spaces and played distinguished roles throughout the United States; while others have remained, with a tenacious loyalty to the early home of their ancestors, playing equally important parts in their native county of Sullivan and in the adjoining and outlying counties. Despite the short period of inundation of European labor, brought in by operators during the heyday of the coal industry, descendants of the founders of the community have maintained the predominately British flavor and attitude of life of their inheritance. This truism may be kept in mind in considering the whole of Sullivan and Vigo: it is well for a stranger in those counties to refrain from criticism of his neighbor, for he may be speaking to a distant relative of the man he is condemning. There is a current saying in those parts that all the descendants of all the old families are related, whether or not they know it.

The purpose of articles such as this is to aid the younger generation in tracing their connections with the early communicants of Little Flock Church and with other pioneer church communities in Sullivan and Vigo.

Following is a list of the ministers of the Little Flock Church during the period of 1824-1919:

1824. Willis Pierson. The minutes merely recorded that "The church agrees to invite our beloved brother Willis Pierson to preach to us for a few months, which invitation is accepted." Pierson died in Kentucky in 1826. His brother Moses, also a Baptist minister, and Elder Joseph Liston—a son of Edmond and Elizabeth (Kester) Liston—were ancestors of the founders of the Pierson lumber companies of middle Indiana. (See John E. Hunt, *The Pound and Kester Families* (Chicago, 1904), 395.

1826. William B. Eldridge. According to the Little Flock minutes of October 8, 1826, "Motion made and seconded to know whether calling on a member to exercise a gift is setting forward a preacher. The Church says it is not. On motion made and seconded Brother William B. Eldridge is liberated to exercise a preaching gift and that he try to preach on next Church meeting day at 11 o'clock." The minutes of November 11, 1826, carried the information that, "After hearing Brother Eldridge the Church says he is liberated to exercise a public gift in the bounds of the church." He left the following year to preach elsewhere, one of his charges being Second Prairie Creek Church, which was not constituted until 1828, in Vigo County. In February, 1834, Elder Eldridge and his wife, Sarah (Anderson) Eldridge, were received as members of Second Prairie Creek Church. There the Eldridges lived during the remainder of their lives. In the minute book of that church, Eldridge's name first appears as moderator in June, 1834, again in April, 1835, and thereafter intermittently through the following two years. From 1837 to December, 1866, he served there in the dual capacity of moderator and pastor almost constantly. In August, 1866, he placed a "request to be released of the pastoral care of the church and also as moderator;" yet, in the September minutes, "the church say retain Brother Eldridge." In December, however, the church elected Philip Randolph to succeed to the moderatorship, and thereafter Eldridge's name disappears from the monthly reports.

Since early 1860 Second Prairie Creek had agreed to call an assistant pastor, and in June, 1860, "Brother S. K. Sparks was chosen" in that capacity.

William G. Eldridge (b. Sullivan County, October 24, 1830), son of William B. Eldridge and a teacher and preacher, married Ruth Welch, a descendant of Paul Kester. William G. Eldridge was received into Second Prairie Creek Church by letter, March, 1859. In June of that year he asked "liberty of the church to exercise in public and by motion and second the Church gives him leave to exercise in the bounds of the Association." In June, 1860, he and his wife Ruth were dismissed by letter by request of his father, William B. Eldridge, the pastor.

Another son of William B. Eldridge, Robert (b. November 27, 1839) married a granddaughter of Thomas and Sarah (Kester) Pound. (See Hunt, 167, 363.)

1827-1831. William B. Stancil. Stancil was one of the leading builders of Union Association, according to Stott (131), although he was not ordained until 1824, the year in which Union was formed. He had become a member of Shiloh Baptist Church, Perry County, in 1821, at the age of 21, and was licensed to preach a year before his ordination. A native of North Carolina, he was brought to Indiana as a boy of eight; ten years later he had married Celia Parker. His life was spent in the manner of the old circuit-riding missionary pastors, fighting the elements as he made his way from one part of the Wabash Valley to another. He died there "in his 85th year" and was buried in Sullivan, where he had assisted in the founding of the First Baptist Church (April 23, 1853) which had sixteen constituent members. He then, according to T. J. Wolfe, *History of Sullivan County* (2 vols., New York, 1909), I, 291, "took up his residence at Sullivan" for the next ten years, and then again, "after a brief interval for four more years." Wolfe says that Stancil lived in Knox County in the early fifties, and as he "passed up and down the Valley to perform his labors," he passed periodically through Sullivan. During these stops, he held services in the Methodist house of worship, where he preached to the small group of Baptists. He "shared some honors with the veteran missionary Isaac McCoy, whose name is closely identified with the early history of the Baptist Church in Indiana," especially in connection with Indian mission work.

[See Elizabeth Hayward, *John McCoy, Life and Diaries* (New York, 1948), for the fascinating story of a family of pioneer Baptist ministers, that of William McCoy and his sons James, John, Rice (or Royce) and Isaac.] Among the churches served by Stancil, besides Sullivan and Shiloh, were Wabash, Maria Creek, Washington, Aikman's Creek, Wilson Creek, Edwardsport, and Second Prairie Creek, where he was the organizing moderator, August 1, 1828. (See Benedict, 870; Stott, 132.)

1831. Abraham Stark. Stark was invited to preach "as often as practicable." According to Stott (181), he "was born in Pennsylvania in 1781, was baptised into membership in the Eighteen-Mile church in Kentucky in 1800; coming to Indiana he was pastor of Union church fourteen years, Second Prairie Creek seven years, Little Flock six years, and for limited terms was pastor of Friendly Grove and Mount Pleasant churches." His name as moderator appears frequently in the early twenties and thirties in the Second Prairie Creek Records. As moderator he assisted in the constitution of Lost River Association in 1825, and served in the same capacity in Union Association, being elected moderator "at nine successive sessions." He died in 1857. He "began his Indiana ministry in the Silver Creek Association in 1815," and he "later distinguished himself in the Curry's Prairie Association near Terre Haute." He was moderator at the founding of the Association in 1834, at Union Church in Vigo County. (See Stott, 177-178.) He was a prominent promoter of "Sunday Schools, weekly instead of monthly meetings, compensation for pastors, and such projects as Franklin College and a Baptist state paper." It was not until the fifties that Currys Prairie officially adopted the Sunday School program. (See Cady, 17, 162, 168.) Stark helped in the constitution and served Second Prairie Creek (constituted, 1828) several years before requesting that the church provide for her minister. In May, 1836, Stark and his wife requested a letter of dismissal from Second Prairie Creek. In October he was replaced by S. K. Sparks. The request was readily met and members were assessed according to their ability to pay. The wife of Abraham Stark was Sarah Stark, his first cousin. (See Hunt, Appendix S, 484, 517, 590). Abraham may have been a brother or possibly an uncle of Margaret Stark (b. 1805 in Kentucky), whose parents were Aaron and Anna (Guntryman) Stark. Margaret was the wife of Ephraim Pound Kester, a grandson of William and Elizabeth (Lacock Ferguson) Kester and also of John and Sarah (Martin) Pound. (See biographical sketch of Elizabeth (Pound) Siner in "Shelburne Baptist Church," *Indiana Magazine of History*, June, 1953.)

1839-1840. William B. Stancil. (Second period.)

1840-1855. Asa Frakes. Frakes' long service would indicate that he was well-liked. He served again from 1865-1867. He was one of the Currys Prairie ordained ministers, serving the sixteen churches of the association. The other ordained ministers of the association were: Elders D. M. Stark, F. R. McKinney, W. B. Eldridge, E. G. Taylor, G[eorge] Crist, and S[amuel] K. Sparks. Frakes' wife was Rebecca Ann Dickerson. Their son William married Mary Liston, a granddaughter of Edmund and Elizabeth (Kester) Liston, daughter of William and Elizabeth (Lacock Ferguson) Kester. Mary was the first cousin of Joseph Liston, prominent Vigo county pioneer from 1811 and Baptist minister for approximately sixty years. One of Joseph Liston's granddaughters married a grandson of Moses Pierson, another Union Church minister. The aforementioned George Crist was a Pound and Kester descendant. S. K. Sparks married into these families. (See Hunt, 395-422, 402, 476; Stott, 178, 180; Vigo county histories, *passim*.)

1855. William B. Eldridge. (Second period.)

1856-1858. D. M. Stark and Thomas McKinney. Stark was "born in eastern Indiana in 1809, and was baptized by his father into the membership of the Union church in 1830. This church called for his ordination in 1844 and he served many of the churches during his twenty-three years of the ministry." (See Stott, 182.) He may have been a relative of Abraham Stark, possibly his son. Abraham had a son Abram, who was a minister. Stark families who for many years resided in Vigo and Sullivan counties were probably descendants of these early ministers. Of Thomas McKinney we find no mention. Possibly he was related to the F. R. McKinney mentioned by Stott as a preacher in 1860. (See McKinneys in Little Flock membership record.)

1858-1861. D. M. Stark. (See above.)

1861-1863. William Winans. Winans is mentioned as one of sixteen ordained ministers serving the twenty-one

Currys Prairie churches in 1880. The others in this list are W. T. Cuppy (brother of Letticia, wife of Paschal Hill), G. P. Fuson, J. B. Arnett, J. M. Turner, G. W. Marlow, G. W. Trent, C. R. Henderson, D. H. Nevins, J. M. Plew, S. M. Stimson, J. W. Stark, W. B. Eldridge, W. P. Sanford, C. B. Allen, and E. Cooprider. (See Stott, 178.) Some of these served Little Flock during these years; some others who served are not mentioned by Stott.

1863-1865. Jacob Smock. Smock was a pioneer minister of Currys Prairie Association, born in Kentucky in 1824 and brought by his parents to Parke county, Indiana, the following year. He was the grandson of William Smock, a Revolutionary War soldier. He was twice married—first to Caroline Milligan, who died in 1879, and second to Dinah Wilson. He was the father of six children by his first wife and of one daughter, Wilma, by his second. (See Stott, 182.)

1865-1867. Asa Frakes. (Second period.)

1867-1869. A. J. Riley. Riley helped in the constitution of Shelburne Baptist Church, in 1870, and served as their first minister. His wife's name was Annie.

1869-1870. Jacob Smock. (Second period.)

This brings the list of ministers up to the time of the division of Shelburne Baptist Church from Little Flock, and eight years beyond the end of the earliest membership record (1821-1862). Since the pastors who succeeded to the centennial year of the church preached within the memory of persons still living, it is hoped that some of these and the survivors in their families may come forth with biographical data. A list of these later pastors, predominated by the large family of Fusons, is as follows:

1870-1877. S. K. Fuson.
1877-1882. G. P. Fuson (brother of S. K. Fuson).
1882-1888. Jacob Smock.
1888-1889. J. L. Weeks.
1889-1891. D. P. Liston.
1892-1885. Henry Fuson.
1885-1888. William T. Cuppy (brother of Letticia [Cuppy] Hill, wife of Paschal Hill).
1889-1899. William Fuson.
1899-   W. A. Fuson.
1900-1902. George Fuson.
1902-1904. James Sanders.

1904-1907. George Fuson.
1907- P. N. Fuson.
1908-1909. Nathan Clark.
1910- J. R. Hinman.
1911- W. H. Coonce.
1912- George Fuson.
1915- Blanchard Davis.
1916- H. R. Baker.
1917- D. Hanna.
1919- James W. Stark.

The following is a list of the members of the Little Flock Baptist Church—the first eleven names of which are the constituent members,—and the dates of their admission to membership in the church:

Tyre Harris—June, 1821
Susannah Harris—June, 1821
John Hodges—June, 1821
Polly Morgan—June, 1821
Mary Hill—June, 1821
Elizabeth Anderson—June, 1821
Robert Anderson, Sr.—June, 1821
Sarah [Froment] Anderson—June, 1821
Betsy Anderson—June, 1821
Sarah Eldridge—June, 1821
Patience Cummins—June, 1821
John Grant—August 11, 1821
Hannah Grant—August 11, 1821
George Rusher—November 16, 1822
John Graham—November 16, 1822
Eliza Anderson—December 7, 1822
Robert Anderson, Jr.—December 7, 1822
Abraham Anderson—April 10, 1823
Benjamin Siner, Sr.—August 7 [?], 1823
Polly [Maladie] Siner—August 7, [?], 1823
Elizabeth Thompson—February 8, 1824
Patience Cummins—"in the constituted."
James Lloyd—March 13, 1824
Margaret Lloyd—March 13, 1824
James Siner—March 13, 1824
Lemuel Magby—Oct. 13, 1822
Isaac Thompson—June 12, 1824

Lemuel Parker—August 17, 1824
Sarah Parker—August 17, 1824
Margaret Daniel—August 17, 1824
Melinda Hill—March 12, 1825
William T. Lloyd—April 9, 1825
Louisa An Lloyd—April 9, 1825
Sinthia Ann Anderson—April 9, 1825
Elijah York—April 9, 1825
[William?] A. Dodd—April 9, 1825
Richard Dodd—June 11, 1825
Priscilla Mise—November 12, 1825
James D. Gardner—January 8, 1826
Desdemonia [Shelburne] Siner— October [——], 1822
John Anderson—February 11, 1826
Sarah Carrithers—May 13, 1826
Huldah Gardner—May 13, 1826
Sally Osburn——May 13, 1826
Sally Nantz—May 13, 1826
Susanna Glover—July 8, 1826
Grove Pomeroy—October 8, 1826
Levi Chambers—October 8, 1826
Champion Shelbourn[e]—October [—], 1822
John Lloyd—November 11, 1826
Eleanor Lloyd—November 11, 1826
Nancy Lloyd—November 11, 1826
Ann Lloyd—November 11, 1826
Alexander M. McDaniel—February 10, 1827

Sally M. McDaniel—February, 10, 1827
Nancy Carrithers—March 10, 1827
Mary Carrithers—March 10, 1827
Dolly Mahan—March 10, 1827
Henry Rusher—March 10, 1827
Katharine Rusher—March 10, 1827
William Rusher—May 12, 1827
Elizabeth Rusher—May 12, 1827
Asenith Rusher—May 12, 1827
Clarissa Pomeroy—July 7, 1827
Ann Harris—November 10, 1827
Elizabeth Osburn—December 8, 1827
Eleanor Lloyd, Jr.—December 8, 1827
Mahala Lloyd—January 12, 1828
Moses Lloyd—January 12, 1828
John Osburn—January 12, 1828
[——] Bridges—January 12, 1828
Sally Bridges—January 12, 1828
Polly Laswell—February 9, 1828
Edward Dodd—February 9, 1828
Cinthia Dodd—April 12, 1828
Elizabeth Lacefield—April 12, 1828
James Rusher—May 10, 1828
Nancy Rusher—May 10, 1828
Aldert [sic] Plough—May 10, 1828
Fanny Plough—May 10, 1828
Jared Rundel—June 8, 1828
Fanny Lloyd—July 12, 1828
Andrew Rusher—August 9, 1828
Charnel Laswell—February 9, 1828
Lydia Laswell—February 9, 1828
Williamson Lloyd—December 13, 1828
Joseph Kelly—May 9, 1829
Mary Kelly—May 9, 1829
Eli Mills—June 13, 1829
Anna Mills—June 13, 1829
Sally Plough—July 11, 1829
Anna Harris—July 11, 1829
Betsy Cummins—March, 1822
Samuel Cummins—March, 1822
Olla Bridges—October 10, 1829
William B. Eldridge—October 13, 1821
Rebecca Daniel—October 13, 1821
William C. Griffith—March 9, 1830
Elin Pitman—October 10, 1830
Mariam Pitman—October 10, 1830
Samuel Osburn—September 11, 1830
James Rusher and wife—September 11, 1830
Joseph Kelly and wife—September 11, 1830
Mariam Pitman—November 13, 1830
Elin Pitman—November 13, 1830
[——]h Hopewell—January 8, 1830
Samuel Oakes—September 7, 1834
Hardy Hill—October 12, 1834
Nelson Signer [Siner]—October 12, 1834
James Bell—October 12, 1834
Alen Pittman—October 12, 1834
Henry Hopewell—October 12, 1834
Mary Hopewell—October 12, 1834
Prudence Reed—June 21, 1834
Dicey Bell—June 21, 1834
Nancy Bell—July 25, 1834
John Pugh—November 22, 1834
Levina Powers—November 22, 1834
Mehelah Cuppy—March 21, 1835
James Martin—December 23, 1837
Shadrach Payne—May 28, 1837
Mary Payne—May 28, 1837
James Lloyd, Jr.—November 25, 1837
James Plew—November 25, 1837
Rebecca Pittman—November 25, 1837
Mary All—June 23, 1839
Sary All—June 23, 1839
Elizabeth All—[June ?] 22, 1839
William Woodsmall—June 25, 1833
Polly Woodsmall—June 25, 1836
Mahalah Pugh—November 22, 1834
Thomas R. Mckinney—May 23 1835
Elizabeth Dicks—[?]
Martha Jane Hill—April 12, 1834
Salley Fox—April 12, 1834
Daniel Clark—May 10, 1834
Melissa Lloyd—March 3, 1834
Champion Shelburn[e]—September 14, 1839
Samuel Cummins

Abraham Stark—June 11, 1831
Sally Stark—June 11, 1831
Elisha Stark—June 11, 1831
Samuel Osburn—October 10, 1830
Mary Jewel—March 12, 1831
William Stark—September 10, 1831
Kisiah Stark—September 10, 1831
Polly Cotton—September 10, 1831
Tamar Cotton—September 10, 1831
Sanford Pitman—September 10, 1831
Elizabeth Pitman—September 10, **1831**
Carline Mills—September 10, 1831
George Hammack—March 9, 1832
Robert Daniel—July 7, 1832
Margaret Daniel—July 7, 1832
Elizabeth Brookbank—October 13, 1832
Rheuben Stout—November 10, 1832
Sarah Stout—November 10, 1832
Katharine Okes—November 11, 1832
William Martin—January 12, 1833
Sarah Martin—January 12, 1833
William Bell—March 9, 1833
Elizabeth Bell—March 9, 1833
William Stark—March 9, 1833
Kesiah Stark—March 9, 1833
[———] Rusher—April 13, 1833
[——— ———?]—April 13, 1833
Lydia Jewel—May 11, 1833
Henry Smith [or Smock]—July 13, 1833
Mary Osburn—July 13, 1833
[——— ———?]—?
Sally Parkes—September 7, 1833
James Plew—August 10, 1833
Richmond Shelburne—September 14, 1839
Meriah Gardner—November 19, 1839
Melvina [Shelburne] Bennett—August 15, 1840
Mary Watson—May 30, 1841
Mahalah Anderson—June 20, 1841
Nancy Pittman—October 16, 1841
Benjamin Dosson—January 15, 1842

Lydia Dosson—January 15, 1842
Joseph Baily—April 17, 1842
Margaret McGrew—April 17, 1842
Jane McKinney—April 17, 1842
Elizabeth P. Lloyd—April 17, 1842
Jacob Marts—April 17, 1842
Rebecca Tincher—April 17, 1842
Jacob Marts, Jr.—April 17, 1842
Martha Marts—April 17, 1842
Sary Borders—April 17, 1842
Jacob Borders—April 17, 1842
John Osburn—April 17, 1842
Plender Osburn—April 17, 1842
Jane Griffith—April 17, 1842
Susan Gardner—May 15, 1842
Letticia D. Plew—May 15, 1842
Alletha M. Plew—May 15, 1842
Mary Peyton——May 15, 1842
Sally Gardner—June 19, 1842
Elizabeth Simpson—June 19, 1842
Jessie [?] Lloyd, Jr.—June 19, 1842
Melisa Lloyd—June 19, 1842
Jas. Lloyd, Sr.—June 19, 1842
Margaret Lloyd—June 19, 1842
Elizabeth Jewel—August 18, 1842
Letty Osburn—August 18, 1842
John Cuppy—September 17, 1842
Eliza Briscoe—September 17, 1842
Stephen Jewel—September 17, 1842
Robert Ewing—December 18, 1842
Lucy Ann Ewing—December 18, 1842
Green T. Gardner—May 20, 1843
Jane Eliot—April 15, 1843
Sarah Lee—February 17, 1844
Paskel [Paschal] Shelburn[e]—September 14, 1844
Thomas Marts—September 15, 1844
Chamberlin Marts—September 15, 1844
Mary Marts—September 15, 1844
Sally Cogshill—September 15, 1844
John Boles—October 13, 1844
Emily Marts—October 19, 1844
Permela Anderson
Meranda Hill
Jane Marts

Elizabeth Combs—March 29, 1845
Sary Kerkham—March 29, 1845
John Belyou
Nancy Laswell—August 20, 1848
Elizabeth Thompson
James Sanford—January 3, 1849
Martha Warner—January 6, 1849
William Higdon—January 6, 1849
John Mcdonall—January 6, 1849
Patten Kirkham—January 7, 1849
Hannah Warner—January 21, 1849
Levi Warner—January 21, 1849
Frances Griffith—April 14, 1849
Nancy Higdon—May 19, 1849
Hannah Marts—May 20, 1849
Mary J. Phillips—[——?]
Serilda [Anderson ?]—[——?] 16, 1849
[Asa ?] Frakes—[——?] 17, 1849
Desdemonia Siner—April 19, 1851
John Cox—April 19, 1851
Fanny M. Gardner—July 19, 1851
Alexander Medonall [McDonall ?]
Thomas Black—August 17, 1851
Melinda Medonall—July 19, 1851
Joseph Liston—September 20, 1851
Margaret Liston—September 20, 1851
Benj. Barney—October 20, 1851
James McClannahan—January 14, 1854
Julia F. Jewell—January 15, 1854
William L. Davis—January 17, 1854
Charles Bunch—January 20, 1854
James Bunch, Sr.—January 20, 1854
Louisa Lloyd—January 22, 1854
Susana Davis—January 22, 1854
Spencer [Shelburne] Siner—January 23, 1854
James Bunch, Jr.—January 23, 1854
Sarah Bunch—January 23, 1854
Mahala Lloyd—January 23, 1854
Elizabeth Jewell—January 23, 1854
Elizabeth [Pound] Siner—January 24, 1854
Levina Payne—January 24, 1854

Sally Bunch
Matilda Lloyd
Lydia Jewell
Mary Jane McClanahan—January 25, 1854
Sally Bunch, Sen.
Ellen Lloyd—January 26
Zerilda McClannahan
Sabry Jewlin—February 18, 1854
Alfred Marlow
Sarah Taylor—September 16, 1854
Mahala Shelburn[e]
Elijah Shelburn[e]—July 1, 1856
Arkansas Shelburn[e]—July 1, 1856
Lucy A. Shelburn[e]—July 1, 1856
Amy Owens—March 3, 1857
Elizabeth J. McGrew—March 6, 1857
Sarah Rowland—March 7, 1857
Elizabeth E. Gardner—August 8, 1857
Nathaniel [?] Haden—August 8, 1857
[——]ah Haden—August 8, 1857
[——] [——]rts—April 5, 1857
[——] Cuppy—June 6, 1857
[——] Mckinney—June 6, 1857
[——] Cuppy—March 9, 1858
[——] [—]etunt [?]—March 12, 1858
[——] [——]ble—March 13, 1858
[——] [——]yd—March 13, 1858
Joseph [——]ble—March 14, 1858
John Lloyd—March 15, 1858
Campbell McKinney—March 15, 1858
Sebourn Kirkham—March 15, 1858
[——] Bardiaman—March 15, 1858
[——] Jewell—March 16, 1858
George R. Mckinney—March 15, 1858
Clifford Lloyd—March 21, 1858
Permelia J. Cox—March 25, 1858
Leavina Marten [?]—April 3, 1858
Stacil Smith—March 21, 1858

A. L. Skinner—January 9, 1866
Cynthia Skinner—January 9, 1866
Mary J. Higdon, Jr. (since Barnett)—January 9, 1866
Cordelia Taylor—January 11, 1866
Samuel McManis—January 11, 1866
Charlotte McManis—January 11, 1866
Mary McManis—January 11, 1866
Joan McManis—January 11, 1866
Mary J. McKinney—January 13, 1866
Minerva Marts—January 13, 1866
B. F. McManis—January 14, 1866
William Skinner—January 15, 1866
Rebecca Skinner—January 15, 1866
Joseph Bailey—February 3, 1866
George Haden—May 5, 1866
Phebe Hodges—September 1, 1866
Letha Emery Cuppy
[——] Julyan
Caroline Scott—April 4, 1868
Mary Marts
Mary G. Marts
Margaret Okes
Sarah Beasley
Margaret Bunch (since Johnson)
Rosy Carter
George Plew
Joshua Carter
Nancy Carter
Ephrim Beasley
Harriett Moore
Laura A. Moore
Emily B. Moore
Stephen P. Beard
Sarah E. Cuppy
Mary J. Carter
Nancy J. Beasly
Sarah E. Higdon (since Thompson)
Samira J. Marts
Huldah Baily
James H. Gardner—November 18, 1865
Louisa J. Taylor
Henrietta Lloyd

Bulah Thompson
William Bolinger—May 7, 1865
Victoria Bolinger—May 7, 1865
John Bolinger
Lizzy Hamilton
Ellen Hill—August 3, 1867
Ruth Lloyd—May 7, 1860
Rachael Scott
Nobel Scott
Bennett Payne
Martha A. Bunch
Synthia Bunch
James W. Thompson
Abel Warner—March 5, 1860
Sarah McCrosky
Samuel Okes
Charles Warner—March 9, 1860
Sarah Mcdonall
Preston Hazelrigg
Beulah Thompson
[——] Bunch, Jr.
Nancy J. Weaver—March 10, 1860
Sarah McGrew
Lorena Siner
John Okes
Harrison Osborn—March 11, 1860
William Warner
John L[awson] Siner—March 12, 1860
Stephen Bridwell
William McGrew
Benjamin Medonnall—March 17, 1860
Alexander Martin
Thomas J. Hazelrigg—May 5, 1860
Elizabeth Smith—May 20, 1860
Rebecca Smith—May 20, 1860
James Smith—May 21, 1860
Melinda Scott—March, 1861
Margaret Thompson—March, 1861
Flese [?] Odell—February 8, 1862
George Marlow—February 9, 1862
Asa Talor
Elizabeth Bunch
Sarah Marlow
F. [?] M. Mckiney
Teresa Okes—12
Manerva Plew
John Coffman
Sam. Tincher—15

Sarah Rowland—16
Sarah Parker—August 3
Sarah J. Case—August 17
Julian Marlow—August 17
Mary Ann Akers—August 20
Katherine Rusher—August 20
Sarah K. Rusher—August 20
Cena Rusher—August 20
Lucinda P. Bunch—August 21
Nancy Walters—August 21
Jackson Rich—August 22
Sarah A. Rich—August 22
John C. Rusher—August 22
Rebecca J. Osburn
Ransom Akers—August 25
Annis Dudley—August 30
James J. Walter [or Hatter]

Shelburn[e] Baptist Church
The Constituent Membership Record, May 7, 1870

Chloe Siner Morgan*

Little Flock Baptist Church, the first Baptist church in Sullivan County, was constituted in June, 1821. Not quite fifty years later, another Baptist church was established a mile distant; and in the course of the following three score years the later church absorbed the earlier. Little Flock Meeting House was built on the prairie and near the village named for the family of William Curry, who is reputed to have built the first cabin on Currys Prairie and started the village of Currysville, within the year that Indiana became a state and Sullivan a county. The wife of William Curry was said to be Clemsy Siner, one of the older daughters of Benjamin and Mary—"Polly" (Maladie or Mallady) Siner—, whose names appear on the Little Flock Record August 7, 1823—July 8, 1826. All efforts to trace the descendants of Clemsy have so far failed, though certain Currys living in Vigo County in later years are listed by historians of that county as descendants of the Curry from whom Currys Prairie took its name. However that may have been, not a single Curry name appears on the Little Flock membership list.

---

* The author of this sketch, Chloe Siner Morgan, is the wife of the late Professor William Thomas Morgan of Indiana University History Department. Mrs. Morgan's teaching experience has included an assistant professorship in the English departments of Indiana State Normal School, Iowa State Teachers College, and a lectureship in the École Normale des Institutrices, Blois, France. She has taught in Indiana University in recent years, and is now Faculty Research Fellow there in English History and Literature.

William in 1825 and 1826 bought land in Honey Creek Township, and evidently preceded his father-in-law into Vigo County. When Benjamin Siner died on his newly acquired farm in Pierson Township, near the site of Union Church, in September, 1826, Polly, as administratrix, presented an inventory of their personal effects and held a sale. Among the purchasers at this sale were William Curry and two other sons-in-law (Eli St. Clair and John Hodges), also two of the older Siner sons, James and Nelson. Nelson, who had married one of the numerous Shelburne family from Virginia, eventually returned to Currysville, where he established a stave factory and store, and became an early postmaster of Shelburn.

Nelson Siner's wife was Desdemona Shelburne, daughter of John Shelburne and Charlotte Wills (also given Charlotte Elizabeth Willis) of Virginia and Kentucky. Among the brothers of "Dessie" who came to Sullivan County, was a bachelor, Paschal, who in his later years buried his gold on one of his farms, then lost his eyesight and thereafter only the pigs were able to find it. But before this enterprising man had come to rest in Little Flock Cemetry, under the marble stone bearing the legend: "Paschal Shelburne, died January 29, 1872, aged 79 years, 8 months, and 28 days," he had founded a town bearing his name—wedged right in between the village of Currysville and Little Flock Church—; and approximately three years before his death he had assisted in constituting a church, Shelburne Baptist Church, within the town which he had founded. Some ten or fifteen years after Little Flock Church had celebrated its centennial, the members tore down their old Meeting House rather than rebuild it, and transferred their membership to Paschal Shelburne's Church within his town.

To those of us who are fifth generation descendants of the founders of Little Flock and third and fourth generation from the founders of Shelburne Church, looking back from the disinterested, historical perspective, the mystery of the existence of two missionary Baptist churches within a mile of each other has ever been inexplicable. Since a third successive building was under discussion in the spring of 1870, when the split occurred, this was likely the outward cause of the division. However, since an examination of the constituent members of the later church reveals that only the Jones', Taylors, Harbolts, Whites and Rileys are unrelated by descent or by "in-law" to the Shelburne, Siner, Hill, and Anderson families, one wonders if this newer church were not the "dream-child" of this aged man without descendants but with so great a family of heirs.

The following is the record of the withdrawal and the the founding:—

Shelburn, May 7, 1870.

According to previous appointment the Brethren and Sisters whose names follow met, being previously dismissed from Little Flock Baptist Church, and after Singing Prayer was offered by Rev. A. J. Riley: 1st, then organized by appointing Brother R[ichmond] B. Shelburn Moderator and J[ames] P[aschal] Siner Clerk.

2nd. then the following names were read for membership in this church.

By letter:

John C. Taylor,

Hardy Hill [m. 1st Mary Shelburne, sister of Paschal and founded the Sullivan County Hill family.]

Ally [Siner] Hodges Hill [daughter of Benjamin and Polly Siner m. 1st John Hodges; 2nd Hardy Hill, above.]

J[ames] P[aschal] Siner [son of Nelson and Desdemona. See sketch in T. J. Wolfe, *History of Sullivan County*, II, 103-4.]

Matte [Hodges] Siner [granddaughter of John and Ally (Siner) Hodges, and wife of J. P. Siner, above.]

E[lijah] W. Shelburne [great nephew of John Shelburne] married granddaughter of John Shelburne, Arkansas, daughter of Spencer.]

Arkansas Shelburn [wife of E. W., above, and sister of Tyrrene Florence Shelburne, first wife of Dr. Joseph Buskirk (originally Van Buskirk).]

B[enjamin] F[ranklin] Siner [son of Nelson and Desdemona.]

Louise [Patton] Siner [daughter of Wm. Patton, and wife of B. F. Siner, above.]

A. J. Riley [minister of Little Flock 1867-1869.]

Annie Riley [wife of above.]

Luella Cuppy [possibly the second wife of Dr. Joseph Buskirk, mentioned above. Dr. Buskirk was an early physican and druggist of Shelburn. By his first wife, Tyrrene Shelburne, he had several children, one of whom—Verne, Berne, or "Hibernia"—followed his father as owner of the drug and general store. He later went to Colorado, became a doctor and banker, and is reputed to have been the originator of the cantaloupe.]

D. C. Taylor

R[ichmond] B. Shelburn [son of John and Elizabeth (Bush) Shelburne. He and Malvina were the only children of Elizabeth Bush.]

Cindarilla [Pound] Shelburn [sister of Elizabeth (Pound) Siner, below, and wife of Richmond B., above.]

S[helbury] D[ale] Siner [son of Nelson and Desdemona. Cared for Paschal Shelburne in his later years.]

Sarah [McClannahan] Siner [sister of Joseph McClannahan. Wife of S. D. Siner, above.]

P[aschal] S[helburne] Hill [son of Hardy and Mary (Shelburne) Hill.]

Letticia M. [Cuppy] Hill [wife of Paschal, above.]

Paschal Shelburn [son of John and Charlotte (Wills) Shelburne, and founder of the town of Shelburn.]

Spencer S[helburne] Siner [son of Nelson and Desdemona, and grandfather of the author of this sketch.]

Elizabeth [Pound] Siner [wife of Spencer S., above. She was the granddaughter of Robert Anderson, Sr., and his wife, Sarah (Froment) Anderson, whose names appear as two of the eleven constituent members of Little Flock Church (1821). Her mother, Elizabeth Anderson, in 1818 married William Pound, son of Thomas and Sarah (Kester) Pound, all constituent members of Second Prairie Creek Church (1828), and earlier of First Prairie Creek Church constituted 1818—the first in Vigo County. Both Thomas and William were deacons and were constant participants in the Baptist activities of Vigo and Sullivan counties. Both Thomas Pound (b. July 28, 1767; d. Feb. 2, 1848) and his wife, Sarah Kester (b. June 24, 1767; d. Feb. 2, 1848) were descendants of "Old Main Line" families.

Thomas Pound of English descent, was the son of John and Sarah (Martin) Pound, whose ancestors were among the first settlers of Piscataway, New Jersey. Sarah Kester was a daughter of William Kester of Germantown, Pennsylvania, and Kingwood, New Jersey, by his second wife, Elizabeth Lacock, who had previously married a Thomas Ferguson and founded a numerous Ferguson family, some of whom later settled in Indiana. The progenitors of William Kester were among the first settlers of Germantown, Pennsylvania. They were of Dutch and Palatine German extraction, and their language was Holland Dutch. See, William Isaac Hull, *William Penn and the Dutch Quaker Migration to Pennsylvania*, 229-35. Three of the children of John and Sarah (Martin) Pound married three of the children of William and Elizabeth (Lacock Ferguson) Kester; and in their old, widowed age, Sarah (Martin) Pound, by that time the Widow Stiglar, married William Kester. Both at the time were living with their children in Kentucky, in the Elk Creek region, where certain of their descendants have remained to this day.

The founder of the Pound family in America came from England to New York or Long Island, and thence to Piscataway, New Jersey. He purchased land in both Piscataway, and in Woodbridge, but died in the former village, February 21, 1690. *John II*, son of John Pound I and his wife Winifred—, died in Piscataway, Middlesex County, New Jersey, 1752. *Thomas Pound*, son of John Pound II and his wife Esther—, was born July 18, 1708, and died between May and August 26, 1752, in Piscataway. This Thomas Pound had a brother (Elijah, born July 18, 1712), who became the ancestor of Dean Roscoe Pound of Harvard, and Professor Louise Pound of the University of Nebraska. Another brother was Joseph (born June 25, 1715.) See, *Compendium of American Genealogy*. John Pound III, son of Thomas Pound I, above, and his wife, Audrey——, was born at Piscataway, New Jersey, *ca.* 1735; and died *ca.* 1790. This John Pound first married Rhoda Cox, and had a son Hezekiah, who became a Revolutionary Soldier, and left descendants who later came to Indiana. John Pound III married, second, the Sarah Martin, previously mentioned, and had six more children, descendants of all of whom came to Indiana. These were the Pound great grandparents of Elizabeth (Pound) Siner of this sketch. This John Pound on July 12, 1770, sold the inherited home plantation in Piscataway, Middlesex County, and probably settled for a time in the adjoining county of Somerset; for it was from there that he served during the American Revolution. (John Pound's service record is as follows: "Official Records of New Jersey: Adjutant General-Revolutionary War Records. Ref. Militia, 2nd year, p. 204. Name: John Pound. Residence: County of Somerset, N. J. Received Certificate no. 1083, Voucher 76 for depreciation of his Continental pay in Somerset Co. Militia, dated May 10, 1784, signed by Wm. Verbryck. Amt.: 0:5:4. 2nd yrs. interest, 0:0:3.") Since conditions in New Jersey were not so happy after the Revolution as they had been previously, and because new promises were luring the Eastern pioneers to the South and West, John and Sarah(Martin) Pound moved with their children to the vicinity of Cumberland, Maryland; and in that region John died, and Sarah either there or in Kentucky, married a Stiglar, and later, as we have noted, William Kester, father-in-law to three of hers and John Pound's children. She and her third husband died in Kentucky.

The ancestry of Sarah Kester, daughter of William and Elizabeth (Lacock Ferguson) Kester is as follows: Paulus Kester and his wife, Geertruid (Streyper)—whose mother was an Isaacs Op den Graaf, which made Geertruid a cousin of Jan and Dirk Op den Graaf, friends of William Penn—followed Geertruid's brother, William Streyper, to Germantown as first settlers there. With them came their three sons. The second of the three was a Burgess of Germantown in 1707, and reputedly a surveyor for William Penn, from whom he received a large grant of land—lost to his heirs through the limitations law. This son, Johannes, married in 1692, Elizabeth Cassell, a daughter of Johannes Cassell, a Mennonite poet who came to Germantown in 1686.

A son of this couple, Paul (b. *ca.* 1700), married Ruth Kitchen, November 17, 1730 (Records Philadelphia First Presbyterian Church). Up to that time, the Kester family had been Quakers. Since Ruth and Paul died when their children were "quite young" the younger children, Rebecca, John, and possibly Samuel, went to Kingwood, New Jersey, to live with their uncle Hermanus. Later, William, the eldest, went there and on November 14, 1756, married his first cousin, Elizabeth Kester, for which they were doubtless expelled from the Kingwood Monthly Meeting. By this marriage, William had one son, Paul, who was a Revolutionary soldier. Elizabeth died, and about 1762, William married Elizabeth Lacock Ferguson, as previously mentioned. They had four children, one of whom was Sarah, who married Thomas Pound in 1786 in Maryland. And so the Pound and Kester families, ancesters of Elizabeth (Pound) Siner, were united, and one of the sons of Thomas and Sarah (Kester) Pound—William (b. June, 1790; d. July, 1870)—married the previously mentioned Elizabeth Anderson in 1818, and they became the parents of Elizabeth Pound (b. June 2, 1832; d. August 8, 1896). Elizabeth on December 25, 1849 (Vigo County Marriage License Records 1818—1850), married Spencer Shelburne Siner, nephew of the founder of Shelburne town and Shelburne Baptist Church.

On October 10, 1886, the elder son of Elizabeth and Spencer—John Hardy Siner (b. June 28, 1857; d. January 16, 1939) married Emma Estella McGarvey (b. October 27, 1866), only child of Ezekiel McGarvey by his third wife, Mary Ann Raines (b. February 14, 1826, at Frankfort, Ky.; married April 12, 1865; d. March 13, 1905), daughter of Margaret (Dampster) Raines and William Pendleton Raines, a soldier of the War of 1812. The author of this sketch is the only child of John Hardy and Emma Estella (McGarvey) Siner.

Since publishing the article: "Minute Book for the Christian Church on Busseron Creek: Record of the Christian Church at Palmers Prairie, Sullivan County, Indiana, 1827? 1831?," *Indiana Magazine of History*, March, 1951, in which appears a brief sketch of the Raines and McGarvey families, three importants facts have come to light. James H. McGarvey, former Sullivan County Auditor, grandson of Ezekiel McGarvey and his second wife, Martha Lou Rainey (Borders McKinley), has pointed out that *Andrew*, father of Ezekiel McGarvey, was a former owner of the land on which Sullivan County Courthouse now stands. Continued search for Andrew's birth and death dates have been without result; but since his name does not appear on the 1830 census, he must have died before that date. Further, a recent search through the Indiana Census Reports reveals that Ezekiel McGarvey was born in Kentucky, and not in Ireland, as family tradition dictated. Also, the minutes of Little Flock Church show proof that Busseron Church, later named Palmers Prairie, was in existence under the former name in 1828, and in friendly relationship with the Baptist churches of Vigo and Sullivan counties. This practically settles the date puzzle of the church. It was probably founded as *The Christian Church on Busseron Creek* in 1827, and changed to *The Christian Church of Palmers Prairie* in 1831, in honor of Henry D. Palmer, member of the House of Representatives of Indiana 1822-1823, and 1823-1824, and reputedly the first minister of the church in question. Palmer appears in the 1830 cenus but not in a later cenus of Sullivan County. (See article by Ray Wyman, on Henry Palmer, the Prairie, and the Church, Sullivan *Union*, October 21, 1937.)

The Little Flock Church minutes, referred to, are of August 8, 1828, and are concerned with the settling of a difficulty arising from the dissatisfaction of and with a constituent member. "The brethren appointed to bear letters to sister churches, requesting helpers reported they had discharged that duty and the following brethren appeared from Prairie Creek: Ebenezer Paddock, Thomas Pounds, Joseph Kester, William Pounds; from Fairbanks: James Drake, Joseph Ransford, Jr.; from Union: Joseph Liston, John Hodges, Abijah Thomas, Zachariah McClure; from Busseron: Brothers West and Simmons . . . . Therefore that brother——may have an opportunity to clear himself if the reports are unfounded . . . . The Church says she will send for helps to Union, Prairy Creek, Fairbanks and Busseron." This does not indicate that Busseron was a Baptist church. At the time and until 1830, when Alexander Campbell was expelled from the Baptist Association, friendliness and co-operation existed between the two denominations. The Vincennes *Western Sun* of September 25, 1830, carried the news that, "A Baptist Association held at Frankfort, Ky. have denounced the Reverend Alexander Campbell [Editor of the *Christian Baptist*] as a heretic, and excluded from communion all who hold his principles."

Of the Anderson ancestors of Elizabeth (Pound) Siner, the author knows little except that they were a Kentucky family, and some of them were Baptist preachers. J. Estelle Stuart King, *Early Abstracts of Wills and Inventories* (1933), includes one abstract that is very probably that of the ancestor of the Currys Prairie Anderson family: "Nelson County, Book A. 1784-1807, p. 181: Anderson, John,

Nov. 7, 1806 . . . 1807. John McGee to settle estate. Sons: John, Robert, James, Samuel, Archibald, David. Widow not named. Daughters: Mary, Jean, Elizabeth."]

Mary L[ucinda] Siner [eldest child of Elizabeth (Pound) Siner and Spencer Shelburne Siner, above; married James C. Redmond of Kansas, Illinois.]

John Riggs [probably the father of William Riggs who married Allie Hill, daughter of Paschal and Letticia Hill, above.]

Johanna Riggs [wife? of John, above.]

John H. Bolinger [brother of the late Charles Bolinger.]

Elizabeth [Siner] Bolinger, [wife of John H. Bolinger, above, and daughter of S. D. Siner and Sarah (McClannahan) Siner, above.]

Cordelia Taylor

Savanah Harbolt

Susa A. Cuppy

Phoebe (Lovelace) Hodges [widow of Harden Hodges, and mother of Matte (Hodges) Siner, above, and of Kate Hodges, wife of Adrian Beecher, a Terre Haute lawyer. Kate and Adrian's son Samuel, a former Terre Haute mayor, practices law in Terre Haute with his son, Samuel, Jr., as partner. Phoebe Hodges later married a Whitney.]

Mary A[lice] Siner [daughter of S. D. and Sarah Siner, above.]

Zerelda [Anderson] McClannahan [wife of Joseph McClannahan, and daughter of John and Elizabeth (Shelburne) Anderson. Elizabeth was a daughter of John and Charlotte (Wills) Shelburne. John Anderson was a son of Robert Anderson, Sr. and Sarah of the Little Flock constituent members, or a brother. The dates on the Anderson tombstones in Little Flock Cemetery would indicate the former relationship. They read: "Robert Anderson, d. July 4, 1835 in the seventy-third year. John Anderson, b. Dec. 5, 1794, d. March 12, 1865. Elizabeth, wife of John, d. Nov. 20, 1867, aged 67 yrs. 8 mo., 8 d."]

Melvina [Shelburne] Bennett [daughter of John Shelburne and his second wife, Elizabeth Bush. She and Richmond Shelburne, above, were half sister and brother to Paschal and the other Shelburne brothers and sisters. Melvina married Adonijah Bennett.]

John W[allace] Hill [son of Hardy Hill and his first wife, Mary Shelburne. He married Jane Russell, sister of Spencer Russell, and their son, Hardy Hill, married Rosella, below.]

Rosella [McClannahan] Hill [daughter of Joseph McClannahan and Zerelda (Anderson) McClannahan, above. The children of Rosella and this Hardy Hill, were descendants of two daughters of John and Charlotte (Wills) Shelburne: Mary and Elizabeth.]

Sarah A[nne] Shelburne [daughter of Richmond and Cinderilla (Pound) Shelburne.]

John Jones

Sarah Jones

C[hampion] S[helburne] Anderson [a son of John and Elizabeth (Shelburne) Anderson, above. His stone in Little Flock Cemetry gives his dates: "b. Nov. 2, 1829, d. June 19, 1918; w. Anne, 1836-1902." A brother, Samuel, d. May 2, 1844, aged 29 years.]

Ann Anderson [wife of Champion S. above.]

Amy F. Taylor

W[illiam] H. Bolinger [son of John and Elizabeth (Siner) Bolinger, above. He married Lola Bailey.]

Victoria Bolinger [sister of William H., above. Married Adam Miller.]

Caroline White

Desdemona [Shelburne] Siner [sister of Paschal Shelburne. See sketch of Nelson Siner, above. Before the Shelburn Baptist Church was constituted, Desdemona was a widow. Nelson had served as postmaster under Abraham Lincoln (1861-1865), keeping the post office in his store. One evening some of his neighbors and customers loafed about the store. Nelson, suspecting their purpose, and also suspecting them of membership in the Knights of the Golden Circle, was careful that they learned nothing. That night they broke into the home of Nelson and Dessie, demanding their money, and threatening to put hot irons to their feet, unless they disclosed its hiding place. They did not get the money, or carry out their dire threat. They took fright and fled, and were later arrested for this and other marauding. The names of these persons and others of their gang appear in a history of Sullivan County. The shock of that terrible night weakened the health of Nelson and his wife, and neither lived many years afterwards. Their stones in Little Flock Cemetry read: Nelson Siner, died February 6, 1868, 58 years, 9 months, 9 days. Desdemona Siner, d. February 7, 1872, 65 years, 8 months." Near them are the stones of their son Spencer and his wife: "Spencer S. d. January 8, 1882, 53 years, 5 months, 13 days. Elizabeth (1832-1896)." Her birth date was June 2, and she died August 8].

This ends the list of constituent members of Shelburn Baptist Church; but the minutes continue with the further account of the organization:—"3rd. Sister Nancy Riley presented a letter from First Prairie Creek Church. 4th. Brother H. H. Richards came forward and related his Christian experience. 5th. By motion the Secretary agreed to call this organization by the name of Shelburn Baptist Church. 6th. By motion and second, adopted the Articles of Faith, Rules of Decorum and Covenant as set forth in Hiscocks *Baptist Church Directory*. 7th. By motion and second, that we go into secret ballot for the election of one deacon. Brother E. W. Shelburn received the majority of the votes and was duly elected. 8th. By motion and second, we hold regular meeting on the Saturday before the fourth Sabbath in each month at 2 o'clock, P.M. 9th. By motion and second the clerk be instructed to write to the following Churches for a recognizing Council: Olive Branch, Little Flock, Mt. Zion, Union, New Harmony, Fair Banks, Sullivan, Hudsonville, Zion; and Rev. G. A. Russell, Hartz Smith, and P. W. Riley. 10th. By motion and second, the Clerk be instructed to post three notices for an election to elect three trustees on Saturday before the fourth Sabbath in May. 11th. Moved to adjourn. R. B. Shelburn, M.D., J.P. Siner, CLK."

The first meeting recorded "Singing Prayer," minutes, etc., May 21, 1870. And on July 23, 1870, the church appointed the following building committee: Bros, Hardy Hill, E. W. Shelburn, Paschal Hill. And motion was made to ask admission into Curries Prairie Association.

Before leaving this topic, the author would like to make several acknowledgements, and leave several thoughts in the minds of those who may see these pages. First, she wishes to acknowledge indebtedness to Charles Thompson, Shelburn attorney and banker, and present member of

Shelburn Baptist Church, who permitted her to copy the original records of Little Flock and Shelburn Baptist churches. Since the older Minute Book is too fragile for frequent use, it should be carefully mended in the modern invisible methods used by Indiana University librarians. Then it should be photostated with the same care, so that copies might be deposited in the Special Collections of Manuscripts in Indiana University, and in the Indiana State Library at Indianapolis. In both libraries these records would be open to any historian or descendant at any time, for further study and writing. Historians and genealogists are becoming ever more attentive to the fact that such church records, along with Bible records, wills, deeds, etc., are more precious than jewels as source material for state and church history, population movements, etc. They give much that census records do not, and are on the whole possibly more accurate, and complete; yet are constantly in danger from fire or other loss.

Second, she wishes to express appreciation for the help given by her Mother, in the way of identifying names and family relationships. As her constant guides on matters of family history she has drawn on notes which she has taken through many years, and especially she has leaned upon John E. Hunt, *The Pound and Kester Families* (Chicago, 1904), and upon William Isaac Hull's *William Penn and the Dutch Quaker Migration to Pennsylvania* (Swarthmore, 1935). She has also consulted other church records and histories of Sullivan and Vigo counties.

It is her hope to publish in the near future the Little Flock Church early membership list, and as much as is available of the genealogies of the descendants of John Shelburne of Virginia, brother of Augustine III, both of whom came to Kentucky, and later, heirs of both came into Indiana, and some to Texas, Colorado, and elsewhere. Any authentic data or traditions will be welcomed, whether on this family or on any of the other families mentioned. This Shelburne family—and incidentally, the correct spelling is with the *e* ending, despite the recently abbreviated form in place names—according to tradition in the branch which remains in Virginia, the Shelby County, Kentucky, branch, and the Indiana branch, is descended from Thomas Shelburne who came from Great Britian to Jamestown, Virginia, in 1607 as one of the "gentleman adventures," who paid with tobacco the passage of one of the young maidens sent over as wives for these early would-be colonists of America. There is also the tradition among all branches, that there was an estate in England or Ireland and a title, lost to the family, and a family coat of arms. Unless the Shelburne title conferred by James II was one revived from earlier times, rather than newly created, there appears to be but slight possibility of substantiating this thesis.

Among the connected families about which the author would welcome further information is that of the Ferguson family descendants of her great, great, great grandmother, Elizabeth (Lacock Ferguson) Kester. She would like also to know the name of Elizabeth's first husband, and if there were any descendants by this marriage. These questions have been raised by the following notes by A. R. Markle, prominent geanealogist of Vigo County families. These notes were published in the Terre Haute *Tribune*, October 4, 1931, as follows:

"197. Ferguson, William (1090). The Ferguson family of Vigo County, Indiana. The greater portion of them came from Thomas Ferguson and his wife Elizabeth, a widow when she married him, and as a widow she married again and help found the family of *Kesters*, pioneers of Vigo County. *Samuel Ferguson*, head of the second generation, born in 1758, married in 1779, had four children: Thomas, Athol, Nancy, and Leitha. He married (2) Elizabeth Blue and had eleven children: Mary, born in 1791; Samuel, born in 1799; Elizabeth, born in 1789, married Joseph Chambers in 1809; Sarah, born in 1793; Levina, born in in 1797; John, born in 1801; William, born in 1803; Malinda, born in 1806; James, born in 1808; Hosanna, born in 1810; Frank, born in 1813. Thomas, eldest son of Samuel (1), born in Maryland in 1780, married in Ohio, in 1808, Elizabeth Lee, and they had James, Anderson, Athol, John, Henry, Nancy, Mary, and Eliza, or Elizabeth. Athol, the second son of Samuel (1), born in Maryland in 1781, married Rebecca Paddock, who had become the "widow Paine," and they had Nancy, Mary, Levina, Julia Ann, Leitha, and William. *Nancy*, third child of Samuel (1), born in 1783, married *Ebenezer Paddock* and they were parents of the mother of the late William Riley McKeen [Terre Haute Banker]. Leitha, the fourth child of Samuel (1), born 1785, nothing known of her in Vigo County, probably that she married in Kentucky or Ohio and did not come with her parents in late 1816 [to Vigo County]. (Many of these lines are carried out and others of the Ferguson name in Vigo County mentioned, with marriages and dates.)" William Riley McKeen (b. in Vigo County, October 12, 1829) was the son of Benjamin (b. in Kentucky, January 1, 1803) and Leathy (Paddock) McKeen, who was born in Ohio. See sketch in H. C. Bradsby, *History of Vigo County, Indiana* (Chicago, 1891), 840.

Hunt, *The Pound and Kester Families*, 589 (Appendix P) sheds further light upon the Ferguson and Paddock familes of Vigo County: "Ebenezer Paddock came from Ohio to Indiana and was an early settler in Vigo County. His wife's name was Keziah Case. His children were: Henry, married Marium; William married Letha Ferguson, daughter of Athel Ferguson, and a niece of Nancy Ferguson, above named; Mary married Benjamin Harris; Rebecca married Elijah Payne, and then Athel Ferguson; Sarah married James Drake; Catherine married Jacob Maddox; Rhoda married Jesse Rozzel; Susan married James Thompson; Rachel was not married."

Hunt, *The Pound and Kester Families*, 82, 94, and 96, throws still further light on the Ferguson-Paddock connections. Two granddaughters of Thomas and Sarah (Kester) Pound married sons of John and Letha (Ferguson) Paddock, above. These were Sarah Kercheval, daughter of William Kercheval, son of Benjamin and Nancy (Pound) Kercheval, daughter of Thomas and Sarah (Kester) Pound, who married William (Ferguson) Paddock. Mary Jane Kercheval, sister of Sarah, married Athel Paddock. Bradsby, *History of Vigo County*, 208, lists the following Vigo County land entry, of September 21, 1825. Athel Ferguson to Thomas Ferguson 300 acres NW 1/4 of SW 1/4 of Section 2, and NW 1/4 of Section 11 Township North 10, Range West 10.

One William Ferguson became a member, on February 10, 1838, of Maria Creek Church near Vincennes. See Membership list: November, 1809-March, 1863. Other Fergusons: David, Sr., David, Jr., Stephen, Lucy, and Leah were members of Palmers Prairie Church.

Vevay Cemetery, Switzerland County

*Francis Jennings**

Midway between Cincinnati and Louisville high on the Indiana bank of the Ohio River and in the shadow of the beautiful hills of Switzerland County is the old town of Vevay settled by courageous Swiss men and women in 1813. Later others also crossed the ocean and made the weary trip to settle in the southern Indiana town. From the epitaphs in the Vevay cemetery, it is evident that many chose to spend the remainder of their life in the new country. Among the inscriptions here reproduced from the old section of the cemetery are the names of both foreign and native-born men and women.

John F. Dufour founder of Vevay Indiana born in Montrieux Switzerland May 15, 1783 came to the U.S. in 1801 he was married to Mary "Polly" Critchefield in Garrard Co Ky. They moved to the Territory of Indiana in 1809. He died in 1850

Mary Dufour his wife was Born in Surry Co. N C. in 1789 Died 1850

John Critchfield, a soldier of the Revolution Born in New Jersey 1752 he emigrated to North Carolina in 1763, to the Territory of Indiana in 1803 and died in 1841

John Dumont. Born in New Brunswick N.J. Jan 8, A.d. 1787 and married to Julia L. Corey in Greenfield N.Y. Aug 12, 1812 he settled in Vevay Indiana A.D. 1813, where he continued to reside until his death, which occurred Feb 2. 1871 He was a learned able and upright Lawyer a Capable, courteous and incorruptible [officer] a wise far-seeing patriotic Legislator who preferred the general weal, to his own popularity and through life a citizen of great public spirit. Devoted to the cause of education morality and freedom. He thus filled all the stations in life, to which he was called, with advantage to others and honor to himself.

Julia L Dumont his wife died Jan 2, 1857 aged 62 years

Martha Manvill mother of Julia L Dumont died June 2, 1849 aged 85 years

Linda wife of Wm Shaw. Daughter of James and Elizabeth Rous Born in Yorkshire, England Dec 6 1805. Died in Vevay, Indiana April 4, 1892

Daniel Dufour Born in Switzerland 1765 came to the U.S. in 1801 Died in 1855

Frances E. his wife Born in Switzerland 1765 came to the U.S. in 1801 Died in 1865

Samuel Protsman Born 1797 died 1875

---

* Francis Jennings is a resident of Vevay, Indiana.

Jemima Prostman Born 1806 Died 1872
Rev. J. D. Griffith Born in Switzerland County Indiana Dec 11, 1823 Died Jan 2 1905
Caroline Vernon Griffith Born in Stokes Co. N.C. Nov 3, 1827 Died Feb 23, 1908
Charles G. Boerner Born in Artern, Kingdom of Prussia, Germany 1827. Died 1900
F. L. Grisard Born in the Canton of Berne Switzerland 1803 came to Vevay Ind in 1818 died in 1881
Zellie Grisard Born in the Canton of Neuchatel Switzerland 1807 Came to Vevay Indiana in 1823 Died 1892
Jean Daniel Moreod Born in Switzerland, Europe 1769 Died 1838
Charles Amie Thieubaud, was Born in The Canton of Neuchatel, Switzerland in 1800 Died in 1871
Thomas Jager, a native of England. Died in 1870 aged 66 yrs 4 ms 27 ds
Ann E. wife of Julius Dufour and only Daughter of Jas. and Nancy Malin 1822 died 1856
Philip Bettens Died June 22, 1844 aged 35 years
Charlotte wife of Philip Bettens Died Dec 24, 1875. Aged 66 years
Henry Weales Born in London, England. Oct 9, 1824 Died June 7, 1904
Martha Weales Born in Chatham, England. Oct 7. 1827. Died Sept 14. 1897
Robert Le Clerc. Born in Detroit Michigan Aug 22, 1809 Died July 22. 1856
Ira A. Mendenhall. Died July 8, A.D. 1845 aged 16 years
Julius McMakin Died at Luna, Ark. Oct 20. 1877 aged 37. years
U. P. Schenck Born in the Canton of Neuchatel Switzerland May 16, 1811. Died in Vevay Ind Nov 16. 1884. Justine his wife Born in the Canton of Neuchatel May 29, 1809 Died in Vevay Indiana Feb. 17. 1889
Jesse Teats, Born in Adelphia Ross Co. Ohio June 19, 1816 Died Dec 17. 1868
Owen Todd. Died Dec 6, 1817 aged 55 years
Elisha Golay Born in Switzerland Europe Oct 17. 1783 Died April 30. 1866.
Susanne Golay his wife Born in Switzerland Europe. Oct 5. 1785. Died Dec 26. 1865. Both came to the U. S. in 1801
Henry Stucy Born in Canton Glarus Switzerland, Jany. 14. 1815. Died May 16. 1843
Afra Stucy, Born in Canton Glarus, Switzerland Dec. 22. 1815. Died Jany. 5. 1894
R. Stearman Died July 27, 1882. Aged 71 years
Levi B. Christie Died Aug. 28. 1877 aged 49 years
Ralph Brown Born Sept 29. 1808 Died Feb 14. 1899. Sarah Brown Sept 11. 1810. died March 6, 1897.
Samuel Ward. Born in Fulton Co. New York (Died) Jan 17. 1824— Aged 26 years
Frederick L. Thieubaud. Died Dec 24, A D. 1846 Aged 79 years. He emigrated from Switzerland A.D. 1817.

Honey Creek Monthly Meeting of Friends
Willard Heiss

It seems fitting in this centennial year of the Western Yearly Meeting of the Society of Friends that some account be given of one of its earliest monthly meetings. The oldest monthly meeting within the boundaries of Western Yearly Meeting is Lick Creek in Orange County, established in 1813; the second is Blue River in Washington County, established in 1815. The third oldest monthly meeting was Honey Creek in Vigo County, which was set off from Lick Creek Monthly Meeting and established September 9, 1820. At this time Honey Creek included all Friends that lived in central and western Indiana; as other monthly meetings were set up, the boundaries of Honey Creek were narrowed to western Indiana and eastern Illinois. On February 14, 1829, the meeting was laid down and the membership attached to Bloomfield Monthly Meeting. The reason for its discontinuance is not known; it has been stated that it was due to the Hicksite controversy, but there is no evidence of this in the minutes.

At the time of the opening of the meeting in Vigo County, two settlements are mentioned: "Honey Creek on the Wabash" and "the settlement on the west side of the Wabash," which was soon established as Union preparative meeting. Meetings set up under Honey Creek were as follows:

Turmins Creek meeting, indulged 1822; preparative 1826 and name changed to *Fairland* meeting. Located in Sullivan County.

Spring Creek meeting, indulged 1822. Location unknown.

Vermillion meeting, preparative and worship 1823; set off as a monthly meeting 1826. Located in Vermilion County, Illinois.

Leatherwood meeting, indulged 1826. Location unknown.

Elevatis meeting, preparative and worship 1826; set off as a monthly meeting 1827 and name changed to *Bloomfield*. Located in Parke County.

The exact location of the Honey Creek Meetinghouse is not known to this writer. Evan Hadley writes of it as being "on the Wabash south of Terre Haute." It was not until April, 1822, that trustees were appointed to hold title to the property. They were William Durham and Moses Hoggatt. Schools were conducted by the Honey Creek and Turmins Creek meetings as early as 1824.

The following records were compiled from a photostat of the Men's Minutes of the Honey Creek Monthly Meeting, September 9, 1820 to May 14, 1825, in the Genealogy Division, Indiana State Library; from the Women's Minutes, October 8, 1825 to February 14, 1829; and from loose pages containing marriage records and removals located at the meetinghouse of the Western Yearly Meeting at Plainfield, Indiana. The abbreviations are those commonly used in transcribing Quaker records.

ABBREVIATIONS

appt to comm	appointed to committee	mcd	marriage contrary to discipline
att mcd	attendance at a marriage contrary to discipline	mem	member
		misc	misconduct
cert	certificate	MM	Monthly Meeting
ch	children	mtg	preparative meeting
compl	complained of	rec	received
con	condemned	rem	removed
dt (s)	daughter (s)	req	request (ed)
dtd	dated	ret	return (ed)
dis	disowned	rocf	received on certificate from
gct	given certificate to		
jas	joined another society	rqct	request certificate to
m	marriage, married, marry	s (s)	son (s)
		w	wife

ABSTRACTS OF HONEY CREEK MARRIAGE RECORDS

10-?-1824 Joel Haworth & Susannah Haworth (this certificate missing)

1-19-1826 Aaron Stanley, Dover MM, Guilford Co., NC, son of Michael & Mary Stanley of the same place, to Mahala Stanley, dt of John & Elizabeth Stanley of Turmins Creek, Sullivan Co.

At Turmins Creek Meetinghouse. Witnesses:

Warmonious Akine	Anselm Hunt	Zimri Hunt
William Dicks	Mary Hunt Jr	Asher Hunt
Nathan Hunt	Mary Hunt	Jonathan Jessop
Anna Dicks	Anna Hunt	James Hunt
Anna Hunt	Elizabeth Dicks	William Hunt
R Davis	Hannah Wilson	Delana Stanley
J Riggs	Sarah Hunt	William Currey
Asael Hunt	Abner Hunt	Jesse Dicks
Solomon Hunt	Abigail Hunt	Joshua Dicks
Aaron Hoggatt	John Stanley	Elizabeth Dicks
Robert Hoggatt	Elizabeth Stanley	Elizabeth Hunt
		Gabriel Wilson

9-12-1827 Ezekial Rubottom, of Elevatis settlement in Parke Co. Ind., son of Simon & Elizabeth Rubottom, to Jane Coate, dt of William & Elizabeth Coate of the same place

At Elevatis Meetinghouse. Witnesses:

Mary Mote	Simon Rubottom	John Rubottom
Mary Hoggatt	Elizabeth Rubottom	Samuel Kelly
Hannah Wilson	William Coate	Samuel Rubottom
John Commons	Elizabeth Coate	Nathaniel Newlin
Thomas Rubottom	Ruth Reynolds	Mahlon Reynolds
Samuel Haworth	Mary Kelly	Jer. W. Siler
Warner Davis	Mahala Rubottom	Betty Holaday

10-17-1827 James Siler, son of Adam & Sarah Siler of Parke Co., Ind. to Hannah Newlin, dt of Nathaniel & Catherine Newlin of same place

At Elevatis Meetinghouse. Witnesses:

Thomas Carty	Nathan Hunt	Abraham Holaday
Duncan Newlin	Elizabeth Davis	Eleanor Newlin
John Newlin	Rebecca Davis	Mary Morrison
Thomas Woody	Abraham Hadley	Enoch Morrison
Hannah Wilson	Nathan Harvey	Jacob Newlin
Samuel Davis	John Marshall	Joseph Hadley
James Cox	Adam Siler	Thomas Rubottom
John Maris	Nathaniel Newlin	Samuel Haworth
Paton Wilson	Philip Siler	William Hunt
Ruth Harvey	Jer. W. Siler	Simon Rubottom
Enoch Kersey	Jacob Hoggatt	

FAMILY REFERENCES IN RECORDS OF
HONEY CREEK MONTHLY MEETING

ALLEN
7-14-1827 Amy & dt Emily rocf Greenplain MM, O, dtd 4-4-1827

ARNOLD
8-14-1824 Raiford, Joseph & s Michael rocf Contentney MM, NC, dtd 3-8-1823; endorsed to Blue River MM

ATKINSON
1-13-1829 Rebecca Crow (formerly Atkinson) rqct Lick Creek MM; 2-14-1829 as mtg was laid down & she having removed, Lick Creek requested to treat with her

BALEY
9-9-1820 Benjamin appt to comm

BARNARD
3-12-1825 Frederick rocf Fall Creek MM, O, dtd 2-21-1824
1-13-1827 Mary rocf [Fall Creek MM, O] dtd 12-24-1826 & directed to Vermillion MM, Ill.

BARNETT
10-8-1825 Betty rocf Dover MM, O, dtd 8-6-1825

BENNETT
2-14-1824 James, of Honey Creek mtg, received on request

BIRKBECK
1-10-1824 Elizabeth, Prudence, Bradford & Charles rocf Guilford MM, Surrey Co., England, dtd 4-12-1818 (copy of original certificate states, "being removed to English Prairie, Illinois Territory," and is addressed to Whitewater MM; there is no notice in that record)

BISHOP
7-12-1828 Ruth & dt Celia rocf Contentney MM, NC, dtd 3-8-1828

BRAY
1-12-1822 John H rocf Lick Creek MM, dtd 11-24-1821

BROWN
7-8-1826 Mary & dts gct White Lick MM

BUCKNER
1-12-1822 Henry, Union mtg compl for mustering; 3-9-1822 dis
6-10-1826 Patsey con att mcd
6-14-1828 Martha compl for att mcd; 9-13-1828 dis

CANADAY
2-9-1822 Henry & ss Frederick & William rocf Springfield MM, Ind., dtd 7-2-1822
6-8-1822 Henry & family gct Lost Creek MM, Tenn.
10-9-1824 Benjamin, Springfield MM req this mtg to treat for mcd; 12-2-1825 con his misc & Springfield MM informed
11-13-1824 Henry & family, who was gct Lost Creek MM, Tenn. & cert was lost, has since ret & settled in this mtg

CASY
9-8-1827   Lavina rocf West Branch MM, O, dtd 4-21-1827
COATE
3-10-1827   Elizabeth & dts Jane, Sally & Elizabeth rocf Union MM, O, dtd 9-2-1826
9-12-1827   Jane m Ezekial Rubottom (see abstract of m cert)
COOK
2-11-1826   Rebecca & dts Mary & Anna rocf Silver Creek MM, dtd 11-26-1825
6-10-1826   Kezia & dts Rebecca, Mary, Elizabeth & Sally rocf Silver Creek MM, dtd 4-22-1826
COONROD
7-8-1826   Rebecca, Union mtg compl for mcd; 9-9-1826 dis
COOPER
5-12-1827   Elizabeth, Horsham MM, Pa., req this mtg to treat for mcd; 2-9-1828 visited with no satisfaction, Horsham informed; 7-12-1828 dis rec from Horsham MM
COX
10-14-1820   John appt overseer at Honey Creek mtg
7-14-1821   John appt treasurer of MM
7-13-1822   William, Honey Creek mtg, compl for mcd & mustering; 11-9-1822 con his misc
3-13-1824   Isaac & ss Richard Albertson & Isaac Parker rocf Contentney MM, NC, dtd 3-8-1823; endorsed to Driftwood MM
12-11-1824   Richard rocf New Garden MM, NC, dtd 8-28-1824
7-8-1826   Mary & dts Mary, Elizabeth, Orpha & Charlotte rocf Contenteny MM, NC, dtd 4-12-1823
8-12-1826   Mary gct Driftwood MM
10-14-1826   Charity & dts Susannah & Mary rocf ———— & endorsed to Vermillion MM
6-9-1827   Ruth & Mary, minor dts of David, rocf Miami MM, O, dtd 1-24-1826
4-12-1828   Deborah, Union mtg compl for mcd
12-13-1828   Zilpha appt overseer at Union mtg
CROW
9-9-1820   Reuben appt to comm
4-14-1821   Joshua appt to comm
7-14-1821   Elizabeth disowned
7-12-1823   Joshua appt overseer at Union mtg in room of Jesse Reynolds
2-12-1825   Joshua gct Lick Creek MM
1-13-1829   Rebecca, *see* Atkinson
DAVIS
5-13-1826   Milly & dts Alice, Elizabeth, Jane, Caroline, Irena, Rumina & Ruhama rocf Lick Creek MM, dtd 4-15-1826
9-8-1827   Elizabeth rocf Exeter MM, Pa., dtd 5-30-1827
                Rebecca & Lydia, minor dts of Joseph, rocf Exeter MM, Pa., dtd 5-30-1827

DAWSON
8-10-1822   John & Daniel Jr rocf Lick Creek MM, dtd 7-27-1822
6-12-1824   John gct Lick Creek MM (already removed)
             Daniel Jr, Union mtg compl for horse racing and fighting; 10-9-1824 Lick Creek MM req to treat with him; 11-13-1824 he has since ret within this mtg; 12-11-1824 dis
5-14-1825   Daniel rocf Lick Creek MM, dtd 3-19-1824

DILLON
2-11-1826   Gulielma rocf Springfield MM, O, dtd 9-24-1825 & endorsed from Milford MM

DIX—DICKS
3-10-1821   Joshua & s Jesse, William & s Eli, Seth rocf New Garden MM, NC
9-12-1823   Joshua "expressed a prospect he had of visiting his children & friends in his native country on his lawful concerns & social affairs, this meeting therefore thinks proper" to grant him a cert
5-8-1824   William (Dicks) appt overseer at Turmins Creek mtg in room of Asher Hunt
12-11-1824   Job (Dicks) rocf New Garden MM, NC, dtd 8-28-1824
12-10-1825   Elizabeth (Dicks) appt to comm
11-11-1826   Hannah appt overseer at Turmins Creek mtg

DRAPER
5-12-1827   Nancy, Union mtg compl for att mcd; 9-8-1827 dis

DURHAM
9-9-1820   William appt clerk for day of opening of MM
3-10-1821   Thomas rocf Newberry MM, Blount Co., Tenn., dtd 1-4-1817
10-13-1821   Thomas gct Lick Creek MM to m
1-11-1823   Daniel rocf Newberry MM, Tenn., dtd 11-2-1822
3-8-1823   William H con his mcd
5-8-1824   Daniel appt overseer in room of Joseph Noblitt
1-14-1826   Jane appt to comm
3-11-1826   Jane con her mcd
3-8-1828   Jane appt overseer at Honey Creek mtg

EVANS
1-12-1822   Daniel, Union mtg compl for mustering; 3-9-1822 dis
2-14-1824   Willis, Union mtg compl for fighting & mcd; 7-10-1824 dis
2-12-1825   Calvin rocf New Garden MM, NC, dtd 7-31-1824
6-10-1826   Elizabeth, Anna & Abigail con att mcd
5-12-1827   Rachel & Nancy, compl for att mcd; 9-8-1827 dis
6-14-1828   Elizabeth & Abigail, compl for att mcd; 9-13-1828 dis

FERRIL
8-14-1824   Rebecca dis

FORSTER
2-10-1821   William rocf New Garden MM, NC, dtd 7-29-1820; endorsed by Lick Creek MM

3-10-1821 William, Honey Creek mtg compl for mcd; 5-12-1821 con his misc; 3-9-1822 compl for taking too much strong drink and for offering to fight; 5-11-1822 dis

GREEN
4-8-1826 Hannah compl of for dancing & deviating from plainness of dress; 7-8-1826 dis

GUIRE
6-2-1821 Axiom, con his mcd; 7-12-1823 appt overseer at Union mtg

HAMILTON
12-13-1828 Gulielma con her mcd

HANDY
8-14-1824 Jane dis

HARRISON
10-14-1820 Henry appt overseer at Union mtg

HASKET
12-8-1821 Ralph, Union mtg compl for mcd & mustering; 3-9-1822 dis

HAWORTH
3-10-1821 Jeremiah & ss Barnabas & Thomas rec on req
12-8-1821 Jonathan & s David rocf Lost Creek MM, Tenn., dtd 4-29-1820; endorsed by Silver Creek MM, Ind., dtd 3-10-1821
12-8-1821 Richard rocf ———, dtd 12-9-1820
3-9-1822 John & ss Mourman, George, Mahlon, John, Allen & Harmon rocf Center MM, O, dtd 8-18-1821
6-14-1823 James & ss George, Jonathan, James, Eli, Mahlon & William rocf Center MM, O, dtd 10-19-1822
9-13-1823 John & ss Joel, Thomas, David, Calvin & James rocf Silver Creek MM, dtd 12-16-1822
12-13-1823 Richard appt overseer at Vermillion mtg
9-11-1824 Joel & Susannah Haworth declared intention to marry; 10-9-1824 given liberty to marry; 11-13-1824 marriage reported
1-8-1825 Samuel & ss Job, Moses, Josiah & Samuel rocf Springfield MM, NC, dtd 12-10-1823
10-8-1825 Joann rocf Center MM, O, dtd 2-18-1825

HENDERSON
2-11-1826 Annas & Asenith rocf Silver Creek MM, dtd 11-26-1825

HOGGATT—HOCKETT
9-9-1820 Moses appt to comm
3-10-1821 Deborah appt elder
4-14-1821 Robert appt to comm
4-12-1823 Robert gct Lick Creek MM to m Mary Johnson
8-14-1824 Moses appt elder
11-13-1824 Jacob (Hockett) rocf Center MM, NC, dtd 9-18-1824

12-11-1824   Aaron con his taking too much strong drink
1-14-1826   Deborah appt to comm
3-10-1827   Mary rocf Lick Creek, MM, dtd 2-17-1826
10-12-1827   Ann rocf Springfield MM, dtd 4-11-1827; endorsed from White Lick MM

HOLLADAY
9-9-1820   Robert appt to comm
11-13-1824   Robert appt overseer at Union mtg in room of Joshua Crow
9-8-1827   Elizabeth appt to comm
12-13-1828   Margaret appt overseer at Union mtg

HOLLINGSWORTH
11-10-1821   Thomas rec by req
———   James & w Rachel & ch George, Ruth, Sarah, Jonathan, James, Eli, Mahlon, Susanna & William rocf Center MM, O, dtd 10-19-1822

HUCKABY
5-10-1823   Lewis, Lick Creek MM req this meeting to treat with him for mcd; 6-14-1823 con his misc, Lick Creek informed; 9-11-1823 rocf Lick Creek MM, dtd 6-28-1823
5-14-1825   Lewis & w gct Lick Creek MM

HUNT
3-10-1821   Anselm, Abner & ss Solomon, Phineas & Elihu, Zimri & ss Nathan & William rocf New Garden MM, NC
6-2-1821   Asher & ss Elihu, Eri & Ira rocf New Garden MM, NC, dtd 2-24-1821
8-11-1821   Asher appt overseer at Turmins Creek mtg
11-13-1824   William rocf New Garden MM, NC, dtd 7-31-1824
12-10-1825   Ann appt to comm
1-14-1826   Jane appt to comm
5-13-1826   Mary appt to comm

JEFFCOAT
10-8-1825   Rebecca appt to comm

JENNY
4-12-1828   Jane, Union mtg compl for mcd & permitting it in her home and supporting a hireling minister; 8-9-1828 con her misc

JESSUP
8-11-1821   Jonathan rocf New Garden MM, NC, dtd 10-28-1820; endorsed by New Garden MM, Ind.
9-8-1821   Jonathan con his mcd
10-12-1827   Hannah, Elevatis mtg compl for mcd; 1-12-1828 dis

JOHNSON
4-?-1827   Anna compl for mcd; 6-9-1827 dis

JONES
 1-14-1826 Mary appt to comm
 1-13-1827 Mary rocf Springfield MM, dtd 8-26-1826

KELLY
 5-13-1826 Mary rocf Union MM, O, dtd 4-1-1826
 10-12-1827 Esther, Mary & Rhoda rocf Union MM, O, dtd 8-4-1827

LACY
 12-8-1821 Evans, Union mtg compl for mcd; 3-9-1822 dis

LAYWOOD
 5-12-1827 Achsah, Union mtg compl for mcd; 9-8-1827 dis

LEWIS
 2-11-1826 Martha rocf Silver Creek MM, dtd 11-26-1825
 6-10-1826 Judith & dts Rachel & Mary rocf Silver Creek MM; endorsed from White Lick MM
 6-10-1826 Anna & dts Maryann & Martha rocf Silver Creek MM, dtd 4-22-1826

LINDLEY
 9-14-1822 Thomas & ss Abraham, William, John & Morton rocf Lick Creek MM, dtd 8-31-1822
 4-12-1825 Jane appt to comm

LINNEY
 7-8-1826   Margaret, Union mtg compl for mcd; 9-9-1826 dis

LOWDER
 3-10-1827 Rachel rocf Lick Creek MM, dtd 2-17-1827

MARDOCK
 7-12-1823 Isaac, a minor, rocf Cherry Grove MM, Ind., dtd 11-14-1822

MARIS
 12-9-1826 Sarah & dts Eleanor Chambers, Katherine, Jane, Rebeccana & Martha Lindley & her grdt Sarah Jane Maris, rocf Lick Creek MM

MENDENHALL
 9-14-1822 William rocf West Branch MM, O, dtd 10-20-1821

MILES
 1-14-1826 Edith compl for mcd; 3-11-1826 dis
 1-12-1828 Mary con her mcd

MILLS
 4-10-1824 John & ss William, Ira, Millikan & John Marshall rocf Lost Creek MM, Tenn., dtd 4-27-1822

MORRIS
 6-14-1823 Eli con his mcd
 12-10-1825 family of Eli given certificate

MORRISON
 11-11-1826 Mary rocf Spring MM, NC, dtd 8-26-1826

MOTE
    12-9-1820   Jeremiah appt to comm
    7-14-1821   William appt to comm
    3-9-1822   David & ss Smith, Zeno, Markus & Linus rocf West
                 Branch MM, O, dtd 10-20-1821
    6-8-1822   William appt overseer at Honey Creek mtg
    10-12-1822   Joseph & family gct West Branch MM
    12-14-1822   Isaiah con his taking too much strong drink
    [6-11-1825] Aaron gct West Branch MM, O (already rem)
    6-10-1826   Sarah compl for att mcd & jas; 9-9-1826 dis

MUSGRAVE
    10-14-1826   Arcada & dts Laricy & Sally Ann rocf Contentney MM,
                 NC, dtd 3-11-26
    6-14-1828   Avis & dts Elizabeth, Rebecca & Charity rocf Contentney
                 MM, NC, dtd 2-9-1828

NEWLIN
    9-9-1820   John appt to comm
    7-14-1821   Nathaniel and William, Union mtg compl for mcd;
                 9-8-1821 dis
    2-12-1825   Jonathan, Union mtg compl for mcd
    11-11-1826   Ruth, Katharine & dts Hannah, Eleanor & Ruth, Sarah &
                 dt Sinai rocf Spring MM, NC, dtd 8-26-1826
    10-17-1827   Hannah m James Siler (see abstract of m cert)

NOBLITT
    9-9-1820   Joseph appt to comm; 2-8-1823 appt overseer at Honey
                 Creek mtg

PEMBERTON
    10-12-1827   Elizabeth & dts Esther, Susannah, Rhoda & Tace Eleman
                 rocf Union MM, O, dtd 9-1-1827

PERVO
    8-12-1826   Jane rec by req

PICKARD
    4-9-1825   William A rocf Lick Creek MM, dtd 10-20-1824
    2-10-1827   Mary appt overseer at Elevatis mtg

PITMAN
    7-12-1823   James & family rocf Deep River MM, NC, dtd 7-5-1821
    10-14-1826   Judith appt to comm

POSTGATE
    1-13-1827   Charity & dt Rachel rocf ——— & directed to Vermillion
                 MM

REYNOLDS
    9-9-1820   David and Jesse appt to comm
    10-14-1820   Mahlon appt clerk of men's mtg; Jesse appt overseer at
                 Union mtg
    3-10-1821   David and Ann appt elders

1-8-1825	Mahlon gct White Lick MM to m
1-14-1826	Ann appt to comm
9-9-1826	Welmet appt to comm
12-8-1827	Rachel appt to comm

RUBOTTOM
2-10-1827	Elizabeth appt overseer at Elevatis mtg
9-12-1827	Ezekial m Jane Coate (see abstract of m cert)

RUNDOLS
5-13-1826	Rachel appt clerk of women's mtg

SHATTOCK
4-12-1828	Sarah, Honey Creek mtg compl for mcd; 6-14-1828 dis

SILER
1-8-1825	Adam & s James, Jeremiah & s Enos C rocf Lick Creek MM, dtd 10-16-1824
10-17-1827	James m Hannah Newlin (see abstract of m cert)

SPENCER
5-12-1827	Mary & infant dt Frances rocf Horsham MM, Pa., dtd 8-30-1826

SPIVY
5-14-1821	Axiom con his mcd
6-10-1826	Milly con att mcd
5-10-1828	Ormely, Union mtg compl for using profane & unbecoming language; 9-13-1828 dis

STANLEY
3-12-1825	John & ss Wiatt, Milton & Harmon rocf Dover MM, NC, dtd 8-21-1824 [1825] Aaron rocf [Dover MM, NC]
1-19-1826	Aaron m Mahala Stanley (see abstract of m cert)
7-14-1827	Delana appt to comm

STEVENSON
10-14-1820	Mahlon appt overseer at Honey Creek mtg
8-14-1824	Mahlon & Ruth appt elders

TAILOR
7-8-1826	Naomey, Union mtg compl for mcd; 9-8-1827 dis

THOMAS
9-8-1821	Stephen & s Daniel rocf Lick Creek MM, dtd 7-28-1821

THOMPSON
3-9-1822	Joseph & ss Isaac, Israel & Joseph rocf Elk MM, O, dtd 2-2-1822

THORNTON
3-12-1825	Thomas & William rocf Silver Creek MM, dtd 1-10-1824; Isaac rocf Silver Creek MM, dtd 8-21-1824
6-10-1826	Katurah rocf Silver Creek MM, dtd 3-25-1826

WATSON
5-12-1827   Rachel con her mcd

WELLS
10-13-1821 Nathan, Union mtg compl for mcd; 2-29-1822 con his misc
9-14-1822   Nathan, Union mtg compl for mustering; 11-9-1822 dis
5-12-1827   Susannah, Union mtg compl for att mcd; 9-8-1827 dis

WILLARD
9-9-1820   Joseph appt comm
9-14-1822   Joseph Jr, Union mtg compl for mcd; 11-9-1822 dis
9-11-1824   Daniel con his mcd
11-12-1825 Penina appt to comm

WILLIAMS
3-8-1823   James & w Julianna & ch Peggy, George, Isaac, Mary, Boaz, Belinda & Dirias rocf Springfield MM, Ind., dtd 9-11-1822
10-8-1825   Arabella appt to comm
6-14-1828   James & ch Peggy, George, Isaac, Mary, Boaz, Malinda (or Belinda), Darius (or Dirias), Ahava & Cynthia gct White Lick MM

WILSON
1-12-1822   Gabriel, Honey Creek mtg compl for mcd; 5-11-1822 dis
3-12-1825   Paton & ss William & Samuel rocf Lick Creek MM, dtd 9-18-1824
1-14-1826   Hannah appt to comm

WRIGHT
7-13-1822   Joshua & w Rebecca & ch Sarah, Isaac, Jonathan, Betsy, Matilda, Jesse & Polly rocf Fall Creek MM, O, dtd 9-22-1821
6-14-1823   Joshua & family gct Newberry MM, O.

Washington County Cemetery Records

Hardin Cemetery Records

Copied by LOIS BROWN CARTER

Aaron Hardin[1]—b. Dec. 17, 1789; d. June 17, 1855.
Sarah (Consort of Aaron Hardin)—b. Feb. 7, 1787; d. May 11, 1863.
Alberter [sic] L. Hardin—b. June 6, 1818; d. May 27, 1843.
Matilda Kelso (Consort of P. D. Kelso)—d. May 29, 1839.
Matilda (daughter of P. D. and M. Kelso)—d. June 10, 1843; age 4 yrs.
Leander Hardin—b. July 24, 1816; d. September 29, 1839.
Mary E. Hardin—b. May 13, 1823; d. August 18, 1827.
John F. Hardin (son of J. M. and M. C. Hardin)—b. Dec. 17, 1860; d. Jan. 21, 1861.
Aaron H. Schoonover (son of R. and M. Schoonover)—b. Oct. 12, 1835; d. Jan. 15, 1856.
Matilda E. Schoonover (dau. of P. and M. Schoonover)—b. June 11, 1844; d. May 11, 1845.
Andrew J. Hardin—b. Oct. 17, 1824; d. Oct. 18, 1865.
A. J. and M. Hardin (twin daughters)—b. Sept. 25, 1856; d. Oct. 23, 1856.
Aaron Leatherwood Hardin—b. Nov. 19, 1825; d. April 27, 1896.
Virginia Ann Patton Hardin (wife of A. L. Hardin)—b. Feb. 7, 1826; d. Feb. 6, 1900.
Mary Louisa Hardin Coombs—b. Sept. 21, 1848; d. Feb. 28, 1924.
William Preston Hardin (son of A. L. and B] Hardin)—b. Sept. 21, 1855; d. August 7, 1856.
Frank L. Hardin—b. May 23, 1857; d. Mar. 11, 1872..
Infant (son of Aaron L. and Virginia Ann Hardin)—b. and d. Aug. 12, 1847.
Albert McClellan Hardin[2]—b. July 1, 1862; d. Sept. 11, 1865.
David P. Hardin—b. July 1, 1862; d. July 4, 1862.
Harley H. Hardin—b. April 27, 1869; d. Sept. 25, 1874.
Aaron E. Hardin—b. Feb. 17, 1853; d. April 6, 1935.
Sallie F. Hardin (wife of A. E. Hardin)—b. April 10, 1853; d. April 13, 1906.
Rene C. Hardin—b. 1891; d. 1917.

[1] Aaron Hardin founded Hardinsburg, Indiana, in 1838. The Centennial anniversary of the following was observed in Aug. 16-17, 1938.
The Hardin Family Cemetery is located in Madison Township, Washington County, Indiana. In addition to members of the Hardin family, some neighbors and friends were buried in the Hardin Cemetery. The burial ground was recently enclosed by a strong wire fence, which was erected by descendants of the Hardin family. Mrs. Lois Brown Carter, who copied the records, is a granddaughter of Aaron L. and Virginia (Patton) Hardin.

[2] Albert McClellan Hardin and David P. Hardin were twins.

Lorenzo M. Hardin[3]—b. 1901; d. 1920, in Germany; Bugler Co. A, Fifth Infantry, Second Brigade of American Forces.

Margaret E. Cravens (daughter of J. A. and S. Cravens)—b. May 7, 1846; d. Nov. 23, 1848.

J. A. Cravens[4]—b. Nov. 4, 1818; d. June 21, 1893; age 74 years, 7 months, 17 days; "Served in Mexican War, in State Senate, and in Congress."

Susan E. Cravens—d. Feb. —, 1895; age 71 years, 5 months, 18 days.

Sarah A. Cravens—b. Dec. 26, 1856; d. August 3, 1876; age 19 years, 7 months, 7 days.

John Cravens[5]—d. Nov. 15, 1879, age 83 years, 7 omnths, 12 days.

Nancy Elizabeth (daughter of Washington and Mary Hislip)—d. June 3, 1863; age 4 years, 8 months, 11 days.

Mary Ida (daughter of Washington and Mary Hislip)—d. Mar. 18, 1871; age 6 years, 2 months, 8 days.

Martha J. Davis[6]—b. Oct. 27, 1861; d. Nov. 26, 1862.

James E. Davis—b. July 27, 1859; d. Sept. 3, 1862.

Charles R. Ellis—b. Oct. 4, 1819; d. Jan. 24, 1861.

Sarah E. Ellis (wife of C. R. Ellis)—b. July 18, 1828; d. April 4, 1862.

Sarah M. Ellis—d. Oct. 9, 1878; age 25 years, 26 days.

William A. Ellis—d. June 17, 1876; age 24 years, 10 months, 14 days.

A. Coulsen Ellis (son of S. G. and F. B. Ellis)—d. September 16, 1887.

Ballard Lond—d. Nov. 6, 1851; age 6 years, 11 months, 3 days.

Elizabeth K. Bogle (wife of John G. Bogle)—d. June 14, 1884; age 59 years, 7 months, 18 days.

Jane (wife of Samuel J. Hagens)—d. January 17, 1828; age 34 years, 11 months, 17 days.

Sarah Suddith—b. 1841; d. 1869.

John A. Roll (son of John and Sarah Roll)—d. Nov. 21, 1867; age 8 years, 2 months, 17 days.

Simeon (son of J. and Sarah Roll)—d. September 15, 1855; age 6 years, 7 months.

---

[3] Lorenzo McIntosh Hardin's name was placed on the Gold Star Honor Roll. *Indiana World War Records: Gold Star Honor Roll* (Indianapolis, 1921), 691. He is classed as a bugler. His record follows:

"Son of Aaron E. and Sarah McIntosh Hardin; born June 12, 1901, Madison Township, Washington County, Ind. Farmer. Entered service September 1, 1919, Louisville, Ky. Trained at Camps Taylor, Ky., and Meade, Md., assigned to Company H, 5th Infantry. Sailed over seas October 17, 1919. Died of pneumonia January 2, 1920, Base Hospital, Coblenz, Germany. Body returned, and buried in Hardin Family Cemetery, near Hardinsburg, Ind."

[4] James A. Cravens of Hardinsburg served two terms in the national House (1861-1865).

[5] Near the grave of John Cravens is a small stone with the initials "J. C.," but nothing more.

[6] Martha J. Davis and James E. Davis were children of Joseph M. and D—— Davis.

Providence Methodist Church Cemetery[1]

Hugh Sherwood, 1770-1846.
Rebecca Sherwood, 1772-1852.[2]
Edward Mulvany, 1903-1906
Albert Mulvany Indiana Pvt. 4 U.S. Art.—Nov. 6, 1921
Marion Cooper—Born Apr. 22, 1837—Died May 17, 1902
Andrew A. H. May—Born July 3, 1886—Died July 24, 1902—Aged 16 Yrs.
Eliza J. Cooper—Died July 20, 1850—Born Feb.-, 1802
Clyde H. Mattox—Born July 3, 1886—Died Sep. 26, 1888
Amela Mattox—Born Feb. 13, 1840—Died Apr. 5, 1870—Aged 20 Yrs.
Thomas Hunt—Killed Dec. 21, 1906—Aged 23 Yrs. 5 Mo.
Leonard H. May—Born Feb. 23, 1846—Died Apr. 5, 1845
James W. Buchanan [no dates]
Wm. F. Mattox—Born Mch. 9, 1873—Died Mch.-, 1902
Matilda Mattox—Born Apr. 11, 1827—Died [date not inscribed]
Valentine Mattox—Born Dec. 3, 1825—Died Feb. 5, 1902
Joseph Matton—Born May 7, 1859—Died Nov. 16, 1901
Missouri Mattox—Born July 18, 1854—Died July 12, 1927—Aged 73 Yrs.
Corneleson [large stone]
    Cora M. 1878-1909
    Ira W. 1896-1913
Francis L.—Son of Wm. & Muhulda Buchanon—Born Sep. 4, 1851—Died Aug. 5, 1856
Sarah—Wife of Newton Collins—1845-1926
Emily Hollowell—Born Dec. 29, 1823—Died June 10, 1899
Wm. Hollowell—Born Mar. 4, 1823—Died July 27, 1904
James M. May—Aug. 24, 1856—Died May 29, 1913
Robert May—Born Aug. 27, 1880—Died June 29, 1906.
Maria—Wife of J. S. May—June 12, 1843-Oct. 17, 1901
John S. May—Born Oct. 19, 1841—Died Apr. 5, 1902
Andrew J. May—Aug. 24, 1856—Died May 29, 1913
Hannah May—Born Mar. 14, 1818—Died Jan. 24, 1884
James M. May—Born Nov. 26, 1815—Died Apr. 16, 1899
William T. May—Sep. 19, 1835—Died Aug. 7, 1912
Clara A. May—Oct. 22, 1840—Feb. 12, 1919
Charley V. May—Son of J. M. & E. A. Tarr—1909-1912
Minnie Marshall—[no dates]
John Marshall—1842-1912
Mary A. Marshall—1844-1912 ....

---

[1] This Cemetery is in Madison Township, Washington County, Ind. It is a part of Section 28, Township 1N, Range 3E. The inscriptions were copied by Mrs. C. P. Lesh and Mrs. Theodore Craven, both of Indianapolis, and Mrs. Harvey Morris of Salem, in June, 1936.

[2] The old markers for the two Sherwood graves, which carried only initials, were replaced by a granite marker with names and dates, as given above. The new marker is the gift of a great-granddaughter of Hugh and Rebecca Sherwood, Mrs. C. P. Lesh of Indianapolis.

Eva M. Marshall—Born Jan. 22, 1870—Died 1875
Rebecca Clements Polson—Died Jan. 2, 1898—Age 67 Y. 24 Das.
John T. Polson—Died Oct. 8, 1862—Age 24 Yr. 3 M. 23 Das.
Thomas Clements—Born Aug. 22, 1845 [?]—Died Nov. 15, 1906
Catherine—Wife—Born June 16, 1842—Died July 18, 1890
Milton Clements—Co. F., 59th Inf. [Government Stone]
Colglazier [large stone]
David Colglazier—Born Feb. 4, 1831—Died Jan. 20, 1898
Ellen—his Wife—Born Mar. 18, 1838—Died May 1, 1903
Clyde Colglazier—Born June 25, 1880—Died Nov. 1, 1881
Infant—Born and died—Apr. 3, 1882
Montgomery [large stone]
George—Born Apr. 4, 1833—Died Feb. 13, 1885—Aged 46 Y. 10 M. 9 D.
Mary E.-wife-Born June 18, 1839 [no date of death]
Maryanne—Wife of A. Agan—Born Sep. 22, 1845—Died Mar. 23, 1884—
    Aged 38 Y. 6 M. 1 D.
Lemuel L. Kimbrel—Died Sep. 13, 1889—Aged 72 Y. 2 M. 14 D.
Mary Kimbrel—Died Feb. 2, 1890—Aged 73 Y. 2 D.
Thomas Sherwood [no dates]
Elizabeth Sherwood [no dates]

This cemetery has a number of new graves, with only undertaker markers. A road to this cemetery has been built recently. The old log church, organized and built in 1844, is to be kept as a "Memorial" to the founders of the Church. The land for the Church and the Cemetery was given by Thomas Sherwood, son of Hugh and Rebecca (Field) Sherwood, and his wife Elizabeth.[3]

The early minutes of the Methodist Church of this community record the naming of the Church. While the building was being erected by the men of the neighborhood, there was not a rainy day, of the many chosen for the work, and on one of the days, near the completion of the Church, a wild turkey flew over the site where the men were working. It was captured by Thomas Sherwood, and was prepared by the women, for the dinner that day, it was decided while eating this fine dinner, that the new Church should be called "Providence", for the many blessings the members had received while constructing it.—M.T.M.

---
[3] The deed is recorded in Book Q, p.81, Salem, Washington County, Ind.

FAMILY BIBLE RECORDS
The Beard Family

On the front page of this Bible[1] is written:

Human Biography
Born, welcomed, caressed, cried, fed, grew, amused, reared, studied, examined, graduated, in love, loved, engaged, quarreled, reconciled, suffered, deserted, sick, dead, mourned, buried and forgotten.

There also appears the statement: "This book belongs to Matthew Symons Junior, bought of William Beard in the 11th month, 1813." And just below is written: "This book belongs to John Beard, son of I. N. Beard and Great Grandson of John Beard the first owner who left Londonderry, Ireland for America A. D. 1770."[2]

John Beard came from Ireland with his wife Martha and two sons, Thomas and Paterick, in the year of 1770 and landed the 18th day of the eighth month of the same year.

Children of John and Martha Beard:
   Thomas—b. Jan. 14, 1768; d. July 28, 1830.
   Paterick—b. Dec. 29, 1769; d. March 12, 1831.
   Jane—b. Feb. 22, 1772.
   Eseble and Martha—died young.
   Sarah—b. July 2, 1778.
   John—b. Aug. 2, 1780; d. Sept. 9, 1809.
   Isaac [N.]—b. Jan. 28, 1783; d. May 26, 1799 in Randolph County, North Carolina.
   Jesse—b. June 29, 1787; d. Dec. 19, 1856.
   William—b. April 7, 1792.
   Martha—wife of John [Beard]; d. June 19, 1816.
   John—son of John and Martha; d. Feb. 13, 1859.
   Mary—wife of John, son of John and Martha; d. Oct., 1860.

Births and deaths of the children of Isaac N. and Matilda Beard:
   Amanda J.—b. July 31, 1833; d. Sept. 21, 1837.
   Martha M.—b. April 7, 1834; d. Sept. 21, 1837.[3]
   Victoria A.—b. May 9, 1839.
   Benton J.—b. July 4, 1841; d. Dec. 19, 1877.
   Mary C.—b. Aug. 29, 1843.
   John W.—b. Sept. 18, 1845; d. June 6, 1924; aged 77 yrs., 8 mos., 18 days.

---

[1] The Bible was printed and published by Matthew Cary, 122 Market Street, Philadelphia, April 23, 1806. The record was copied by Mrs. Ira E. Tranter, Franklin, Ind.

[2] The following questions are found written in this Bible: "Where John Beard and his wife Martha first landed in this country before going to North Carolina? Where Martha Beard, his wife, was buried? The location of the cabin of Thomas Beard in Washington Township."

[3] Martha and Amanda died the same day of influenza and were buried in the same coffin.

Levi W.—b. Nov. 19, 1848.
Sisy—b. Nov. 22, 1850; d. Sept. 23, 1852.
Malinda—b. Dec. 1, 1852.
Ida May—b. Dec. 25, 1854.
Matilda—wife of Isaac N. Beard; d. of cancer, Feb. 11, 1871.

THE JAMES DODD FAMILY[4]

James Dodd—b. December 16, 1779; d. June 24, 1861; m. April 8, 1816, Alce (Elcy, Elsy) Dodd[5]; d. May 16, 1798; d. January 10, 1864.

Children of James and Alce Dodd:
Mahethalem—b. March 2, 1817.
Josinah—b. Aug. 27, 1818.
Joseph—b. Oct. 7, 1820.
Carson—b. Oct. 19, 1822.
Mary Ann—b. Feb. 14, 1825.
Joshua—b. June 13, 1827.
John Allen—b. Sept. 26, 1829.
Sarah Allen—b. June 13, 1832.
William—b. Jan. 20, 1835.
Marshall—b. June 30, 1837.
Rebecca Hickman—b. Oct. 20, 1839.

THE GAGE FAMILY

Thomas Gage (grandfather of James Gage).[6]
Phillip Gage (father of James Gage).
Joseph Shotwell (maternal grandfather of Easter Gage).
Jacob Shotwell (father of Easter Gage).
James Gage—b. Dec. 15, 1769.
Easter Gage—b. May 10, 1765.

Children of James and Easter Gage:
John Craig Gage—b. May 10, 1792.
Gennet Gage—b. Aug. 3, 1800.
Abel Gage—b. March 16, 1802.
Simon Gage—b. July 22, 1805.
Abel Gage—b. March 13, 1807.

---

[4] This record was contributed by Eugene Studebaker Wierbach of Muncie, Ind. Mr. Wierbach would like to know the parentage of James Dodd and the places where his children settled.

[5] The marriage took place in Monongalia County, West Virginia.

[6] The Bible containing this record is in the possession of Miss Byrd Hickman of Springport, Indiana. The record was copied in August, 1939. At this time, no connection between the Gage family and the Hickman and Moore families of Henry County, Indiana, had been found. It is surmised that the Bible belonged to another family previous to the Hickman-Moore ownership. The fact that the Gage family record is found in the same Bible with the Hickman and Moore families is somewhat confusing.

The Valentine Boruff Family[1]

Ann Boruff—b. Sept. 1, 1798.
Samuel Boruff—b. March 25, 1800.
Margaret Boruff—b. Dec. 27, 1802.
Charity (Catsy) Boruff—b. Sept. 15, 1804.
Christopher Boruff—b. last day of Feb., 1806.
William Boruff—b. Feb. 12, 1808.
Daniel Boruff—b. Jan. 10, 1810.
Sarah Boruff—b. Aug. 4, 1812.
Valentine (Felty) Boruff—b. Oct. 22, 1816.
John Boruff—b. Oct. 4, 1818.

On the inside of the front cover of the old Boruff Bible[2] is found in German the statement:

"Valentine Boruff died 50 years ago this fall, 1906, and was 82 years old when he died. Grandpa Boruff."[3]

---

[1] Record sent in by Oscar Boruff, Owensburg, Indiana.

[2] The title-page of the old Bible of the Valentine Boruff family carries the following:

I.
Das Neue Testament
Unsers Herrn und Heilandes Jesu Christi,
Nach der Deutschen Uebersetzung
D. Martin Luther.
Zweite Auflage.
Germantaun
Gedruckt bey Michael Billmeyer
1795.

II.
Kirchen Gesang—Buck
D. Ambrosu Lobwasser
Philadelphia

III.
Geistleches Blumen Gartlein
Germantown
Debruckt und Zufinden bey
Michael Billmeyer

1800.

[3] This entry was made and signed by Andrew Jackson Boruff (1857-1925). The statement that Valentine Boruff died in 1856, aged eighty-two years, indicates that he was born in 1774. The Census of 1850, however, gives his age at that time as seventy-three, which would make his birthdate 1777. The place of his birth as given in the Census of 1850 was Pennsylvania. He died in Mercer County, Illinois. His wife's name was Margaret (Mallicote?) Boruff. The date of her birth is unknown; she died in 1842. Valentine and Margaret Boruff came from Campbell, or Claiborne, County, Tennessee, to Monroe County, Indiana, in 1829 or 1830. The 1830 Census shows them living in Monroe County, Indiana. About 1834 they went to Mercer County, Illinois, and in 1841 they purchased a farm from the United States Government. The description of the land is given as follows: East 1/2, S.W. 1/4, Sec. 9, Tp. 15 N, Range 5 W. This land passed from Valentine I, to Valentine II, then to the present (1937) owners, Anna Monson Boruff and her son Maynard.

The Easom Hannan Family

Marriages:

Easom Hannan[1] was married in the year of our Lord and Saviour, September 15th, 1783, to Mary Greenlee, daughter of William Greenlee of Botetourt County, Virginia.

Edward G. Hannan, son of Easom Hannan, was married in the year of our Lord and Saviour, August 4th, 1825, to Jane Maxwell, daughter of Capt. Audley Maxwell of Tazewell County, Va.

James William Hannan, son of Edward G. Hannan, was married on the 21st day of March, 1850, to Miss Rosana Parks, daughter of Benjamin Parks, all of Miama County, Ohio.

Emma F. Hannan was married to Henry Stover, March 4th, 1872.

Eliza Jane Hannan married William R. Brady, Beb., 1875.

Mary Carolina Hannan married George W. Bryan, Dec. 20, 1876.

Clara Alice Hannan married William R. Myers, ——, 1882.

Edward Parks Hannan married Elizabeth Frances Hunt, Dec. 21, 1884.

John Barnard Hannan married Mary Marjory Effie McCreary, Sept. 17, 1890.

Joseph Bennett Hannan married Ella Young, March 19, 1903.

Births:

Edward G. Hannan was born in the year of our Lord and Saviour, April 11th day, 1800.

Jane Hannan was born in the year of our Lord and Saviour, February 26th, 1803.

James William Hannan was born, May 19th, 1826.

Sarah Ann Hannan was born, November 15th, 1828.

Silas Reynolds Hannan was born, March 19th, 1831.

Mary Jane Hannan was born, June 2nd, 1833.

Audley Mathews Hannan was born, December 28th, 1835.

Rebecca Maxwell Hannan was born, August 30th, 1838.

Nancy Matilda Hannan was born, January 1st, 1845.

Rosana Parks was born, February 17th, 1829.

Deaths:

Silas Reynolds Hannan departed this life, November 13th day, 1833.

Jane Hannan departed this life, August the 22nd day, 1847.

Edward G. Hannan departed this life, July 27th, 1850.

Nancy Matilda Hannan departed this life, July 8, 1887. (Daughter of James Wm. Hannan).

James William Hannan died, December 19, 1904.

Roseana Hannan died, June 28th, 1910.

Nancy Matilda (Hannan) Bay died, March 31, 1931.

---

[1] Easom Hannan was married in Botetourt County, Virginia, but in that section which later became Roanoke County. He lived and died tthere, and is the Revolutionary ancestor of Mrs. Robert E. Brown (Indianapolis, Ind.), in whose possession the Bible containing these records has been placed. The Bible was published and sold by Edmund Cushing, Lunenburg, Mass., 1828.

The Powers Family

Births:
William D. Powers—b. Sept. 29, 1779.[1]
Sarah Beeks—b. Dec. 17, 1792.
Mary Hoakeland Powers—b. July 30, 1814.
Arabella C. Powers—b. March 2, 1816.
Wm. H. Powers—b. March 11, 1818.
James H. Powers—b. Aug. 30, 1819.
Martin John Powers—b. Nov. 19, 1820.
Richard Peter Powers—b. Apr. 19, 1823.
Jane McRay Powers—b. March 27, 1825.
Richard Nelson Powers—b. Aug. 5, 1827.
Eliza Katherine Powers—b. Oct. 5, 1830.
Nancy May Powers—b. Dec. 4, 1832.
Sarah Isabella Powers—b. Apr. 24, 1835.

Marriages:
Wm. D. Powers m. Sarah Beeks, April 26, 1810.
Wm. H. Powers m. Sarah Clentine, Oct. 1, 1844.
Richard Nelson Powers m. Malissa Sharp, Aug. 5, 1847.
James A. Hume m. Mary H. Powers, Nov. 20, 1834.
Jonathan Kershner m. Jane McKay Powers, July 4, 1847.
Richard N. Powers m. Frances E. Tucker, July 26, 1855.
Daniel W. Tucker m. Eliza K. Powers, April 29, 1867.

Deaths:
Richard Peter Powers—d. Oct. 24, 1824.
Nancy May Powers—d. May 23, 1838.
Sarah Isabella Powers—d. May 31, 1838.
William D. Powers—d. Aug. 27, 1857.
Sarah Powers, wife of Wm. D. Powers—d. Oct. 29, 1869.
Arabella C. Powers—d. Dec. 27, 1859.
Martin John Powers—d. Oct. 6, 1886.
Richard N. Powers—d. April 7, 1896.
Elizabeth K. Powers Tucker—d. Aug. 10, 1906.
Malissa Powers, wife of Richard N. Powers—d. March 7, 1854.
Mary Powers, wife of Martin John Powers—d. Jan. 25, 1887.
Frances E. Powers, wife of Richard N. Powers—d. March 15, 1928.

---

[1] William D. Powers, and his wife Sarah Beeks, lived in Indiana in 1827. Sarah was the daughter of Christopher and Catherine (Barnes) Beeks. One sister, Nancy Beeks, married George May, and lived in Bartholomew Co., Ind. Another sister, Catherine Beeks, married George Smith in 1817, and removed from Ohio to Albany, Delaware Co., Ind. See Query 10, December, 1936, p. 433, *Indiana Magazine of History.*—Katherine K. Adams, 1837 Greenleaf Ave., Chicago, Ill.

Stephen Harvey Family

Record of Stephen Harvey, Jr.:[1]

Stephen Harvey was born (not legible).
Jemima Weatherby was born November the 26th day 1784 [married Stephen Harvey].
Rachel Harvey was born October 22, 1806, on the fourth day of the week.
Perlina Harvey was born February the 27, 1808, on the seventh day of the week.
Delano Harvey was born December the 2, 1809, on the first day of the week.
Samuel Harvey was born November the 14, 1810, on the fourth day of the week.
Stephen Harvey was born October the 6, 1811, on the third day of the week.
Stephen Harvey deceased on April 20th Day, 1811.
Jemima Harvey [widow of Stephen Harvey,] and David Fitz Randolph were mar. (not legible)
Note: The children of Stephen and Jemima Harvey were born in New York. The last two, at least, were born in Seneca or Tompkins County. This family lived in Sehlby County, Ind., for many years. Jemima died in Polk County, Iowa, Sept., 1852. They moved to Shelby County, Ind., in 1821.

Record of Stephen Harvey, Jr.:

Stephen Harvey was born October the 6th, 1811
Elizabeth (ink faded) was born Jan. the 2nd, 1811;
married October the 31, 1833.
Nancy Ann Harvey was born April the 24th, 1836, on the 2nd day of the week.
Lewis Harvey was born June the 12, 1837, on the 2nd day of the week.
Elizabeth Harvey deceased November 9, 1838.
Susan Lee was born July the 10th, 1827.
Stephen Harvey and Susan Lee were married July the 27, 1842.
Samuel Harvey was born May 24, 1843.
Elizabeth Harvey was born October the 27th, 1844.
Maria Harvey was born June the 7th, 1846, on the 7th day of the week.
Jemima Harvey was born January the 12th, 1848, on the 4th day of the week.
Theophilus Harvey was born Dec. the 26th day, 1851.
Richard Harvey was born January 25th, 1855.
Sarah Jane Harvey was born December the 25th day, 1856.

---

[1] This record was copied by Mrs. Lawrence Jack, 2625 Garfield Road, Spokane, Washington. Mrs. Jack is Corresponding Secretary of the Eastern Washington Genealogist Society. The entries in the original record are badly faded, and some records are torn out.

Hannah Viretta Harvey was born December the 25th day, 1861.
Samuel Harvey died February, 1843 [1844].
Richard Harvey died August the 10th, 1855.

ROBERTSON FAMILY[1]

Charles Robertson was married to Miss Nancy Ford on Sept. 15, 1798.[2]

Children:

Sally and Franky Robertson (twins)—b. Aug. 24, 1799.
Eliza Robertson—b. July 15, 1800.
Alexander Robertson—b. April 10, 1802.
Matilda Robertson—b. Feb. 9, 1805.
James Robertson—b. Aug. 11, 1807.
Margaret Robertson—b. Dec. 14, 1809.
Reuben Robertson—b. May 30, 1812.
David Robertson—b. Sept. 6, 1814.
William Robertson—b. Dec. 13, 1817.

Reuben Robertson was married to Elvira Littell, daughter of Elder John T. Littell on May 23, 1833.

Elvira Littell was born Nov. 24, 1815.

Children:

Robert Alexander Robertson—b. Feb. 19, 1834.
John Thompson Robertson—b. Sept. 3, 1835.
Nancy Malissa Robertson—b. Feb. 4, 1837.
Mary Matilda Robertson—d. Oct. 16, 1839, age 2 mo., 6 d.
Charles Milburn Robertson—b. Sept. 20, 1841.
Sarah Jane Robertson—b. Dec. 5, 1843.
Reuben Edgar and Elvira Isadore Robertson (twins)—b. Feb. 25, 1851.
Joseph Orlando Robertson—b. Oct. 8, 1853.
Margaret Emma Robertson—b. July 4, 1855.

Deaths:

Departed this life, Our Mother, Nancy Robertson, Mar. 2, 1860; aged 83 years, 8 mo., 8 days; who lived the life of a Christian, died in the triumph of the Christian faith, and is now enjoying the reward of her labors.

Robert Alexander Robertson—d. Oct. 16, 1835, age 1 yr., 7 mo., 23 d.
Mary Matilda Robertson—d. Oct. 16, 1839, age 2 mo., 6 days.
Elvira Isadore Robertson—d. July 4, 1853, age 2 yr., 4 mo., 9 d.
Reuben Edgar Robertson—d. July 8, 1853, age 2 yr., 4 mo., 13 d.
Joseph Orlando Robertson—d. Aug. 1854; ―――――.
Margaret Emma Robertson—d. Oct. 13, 1858, age 3 yr., 2 mo., 19 d.
Elder Charles M. Robertson—d. Dec. 10, 1883, age 41 yrs., 2 mo., 20 d.

---

[1] From the Bible of Reuben Robertson, published 1833, now in ossession of his grandson, James Arthur Robertson, Salem, Indiana. Copied by Lulie Davis, 306 So. High St., Salem, Indiana.
[2] This date is incorrect—should be Dec. 14, 1797.

Complete List of Robertsons buried in Robertson Cemetery:[3]

David Robertson—d. July 25, 1865; age 50 yrs., 10 m., 19 days.
Margaret, wife of D. Robertson—b. Feb. 23, 1815; d. May 13, 1883.
Nancy, wife of Charles Robertson—d. Mar. 2, 1860; age 83 yrs. 8 mo., 8 days.
James N. Wood—b. Feb. 20, 1839; d. May 5, 1869.
John M. Wood—b. July 24, 1808; d. Mar. 28, 1869.
Margaret, wife of John M. Wood—b. Dec. 14, 1809; d. Oct. 10, 1862.
Alexander Robertson—b. Apr. 10, 1803; d. Mar. 23, 1864.
Charlie, son of Nancy and George W. Stout—b. Aug. 7, 1870; d. Feb. 5, 1874.
Micah Burns—b. Sept. 24, 1794; d. Sept. 21, 1876.
Frances, wife of M. Burns—b. Aug. 24, 1799; d. July 21, 1874.
Reginald Howard Burns—b. Feb. 27, 1889; d. Aug. 6, 1890.
Marion Regina Burns—b. Feb. 27, 1889; d. Aug. 6, 1890.
Oscar L. Robertson—son of C. B. and M. C. Robertson. d. Nov. 18, 1878; age 6 mo., 16 days.
Charles B. Robertson—b. Nov. 1, 1842; d. June 27, 1888.
Mary, wife of C. B. Robertson—b. Mar. 5, 1853; d. Jan. 21, 1884.

ELISHA B. LEE FAMILY

Age Paper of Elisha B. Lee:

Elisha B. Lee was born March the fourth day, 1796.
Maria Everson was born November the 15 day, 1799.
Elisha B. Lee and Maria Everson were married September the 9 day, 1819.

Richard M. Lee was born, June the 27 day, 1820.
Sophia Lee was born, February the 15 day, 1822.
Joseph K. Lee was born, June the 13 day, 1824.
Susanna Lee was born, July the 10th day, 1827.
William W. Lee was born, March the 26th day, 1830.
Lavinna Lee was born, February the 27th day, 1832.
Elizabeth Rudisill Lee was born, April the 19th day, 1835.
Maria Lee was born, May the 20th day, 1839.
John N. Lee was born, April the 4th day, 1839.
Eliza Ann Lee was born, June the 10th day, 1841.

Elisha B. Lee and Harriet Hughes were married, October the 1st day, 1844. [The first wife died from child-birth, May 29, 1844].

Martha Hughes was born, March the 1st day, 1840.
Thomas G. Hughes was born, January the 28 day, 1843.
George Snyder Lee was born, July the 22d day, 1845.
Marshall Lee was born, September the 19th day, 1847.
Charles W. Lee was born, May the 6th day, 1849.
Harriet Lee was born, September the 10th day, 1852.
Mary Francis Lee was born, July the 9th day, 1855.
Sarah Isabel Lee was born, February the 2d, 1857.

---

[3] The Robertson Cemetery is in Wood Township, Clark County, Indiana. It is located on the farm acquired from the Federal Government by Charles Robertson. It was later owned by David Robertson, son of Charles, then by David's son, Charles B. Robertson. The next owner, William Todd. Copied by Lulie Davis.

Sophia Everson departed this life, April the 15th day, 1820.
Amos R. Everson departed this life, September the 28th day, 1829.
Maria Lee departed this life, May the 29th day, 1844, and the child the same day.
Levina Lee dearted this life, July the 2d day, 1845.
Eliza Ann Lee departed this life, July the 15th day, 1845.
George Snyder Lee departed this life, August the 10th day, 1851.
Harriet Hughes Lee departed this life, September the 22nd, 1862 [Second wife of Elisha B. Lee].
Mary Lee departed this life, March the 10th dnay, 1868.
Elisha B. Lee and Martha Keefe were married, Nov. the 8th, 1868.
    Ella Lee born, January the 18th day, 1870.
    Ella Lee departed this life, Jan. 4th day, 1872.
    Elmer O. Lee was born on June 17, 1872.
Elisha B. Lee departed this life, September the 5th day, 1872, and is buried in the old Harvey graveyard in Delaware Twp., Polk County, Iowa. He was o soldier in the war of 1812. [This entry is written in a different hand].

Hudelson and Bradley Families

The first Hudelson family record was copied from the Bible of John Montgomery Hudson, who died in Henry County, Indiana, on August 22, 1843, aged 73 years. His wife, Catherine, died on February 1, 1852. The second Hudelson family record was copied from the Bible of William Hudelson, who lived at Knightstown, Indiana. William was born on July 16, 1802. He married Margaret Bradley (born May 20, 1800) on June 2, 1825. William died in Henry County on December 27, 1886. The Bradley family record was also copied from the William Hudelson Bible. Thomas Bradley was born on March 15, 1761. He married Philadelphia Ficklin(born December 15, 1768) on March 5, 1788. These records were sent in several months ago by Edwin Garner Chapman of Minneapolis, Minnesota. Mr. Champan died on July 12, 1937.

Children of John Montgomery and Catherine Hudelson:

James Hudelson—b. Jan. 25, 1797; d. Feb. 7, 1873; m. Elizabeth Vanderen.

Mary Hudelson—b. Nov. 3, 1798; d. Mar. 7, 1799.

John Miller Hudelson—b. Jan. 1, 1800; d. Oct. 18, 1873; m. Matilda Ann Hinds.

William Hudelson—b. Jul. 16, 1802; d. Dec. 27, 1886; m. Margaret Bradley.

Samuel Hudelson—b. Nov. 7, 1804; d. May 11, 1853; m. Mancy Jane Templeton.

Robert Irwin Hudelson—b. Sept. 4, 1807; d. Mar. 18, 1855; m. Phebe Shipman Cary.
Alexander Hudelson—b. Feb. 24, 1811; d. Mar. 1, 1834; did not marry.

All of the above, except William, are buried in the Shiloh cemetery, near Carthage, Rush Co., Indiana. William Hudelson is buried in the cemetery at Knightstown, Indiana.

Children of Thomas and Philadelphia Ficklin Bradley:
Robert Bradley—b. June 26, 1790; m. Nancy Pulliam.
William Bradley—b. Feb. 1793; m. (1) Sally Deakins and (2) Sally W. Jenkins.
Henry Bradley—b. Jul. 7, 1795; m. Maria Jenkins.
Fames Ficklin Bradley—b. Feb. 10, 1798; m. Nancy Keller.
Margaret Bradley—b. May 20, 1800; m. William Hudelson.
John Bradley—b. Feb. 20, 1805.
Jephthah Dudley Bradley—b. Feb. 20, 1808; m. Eliza Suggett.
Joseph Leland Bradley—b. Aug. 11, 1810.

Thomas Bradley and his wife Philadelphia Ficklin, as well as the parents of the latter (Thomas and Mary Herndon Ficklin), all rank as Revolutionary patriots, having been among the defenders of Bryan (Bryant's) Station, Kentucky, which was one of the last engagements of the Revolutionary War.

Children of William and Margaret Bradley Hudelson:
John L. Hudelson—b. Feb. 20, 1836; m. Esther Ann Winder.
Mary C. Hudelson—b. May 6, 1827; m. G. W. Stevenson.
James T. Hudelson—b. Dec. 18, 1828; m. Nancy Strattan.
Ann Mariah P. Hudelson—b. Mar. 27, 1830; m. William Penn Hill.
Jephthah A. Hudelson—b. Apr. 11, 1832; m. Ann Yetter.
William H. Hudelson—b. Apr. 21, 1835; m. Jane Johnson.
Jane Montgomery Hudelson—b. Mar. 27, 1837; did not marry.
Robert Samuel Hudelson—b. Feb. 20, 1838; died young.
Rufus Irwin Hudelson—b. Sept. 19, 1840; m. Eliza Armstrong.
Margaret Elizabeth Hudelson—b. Jul. 9, 1843; m. Adam J. Johnson.
Sarah Bradley Hudelson—b. Jul. 1, 1846; did not marry.

THE HAWKINS AND WEST FAMILIES

James Hawkins (born Jan. 16, 1766) married Rachel Lytle (born Feb. 19, 1769) on Apr. 6, 1789, in Lincoln County, North Carolina, where both were born. They moved to the Abbeville District of South Carolina where all their children were born. In April, 1834, James Hawkins, then 68 years of age, came to Bartholomew County, Indiana. This was several years after three of his children had married and moved to

Indiana. The Hawkins and West genealogical data were all copied from old Bible records and sent in by Mrs. Lawrence Jack, S. 2625 Garfield Road, Spokane, Washington.

Children of James and Rachel Lytle Hawkins:

Elizabeth Hawkins—b. Apr. 25, 1790; m. Moses Pruitt; moved to Ind., 1815.

Mary Hawkins—b. Oct. 20, 1792; m. William West; moved to Franklin Co., Ind., 1816.

John Hawkins—b. Dec. 3, 1794; m. Nancy Hackleman; moved to Franklin Co., Ind., 1815.

Rebecca Hawkins—b. Nov. 1, 1796.
Margaret Hawkins—b. Mar. 4, 1799.
Rachel Hawkins—b. Mar. 3, 1801.
James Hawkins—b. Aug. 27, 1803.
Mathew Hawkins—b. ———.
William Lytle Hawkins—b. Oct. 30, 1805.

Robert West lived to be 112 years old. Benjamin West [presumably the son of Robert West] m. Nancy Hawkins.

Benjamin lived to the age of 85 and Nancy to 84. William West was born in South (?) Carolina on Apr. 17, 1791. He married (1) Mary [Polly] Hawkins (daughter of James and Rachel Hawkins) on Nov. 13, 1813, in South Carolina. Mary died on Oct. 1, 1822, and was buried in the old Wiley Graveyard in Franklin County, Indiana. They had migrated to Indiana in 1816. William West married (2) Martha Findley. He died on Mar. 29, 1862, and was buried in the old Wiley Graveyard.

Children of William and Mary (Hawkins) West:

James Lytle West—b. Dec. 27, 1815, Abbeville District, S. C.
Mathew West—b.———; d. 12 yrs. of age; buried in Franklin Co., Ind.
Benjamin Harrison West—b. Jul. 18, 1818, Franklin Co., Ind.
John Quincy West—b. Apr. 2, 1820, Franklin Co., Ind.
Rachel West—b. Jul. 14, 1822, Franklin Co., Ind.

There was one child by the union of William West and Martha Findley, George Anne West (born Sept. 28, 1828). Two of the children of William West, Rachel West and James Lytle West married into another family of the same name, as recorded below. The family of Townsend West and Susan West was not related to the South Carolina Wests, but belonged to the Fairfax County, Virginia, Wests.

Record of Marriages:

James Lytle West—m. Susan West, Mar. 15, 1838.
Rachel West—m. Townsend West, ————.
Benjamin Harrison West—m. Sarah I. Carmichael, Apr. 21, 1847.
John Quincy West—m. Mary E. Doerflier, Dec. 17, 1861.

Record of Deaths:

Rachel (West) West—d. Dec. 3, 1847.
Benjamin Harrison West—d. Nov. 18, 1868 (buried in old Wiley Graveyard).
John Quincy West—d. Dec. 16, 1874.

James Lytle West (born in Abbeville District, S. C., Dec. 22, 1815) married Susan West (born in Wood County, Va., [Now W. Va.], Oct. 10, 1816) on Mar. 15, 1838, in Franklin County, Indiana. Here their children were born, except the youngest, who was born in Polk County, Iowa.

Children of James Lytle and Susan (West) West:

Milton Hawkins West—b. Mar. 1, 1839.
Maria Woodyard West—b. May 12, 1841.
Francis Marion West—b. Mar. 12, 1845.
Alexander Miller West—b. Mar. 20, 1847.
Rebecca Pruitt West—b. Jan. 8, 1850.
William Harrison West—b. Apr. 19, 1852.
John Townsend West—b. Sept. 10, 1855.
Benjamin Franklin West—b. Jul. 19, 1858.

THE ARTHUR BARRETT FAMILY

Arthur Barrett—b. 10, September, 1742; d. March 7, 1828.
Elizabeth Baldwin—b. September 14, 1756; d. July 10, 1811.
Sarah Barrett—b. April 17, 1774; d. July 28, 1834.
Thomas Barrett—b. August 18, 1775.
Ann Barrett—b. January 20, 1777.
Arthur Barrett, Jr.—b. December 7, 1778; d. November 28, 1844.
David Barrett—b. May 4, 1780; d. November 27, 1844.
Isaac Barrett—b. February 5, 1782.
Elizabeth Barrett—b. October 25, 1783.
Hannah Barrett—b. July 24, 1785.
Aeneas Barrett—b. June 3, 1787; d. December 4, 1844.
Rachel Barrett[6]—b. February 11, 1789.
Rebekah Barrett—b. June 14, 1791; d. November 1847.
Susanah Barrett—b. March 11, 1793.
William Barrett—b. July 14, 1795; d. August 1, 1801.

---

[6] My direct ancestress in this family, Rachel Barrett, married and moved to Randolph County, Indiana, in 1833, coming from Harrison County, Ohio, and prior to that from Frederick County, Virginia. Her father, Arthur Barrett, was born in Chester County, Pennsylvania. This record was written on a sheet of paper and marked "From Eage Book 1852." The record is now in my possession.—Mrs. Herbert E. Brown, Indianapolis, Indiana.

The Rev. William Hunt Family

Births:

Rev. Wm. Hunt—b. June 1, 1789.
Mary R. Hunt—b. Mar. 2, 1800 [m. Rev. William Hunt]
Matilda Hunt—b. June 17, 1819.
Levina Hunt—b. Nov. 20, 1820.
Eliza B. Hunt—b. May 18, 1823.
John Wesley Hunt—b. Mar. 19, 1825.
William F. Hunt—b. Oct. 11, 1827.
Giles S. Hunt—b. Feb. 5, 1830.
Mary Jane Hunt—b. May 23, 1832.
Mercy Ann Hunt—b. Apr. 29, 1835.
Elviney Hunt—b. Jan. 16, 1838.
Basil Hunt—b. Apr. 3, 1765; d. June 28, 1828.
Sara (Denton) Hunt [wife of Basil Hunt]—b. October 28, 1770.

Deaths:

Sarah (Denton) Hunt [widow of Basil Hunt]—d. October 26, 1855.
Giles S. Hunt—d. April 1, 1842.
William F. Hunt—d. September 3, 1845.
Rev. Wm. Hunt—d. February 15, 1845.
Mary R. Hunt [widow of Rev. Wm. Hunt]—d. March 15, 1877.

Rev. William Hunt was one of the early circuit riders of the Methodist Church in Indiana. He began his work in Randolph County, Indiana, about 1815. His father, Basil Hunt, was in East Tennessee, that part which later became Washington County, and signed the petition of 1787 for separation from North Carolina. I believe that he and his parents may have come from Hampshire County, Virginia. I would appreciate any information concerning them. Basil Hunt, born 1765, according to the Bible record, was the son of John Wesley Hunt.

The Samuel Holly Family

Births:

Samu.l Holly—b. August 7, 1762; d. July 16, 1831.
Deborah Holly[1]—b. June 17, 1764; d. May 7, 1840.
Mary Holly—b. January 2, 1790.
Charity Holly—b. October 31, 1791; d. March 14, 1792.
Jeremiah Holly—b. November 21, 1793; d. August, 1795.
Jemeriah Holly (2nd)—b. November 14, 1802.
William Pearcy—b. March 4, 1784, Thursday.
Polly [Mary] Holly[2]—b. January 2, 1790, Saturday.

Charity Johnson Pearcy—b. November 21, 1812.
Elizabeth Ann Pearcy—b. September 3, 1820; d. September 21, 1820.
Jeremiah Holly Pearcy—b. March 21, 1823, Friday.
Elizabeth Esther Pearcy—b. May 26, 1825, Thursday.
Mary Ann Pearcy—b. June 18, 1833, Tuesday.
Samuel H. Pearcy—b. March 13, 1829.
Mary H. Pearcy[3]—b. April 18, 1833.
Sarah Esther Pearcy—b. May 7, 1854.
Charity L. E. Pearcy—b. July 15, 1857.
Stanton W. Pearcy—b. April 14, 1859.
William Thomas Pearcy—b. July 16, 1861.
Jemima Elva Pearcy—b. October 2, 1863.
John K. Pearcy—b. October 11, 1866.
Mary V. Pearcy—b. August 31, 1868.

Children of Joseph and Gartrew [Gertrude] Ketcham.[4]

Daniel Ketcham—b. February 12, 1742.
Martha Ketcham—b. September 28, 1743.
Abigail Ketcham—m. June 20, 1745.
Joseph Ketcham—b. March 30, 1751.
Daniel Ketcham (2nd)—February 17, 1753.
Abigail Ketcham—February 7, 1755.
Elizabeth Ketcham—October 12, 1756.
Mary Ketcham—October 28, 1759.
Deborah Ketcham—June 17, 1764 (m. Samuel Holly).

Deaths

Jeremiah Holly Pearcy—d. July 19, 1828.
Charity Liveley—d. April 7, 1845, aged 32 y., 7 m., and 7 d.
Mary Ann Yount—d. July 23, 1852.
William Pearcy—d. June 29, 1852, aged 62 years.
Earl V., son of John and Corda Pearcy—d. October 17, 1893, aged 17 m.
Mary H. Pearcy—d. October 1, 1906, aged 74 y., 5 m., and 17 days.
Mary Val, wife of A. Nichols—d. May 9, 1909, aged 40 y. and 9 m.
Samuel H. Pearcy—d. February 7, 1920.[5]

---

[1] Wife of Samuel Holly. Maiden name, Deborah Ketcham. Samuel and Deborah both died in Shelby County, Kentucky.

[2] Wife of William Pearcy. The marriage occurred in Shelby County, Kentucky, in 1812. They moved to Green Township, Morgan County, Indiana.

[3] Wife of Samuel Holly Pearcy. Maiden name, Mary Hannah Huges. The marriage occurred in 1852. Samuel and Mary Pearcy are both buried in the Centennial Cemetery, in Morgan County, Indiana.

[4] Joseph Ketcham—b. May 11, 1715; m. Gartrew (or Gertrude) Johnson. They accompanied their son Daniel (second son of the name) when he left Maryland for the West in 1784. They came down the Ohio on a flatboat. Joseph and his wife settled in Shelby County, Kentucky, and died there. Their son Daniel and his wife (Keziah) also lived there until death.

[5] The Bible from which the above records were copied was published by N. Bangs and J. Emory for the Methodist Episcopal Church, in New York in 1827. Azar Hot was the printer. The Bible is now owned by William T. Pearcy of Indianapolis. The records were copied in 1937 by Mrs. Charles R. Emery, 1316 So. Walnut St., Bloomington, Indiana.

THE EPHRAIM TUCKER FAMILY

Marriages:

Ephraim Tucker and Winnafred Hood—m. 1814.
Amos Morris and Sarah Howard—m. Sept. 28, 1816.
William H. Tucker and Melinda Morris—m. Nov. 13, 1845.
William H. Tucker and Aurilla Morris—m. Sept. 21, 1851.

Births:

Amos Morris—b. Sept. 15, 1792.
Sarah Howard—b. Sept. 15, 1796.
Ephraim Tucker—b. Dec. 16, 1792.
Winnafred (Hood) Tucker—b. Sept. 26, 1792.
William H. Tucker—b. March 5, 1825.
Melinda (Morris) Tucker—b. Oct. 5, 1825.
Aurilla (Morris) Tucker—b. Feb. 9, 1832.
  1. Amos M. Tucker—b. Nov. 1, 1846.
  2. Ephraim Tucker—b. Dec. 22, 1849.
  3. Ethan A. Tucker—b. Oct. 7, 1852.
  4. Sarah M. Tucker—b. Dec. 5, 1854.
  5. Emily A. Tucker—b. June 15, 1856.
  6. Edward W. Tucker—b. March 12, 1859.
  7. **James A. Tucker—b. March 23, 1861.**
  8. **Dora A. Tucker—b. Feb. 2, 1864.**
  9. **Melinda Tucker—b. Nov. 2, 1866.**

Deaths:

Winnafred Hood Tucker—d. March 17, 1853.
Ephraim Tucker—d. April 3, 1873.
Amos Morris—d. Nov. 24, 1869.
William H. Tucker—d. Dec. 31, 1898.
Aurilla Morris—d. March 16, 1909.
Sarah Howard Morris—d. Sept. 15, 1886.
Melinda Morris Tucker—d. April 11, 1851.
Sarah M. Tucker—d. July 14, 1855.
Melinda Tucker—d. Feb. 5, 1873.
Amos M. Tucker—d. Feb. 20, 1873.
Earl Williams, son of Emily Tucker Williams and Richard Williams, died Dec. 18, 1922.[7]

---

[7] The Bible from which the above records were copied was published in 1872 by Chase, Lockwood and Brainard, Hartford, Conn. The Bible is now owned by James Albert Tucker, son of William H. and Aurilla Morris Tucker. The emigrant of this Tucker line was John, who settled first in Hingham, Mass., and went later to Southold, Long Island. William H. Tucker married (1) Melinda Morris and (2) her sister, Aurilla Morris. These records were copied by Mrs. Ira E. Tranter, 448 E. Madison St., Franklin, Indiana.

Roberts Family Bible Record.

The Roberts Family Bible was presented to the Washington County Historical Society, Salem, Indiana in July, 1925, by Mrs. Rose Cornwell Oden, a grand-daughter of James Q. Roberts, nephew of Robert R. Roberts, first bishop of the Methodist Church of Indiana. The Bible was published by B. Waugh & T. Mason, for the Methodist Episcopal Church at the Conference Office, 14 Crosby Street, New York, 1832, and presented to James Q. Roberts, by his uncle, Bishop Roberts, in the year 1833. James Q. Roberts was one of the three nephews that accompanied the family of the Bishop to Indiana from Pennsylvania in November, 1819, to make their home here.

Family Record as written by James Q. Roberts:
James Q. Roberts was born 21 January, A.D. 1804.
Mary Marshill was born 23 December A.D. 1809.
We were married the 25th February 1830.

Transcript of the Records of my Father's Family.
Father and Mothers Ages and Marriage.
John Roberts was born 13 Jany A.D. 1763 (brother of Bishop Roberts)
Mary Shannon was born 6 Jany A.D. 1769—and were married 12th September A.D. 1786.

Transcribed by James Roberts—May 2nd A.D. 1840. Fayette County State of Pennsylvania.
Father died 20th January 1812
Mother died 6th March 1832
Thomas died 11th October 1832
Saml died 15th August 1833

Children

1. Thomas Roberts was born 30th May A.D. 1787
2. Sarah Roberts was born 18th August 1788
3. Samuel Roberts was born 16th February 1790
4. Elizabeth Roberts was born 11th June 1793
5. Robert Roberts was born 19th January 1795
6. Charlotte Roberts was born 19th January 1795
7. Mary Roberts was born 23rd August 1796
8. John Roberts was born 24th June 1798
9. Shannon Roberts was born 3rd February 1800
10. Louis Roberts was born 13th September 1802
11. James Roberts was born 21st January 1804
12. Rebecca Roberts was born 2nd May 1805
13. George Roberts was born 9th December 1806—Died Dec. 27, 1841
14. Esther Roberts was born 17th April 1808
15. 2nd Thomas Roberts was born 12th February 1810
16. Martha Roberts was born 16 September 1812.

Benjamin King Family Records.

Compiled by Mrs. C. P. Lesh of Indianapolis; typed record "King Family of Virginia and of Harrison Co. and Washington Co., Indiana;" filed in State Library and in Washington County Historical Society archives.

Benjamin King, youngest son of Thomas and Sarah King was born in Louisa County, Virginia, on Sept. 11, 1767. He was married in Culpepper Co., Va., on Nov. 4, 1894, to Martha, daughter of George and Deborah Haywood. She was born Aug. 7, 1774, and died in 1820, in Harrison Co., Ind. George and Deborah Haywood, in 1795, bought 309 acres of land adjoining that of Thomas King, which later became the property of Benjamin King.

Oct. 30, 1802, Benjamin and Martha King sold to George Washington Truehard 222 and one-half acres lying on both sides of Pamunky River [in Virginia] and on Oct. 2, 1802, George and Deborah Haywood [sold] their plantation, adjoining the King farm, to James Michie. Early in 1803, both families removed to Jefferson Co., Ky., where they appear on tax returns, filed at Historical Society at Frankfort, Ky. On July 8, 1799, Governor of the state of Virginia, gave a bond to Benjamin King permitting him to preach and marry. Benjamin King bought 110 acres of land on Chenoweth Creek, in 1806, Jefferson Co., Ky. Benjamin King and family moved to Posey township, Harrison Co., Indiana, in 1808, and June 2, 1813, sold balance of plantation in Louisa County, Va., "2/12 of land wherein Thomas King lived and died," to his brother Thomas King, Jr. (Deed filed at Louisa, Va.)

The Haywoods died in Jefferson County, Ky., as they do not appear in tax lists after 1814. Martha Haywood King died in Indiana in 1820, and Mar. 23, 1820, her husband set aside land for a Methodist Church and Cemetery, naming John Hancock, Samuel Hancock, Thomas Polson, John Royse and Eli Wood as trustees (Book D, page 93, Corydon, Ind.)

Benjamin King married Elizabeth Wood, June 13, 1822, and after death of this wife, married Rebecca Ramsey, Aug. 1, 1842. He was one of the pioneer ministers of the state and endured many privations and hardships, especially during the war of 1812. The land he bought in different surveys both in Harrison and Washington county was around the present town of Fredericksburg, Ind., on Blue River. He built one of the first grist mills in the state, on the west side of Blue River below Fredericksburg. The Methodist Church and Cemetery are on the east side of the river about one and a half miles below Fredericksburg. Benjamin King died in February, 1852. His will, filed in Book "C", pp. 13 and 14, at Corydon, Ind., is as follows:

"In the name of God, Amen, I, Benjamin King—of the county of Harrison and State of Indiana, being of sound mind and memory, blessed be God, on the seventeenth day of March, 1848, make this my last will and testament in the following manner, to wit: first, I give my soul to God and my body to the dust. I desire to be laid in woolen by the side of my first wife, in one half chain of ground reserved for a burying ground forever: Secondly, each and every one of my legatees, have received their full portion, as will be hereafter named, to wit: Elisha B. King; Zilla Polson; George T. King; Martha Hancock; Nancy P. Polson; James King; McKendrie King; Robert King; Deborah Cooper and William King or his heirs, all of whom have received their portion, claims, or allowances of my estate both personal and real. The meeting house and lot known as King's Meeting house, I will to the Methodist Episcopal Church of Indiana—to the trustees of the same, viz: Benjamin King, Jr., David W. Sticker, and John Roberts as trustees in trust for the same, and their successors ever. Thirdly, I will, bequeath, and deliver to Benjamin King, Jr. all of my personal and Real Estate—Bay mare, according to the first date. For which consideration he is to support me comfortably and creditably during my natural life for which, he and his heirs are to have all my estate forever.

"In testimony where-unto, I have set my hand and seal this year and date first above written and in the presence of William Hancock and John A. Cromer. (Signed) Benjamin King."

"Still further, I bequeath and give unto William King's daughter, the only child he left at his death, five dollars, this third day of Nov. 1849."

Probated Feb. 13, 1852.

The old mill run by water power was sold by Benjamin King, Jr. and George King to a Mr. Green, who tore it down and moved it to Fredericksburg.

Children
of Benjamin and Martha (Haywood) King

1. Elisha Budd King, born Nov. 9, 1795. He mar. (1) July 30, 1821—Rebecca Rawlings. They had one daughter—Sarah Jane, born Sept. 1822, when the mother died. Elisha mar. (2) Sarah Butlerton—she died Jan. 1, 1835, leaving five children. Elisha mar. (3) Ann Miller. They had six children.

2. Zilla King was born Jan. 7, 1797. She was married to Thomas Polson, Nov. 30, 1817, in Harrison county, Indiana. They had 11 children.

3. George Thomas King, born Louisa County, Va. Aug. 20, 1798. He mar. (1) Sallie Graham Jan. 25, 1824. She died Feb. 14, 1857. They had 6 children. George Thomas King, mar. (2) Jane Ann Haines, Nov. 30, 1837—no children. He mar. (3) Juley E. Bates—four children by this marriage.

4. William King, born Feb. 22, 1800, mar. July 6, 1840 Mary Jane Dodds. He mar. (2) Margaret Dodds Apr. 21, 1847. They had one daughter, mentioned in will of Benjamin King.

5. Martha Haywood King, born Sept. 7, 1801, in Louisa County, Va., mar. John Hancock of N. C. Jan. 27, 1820. They had 7 children.

6. James King, born Jefferson County, Ky., May 23, 1803. He mar. Sept. 29, 1825, Tabitha Sherwood, of Washington County,

Ind. They had 11 children. James King and his wife are buried in Crown Hill Cemetery, Indianapolis.
7. Benjamin King, Jr. born May 16, 1806, in Jefferson Co. Ky., mar. Feb. 13, 1832 Lydia Sherwood, of Washington Co., Ind. They had nine children.
8. Nancy Price King, born Mar. 8, 1808, mar. Benjamin Polson, Sept. 23, 1826. They had 3 children. Nancy died at Paoli, Ind. in 1840.
9. Wesley King born Feb. 20, 1810, died in 1841.
10. McKindree King, born May 1, 1812 Harrison Co. Ind. mar. Oct. 1, 1833 Mary Cole. Eight children. McKindree King died Feb. 12, 1849.
11. Robert King, born Harrison Co. Ind. Sept. 24, 1813, mar. Elizabeth Jolly, Dec. 29, 1835. Twelve children. Robert King died Aug. 21, 1877, Hardinsburg, Ind.
12. Deborah King, born May 15, 1816, Harrison Co., Ind. She mar. Samuel Cooper, Aug. 18, 1835. Nine children.
13. Mary King, born Mar. 9, 1818; died Mar. 26, 1818.

[Note—Records of the families of the children of Benjamin King and his parents Thomas and Sarah King of Virginia are given in his fine Genealogy of the *King Family of Virginia and Indiana*—M. T. M., Editor.]

Shipman Family Bible Record[1]

John L. Shipman, born Nov. 20, 1825; died Jan. 27, 1870, aged 44 years, 2 months, 7 days.
Lucinda E. Shipman [Lucinda Evelyn Graham] was born May 27, 1827; died April 26, 1898, aged 70 years, 10 months, 29 days.
Durett F. Shipman, born Nov. 6, 1852; died Aug. 19, 1872, aged 19 months, 1 day.
Anna Vesta Shipman, born Dec. 8, 1851; died Sept. 9, 1872, aged 20 years, 9 months, 1 day.
Charles S.[2] [Samuel Charles] Shipman, born Sept. 12, 1850; died Aug. 2, 1851, age 10 months, 3 weeks.
Edward W. Shipman [middle name Walter], born Jan. 19, 1856; died Oct. 1, 1861, aged 4 years, 3 months, and 22 days.
Charles Shipman [a second Charles], born Nov. 14, 1857; died Aug. 18, 1859, aged 19 months, 4 days.
Cassius C. Shipman, born July 1, 1860; died March the 29, 1881, age 20 years, 9 months.
James David Shipman, born Nov. 25, 1862; died Mar. 3, 1931, at Brooklyn, N. Y.[3]

---

[1] The Shipman Bible is in the possession of Mrs. Sylvan L. Mouser (616 E. 47th St., Indianapolis) who copied the records.

[2] The name was first written "S. C." Shipman and then changed to "Charles S."

[3] Harry Shipman, the only living child of John L. and Lucinda E. Shipman, is not included in this Bible record. The Cemetery inscriptions correspond with the Bible record. In copying the inscriptions, it was found another Shipman family was buried in the New Albany Cemetery but no connection between the families has been discovered. Their names are: Wm. Charles Shipman (1813-1874) and Lucinda Shipman (1819-1894).

Kendrick Family Bible Record[1]

Marriages.

William Kendrick and Anne Taylor .... October 18, 1810.
Lavenia Kendrick and William Fryar .... May 5, 1831.
John Kendrick and Lavina McWhinney .... April 14, 1834.
Temperance Malvina Kendrick and Samuel W. Holmes .... May 11, 1837.
William Houston Kendrick and Jeanette Meredith .... Mar. 19, 1842.

Births.

William Kendrick	Jan. 2, 1785
Anne Kendrick	Mar. 15, 1789
James H. Kendrick	May 12, 1811
Lavenia Kendrick	Dec. 4, 1811
John L. Kendrick	Mar. 12, 1813
William H. Kendrick	Dec. 21, 1815
Mary Jane Kendrick	Nov. 24, 1816
Temperance Kendrick	Nov. 17, 1817
Oscar Kendrick	Feb. 23, 1820
Franklin Kendrick	Jan. 16, 1822
Susan Kendrick	Dec. 21, 1824
Wesley Kendrick	Apr. 1, 1826
Matthew Kendrick	Nov. 21, 1830
Stephen L. Kendrick	July 24, 1831

Deaths.

Mary Jane Kendrick	Nov. 26, 1816
Franklin Kendrick	Oct. 27, 1823
Susan Kendrick	Apr. 9, 1827
Matthew Kendrick	Oct. 1, 1831
Stephen L. Kendrick	Feb. 26, 1843
Wesley Kendrick	Sept. 27, 1850
Anne Kendrick	Apr. 16, 1852
William Kendrick	July 10, 1857
Oscar Kendrick	Mar. 5, 1868
Lavenia Kendrick Fryar	Dec. 6, 1885
William H. Hendrick	Nov. 26, 1899

---

[1] This record was sent in by E. C. Chapman (4375 Wooddale Ave., Minnaepolis, Minn.), the copy being furnished by William Meredith Kendrick (972 Middle Drive, Woodruff Place, Indianapolis). Mr. Kendrick says in a letter: "The *Meredith* in my name comes from Grandmother Kendrick whose maiden name was Jeanette Meredith, and who came from Wayne County, Indiana.

The Tannehill Family

A copy of family records as found in an old Bible in the possession of Mrs. Fern Phipps Sprunger, 513 West Walnut Street, Portland, Indiana, and copied by Mrs. Hazel Grimes Finch, Registrar of the Mississinewa Chapter, Portland, Indiana. This Bible was printed in Philadelphia, for Mathew Carey, No. 118 Market Street, October 27th, 1802.

Children of Samuel Tannehill:
(First record)

Mary Tannehill—b. July 24, 1756.
James Tannehill—b. Mar. 19, 1759.
Rachel Tannehill—b. Feb. 5, 1764.
Christine Tannehill—b. Dec. 14, 1766.
Samuel Tannehill—b. Dec. 17, 1768.
Ruth Beall Tannehill—b. Dec. 23, 1770.
William Tannehill—b. May 19, 1773.
Ninian Tannehill—b. July 13, 1775.
Zachariah Tannehill—b. Jan. 13, 1777.

(Second record)

Samuel Nogle—b. 1789.
Anna A. Danning—b. 1806.
James Foglesong—b. Dec. 21, 1818. His hand and pen.

Children of John Birdsong and his wife Ruth:

David Birdsong—b. Jan. 4, 1806.
Otho Birdsong—b. June 6, 1809.
Mary Birdsong—b. Apr. 11, 1811.
Elizabeth Birdsong—b. Jan. 9, 1813.
Ruth Birdsong—b. May 24, 1815.
Matilda Birdsong—b. Jul. 4, 1817.
Susanna Birdsong—b. Mar. 11, 1819.
James Birdsong—b. Dec. 29, 1820.
John Birdsong—b. June 21, 1823.
Mahaly Birdsong—b. August 14, 1825.
Okey Birdsong—d. Apr. 25, 1883.
Otha Birdsong—d. Apr. 25, 1843.

Children of Henry Nogle:

Ruth Nogle—b. Dec. 26, 1788.
Samuel Nogle—b. Aug. 28, 1789.
Mary Nogle—b. Dec. 15, 1791.
Henry Nogle—b. Sept. 31, 1793.
James Nogle—b. No. 2, 1797.
James Nogle—b. N ov. 2, 1797.
Elizabeth Nogle—b. July 11, 1801.

Ichabod Spencer—b. 1774; d. Oct. 23, 1850, aged 76 years, 9 months, 13 days.

Ruth Spencer, wife,—b. 1788; d. Oct. 16, 1864. Aged 76 years, 2 months and 10 days.

Mahala Spencer—dau. Ichabod and Ruth Spencer; m. Alonzo A. Baker. Alonzo A.—b. Dec. 16, 1816, in Herkimer County, N.Y.; d. May 6, 1884. Thirteen children.

(On page four of this Bible the name James Nail, with no dates, appears in three places).

THE RISH FAMILY

An exact copy of records taken from a Bible no win possession of Adah L. Miller of Portland, Indiana, Yount Apartments. Inside of the front cover appears the entry: "Isaac G. Barrick was born February 2, 1829." On the first page is found another entry: "William Badger was born January 15, 1775."

Marriages:

Margaret Rish—m. John Shriver, Jul. 14, 1839.
Hannah Rish—m. Ezekiel Wolf, May 8, 1842.
Rachel Rish—m. John Coulson, Nov. 3, 1842.
Joseph Rish—m. Catherine Kreiling, Jul. 4, 1844.
Catherine Rish—m. Nimrod Barrick, Dec. 23, 1850.
Sarah Rish—m. Isaac Barrick, Jan. 23, 1850.
Christina Rish—m. Nimrod Wildman, Nov. 25, 1852.
Ann Jane Rish—m. Manuel Reed, Jul. 24, 1853.

On blank pages between Old and New Testament, the following are recorded:

Ann Jane Mitchell—b. Jul. 22, 1822.

Simeon Rish—b. Jan. 5, 1780; son of Jacob and Margaret (Kissinger) Rish.

Anne Rish—b. Dec. 23, 1798; dau. of William and Catherine (Furgerson) Badger. William Badger—b. in Va. Jan. 15, 1775; d. ————, 1857. Married by Geo. Brown. Esq. of Columbiana County, Ohio— Simeon Rish to Ann Badger, April 4, 1816.

Children of Simeon and Anne Rish:

Joseph Rish—b. Jul. 19, 1815.
Hannah Rish—b. Aug. 7, 1818.
Margaret Rish—b. Sept. 10, 1820.
Betsey Rish—b. May 13, 1823.
Cristina Rish—b. July 24, 1825.
Rachel Rish—b. Feb. 8, 1827.
Cathern Rish—b. Jan. 2, 1829.
Sarah Rish—b. April 17, 1831.
Ann Jane Rish—b. Apr. 15, 1833.
Mary Rish—b. Mar. 10, 1837.

James Robertson Rish—b. Apr. 26, 1839.
Tamar Rish—b. Nov. 24, 1842.

Deaths

Elizabeth Rish—d. Aug. 12, 1832.
Mary Rish—d. April 24, 1843.
Tamar Rish—d. Sept. 21, 1845.
Simeon Rish—d.—Mar. 1, 1848.
Joseph Rish—d. Mar. 25, 1848.
Catherine Barrick—d. Sept. 4, 1849.
Mary Ann Barrick—d. Sept. 17, 1849.

THE ADAM WIBLE FAMILY

(Contributed by E. S. Harvey of Kokomo, Indiana, the records being supplied through the courtesy of Franklin J. Hole, Monrovia, Kansas.)

Adam Wible married Hannah Harris on January 1, 1788. Hannah was born on July 1, 1767. She died on January 15, 1794. On December 16, 1795, Mr. Wible married Jane Vancleave, who was born on January 29, 1777. (Vancleave records indicate that the birth year was 1778).

Children of Adam and Hannah (Harris) Wible:

Susannah Wible—b. Oct. 4, 1788; d. Aug. 22, 1812.
John Wible—b. June 26, 1790; d. Aug. 16, 1815.
Joseph Wible—b. June 14, 1792; d. July 10, 1800.
Samuel Wible [twin of Joseph]—b. June 14, 1792; d. [Jul. —, 1888].
Dorsity Wible—b. Aug. 23, 1793; d. Jul. 10, 1800.

Children of Adam and Jane (Vancleave) Wible:

Ruth Wible—b. [page torn], 1796; d. (date unknown).
Margarite Wible—b. Aug. 23, 1798; d. Dec. 11, 1798.
Charlotte and Polly Wible (twins)—b. Oct. 6, 1799.
Joseph C. Wible—b. May 26, 1803; d. (date unknown).
Margarite Dorsity Wible—b. Dec. 15, 1805.
Benjamin Vancleave Wible—b. Feb. 7, 1808.
Sirena Wible—b. Feb. 22, 18 [illegible] d. Aug. 20, 1811.
Eliza Elizabeth Wible—b. Jan. 18, 1812.
Adam [J.] Wible—b. June 29, 1814 (probably 1813).
Benjamin M[iller] Wible—b. Aug. 12, 1814.
John Vancleave Wible—b. Mar. 27, 1816.
Isaiah [B.] Wible—b. Dec. 30, 1817.
Hugh Conway Wible—b. Mar. 20, 1821.

Samuel Wible (youngest son of Adam and Hannah Harris Wible) was born in Nelson County, Kentucky, on June 14, 1792. He married Polly Rigney on May 15, 1815. Polly was born in Surrey County, North Carolina on December 19, 1796.

She was the daughter of William Rigney (b. August 27, 1768) and Amariah (Potter) Rigney (b. Nov. 18, 1772). William Rigney and Amariah Potter were married on September 22, 1791. Samuel Wible died on July —, 1888. He entered land in Orange County, Indiana in 1818.

Children of Samuel and Polly (Rigney) Wible:

John Mayhugh Wible—b. Aug. 27, 1816; killed by Morgan's raiders at Salem, Indiana, Jul. 10, 1863.

Hannah Wible—b. May 23, 1819; d. Jan. 13, 1852.

William Rigney Wible—b. Jan. 26, 1821; d. Sept. 21, 1897.

Mary Dow Wible—b. Feb. 23, 1823; d. Aug. 15, 1907; m. James Harvey Hale.

Adam Wible—b. Jan. 17, 1825.

Samuel Harris Wible—b. Dec. 8, 1828; d. Jan. 2, 1843.

BIBLE RECORD OF THE MATTHEW SYMONS FAMILY

Matthew Symons,[1] son of John and Ann Symons, b. Dec. 7, 1766.

Sarah, wife of Matthew Symons and daughter of Thomas and Elizabeth Gilbert, b. Dec. 17, 1772.

Children of Matthew and Sarah (Gilbert) Symons:
Samuel Symons, b. March 22, 1790.
John Symons, b. Oct. 23, 1791.
Thomas Symons, b. March 25, 1794.
Matthew Symons, b. Feb. 11, 1798.
Ann Symons, b. April 23, 1800.
Elizabeth Symons, b. Feb. 22, 1803.
Prudence Symons, b. May 20, 1805.
Mary Symons, b. Aug. 7, 1806.
Sarah Symons, b. Oct. 6, 1812.
Margaret Symons, b. Aug. 15, 1815.
Elizabeth Symons, [2] d. Oct. 27, 1832, aged 88 yrs., 5 mos., and 5 days, wife of —— Symons, Sr.

---

[1] This record, contributed by Mrs. Ira Tranter, 448 East Madison Street, Franklin, Indiana, was copied from the Beard Bible, printed and published by Matthew Carey, 122 Market Street, Philadelphia, April 23, 1806.

[2] Possibly an aunt of Matthew Symons, the wife of a brother of John Symons.

Bible Records of the Taylor Family

Contributed by Alameda McCollough[*]

The Bible records that are printed here are those of the Taylor family. Stephen O. Taylor, I, was a pioneer of early Lafayette. Born in New York City in 1793, the son of a shoemaker on Golden Street, he migrated to Montgomery County, Ohio, as a young man, where near Dayton he married Elizabeth Diltz. In 1826 they went to Kentucky and remained two years. Taylor's interest in stock raising, kindled in that state, was to continue to the next generation. In 1828 the family came to Indiana with a start of some good livestock and located for a time in what is now Jackson Township, Tippecanoe County. A year later (1829) they settled in Lafayette, a crude, languishing village on the east bank of the Wabash. It was a good move, for the steamboat trade was beginning to come to the upper reaches of the river. The Taylors soon established themselves as innkeepers, and their National House, close to the public square on Main Street, became one of the first three hotels in the town. Prior to Stephen's death in 1844, the Taylors had also operated the Wabash House in what later became known as the Lahr Hotel, a name this hotel still uses. The hostel tradition was continued by Taylor descendants, and several of them followed that business in other states. A portrait of Elizabeth Diltz Taylor, 1798-1865, hangs in the Tippecanoe County Historical Museum at Lafayette.

Stephen O. Taylor, II, born in 1836 or 1837 and the youngest son of Stephen and Elizabeth Taylor's nine children, carried on his father's interest in livestock, particularly horses. He was considered an excellent judge of horseflesh, and during the Civil War furnished a large number of animals to the government. The Taylor livery establishment on South Third Street, which the second Stephen O. Taylor opened in 1856, became an extensive business that continued until his death in 1906. For fifty years it was a gathering place for horsemen in the Lafayette area.

RECORD FROM THE FAMILY BIBLE OF STEPHEN O. TAYLOR, I:

Births

Stephen Taylor	was born	Dec. 9, 1793
Elizabeth Taylor	" "	Feb. 13, 1798
Kelson Taylor	" "	Nov. 1, 1818
Clinton Taylor	" "	Sept. 24, 1821
Vincent Taylor	" "	Sept. 24, 1823
Lyman Taylor	" "	Sept. 18, 1826
Eliza Taylor	" "	Nov. 4, 1828[1]
Daniel Taylor	" "	April 22, 1831
Ingram Taylor	" "	Sept. 3 [?] 1833
Stephen Taylor	" "	Mar. 20, 1836[2]
Emeline Taylor	" "	May 15, 1838

Marriages

Stephen Taylor was married to Elizabeth Delts [Diltz] January 26, 1818

Deaths

Eliza Taylor	died	Sept. 27, 1838
Stephen O. Taylor	"	Nov. 3, 1844
Emeline Taylor	"	Oct. 8, 1847
Vincent Taylor	"	Jan. 30, 1854
Elizabeth Taylor	"	Feb. 13, 1865
Clinton Taylor	"	1876

RECORD FROM THE FAMILY BIBLE OF STEPHEN O. TAYLOR, II:

Births

Stephen O. Taylor	was born	March 20, 1837
Laura J. Shively [Taylor]	" "	October 4, 1841
Lillian Mercer Taylor	" "	January 9, 1863
Henry C. Taylor	" "	June 1, 1864
Wm. Gates Taylor	" "	September 13, 1867
Harvey Hall Taylor	" "	March 18, 1870

Marriages

Stephen O. Taylor and Laura J. Shively were married Oct. 12, 1858
Samuel Judson Carpenter and Lillian Mercer Taylor were married Oct. 21, 1903
Henry Hall Taylor and Janet Milne were married Nov. 11, 1918

Deaths

| Stephen Oliver Taylor | died | May 17, 1906 |
| William Gates Taylor | " | 1919 |

---

[1] Possibly 1827; the date is blotted.
[2] The 6 in this date has been marked over with what appears to be a 7.

ATKINSON GENEALOGY
Contributed by
FLORENCE M. BOSWELL

Several Atkinsons came to America in the early colonial period. Luke Atkinson was a signer of the New Haven Compact and an early settler and leading citizen of New Haven, Connecticut. Theodore and Thomas Atkinson, who were brothers, came from Lancaster, England, in 1636, and settled in Boston. Thomas and John Atkinson, brothers, were born in Yorkshire, England, the sons of John Atkinson. These brothers emigrated to Pennsylvania in 1681, where they were among the founders of Bucks County. The family belonged to the Society of Friends. Other Atkinsons settled in New Jersey near Burlington. The head of this branch was William, who married Elizabeth Curtis. Descendants of this family moved westward, and Atkinsons are found in many western and southern states. The family whose lineage is traced below is thought to have descended from the Pennsylvania line. The record as given includes only the part for which proof has been found. This begins with Henry and Ann Atkinson, of old Craven County, North Carolina.

Chief sources for the information on this genealogy include William L. Saunders (ed.), *The Colonial Records of North Carolina*, IV (Raleigh, N. C., 1886); William Wade Hinshaw (comp.), *Encyclopedia of American Quaker Genealogy* (2 vols., Ann Arbor, Michigan, 1936), I; Columbia County, Georgia, Records; Chatham County, North Carolina, Court Records; Lucas County, Iowa, Deed Records; and family Bible records.

ATKINSON

I. Henry Atkinson m. **Ann———**.
   Was granted 130 acres of land in old Craven County, North Carolina, 5-21-1741 (*North Carolina Colonial Records*, IV, 594).

II. Thomas Atkinson, son of Henry and Ann Atkinson, b. 9-18-1741; m. first to Ruth Cruze, dau. of John and Ann Cruze, d. 1-17-1779 (Hinshaw, *Quaker Genealogy*, I, 346).
   Children of Thomas and Ruth (Cruze) Atkinson:
   1. John, b. 11-25-1766, N. C.; m. 1-17-1793 Mary Woody.
   2. Thomas, Jr., b. 8-30-1769, N. C., d. 4-3-1844, Orange Co., Ind.; m. 7-24-1795 Margaret Kennedy, b. 8-28-1762, d. 7-28-1833.

Children of Thomas, Jr., and Margaret (Kennedy) Atkinson:
  a. John, b. 10-9-1796, d. 8-14-1884; m. 2-3-1819 Milly Dawson, b. 12-29-1794, d. 4-8-1884.
  b. Robert, m. 1847 Margaret Truax.
  c. Arthur, m. Mary Jane Pinnich.
  d. Henry, m. Lydia Dixon.
  e. Thomas, m. 12-29-1836 Rachel Vance.
  f. Ruth.
  g. Mary Ann, b. 1-31-1805, d. 7-31-1848; m. John Ditto.
  h. Margaret, b. 8-28-1806; m. Nathaniel Vest.
  i. Hiram, d. single.
3. Mary, b. 4-5-1771; m. 1812 Hugh Woody.
4. Ann, b. 2-28-1773; m. 1799 ――――Lynch.
5. Robert, b. 2-17-1775; m. 1797 Hannah Dunn.

Thomas Atkinson, Sr., m. second, 9-5-1781, Ruth Harvey, b. 12-25-1755, dau. of Isaac and Martha Harvey (Columbia County, Georgia, Records).

Children of Thomas and Ruth (Harvey) Atkinson:
6. William, b. 7-18-1782, Orange Co., N. C.
7. Elizabeth, b. 9-29-1784, Orange Co., N. C.
8. Henry, b. 2-11-1786, d. 10-30-1800.
9. Martha, b. 6-10-1787.
10. Rachel, b. 10-12-1788.
11. Isaac, b. 2-7-1790, d. 6-27-1799.
12. Ruth, b. 5-25-1791.
13. Edith, b. 6-29-1793.
14. Nathan, b. 4-3-1795, d. 11-22-1800.
15. David, b. 8-21-1797.

III. John Atkinson, son of Thomas and Ruth (Cruze) Atkinson, b. 11-25-1766, N. C., d. 1830, Chatham Co., N. C.; m. 1-17-1793 Mary Woody, b. 9-12-1772, dau. of James and Mary Woody, d. 12-1-1859 (Hinshaw, *Quaker Genealogy*, I, 346. Will of John Atkinson, 10-24-1829, probated May term, 1830, Chatham County, North Carolina, Court Records, Book B., 181-81).

Children of John and Mary (Woody) Atkinson.
1. James, b. 10-23-1793; m. 1-29-1817 Rachel Thomas.
2. Ruth, b. 11-20-1794; m. 2-10-1814 Solomon Stout.
3. Thomas, b. 8-28-1796.
4. Hugh, b. 2-27-1798; m. 11-12-1818 Hannah Barker.
5. Sarah, b. 2-26-1800; m. 12-11-1828 Nathaniel Newlin.
6. Robert, b. 4-3-1802; m. 1830 Mary Curl.
7. Charity, b. 9-20-1804.
8. John, b. 1-10-1807; m. 11-20-1830 Ann Vestal.
9. Mary, b. 2-3-1810.
10. Samuel, b. 5-9-1812; m. 10-15-1835 Rebecca Hornaday.
11. Elihu, b. 7-16-1815.

IV. James Atkinson, son of John and Mary (Woody) Atkinson, b. 10-23-1793, Chatham Co., N. C.; m. 1-29-1817 Rachel Thomas, b. 6-19-1797, dau. of Lewis and Agnes Thomas of Orange Co.,

Ind. (Hinshaw, *Quaker Genealogy*, I, 346, 1068, 1071-72. Certificate of removal, and Records of Lick Creek Monthly Meeting, Orange County, Indiana. Lucas County, Iowa, Deed Record Book A, 33-34).
Children of James and Rachel (Thomas) Atkinson:
 1. Joseph.
 2. Maggie, m. ———Young.
 3. William.
 4. Sarah, m. ———Morris.
 5. Lewis, b. 10-6-1830, Orange Co., Ind., d. 1-21-1882, Cuba, Ill.; m. 1-7-1856 Angaline McNew, b. 12-15-1839, d. 8-22-1890.
 6. Rebecca, b. 1833, Orange Co., Ind.; m. ———Harpold.
 7. James, b. 1834, Orange Co., Ind.
 8. Stephen, b. 1836, Orange Co., Ind.; m. 9-26-1856 Mary McNew.

V. Lewis Atkinson, son of James and Rachel (Thomas) Atkinson, b. 10-6-1830, d. 1-21-1882; m. 1-7-1856 Angaline McNew, b. 12-15-1839, d. 8-22-1890 (Hinshaw, *Quaker Genealogy*, I, 1071-72. Lucas County, Iowa, Deed Record Book D, 134. Bible records).
Children of Lewis and Angaline (McNew) Atkinson:
 1. Lucinda, b. 10-7-1856, Chariton, Iowa, d. 3-15-1927, Cuba, Ill.
 2. Thomas, b. 3-1-1858, Chariton, Iowa, d. 12-14-1922, Cuba, Ill.; m. Alice Winship, b. 11-23-1860, Colchester, Ill., d. 10-3-1935, Cuba, Ill.
    Children of Thomas and Alice (Winship) Atkinson:
     a. William Franklin, m. Sarah Whitworth, Cuba, Ill.
     b. Clara Ann, m. 2-3-1901 Cyrus Bishop, Cuba, Ill.
     c. James Lewis, m. Mary Mordue, Cuba, Ill.
     d. Ethel Judith, m. Joseph Goett, Cuba, Ill.
     e. George Henry, b. 1896, d. 1903, Cuba, Ill.
     f. Jane Vanessa, b. 1898; m. 5-7-1915 Jake Vondelo, Cuba, Ill.
 3. William Riley, b. 3-7-1860, Nodaway, Missouri, d. 7-17-1936, Cuba, Ill.
 4. Mary E., b. 4-10-1861, Chariton, Iowa, d. 8-6-1863.
 5. Lewis L., b. 4-10-1863, Chariton, Iowa, d. 9-10-1864.
 6. Effie S., b. 8-10-1879, Cuba, Ill., d. 8-10-1879, Cuba, Ill.
 7. Lilly, b. 7-13-1880, Cuba, Ill., d. 8-3-1880, Cuba, Ill.

VI. William Riley Atkinson, son of Lewis and Angaline (McNew) Atkinson, b. 3-7-1860, d. 7-17-1936; m. 3-10-1881 Mary Elizabeth Zimmerman, b. 2-6-1863, Blyton, Ill., dau. of Cornelius and Charlotte Herriford Zimmerman.
Children of William Riley and Mary Elizabeth (Zimmerman) Atkinson:
 1. William Franklin, b. 3-13-1882, Cuba, Ill., d. 10-4-1882, Cuba, Ill.
 2. Lucinda E., b. 5-23-1884, Cuba, Ill.; m. 8-6-1906 Matthew Felix.

3. Florence Myrtle, b. 9-14-1886, Cuba, Ill.; m. 7-18-1918 Arthur Wilson Boswell, son of Cyrus Clinton Boswell and Virginia Elizabeth (Fox) Boswell.
4. Stephen Floyd, b. 9-26-1889, Cuba, Ill.
5. Cornelius Wesley, b. 9-26-1889, Cuba, Ill.; m. 5-20-1935 Grace MacJordan.
6. Mary Ula, b. 8-12-1898, Cuba, Ill.; m. 3-20-1916 Elmer Hageman.
7. Velma Mabel, b. 12-20-1900, Cuba, Ill., d. 7-4-1940, Cuba, Ill.; m. 10-13-1917 Ralph Wells.
Children of Ralph and Velma Mabel (Atkinson) Wells:
  a. Florence Lou Wells, b. 5-4-1919, Cuba, Ill.; m. 12-6-1941 Kenneth Atkins.
  b. Mary Ellen Wells, b. 1-18-1921, Cuba, Ill.
  c. Felix Robert Wells, b. 3-31-1922, Cuba, Ill.

The Bond Family
By Edwin C. Chapman

Bond families live in the following Indiana Counties; Wayne, Henry, Randolph, and LaPorte. Many of them are descended from Joseph Bond, an English Quaker, who came to America by or before 1735, landing in Philadelphia. He seems to have settled in Bucks County, Pennsylvania, and there to have married Martha Rogers also of English origin. She came to America along with her family on the same ship that brought Joseph Bond. The two families may have been acquainted in England, or it may be that the association on shipboard led to the later marriage. At any rate, the marriage took place about 1739. To Joseph and Martha Bond, who lived on a farm, were born five children while they lived in Pennsylvania. The family became members of the Monthly Meeting of Friends in Bucks County.

About 1750, when many Friends were migrating to North Carolina, Joseph Bond with his family went to that colony. They settled in Guilford County and became members of Center Monthly Meeting. Two additional children were born in the new home, bringing the number to seven. It is not certain when either Joseph Bond or his wife died, but there is a tradition among descendants that both died about 1760 and were buried in unmarked graves in the Guilford Cemetery.

Most of the Bond children lived to rear large families. Some of them remained in North Carolina. As was natural, some of them moved westward to Tennessee. One at least came to Indiana, where he died in 1821. This was Edward Bond who was the father of nine children, most, or all, of whom came to Indiana during 1809 and 1810 when many Friends migrated to the Territory.

Genealogical records relative to various members of the Bond family follow:

Joseph Bond.

Son of Benjamin Bond and his wife Ann Paradise; born in Wiltshire, England, at or near the village of Devizes, 8th month, 6th day, 1704; died in Guilford County, North Carolina, about 1760; settled in Bucks County, Pennsylvania, in 1735; married Martha Rogers, an English girl; migrated to North Carolina about 1750; seven children, five born in Pennsylvania and two in North Carolina.

Children of Joseph Bond.

1. Edward	b. Sept. 26, 1740	m. Ann Mills
2. Benjamin	b. . . . . . , 1742	m. Mary Walton
3. Ruth	b. . . . . , 1744 (or 5)	m. Benjamin Walton
4. Stephen	b.	m. . . . .
5. Ann	b.	m. . . . .
6. Samuel	b. Dec. 2, 1753	m. Elizabeth Beales
7. John	b. May 30, 1755	m. (1) Jane Beeson
		(2) Elizabeth Beeson

Edward Bond.

Son of Joseph Bond and his wife Martha Rogers; born in Bucks County, Pennsylvania, Sept. 26, 1740; moved with his parents to Guilford County, North Carolina, about 1750; died in Indiana, May 6, 1821, having removed to Indiana Territory about 1810; married Ann Mills in Guilford County, North Carolina, Aug. 16, 1764. Ann Mills was the daughter of John and Sarah (Beals) Mills; born in Guilford County, North Carolina, in May, 1745; died in Indiana, April 3, 1826.

Children of Edward Bond and his wife Ann Mills.

1. Benjamin	b. July 4, 1765	m. Williams
2. Keziah	b. June 29, 1767	m. . . . .
3. John	b. June 15, 1769	m. Mary Huff
4. William	b. Nov. 16, 1771	m. Charlotte Hough
5. Edward	b. Jan. 24, 1774	m. Anna Huff
6. Anna	b. Sept. 19, 1776	m. Abram Bunker
7. Jesse	b. Nov. 24, 1779	m. Phebe Commons
8. Joshua	b. Nov. 28, 1781	m. Ruth Coffin
9. Joseph	b. Feb. 20, 1785	m. Sarah Mendenhall

Edward Bond, Jr.

Son and fifth child of Edward Bond and his wife Ann Mills; born in Guilford County, N.C., Jan. 24, 1774; died in Wayne County, Indiana, March 14, 1856; married Anna Huff in Guilford County, N.C., May 17, 1795. Anna was the daughter of Daniel Huff and his wife Elizabeth Christie; born Feb. 18, 1777, in Guilford County, N.C.; died Sept. 22, 1839, in Wayne County, Indiana.

In 1811, the family of Edward Bond, Jr., now consisting of wife and seven children moved to Indiana and settled in Wayne County where the town of Webster now is. There the family continued to live until the death of the parents.

Children of Edward Bond and his wife Anna Huff.

1. Daniel	b. Oct. 5, 1796	m. Mary Hussey
2. Benjamin	b. Nov. 15, 1797	m. Ellen Goldsmith
3. Keziah	b. July 17, 1799	m. Lewis Underwood
4. Elizabeth	b. May 6, 1801	m. Soloman W. Roberts
5. Rachel	b. Dec. 1, 1804	(unmarried) d. Feb. 1, 1851
6. Edward	b. Jan. 11, 1809	(unmarried) d. Dec. 22, 1840
7. John	b. July 3, 1810	(unmarried) d. June 28, 1829
8. Huldah	b. May 22, 1812	m. Barnabas Payne
9. Anna	b. May 1, 1815	m. Jonathan Garrett
10. Elias	b. June 25, 1817	m. Lydia Hutchins
11. Gideon	b. Aug. 18, 1820	(no issue) d. July 11, 1839

Daniel Bond.

Son of Edward Bond, Jr., and his wife Anna Huff; born in Surry County, N.C., May 10, 1796; died in Randolph County, Indiana, August 17, 1839; came with his parents to Indiana in 1811; married Mary Hussey in 1819. Mary was the daughter of Christopher Hussey and his wife Sarah Brown, of Ohio; born March 13, 1797; died in Randolph County, Indiana, Sept. 30, 1837.

Children of Daniel Bond and his wife Mary Hussey.

1. Christopher   b. June 28, 1821   m. Sarah Rinard
2. Levina   b. March 11, 1824   m. John Hull
3. Sarah   b. May 31, 1826   m. Zimri Hollingsworth
4. Cyrus   b. Aug. 8, 1828   m. Mary D. West
5. Eunice   b. June 28, 1830   m. Henry Nugent
6. Simon   b. Oct. 21, 1832   m. Susannah Harris
7. Pleasant   b. June 27, 1835   m. Martha Wilson
8. Peninah   b. June 11, 1837   (unmarried) d. April 11, 1858

Simon Bond.

Son of Daniel Bond and his wife Mary Hussey; born in Wayne County, Indiana, Oct. 21, 1832; died in California, Jan. 17, 1898; married Susannah Harris in Indiana, probably in 1853 or 1855. Susannah was the daughter of Benjamin Harris and his wife Lydia Hiatt; born about 1835 in Indiana.

Children of Simon Bond and his wife Susannah Harris.

1. Mary Elmetta   m. Cornelius Harris
2. Charles Sumner   m. Julia Boyd
3. M. Ella   m. Dr. Melville F. Johnston
4. Martha Emma   m. . . . .
5. Susan Myrtle   (deceased)

Charles Sumner Bond is a physician and resides in Richmond, Indiana. Dr. Melville F. Johnston also resides in Richmond.

Joseph Bond.

Youngest of the children of Edward Bond and his wife Ann Mills; born in Guilford County, N.C., Feb. 20, 1785; died in Wayne County, Indiana, August 18, 1864; married Sarah Mendenhall in Guilford County, N.C., Dec. 14, 1809. Sarah was the daughter of Aaron Mendenhall and his wife Marion Rich; born in Guilford County, N.C., Dec. 19, 1790; died in Wayne County, Indiana, Feb. 18, 1848. Before the birth of any children, the family moved to Wayne County, Indiana, about 1810 and settled in Middlesboro.

Children of Joseph Bond and his wife Sarah Mendenhall.

1. Aaron	b. Aug. 8, 1811	m. Amy Wright
2. Isaac	b. Nov. 4, 1812	m. Sarah Hiatt
3. Achsah	b. Dec. 10, 1814	m. Sylvanus Jones
4. Dinah	b. Dec. 2, 1816	m. Joseph Hiatt
5. Mahlon	b. Nov. 2, 1818	m. (1) Susan Mullin
		(2) Martha P. Bennett
6. Marian	b. Nov. 17, 1820	m. Charles Bond
7. Ann	b. Dec. 8, 1822	m. Elihu Jones
8. Peter	b. Oct. 17, 1824	m. Martha Fulghum
9. Susannah	b. Feb. 25, 1828	m. John Brown
10. Esther	b. July 21, 1834	m. Jonathan Jay

Peter Bond.

Son of Joseph Bond and his wife Sarah Mendenhall; born in Wayne County, Indiana, Oct. 17, 1824; died there Aug. 31, 1881; blacksmith by trade; married Martha Fulghum in Indiana, Sept. 5, 1850. Martha was the daughter of Frederick Fulghum and his wife Piety Parker; born Dec. 11, 1831; survived her first husband Peter Bond; married (2) David Little; and married (3) Alpheus Test. It is believed that no children were born of these later marriages.

Children of Peter Bond and his wife Martha Fulghum.

1. Erastus	b. Oct. 21, 1851	m. Mary Hortense Murray
2. Fredericka J.	b. June 11, 1855	(unmarried) d. Nov. 21, 1875
3. Miriam	b. Nov. 1, 185-	(unmarried) d. Oct. 24, 1864
4. Charles F.	b. April 18, 1860	m. . . . .
5. Josiah Rockwell	b. Sept. 16, 1862	m. [?]; d. Aug. 6, 1864
6. Marianna	b. Jan. 4, 1866	m. W. J. Hippard
7. Sarah M.	b. Oct. 27, 1870	m. [?]; d. June 16, 1874
8. Henry Herbert	b. June 12, 1874	m. Joseph Froggatt

The Christian Bowman Family
George W. Bowman

If it is important that church and state keep careful records of historical facts and incidents, it is vitally more important that the family, the greatest of the three and the foundation of the others, keep careful records. Family Bibles fade and become illegible, fall to pieces, and are lost to posterity. It is a great satisfaction to trace one's forebears back to the time when the land was a trackless wilderness and ascertain to which branch of those early pioneers one belongs, how he is related to the others, and from what type of stock he is descended. Henry Ward Beecher said: "The dry branches of genealogical trees bear many pleasant and curious fruits for those who know how to search after them."

The surname *Baumann* (Bowman) is a common one in German-speaking countries. There have been several changes in the spelling of the name from medieval times to the present. For instance, *Buman* was used until 1617; then *Buwman* and *Bouwann*, until 1650; and later *Baumann* or *Bauman*. This last spelling was changed to *Bowman* in the case of early American members of the family as English officials, in entering court records of legal documents, spelled the *Bau* as it sounded—that is, *Bow*. *Baughman*, *Boughman*, and *Bachman* are less frequent spellings.

All of the early emigrant Baumanns were Palatines of Swiss-German origin, coming from the Rhine district. Although there are records in the early eighteenth century of the landing of relatively few members of this family, Wendell, Christian, George, Daniel, and Hans are mentioned. From 1750 on, the name appears frequently. The lives of those mentioned are closely connected; their sources, arrivals, religion, locations, and dealings being closely associated, as records prove.

In July, 710, about 3,000 Palatines, having migrated to Ireland, were sent to New York as bond servants of the crown under Governor Robert Hunter. They settled at Livingston Manor and on the opposite side of the Hudson at Saugerities or Schoharie, a tract voluntarily presented to Queen Anne by Indian sachems for the homeless Palatines. Because of their condition of servitude at the first two places mentioned and because of refusal to let them leave, some fifty families fled to Schorie in the fall of 1712 and the rest followed in March, 1713. Hardly established in the several settlements, they again found themselves in trouble with the "Gentleman in Albany." Continual conflicts made life a burden in Schorie; and despairing of justice in 1722, a large number accepted offers from Pennsylvania to settle there.

About two-thirds of the Schoharie people were not willing to buy land or settle on the Mohawk at the Governor's pleasure, so they started for Pennsylvania. From Schoharie they cut through the forests to the head waters of the Susquehana, working down the river to the mouth of the Swatara and then ascended this river to the mouth of the Tulpehocken, where they settled. This was then the most remote outpost of white colonization in Pennsylvania. During this period many other Palatines sailed directly from Rotterdam and Amsterdam or came on ships touching these ports *en route* from England and bound for New York, Boston, or Philadelphia. Some setting out for one destination landed at another after many weary weeks of buffeting.

Jost (Joist) Hite (Heydt), setting out from Strassburg, the principal town of Alsace in 1710, landed at New York with sixteen families in *Brigatine Swift* and *Schooner Friendship*, ships built or purchased by Hite for this journey. They then went to Kingston. In 1716 or 1717 Hite and the families with him settled at Germantown, near Philadelphia. Becoming angry with the Governor of the province, partly because he would not give protection from the Indians, Hite purchased land in 1731 from the VanMeters in Virginia, and, in 1732, he with his family, his sons-in-law, Jacob Chrisman, George Bowman and their families started from York, Pennsylvania, for the Shenandoah Valley of Virginia—sixteen family groups in all. Other families were migrating to the Valley. Christian Bowman entered land in 1731 or 1732. Cutting their road through the forests, they crossed the Potomac near Harper's Ferry and entered the rich and beautiful valley. Hite settled near Winchester; Christian Bowman, near Edenburg; some, near the present Stephens City; and others, at distances of a few miles apart down the valley. The later towns of Strasburg and Shepherdstown were founded by Peter Stover and a man named Shepherd or Schaeffer.[1]

Christian Bowman, ancestor of the writer, was a native of the vineyard section of the Rhenish Palatinate. According to word of mouth, he and George Bowman, Hite's son-in-law, and probably Wendell Bowman, were related.

---

[1] Census of 1790, Pennsylvania, under heads of families, gives: Daniel and Christian Bowman, Lancaster Co.; Christian Bowman, Dauphin Co.; Christopher Bowman and Christopher Bowman, Jr., Berks Co.; Christian Bowman, Northampton Co.; Christian Bowman, York Co. The difficulty of keeping the Christian Bowmans straight is enhanced by the number bearing the name.

So far the parentage of Christian has not been established nor the name of his wife ascertained. Tradition tells us that Christian and George came from York (Pennsylvania) into the Shenandoah Valley of Virginia at the same time and perhaps they had been together throughout their travels. Court records show the purchase of land by Christian Bowman in May 1737; probate records show his will in 1764 and there are other ferefences to him and his neighbors.

The Bowman family was Lutheran. In early times it had belonged to the Reformed Church, but lated it accepted both of these religions and the Anabaptist, Mennonite, and primitive Baptist (Dunker) in addition. The older members of this family today are Reformed Presbyterians. The occupation of the Bowmans of earlier times was chiefly farming, but today they may be found as representative citizens in practically every walk of life. We find also that war records contain the names of members of the Christian Bowman family. In the Revolutionary War those of the first generation of Palatine emigrants were listed; in the Civil War we find them in both the northern and the southern armies—the proverbial brother against brother. In the Spanish and World Wars they were represented, some again making the supreme sacrifice.

Christian Bowman, born in Europe, came to the Shenandoah Valley, Virginia. He purchased land from William Russell, May 26, 1737. He obtained 675 acres south of Strasburg on the south side of North River at the mouth of Trembling Run. He established a home and spent the rest of his life as a farmer. Later he purchased other land, and at the time of his death, about Jan., 1764, he possessed much real estate. His wife preceded him in death.

Children

Jacob Bowman—m. Elizabeth Keller (?); d. 1774 (possibly not till 1778). Lived for a while at and near Strasburg, Va. His wife was administratrix of his will. His children were Peter and Jacob. His widow, Elizabeth, m. Philip Huffman of Strasburg.

Henry Bowman—d. 1814. Lived on land allotted him

in the division of his father's estate on the south side of the river, opposite Narrow Passage. Children: Isaac, Elizabeth, Benjamin, Stephen, Rebecca, John, and Henry, Jr.

Daniel Bowman—d. 1826; m. Anna Marie (Mary) Wakeman, Dec. 22, 1774. Anna Maria was the daughter of Conrad Wakeman. Children: Henry, Benjamin, Jacob, Samuel, Barbara, Christian, Joseph, George, Daniel, Anne. (Certified Revolutionary record for Daniel).

Christian Bowman, Jr., lived for a time on land willed him by his father, being part of the 675 acre tract near Strasburg. Litle is now known of him. (Record from War Department, for Revolutionary War service).

David Bowman lived between Woodstock and Edinburg on land received from his father (now owned by the Huffmans). This he sold to Phillip Hoffman (Huffman) and is supposed to have lived many years afterwards on land owned by the late John Barton, east of Hamburg. David had a son, John (d. 1849), who lived at same place as his father. John left a will (Will Book Y, page 411), dated 1847 and probated 1849.

Benjamin Bowman received one-third of a 525 acre tract opposite Narrow Pass.[2] Was killed by Indians.

Samuel Bowman (no record).

John Bowman received one-third of 525 acres opposite Narrow Pass. He married Barbara ——— and died prior to 1816 or 1818. (Will Book Y, page 115-8 names children).

Mag[d]alene Bowman (no record).

Catherine Bowman married Jacob Stover, brother of Peter Stover, founder of Strasburg. Her children were: a daughter (married Reuben Boehm), Barbara, John, Christian.

It is possible and likely that the first Christian Bowman was buried in the old cemetery located at Harmony Hall on the old Bowman Fort farm. True copy of will of Christian Bowman is on file in the Clerk's office of Frederick County, Virginia.[3]

The plantation where Jacob Bowman was living was bequeathed to him by the will of Christian Bowman and the plantation on which the father was living he gave to

---

[2] Thomas K. Cartmell, *A History of Frederick County* (Winchester, Va., 1909), 75.
[3] Will-book No. 3, Folio 166, probated Feb. 7, 1764.

Christian Bowman, Jr. These two sons were to "pay to the rest of their brothers and sisters so much back as to all share equal." The children named in the will were: Christian, John, Daniel, Henry, Benjamin, Samuel, Catherine, and Magdalene. Executors named were: Jacob Bowman, Peter Stover, Henry Funk, and Jacob Stover (son-in-law). The witnesses who signed the will were: Simon Harr, Hennich Funk, and Peter Staufer [Stover] Jr. The maker of the will signed his name *Chrystian* Bowman.

At a court held for Frederick County, February 7, 1764, there were present Henry Funk and Jacob Stover, executors. Witnesses, Simon Harr and Peter Stover.

In the settlement of the estate these sons appear as distrubutees:

>Henry Bowman
>Benjamin Bowman
>Daniel Bowman[4]
>Samuel Bowman
>(Jacob, Christian, and John were not listed.)

Purchasers at sale were:

>David Bowman
>Paul Bowman
>John Bowman
>Christian Bowman
>Jacob Bowman
>Peter Bowman[5]

---

[4] The line of Daniel Bowman (wife, Anna Wakeman), through his son Daniel Bowman, Jr., who came to Indiana, will be continued in the June issue of the *Indiana Magazine of History*.—M. T. M.

[5] In 1763 rents were paid to the executors by Peter Bowman and also by George Bowman. From old deeds, we find that Jacob Bowman was the eldest son of Christian Bowman. Peter was the eldest son of Jacob Bowman.

The Daniel Bowman Family

George W. Bowman

Daniel Bowman,[1] the elder, son of Christian Bowman, married Anna Wakeman, Dec. 22, 1774, in Virginia. They were married by Simon Harr, a Lutheran minister. Daniel

---

[1] The first installment of the Bowman family history was published in the March issue of 1938.

Bowman made a will[2] dated 1824, probated 1828, Shenandoah County, Virginia, in which he devises and bequeaths to his wife, Anna Maria (or Mary); to his son Henry, he devises his home farm on the river near Woodstock; to his son John, land upon which he then lived; to his son Benjamin, all claims for advances made to pay for Benjamin's land; he then provides for the distribution of his entire estate among his ten children, each one to have an equal share, but he does not mention them by name. Henry Bowman was named executor, and as such made a settlement in 1830, covering items of 1828-30. In this settlement distributions were made to:

Daniel Funkhauser and wife (name not given).
Eberhard Midinger and wife (no name).
Abraham Smutz (Smoot) and wife Mollie.
Mrs. Anna Fravel (widow of Benjamin Fravel).

The ten children are again mentioned, but the four named are to receive their shares of the inheritance later from payments on the lands as they come due. The ten children were Henry, Benjamin, Jacob, Samuel, Barbara, Christian, Joseph, George, Daniel, Jr., and Ann.

Shenandoah County records show a quit-claim deed of Daniel, Jr., to his brother Henry, administrator of his father's estate. Daniel Bowman, Jr., son of Daniel and Anna (Wakeman) Bowman, left Stony Creek, Virginia, with his wife and six children in the early eighteen-hundreds with the great western migration. The western migration followed the trail of Daniel Boone down the valley and on beyond the Cumberlands to Tennessee, Kentucky, and other western areas.

Daniel Bowman, Jr., and his wife, with their family, made the journey and ultimately reached Shelby County, Indiana, where they settled about 1816. All remained in this county with the single exception of the oldest son, John, who returned to Virginia. Daniel, Jr., was born in Virginia in 1779 and married Anna Reeser on Mar. 5, 1799. He died on July 27, 1843. Anna was born on Sept. 30, 1775. Her certificate was a Pennsylvania-German fractur-script. Daniel was buried in the old Bowman-Dake Family Cemetery, in Shelby County, Indiana, near London. He left no will. The

---

[2] The service of Daniel Bowman, Sr., in the Revolutionary War is noted in the "List of Virginia Revolutionary Soldiers," compiled by H. J. Eckenrode. On May 13, 1784, a warrant was issued to Daniel Bowman for the sum of 4£, 5s, and 4d. (Certified copy from the Virginia State Library, Richmond). See John H. Wayland, *History of the Shenandoah Valley* for a reference to Daniel Bowman.

children were John, Mary Magdalene, Catherine, Ann, Fred and Christopher. All of them were born in Virginia.

The family Bible was finally located after much search. It was **found in a family of descendants**, who had not borne the name Bowman for four generations. Photostatic copies of the **fly-leaf and family dates were made**. A literal copy of records follows:

> To we two, man and wife, Daniel and Anna Bauman, a son was born on the 13th day of September, 1799, his name was Johannes Bauman.
> and on August 3rd, 1801, a daughter was born, her name was Kathrine Bauman.
> another time on November 23rd, 1803, another daughter was born, her name was Magdalina Bauman [Mary?]
> another time on February 3rd, 1806, another daughter was born, her name was Irma Bauman.
> another time on the morning of December 13th, 1810, a son was born, a sweet boy, his name was Frederich Bauman.
> another time on January 17th [13?], 1813, another son was born, his name was Christian [Christopher] Bauman.

A tradition in the Bowman family relates how each evening an Indian Chief brought up the cows for Anna Reeser Bowman and sat upon her doorstep, waiting for a bowl of mush and milk; also that he captured a fawn for her, to which a bell was tied so that the beautiful, young animal would not be shot by his braves or by hunters.

Christian Christopher Bowman

Christian Christopher Bowman, the writer's grandfather, was born in Virginia on Jan. 13, 1813. He married Katherine Scott on Mar. 26, 1835. She died on July 22, 1838, leaving three children—John, Anne, and Daniel. Of these three, John was born on Dec. 9, 1835. He was a successful farmer in Shelby County, Indiana, and a captain of infantry during the Civil War. He died in November, 1909. Christian Christopher Bowman was married a second and a third time. The second wife was Phoebe Imel, the marriage taking place on March 4, 1840. This second Mrs. Bowman died on July 20, 1842, leaving one son Henry who died soon after his mother. The third wife had, like her new husband, been twice married before. Her maiden name was Elizabeth Williams, and she was born on July 26, 1814. Her first marriage was to William Tinkle. There were two children by this marriage—William, who died without issue, and Mary Elizabeth who married Isaac White and left no issue. Elizabeth (Williams) Tinkle, widow of William Tinkle, married William Barlow. There were three children by this marriage—Martha (who married Adam Fansler, and had two sons), James and William. Christian Christopher and Elizabeth Bowman had four children—Frederick, George, Catherine and Christopher. The last two died in infancy. The mother died on Sept. 25, 1861, and the father, on April 18, 1885.

Frederick Bowman, son of Christian Christopher and Elizabeth Bowman, was born on Feb. 24, 1851. He married Mary Padrick. There were two daughters—Fannie, who married C. Herman Jose, and Addie, who married Adrian Carpenter. Frederick's second marriage was to Ida Cosler, and their children were: Eva, who married William Hogle; Raymond, who married Anna Buenagle; and Frederick Bowman, Jr. The father, Frederick Bowman, Sr., died on Aug. 11, 1899.

George Washington Bowman, second son of Christian Christopher and Elizabeth Bowman, was born on Jan. 25, 1855, and married Margaret Emma White on Mar. 19, 1884. They had one son, George Washington Bowman, Jr., who was born at Indianapolis on Nov. 30, 1889. Margaret Emma White, daughter of Isaac M. and Alvira (McCartney) White, was born on May 10, 1863. George W. Bowman Sr., was a wholesale confectioner. He died on Sept. 12, 1910. George Washington Bowman had one daughter, Julia Elizabeth Bowman, who was born on Dec. 2, 1911. She married Edgar Hollis Leedy on July 2, 1929. Lillie Catherine Keller, who was born on Sept. 5, 1886, was a daughter of Joseph H. and Charlotte (Wenzel) Keller.[3]

---

[3] The record of the Bowman family has been carefully proved. Many photostats of wills, Bible records, maps, and other documents have been collected. Pictures of members of the family and of their homes have been collected. An unusual chart showing eight generations and bringing the family lineage down to the present time has been prepared. Credit for research done relative to the history of the Bowman family should be given to the following: P. S. Rhodes, Woodstock, Va.; John Bowman, Edinburg, Va.; James L. Bowman, Carmanguar, Alberta, Canada; D. H. M. Bowman Toledo, O.; Wirt George Bowman, Palm City, Cal.; and Dr. John H. Wayland, Harrisonburg, Va.

The Henry Bryan Family
By Emily King Anderson

Henry Bryan and two sisters, all single, came from New Castle County, Delaware, after the Revolutionary War and bought land about three miles southwest of the present town of Centerville, Indiana. They talked very little about their past. They were wealthy, or had been, in Delaware, where they were merchants, importing fine dress materials, furs, etc. When they came west they brought great trunks full of fine silks, paisley shawls, and other such luxuries, which were not displayed but kept packed for years. They had been loyal to England, that is, Tories, while their neighbors on all sides were for independence, but were all on good terms. Henry Bryan's brother, John Bryan, settled in Beaver County, Pennsylvania.

A family by the name of Crawford, whose head had fought in the Revolutionary War, lived on the farm next to them after they settled in Indiana. Henry Bryan married one of the daughters. He was a well educated man. He surveyed the land for the location of the town of Centerville. He built a schoolroom on his farm, where his small girls were taught in regular sessions, and he was their teacher. Other children in the neighborhood were invited to attend school free of charge. He continued this school until his girls were ready for the higher grades.

Eliza Bryan, one of the daughters, lived in Centerville across from the Methodist Episcopal Church for many years. I have been in her parlor several times; it was furnished with old-fashioned haircloth mahogany chairs and sofa and velvet carpet. She went to Indianapolis later to live with a sister where she died.

Martha, another daughter of Henry Bryan, who must have been beautiful when young, married a young lawyer, Jacob B. Julian. They started housekeeping in two rooms in Muncie, Indiana, but later returned to Centerville. Jacob Julian had a taste for landscape gardening and could see possibilities in a vacant lot. He selected a knoll in the west part of Centerville, built a substantial brick house with a large latticed porch at the back of the kitchen, and laid off winding gravel walks in the large yard, with clusters of shrubbery at the turns. He planted rare bulbs and shrubs, including Jack Parlneyron roses and many kinds of trees, especially evergreen and fruit trees. The persimmon trees set out by him multiplied into a grove at the west side of the lot.

This home was sold to Oliver P. Morton, after which Mr. Julian bought the whole block enclosed by what is now Morton Avenue on the west, the Pennsylvania Railroad on the north, First Street on the east, and Plum Street on the south. He made a gravel walk from the house at the east part of the lot to Morton Avenue, with rare rose bushes on each side, and smoke bushes and other shrubs just at the right places. A walk wound down the hill to Paddy's Run. There was a perennial spring at the edge of the branch with stepping stones leading to the circular-cut stone. A group of thick evergreens was planted so as to enclose an oval space, within which was a seat just large enough for two persons. This was called "Lovers Retreat."

A class of young girls gave a moonlight picnic in the Julian place one beautiful moonlight night. Over one hundred guests were invited, many of them coming from Richmond. Two young girls served buttermilk from an artistic fountain. I think they called it the Fountain of Youth. There were long tables in the yard with cake, pie, chicken, and other good things to eat. An orchestra furnished music for dancing.

Mary, the oldest daughter of Jacob B. and Martha Bryan Julian, married James E. Downey of Indianapolis. She had been teaching a Sunday School class of young girls and invited them to come and look at the wedding preparations, her dresses, presents, and the tables already set for the feast. She also gave each one a piece of her beautiful wedding dress, which some of them have kept to this day, and a piece of cake to dream over. The Downeys afterwards lived in Irvington and were the parents of nine children, Julian Bryan Downey being the oldest. A daughter, Rebecca, is the wife of Professor Alfred Holmes White of the University of Michigan. Rebecca, Julian next younger than Mary, married James L. Mason, a lawyer of Greenfield. Both these weddings took place in Centerville.

Martha, the youngest child, was a beautiful girl, a leader in school and society. She spent a winter in Washington with her uncle, Congressman George W. Julian, which meant a round of pleasure for her. I attended her wedding in the beautiful new home in Irvington. She married Edgar A. Brown, an attorney of Indianapolis, soon after her family moved from Centerville. They had two children, a boy, George, now in the real estate business in Indianapolis, and a daughter, Juliet, wife of Dr. Christopher B. Coleman, director of the Indiana Historical Bureau.

John F. Julian, the oldest child, and only son of Jacob and Martha Julian, practiced law with his father both in Centerville and Indianapolis. He was named for John Finley, early Indiana poet, author of "The Hoosier's Nest," who resided in Centerville and was an intimate friend of the family.

The John Bryan Family

By President WILLIAM LOWE BRYAN

Henry Bryan, subject of Mrs. Anderson's sketch, was a brother of my grandfather, John Bryan. They were the sons of my great-grandfather, Henry Bryan, who at the time of the War of the Revolution lived on the Brandywine in Newcastle County, Delaware, near Chads Ford, which is in Pennsylvania. There is a family tradition that two daughters of Henry Bryan, the elder, were captured by British troops, taken to British headquarters, and then courteously conducted to their father's home. There is another tradition that Washington visited the Bryan home and ate at their table. Some years ago I saw a table which was piously believed to be the Washington table, along with many other beautiful inheritances in mahogany and silver in the home of Miss Walpole, granddaughter of Henry Bryan, the younger. Finally, there is the tradition that Hessian troops invaded the Bryan home, ate whatever could be found, and as a joke which little Henry Bryan could not enjoy but never forgot, carried away his hat.

My grandfather, John Bryan, born in 1763, spent most of his adult life in Beaver County, Pennsylvania, where he had a typically large family. From his children have come very many descendants, of whom many still survive in various parts of the United States and beyond.

My father, John Bryan, was born in Pennsylvania in 1811. He became a minister of the United Presbyterian Church. He preached at various places, including New York City, but principally in eastern Ohio and in Bloomington, Indiana. He died in 1887.

I shall record nothing of him here except that from his college days he was foe of slavery and foe of the liquor traffic through years when it was dangerous even in the North to be an open foe of slavery and dangerous even for a minister to be the foe of the liquor traffic.

When my father was about fifteen he spent considerable time at the home of his uncle, Henry Bryan, in Centerville, Indiana. He maintained intimate acquaintance with his uncle's family and cherished through life the friendship of his cousins, Eliza and Martha Bryan, who became Mrs. Walpole and Mrs. Julian. They are referred to in Mrs. Anderson's paper.

My cousin, Reverend Dr. James O. Campbell, has prepared a formidable volume about our Bryan clan. The book includes the names of hundreds of the dead and the living.

As a final note I may add that I have not found the name Bryan in any Scotch or Scotch-Irish list of names. The name Bryan is found in English records as far back as the thirteenth century and frequently thereafter.

SOME OF THE BUNDY FAMILY AS PIONEERS IN AMERICA

Alice Ann Bundy

In the middle of the seventeenth century many Quakers were drawn to America by the hope of religious tolerance. Among the occasional clusters of Quaker homes at favorable sites along the Atlantic coast was a nucleus on the lowlands bordering Albemarle Sound in what was incorporated as Albemarle County in Carolina about 1666. These permanent settlers pushed the frontiers of the Virginia colony to the south after the good land had become scarce, drifting individually, or by families into the fertile spots bordering the rivers, evidently in the latter part of the 1650's.[1]

Geographical factors largely determined the direction of this small migration. Many of the streams of southeastern Virginia find their way to the Albemarle Sound. These water

---

[1] *The North Carolina Historical and Genealogical Register* (3 vols., Edenton, North Carolina, 1900-1903), I, 307; Catherine Albertson, *In Ancient Albemarle* (Raleigh, North Carolina, 1914), 46.

courses offered a route to fertile unsettled lands with less danger and greater ease. Their chances of escape were better if attacked by tribes of Indians or wild beasts from the impenetrable Dismal Swamp, or the dense forests and thick undergrowth of the interior. An abundance of fish in the streams was a partial guarantee of a food supply, and purer water could be obtained along the streams, then too, the rich bottom lands were more easily cleared, and the higher lands were more desirable sites for building homes. Furthermore, the soil, climate, flora, and fauna were similar to that of the southern part of the Virginia colony. It is quite possible that the revision of the colonial laws of the colony of Virginia stimulated a portion of them to seek homes in the unsettled lands to the southeast, for in 1662 the Church of England was re-established and severe laws were passed against the Quakers and other separatists. It seems, however, that there was only a small percentage of Quakers among the earliest settlers. George Fox, the founder of the Quaker faith, visited the settlement in 1672 and organized Quaker groups that became influential in the life of the colony.[2]

They bought their land of the Indians, and when Charles II, 1663, included the Albemarle region in the grant of the Lords Proprietors, they took out patents for their newly-settled plantations in a land infested with malaria and remote from any colonial settlement. When William Edmundson, an early follower of George Fox, traveled from Virginia to Albemarle in 1671, he found his way through "all wilderness with no English inhabitants or pathways, but some marked trees" to guide the traveler.[3]

It is evident that among these adventurous colonists were some members of the Bundy family, a family of French descent that originally spelled their name Bundeie. According to the family tradition their ancestors were among the French Huguenots driven out of France by the Catholic persecutions,

---

[2] Mrs. Watson Winslow, *History of Perquimans County, North Carolina* (Raleigh, North Carolina, 1931), I; William W. Hening, *The Statutes at Large; being a Collection of all the Laws of Virginia* (13 vols., Richmond, Virginia, 1809-1823), II, 41-55, 180-182; William L. Saunders (ed.), *The Colonial Records of North Carolina* (10 vols., Raleigh, North Carolina, 1886-1890), I, xix.

[3] Albertson, *In Ancient Albemarle*, 46-47; William Edmundson, *A Journal of the Life, Travels, Sufferings, and Labour of Love in the Work of the Ministry of William Edmundson* (London, 1774), 66.

who settled in Wales, and about the middle of the seventeenth century some of the more venturesome sailed from Pembroke, Wales, for America. Members of the family residing in Worcestershire in southwest England adopted as the family crest, a hand, holding an eagle's leg and had as their motto, *Certum pete finem."* (Aim at a sure end.)[4]

The Bundys settled on plantations reaching out from both banks of Little River, that forms a natural boundary between Pasquotank County and Perquimans County where some of their descendants were living two hundred years later. Caleb and Jean (Jane), his wife, sold a plantation on Perquimans River "towards the head thereof" February 25, 1692-3. Williams sold one hundred acres on the north side of the Perquimans River, November, 1694. The following grants of land in Pasquotank Precinct (later Pasquotank County) were made to members of the family. William received a grant of 130 acres in 1694, Caleb, 175 acres, and Samuel, 110 acres. Samuel received a grant of 351 acres on Little River in 1716. A grant was made in 1714 to Caleb "which lapsed in John Bundy's name" in 1727. Samuel received a grant of 588 acres in 1739 and William a grant of 483 acres.[5]

The Bundys seem to have been active members of the Quaker church and to have participated in the civic and political life of the colony. William Bundy was a member of the first Quaker organization in Perquimans Precinct which met at the home of the members. William's wife, Elizabeth, whom he probably married before coming to Carolina, died March 4, 1676. Seven years later at a quarterly meeting held at the home of Christopher Nicholson, William Bundy and Mary Pearre, widow of John Pearre and daughter of Joseph Scott, published their intention of marriage. They were married at her home "Desember 15, 1683." William

[4] George Washington Smith, *A History of Southern Illinois* (2 vols., Chicago, 1912), II, 744; S. H. Bundy, Dongola, Illinois, to J. A. Bundy, Iroquois, Illinois, June 11, 1895; Manuscript read at the Fiftieth Wedding Anniversary of John and Mary Moore Bundy, Monrovia, Indiana, March 10, 1881; Arthur Charles Fox-Davies, *Fairbairn's Book of Crests of the Families of Great Britain and Ireland* (2 vols., Edinburgh, 1892), I, 36.

[5] Winslow, *History of Perquimans County, North Carolina*, 43-45, 327-328; Records of the Secretary of State, State Department, Raleigh, North Carolina, Book I, 11, 140, Book VIII, 30, 116, 290.

Bundy is recorded as being a witness at several weddings in 1680. His signature appeared on a remonstrance dated September 25, 1679, which was addressed to the Duke of Albemarle by the Quakers, most of whom had been inhabitants of Carolina since 1663. The court records show that he assigned to Mary Scott all his interests to an Indian named Sanders, April 6, 1680. He served as one of the justices at a court held for the Precinct of Perquimans at the home of Mary Scott, the first Monday in January, 1690-1. In every precinct the court consisted of a judge and four justices. To be an eligible candidate for justice, a man must have been an inhabitant of the precinct and own 300 acres of land. At that time there were four precincts in Albemarle County —Perquimans, Pasquotank, Currituck, and Chowan. Albemarle County was abolished in 1729 when each of the precincts became a county. He is listed among the Quakers who were sentenced and imprisoned for refusing to bear arms, serving a six months' term in 1680.[6]

Caleb Bundy married Jane (Jean) Maners at "ye quarterly meeting," July, 1690. At a meeting of the Quakers, March 1, 1703, their home was selected as the place for holding their monthly meetings. At their regular monthly meeting May 4, 1706, this organized group of Quakers decided to build a church between the home of Caleb Bundy and William Brother's Creek, and "unanimously agreed that it should be left to the Discression of the afsd Caleb Bundy Stephen Scott & Henry Keton to choose a proper place and also to go through with the Building of the said Meeting House." The committee chose a site on the banks of Symon's Creek, an arm of Little River, the oldest Quaker meetinghouse in the State of North Carolina of which there is a record. It has not been possible to fix accurately the location of the early Quaker churches in Pasquotank County. It seems to be the consensus of opinion that the site of this church was one mile from Symon's Creek on the road from Nixonton to Weeksville.

[6] William W. Hinshaw, *Encyclopedia of American Quaker Genealogy* (3 vols., Ann Arbor, Michigan, 1936-1940), I, 1, 38; Winslow, *History of Perquimans County, North Carolina*, 3, 32, 327; *The North Carolina Historical and Genealogical Register*, III (1903), 365, 436-437; Albertson, *In Ancient Albemarle*, 13; Saunders (ed.), *The Colonial Records of North Carolina*, I, 252-253.

Samuel and Caleb Bundy are listed as members.[7]

Mrs. Winslow in her *History of Perquimans County* describes an old cemetery where the Bundys who settled on Little River were probably buried.

Little River Meeting House is just beyond the village of Woodville, and it is spoken of as being "at the head of Little River" where today a Quaker burying ground can be seen on a small eminence on the right side of the road going toward the Weeks home across Little River, on the Pasquotank side. A large sycamore tree marks the location and many small grave stones lift their mute testimony for all to see. Here in tranquil peace lie numbers of old residents of Quaker faith.[8]

Caleb Bundy served as a member of the House of Burgesses, the lower house of the legislative body, for several terms. An address from the House of Burgesses to the governor and council, bearing no date but evidently about 1703, bore the signature of Caleb Bundy and others. When Queen Anne came to the throne of England in 1704, Parliament passed a law requiring all public officials to take an oath swearing allegiance to the new sovereign. Since in the early days of the colony of Albemarle the Quakers were more numerous than any other religious group, they were exempted from taking the oath to hold public office, cleaving religiously by the teachings of the New Testament, "Swear not at all" and were given the privilege of taking its equivalency, an affirmation. The deputy-governor, a staunch member of the Church of England, was anxious to establish the Church of England in Carolina by law, but as long as the Quakers had a potent influence in the legislative body and higher offices, the law could not be passed. For that reason Robert Daniels, the deputy-governor, demanded that all persons holding public office should take the oath of allegiance which resulted in driving the Quakers from the Assembly.[9] Mean-

---

[7] Winslow, *History of Perquimans County, North Carolina*, 327; *The North Carolina Historical and Genealogical Register*, III, 204; Saunders (ed.), *The Colonial Records of North Carolina*, I, 596, 656; Hinshaw, *Encyclopedia of American Quaker Genealogy*, I, 92; Stephen B. Weeks, *Southern Quakers and Slavery* (John Hopkins University Studies in Historical and Political Science, XV, Baltimore, Maryland, 1896), 67.

[8] Winslow, *History of Perquimans County, North Carolina*, 29.

[9] *The North Carolina Historical and Genealogical Register*, II (1901), 223; Albertson, *In Ancient Albemarle*, 38-39; Samuel A. Ashe, *History of North Carolina* (2 vols., Greensboro and Raleigh, North Carolina, 1908-1925), I, 158-159.

while, the following proclamation was issued giving the reason for ordering another election: "Whereas Caleb Bundy Jeremiah Symonds Augustine Scarborough & John Hawkins Chosen Burgesses for this present Assembly . . . have refused to take the Oaths appointed by Law."[10] The date of the proclamation was 1709 or 1710, as Caleb Bundy was a member of the House of Burgesses, October 11, 1709.

Caleb mentions a brother Samuel in his will. Mary Bundy married Nicholis Simons, June, 1602. The same year Hannah Bundy married John Larance, son of William Larance. Very likely Mary and Hannah were sisters of the three brothers, William, Caleb, and Samuel, sons of William Bundy. It seems that William Bundy, a cordwainer, settled in Perquimans Precinct where he died, March 27, 1692. William, his son, a planter, died in Pasquotank Precinct, July 28, 1700. There is a record of the birth of Samuel, February 4, 1676, to William and Elizabeth. One daughter, Mary, is mentioned. William and Mary had one daughter, Sarah. Samuel married Tamer Symons in 1696 at the home of Henry White in Perquimans Precinct. Two of his children were Jeremiah and Samuel. Caleb died, March 4, 1721. His will was probated in Pasquotank Precinct Court, April 27, 1721, in which he bequeathed to each of his heirs a tract of land. John was given the land he had purchased of Thomas Stanton, Benjamin received the farm where his father lived, Samuel was willed the land "lying up Little River," and Mary, the daughter, received a tract of land that he had bought from his brother Samuel. In the will he mentioned a granddaughter Liday, daughter of his son William. He named as his executors his sons, John and Benjamin. His son Caleb died in January, 1721, leaving a will in which he named his brothers, William and John, as his beneficiaries. His wife, Jane, died in 1719. His son, William, who married Ann Keaton, died in February preceding Caleb's death, and Mary passed on a few days after the death of her father."[11]

---

[10] *The North Carolina Historical and Genealogical Register*, III, 136; *ibid.*, I, 304.

[11] J. Bryan Grimes, *Abstract of Wills* (Raleigh, North Carolina, 1910), 55; *The North Carolina Historical and Genealogical Register*, I, 443, III, 204, 364; Hinshaw, *Encyclopedia of American Quaker Genealogy*, I, 131; Winslow, *History of Perquimans County, North Carolina*, 45, 327-329.

The spirit of freedom overflowing with energy and self-reliance of the sons of William Bundy seems to have been handed down to the next two or three generations. At the close of the eighteenth century and the early part of the nineteenth century a number of their descendants joined the heavy migration from the Tidewater section of the Carolinas to the "uplands" or Piedmont region, and many of them were traveling by packhorse over nature's thorough-fares, crossing the Appalachian Highlands and following the streams that directed them into the fertile lands to the west. William Bundy and relatives crossing the Appalachian Highlands, where the barriers had been carved by the interlocking of the eastward moving rivers and westward flowing streams, found their way to middle Tennessee and settled near the present site of Nashville in 1792. This was two years after Congress had passed an act providing for the government of the western land ceded by North Carolina to the federal government, which was known as the Southwest Territory. In a few years one of his brothers, accompanied by two cousins emigrated from the Southwest Territory to Walnut Prairie, Illinois. S. H. Bundy of middle Tennessee moved to Williamson County, Illinois, in 1852. Several Bundy families were among the pioneers that found their way to the border of Indiana and followed the course of the Whitewater River into the east central part of the state. Christopher Bundy, the great-grandfather of the late Major General Omar Bundy, who was born in Pasquotank County, joined the tide of emigrants to the upland country. About 1818, he left Guilford County, North Carolina, and stopped in Wayne County, Indiana. Later, he entered land in Henry County, Indiana, where he died in 1835. George Bundy came to Wayne County, Indiana, before 1823, and his brother Josiah was among the early settlers from North Carolina that located south of Carthage. Other Bundy families that were pioneers in this section were the children of Nathan and Ruth Morris Bundy of Perquimans County, North Carolina. Elias Bundy, father of the late William Bundy of Carthage and grandfather of Elias Bundy, at one time an attorney-at-law, Marian, Indiana, moved from Perquimans County, North Carolina, and entered 160 acres of land south of Carthage in 1832. Ely Bundy followed his relatives to Henry County, Indiana, in 1824. William Bundy and family transferred their membership to the Whitewater Monthly

Meeting in 1818. Ephriam Bundy joined his kinsman in Wayne County in 1829. Charles, his wife, Pheriba, and children were granted certificates to Milford Monthly Meeting in 1838. Abraham Bundy, son of Moses and Jane Bundy of Perquimans County settled in Washington County in 1816. The same year John Bundy joined the pioneers in Washington County, Indiana, and moved the church membership of his family to the Blue River Monthly Meeting. Another pioneer that came to Washington County was William, son of Moses and Elizabeth Bundy. In 1813 Gideon Bundy moved from North Carolina to Harrison County, Indiana. William P. Bundy and bride, John Bundy and family transferred their church membership to the West Union Monthly Meeting, Morgan County, Indiana. Joshua Bundy and family joined the Quakers that were worshiping at the Wheeler Monthly Meeting, Ohio. William, his wife, Mary, and their daughters migrated to a Quaker settlement that attended the Concord Monthly Meeting, Ohio. In 1815 Zodak and Rebecca and their children transferred their church membership to the Fall Creek Monthly Meeting, Ohio.[12]

The story is told that a North Carolinian tribe of Indians, splitting a bezoar, or madstone, gave half of it to the head of a Bundy family for some good turn the white friend had given them in 1815 and kept the other half for their own use. This stone, used for the bites of snakes, dogs, and wolves, was brought by a pioneer Bundy family to Indiana and is said to be kept in a vault.[13]

Caleb, whom records indicate was the third son of John and Elizabeth Keaton Bundy, owned and operated a farm near Little River Bridge, Pasquotank County, North Carolina. He married Elizabeth Henby in 1745. Their children were Dempsey, John, Miriam, Samuel, and Sarah. Elizabeth died November 5, 1762. Caleb's second wife was Miriam Morgan, one authority states that her maiden name was Nicholson.

---

[12] S. H. Bundy, Dongola, Illinois, to J. A. Bundy, Iroquois, Illinois, June 11, 1895; Letter from William Bundy, Carthage, Indiana, October 17, 1918; Letter from Zella White, Salem, Indiana, December 7, 1941; Letter from Clarence H. Smith, Curator, Henry County Historical Museum, New Castle, Indiana, October 5, 1941; Hinshaw, *Encyclopedia of American Quaker Genealogy*, I, 133-134, 710-711, 802, 873, 1008.

[13] Hassoldt David, "The Snake Stone of Nepal," *Travel* (New York, 1901-), LXXX (1943), 13.

The children of Caleb and Miriam were Benjamin, Caleb, John, Jeremiah, James, Hannah, Moses, Samuel, and Christopher. In a sketch of the family the following was read at the celebration of the golden wedding of John and Mary Moore Bundy at Monrovia, Indiana, March 10, 1881:

We are indebted to Joseph Bundy, son of Moses [one of the above-named brothers] for a description of the old homestead. He is an old man now in his 84th year, living at High Point, North Carolina, and quietly waiting his summons to that Better World. He was a member of his grandfather's family in his boyhood and seemed living over again his childish joys whilst telling of the large old-fashioned house built upon a stone basement, which served as a cellar in which was stored many barrels of wine and cider and great heaps of apples. And very often some of his large family of boys would serve as cooks whilst the rest were in attendance at meeting and quite often expecting some traveling Friends as guests as they lived near the meeting house.

Many of the descendants of the fourteen children, three daughters and eleven sons, of Caleb Bundy were part of the stream of emigrants that left the Tidewater region and sought homes in the more favorable uplands of North Carolina in Guilford County, Randolph County, and surrounding section, from whence they followed along the streams of North Carolina to their sources and crossed over to the trails following rivers and buffalo trails leading westward. Among these were the descendants of Jeremiah Bundy.

Jeremiah, fourth son of Caleb and Miriam Bundy, married Betsey (Elizabeth) Low, daughter of one of Caleb Bundy's neighbors, and member of a pioneer family in Albemarle County in 1797. He settled in the lowland along Albemarle Sound. In late 1806 or early 1807 he died, leaving the widow and eight children, four boys and four girls. In the December term of court, 1807, the dower of the widow was laid off. John Bundy served as administrator with Benjamin as security. The administrator made his final statement in 1809. Leaving the eldest daughter, Milliscent, with her grandmother Bundy, the widow with seven children joined some neighbors that were emigrating to the uplands of North Carolina. She was not financially able to support the children. For that reason she "bound out" five of them. She married Joseph Stafford on May 11, 1812.[14]

[14] Winslow, *History of Perquimans County, North Carolina*, 329; Manuscript read at the Celebration of the Fiftieth Wedding Anniversary of John and Mary Moore Bundy, Monrovia, Indiana, March 10, 1881; Court Records, Pasquotank County, North Carolina, 75,014, State Department of Archives and History, Raleigh, North Carolina; Marriage Certificate, State Department of Archives and History, Raleigh, North Carolina.

After the death of her second husband, she again became a part of the westward movement. She and Fielden and Martha Bundy Brown, her daughter, were on the frontier in Hamilton County, Indiana, in 1851. As they crossed southern Indiana they visited her sons east of Vernon. Her two sons, Phineas and Ephriam, and their families joined them on the edge of the frontier in Hamilton County. The spirit of pioneering urged them until the three families had reached Sauk County, Wisconsin, in 1855. The mother passed on in 1858. Her funeral was held in Ephriam Bundy's hewed log house, and she was buried at the edge of a forest in a pioneer graveyard which is now abandoned.[15]

Phineas, the second son, married Nancy Reynolds in North Carolina, and joined his brother, Miles, in one of the early settlements in Jennings County, Indiana. His wife died in 1825 at the birth of their only child, William. When William was three months old, his father carried him on horseback from Vernon, Indiana, to his former home in North Carolina. A year later he married Nancy Turner and returned to Vernon, Indiana. He entered the marriage contract five times. All of his living sons served in the Civil War. John, Phineas, and James served in the infantry and Dr. Miles served as a surgeon. James was killed in service. His daughters were Elizabeth, Rebecca, Ruth Ann, and Martha. He died February 12, 1887, and was buried at Valton Cemetery, Sauk County, Wisconsin.[16]

Ephriam Bundy died June 12, 1888, and was buried in a new cemetery about a mile from where his mother was buried. He had a large family. The eight children were Christopher, Pheriba, Martha, Jabez, Mary, Eva, Miriam, and William. The latter served in the Civil War, was graduated from Ripon College, and was employed as a teacher in the Wisconsin public schools.[17]

Martha Brown had three children, Mary Brown Cook, Charlotte Brown Pickering, and Jabez. A daughter and two sons of Jabez Brown founded Browns' Preparatory School in Philadelphia, Pennsylvania, which has served that section

[15] Elizabeth Bundy Stafford, Sauk County, Wisconsin, to Miles Bundy, Sr., Vernon, Indiana, 1855; Letter from Eva Bundy Berry, daughter of Ephriam Bundy, Rockford, Illinois, March 20, 1929.

[16] Letter from Fred Small, grandson of Phineas Bundy, Wonewoc, Wisconsin, March 3, 1932.

[17] Letter from Eva Bundy Berry, Rockford, Illinois, March 20, 1929.

for more than fifty years. Later, on the Wisconsin frontier these descendants of Jeremiah Bundy endured the usual hardships of pioneer life. One winter when the settlers "ran short of flour, Phineas Bundy and a neighbor drove sixty miles through a deep snow to Portage to get a supply."[18]

John Bundy, another son of Jeremiah and Betsey, was "bound out" to John Hodges who died when he was about eleven years old. Then he was "bound out" to Joseph Newby with whom he lived until his marriage in his twenty-fifth year to Mary Moore. Their children were William P., Samuel C., Jesse M., Daniel W., Martha, Elizabeth, Sarah Jane, Semira, Mary, and John Elwood. The children were all born in North Carolina. Some of them attended Guilford College, and later most of them came to Indiana. John Elwood taught in Earlham College and was dean of the Richmond group of painters. John and Mary Moore Bundy sold their possessions in North Carolina in 1866 and came to Monrovia, Indiana, to make their future home, stopping on their way for a visit with Miles Bundy.[19]

Pheriba Bundy married Ephriam Pool, May 24, 1812, in Randolph County, North Carolina. According to the United States Census for 1820, they were living east of Vernon, Indiana. They must have joined those who were pushing the frontier northward for according to the Census of the United States for 1830, an Ephriam Pool was living in Wayne County, Indiana. The eldest daughter whose name was very likely Miriam, not Milliscent, married John Nixon, April 19, 1816, in Wayne County, Indiana. Hannah married Andrew Whisenhunt in September, 1819, in North Carolina where they continued to reside. According to the family history, handed down, their sons served in the Confederate Army.[20]

Miles, the eldest child of Jeremiah and Betsey, was "bound out" at the age of eleven. In the spring of 1816, he

---

[18] Letter from Melissa Brown, granddaughter of Martha Bundy Brown, Madison, Wisconsin, March 11, 1932; Letter from Fred Small, Wonewoc, Wisconsin, March 3, 1932.

[19] Manuscript read at the Celebration of the Fiftieth Wedding Anniversary of John and Mary Moore Bundy, Monrovia, Indiana, March 10, 1881.

[20] Marriage Certificate, Randolph County, North Carolina, Department of Archives and History, Raleigh, North Carolina; Mrs. Irene Macy Strieby, "Wayne County Marriage Records, 1811-1817," *Indiana Magazine of History* (Bloomington, Indiana, 1905-), XL (1944), 96.

ran away and joined some neighbors who journeyed westward, following the Wilderness Road to its terminal, Louisville. Here they crossed the Ohio River on a ferry and found their way to a settlement near Charlestown, Clark County, where they stopped at the homes of the Pools, Benjamin and Thomas. He joined Joseph Pool whose family followed the trail on packhorses to Vernon which had been platted the previous year, 1815. The town consisted of three cabins, surrounded by a clearing here and there with a cabin in the center. Joseph Pool chose a site for his round log cabin near a spring on the south side of the South Fork of the Muscatatuck in the forest three miles east of Vernon in which they lived until 1824 when he erected a large two-story house from brick he burned on the site. Just across the creek from the Pool cabin was a camp of some of the Delaware whose camps extended for several miles along the stream. They were under the control of White Eyes and Big John. In the spring of 1817, they abandoned their camps and set out for the West. Just before leaving some of the tribe came to the Pools and demanded meal.

Their first year was full of hardships and privations. In the fall of 1816, their horses got loose and the last of their corn meal had been made into corn pone. Joseph Pool and his thirteen year old daughter, Emilia, walked and carried the packsaddles forty miles to the settlement in Clark County where they found the horses and obtained meal. Jemima, the second child, said when reminiscing in her advanced age that "it was awful" while they were gone, for the mother and the children lived on frost-bitten pumpkins, the children cried and the wolves howled around the cabin. The summer was cool, frost came early and the winter of 1816-1817 was severe. One week in January the ice froze eighteen inches thick on the Muscatatuck Creek. Then a thaw came and the creek was almost clear of ice and again it was frozen sixteen inches or more thick. Scars that were made on the trees by the floating ice could be seen for many years.

Miles Bundy married Emilia (Milly) Pool, the eldest child of Joseph and Hannah Hooker Pool in 1819 and lived in a cabin across the Muscatatuck from the Pools for thirteen years. They obtained a living by tilling the "clearing" and killing wild game. There were plenty of deer, and turkeys were easily caught in rail pens. In the fall when the beechnuts were ripe, the passenger pigeons came in such large flocks that they darkened the air and at night they would roost in the trees at their regular roosting places in such numbers that the limbs of the trees were often broken. They obtained many of them for food with clubs at night. Every spring they made maple sugar. One spring the young wife cared for two children and made two hundred pounds of sugar. She placed the baby, Elizabeth Bundy (Patrick) in a sugar trough and carried Jeremiah so far from the boiling sugar water that he could not reach the fire under the sap before she returned from gathering sap. Hogs were fattened on the bountiful mast and part of the drove was driven to market at Madison. In a few years, the Vawter slaughter house was built in Vernon from which salt pork was shipped by rail to Madison and from that place by flatboat to New Orleans.

The father cut millstones and in this way was able to accumulate a small capital. He formed a partnership with "Jim" Spaulding and erected a gristmill run by water power two miles farther up the creek which was later known as the Wilson Mill. Then the family moved to the site of the new mill. Their savings increased and in 1839 they purchased two hundred or more acres of timberland on Crooked Creek, paying $1.25 an acre for government land. A cabin was built which burned to the ground in 1840. That year with the help of his seven sons, he built one of the largest sawmills in the county. The dam was made of limestone rocks and timber, the huge frame of hewed timber. During the spring months, the mill was run night and day while the stream was being fed by rains and the melting snow. During the summer months, his sons, John and Miles, hauled thousands of feet of poplar, walnut, and ash lumber with ox teams over the dirt road to Vernon from which point it was shipped by rail to Madison to be loaded on boats for the market at New Orleans. When the little Crooked Creek was out of its banks in 1876, the dam broke and was never rebuilt for the supply of timber was exhausted, steam-driven mills were taking the place of the older water-power mills.

Another hard year was 1833 when a killing frost came the night of June 15. The tender new twigs on the beech trees were about a foot in length and an abundant crop of green peaches about the size of a quail's egg hung on the trees. The leaves, twigs, and fruit fell, and many of the trees and shrubs were killed. On large areas in the flats or level swamplike land the timber was killed which was afterward known as the "frost deaden'."

They were among the first members of the Baptist church which was organized at Vernon in 1817. On horseback the father and mother each carried two children along the unimproved dirt road roughly paralleling the North Fork of the Muscatatuck to Vernon to listen to the sermon of John Vawter, or of Reverend Jesse Vawter. They were among the organizers of the Ebenezer Church, a Methodist church erected on a plot of land adjoining their farm. Their large family of young people made the home a place for social gatherings such as quiltings, dances, stirring off sugar, etc., which were attended by the Moncriefs, Hiltons, Royles, Patricks, and Hinchmans. In cases of illness, Dr. Pabody, the first physician to join the settlement at Vernon, was called. Dr. Gunn's book was often consulted and a generous supply of "Smith's Ager Tonic" was kept on hand.

The parents could write a legible hand, in fact, both of them had had instructions in the three R's. The father helped "to raise" the first log schoolhouse on Crooked Creek, which was equipped with puncheon floor, long benches, and a fireplace. He was appointed in 1841 as one of the three school commissioners. In this position he served for a number of years. Many evenings all the thirteen children would gather around the fireplace and by a flickering yellow poplar torch drill for the neighborhood spelling school. Around this fire was kindled the desire for learning that enabled one son to become judge of the circuit court for a number of years, another enter the ministry, and several to serve the community as teachers. Most of the grandchildren and many of the great-grandchildren entered the professions.

The news came in 1863 that Morgan and his men were coming, and that, no doubt, there would be an attack on Veron. The father hid the horses in a deep hollow, commonly known as a sinkhole. The small amount of "shin-plasters" and bills were placed in a box and secreted in a knothole in an apple tree. The two young sons, Miles and Clay, joined the handful of old men and boys that had assembled to protect Vernon. Various verbal reports reached the home as to the number killed in a battle. Later, an authentic report came that the inhabitants of Vernon with some of their treasures sought safety outside of the town, and a few volunteers were formed in line of battle south of town. They refused to surrender to Morgan who moved his forces south through the county towards Dupont.

Miles not only endured the hardships that fell to the farmer-lumbermen and other citizens during the Civil War, but death claimed his wife and daughter, Mary Ann. His youngest son Frank, accidently shot himself. Shortly after the war closed, Clay passed on. His children were Jeremiah, Nancy, Joseph Pool, Elizabeth (Betsy), George, Hannah, Mary Ann, Emilia, John, Jane, Miles, Henry Clay, Benjamin Franklin. Jason, the eldest, died at the age of a few months and was buried in the Baldwin Cemetery, one of the oldest in the county.[21]

The family of Jeremiah Bundy endured the hardships and privations that were experienced by all the members of the small groups who pushed the frontier northward across the Northwest Territory and helped to block out the territory for settlement. Yet theirs is a record of longevity. The mother reached the eighties, and Martha died at the age of ninety-one. Miles, Phineas, and Ephriam passed on in the eighties. Records indicate that John and Hannah also enjoyed long lives. The family was a part of the migration from North Carolina to the Old Northwest, particularly to Indiana.

[21] Personal interview with my father Miles Bundy, Jr.

Descendants of the Dumonts of Vevay*

LUCILLE DETRAZ SKELCHER
and
JANE LUCILLE SKELCHER

The seven children of John and Julia L. Dumont who grew to maturity were: Ebenezer, Martha, Mary, Peter Cory, Aurelius, Marietta, and Julia. Three boys, John, Henry and Cornelius, each lived to be about ten years of age, and a fourth, Edgar, was drowned at the age of thirteen.[1] The parents were married in 1812, and, after living in Cincinnati for a short period, they came to Vevay some time before the birth of the first son on November 23, 1814.

* This article is a sequel to "Julia L. Dumont of Vevay," by the same authors, which appeared in the September, 1938, issue.

[1] See "Julia L. Dumont of Vevay," *Indiana Magazine of History* (Sept., 1938), XXXIV, 306, Note. 9.

Ebenezer Dumont

Ebenezer Dumont was a teacher, lawyer, banker, soldier, and member of the national House of Representatives. He taught school while studying law. He married Mary Ann Cheek in 1838 or 1839. During the Mexican War he served as a lieutenant colonel. From 1852 until the institution wound up its business, Mr. Dumont served as the President of the Indiana State Bank. At the beginning of the Civil War, he became the colonel of the Seventh Indiana Regiment, but, in September, 1861, was promoted to the rank of brigadier general. His brigade was often commended by superior officers. In 1863, when stationed at Nashville, he led a force in pursuit of John Morgan who barely escaped at Lebanon, Tennessee. Having been elected to Congress in 1862, General Dumont resigned from the army in February, 1863. He was an experienced legislator having earlier served in the Indiana legislature. He was well read and quite a student of the Bible. He was an entertaining speaker and popular with his colleagues. When it was known that he was to speak, seats were sure to be filled. His drawling humor was much in evidence in his speeches.[2] He served two terms in the House, but was not a candidate for a third term in 1866. He was appointed governor of Idaho Territory in 1871, accepted, and was preparing to leave to take up the duties of the office when he died in April of that year.

Ebenezer Dumont had a family of seven daughters, towards whom he is said to have played the part of a strict Victorian father. His eldest daughter was Fanny. She married David Braden in 1858, who became a captain in the Civil War. She lived to be ninety-four years old, dying in 1934. During the Civil War, she took her two children to Nashville, Tennessee, to be near her husband who was ill. At the time of her death, she was survived by two daughters, Mrs. William Caldwell, and Mrs. H. T. Dwiggins, and two sons, David and James Braden. James Braden was killed in an airplane crash early in 1937. Her grandchildren are said to have numbered seven and her great-grandchildren ten. At

---

[2] His speeches as printed in the *Congressional Globe* bear out this statement. For example, see his speech of Feb. 16, 1867 (*Cong. Globe*, 39 Cong., 2 Sess., Appendix, 162-166.) This was a speech in which the Representative from Indiana criticised the Supreme Court for the decision in the Garland case, "to the effect that the act of Congress requiring attorneys-at-law to take what is familiarly called the ironclad oath is unconstitutional and void and cannot be enforced. . . ." (*Ibid.*, 162). It is not the purpose here to indicate the content of the speech, but to illustrate the

least one son, Frederick Braden, died before his mother. Her daughter, Mrs. William Caldwell, had three sons, Dumont, Braden, and Wallace Caldwell.

Ebenezer's second daughter, Julia Dumont, was given the name of his mother. In 1862, she married Major Jonathan W. Gordon. He served in the Mexican War and also in the Civil War for about three years. Julia was Major Gordon's second wife. They had five daughters, and one son named John C. Gordon. Mrs. Gordon died in 1928.

Ebenezer's third daughter was Martha Cory Dumont, who married H. E. Drew. The fourth daughter, Emma Dumont married Matthew D. Watson. They had at least two children, a daughter who married George M. Cole, and a son, Lieut. Thomas Dumont Watson. The fifth daughter of Ebenezer, Isabelle Dumont, married John W. Williams. She was still living in 1934. The sixth daughter, Anna Dumont, married R. E. Springeteen. The seventh and youngest, Jessie Dumont, married William S. Whitney. She also was still living in 1934.

MARTHA DUMONT

Martha Dumont, eldest daughter of John and Julia L. Dumont, married William B. Campbell in 1834. He was one of the early teachers of Switzerland County. While studying law at Oxford, Ohio, William's father died during the great Ohio River Flood of 1832. The young man soon after went with his brother-in-law, William Protsman, to Cincinnati to buy the Protsman farm north of Vevay. Making the trip on horseback, they beat Joseph Malin who traveled by steamboat bent on purchasing the same farm. William Campbell built the brick house on Main Street in Vevay where Nelson Haskell

---

humor of Dumont. The whole speech abounds in humorous sallies which there is not space to quote. Before opening his remarks, the gentleman from Indiana asked the Clerk of the House to read the following paragraph:

"A hotel keeper in Washington posted this notice: 'Members of Congress will go to the table first, and then the gentlemen. Rowdies and blackguards must not mix with Congressmen, as it is hard to tell one from the other.'"

The quoted notice is not related to the speech that followed, and was evidently used to wake up the audience as the Congressman intimated.

In another part of the speech, Dumont told a story from back home in Indiana, which is worth repeating. Here it is:

"A constituent of my colleague [John H. Farquhar], in whose district I once lived, was elected justice of the peace, and thereupon, believing his was one of the few immortal names not born to die went to the clerk of the court to file his bond and be qualified. He exhibited his commission and said he had come to file his bond and be sworn into office. 'Hold up your hand,' responded the gruff old clerk, who, when enraged and indignant, was a little rough and profane; 'I'll swear you in; all h—l can't qualify you.'" (*Ibid.*, 165).

now resides. He kept a store and sold the first lucifer matches put on the market in the town. He became prosperous and at one time owned considerable property in Vevay. He lost most of it through signing surety bonds. After meeting reverses, the Campbell family moved to Lawrenceburg, where Mr. Campbell practiced law and collected taxes. He died about 1846, and Mrs. Campbell returned to Vevay with her children. She kept house for her father, John Dumont, after the death of her mother. She died in 1869, about a year before her father passed away.

William and Martha Dumont Campbell had five children. One of the daughters was Annette Campbell, who died when a young woman. She was a school teacher and wrote poetry, some appearing in the *Philotheamean Gem*, an early Vevay high school paper. The only son, William Lamb Campbell, was born in 1836. He became a lawyer and was also a newspaper man. He was extremely well versed in the law, so that other lawyers consulted him on doubtful points connected with their cases, and called him the "lawyer's encyclopedia." He was, however, quite impractical and gave much of his legal advice without charge. He served in the Civil War and figured in *The First of the Hoosiers* and *The Last of the Flatboats* by George Cary Eggleston.[3] In the eighteen-eighties he went to California for his health and edited a paper in Los Angeles for some time. He died there in 1922. He was married twice, his first wife being an Indianapolis woman. They had one daughter, Mary Louisa. She married a man named Bigelow and they had three children, May, Fran, and Lawrence Campbell. After his separation from his first wife, William L. Campbell married again. His second wife's Christian name was Mary. They had one daughter, Juliette Dumont Campbell, born in 1890. She also evidenced talent in writing. She married a man by the name of Armstrong, and had five children: Mary Janet, Ethel Pearl, Ruth Loretta, John Forrest, and William Campbell.

Juliette Dumont Campbell, another of the daughters of William and Martha (Dumont) Campbell, married Joseph Shipp, an Indianapolis business man. She died in 1891, leaving two daughters, May Louisa and Margaret Shipp. May

---
[3] *The First of the Hoosiers* (Philadelphia, 1703), 183-186; *The Last of the Flat Boats* (Boston, 1900). William L. Campbell, Edward Eggleston, and George Cary Eggleston were the originals of "Irving Strong," "Ed Lowry" and "Phil Lowry," respectively, in *The Last of the Flatboats*.

Louisa did some writing, delivered occasional lectures and gave private lessons at her home in language and history. Margaret also did some private tutoring and was a teacher in a private school. She is a Vassar graduate. Both of these sisters are still living in Indianapolis. Neither ever married.

Eliza Maria Campbell, a third daughter of William and Martha Campbell, married a physician, a Dr. Henderson. Their only child, a daughter, Juliette Cory, married Frank Leslie. Three children were born to the Leslies. One, a daughter, Eliza Maria, died in infancy. The elder son, William Leslie, born in 1903, became a doctor. The younger son was named John Dumont Leslie. About ten years ago he left home and has not been heard from since. Eliza Maria Henderson died in 1929.

Mary Louisa Campbell was the eldest daughter of Martha and William Campbell. In 1855, she married Francis Rodolph Detraz, a builder and cabinet-maker of Vevay. At one time, he was also Vevay's principal ice dealer. He built the house now occupied by Lincoln Means. Mary Louise Detraz died in 1874, leaving five children, a daughter and four sons. The daughter, Martha Antoinette, was the eldest, and after her mother's death took her place in looking after and caring for her father and three of her brothers. Next to the youngest brother, having made his home with his Grandmother Detraz for several years, due to his mother's ill health, continued to do so after her death. Martha Detraz never married.

The eldest brother of Martha Detraz, William Benjamin, died in 1888 at the age of twenty-nine. The second brother, Eugene Rodolph, and the youngest or fourth, Clarence Aime, made up the firm of the Detraz Brothers who were in the lumber, building, and planing-mill business in Vevay for over thirty years. Many of the buildings in and around the little city were planned and built by them. These include the present *Reveille* building, the Dickason & Weales Garage, the Frank Riley and Forrest Griffith homes, and also the house where they themselves lived so long, now occupied by Mr. and Mrs. Herman L. Fox. The third of the four brothers, Samuel Francis Detraz, married Amy Lewark in Pendleton, Indiana, where he and his brothers had gone to build and establish a planing mill. Samuel's brothers never married. This Samuel F. Detraz was an architect and builder. He planned the Vevay Deposit Bank building, which his brothers erected. Martha Detraz died in 1927, Eugene in 1933, Clarence in 1935. Samuel Francis Detraz died earlier, in 1911. He was generally known as "Frank" Detraz. He left three children, Lucille, Louisa and Orville Detraz. Orville married Mildred Bliss in 1927. They have two sons, David Francis and Orville Richard Detraz, and at the present time they reside in Rock Island, Illinois, where the father is the head of the contract section of the Rock Island division of the United States River Survey. Louisa Detraz is the wife of Herman L. Fox, a grain dealer. They reside in Vevay with their sons, Jack Warren and Newell Fox. Lucille Detraz married Sydney Palmer Skelcher, a florist, in 1916. There is one daughter, Jane Lucille Skelcher. Since Mr. Skelcher's death in 1935, the widow and daughter have resided in Vevay.

Mary Dumont

The second of the Dumont daughters was Mary, who married William S. Lamb in 1837. He became county clerk of Perry County, Indiana, in 1840 or 1841. This daughter died before her mother, Julia L. Dumont, whose death occurred in 1857.

Peter Cory Dumont

Peter Cory Dumont was the second son. He outlived both his father and mother. He married but his wife's name has not been discovered. There were seven children, two sons and five daughters. A daughter Abbie married a man named Farwell, and they later lived in Texas. One of her brothers was John F. Dumont and the other William Dumont. The latter died in early manhood, but was married and left two children. The daughters of Peter Cory Dumont besides Abbie were: Mary A., who married a Mr. Parks; Julia Louise, who married a Duffy; Mary; and Eunice. No information can be furnished about the last two.

Aurelius Dumont

Aurelius Dumont was the third and youngest of the sons of John and Julia L. Dumont to reach maturity. He was graduated from Hanover College and elected to the office of county auditor soon thereafter. He was just well started on what promised to be a brilliant career as a lawyer, when he died at the age of twenty-six. He married Harriet Dufour, a refined young woman of Vevay who died soon after her husband.[4]

MARIETTA DUMONT

Marietta Dumont, the third daughter, married Robert N. Lamb in 1847, who was the original of "Lawyer Barlow" in Edward Eggleston's novel *Roxy*, in which Aurelius and Harriet Dufour Dumont were made the leading characters.[5] When elected county auditor, Aurelius Dumont invited Robert Lamb to serve as an assistant in the office for a part of each day and read law with him during his time off. It was not long until the assistant was practically placed in charge of the auditor's office, while the man chosen to fill the place devoted his time to his growing law practice. The young attorney was instrumental in obtaining for his assistant the position as deputy sheriff. Though his duties were doubled, Lamb still read law at intervals and was admitted to the bar. He then became a law partner of his friend Dumont. In 1848, Mr. Lamb was elected to the office of prosecuting attorney, and, following the death of young Dumont was appointed to complete his term as auditor. In 1850, Mr. Lamb was defeated, but in 1855 he won the race for auditor. He held the office till 1859, while he continued to practice law.

In July of 1861, Robert N. Lamb was appointed assistant quartermaster with the rank of captain and served in the Union army until discharged on account of ill health in the fall of 1862. He was then sent to the legislature. In 1864, he became judge of the local circuit court. In 1868, he ran for Congress but was defeated. Later the family moved to Indianapolis where Mrs. Marietta (Dumont) Lamb died in 1876. A few years later Mr. Lamb became president of the First National Bank of Indianapolis.

Robert N. and Marietta (Dumont) Lamb had two children who died in infancy, a third child, Laura who died at the age of nine, and two daughters that grew up. The eldest of the two, Elizabeth Lamb, married a lawyer named Thompson. He later became a judge. She, like her grandmother, wrote some poetry. She also used to lecture at women's

---

[4] For further matter relative to Aurelius Dumont and his wife, see "Julia L. Dumont of Vevay," *loc. cit.*, 306.

[5] Harriet Dufour Dumont, was the original of "Roxy" and Aurelius Dumont was the original of "Mark Bonamy."

club metings and was a very gifted, but eccentric woman, especially in matters of dress. She had one son, Mac (or Max) Thompson. The second daughter of Robert and Marietta Lamb to reach maturity was named Marietta. She married a Dr. Charles E. Ferguson, an Indianapolis physician. Mrs. Ferguson died within the past year, but Dr. Ferguson is still living. They had one daughter, also named Marietta, who was married twice, first to a man named Holloway, and later to a Mr. Covall.

JULIA DUMONT

Julia, the fourth and youngest of the four Dumont sisters was her mother's namesake. She was a teacher, holding forth in the old schoolroom after the death of her mother. In fact, she had served an apprenticeship by helping her mother. In 1859, she married the Rev. Archibald S. Reid, who was both a teacher and preacher. As late as 1870, Mrs. Reid advertised the opening of a school. School terms were often quite short even after the establishment of a public system, and it was not uncommon for extra subscription schools to follow. Mrs. Reid collected all of the unprinted writings of her mother, Julia L. Dumont, intending to have them published, but after the Reid family left Vevay, most of the collected manuscripts were destroyed in a fire. The Reids had one son, John Dumont Reid, who became a minister. In 1891, this son married Bessie Gertrude Bayse in Minnesota. Two children were born of this union, a son Kenneth Dumont Reid (1892), and a daughter, Margaret Reid (1896).[6]

---

[6] Information regarding the descendants of John and Julia L. Dumont was found on the gravestones of the Vevay Cemetery, in the records of Switzerland County, in the files of the Vevay *Reveille*, and in Perret Dufour's *History of Switzerland County*. Other facts were obtained from clippings in scrap-books belonging to Julie LeClerc Knox and the Switzerland County Historical Society. A letter from William Lamb Campbell to his nephew, Clarence A. Detraz, written at Los Angeles on Mar. 2, 1901, contains much data relative to the ancestry of Julia L. Dumont and her descendants. Many of the statements in the above article are based on carefully preserved and oft repeated family traditions.

The Engle Family, Randolph County, Indiana
Jennie M. Engle Staudt*

In 1683 four brothers came to America from Cambridgeshire, England, which is about sixty-four miles from London. Three of them settled in Pennsylvania. It is presumed that these three brothers first settled in Bristol Township.

[1] Robert Engle, immigrant, direct ancestor of the Randolph County, Indiana, Engle family, settled in Evesham Township, Burlington County, New Jersey. He married Jane Horne on the fourth day of the fifth month in 1684. One child, a son, John, was born to this union. [2] John married but at this moment his wife's name is not known. [1] Robert Engle, the immigrant to New Jersey, died in 1696.

John's son, [3] Robert, married Mary, the daughter of Samuel and Jane Ogborn. They had five children and their son [4] Robert married Rachel Vimcum. [4] Robert was born in 1708 and died in 1774, at the age of sixty-six. His children were [5] Robert, Joseph, Abraham, Rachel, and Sarah.

[5] Robert married Jane Sharp on September 19, 1739. Only one child of theirs is mentioned, their son, [6] Isaac Engle, born March 18, 1773, who married Sarah M. Price, daughter of Thomas and Hannah Price. Sarah M. Price was born on March 17, 1774. Both Isaac and Sarah were born in Burlington County, New Jersey, and were married there.

[6] Isaac and Sarah Engle were the parents of these children: Hannah, Robert, Sarah, Isaac, Rachel A., Prudence, Susan, [7] William, Lydia A., and Phoebe.

[7] William, the ninth child of Isaac and Sarah M. Price Engle, was born December 13, 1811, in Burlington County, New Jersey. When he was fourteen years old the family went to Warren County, Ohio. William Engle was raised on a farm and endured all of the hardships common to pioneer life. He received a fair business education from the common schools. He was married to Lutitia Cabe on February 13, 1834.

---

* Mrs. Jennie M. Engle Staudt is a resident of Union City, Indiana. The sources of this family history are: E. Tucker, *History of Randolph County, Indiana* (Chicago, 1882); Francis Bazley Lee (comp.), *General and Memorial History of the State of New Jersey* (4 vols., New York, 1910), II.

Lutitia Cabe Engle, born in Bucks County, Pennsylvania, November 29, 1813, was the daughter of Elias and Sarah (White) Cabe. Elias Cabe was born in Bucks County, Pennsylvania, in 1768, the son of Thomas and Rebecca (Van Horne) Cabe, of Dutch descent. Sarah White Cabe was born in Bucks County, Pennsylvania, and was a daughter of George and Mary White, who were natives of Pennsylvania. Lutitia Cabe Engle had one brother and five sisters, whose names were: Mary, Charlotte, Abigail, Sarah, Margaret, and Thomas.

Lutitia Cabe's union with William Engle was blessed with twelve sons, whose names and birth dates are as follows:

Isaac	December 11, 1834
Wesley	April 21, 1836
Robert	September 21, 1837
Elias	December 9, 1838
William	December 18, 1841
Samuel	March 22, 1843

(All of the above were born in Warren County, Ohio, not far from Waynesville.)

Calvin Stratton	September 9, 1844
James S.	September 18, 1846
Daniel H.	May 11, 1849
Albert H.	May 26, 1851
Price	October 5, 1852
Josiah (Si)	October 30, 1854

(The last six sons were born at the Old Engle Home in Washington Township, Randolph County, Indiana.)

The Engle boys, as they were generally known, were farmers, stock raisers, schoolteachers, and carpenters. James S. Engle was judge of Randolph County. Calvin S. Engle was auditor. After the Civil War five of these boys migrated to the West. Three married in the West and the Southwest. All came to live in later years at home. Calvin S. and family, his wife and two daughters, in 1883 came by invitation from his father to operate what is known as the Engle Home Place. Calvin S. Engle brought with him the first Holstein herd known in that section of the county and took many blue ribbons at the county fairs. He had full-blooded Clydesdale horses also.

Isaac Engle, Wells County, married Ann Hopkins. Wesley, Randolph County, was married twice. His first wife was Martha Johnson, the mother of Molly Engle Bright.

(Molly was the oldest grandchild of William and Lutitia Engle.) Wesley's second wife was Catherine Sheppard.

Robert, Randolph County, was married twice. His first wife and the mother of his children was Datia Ferguson. His second wife was Elizabeth Stevenson. Robert Engle served in the regular army, being drafted in 1864. He served his country faithfully to the end of the Civil War.

Elias Engle married Ruth A. Thornburg, Jefferson County, Kansas. He served his country in the Morgan Raid. William, who entered the Sixty-ninth Regiment of the Volunteer Infantry, died on his way to the hospital in St. Louis, Missouri, after having been wounded in the Battle of Shiloh.

Samuel died in infancy at the age of two years.

Calvin Stratton Engle was named for a Dr. Stratton, the pioneer physician who brought him into the world. He married Ellen Greeley of Faribault, Minnesota. He was the seventh son and the first child born at the old Engle Home Place in Indiana. Calvin enlisted in the Sixty-ninth Regiment, but being under age and having an attack of measles, his father brought him home. After he returned to health, he re-enlisted in the Fifth Indiana Cavalry. He was taken prisoner at Macon, Georgia, and was confined in southern prison pens (in Charleston, South Carolina, and in Andersonville Prison, near Americus, Georgia) and endured all of the hardships of prison life for ten months. He was honorably discharged at the close of the war.

James S. Engle enlisted in the Union forces for 100-day service. He was married in 1875 to Alice Monks, of Randolph County.

Daniel married Martha Sharp. Albert married first Harriet (Hattie) Deboy; his second wife was Mary Hardwick (Hardrick).

Price married Esther Patton, then of Iowa. Josiah (Si) married Amanda Hoover.

All but one of William and Lutitia Cabe Engle's twelve sons lived to manhood, that one being Samuel. All married but two, Samuel and William. All the married sons except James S. had children.

Calvin S. and Albert H. Engle made the first telephone in their section. The wires were placed in old clock faces and strung over a mile, over fields and through woods. This lasted several years until the children were old enough to do the errands.

William Engle cast his first vote for Benjamin Harrison, being a Republican. Mr. and Mrs. Engle were members of the United Brethren Church more than forty years. William Engle was a public-spirited man, and served as trustee several times. He was interested in every movement calculated to advance the interest of the country at large or of his immediate community. He died in Washington Township, Randolph County, Indiana, December 18, 1884. He was buried at Union Chapel Cemetery, west of the villiage of Carlos. His wife, who died in 1900, was buried there also.

The family of William and Lutitia Cabe Engle has entered its sixth generation (1951-1953), spreading over Indiana, the Southwest and West. The three immigrants who crossed the Delaware River into Pennsylvania have spread their name all through Pennsylvania and through Ohio, in Sidney, Piqua, Dayton, and elsewhere throughout the state.

The Fauntleroy Family
Mary Emily Fauntleroy

The name of this family has been spelled Enfans du Roi, Enfans le Rois, and for many centuries Faunt le Roy; only in the past century has it been written as one word—Fauntleroy. The family was established in Dorsetshire, England, at a very early period, and was closely affiliated with the supporters of the early Normans, Plantagenets, and Lancaster kings.[1] They were people of education, heavy landowners, charitable, supporters of the Church. They were in high standing in that part of England, where the family had been seated, and enjoyed the distinction of antiquity.

Arms were granted members of the Fauntleroy family by the College of Arms of England in 1600. Copies of this grant are found in the British Museum, London. The Shield was marked with the heads of three golden-haired boys. The Crest was added during the reign of Queen Elizabeth, the Fleur-de-lis between two azure wings above the shield. The Motto (or scroll) was "beneath the shield 'Fauntleroy.'"

---

[1] The typed record of the Fauntleroy family, compiled by Mary Emily Fauntleroy (30 pp. with chart and photographs) has been filed in the Genealogy Section of the Indiana State Library, Indianapolis, by the Society of Colonial Dames of Indiana.

The English authorities consider the coat of arms just a pictorial device designed in Early England, illustrating the name with direct evidence as to its Norman or French origin. The ancient Anglo-Normans had for their coat of arms the same as that of the Fauntleroys. The name le Roy appears quite frequently in the ancient Norman rolls.

Walter Fauntleroy, born about 1273, married Juliana de Thornhull, daughter of Robert de Thornhull, of Sherborne, Dorsetshire, England. The history of the de Thornhull family begins as early as 1200 with definite records from John de Thornhull and his two sons, Ralph and Walter. It is recorded that Walter granted to his brother Ralph the estate of Alveston Manor in the year 1227. This name, Alveston Manor, appears later in the records of the Fauntelroy estates. Walter de Thornhull had a son Walter de Thornhull, Jr., who was married in 1274 to Cecelia Antioch, and died in 1307. Their son, Robert de Thornhull, married in 1294 (wife's name not given), and their daughter, Juliana, married Walter Fauntleroy, as stated above.

Walter and Juliana (de Thornhull) Fauntleroy were the parents of two sons: John, recorded as being a witness in a law suit in 1333, and Adam, recorded as living at Alveston, part of the Fauntleroy estate, in 1340. Adam had but one son, whose name was John (living in Fauntleroy Marsh in 1373). This John had five sons: John, William, Nicholas, Richard, and Robert. John Fauntleroy (only son and heir of Adam Fauntleroy) was born in 1370 and died in 1440. John was married in 1397 to Joan Walyes (born in 1374; daughter of John Walyes). John Wayles was a man of wealth and prominence, and did homage to the Bishop of Sarum in 1428.

John Fauntleroy (the fourth), Sir Knight, and his wife Joan Walyes had but one son, John (the fifth), called John, Jr., who inherited his father's great wealth and much property from his mother's family. John Fauntleroy (the fifth) married Elizabeth Wadham of Merrifield, Somerset County, England. They had seven children: Peter, Bridget, William, John, Elizabeth, Agnes, and Tristram (spelled also Tristam). This seventh child, Tristram Fauntleroy, was born in 1452 at Fauntleroy Marsh, and died at "Priory," in Hampshire. He married Mrs. Joan Holt Viliers, widow of Robert Viliers of Crondall, Wiltshire, who had two children by her first marriage (William Viliers, who became a priest, and a daughter who married George Brooks). Tristram and Joan Fauntleroy had two sons, Byron and John. Tristram Fauntleroy died in 1538 at the "Priory," a short distance from Michel Marsh Church given to him for his services to Henry VIII in the settlements of church and state during the Reformation. He was master and squire of the Manor of Michel Marsh Church, one of the oldest in England. This church was restored about 1825. His portrait is shown in one of the restored windows, with the notation "Tristram Fauntleroy, who by his generosity and services to the State and Church has left a living memory." There are also two stone tablets on the wall of the chancel of the Church, and a much larger tablet in the church to the memory of Tristram and Joan Fauntleroy.[2]

After the death of Tristram Fauntleroy, his wife Joan and their two sons, Byron and John, resided at Crondall, Hampshire, on the estate that she inherited from her father. Byron, the eldest son, was heir and executor of his father's will made in 1538. His inheritance embraced Michel Marsh Manor and many other places. John Fauntleroy, the second son, married Margaret Moore. He died in 1598, his wife on April 5, 1613. Both are buried at Crondall, Hampshire, England.

Their son William Fauntleroy, of Crondall, eldest son and heir, married Frances ——— (buried May 24, 1636), and their son John was baptized January 13, 1588. John married Phoebe Wilkinson at Crondall in 1607. They had thirteen children. The second son, Moore Fauntleroy, first married Dorothy Colle on December 22, 1639. She died leaving two daughters who remained in England when Moore came to America. His first voyage to America was in 1641, but it was in 1643 that he left England for good for political reasons and settled in upper Norfolk County, Virginia. His home was called "Roger's Nest." He was commissioned captain in 1645 and major in 1647 in the county militia. He was granted a land patent February 20, 1643, and served in the House of Burgesses 1644-1648.

Moore Fauntleroy moved to the Northern Neck of the Virginia Tidewater in 1648, and settled on a tract of land

---

[2] Photographs of the portrait of Tristram Fauntleroy and the tablets mentioned are shown in the record mentioned in note 1. They were secured by Miss Fauntleroy while visiting in England, as was also a copy of the will of Tristram Fauntleroy, who died in 1538. She writes, "It is rather unusual to possess a portrait of an ancestor of four hundred years ago."

at Naylor's Hole, on the north bank of the Rappahannock River, extending from the Rappahannock to the Potomac River in Lancaster County, Virginia. Of this large tract of land, five hundred acres was granted and confirmed by Act I, Grand Assembly of Virginia, March 23, 1660, in the twelfth year (reckoning from the execution of Charles on January 30, 1649) of the rein of King Charles II. This property was successively a part of Lancaster, Old Rappahannock, and Richmond counties. Moore Fauntleroy was justice and Burgher from Lancaster 1651, 1652, 1656, and from Rappahannock, 1656. He owned large tracts of land, many slaves, and several vessels, and transported many settlers from England. He died in 1667 at Crondall, a part of Naylor's Hole. He was buried there. His second wife was Mary Hill, daughter of Thomas Hill of Rappahannock County, Virginia. The marriage occurred in 1648. The coat of arms was given to him on December 8, 1633.

Moore Fauntleroy and his wife Mary Hill had a family of two sons and one daughter: William, Moore, and Elizabeth. William was born in 1658 at Crondall, Rappahannock County, and died in 1686. He was married in 1678 to Katherine Griffin (b. March 16, 1664; d. 1703; dau. of Col. Samuel Griffin of Northumberland County, Virginia). William and Katherine Griffin Fauntleroy had three sons: Col. William Fauntleroy, Col. Griffin Fauntleroy, and Moore Fauntleroy.

Col. William Fauntleroy (third) born on March 31, 1684, lived at Naylor's Hole, Richmond County, Virginia. He was married in 1712 to Apphia Bushrod, daughter of Col. John Bushrod, of Bushfield, Westmoreland County, Virginia. He was a member of the House of Burgesses from Richmond County, 1736-1749. His will was dated December 5, 1757, at Naylor's Hole. He died in 1757.

Children of Col. William and Apphia (Bushrod) Fauntleroy:

William (Lieut. Col.)—b. 1713; d. 1793; m. (1) Elizabeth ———, (one child);[3] m. (2) Margaret Murdock; 12 children.

---

[3] Elizabeth (Betsy) dau. Lieut. Col. William and Elizabeth Fauntleroy; b. 1736; m. (1) John Adam; m. (2) Capt. Bowler Crooke; d. 1792. This Betsy, the "Lowland Beauty," made an impression upon the youthful and susceptible heart of George Washington.

Moore (Capt.)—b. 1716; d. 1791; m. (1) Ann Neal; (2) Elizabeth Mitchel.

John—b. 1724; d. 1766; m. (1) Judith Littlepage; (2) Elizabeth Waring, daughter of Thomas Waring.

Hannah—m. Capt. Maxmillian Robinson.

Apphia—m. Col. William Dangerfield.

Katherine—m. John Lewis.

Mary—m. Robert Brooks.

Ann—m. John Pettet.

Sarah—m. James Gray.

Children of Lieut. William and Margaret (Murdock) Fauntleroy:

Apphia—d. young.

William (M.D.)—b. 1742; d. 1775; student at the "Temple," Edinburgh, Scotland, and in London.

Moore (M.D.)—b. 1743; d. 1802; student with his brother William at Edinburgh; inherited the old plantation at Naylor's Hole.

John (Capt.)—b. 1745; d. 1798; m. Mrs. Judith (Ball) Griffen (dau. of Col. James Ball of Bewly).

Griffen Murdock (Capt.)—b. 1747; d. 1794; m. Ann Belfield of Mars Hill (dau. of John Belfield, a Revolutionary soldier). Griffen was an officer in the Revolution, first lieutenant in the Virginia Militia, April 5, 1779, and later made captain.

Jane—b. 1748; m. Col. Thomas Turner of Washingham, Westmoreland County, Virginia.

Sally—b. 1752; m. ——— Turner.

Molly—b. 1753; d. young.

Joseph—b. 1754; d. 1815; m. Elizabeth Foushee Fauntleroy (dau. of Capt. Bushrod and Elizabeth Foushee Fauntleroy).

Henry (Capt.)—b. 1756; killed in the battle of Monmouth, New Jersey, June 28, 1778.

Robert—b. 1758; d. 1832; m. Sarah Ball.

Apphia (first Apphia died in infancy)—b. 1760; m. Capt. John Champe Carter.

Children of Capt. Griffen Murdock and Ann (Belfield) Fauntleroy:

Margaret—m. Capt. Thomas Yerley of Frederick County, Virginia.

Belfield—d. young.

Mary—m. John Campbell of Kiran, Westmoreland County, Virginia.

Ann—m. Raphael Thompson, renowned artist; removed to Kentucky.

Elizabeth—b. 1790, Mars Hill, Richmond County, Virginia; m. Thomas Jones of Bathurst; d. August 31, 1865, in Frederick County, Virginia.

Joseph—b. 1787, Mars Hill; d. 1832 at New Harmony, Indiana; m. Emily Carter Fauntleroy (first cousin; a dau. of Joseph and Elizabeth Foushee Fauntleroy; moved to New Harmony in 1827, attracted by the inducements of the Robert Owen movement and founding of New Harmony; were accompanied to New Harmony by four brothers of Emily Carter Fauntleroy; namely, William Moore Fauntleroy, Laurence Butler Fauntleroy, Joseph Murdock Fauntleroy, and Robert Henry Fauntleroy. Joseph who married his cousin Elizabeth Foushee Fauntleroy, had eleven children, several of whom died young. Of the brothers of Emily Carter Fauntleroy, wife of Joseph Fauntleroy, coming to New Harmony, the record of Robert Henry Fauntleroy will be given.

Children of Joseph and Emily C. (Fauntleroy) Fauntleroy:[4]

Eliza Griffin—b. April 8, 1812, near Danville, Kentucky; m. George W. S. White; buried in Evansville on October 1, 1875; lived in New Harmony. George W. S. White was the son of Isaac White of Tippecanoe fame.

Emily C.—b. December 6, 1813, at Greenville, Virginia; m. Nelson Nettleton, a man of means and prominence in early New Harmony; one daughter, Virginia; one son, Fauntleroy Nettleton.

Thomas Moore—b. September 22, 1815; died unmarried.

Frederick—b. February 7, 1818, at Greenville, Virginia; m. Marry Trotter in Texas, where they lived. They had four sons and one daughter.

Henry—b. January 2, 1820, at Greenville, Virginia; m. Isabella Smythe, of Vincennes, Indiana; moved to Chicago, bought land, and became quite wealthy; had three sons (Thomas, in whose honor the story, *Little Lord Fauntleroy*, was named, Samuel Smythe, and Eugene Smythe).

---

[4] Miss Fauntleroy's record, mentioned in notes 1 and 2, tells that Joseph and Emily Carter Fauntleroy were married on March 12, 1811. They lived near White Post at Salem, Virginia, and in 1827 moved to New Harmony.

Josephine—b. Nov. 25, 1821, at Greenville, Virginia; m. (1) ―― Baker; m. (2) ―― Faith; m. (3) ―― Fisher. Josephine had one daughter by her first marriage, Emily, who married and lives in Louisville with her two daughters.

Ferdinand—b. March 16, 1824, at Greenville, Virginia; m. Chloe Biscoe in Texas; six children; one grandchild, Schuyler William (living in Memphis, Tennessee).

William Theodore—b. July 7, 1826, at Greenville, Virginia; m. Rachel Homer in 1855, English by birth, a teacher for many years, a charter member of the Minerva Club of New Harmony, and later made an honorary member of the General Federation of Women's Clubs; b. 1830; d. 1914; husband died in 1906; both buried in New Harmony Cemetery; children: Ida Eliza (b. August 10, 1856; m. Dr. I. C. Watts, of Bowling Green, Kentucky; d. 1896; buried at Evansville in the Dr. Isaac White cemetery lot); Homer (b. 1866; m. (1) Hanse Goodloe; m. (2) Maud Miller in 1905; one son by the first marriage; Mary Emily—b. April 14, 1858; living in New Harmony).

Virginia—b. August 22, 1839, in New Harmony; m. John Preaus (a brilliant man who came from Prussia); charter member of the Minerva Society of New Harmony; bright mind and very beautiful; removed to Louisiana in 1873; five children.

Robert Henry Fauntleroy—tenth child of Joseph and Elizabeth (Foushee) Fauntleroy and brother of Emily Carter Fauntleroy, was born March 23, 1806, and died December 13, 1848. He came to New Harmony in 1827, and married Jane Dale Owen, daughter of Robert Dale and Caroline Owen in New Harmony on March 23, 1835. Robert Henry Fauntleroy[5] was appointed to the staff of the United States Coast and Geodetic Survey, and became chief of the Coast Survey in 1846. He also made the first survey of the Miami River, and built five bridges near New Harmony.

---

[5] George Browning Lockwood, *The New Harmony Communities* (Marion, Ind., 1902), 267. For Robert Owen's marriage, see *ibid.*, 65-66; Arthur H. Estabrook, "The Family History of Robert Owen," in *Indiana Magazine of History* (March, 1923), XIX, 63-101. *See also* the general index to the *Indiana Magazine of History* (1905-1929) for references to New Harmony and the Owen family.

Children of Robert Henry and Jane Dale (Owen) Fauntleroy:

Son—b. and d. in infancy in New Harmony, date unknown.

Constance Owen Fauntleroy—b. January 15, 1836; d. May, 1911; m. Rev. James Runcie, a clergyman of the Episcopal Church; writer of prose and verse; organized the Minerva Society in New Harmony; husband d. in St. Joseph, Missouri, and was buried there; children: Blessing Constance, (m. Elliot St. John Marchall); Elinor Dale, (d. Dec. 1834); James F. (d. 1836); Perc Owen, (unmarried).

Elinor Owen Fauntleroy—b. July 15, 1838; d. Nov. 19, 1909, in San Francisco; m. George Davidson (b. May 9, 1825, in Nottingham, England; assistant to Robert Henry Fauntleroy in the United States Coast and Goedetic Survey; named many of the bays, inlets, and peaks of the Olympic Mountains after the Fauntleroy family; complete list of his work on file in the New Harmony Library; four children).

Arthur Robert Fauntleroy—b. Jan. 11, 1842; d. Dec. 1884 of pneumonia, in Milwaukee, Wisconsin, while on government work; followed closely along the scientific work of his father; lived in New Harmony; loved and respected; never married.

Edward Owen Fauntleroy—b. 1841; d. 1866, in San Francisco; was associated with his brother-in-law, George Davidson, and was his assistant in the western survey; never married.

It seems rather remarkable that this line should reach from 1273, Walter Fauntleroy, down to 1939, still carrying the original name (Mary Emily Fauntleroy), and it is interesting to know that I am descended from two brothers, of the early 1600's; the two lines having connected twice after several generations. I have four Fauntleroys for my grandparents and four Fauntleroys or my great-grandparents. Through this line of descent, I have been elected to the Society of Colonial Dames of America on many lines, and the Daughters of the American Revolution on four lines. I am a charter member of the Society of Indiana Pioneers on five lines. I had the privilege, because of my inheritance, of purchasing the Old Fauntleroy Home in New Harmony. In 1924, I sold this home to the Indiana Federation of Women's Clubs and it has become a shrine for all club women.

GILMAN FAMILY HISTORY
by
PANSY MODESITT GLEASON
Submitted by
FLORENCE CRAWFORD

The first of the family in America was *Edward Gilman* and his wife, *Mary*, who with their children left Gravesend, England, April 26, 1638, in the "Diligent" of Ipswich. They landed in America at Boston, August 10, 1638. Their children were Mary, Edward, Sarah, Lydia, John, Moses, and Jeremiah.

John (the Hon. John) s. of Edward, b. 1624, d. 1709; settled in Hingham, Massachusetts, the Exeter, New Hampshire, records indicate that he was living there in 1650, entered lumber business, elected a Selectman, when New Hampshire was separated from Massachusetts in 1680 he was appointed a Councillor, which office he held three years, elected a member of House of Representatives and in 1693 was Speaker; wife was the dau. of an English merchant; they had sixteen children.

Nicholas (Col. Nicholas), s. of John, b. 1672, d. 1741, m. Sarah Clark (dau. of Nathaniel and Elizabeth Clark of Newbury, Massachusetts), two sons were mentioned: Daniel[1] and Nicholas (Reverend Nicholas).

Nicholas (Reverend Nicholas), s. of Colonel Nicholas, b. 1707, d. 1748, m. 1730, Mary Thing (b. 1713, d. 1789, dau. of Bartholomew[2] and Sarah Kent Thing), attended Latin School at age of eight at Newbury, Massachusetts, was graduated from Harvard at age of 17 in 1724, began to preach at Kingston, New Hampshire, October 30, 1727, was ordained at Durham, New Hampshire, March 3, 1742.

Joseph, s. of Reverend Nicholas, b. May 5, 1738, in Exeter, New Hampshire, d. May 14, 1806, at Marietta, Ohio, m. (1) Jane Taylor (d. 1760), (2) Rebecca Ives (b. June 23, 1745, d. May 20, 1823, m.

---

[1] Daniel, s. of Colonel Nicholas, b. 1702, d. 1780, m. (1) Mary Lord, (2) Abigal Sayer; had two sons: Nicholas and John. Nicholas, s. of Daniel, b. 1731, d. 1783, m. Ann Taylor; children included John Taylor, Nicholas, and Nathaniel. John Taylor, s. of Nicholas, b. December 19, 1753, d. September 1, 1828, served in provincial army, delegate from New Hampshire in the convention at Hartford called to take measures for the defense of the country, member of Continental Congress, 1782-1783, state treasurer, 1791, governor, 1794-1805, 1813-1816, member of state legislature, 1810, 1811. Nicholas, s. of Nicholas, b. August 3, 1755, d. May 2, 1814, served as adjutant in Colonel Scammell's regiment during the Revolution, was a member of Washington's military family, took account of prisoners surrendered by Lord Cornwallis at Yorktown, member of Philadelphia convention that framed the Constitution of the United States, member of Congress, 1786-1797, presidential elector, 1793 and 1797, United States Senator, 1805-1814.

[2] Bartholomew was the s. of Jonathan and Mary Gilman Thing, who had six children, one of whom was Tristam, an early and noted minister of Maine.

September 22, 1763; dau. of Benjamin and Elizabeth (Hale) Ives of Beverly, Massachusetts); appointed treasurer of Rockingham County, New Hampshire, justice of the peace, 1779, senator, 1785, member of Governor's Council in 1787; in 1788 went with wife and one son to Marietta, Ohio, where he became one of the judges of the Northwest Territory.

Benjamin Ives, s. of Joseph, b. July 29, 1766, in Exeter, New Hampshire, d. October 13, 1833, in Alton, Illinois, while on a visit to a son, m. February, 1790, at Plymouth, Massachusetts, Hannah Robbins (dau. of the Reverend Chandler Robbins[3]), they had nine children, among whom were Ichabod W., Chandler Robbins,[4] Winthrop Sargent,[5] and one daughter who married Samuel Long; came with his parents to Marietta, Ohio, in 1788; in 1824 came to Terre Haute, Indiana, and established a pork-packing business, building the first

---

[3] Chandler Robbins, b. at Branford, Connecticut, August 24, 1738, d. at Plymouth, Massachusetts, June 30, 1799, was graduated from Yale, 1756, taught in Indian Schools at Lebanon, studied theology, was ordained pastor of Congregational Church in Plymouth, Massachusetts, was awarded D. D. degree by Dartmouth College in 1792 and by University of Edinburgh in 1793, published reply to John Cotton's Essays on Baptism and other books. His father Philemon was the pastor of the church at Branford, Connecticut, 1732-1781. An uncle of Chandler Robbins, Ammi Ruhamah Robbins, was a graduate of Yale, the pastor of the Congregational Church at Norfolk, Connecticut, who joined General Philip Schuyler's brigade at Albany, New York, as chaplain. Thomas Robbins, s. of Ammi Ruhamah, was also a clergyman, and a founder of the Connecticut Historical Society to which he gave his private library valued at $10,000, and containing a pine chest that was brought over on the Mayflower, on the lid of which the passengers signed their compact. Chandler Robbins, a grandson of Chandler, was b. at Lynn, Massachusetts, February 14, 1810, d. at Weston, Massachusetts, September 11, 1862, was a graduate of Harvard, 1829, and of the Divinity School in 1833, was pastor of the Second Church in Boston of which Ralph W. Emerson had been in charge, active in building a new church edifice on Roylston Street, was chaplain of Massachusetts Senate in 1834 and of the House of Representatives in 1850, was awarded the D. D. degree by Harvard in 1855.

[4] Chandler Robbins Gilman, s. of Benjamin Ives Gilman, was b. September 6, 1802, at Marietta, Ohio, d. September 26, 1865, in Middletown, Connecticut; moved with his father to Philadelphia, where he received the M.D. degree; later moved to New York where he spent the remainder of his life; was professor of Physiology and Surgery after 1841; with a relative, Charles Fenne Hoffman, he had charge of the *American Monthly*, and wrote several books.

[5] Winthrop Sargent Gilman, s. of Benjamin Ives Gilman, m. Abia Swift Lippencott; they had thirteen children among whom were two sons, Theodore and Arthur. Theodore was b. January 2, 1841, at Alton, Illinois, m. Elizabeth Drinker Paxton in 1863; was educated at private schools and at Williams College where he received the A.B. degree in 1862, and the A.M. degree in 1864; in Wall Street forty years in municipal, railroad, and industrial business; a deacon and an elder in the Presbyterian church; is a member of the Sons of the American Revolution; has two daughters and two sons. Arthur Gilman was b. June 22, 1837, d. Dec. 27, 1909, m. (1) Amy Cooke Ball, of Lee, Massachusetts, April 12, 1860, and (2) Stella Houghton Scott, July 11, 1876; became an editor and author of note in the fields of history and English literature; was instrumental in the founding of the "Harvard Annex," which became Radcliffe College; published *The Gilman Family*, (1869).

brick building in the town on the northeast corner of First and Mulberry Streets, which he used as an office; he sold the business to Joseph Miller, going to St. Louis, where he entered business with his brother under the name of Gilman Brothers.

Ichabod W., s. of Benjamin Ives, b. 1793, d. 1879, m. (1) Lydia Mattox (d. 1850), (2) Nancy Rhodes Andrews (m. in 1852); enlisted in War of 1812 in Clermont County, Ohio, February 5, 1813, under Captain Daniel Hasbrook; came to Indiana in 1832 and settled first in Shelby County, and later in Greene County; died at Hymera, Sullivan County, Indiana; a son and a daughter are mentioned.

Elijah Mattox, s. of Ichabod, was b. in Clermont County, Ohio, August 25, 1825, m. Helen Louise Reeves (dau. of Eden and Phoebe (Hawkins) Reeves) in April, 1848; came with his father's family to Shelby County, Indiana, in 1832, where he attended school; came to Terre Haute, Indiana, in 1834, where he learned the cooper trade; had six children: Henry (d. in infancy), Helen Louise (b. February 2, 1850, in Terre Haute, Indiana, m. October 10, 1871, James Bartram Reynolds, who was b. December 18, 1846, in Freeport, Pennsylvania, and d. September 29, 1902), Anna, Frank (m. Alice Lee), Harry Bryant (m. Virginia Feltus, served several terms in the city council, and carried on the largest stave and barrel industry in the city until his death), and John A. (d. in infancy).

Mary Ellen, dau. of Ichabod W., was b. in Clermont County, Ohio, January 29, 1829, m. in 1849 James W. Gibson; came with her father's family to Shelby County, Indiana, in 1832; attended schools in this county; had seven children: Josephine (b. September 8, 1850, d. May 31, 1927), Lucetta (b. April 21, 1852, d. April, 1931), Martha (b. March 17, 1854, d. 1922), Frank C. (b. October 30, 1855, d. November, 1928), Charles H. (b. April 15, 1860), Kate (b. December 21, 1862, d. 1884), and Jessie M. (b. December 15, 1870).

Graham Genealogy

Contributed by

MRS. SYLVAN L. MOUSER

Although this genealogy begins with Hugh Graham, it is principally concerned with his son, John Kennedy Graham, and his descendants. For further information on the Pennsylvania branch of the family, descendants of John Kennedy's brother, Robert Findley, see John W. Jordan, *Genealogical and Personal History of Western Pennsylvania* (3 vols., New York, 1915), II, 820.

John Kennedy Graham was born January 30, 1783, in Bedford County, Pennsylvania. Some time before 1810 he came to Indiana Territory, married Elizabeth Weach, and settled first in what is now Clark County; later he moved to the site of the present New Albany. In 1816 he was elected to the convention which met in Corydon to frame the state's first constitution. He also served in the House of Representatives of Indiana in the sessions of 1816-1817, 1825, and 1827-1828, and in the Senate, 1825-1826. A surveyor by profession, he laid out the city of New Albany in 1813 and ran the boundary lines for some of the newly formed counties; he did some of the surveying of the Michigan Road and the Wabash River as well. In August, 1841, he died at his home near New Albany.

I. Hugh Graham, b. c. 1745, Lancaster Co., Pa.; his ancestors were Scotch-Irish Seceders; m. c. 1769, Margaret Kennedy, of Scotch-Irish descent.
Children: a, Robert Findley, b, Jane, c, Elizabeth, d, Thomas, e, John Kennedy.

II. A. Robert Findley Graham, b. Lancaster Co., Pa., 4-2-1771; m. Margaret Gilchrist, dau. of Col. Thomas Gilchrist; moved to Butler Co., Pa., after 1800, and to Allegheny Co., Pa., after 1815, near Elizabeth, Pa.; 9 children: 2 sons, 7 dau.; 4 dau. d. in childhood.
Children: a, Thomas G., b, Susan, c, Margaret, d, Mariah, e, John Kennedy.
B. Jane Graham, d. young; never married.
C. Elizabeth Graham, m. McConnelsburg, Pa., c. 1807, William Gamble, no descendants.
D. Thomas Graham, m. 1812, Mrs. Carry or Curry, Charleston, S.C.; d. 5-21-1821; no children.
E. John Kennedy Graham, b. Bedford Co., Pa., 1-30-1783, d. 8-21-1841; m. 1st, 7-15-1810, Elizabeth G. Weach or Wetch or Veach, b. Ky., c. 1782, d. 8-19-1822, dau. of ―――― Weach and his wife Jane Wetherall, moved to Ind. c. 1808.
Children: a, Ferdinand, b, Menander, c, Eliza Jane, d, Louisa, e, Angeline, f, Amanda, g, Harry.
John Kennedy Graham m. 2nd, 4-16-1823, Mary Ann Huff, dau. of James Huff of German descent and Jane Gillot of French Huguenot descent, b. 1796, Seneca Co., N. Y., d. 5-5-1873; moved to Ind., 1816.
Children: h, Emma, i, Julia Ann, j, Lucinda Evelyn, k, Albert, l, John Kennedy, Jr., m, Caroline A., n, Maria T., o, James Madison.

III. A. Ferdinand Graham, b. Clark Co., Ind., 10-5-1811, d. New Albany, 12-20-1871; m. 10-5-1835, Abbie Ayers Day, dau. of John Day and Mary K. Ayers, b. Preble Co., Ohio, 7-9-1815, d. 1-18-1896.
Children: a, Mary Elizabeth, b, Ann Eliza, c, Abby Evelyn, d, Cornelia Day, e, John Kennedy, f, Bourbon Reese,

g, Amzi Alexander, h, Silas Ferdinand, i, Theodore Ezekial, j, Charles Smith, k, Jenny Campbell, l, Edward Forrester.
- B. Menander Graham, b. 1-22-1813, d. 1-12-1838; m. 10-5-1837, Lavinia McClung; no children.
- C. Eliza Jane Graham, b. 6-16-1814, d. 3-20-1851; m. 9-10-1833, Martin Very, s. of Francis Very, Jr., and Rhoda Lawrence, b, Vt. 2-22-1807, d. 6-18-1870. Mr. Very m. 2nd, Julia Ann Graham.
  Children: a, John Kennedy, b, Menander Clark, c, William G., d, Martin Luther, e, Ruby Evelyn, f, Mary Louisa, g, Jerusha Anna, h, Florence Amanda, i, Martha Angeline.
- D. Louisa Graham, b. 5-5-1816, d. 1-28-1895; m. 4-27-1837, James Guest, d. 11-19-1869.
  Children: a, Eliza Jane, b, John, c, Penina, d, James Hervey, e, Maria Louisa, f, Amanda Graham, g, William.
- E. Angeline Graham, b. 11-9-1818, d. 5-5-1872; m. John Mann, b. 5-28-1814, d. 4-9-1895; no children. She was his second wife.
- F. Amanda Graham, b. 3-21-1820, d. 4-14-1852; m. John Mann (see above); no children. She was his first wife.
- G. Harry Graham, d. in infancy.
- H. Emma Graham, b. 8-21-1824, d. New Albany, 9-14-1908; never married.
- I. Julia Ann Graham, b. 1-1-1826, d. 1-3-1911; m. Martin Very (see above).
  Children: a, Charles F., b, Emily Prime, c, Eliza Ada, d, Nathaniel L., e, Edward Everett, f, William Guest, g, Francis Townley.
- J. Lucinda Evelyn Graham, b. 5-27-1827, d. 4-25-1898; m. 1-1-1850, John L. Shipman, s. of Samuel Shipman and Lavina Ann Hatfield, b. New Albany, 11-20-1825, d. 1-27-1870.
  Children: a, Samuel Charles, b, Anna Vesta, c, Durett F., d, Edward Walter, e, Charles, f, Cassius C., g, James David, h, Harry.
- K. Albert Graham, b. 3-27-1829, d. 6-18-1832.
- L. John Kennedy Graham, Jr., b. 3-26-1831, d. 7-1-1832.
- M. Caroline A. Graham, b. 8-3-1834, d. 6-22-1906; m. 11-8-1860, James H. Belton, b. Saugerties, N. Y., 1832, d. 10-22-1915; moved to North Platte, Nebr.
  Children: a, Carolyn Belle, b, Mary.
- N. Maria T. Graham, b. 9-2-1836, d. 1-14-1924; m. 9-15-1857, Thomas L. Grant.
  Children: a, La Belle Lenore, b, William Lewis Talbott.
- O. James Madison Graham, b. 8-28-1838, d. 3-11-1915; m. 10-22-1871, Mrs. Mary J. Akin (Price), dau. of William Akin and Emeline Genung, b. 2-?-1844, d. after 1930.
  Children: a, James Madison, Jr., b, Ida, c, Hubert, d, Earl A., e, Minnie, f, Chester.

IV. A. Mary Elizabeth Graham, dau. of Ferdinand Graham and Abbie Ayers Day, b. near New Albany, Ind., 8-7-1836, d. 10-10-

1919; m. 5-16-1855, Rev. Francis Walker, s. of James Walker and Eleanor Turner, b. New Richmond, Ohio, 10-23-1831, d. 3-25-1914.

Children: a, Herbert Graham, b, Ferdinand Graham, c, Nellie Adda, d, Ernest Graham, e, Clarence, f, Abbie Evelyn, g, Leland Francis, h, Francis Ingold, i, John Mann, j, Earl Cranston, k, Harriet Day.

B. Ann Eliza Graham, dau. of Ferdinand Graham and Abbie Ayers Day, b. 12-26-1837, d. 12-22-1894; m. 1861, Lewis E. Carson, b. 12-20-1824, d. 12-31-1901. Mr. Carson was married 3 times; his 3d wife was Rebecca Graham.

Children: a, Julian, b, Lewis, Jr., c, William, d, Nellie, e, Abby.

C. Abby Evelyn Graham, dau. of Ferdinand Graham and Abbie Ayers Day, b. 3-2-1839, d. 8-12-1840.

D. Cornelia Day Graham, dau. of Ferdinand Graham and Abbie Ayers Day, b. 11-16-1840, d. 8-13-1842.

E. John Kennedy Graham, s. of Ferdinand Graham and Abbie Ayers Day, b. 12-4-1842, d. 5-20-1918; m. 1st, 10-6-1864, Nancy Swartz, d. 2-29-1872.

Children: a, Charles Francis, b, John Williams, c, Rebecca Catherine.

John Kennedy Graham m. 2nd, 12-10-1874, Juliet Isabel Stevenson, who is still living in New Albany.

Children: d, Harriet Day, e, George Stevenson, f, Ferdinand, g, Nannie.

F. Bourbon Reese Graham, s. of Ferdinand Graham and Abbie Ayers Day, b. 10-15-1844, d. 7-3-1899; m. Clara B. Loveland, dau. of Ebenezer Pratt Loveland and Jane Hood.

Children: a, Maude A., b, Robert.

G. Amzi Alexander Graham, s. of Ferdinand Graham and Abbie Ayers Day, b. 9-26-1846, d. 10-12-1923; m. Emma Anderson.

Children: a, Edgar, b. Houston, c, Wallace, d, Mary, e, Nellie.

H. Silas Ferdinand Graham, s. of Ferdinand Graham and Abbie Ayers Day, b. 9-8-1848, d. 3-14-1850.

I. Theodore Ezekial Graham, s. of Ferdinand Graham and Abbie Ayers Day, b. 12-11-1850, d. 2-16-1851.

J. Charles Smith Graham, s. of Ferdinand Graham and Abbie Ayers Day, b. 12-18-1851, d. 1-29-1852.

K. Jenny Campbell Graham, dau. of Ferdinand Graham and Abbie Ayers Day, b. and d. 11-11-1853.

L. Edward Forrester Graham, s. of Ferdinand Graham and Abbie Ayers Day, b. 7-4-1855, d. 4-10-1933; m. Sallie Inwood, d. 1932.

Children: a, Edna, b, Albert.

M. John Kennedy Very, s. of Martin Very and Eliza Jane Graham, b. 8-12-1836, d. 6-13-1917; m. Troy, Kan., Anna Tyre. Rhoda Miller.

N. Menander Clark Very, s. of Martin Very and Eliza Jane Graham, b. 8-12-1836, d. 6-13-1917; m. Troy, Kan., Anna Tyre.

Children: a, Hettie, b, Lora.

O. William G. Very, s. of Martin Very and Eliza Jane Graham, b. 8-27-1838 or 8-12-1838, d. 9-13-1846.

P. Martin Luther Very, s. of Martin Very and Eliza Jane Graham, b. 2-23-1840 or 2-27-1840, d. 4-13-1840.
Q. Ruby Evelyn Very, dau. of Martin Very and Eliza Jane Graham, b. 1-26-1841, d. 8-10-1900; m. Palermo, Kan., 8-23-1870, Daniel Landis, s. of William Landis and Penelope Witherspoon, b. Allen Co., Ky., 8-30-1834, d. 9-19-1905.
Children: a, Hugh Graham, b, Anna Mary, c, Flora Mattie, d, Penelope Witherspoon, e, Ruby Lawrence.
R. Mary Louisa Very, dau. of Martin Very and Eliza Jane Graham, b. 1-27-1843, d. c. 1926; m. 6-25-1873, John Mann, s. of Peter Mann and Sara Lyons (who moved to Utica, Clark Co., Ind., in 1818, and Floyd Co., 1823), b. New York, 5-28-1814, d. 4-9-1895. She was his third wife.
Children: a, John Horace, b, Robert Dixon, c, Mary Angeline, d, Wallace Blakely, e, Jesse Menander.
S. Jerusha Anna Very, dau. of Martin Very and Eliza Jane Graham, b. 3-22-1845, d. 9-30-1901; m. Troy, Kan., 6-8-1876, Charles Edwin Cook, b. Litch Co., Conn., 2-22-1835, d. 8-27-1907.
Children: a, Edwin M., b, Norman, c, Mattie, d, James, e, Louis Graham.
T. Florence Amanda Very, dau. of Martin Very and Eliza Jane Graham, b. 8-27-1847; m. 10-6-1875, Dr. S. H. Blakely; no children.
U. Martha Angeline Very, dau. of Martin Very and Eliza Jane Graham, b. 12-31-1849, d. Derby, Kan.; m. 12-27-1883, Henry Mastyn Deming.
Children: a, Theodora, b, Elizabeth Graham, c, Lawrence.
V. Eliza Jane Guest, dau. of James Guest and Louisa Graham, b. 3-24-1838, d. in infancy.
W. John Guest, s. of James Guest and Louisa Graham, b. 10-31-1839, d. 1-21-1862; never married.
X. Penina Guest, dau. of James Guest and Louisa Graham, b. 5-31-1841, d. in infancy.
Y. James Hervey Guest, s. of James Guest and Louisa Graham, b. 9-21-1843, d. 5-15-1910; m. 6-11-1873, Hattie N. Davis.
Children: a, Daisy Louise.
Z. Maria Louisa Guest, dau. of James Guest and Louisa Graham, b. 12-21-1845, d. 7-22-1933; m. 5-27-1874, Dr. John Newton McCord, d. 9-21-1891. She was his 2nd wife.
Children: a, James Newton, b, Mary Louise.
AA. Amanda Graham Guest, dau. of James Guest and Louisa Graham, b. 6-14-1850, d. St. Louis, Mo., 12-16-1935; m. 10-7-1894, William T. Taylor, d. 11-1-1915; no children.
BB. William Guest, s. of James Guest and Louisa Graham, b. 1-6-1853, d. 6-13-1864.
CC. Charles F. Very, s. of Martin Very and Julia Ann Graham, b. 3-9-1854, d. c. 1930; m. 2-18-1903, Mary Marshall; moved to Colo. before 1910; no children.
DD. Emily Prime Very, dau. of Martin Very and Julia Ann Graham, b. 4-28-1856, d. 3-25-1874; not married.
EE. Eliza Ada Very, dau. of Martin Very and Julia Ann Graham,

b. 1-19-1858; m. Prof. O. O. Charlton, resided in Kan., Okla., and Texas.
Children: a, Julia Graham, b, Wilbur.
FF. Nathaniel L. Very, s. of Martin Very and Julia Ann Graham, b. 7-23-1860, d. 9-25-1881 or 9-29-1881; resided in Kan.; no children.
GG. Edward Everett Very, s. of Martin Very and Julia Ann Graham, b. 5-3-1863, d. 2-14-1864.
HH. William Guest Very, s. of Martin Very and Julia Ann Graham, b. 5-24-1865, d. 8-30-1882.
II. Francis Townley Very, s. of Martin Very and Julia Ann Graham, b. 5-5-1868, d. 4-23-1909 at Hiawatha, Kan.; m. 1st, Carrie McDavy, 2nd Elizabeth French, b. 10-23-1872.
Children by first wife: a, Edwin, b, Earl.
JJ. Samuel Charles Shipman, s. of John L. Shipman and Lucinda Evelyn Graham, b. 9-12-1850, d. 8-2-1851.
KK. Anna Vesta Shipman, dau. of John L. Shipman and Lucinda Evelyn Graham, b. 12-8-1851, d. 9-9-1872; never married.
LL. Durett F. Shipman, s. of John L. Shipman and Lucinda Evelyn Graham, b. 11-6-1852, d. 8-19-1872; never married.
MM. Edward Walter Shipman, s. of John L. Shipman and Lucinda Evelyn Graham, b. 1-19-1856, d. 10-1-1861.
NN. Charles Shipman, s. of John L. Shipman and Lucinda Evelyn Graham, b. 11-14-1857, d. 8-18-1859.
OO. Cassius C. Shipman, s. of John L. Shipman and Lucinda Evelyn Graham, b. 8-1-1860, d. 3-27-1881; never married.
PP. James David Shipman, s. of John L. Shipman and Lucinda Evelyn Graham, b. 11-25-1862, d. 1931; m. Clara Hager; he was her 2nd husband.
Children: a, Myrtle May, b, Charles, c, Durett Howard.
QQ. Harry Shipman, s. of John L. Shipman and Lucinda Evelyn Graham, b. New Albany, 10-10-1868, still living; m. 1st and divorced Emma Rogers; no children. Harry Shipman m. 2nd, 1-10-1899, Luella Smith, dau. of Elmore Smith and Maria Louisa Gregg, b. Galena, Ind., 1-4-1869, d. 12-22-1940.
Children: a, Evelyn Mae, b, Clarence Taylor, c, Leila Belle.
RR. Carolyn Bell Belton, dau. of James H. Belton and Caroline A. Graham, b. c. 1860, d. Cal., 1930; never married.
SS. Mary Belton, dau. of James H. Belton and Caroline A. Graham, still living; m. North Platte, Nebr., William Henry McDonald.
Children: a, Janet.
TT. La Belle Lenore Grant, dau. of Thomas L. Grant and Maria T. Graham, b. 1859, d. in infancy.
UU. William Lewis Talbott Grant, s. of Thomas L. Grant and Maria T. Graham, b. 1-17-1875, d. 4-13-1927; m. 6-26-1911, Leona Dumar.
Children: a, John William (lived only a few hours).
VV. James Madison Graham, Jr., s. of James M. Graham and Mary J. Akin Price, b. 1872, d. 10-18-1914; m. 1st, Zenia ———.
Children: a, Ula.
James Madison Graham, Jr., m. 2nd, Laura Denison; 2 daughters, names unknown.

WW. Ida Graham, dau. of James M. Graham and Mary J. Akin Price, b. 1874; m. 1-12-1892, Benjamin Blackiston, Jr., s. of Benjamin Blackiston, Sr., and Caroline Very.
Children: a, Beatrice Amelia, b, Adelaide, c, Carolyn Mae, d, Winfred Graham, e, B. Roland, f, Marjorie Mae, g, Isabelle, h, Mary Evelyn, i, Benjamin Curtis, j, Dorothy Jean.
XX. Hubert Graham, s. of James M. Graham and Mary J. Akin Price, d. 9-17-1915; m. 10-30-1903, Jennie Conner, dau. of James Harvey Conner and Sarah Elizabeth Davis, still living.
Children: a, Hubert, Jr., b, Virginia, c, Jane Whitelaw.
YY. Earl A. Graham, s. of James M. Graham and Mary J. Akin Price, b. 11-6-1875, d. 12-7-1915; m. 8-12-1904, Grace Conner, dau. of James Harvey Conner and Sarah Elizabeth Davis, still living.
Children: a, Katherine Conner, b, Donald.
ZZ. Minnie Graham, dau. of James M. Graham and Mary J. Akin Price, still living; m. 11-2-1913, Charles Zapp; no children.
AAA. Chester Graham, s. of James M. Graham and Mary J. Akin Price; m. Edna Miller, dau. of E. A. Miller and Estelle Ricketts; r. New Albany.
Children: a, Stuart.

V. A. Herbert Graham Walker, s. of Rev. Francis Walker and Mary Elizabeth Graham, b. 3-24-1857, d. 6-1-1923; m. 9-28-1892, Clara Perry.
Children: a, Kingsley, b, Gene (girl), c, Eunice.
B. Ferdinand Graham Walker, s. of Rev. Francis Walker and Mary Elizabeth Graham, b. Mitchell, Ind., 2-16-1859, d. 6-13-1927; m. 11-13-1884, Mary Watkin.
Children: a, Stanley Ward.
C. Nellie Adda Walker, dau. of Rev. Francis Walker and Mary Elizabeth Graham, b. Leesville, Ind., 12-17-1860, d. 8-14-1862.
D. Ernest Graham Walker, s. of Rev. Francis Walker and Mary Elizabeth Graham, b. Brownstown, Ind., 11-12-1862, d. 12-?-1916; m. Mary Newman of Clemson College, S. C.
Children: a, Marion, b, Elbert, c, Ernestine.
E. Clarence Walker, s. of Rev. Francis Walker and Mary Elizabeth Graham, b. Newburg, Ind., 2-14-1865, still living, New Albany; never married.
F. Abbie Evelyn Walker, dau. of Rev. Francis Walker and Mary Elizabeth Graham, b. Gentryville, Ind., 12-5-1867, d. 10-27-1918; never married.
G. Leland Francis Walker, s. of Rev. Francis Walker and Mary Elizabeth Graham, b. Cannelton, Ind., 9-9-1869, d. 1-5-1870.
H. Francis Ingold Walker, s. of Rev. Francis Walker and Mary Elizabeth Graham, b. Cannelton, Ind., 3-16-1871; m. Colorado Springs, Colo., c. 1904, Flora Lee Dula.
Children: a, Margaret McKee, b, James Francis.
I. Rev. John Mann Walker, s. of Rev. Francis Walker and Mary Elizabeth Graham, b. Washington, Ind., 2-3-1874, still living; m, 10-5-1904, E. Nora Severinghaus, d. c. 1937.
Children: a, Mary Alden, b, Louise.

- J. Earl Cranston Walker, s. of Rev. Francis Walker and Mary Elizabeth Graham, b. New Albany, 1-21-1876, r. Altadena, Cal.; m. Louisville, Ky., Florence Jacobsen.
  Children: a, Myrtle Alden.
- K. Harriet Day Walker, dau. of Rev. Francis Walker and Mary Elizabeth Graham, b. 4-2-1880, r. New Albany; never married.
- L. Julian Carson, s. of Dr. Lewis E. Carson and Ann Eliza Graham; m. ———; one child, name unknown.
- M. Lewis Carson, Jr., s. of Dr. Lewis E. Carson and Ann Eliza Graham; m. ———.
  Children: a, Hilda.
- N. William Carson, s. of Dr. Lewis E. Carson and Ann Eliza Graham, d. boyhood.
- O. Nellie Carson, dau. of Dr. Lewis E. Carson and Ann Eliza Graham.
- P. Abby Carson, dau. of Dr. Lewis E. Carson and Ann Eliza Graham.
- Q. Charles Francis Graham, s. of John Kennedy Graham and Nancy Swartz, b. 8-27-1865, still living; m. 11-12-1891, Louisa L. Bettmann, d. 1-6-1942.
  Children: a, Charlotte Louise, b, William John, c, Edward Herman, d, Marguerite Clara, e, Frederic Charles.
- R. John William Graham, s. of John Kennedy Graham and Nancy Swartz, b. 5-13-1867, still living; never married.
- S. Rebecca Catherine Graham, dau. of John Kennedy Graham and Nancy Swartz, b. 11-12-1868, d. 7-12-1942; m. 8-12-1896, Dr. Lewis E. Carson. She was his third wife.
  Children: a, Winifred.
- T. Harriet Day Graham, dau. of John Kennedy Graham and Juliet Isabel Stevenson, b. 11-10-1875, d. 12-12-1875.
- U. George Stevenson Graham, s. of John Kennedy Graham and Juliet Isabel Stevenson, b. 5-15-1877, still living; never married.
- V. Ferdinand Graham, s. of John Kennedy Graham and Juliet Isabel Stevenson, b. 6-29-1883; never married.
- W. Nannie Graham, dau. of John Kennedy Graham and Juliet Isabel Stevenson, still living; never married.
- X. Maude A. Graham, dau. of Dr. Bourbon Reese Graham and Clara Loveland, r. Cal.; m. William A. Banta; no children.
- Y. Robert Graham, s. of Dr. Bourbon Reese Graham and Clara Loveland; m. ———.
  Children: 2 or 3, names unknown.
- Z. Edgar Graham, s. of Dr. Amzi Alexander Graham and Emma Anderson, b. c. 1875, d. 8-23-1892; never married.
- AA. Houston Graham, s. of Dr. Amzi Alexander Graham and Emma Anderson; m. ———.
  Children: names unknown.
- BB. Wallace Graham, s. of Dr. Amzi Alexander Graham and Emma Anderson; m. ———; no children. Houston and Wallace Graham are twins.
- CC. Mary Graham, dau. of Dr. Amzi Alexander Graham and Emma Anderson; m. Brady Brown.
  Children: a, Mary, b, Emily, c, Brady, Jr.

DD. Nellie Graham, dau. of Dr. Amzi Alexander Graham and Emma Anderson, d. childhood.
EE. Edna Graham, dau. of Edward Forrester Graham and Sallie Inwood; m. ——— Osborn.
Children: 2 dau., names unknown.
FF. Albert Graham, s. of Edward Forrester Graham and Sallie Inwood, r. Detroit, Mich.
GG. Hettie Very, dau. of Menander Clark Very and Anna Tyre, d. 6-21-1896; never married.
HH. Lora Very, dau. of Menander Clark Very and Anna Tyre, b. 1880; m. 1905, W. F. Culp, r. Troy, Kan.
Children: a, Dorothy, b, Annie, c. Franklin, d, Louis Max.
II. Hugh Graham Landis, s. of Daniel Landis and Ruby Evelyn Very, b. Doniphan Co., Kan., 6-25-1871, r. Los Angeles, Cal.; m. 1895, Naomi Carter.
Children: a, Ruth, b, Helen.
JJ. Anna Mary Landis, dau. of Daniel Landis and Ruby Evelyn Very, b. Doniphan Co., Kan., 11-16-1873, d. 1-1-1917; m. Lee Bumgardner.
Children: a, Florence Louise, b, Nellie Lee, c, Jesse Edward, d, James.
KK. Flora Mattie Landis, dau. of Daniel Landis and Ruby Evelyn Very, b. Doniphan Co., Kan., 12-23-1880, d. 2-4-1895; never married.
LL. Penelope Witherspoon Landis, dau. of Daniel Landis and Ruby Evelyn Very, b. Doniphan Co., Kan., 8-27-1884, r. Albuquerque, N. M.; m. 2-18-1918, Albert E. Bebermeyer.
Children: a, Landis V., b, Virginia.
MM. Ruby Lawrence Landis, dau. of Daniel Landis and Ruby Evelyn Very, b. Ottawa, Kan., 12-18-1886, d. 1-17-1938; m. 11-19-1907, Henry Duffy.
Children: a, Daniel Henry, b, Lawrence Albert, c, Harold Aloyseus, d, Paul Joseph, e, Cecil, f, Ruby Evelyn, g, Hugh Maurice, h, Vera Penelope, i, Josie Marie.
NN. John Horace Mann, s. of John Mann and Mary Louisa Very, b. 1873, d. 6-2-1892; never married.
OO. Robert Dixon Mann, s. of John Mann and Mary Louisa Very; m. Mary Rager.
Children: a, Robert J., b, Ruth, c, Kenneth, d, Lewis.
PP. Mary Angeline Mann, dau. of John Mann and Mary Louisa Very, d. 8-21-1937; m. 6-?-1923, Chester Winstandly; no children.
QQ. Wallace Blakely Mann, s. of John Mann and Mary Louisa Very, d. 5-14-1914; never married.
RR. Jesse Menander Mann, s. of John Mann and Mary Louisa Very, b. 8-13-1887, r. Monte Vista, Colo.; m. 6-?-1922, Marian Frances Wilbur.
Children: a, Mary Louise.
SS. Edwin M. Cook, s. of Charles Edwin Cook and Jerusha Anna Very, b. 10-7-1877, still living; m. Effingham, Kan., 6-30-1903, Ida Thompson.
Children: a, Bertha Lena, b, Orlena Rusha, c, Clarence Edwin.

TT. Norman Cook, s. of Charles Edwin Cook and Jerusha Anna Very, b. 9-24-1879; m. 12-27-1904, Nellie Cook (no relation); no children.
UU. Mattie Cook, dau. of Charles Edwin Cook and Jerusha Anna Very, b. 6-17-1881, d. 6-20-1881.
VV. James Cook, s. of Charles Edwin Cook and Jerusha Anna Very, b. 10-2-1882, r. Effingham, Kan.; m. 8-25-1929, Bertha Wilkins; no children.
WW. Louis Graham Cook, s. of Charles Edwin Cook and Jerusha Anna Very, b. 3-16-1885, r. Oskaloosa, Kan.; never married.
XX. Theodora Deming, dau. of Henry Mastyn Deming and Martha Angeline Very.
YY. Elizabeth Graham Deming, dau. of Henry Mastyn Deming and Martha Angeline Very, r. Mulvane, Kan.; m. Ray Palmer. Children: 2; names unknown.
ZZ. Lawrence Deming, s. of Henry Mastyn Deming and Martha Angeline Very.
AAA. Daisy Louise Guest, dau. of James Hervey Guest and Hattie N. Davis, r. New York City; m. 1st, ———, 2nd, ——— Rice.
BBB. James Newton McCord, s. of Dr. John Newton McCord and Maria Louisa Guest, b. Vandalia, Ill., 2-20-1877, r. West Orange, N. J.; m. Mabel Decker.
Children: a, Doris Jacqueline.
CCC. Mary Louise McCord, dau. of Dr. John Newton McCord and Maria Louisa Guest, b. Vandalia, Ill., 8-4-1879, r. Robinson, Ill.; m. 6-25-1908, Thomas A. McComb.
Children: a, Dorothy Louise.
DDD. Julia Graham Charlton, dau. of Prof. O. O. Charlton and Eliza Ada Very, b. c. 1880, r. Dallas, Texas.
EEE. Wilbur Charlton, s. of Prof. O. O. Charlton and Eliza Ada Very, b. c. 1883, d. c. 1886.
FFF. Edwin Very, s. of Francis Townley Very and Carrie McDavy, b. 1889, r. San Diego, Cal.; never married.
GGG. Earl Very, s. of Francis Townley Very and Carrie McDavy, b. 1891, d. 1911; never married.
HHH. Myrtle May Shipman, dau. of James David Shipman and Clara Hager, b. New Albany, Ind., c. 1895; m. 1920, William H. Meeker, III.
Children: a, William H., IV, b, Robert.
III. Charles Shipman, s. of James David Shipman and Clara Hager, d. c. 1938; m. 1st, Etta ———, 2nd, Izetta ———; no children.
JJJ. Durett Howard Shipman, s. of James David Shipman and Clara Hager, b. 5-27-1899, r. Brooklyn, N. Y.; m. Madeline ———; no children.
KKK. Evelyn Mae Shipman, dau. of Harry Shipman and Luella Smith, b. New Albany, Ind., 10-20-1899, r. Indianapolis, Ind.; m. 7-3-1929, Dr. Sylvan Leslie Mouser.
Children: a, Robert Winston.
LLL. Clarence Taylor Shipman, s. of Harry Shipman and Luella Smith, b. Madison, Ind., 7-20-1901, r. Indianapolis, Ind.; never married.

MMM. Leila Belle Shipman, dau. of Harry Shipman and Luella Smith, b. and r. Indianapolis, Ind., 12-19-1904; m. 8-18-1934, Wallace Pickens Daggy, s. of Eugene L. Daggy and Charity Pickens, b. Spencer, Ind., 12-15-1902.
Children: a, Richard.
NNN. Janet McDonald, dau. of William Henry McDonald and Mary Belton, b. and r. North Platte, Nebr.
OOO. Ula Graham, dau. of James Madison Graham, Jr., and Zenia ———, r. Cal.; m. Walter Meyer, one dau.
PPP. 2 dau. of James Madison Graham, Jr., and Laura Denison;
QQQ. Names unknown.
RRR. Beatrice Amelia Blackiston, dau. of Benjamin Blackiston, Jr., and Ida Graham, b. 12-11-1892; m. 1923, Merse Murphy.
SSS. Adelaide Blackiston, dau. of Benjamin Blackiston, Jr., and Ida Graham, b. 9-14-1894, r. Mt. Tabor Road, New Albany, Ind.; m. 1919, Roy D. Blanton.
Children: a, Elaine, b, Marilyn.
TTT. Carolyn Mae Blackiston, dau. of Benjamin Blackiston, Jr., and Ida Graham, b. 2-12-1897; m. 10-5-1920, Herrin Dillard.
Children: a, Donald.
UUU. Winfred Graham Blackiston, s. of Benjamin Blackiston, Jr., and Ida Graham, b. 6-27-1899; m. 1925, Ida Smith.
VVV. B. Roland Blackiston, s. of Benjamin Blackiston, Jr., and Ida Graham, b. 9-14-1901; m. 1-31-1924, Charlotte Smith.
Children: a, Betty Jane.
WWW. Marjorie Mae Blackiston, dau. of Benjamin Blackiston, Jr., and Ida Graham, b. 4-26-1904; m. c. 1921, Charles Thorne.
Children: a, Doris Jean, b, Aletha.
XXX. Isabelle Blackiston, dau. of Benjamin Blackiston, Jr., and Ida Graham, b. 9-27-1906; m. 1932, Charles Dickerson.
Children: a, Ruth Joyce.
YYY. Mary Evelyn Blackiston, dau. of Benjamin Blackiston, Jr., and Ida Graham, b. 1-14-1909; m. 1935, James Hoglen.
ZZZ. Benjamin Curtis Blackiston, s. of Benjamin Blackiston, Jr., and Ida Graham, b. 5-27-1912; m. 1933, Stella Ramsier.
AAAA. Dorothy Jean Blackiston, dau. of Benjamin Blackiston, Jr., and Ida Graham, b. 7-16-1914; m. 1934, John Ernest Stevens.
BBBB. Hubert Graham, Jr., s. of Hubert Graham and Jennie Conner; m. 1936, ———.
CCCC. Virginia Graham, dau. of Hubert Graham and Jennie Conner.
DDDD. Jane Whitelaw Graham, dau. of Hubert Graham and Jennie Conner.
EEEE. Katherine Conner Graham, dau. of Earl A. Graham and Grace Conner, r. Baltimore, Md.; m. 5-19-1937, Kenneth Lloyd Thompson; no children.
FFFF. Donald Graham, s. of Earl A. Graham and Grace Conner, r. New Albany, Ind.; m. Mary Jane Newhouse.
Children: a, James Madison, b, John Kennedy.
GGGG. Stuart Graham, s. of Chester Graham and Edna Miller, b. c. 1918.

VI. A. Kingsley Walker, s. of Herbert Graham Walker and Clara Perry, r. Louisville, Ky.; m. Grace Funk.
Children: a, Marguerite, b, Betty Jean.
B. Gene Walker, dau. of Herbert Graham Walker and Clara Perry, r. Warren, Pa.
C. Eunice Walker, dau. of Herbert Graham Walker and Clara Perry, r. Scarsdale, N. Y.; m. Gerald Vibberts.
Children: a, Kingsley.
D. Stanley Ward Walker, s. of Ferdinand Graham Walker and Mary Watkin, b. 1-12-1890, r. N. Y.; m. Emily C. McDonald.
Children: a, Stanley (girl).
E. Marion Walker, s. of Ernest Graham Walker and Mary Newman, r. Leesburg, Fla.; m. Olive ———.
Children: a, Marian Graham.
F. Elbert Walker, s. of Ernest Graham Walker and Mary Newman; m. ———.
Children: a, Elbert, Jr., b, son (name unknown).
G. Ernestine Walker, dau. of Ernest Graham Walker and Mary Newman, b. c. 1913, r. Albany, Ga.; m. Mercer Sherman.
H. Margaret McKee Walker, dau. of Francis Ingold Walker and Flora Lee Dula, r. Wilmette, Ill.
I. James Francis Walker, s. of Francis Ingold Walker and Flora Lee Dula, b. c. 1904.
J. Mary Alden Walker, dau. of Rev. John Mann Walker and E. Nora Severinghaus, b. Louisville, Ky., 9-21-1905.
K. Louise Walker, dau. of Rev. John Mann Walker and E. Nora Severinghaus, b. Indianapolis, Ind., 9-17-1911.
L. Myrtle Alden Walker, dau. of Earl Cranston Walker and Florence Jacobsen, r. Altadena, Cal.; m. 4-18-1931, Dr. John Eugene Lotspiech.
Children: a, Graham Alden.
M. No name for child of Dr. Lewis E. Carson and Ann Eliza Graham.
N. Hilda Carson, dau. of Lewis Carson, Jr., and ———, r. Prairieton, Ind.
O. Charlotte Louise Graham, dau. of Charles Francis Graham and Louisa L. Bettmann, b. 4-21-1893; m. 6-24-1913, Claude B. McBride.
Children: a, Florence Virginia, b, Marguerite Blanche.
P. William John Graham, s. of Charles Francis Graham and Louisa L. Bettmann, b. 8-2-1895; m. 9-2-1926, Lovenia Bigler.
Children: a, Bruce Alden.
Q. Edward Herman Graham, s. of Charles Francis Graham and Louisa L. Bettmann, b. 10-11-1897; never married.
R. Marguerite Clara Graham, dau. of Charles Francis Graham and Louisa L. Bettmann, b. 9-19-1900; m. 6-27-1925, Basil B. Barnett.
Children: a, Richard Warren, b, Madge Jean.
S. Frederic Charles Graham, s. of Charles Francis Graham and Louisa L. Bettmann, b. 11-15-1903, d. 6-?-1913.

T. Winifred Carson, dau. of Dr. Lewis E. Carson and Rebecca Catherine Graham, b. Prairieton, Ind., 1-8-1901, r. Paoli Pike; m. 12-24-1920, William Phillip Holz, b. 2-24-1899.
Children: a, William Phillip, Jr., b, Robert Graham, c, Sherley Jean, d, Arthur.
U. 2 or 3 children of Robert Graham and ———, r. Texas; names
V. unknown.
W. Children of Houston Graham and ———; names unknown.
X. Mary Brown, dau. of Brady Brown and Mary Graham, m. c. 1936.
Y. Emily Brown, dau. of Brady Brown and Mary Graham; m. —.
Z. Brady Brown, Jr., s. of Brady Brown and Mary Graham, m. —.
AA.
BB. 2 dau. of ——— Osborn and Edna Graham; names unknown.
CC. Dorothy Culp, dau. of W. F. Culp and Lora Very; m. ———.
DD. Annie Culp, dau. of W. F. Culp and Lora Very; m. ———.
EE. Franklin Culp, s. of W. F. Culp and Lora Very.
FF. Louis Max Culp, s. of W. F. Culp and Lora Very, b. c. 1925.
GG. Ruth Landis, dau. of Hugh Graham Landis and Naomi Carter, b. 4-10-1900; m. ———; one child.
HH. Helen Landis, dau. of Hugh Graham Landis and Naomi Carter, d. 4-6-1911, in childhood.
II. Florence Louise Bumgardner, dau. of Lee Bumgardner and Anna Mary Landis, b. 7-7-1907.
JJ. Nellie Lee Bumgardner, dau. of Lee Bumgardner and Anna Mary Landis, b. 5-7-1911.
KK. Jesse Edward Bumgardner, s. of Lee Bumgardner and Anna Mary Landis, b. 10-10-1913.
LL. James Bumgardner, s. of Lee Bumgardner and Anna Mary Landis, b. 4-29-1916.
MM. Landis V. Bebermeyer, s. of Albert E. Bebermeyer and Penelope Witherspoon Landis, b. 6-17-1911; m. 6-17-1934, Helon Kelley.
Children: a, Landis Eugene, b, Carol.
NN. Virginia Bebermeyer, dau. of Albert E. Bebermeyer and Penelope Witherspoon Landis, b. 4-3-1913.
OO. Daniel Henry Duffy, s. of Henry Duffy and Ruby Lawrence Landis, b. 9-14-1908.
PP. Lawrence Albert Duffy, s. of Henry Duffy and Ruby Lawrence Landis, b. 11-20-1909, d. 10-1-1925.
QQ. Harold Aloyseus Duffy, s. of Henry Duffy and Ruby Lawrence Landis, b. 7-31-1911.
RR. Paul Joseph Duffy, s. of Henry Duffy and Ruby Lawrence Landis, b. 10-20-1912.
SS. Cecil Duffy, s. of Henry Duffy and Ruby Lawrence Landis, b. 1914.
TT. Ruby Evelyn Duffy, dau. of Henry Duffy and Ruby Lawrence Landis, b. 2-23-1916.
UU. Hugh Maurice Duffy, s. of Henry Duffy and Ruby Lawrence Landis, b. 3-9-1919.
VV. Vera Penelope Duffy, dau. of Henry Duffy and Ruby Lawrence Landis, b. 8-26-1921.

WW. Josie Marie Duffy, dau. of Henry Duffy and Ruby Lawrence Landis, b. 3-30-1927.
XX. Robert J. Mann, s. of Robert Dixon Mann and Mary Rager; m. ———; one dau.
YY. Ruth Mann, dau. of Robert Dixon Mann and Mary Rager, r. Louisville, Ky.
ZZ. Kenneth Mann, s. of Robert Dixon Mann and Mary Rager, r. Louisville, Ky.
AAA. Lewis Mann, s. of Robert Dixon Mann and Mary Rager, r. Louisville, Ky.
BBB. Mary Louise Mann, dau. of Jesse Menander Mann and Marian Frances Wilbur, r. Los Angeles, Cal.; m. 1-23-1943, Edgar Elton Davenport.
CCC. Bertha Lena Cook, dau. of Edwin M. Cook and Ida Thompson, b. 10-9-1908, r. Laramie, Wyo.; m. 5-12-1934, John Hamon. Children: a, Marjorie Jean, b, Charles Edwin, c, Nancy Joe.
DDD. Orlena Rusha Cook, dau. of Edwin M. Cook and Ida Thompson, b. 3-17-1912, r. Arlington, Va.; m. 5-12-1934, Thomas Elliott Hall.
Children: a, Larry.
EEE. Clarence Edwin Cook, s. of Edwin M. Cook and Ida Thompson, b. 11-8-1914, r. Wichita, Kan.; m. Hay, Kan., 7-1-1939, Doris Burns; no children.
FFF. 2 children of Ray Palmer and Elizabeth Graham Deming;
GGG. names unknown.
HHH. Doris Jacqueline McCord, dau. of James Newton McCord and Mabel Decker, b. 11-29-1914, r. N. J.; m. 6-27-1937, Robert Ball.
III. Dorothy Louise McComb, dau. of Thomas A. McComb and Mary Louise McCord, b. Chicago, Ill., 9-23-1909, r. Robinson, Ill.; m. 6-3-1939, Paul Otey.
Children: a, one adopted, b. 12-14-1942.
JJJ. William H. Meeker, IV, s. of William H. Meeker, III, and Myrtle May Shipman, b. Brooklyn, N. Y., c. 1922.
KKK. Robert Meeker, s. of William H. Meeker, III, and Myrtle May Shipman, b. Brooklyn, N. Y., c. 1927.
LLL. Robert Winston Mouser, s. of Dr. Sylvan Leslie Mouser and Evelyn Mae Shipman, b. Indianapolis, Ind., 10-21-1931.
MMM. Richard Daggy, s. of Wallace Pickens Daggy and Leila Belle Shipman, b. and d. 5-31-1938.
NNN. (girl) Meyer, dau. of Walter Meyer and Ula Graham, r. Cal.
OOO. Elaine Blanton, dau. of Roy D. Blanton and Adelaide Blackiston.
PPP. Marilyn Blanton, dau. of Roy D. Blanton and Adelaide Blackiston.
QQQ. Donald Dillard, s. of Herrin Dillard and Carolyn Mae Blackiston, b. 6-28-1928.
RRR. Betty Jane Blackiston, dau. of B. Roland Blackiston and Charlotte Smith.
SSS. Doris Jean Thorne, dau. of Charles Thorne and Marjorie Mae Blackiston, b. 6-?-1921.
TTT. Aletha Thorne, dau. of Charles Thorne and Marjorie Mae Blackiston.

UUU. Ruth Joyce Dickerson, dau. of Charles Dickerson and Isabelle Blackiston, b. 3-12-1933.
VVV. James Madison Graham, s. of Donald Graham and Mary Jane Newhouse, b. c. 1940.
WWW. John Kennedy Graham, s. of Donald Graham and Mary Jane Newhouse, b. 1942.

VII. A. Marguerite Walker, dau. of Kingsley Walker and Grace Funk, b. c. 1918, r. Louisville, Ky.; m. 3-7-1935, J. B. Stratton, Jr.
Children: a, Herbert, b, John Kingsley, c, Thomas Franklin.
- B. Betty Jean Walker, dau. of Kingsley Walker and Grace Funk, b. c. 1924 (or 1926), r. Louisville, Ky.
- C. Kingsley Vibberts, s. of Gerald Vibberts and Eunice Walker, b. c. 1932, r. Scarsdale, N. Y.
- D. Stanley Walker, dau. of Stanley Ward Walker and Emily C. McDonald, b. 10-?-1924, r. N. Y.; m. Charles Clinton Lush.
- E. Marian Graham Walker, dau. of Marion Walker and Olive ———, b. Leesburg, Fla., 3-13-1936.
- F. Elbert Walker, Jr., s. of Elbert Walker and ———, b. c. 1922.
- G. (boy) Walker, s. of Elbert Walker and ———.
- H. Graham Alden Lotspiech, s. of Dr. John Eugene Lotspiech and Myrtle Alden Walker, b. 2-4-1933, r. Altadena, Cal.
- I. Florence Virginia McBride, dau. of Claude B. McBride and Charlotte Louise Graham, b. 12-25-1916; m. 4-17-1940, Justin Salyards.
Children: a, Gregory Mark.
- J. Marguerite Blanche McBride, dau. of Claude B. McBride and Charlotte Louise Graham, b. 2-26-1923.
- K. Bruce Alden Graham, s. of William John Graham and Lovenia Bigler, b. 9-11-1927.
- L. Richard Warren Barnett, s. of Basil B. Barnett and Marguerite Clara Graham, b. 9-23-1926.
- M. Madge Jean Barnett, dau. of Basil B. Barnett and Marguerite Clara Graham, b. 2-8-1931.
- N. William Phillip Holz, Jr., s. of William Phillip Holz and Winifred Carson, b. 4-22-1925.
- O. Robert Graham Holz, s. of William Phillip Holz and Winifred Carson, b. 11-16-1926.
- P. Sherley Jean Holz, dau. of William Phillip Holz and Winifred Carson, b. 6-30-1930, d. 10-24-1930.
- Q. Arthur Holz, s. of William Phillip Holz and Winifred Carson, b. 8-18-1933.
- R. No name for child of Ruth Landis and ———.
- S. Landis Eugene Bebermeyer, s. of Landis V. Bebermeyer and Helon Kelley, b. 5-16-1935.
- T. Carol Bebermeyer, dau. of Landis V. Bebermeyer and Helon Kelley, b. 3-26-1938.
- U. (girl) Mann, dau. of Robert J. Mann and ———.
- V. Marjorie Jean Hamon, dau. of John Hamon and Bertha Lena Cook, b. Fredonia, Kan., 9-2-1935.

W. Charles Edwin Hamon, s. of John Hamon and Bertha Lena Cook, b. Fredonia, Kan., 10-16-1938.
X. Nancy Joe Hamon, dau. of John Hamon and Bertha Lena Cook, b. Thermopolis, Wyo., 10-16-1942.
Y. Larry Hall, s. of Thomas Elliott Hall and Orlena Rusha Cook, b. 6-1-1942.
Z. Robert Jonathan Ball, s. of Robert Ball and Doris Jacqueline McCord, b. 7-11-1942.

VIII. A. Herbert Stratton, s. of J. B. Stratton, Jr., and Marguerite Walker, d. in infancy.
B. John Kingsley Stratton, s. of J. B. Stratton, Jr., and Marguerite Walker, b. 1-3-1938.
C. Thomas Franklin Stratton, s. of J. B. Stratton, Jr., and Marguerite Walker, b. 4-6-1940.
D. Gregory Mark Salyards, s. of Justin Salyards and Florence Virginia McBride, b. 2-1-1941.

SIMON HADLEY AND HIS DESCENDANTS

Mrs. Irene M. Strieby

The Genealogy Section of the Indiana State Library is the recipient of "Simon Hadley and His Descendants," a compilation of hundreds of typewritten pages assembled in four volumes bound in "Quaker" gray. In addition to the genealogical records there are photographs of people and places, newspaper clippings, copies of census, court, Bible and church records, early wills, and marriage agreements signed by witnesses. Interesting anecdotes and bits of family history and biography, as well as personal letters are found among the pages, leading descendants to anticipate something greener for their family tree.

Supplemented by material listed above, the family records are based primarily on questionnaires sent out by the compiler, Kingston Goddard Hadley, of Media, Pennsylvania. It is evident that he devoted many years of his life to this work, following every clew received to enable him to make the family records complete to 1937. Many years ago Mordecai Hadley, of Indiana, wrote a partial genealogy of the family which the compiler had the privilege of copying. He states that he used a chart made by Walter Brooks Hadley as well as data sent by others who had attempted to trace their own lines back to the immigrant ancestor. To these he gives credit in his preliminary notes.

An examination of the volumes reveals the fact that the original plan was to assign to each descendant a number keyed to generations down from Simon Hadley. As more information reached the compiler he was unable to carry out the plan; however, these numbers are helpful in keeping family groups together. Families of daughters are carried through several generations, a feature not customary in the usual family history. Birth, death, and marriage dates always are included when the facts are available. Much collateral data appear making buried treasure for the genealogist. It is amazing to realize that the compiler was able to assemble the information, once it was collected. In its present form the genealogy is difficult to use; it is hoped that some descendant will supplement this labor of love with an adequate index.

Simon Hadley, the father of Simon Hadley, the immigrant, owned an iron smithy in King's County, Ireland, and was also interested in some fishery property in Dublin. He was born about 1640 and his first wife was Catherine Talbot (?), of Dublin. She seems to have been the first of the name to join the Society of Friends; her death is recorded in the Minutes of the Moate Granoge Register. After her death Simon Hadley married a second time; this marriage was "out of unity" and caused his disownment from the society. He died on June 6, 1711, leaving four children —John Hadley, Elizabeth Hadley Miller, Jane Hadley Kiernan, and Simon, the immigrant.

Simon Hadley II (c. 1675-1756) came from County West Meath, Ireland, to America, in 1712, accompanied by his wife, Ruth Keran, and six children born in Ireland. He settled in New Garden Township, Chester County, Pennsylvania, in what was then known as the Manor of Steyning. The land extended into Newcastle County; when the Deleware state line was drawn, it passed through his land and placed his residence in Mill Creek Hundred, Newcastle County, Delaware. Tradition says that the British Army camped upon a section of this land on the night before the Battle of the Brandywine.

About him lived many of the early families, most of whom were of English origin, who came to Penn's colony by way of Ireland. These Friends of Steyning Manor built a meeting house in 1713; Simon Hadley was one of the four trustees, and was chosen overseer of the New Garden Meeting in 1733. In 1726 he was appointed a justice of the peace and also served at various times as judge of the county court. His name appears on a petition from Concord Quarterly Meeting—3rd month, 13th day, 1734—addressed to King George II, of England, relative to the boundary disputes between the Penns and Lord Baltimore.

Many descendants have gone back to Simon Hadley's Pennsylvania home during the past decade. The old house is a two-and-one-half-story stone structure covered with yellow stucco. A pen and ink sketch shows the gabled roof, the quaint-pointed windows, and the white stone slab sunk in the front wall on which are carved the initials, S (and) R. H, 1717, the year that Simon and Ruth built this home. The interior of the house includes a lovely old mantle and a colonial stairway. The stone foundations of the carriage shed remain; the old barn with its gabled roof and stone foundations, with new exterior timber as well as an addition, are on the same hilltop as the house. A short distance away is the meeting house, with its burial ground, the final resting place of this progenitor of the Quaker Hadleys in America.

Simon Hadley's will is on file in the courthouse at Wilmington, Delaware. It is a lengthy one; a copy is included as the inventory which has been printed in the *Calendar of Delaware Wills, Newcastle County, 1682-1800*, compiled by the Colonial Dames. His bequests were sixty, exceeding any on record to that date, and, in addition to large grants of land, he willed $15,000 to his children and grandchildren. Even the children of his second wife, Phoebe Grubb, are named and remembered.

The children were Joseph, born in 1698, who married Amy Gregg; Deborah, born in 1701, who married (1) Benjamin Fredd and (2) Jacob Howell; Joshua, born in 1703, who married (1) Mary Rowland and (2) Patience Brown; Simon, born in 1705, died unmarried; Hannah, born in 1710, who married (1) Thomas Dixon and (2) John Stanfield; Ruth, born in 1712, who married Thomas Lindley; Catherine, born in 1715, who married Robert Johnson; Anne, born in 1718, who married Richard Gregg.

During the year 1746, Joshua Hadley bought 400 acres of land in Augusta County, Virginia. Later, he bought additional tracts, records of which are included. After a few years in Virginia, the family moved to Orange County, North Carolina, where other members of the family were living. Records of many births, marriages, and deaths of the family are recorded in the Cane Creek Monthly Meeting Minutes many of whose first members were families from Pennsylvania when the meeting was authorized in 1751. From Cane Creek Meeting the family spread out to neighboring counties. Some members remained after the great migration of the Quakers westward between 1800 and 1850. Those still there make occasional pilgrimages to the Joshua Hadley marker, erected in 1932 at the Spring Friend's Church about twelve miles south of Graham, the county seat of Alamance County. On the top of an old mill stone is a large stone from the chimney of Joshua Hadley's first house; on top of it is a rock from the family hearth.

Hadleys married Hadleys from generation to generation and, in addition to the collateral families already mentioned, they were closely allied with the families of Pyle, Mendenhall, Newlin, Harvey, Jackson, Chambers, Maris, Hinshaw, Marshall, Pickett, Andrew, McCracken, Holliday, Chamness, Woody, and Macy, as well as many others familiar to users of Hinshaw's *Quaker Genealogy*. Descent from Charlemagne and English royal lines is traced for those descended through Patience Brown, the great-granddaughter of William Clayton, who came to New Jersey on the ship Kent in 1677 and who was acting governor of Pennsylvania in 1684-1685.

The name Hadley is a place name, derived from two Anglo-Saxon words meaning "a wild heath where cattle graze." In America we have a Hadley village in seven states, a Hadley Station, a Hadley Chapel, and Hadley townships in both the North and the South. The spot called Hadley, in Chatham County, North Carolina, is presumed to have been the location of Joshua Hadley's mill, possession of which probably aided members of the family to render material aid to our continental troops.

In every line from Simon and Ruth, one finds given names repeated. There are Simons by the dozen. Jonathan, too, was a popular name; one who lived near Guilford Courthouse, because of his loud voice, was called "Whispering Jonathan" to distinguish him from "Jonathan-up-the-creek" and "Jonathan-down-the-creek." Jeremiah, James, Joshua, John, and Joseph were other favorites. Hence we have

"Gentleman John," "Hill Jerry," "Lame Joseph," "Joshua the Miller," and "Little Newt," the latter for James Newton Hadley. There were the "T. Hadleys," too; eight sons of Simon and Elizabeth Thompson, buried at Mill Creek, Hendricks County, Indiana, had the middle initial "T" for Thompson to carry on the mother's name.

Hadley families are in every state from Pennsylvania south, southwest, and west to the coasts. The four volumes record the trek of a family of indomitable pioneers pushing farther and farther into newer territory. Many of the descendants of Joshua and his first wife, Mary Rowland, espoused the cause of the Revolution, later moving into every Southern state, whereas the majority of Simon's descendants came north and west via the Carolina gateway. By far the greatest concentration before 1850 was found in south central Indiana, with Morgan and Hendricks counties as the nucleus. Iowa was another gathering place whence they pushed farther westward.

Descendants are legion. To be convinced one has only to examine the obituary columns of the *American Friend* where as many as three of the names in as many different parts of the country have been listed at the same time. There is a Hadley Genealogical Society in California where descendants of Simon even admit to membership descendants of the Hadleys, of Ipswich, Massachusetts. Among the family there have been governors, ministers, judges, physicians, lawyers, army officers, ministers, and even Hollywood is represented by "Buddy" Rogers. In Hendricks County, Indiana, there was an unbroken record of seventy-five years in which Hadleys served in public office.

The donor of these volumes is Chalmers Hadley, author of the *Quaker Family of Hadley*, published in 1916, which Mr. Kingston Hadley drew upon in compiling the earliest records of the Hadleys in England, Ireland, and in America. He is descended from William Hadley, son of Thomas and Mary Newlin Hadley, who married Ann Harvey, the daughter of Eli and Mary Stanfield Harvey. Their youngest son was Evan Hadley, born in 1845, who married Ella Quinn. He attended Earlham College and Long Island Medical College, was a Professor of Medicine at the Medical College of Indiana, and a one-time superintendent of the City Hospital. For thirty years he was a practicing physician of Indianapolis, later retiring to Mooresville, near his birthplace. Evan Hadley had four sons, Paul Hadley, our well-known Indiana artist; Evan, who lives with Paul in Mooresville; Harvey, a physician of Richmond, Indiana; and Chalmers Hadley, to whom the compiler gave the books in the hope that some day they would be printed.

Chalmers Hadley was born in Indianapolis, and married Florence Hendrie, daughter of Charles Francis and Sarah Crocker Adams Hendrie, in Denver where he was librarian of the public library, 1911-1924. Prior to 1911 he had been engaged in newspaper work in Philadelphia and Indianapolis, was secretary and state organizer for the Indiana Public Library Commission of Indiana, secretary and executive officer of the American Library Association, and its president in 1919-1920. Since 1924, he has been librarian of the Cincinnati and Hamilton County Public Library, living at his suburban home, "Birdwhistle." His interests have been wide, but he has ever maintained his enthusiasm for genealogy and his Indiana home.

The Anthony Halberstadt Family
Loring C. Halberstadt

Anthony Halberstadt was born in Hessen-Kassell, Germany, about two hundred years ago, and came to America during the Revolutionary War, as a Hessian soldier fighting for England. He was captured at Trenton, when Washington crossed the Delaware and surprised the British early in the morning of Dec. 26, 1776. After the war, he settled in Berks County, Pennsylvania, where he married and reared a family of four children.[1] About 1800, he and his family came to Pittsburgh, took a flatboat down the Ohio to Fort Washington (near Cincinnati), and then moved by ox-team to Cedar Grove, near Brookville, in Franklin County, Indiana. There, the family cleared some land and built a home.

---

[1] *Atlas of Franklin County, Indiana* (Chicago, 1882), 12, 99; Charles M. Thompson, *Sons of the Wilderness: John and William Conner* (Indianapolis, 1937), 50.

According to land records, Anthony Halberstadt entered land on January 20, 1806, in Franklin County, Indiana. This consisted of 160 acres (N. E. Quar., Sec. 10, Tp. 8, R. 2W.) The Mounds Hotel, three miles south of Brookville, Indiana, is located just across the Whitewater River from this location. In 1813, Anthony Halberstadt sold 90 acres for $600 to John Case. In June, 1813, he sold 50 acres to John Laforge for $140. On March 6, 1816, he sold to Zachariah Cooksey, a Revolutionary soldier, buried near the farm, the last 20 acres for $80.[2] Further records concerning this early family have not been found. It is believed the family moved to a location near Lawrenceburg after 1816. Mary Halberstadt was married to Robert Buchanan in the old Franklin County neighborhood in January, 1817, a fact which strengthens the probability that the family did not make a long migration in 1816.

Children of Anthony and ——— Halberstadt:[3]

Thomas Halberstadt was born on June 7, 1789, and lived till November 17, 1857. He married Leahneah Kentley (b. Nov. 15, 1794; d. Dec. 21, 1869) on November 17, 1814. Lewis Deweese, a Baptist minister living near Cedar Grove performed the ceremony. Fifteen children were born to this union.[4]

Esther Halberstadt was born on July 4, 1794, and died on May 27, 1875,[5] at Florence, Kentucky. She was married to Wesley Herndon (b. Jan. 2, 1794, at Madison Court House, Va.; d. Oct. 9, 1854) in Franklin County, Indiana, on May 26, 1813, by Lewis Deweese. Ten children were born to this union.

Mary Halbertsadt was married to Robert Buchan in Franklin County on January 9, 1817, by Lewis Deweese. No record of Mary's birth or death has been found.[6]

John Halberstadt was married to Mary Guilbert on February 13, 1816, by William Tyner, a Baptist minister.[7] Five

---

[2] Land records of Franklin County, Indiana (Brookville).

[3] Bible records of the family is in the old Halberstadt family Bible, which is now in the possession of Loring C. Halberstadt of Terre Haute, Indiana.

[4] For data relative to early Halberstadt marriages, see Marriage Records, Franklin County (Brookville), Indiana.

[5] *Boone County Journal* (Ky.), May 27, 1875.

[6] Anyone having any information concerning Mary (Halberstadt) Buchanan or her descendants, is asked to write to the author (Loring C. Halberstadt, Terre Haute, Indiana), as he desires to compile a complete history of the Halberstadt family.

[7] Rev. William Tyner's wife is buried near an old church, located on a high hill, three miles from Brookville. This brick church is one of the oldest in the state. The author does not know of an older church still standing in Indiana.

children were born to this union. John Halberstadt entered land in Franklin County in 1817. In 1838, he petitioned the court for a clear title to some land, acquired from the Mc-Cleary heirs.

Children of Thomas and Leahneah (Kently) Halberstadt:

Hester—b. Sept. 15, 1815; d. May 11, 1855; m. Dec. 23, 1852, to John Duncan.

Lipporah—b. Aug. 24, 1817; d. June 6, 1907; m. April 7, 1839, to Henry Peterson; descendants live in Illinois.

Mary Ann—b. Jan. 20, 1820; m. 1839, to Elisha Davis.

Anthony—b. Feb. 14, 1822; d. Jan. 31, 1865; m. Feb. 19, 1846, to Hannah H. Hays, by J. Rosecrans; license issued at Lawrenceburg, Indiana, Feb. 17, 1846; descendants live in the vicinity of Brookville.

Mariah—b. June 9, 1823; d. May 23, 1854.

Thomas—b. Jan. 19, 1825; d. Dec. 17, 1869; m. Aug. 19, 1847, to Mary Ann Jones by Jesse Wilson; license issued July 17, 1847, at Lawrenceburg, Indiana; descendants live in the vicinity of Terre Haute, Indiana.

Robert—b. June 15, 1828; m. Sept. 4, 1851, to Joanna Guilder; descendants live in the vicinity of Brookville, Indiana.

David Oliver—b. Oct. 5, 1829; d. Oct. 17, 1858, in Jackson Tp., Sullivan Co., Ind.; buried in Ebenezer cemetery, near Shelburn, Indiana.

Sarah—b. June 15, 1831; m. Dec. 25, 1853, to John B. Godwin; children: William, Lena, Lib (Elizabeth), Lucy, Ida; this branch of the family lives in Kansas.

Samuel—b. Oct. 23, 1832; d. July 16, 1858, in Jackson Tp., Sullivan Co., Ind.; buried in Ebenezer Cemetery.

Hannah—b. April 16, 1834; m. Nov. 17, 1857, to David Bronson; descendants live near Bridgeton, Indiana.

Theodore—b. Aug. 30, 1835; d. Oct. 7, 1909; m. Aug. 13, 1862, to Nancy Thayer; buried at Farmersburg, Sullivan County, Ind.

Elvira—b. Feb. 16, 1837; m. Nov. 11, 1855, to Francis Godwin; children: Ruth, Melvin, Ossa, Stella; this branch of the family lives in Arkansas.

William Henry—b. Dec. 22, 1839; killed in the Civil War on March 25, 1863.

Unnamed infant, twin of Theodore—b. Aug. 30, 1835; d. at age of one month.

Children of Esther (Halberstadt) and Wesley Herndon:[8]

Anthony—b. Feb. 14, 1814; d. June 13, 1814.

William—b. June 15, 1816, at Cedar Grove, Franklin Co., Ind.; d. March 17, 1895; m. Feb. 13, 1839, to Lucy Jane Pitts (d. Dec. 28, 1896) at Charlottesville, Va.; children: Mary (m. Mason Fletcher), J. Pitts (m. Rose——and had one child, Rose); Robert (d. 1888), Jennie (m. ——Moxley); Lucy (b. 1857; d. 1882, m.—— Collier), Martha, b. 1863 (m. —— Connelly; had two children, Margie and Robert), Willie.

Elizabeth—b. July 20, 1818; m. Feb. 14 1835, to Jesse Kirkpatrick; children: John, Joseph, Benjamin, Archie, Thomas, Augusta, Frank, Esther (m. William Piper).

Amanda—b. Sept. 13, 1821; d. Nov. 11, 1887.

Mary—b. Dec. 1823; d. Aug. 1, 1829.

Sara Ann—b. Feb. 20, 1827; d. July 25, 1829.

Jane—b. May 18, 1829; m. June 15, 1857, to John Roland.

Mellison—b. Dec. 29, 1831; m. 1856, to Louis Conner Yager (b. Sept. 25, 1830; d. Oct. 5, 1885).

Elijah Kirtley—b. March 16, 1835; d. Nov. 21, 1910; m. June 14, 1859, to Margaretta Haydon (b. Feb. 5, 1841; d. Jan. 11, 1918).

Archeable—b. April 25, 1837; d. Sept. 29, 1837.

Children of Mellison (Herndon) and Louis Conner Yager:

Ernest—b. March 6, 1857; d. Jan. 16, 1931; m. Ella Barton.

Gertrude—b. Oct. 1, 1858; m. John Aylor; children: Ira, Jenny, Willa.

Ola—b. Jan. 27, 1863; d. Jan. 4, 1927; m. Perry Carpenter; children: Clarence, Edith, Edwin.

Anne—b. Aug. 17, 1874; d. April, 1900.

Mary—b. March 13, 1867, d. July 23, 1869.

Grace—b. Aug. 8, 1876; m. T. B. Castleman; children: Clay and Osceola.

Louis C.—b. Aug. 4, 1860; m. Oct. 29, 1885, to Margaretta Herndon. Children: infant (b. Nov. 8, 1886; d. Nov. 24, 1886), Elsie (b. Jan. 25, 1888; m. Albert Riggs; 3 children), Virginia (b. Jan. 30, 1895, m. Frank Landers; one child,

---

[8] Records for the family of Wesley and Esther (Halberstadt) Herndon were contributed by Louis C. Yager, Jr., Indianapolis, Ind.

Mary Louise), Eloise (b. Jan. 3, 1902; m. Walter Forman; children, Phyllis and Eleanor), Grace (b. No. 8, 1909).[9]

Children of Elijah Kirtley and Margaret (Haydon) Herndon:[10]

Ida—b. July 14, 1860; m. John Hall; children: Kirtley and Kathrine.

Ollie—b. Jan. 22, 1863; d. Oct. 30, 1935; m. Charles Y. Gray; one child, Nellie.

Laura—d. in infancy.

Margaretta—b. June 17, 1866; d. July 5, 1938; m. Louis C. Yager, Jr.[11]

Eeila Corinne—b. Dec. 17, 1868; m. J. W. Leathers; children: John, Corinne, Herndon.

Emma Buford—b. Oct. 1, 1874; m. Joseph Drexilius.

---

[9] These are grandchildren of Wesley and Esther (Halberstadt) Herndon and great-grandchildren of Anthony Halberstadt.

[10] See preceeding note.

[11] Louis C. Yager, Jr., was the son of Louis Conner and Mellisson (Herndon) Yager. The mother of Louis C. Yager, Jr., was a sister of Elizabeth Kirtley Herndon, whose daughter was Margaretta Herndon. Louis C. Yager, Jr., therefore, married his first cousin.

Governor J. Frank Hanly: Genealogical Notes

HARRY O. GARMAN

J. Frank Hanly was born on April 4, 1863, in a log cabin in St. Joseph Township, Champaign County, Illinois. In 1866, his father, Elijah Hanly (1829-1885)[1] moved to another cabin home about one mile south of the birthplace of J. Frank. This new home was in the same county, but in Sydney Township.[2] Both of these pioneer homes were in the valley of Salt Creek, which joins the Vermillion River at Danville, Illinois. At eighteen years of age, J. Frank Hanly began making Republican speeches in Illinois, and continued public speaking through the remainder of his life. He spoke in

---

[1] The parents of Elijah Hanly and grandparents of J. Frank Hanly were: Israel and Rachel (Gilet) Hanly. Israel Hanly was born in 1804 and died in 1860.

[2] The tract of land on which stood the home where J. Frank Hanly was born was a part of Section 34, Township 19N, Range 10E. The next home of the Hanly family was situated on a tract that formed a portion of Sec.3, Tp.18N, R10E. These were two of several home places occupied by the family of Elijah and Anne E. (Calton) Hanly, parents of Governor Hanly. It required much time and money to locate exactly the sites of these two homes. Each was a log cabin in the woods. After the sites were located in the fields of today, it was possible to find pieces of brick from the chimney, some charcoal, and pieces of dishes, old milk crocks and jugs.

every state of the United States, and was on his way to make a speech when he was killed in a railroad wreck near Dennison, Ohio, on August 1, 1920. He was elected Governor of Indiana in 1904, and served from 1905 to 1909. At the time of his election, he lived in Lafayette, Indiana. The maiden name of Governor Hanly's wife was Eva A. R. Simmer (1860-1927).

Children of Elijah and Anna E. (Calton)[3] Hanly:
George Hanly—b. 1849; d. 1857.
L. Hanly—b. 1852; d. 1854.
Lyman Hanly—b. 1854; d. 1884.
Willis Hanly—b. 1856; d. 1871.
Mary Hanly—b. 1858; d. 1876.
Rachel Hanly—b. 1860; d. 1918.
Gov. J. Frank Hanly—b. 1863; d. 1920.

Children of J. Frank and Eva A. R. (Simmer) Hanly:
Ethel Elfride Hanly—b. July 24, 1882, Warren County, Ind.; m. Harry O. Garman, Dec. 19, 1904, at Lafayette, Ind.
Lyle Alice Hanly—b. Nov. 12, 1883; d. July 9, 1884.
Owen Pugh Hanly—b. Aug. 29, 1886; d. Oct. 26, 1891.
Inda May Hanly—b. Sept. 13, 1888; d. at birth.
Cecil Rabb Hanly—b. Sept. 24, 1896; d. Mar. 7, 1899.

Children[4] of Harry O. and Ethel Elfride (Hanly) Garman:
Esther Hanly Garman—b. Oct. 8, 1905; d. Oct. 9, 1905.
Harry Franklin Garman—b. Sept. 18, 1907; d. at birth.
Harry Hanly Garman—b. Feb. 19, 1915.
Helen Louise Garman—b. Feb. 8, 1918.

---

[3] Anna E. (Calton) Hanly was born in 1829 and died in 1891.
[4] Grandchildren of J. Frank and Eva A. R. (Simmer) Hanly.

The Hardy Family
Marion D. and Ruth V. Weston

Thomas Hardy, brother of John Hardy of Boston, came to America from England with Governor Winthrop in 1630. He was one of the twelve founding the town of Ipswich, Mass. He built the first frame house there in 1634. Later he moved to Rowley and purchased one thousand acres of land along the Merrimac river, comprising for the most part what is now known as Groveland, but which, at the time Thomas Hardy made his purchase, belonged to the Rowley settlement, formerly known as the Rogers Plantation. He settled on this large tract of land about 1662, and the annual meeting of the Hardy Family Association, August 21, 1937, commemorated the two hundred seventy-fifth anniversary of this event.

The Second Congregational Church of Groveland was host to the Hardy Family Association and brought members of the Hardy Family from all parts of the United States and Canada. In June, 1726, Daniel Hardy, a grandson of Thomas, called the first meeting of the "second" or "east" parish, which was set apart from the Bradford parish, of which Thomas Hardy and his wife were charter members, for the purpose of making plans for building a meeting house; the result was that in 1727 the new parish, now the Groveland Second Congregational church, was organized. Of the first one hundred one members, thirty-three were members of the Hardy Family. The year 1937 marked the two hundred tenth anniversary of the founding of this church. It is said that more of the Hardy name claim descent from Thomas Hardy of Groveland than from any other early settler of that name. A number of descendants still live at Groveland and at nearby Georgetown. Our grandmother, Caroline Matilda Hardy, married Flint Weston and lived in Georgetown, Massachusetts, but her parents, four brothers, and a sister, more than a hundred years ago, left their home on King Street, Georgetown, to found new homes on the banks of the Ohio river, settling in Kentucky and southern Indiana.

During July of 1937, a motor trip of more than 3,000 miles included a visit to the Great Lakes Exposition at Cleveland, attendance at the annual convention of the National Education Association at Detroit, and the devotion of some time to genealogical research in Indiana and Kentucky. In 1817, Nathaniel Hardy, oldest of the four brothers and the pioneer emigrant of the family, took the journey alone on horseback, carrying with him his beloved bass viol. Residing for a few years in Indiana, he later made Louisville, Kentucky, his permanent home. There he became a very prosperous merchant. Descendants of this great uncle were visited in Louisville and Anchorage, Kentucky, by the writers.

Descendants of another great uncle, Bartlett Hardy, were traced to Indianapolis. Near Salem, Indiana, in a family burial plot on the Hardy farm four miles west of town, was found the site of the graves of our great grandparents, Joseph and Lucretia Hardy; perhaps others of the family were buried there, too, but only one inscription could be read—

"Ruth B. Sawyer—Wife of Dr. Niles Hardy—Died Oct. 22, 1854." Deeds for the Hardy farm were found at the Court House in Salem, Indiana, showing that this land was sold in 1854 to Thomas and Alfred Trueblood. In the Clerk's office of Washington County in Book A, page 559, is the will of Joseph Hardy, dated July 1, 1842, and probated July 14, 1847.

Nathaniel Hardy was born on May 24, 1795, at Bradford, and was the first of the Hardy family to come West as has been stated. He met Samuel Peck from Rehoboth, Massachusetts, and they became good friends. Samuel Peck was engaded to Melinda Hyde, who was born Nov. 4, 1798, at Lisbon, Connecticut, but was now living in Clark County, Indiana, whence Samuel Peck invited Nathaniel Hardy to accompany him to visit the Hyde family. Here young Hardy met the youngest daughter, Mary Hyde, a very beautiful girl. They were married on May 13, 1821. The Hyde Genealogy states that Nathaniel Hardy was of Charleston, Indiana (Clark Co.), at this time. They went to live in a log cabin on the Ohio river, near Charleston, where Nathaniel sold supplies to river steamers. Here their daughter, Caroline Matilda Hardy, was born on March 22, 1823. A descendant of this daughter sent to us through the kindness of Miss Harriet Reid of Salem, Indiana (a descendant of Samuel Peck and Melinda Hyde), a picture of this cabin with the following information: "I am sending you a picture of the old log house, on the Ohio river at Charleston Landing. The house was swept away by the flood of 1913. It was built without nails, of huge timbers, and Santa Claus could have gone down the chimney with ease." A picture was also sent of the house in Louisville, Kentucky, built about 1840 (perhaps earlier) by Nathaniel Hardy, then a successful merchant of Louisville. He died there on May 4, 1848, having married as his second wife—Charlotte Howard of Louisville in 1830. His daughter Caroline Matilda, was married on April 3, 1844, to A. D. Miles of Louisville. They had two daughters, Mary Howard, born on Jan. 20, 1846, and Sarah Lilly, born on Sept. 14, 1847.

Melinda Hyde, older sister of Mary Hyde Hardy, married Samuel Peck on April 2, 1820, at Providence (now Borden), Indiana. They settled at Salem, Indiana, about 1823. He was a captain of the local militia and Probate Judge for several years. Another of the Hyde sisters, Rhoda Hyde, married

Samuel Day of Salem on Dec. 25, 1824. In the spring of 1823, Mary Hyde Hardy and her infant daughter went to visit her family who lived in Salem, and there she died on May 3, 1823. Her grave is in Crown Hill Cemetery, with the following inscription on the tombstone:

Mary C. Hardy—Wife of Nathaniel Hardy—Departed this life, May 3, 1823.[1]

The night of Mrs. Hardy's death, her husband, Nathaniel Hardy, according to his own report, dreamed that she was dead and looked at his watch. In the morning a man came on horseback to report her death, which occurred at the exact time of the dream. The young daughter, Caroline Matilda Hardy, is said to have lived with her grandmother and aunts in Salem until the time of her father's second marriage in 1830.

These early contacts with Salem explain why Nathaniel Hardy chose Washington County, Indiana, as the town in which to purchase land and build a home for his parents and his invalid brother and family. Nathaniel Hardy went in 1838 to accompany them to this new home.[2] The returning party included his parents, Joseph and Lucretia Hardy; his brother, Bailey; his wife Ursula; and five children, among them his own son, Nathaniel, who later became a physician in Salem. With them also came his sister Mehitable and her husband, Johathan Wedgewood. At one time they lived on the road west of the Hardy farm. Niles Hardy, brother of Nathaniel Hardy, does not seem to have come with the family on the "Canal Boat" trip, but must have joined the family sometime during the year 1838. The fourth brother, Bartlett Hardy, had gone to New Albany and Louisville long before 1838 and apparently never lived near Salem. Our father, Bartlett Hardy Weston, was named for this great uncle.

THE JOSEPH HARDY FAMILY

Joseph Hardy was born in Bradford, Massachusetts, on June 24, 1771, and died on Jan. 30, 1843, in Washington County, Indiana. Lucretia Bartlett, wife of Joseph Hardy, was born in Worcester, Mass., on July 24, 1767, and died in Washington County in 1853.

[1] The figures of the year are not clear, but the record from the Hyde Genealogy now in possession of Mrs. Horace Campbell of Frankfort, Indiana, states "Mary Clark Hyde, born September 3, 1800, at Lisbon, Connecticut, died May 3rd, 1823."
[2] The writers are fortunate to have two letters written to his only sister, our grandmother, Caroline Matilda Weston, who was left with her family in Massachusetts.

Children of Joseph and Lucretia (Bartlett) Hardy:

Nathaniel Hardy—b. May 24, 1795, in Bradford, Mass.; d. May 4, 1848, Louisville, Ky.; m. (1) Mary Hyde, May 13, 1821, probably in Clark County, Indiana. She was born Sept. 3, 1800, at Lisbon, Conn., and died May 3, 1823, in Washington County. She was buried in Salem Cemetery. One daughter Caroline Matilda Hardy, born March 22, 1823, married A. D. Miles of Louisville, Ky., April 3, 1844. They had two daughters, Mary Howard (Gleason), and Sarah Lilly (Sherrill). Nathaniel married (2) Catherine Howard of Louisville. They probably had at least one son, James Edward Hardy.

Bartlett Hardy—b. 1797, Mass.; d. 1854. Two daughters who located in Indianapolis, Ind., having descendants in that city. Bartlett Hardy married Louisa McDonald of Ky.

Bailey Hardy—b. 1802, in Mass.; d. March 16, 1850, Washington, Ind. He is probably buried in the Hardy Family Cemetery west of Salem, Ind. He married Ursula Knap. They had five children. One son, Nathaniel, was born in 1828. He became a physician and practiced in Washington County, Ind., before 1855.

Niles Hardy, b. 1804, in Mass., d. 1857, at Salem, Ind.; buried at Crown Hill Cemetery; m. (1) Isabella Knap; three children. One, Edward Mino Hardy, lived at Morristown, Tenn. Niles Hardy m. (2) Ruth B. Sawyer, July 20, 1840, in Salem, Ind. She died Oct. 22, 1854. married (3) Maria Bliss Dickson, 1856, in Salem, Ind. Dr. Lawrence Paynter, of Salem, in his *Medical History of Washington County*, published in 1931, states that Niles Hardy was a graduate of some Medical School in Ohio and practiced in Salem in the late fifties. He was a jeweler and an excellent musician.

Mehitable Hardy, born May 18, 1807, Mass., died Oct., 1850, in Louisville, Ky. She married Johanathan Wedgewood of Newmarket, New Hampshire. They came with the Hardy family to Washington County, Indiana, in 1838 and lived in this county several years. We do not have the descendants.

Caroline Matilda Hardy, born July 18, 1810, Mass., died 1880, Georgetown, Mass. She married Flint Weston and lived and died in Georgetown, Mass. They were the grandparents of Marion D. and Ruth V. Weston of Georgetown, Mass., authors of this brief family history.

The Harshbarger Family of Montgomery County
JESSIE C. WATSON

About twenty-five years ago William Anderson, a descendant of the Harshbarger family, compiled the history and genealogy of the family, a record of one hundred ten pages. The data relative to the Montgomery County, Indiana, line of the Harshbarger family are taken from this manuscript record.

The name *Harshbarger* is an Americanized form of the Swiss-German name *Hirschberger*. Jacob, the emigrant, was born in Basle, Switzerland, about 1722. He went to Holland in 1750, married Maria Eva Petra, and remained there four years to earn his passage money to America by weaving, being an expert in this art. The young couple sailed for America in 1754, with a baby daughter. This child died on shipboard. Jacob and Maria Eva landed at Philadelphia, and later established a home in Lancaster County, Pennsylvania.

They had at least three sons: Christian—b. 1755; d. 1827; m. (1) Barbara Ammen and (2) a widow, Mrs. Garman. Jacob—b. 1757; d. 1850; m. (1) Margaret Keller and (2) a widow, Mrs. Sellebarger. Samuel—b. 1759; d. 1849; M Elizabeth Gish. Little is known of the youth of these three sons. All of them left Lancaster County, Pennsylvania. Their children all lived in Virginia, but Jacob resided for a long period in Maryland. Christian lived several years in Pennsylvania, near his wife's people. After the Revolutionary War, Barbara's father bought 1512 acres of land in southwestern Virginia. In 1784, he took his family, including Christian and Barbara (Ammen) Harshbarger, to the new home on Mill Creek in Virginia. This was about three miles from Fincastle. Barbara died in 1803, leaving a family of eight children:

Child—b. 1780; d. in infancy.
Catherine—b. 1781; m. John Deardorf.
Samuel—b. 1783; m. three times.
Child—b. 1785; d. in infancy.
Jacob—b. 1786; m. Elizabeth Beckner.
Mary—b. 1789; m. John Beckner.
Rebecca—b. 1791; m. Jacob Gish.
Elizabeth—b. 1794; m. John Stair.
Susan—b. 1797; m. David Gish.
Anna—b. 1799; m. John Riddle.

as most of the Harshbargers were and are today, and he helped to organize a Dunkard Church on Cornstalk Creek shortly after coming to the county. Like many of his family, he held tenaciously to German customs and language, keeping the record of births in his family by date, month, and sign of the Zodiac. Many of his descendants may be found near Ladoga at this time.

Children of Jacob and Salome (Ammen) Harshbarger:
    Son—b. 1815; died young.
    Lydia—b. 1816; m. William Myers.
    John—b. 1818; d. 1830.
    Samuel—b. 1820; m. Elizabeth Graves. Lived in Missouri.
    Catherine—b. 1821; m. Zachariah Mahorney of Ladoga, Ind.
    Salome—b. 1824; m. M. B. Anderson.
    Elizabeth—b. 1826; m. S. P. Frame. Lived in Missouri.
    Ann—b. 1830; m. William Frame of Ladoga, Ind.
    Jacob—b. 1828, m. Mary Myers of Ladoga, Ind.
    Mary—b. 1833; m. D. H. Himes of Ladoga, Ind.

Catherine and Susana Harshbarger, daughters of Samuel and Elizabeth (Gish) Harshbarger, who married Jacob and John Bonsack, did not come to Indiana, but went into Tennessee from Virginia, and their families scattered westward.

Mary (Maria) Harshbarger, daughter of Samuel and Elizabeth (Gish) Harshbarger, who married Joseph Nofsinger, had seven children:

    Salome Nofsinger—b. 1813; m. Joel Britts. Went to Kansas.
    William—b. 1815; m. (1) Mary Myers and (2) dau. of Gen. Tilghman Howard of Rockville, Ind.
    Elizabeth—b.1817; m. Joshua Baker. Went to Kansas.
    Mary—b. 1819; m. Daniel Hale.
    Peter—b. 1823; m. Phoebe LaFollette. Moved to Kansas.
    Jacob—b. 1825; m. Mary Spears. Moved to Wisconsin.
    Susan—b. 1825; m. George LaFollette.

Samuel, son of Samuel and Elizabeth (Gish) Harshbarger, married Elizabeth (Myers) Harshbarger. Their nine children were:

    Sarah Harshbarger—b. 1827; m. Robert Miller.
    Nancy—b. 1829; mar. Clark Byrd.
    John—b. 1832; m. Susan Clark.
    Joel—b. 1834; m. Minerva Daugherty.
    Samuel—b. 1837; m. Mary LaFollette.
    William—b. 1839; m. Anna Peffley.
    David—b. 1842; m. Sarah Davidson.
    Lizzie—b. 1844; m. Nathan Kessler.
    Salome—b. 1847; m. David Peffley.

The record of this family has been carried through several generations. The Montgomery County line has been copied and can be used later if space permits. Jacob Harshbarger, son of Jacob and Salome (Ammen) Harshbarger, married Mary Myers, and was probably the best known member of this large Harshbarger family in Montgomery County. He was born in Virginia in 1828, and came to Ladoga with his parents when three years old. He was a successful farmer, president of the Ladoga Bank, and, unlike most of his family, was a member of the Christian Church. His father assisted in establishing the Dunkard Church on Cornstalk Creek, later located a short distance north of Ladoga. Today there is a marker on the Crawfordsville-Ladoga County improved road, just north of Ladoga, pointing to "The Church of the Brethen", the Dunkard Church, which seems quite as prosperous as any other denomination. Many descendants of this Harshbarger family, still members, and one or two of the older women, are said to appear at Sunday services in their Dunkard bonnets.

The old Harshbarger Cemetery, on Cornstalk Creek, is across the road from one of the old Harshbarger farms, is still used, and fairly well kept. It is hoped that our D.A.R. Chapter will copy the records in this cemetery, for it seems certain that we shall find the graves of many pioneers of this district. Samuel Harshbarger the son of the emigrant, who died in 1849, is buried there.

The Benjamin Vancleave Family
EDWARD S. HARVEY

Benjamin Vancleave, son of Aaron Vancleave and Rachel Schencks, was born in Monmouth County, New Jersey, on November 15, 1741, and died in Shelby County, Kentucky, July 27, 1819.[1] He was married in Rowan County, North Carolina, on July 14, 1765, to Ruth Monson, who was born on July 10, 1746, and died of cancer in Shelby County, Kentucky, on December 5, 1823. The Children of Benjamin and Ruth (Monson) Vancleave were:

[1] The names and birth dates of Benjamin Vancleave's family, except Thomas, were written on a piece of brown paper, found among the effects of his son Samuel Vancleave ("Preacher Sammy") of Crawfordsville, Ind., who was killed by a fall from his horse on August 25, 1843. This paper was preserved by Lucy Vancleave, a sister of the Rev. Johnathan Vancleave, and is now in the ossession of Mrs. America Saylor of Crawfordsville.

Mary Vancleave—b. May 22, 1766; m. in Lincoln Co., Ky., June 9, 1784, to Col. Johnathan Ryker, son of Gerardus Ryker and Rachel Demaree.

Aaron Vancleave—b. Dec. 15, 1768; m. in Shelby Co., Ky., Mar. 4, 1794, to Elizabeth Vancleave, daughter of John Vancleave, Sr., and Mary Sheppard.

Samuel Vancleave—b. Feb. 25, 1770; d. in Montgomery Co., Ind., Aug. 25, 1843; m. (1) about 1791, to Elizabeth Wood and (2) in Shelby Co., Ky., Dec. 31, 1823, to Sarah Garner, who was born in 1784, and died at Blakesburg, Iowa, Apr. 6. 1859.

Rachel Vancleave—b. May 7, 1772; d. Apr. 3, 1819. She is buried in the Old Union Cemetery, Montgomery Co., Ind.; m. (1) Aug. 3, 1788, in Jefferson Co., Ky., to Hugh Conoway and (2) in Shelby Co., Ky., Dec. 20, 1810, to Henry Smith.

John Vancleave—b. Apr. 15, 1774; d. July 23, 1833; m. in Shelby Co., Ky., Nov. 18, 1794, to Margery Kerns, daughter of Peter Kerns and Anna Jordan. Peter Kerns and his wife Anna came from Ireland when Margery was seven months old. Margery's mother dipped her in the sea, as she had been taught that this was a cure for sea sickness.

Jane Vancleave—b. Jan. 29, 1778; d. Jan. 15. 1833; m. in Shelby Co., Ky., Dec. 17, 1795, to Adam Wible.

Eunice Vancleave—b. at Ft. Boonesborough, Ky., Nov. 15, 1779; m. in Shelby Co., Ky., Sept. 23, 1794, to John Vancleave, Jr., son of John Vancleave and Mary Sheppard.

Sarah Vancleave—b. Dec. 15, 1781; m. in Shelby Co., Ky., Aug. 11, 1802, to John Benjamin Vancleave, son of Aaron Vancleave, Jr., and Rachel Brent.

Ralph VanCleave—b. Mar. 18, 1784; d. Feb. 2, 1855; m. in Shelby Co., Ky., Feb. 27, 1805, to Elizabeth Stubbins, who was born Feb. 12, 1783 and died Nov. 23, 1848.

Benjamin Vancleave—b. Feb. 9, 1787; d. Oct. 27, 1855; m. in Henry Co., Ky., Dec. 18, 1809, to Mary Stephenson Mount, daughter of Matthias Mount. Mary was born Dec. 15, 1791, and died Apr. 29, 1875 After the death of his first wife, Benjamin Vancleave was again married.

William Vancleave—b. May 3, 1789; d. Feb. 26, 1815. He was a Drum Major at the Battle of New Orleans. He died in New Orleans of the Yellow Fever. He was married in Shelby Co., Ky., Sept. 24, 1811, to Mary Mount.

Hope (or Hopey) Vancleave—m. Johnathan Wood. No other data.

Thomas Vancleave—b. about 1799.

Boone-Mayfield Family in Indiana
REUBEN N. MAYFIELD, M.D.

Nine miles west of Bedford, Lawrence County, Indiana, on Indian Creek, there is an natural bridge at the Dry Ford where the creek, one hundred feet wide, runs under the bluff four hundred feet high, and forms a natural bridge, eight hundred feet wide and a half mile long.

As one goes south towards the Dry Ford, he will see on the right a high, almost perpendicular bluff, which is the north face of the Natural Bridge. At the old Dry Ford Crossing, to the left he will see no water (except after a freshet) in the channel. When one crosses, at the right, he will see the approach to the Natural Bridge.

The Pioneers built a fairly good road over the top of the bridge to the Boone-Mayfield settlement on the West side. This road is not now in use. The south side of the Natural Bridge is not as precipitous as the north side.

A half mile farther south at the Mayfield Crossing, where the author was born, there is very little water in the creek. This water comes from Big Blue Spring, and when there is high water for a few days, pedestrians have trouble in crossing until the water "runs down" when they can easily cross. At the present time, there are three bridge across Indian Creek within a distance of three quarters of a mile—one at the old bridge, one at the Dry Ford, and one at the Mayfield Crossing.

Our ancestors, Jeremiah and Joyce (Neville) Boone, came more than a hundred years ago (1817) and settled three miles north of this freak of nature. (Twp. 5 N., R. 2 W., Lawrence Co., Ind.) The ancestry of Jeremiah Boone follows:

George Boone, III—b. 1666, father of
George Boone, IV—b. 1690 (in England) father of
Josiah Boone—b. 1726 or 1727; d. 1814 at Glenn Creek (five miles south of Frankfort), Ky.; m. Hannah Hite 1750.

Children of Josiah and Hannah (Hite) Boone: George, b. 1751; Noah, died young; Josiah, Jr., b. 1758; Jeremiah, b. Feb. 1760; Allison, died young; Ruth, b. 1770 and m. Pluright Sisk, 1790; Deborah (twin of Ruth), never married; Ruhema, m. William Thompson. Heirs of Josiah, Sr., given in legal document: George, Josiah, Jr., Jeremiah, Ruth, Deborah, Ruhemah.

Jeremiah Boone (listed above) died in 1832. He married Joyce Nevil on May 9, 1787, at Stanford, Kentucky. She was born in 1768 and died in 1861. She was the daughter of James and Sarah Joyce Nevil. James Nevil was born in Prince William County, Virginia, in 1741. He served in the Revolutionary War under Col. Edmonds and Capt. Martin Pickett as shown by the records of the Pension Bureau and other records. In 1779, James Nevil went to Linncoln County, Kentucky. Here he learned that the British and Indians were on the warpath. The settlers were preparing for their first invasion into what is now Ohio. After the invasion into the Indian country, the troops returned to Harrodsburg, Kentucky. The Indians came into Kentucky and, in the fighting, a number of Kentucky soldiers were killed, including Colonels Todd and Trigg. This left Col. Daniel Boone in command of the local troops. He retreated, then rallied his troops and called for volunteers. Many responded, among them Capt. Sam Kirkham and Jeremiah Boone.

When James Nevil (or Neville) and family arrived at the little place Asaphs (afterwards changed to Stanford), they began to see familiar names: Col. Daniel Boone, the surveyor, Sam Kirkham on the Grand Jury, and the name of Abraham Lincoln on the court record. Jeremiah Boone made visits to the Nevil home often. Capt. George Mayfield and Lieut. Isaac Mayfield were also with the troops. James Nevil and wife and Jeremiah Boone and family lived neighbors on Dix River from 1789 to 1796. Jeremiah bought three farms on Pitman Creek, Northeast of Somerset, Kentucky, in 1800. The children of Jeremiah and Joyce (Nevil) Boone were:

Sarah Boone—m. Isaac Wagner, at Somerset, Ky. (A descendant of this line is Mrs. Arthur P. McGee of Charleston, S. C.)

Elijah Boone—m, Jennie Wagner. (Children: William, Jeremiah, Bethuel, Artemacy, Isaac, Joyce, John.)

Simon—(no data).

Charlotte Boone—m, Reuben Mayfield at Somerset, Ky., Oct. 27, 1814. Charlotte—b. 1794; d. 1883.

Mahala—m. John Dishman. (A descendant is Mrs. Pearl Brown Thomas of Jasonville, Ind.)

Hannah Boone—m, (1) Adam Morrow (Mrs. F. P. Lemon, Shoals, Ind., is a daughter) and (2) John Beaty, Owensburg, Ind. (Children: Dr. Marshall Beaty; Luther—m. Victoria Short Owens; Ella, m, Charles Whitted.)

Noah Boone—m, Jane Rhoads. (Children: Clementine, m, Wesley Armstrong; Jeanette, m, Abner Armstrong (brother of Wesley); Louise, m, John Short, son of Ezekiel Short; Daniel, m, Nannie M. Huston; Virgil, m, Luicinda Rector).

The Mayfield Family

Reuben Mayfield (1792-1861) married Charlotte Boone (above). He was a soldier in the War of 1812, serving with Capt. Sam Tate, Maj. Taul, Gen. John E. King, and Governor Shelby at the Battle of the Thames. He was the son of John Mayfield, Jr. (1768-1813) and, in 1790, married Mary Wolfe (1770-1848). John Mayfield was a pioneer doctor. Mary's father Henry, and his father Henry, Sr., fought at Fort Washington, New York, where Henry Wolf, Sr., was killed. John Mayfield, Jr., son of John Mayfield, Sr., was born in Albemarle County, Virginia, in 1745, and died in Pulaski County, Kentucky, in 1816. He served during the entire Revolutionary War. His last service was with Gen. Daniel Morgan at Buckingham, Virginia. John Mayfield married Clarinda Pleasants (1749-1821) in 1767. The Mayfield Coat-of-Arms was granted to Owen Mayfield, Mayor and Alderman of Cambridge, England, in 1684.

Alexander Campbell Mayfield, son of Reuben and Charlotte (Boone) Mayfield was born on May 6, 1831, in Linton, Indiana. He was the ninth child in a family of twelve children and was reared on his father's farm in Lawrence County, Indiana. He married Winnie Short on Jan. 12, 1854, in the Short Home in Springville, Indiana (Lawrence Co.). She was the daughter of Milton and Mary (Tate) Short. Mary Tate was the daughter of Robert and Winnie (Atkinson) Tate, and granddaughter of John and Mary (Bracken) Tate. John Tate, Revolutionary soldier and sheriff of Russell County, Virginia, died in 1828. All of his children migrated to Kentucky, except Joseph. Milton Short, father of Winnie (who married Alexander Campbell Mayfield), was the son of wesley and Rebecca (Owens) Short. Wesley was the son of John and Mary (Hansford) Short. John Short was born in 1756 in Tigart Valley, Virginia (now W.Va.). He was also a Revolutionary soldier. He is buried near Springville.

Children of Alexander Campbell and Winnie (Short) Mayfields
Ila Mayfield—b, 1854; m. John Evans.
Mary Charlotte Mayfield—b. 1857; m. Buenos Wheat Bailey.
Reuben Newton Mayfield—b. June 13, 1859; m. Patti Ayres, Feb. 27, 1908.
Inda Mayfield—b, 1868; m. John Slater.

Patti Ayres, who married Dr. Reuben Newton Mayfield, was a daughter of John Ayres and Alice (Boyd) Ayres. Patti was born in England on June 8, 1876, and died January 14, 1821. The maiden name of the mother of Alice Boyd was O'Neil. She was descended from the Earl of Tyrone. Patti Ayres Mayfield was a noted concert singer, who toured extensively in the United States, Mexico and elsewhere.

Alexander Campbell Mayfield, was a farmer, and during his lifetime, owned several farms in Lawrence County, Indiana. A ninety acre farm was given to him by his father

Reuben Mayfield, and the last two farms owned by him were near Springville, Indiana. He resided with his family many years on the farm one mile east of this town, and his children usually walked to and from the school in Springville, even during the cold winter weather. In 1861, he moved to Springville, and lived for about twenty-three years, either here, or on the old Mayfield farm. In 1884, he migrated with his son-in-law Buenos Wheat Bailey to Ferndale, Washington, and died there in 1885. His wife, Winnie Short Mayfield was born on December 10, 1836, in Lawrence County, Indiana. She died in 1919 in Ferndale, Whatcomb County, Washington.

All my ancestors had an English Coat-of-Arms. Solomon Boone recorded the Boone Arms in the records of Bristol, Pennsylvania, in 1690. The name *Bohun* is of Norman origin. The first family from Normandy settled in Lincolnshire, England, and afterwards some of the name settled in Devonshire. It is from this latter family that the American Boones are directly descended. The Bohun coat of arms, used before the fourteenth century, was probably granted by a Norman-English King. It is not until the middle of the sixteenth century that we find the names *Bohun* and *Boone* spelled both ways in the same document.[1]

[1] The Mayfield Coat-of-Arms was granted to Owen Mayfield, Mayor and Alderman of Cambridge, England, in 1684. John and Robert Tate had been Lord Mayors of London in early days. The Boones, the Shorts and de Nevilles (French), were followers of William the Conqueror. George Boone III, was the grandfather of Josiah Boone, Sr., and also of Daniel Boone. A short history of my ancestor, I filed in the Library of Congress in 1901. In 1931-2-3, I wrote fifty chapters for the *Mountain Branch Vet*, published at Johnson City, Tenn., on the Life of Daniel Boone. These are on file in the Astor and Congressional Libraries. In 1934, I had made ten dozen portraits of Daniel Boone, taken from the only life painting ever made of him. They were placed in all the large libraries of the country and in all the libraries along the Wilderness Road.—Reuben N. Mayfield.

Editor's Note: Dr. Reuben Newton Mayfield was born in Lawrence Co., Ind., and educated in the local schools. He taught eight years in high school. He was graduated with the degree of M.D., in 1880, from Long Island College Hospital, N.Y., and from the Rush Medical College, Chicago, in 1883, devoting his life to medicine and surgery. In 1885, he went to Colorado, where he enlisted in the Colorado State Militia, in 1886. On June 1, 1889, he was appointed Major and Surgeon. He was placed on the retired list, May 6, 1912, at his own request. He was in active service during many of the long series of mining strikes in Colorado. He was a professor of Pathology, Hygiene and Clinical Medicine at the University of Colorado for some time, and Surgeon for the Union Pacific R.R. from 1886-1891. He traveled extensively in Europe and Mexico. While in England, he visited the old town of Mayfield, England, and many of the historical places in that country, where his ancestors once resided. He has spent many years in careful research, proving his family lines, and we are fortunate in having the privilege of recording from his many notes and research this Indiana family ancestry. Dr. Mayfield has resided in Seattle, Washington, for the last twenty-five years.—Martha Tucker Morris.

The Isaac Harvey Family
Ethel Jones McEwen

Isaac Harvey, son of William and Judith Harvey, was born in Pennsylvania on September 21, 1718. His parents were born in England. They were married on June 12, 1714. The mother was a widow when she married William Harvey, her first husband being Peter Osborn. William and Judith Harvey came to Pennsylvania soon after their marriage, where they built the house in which Isaac was born. The Harvey home was on the Brandywine not far from Chadds Ford, where Washington's troops fought the British on September 11, 1777. Before the Revolutionary War, the home had passed into the hands of William Harvey, Jr., a brother of Isaac. During the Battle of Chadds Ford a cannon ball struck the house and lodged in the wall. The building, which still stands, remained in the hands of the Harvey family until 1926.

Isaac Harvey married Martha Newlin, daughter of Nathaniel and Jane (Woodward) Newlin, who was born on September 18, 1721. They lived in Chester County Pennsylvania. She died in North Carolina on November 23, 1906. Her husband had passed away on April 3, 1792.

Children of Isaac and Martha (Newlin) Harvey:

1. William Harvey—b. Nov. 29, 1749; d. Mar. 3, 1781; m. Elizabeth Carter about 1762. Elizabeth—dau. Nathaniel and Ann (McPherson) Carter; b. June 16, 1737. Eight children.
2. Hanna Harvey—(no record).
3. Martha Harvey—b. (date unknown); d. 1825; m. (1) ——— Shy; (2) Jesse Towell, at Spring Meeting, N.C., on July 5, 1795.
4. Rachel Harvey—b. (date unknown); m. Joseph Hadley, son of Joshua and Patience (Brown) Hadley of Chatham, at Cane Creek Meeting, N.C. Joseph—b. Oct. 5, 1745.
5. Edith Harvey—b. (date unknown); m. (1) John Reynolds (2) George Madden, son of Barnabas Madden. George Madden—b. 1759; d. 1823; soldier in Revolutionary War.
6. Caleb Harvey—b. 1754; m. Mary Mooney, Jan. 21, 1779, at Cane Creek Meeting, N.C.
7. Ruth Harvey—b. Dec. 25, 1755; m. Thomas Adkinson, 1781, at Cane Creek Meeting, N.C.
8. Nathan Harvey—b. Sept. 21, 1759; m. Agnes Hoggatt. Agnes —b. Dec. 25, 1756; dau. Anthony and Mary (Agnes) Hoggatt.
9. Isaac Harvey—b. (date unknown); d. in Ohio; m. Lydia Dicks (Dix), Aug. 11, 1784. Lydia—dau. Zachariah and Ruth (Hiatt) Dicks.

The children of Edith Harvey (daughter of Isaac and Martha Newlin Harvey) and her second husband, George Madden, were: Eli, George, Elizabeth, Edith, and Martha. The last named daughter, Martha Madden, married John Towell, son of Jesse and Hanna Rice Towell. The second son of John and Martha Madden Towell was Jesse Towell, who was born on December 27, 1800. He died on March 3, 1833, in Orange County, Indiana. On February 2, 1826, he married Sarah Ann White of Washington County, Indiana. Sarah Ann was the daughter of Caleb and Parthenia White. She was born on May 17, 1803, and died on February 11, 1857. Parthenia Towell (daughter of John and Sarah Ann Towell) was born on August 16, 1828, and died on June 22, 1885. She married Jonathan Lindley Jones on March 23, 1848. Their son, William Jesse Jones, was born at Paoli, Indiana, on December 12, 1855, and is still living. He married Alice A. Wagner on May 22, 1883. She was born at Rochester, New York, on May 11, 1859, and died at Danville, Illinois on December 12, 1919.[1]

Isaac Harvey, Sr. (son of William and Judith Harvey) was a soldier in the Revolutionary War, though he was born in 1718. His name is included in the list of white male inhabitants of the Township of Upper and Lower Chichester in the proper classes.[2] The will of Isaac Harvey, Sr., dated "Fourth Day Fourth Month, 1800," of the County of Orange and State of North Carolina, gives:

> To my beloved wife Martha Harvey my House where I now live with all of my household Goods and a Sufficient maintenance out of the produce and Income of my Lands, with sufficient firewood to be cut and brought to the Door during her natural life . . . .

Children mentioned in the will: Isaac, Caleb, Hannah, Rachel, Martha, Ruth; children of deceased son, William, and of deceased daughter, Edith Madden. To his son Nathan, after

---

[1] The writer of this family history (Ethel Jones McEwen) is a daughter of William Jesse and Alice A. (Wagner) Jones.

[2] Newlin Township, 6th class, Pennsylvania Archives, Fifth Series, vol. 5, page 792. This record was accepted by the D.A.R. on June 20, 1933, as a supplemental record. The D.A.R. number of the writer (Ethel Jones McEwen) is 256,026, on the service of Daniel Bonine. The record of George Madden (m. Mrs. Edith Harvey Reynolds, widow of John Reynolds) was accepted Feb. 14, 1934. There are many descendants of Isaac Harvey who will be interested in these records. Descendants of Edith Harvey Madden are entitled to both records.

decease of his wife Martha, he bequeathed land, plantation houses and household goods, after all debts were paid. This son, Nathan Harvey, was named executor in the will, which was witnessed by James Newlin and H. Hastings.[3]

[3] The genealogical information presented in this article is based on Bible, family and church records, and on tombstone inscriptions. Many of the family lines have been traced down to the present generation. *Encyclopedia of American Quaker Genealogy*, I, by William Wade Hinshaw, verifies many of these records.

The Enoch Smith Family

JAMES H. TAYLOR

William and Joice Smith were the parents of Enoch Smith, who was born on June 7, 1772, in Shenandoah County, Virginia, and died on August 24, 1824, in Clark County, Kentucky. Enoch Smith reached Kentucky before he was married, but it is not clear whether his parents left Virginia or not. He probably had brothers and sisters, but of them, we have no definite information. After coming to Kentucky on April 29, 1829, he married Nancy Poston. She was the daughter of Elijah (or Elias) Poston and his wife Susannah. The Poston family had come to Bourbon County, Kentucky, from Maryland, when Nancy was a young girl.

Children of Enoch and Nancy Poston Smith:

1. Susannah Smith—b. Dec. 16, 1797.
2. William P. Smith—b. Sept. 4, 1799; d. Sept. 23, 1873; m. (1) Sophia Greer (2) Elizabeth Tull (no children). (3) Mrs. Elizabeth Smith Thompson, daughter of George and Nancy (Sharp) Smith of Shelbyville, Ky. Mr. Smith was a distant cousin of his third wife. No children born of this third marriage.
3. Daniel Smith—b. July 7, 1801; d. Jan. 15, 1872; m. Eliza Ann Gardner, Jan. 15, 1824. Eliza—b. May 31, 1806; d. Dec. 27, 1884. Ten children.
4. Cynthia Smith—b. Nov. 3, 1803.
5. Ann Smith—b. Nov. 28, 1805.
6. Jepthah Smith—b. Nov. 7, 1807.
7. Harvey Smith—b. May 24, 1810.
8. Jefferson Smith—b. Feb. 24, 1812.
9. Lydia Smith—b. Oct. 13, 1813.
10. Emily Smith—b. Aug. 12, 1815; D. Dec. 27, 1815.
11. Sanford Smith—b. Dec. 25, 1816.
12. Malinda Smith—b. Aug. 23, 1821; m. Truston Woolen; lived near Georgetown, Ky. Mrs. Woolen visited cousins at Fountaintown, Ind., about 1875-80, and had with her two daughters, Sally and Amelia, then grown, but not married.

Sometime prior to 1834 Johannes Hensel died. By this time his family had received letters from German and French immigrants who were residing in the United States. These friends from across the ocean were writing back to their friends and relatives in Germany telling them of the vast resources in their new home. Often the people in Germany had food shortages—some died from starvation. These letters from the United States told of a land of plenty—where the thrifty could own their own land and could raise more than enough for themselves.

As more and more letters from the United States brought favorable reports of the living conditions there, the three Hensel girls decided to leave their native land and immigrate to the United States. By this time the two oldest girls had married and had families of their own. Anna, who had married Conrad Bickel, was the mother of three children: Conrad, Johannes, and Anna. Elizabetha had married Johannes Rupp and had one son, Heinrich. The youngest daughter was nineteen and unmarried. The three girls persuaded their mother to make the trip to America with them. They disposed of what personal property they could not take with them and had the necessary papers for the journey filled out by August, 1837. Early the following month they boarded a sailing vessel for New York. On the voyage over, Anna Hensel Bickel's oldest son, Conrad, became sick and died; he was buried at sea. Upon arriving in New York, the party continued their journey until they reached the homes of German friends in Louisville, Kentucky. The trip was completed to Louisville by mid-December, 1837. Here the men secured employment as gardeners. On January 1, 1838 the youngest daughter, Catharina Hensel, was married to Johannes Seitz. Elizabetha Hensel, who had been married in Germany wanted her marriage recorded in this country and so appeared with her husband Johannes Rupp before George Brandan, justice of the peace, and repeated her marriage vows. (See Jefferson County Marriage Records, Louisville.)

Louisville was only to be their temporary home until each could look around for a suitable farm to buy. By 1839, the two sons-in-law, Johannes Seitz and Johannes Rupp, had selected farms in Franklin Township, Harrison County, Indiana, about fifteen miles west of Louisville. This land had previously been settled by English people, but a few French and German immigrants had bought farms in the neighborhood. The latter followed their own customs and spoke their native tongue. This apparently annoyed the English and more and more of them offered their farms for sale. These were immediately purchased by German immigrants. Thus during the period from 1830 to 1850 practically the entire population of eastern Harrison County, from Lanesville to New Middletown, changed from English to German.

After moving to Harrison County, the Hensel daughters and their families attended the St. Paul Evangelical Lutheran Church in western Franklin Township. This church was better known as Siegwalds. Here they worshipped for almost a decade until the pastor who was then serving the church wanted the congregation to change to another denomination. These German settlers had been reared in Lutheran churches and were not to be easily persuaded to change. So during the latter part of the 1840's the Bickel, Rupp, and Seitz families and many of their friends withdrew their membership from the Siegwald Church and commenced worshipping in homes throughout their community. These services were often conducted in the home of Conrad and Anna Hensel Bickel or in the home of John Gimble. When no itinerant Lutheran pastor was available, one of the men of the congregation would read the scripture and conduct the service by reading from Arndt's True Christianity or from one of Martin Luther's sermons. Soon this group organized themselves into a congregation known as St. Peter's Evangelical Lutheran Church, and plans were made to erect a church building.

On May 31, 1851, Thomas Enfield (or Infield) and wife, Sarah, deeded one acre of land to John Seitz, John Rupp, and Frederick Ellwanger, trustees of the Evangelic Lutheran Church St. Peter. Henry Rupp, son of John Rupp, went around the community to notify all the members of the log rolling for the new church. With the help of a team of oxen, the trees were felled and logs rolled together to erect the building which was 24 by 36 feet. This log structure remained standing until 1920. It was located near the front or east of the present cemetery.

Seven years later John Rupp and his wife deeded part of their farm for a parsonage. A further purchase of land adjoining the cemetery was made on March 14, 1879, from Jacob Richert, Sr., and wife. This was conveyed to Jacob Richert, Sr., John Richert, and John Bickel, Sr., trustees of the church. This is the land on which the present brick church building was erected; this building was dedicated on May 26, 1881.

After the erection of the brick structure, the old log church continued to be used for school purposes. Here the pastor taught the children to read and to write the German language. The children also learned the catechism, songs, and scriptures in German. That language was used in the confirmation service until about 1898. Preaching services continued in German until about 1917 when the sentiment growing out of the First World War caused its discontinuance.

This first log church was very plain and simple—no bell or belfry—one double door but no windows in the front. There were three windows on each side. The ceiling was low and the benches straight and plain. The backs of the benches had a drop-leaf table arrangement which could be raised on school days so that the children would have a place to study and write. An isle led down the middle of the church to the altar and pulpit which was on a low platform. A little organ which was pumped by foot furnished the music.

From the time the Hensels came to America, Anna Catharina Hensel, the mother, resided in the homes of her daughters and sons-in-law. The major part of her time was spent with her daughter, Mrs. Conrad Bickel. It was here that she died on February 7, 1862 in her 79th year. The stone on her grave, just north of the first church building, was inscribed in German: "Hier Ruht Catharina John Hensel's Ehe Frau Geboren Am 15 Oct. 1783 Gestorben Am 7 Feb. 1862."

Although Catharina Müllerin Hensel died in 1862 her descendants have continued to perpetuate St. Peter's Church. Through her three daughters, her descendants have increased and multiplied until it would be safe to draw the conclusion that all during the history of St. Peter's the majority of its members have been descendants of this Catharina Müllerin and her husband Johannes Hensel. It is then quite proper that she lie buried in the churchyard at St. Peter's where she has kept the spiritual light burning down through many years through her children, grandchildren, great-grandchildren, and those who follow after.

Descendants of Conrad and Anna (Hensel) Bickel

Anna, the oldest daughter of Johannes and Anna (Müllerin) Hensel, was born June 22, 1807 in Germany, and died Jan. 19, 1897 in Webster Township, Harrison County. She was married in Germany to Conrad Bickel who was born Nov. 18, 1806 and died Feb. 12, 1876. Both are buried in St. Peter's Lutheran Church Cemetery. Upon arriving in the United States they lived in Louisville for a year, and then (on Jan. 23, 1839) purchased from Daniel Row 80 acres of land in the southeast corner of Franklin Township, Harrison County.

Conrad Bickel was a shoemaker and made leather boots, ladies' shoes, and children's footwear for the people of his community. He had his work bench at his home and people came from miles around to be measured for shoes or boots. All the stitching and leather work was done by hand over wooden shoe lasts.

Conrad and Anna Bickel had five children:
1. Conrad, Jr. died on the way to the United States
2. Johannes, b. Nov. 17, 1826; d. Feb. 28, 1899; m. Louisa Richert, daughter of Jacob and Catharine (Foreman) Richert, Feb. 24, 1851. Her death occurred Dec. 19, 1883, age 50. Johannes and Louisa Bickel had 13 children:
    a. Johannes Conrad 1852-1855
    b. Johannes Friederick 1854-1879; married Mary Lottich
    c. Katherine Elizabeth 1856-1931; married John Seitz, son of Johannes and Catherine (Hensel) Seitz
    d. John George 1859-1927; married Anna Wernert
    e. Catherine Marie 1860-1898; married John Miller
    f. Marie Louise 1863-   ; married Jacob Schneider
    g. Henry William 1865-1946; married Sophia Haken
    h. Jacob 1868-   ; married Ida Vogt
    i. George Philip 1870-1880
    j. Andreas Henry (twin) 1872-1880
    k. Annie Elizabeth (twin) 1872-1943; married George Felker, son of Philip and Elizabeth (Seitz) Felker
    l. Elizabeth Susana 1874-   ; married William B. Gleitz
    m. Daniel 1877-1879
3. Annie Elizabeth, third child of Conrad and Anna Bickel, b. Dec. 3, 1828 in Germany; d. Dec. 5, 1897. She was married to John Frederick Ellwanger on Dec. 3, 1846. He was born in Germany June 25, 1815, and came to Louisville in 1824. He died on his farm in Webster Township, Harrison County, Feb. 10, 1903. Frederick and Annie Ellwanger had 12 children:
    a. Johann F. 1847-   ; married Caroline Hoffield
    b. Manual 1848-1848; buried in Louisville
    c. Mary K. 1849-1916; married George H. Kraft
    d. John Henry 1851-1925; married Laura Weller

e. Louise 1853-1855
   f. Elizabeth K. 1856-   ; married William Lottich
   g. Conrad G. 1858-1903; married Clemma Hunt
   h. Catharine Marie 1860-1928; married Philip Lottich
   i. George J. 1862-1927; married Carrie Zollman
   j. William P. 1864-   ; married Annie Moesser
   k. Susie Lydia 1868-1948; married Philip Richert
   l. Charlotta F. 1870-   ; married William Voelker

4. George, fourth child of Conrad and Anna Bickel, b. Apr. 16, 1839 in Harrison County; married Mrs. Emma Boone Moore, daughter of Craven and Sallie (Newman) Boone, on Feb. 5, 1882. She was born Feb. 21, 1855; died Aug. 28, 1928 and is buried in Louisville. George Bickel served as deputy sheriff of Harrison County. One day he disappeared and was never heard of again. He and Emma Boone Bickel had 2 children:
   a. Nellie; married ——————— Lancaster
   b. Claude

5. Catherine M., fifth child of Conrad and Anna Bickel, born June 16, 1844 in Harrison County; died Feb. 27, 1896. Married John Richert, son of Jacob and Catharine (Foreman) Richert, Feb. 12, 1863. John Richert was born Mar. 16, 1839; died May 16, 1919. He and Catherine lived on a farm near St. Peter's Church. They had 10 children:
   a. Elizabeth Richert 1863-   ; married John Scharf
   b. Annie 1865-   ; married Frederick Schneider
   c. Catharine 1868-1935; married Jacob Vogt
   d. Susie 1870-   ; married Conrad Lottich
   e. Frederick 1872-1938; married Pearl Brown
   f. Salome 1875-   ; married Robert Kirkham
   g. Charles 1877-1913; married Edna Meyer
   h. Minnie 1880-   ; married Edgar Nance
   i. Adeline M. 1883-1940; married Benjamin Kirkham
   j. Frank 1886-   ; married Mrs. Edna (Meyer) Richert

Descendants of Johannes and Elizabetha (Hensel) Rupp

Elizabetha, the second daughter of Johannes and Anna (Müllerin) Hensel, was born Aug. 4, 1810 in Germany. She was married to Johannes Rupp, born the same year in the Province of Hessen, Germany. After coming to the United States he made several purchases of land in Franklin Township, Harrison County, and became a prosperous farmer. Elizabetha died Mar. 18, 1873, her husband on Sept. 8, 1888; both are buried in St. Peter's cemetery. They had one son, Henry, born Jan. 31, 1834, in Germany.

As Henry Rupp grew up, he developed a talent for woodworking and opened a shop where he made and sold furniture to the people of the neighborhood. Much of his furniture is in use today in the homes of the community. In addition, he made coffins and conducted an undertaking business for fifty years. Henry Rupp married Catherine Marie Bickel, daughter of Weigand Bickel, Nov. 22, 1855. She died Nov. 1878. They had 5 children:

a. Elizabeth K. 1861-1864
   b. Catherine 1863-1933; married Frank Dammann
   c. Frederick J. 1866-1905; married Mary Gunthert
   d. George J. 1869-   ; married Amanda Ehrhart
   e. Anna Louise 1873-1874

Following the death of his first wife, Catherine, Henry Rupp married Lisa (Elizabeth) Katherine Friedericka Moesser on Jan. 15, 1880 in Shelby County, Kentucky. She was born Jan. 20, 1855 in Cincinnati of German parents and had lived in Harrison County, Indiana, before moving to Kentucky. Henry and Elizabeth had 5 children:
   a. Emma 1880-   ; married Charles E. Gleitz
   b. Charlotte 1882-   ; married William Maurice Griffin
   c. Charles J. 1884-   ; married (1) Mary G. Shuck; (2) Nora E. Bickel
   d. Maria 1886-   ; married Grover C. Tindall
   e. Minnie 1890-   ; married Robert J. Richert

Henry Rupp died May 19, 1918, and his wife, Elizabeth Moesser Rupp, died Dec. 27, 1929. Both are buried in the cemetery adjoining St. Peter's Lutheran Church.

Descendants of Johannes and Catherine (Hensel) Seitz

Catherine M. Hensel, third daughter of Johannnes and Anna (Müllerin) Hensel, was born in Germany Aug. 24, 1818, and was married to Johannes Seitz, son of Philip Seitz, shortly after her arrival in Louisville. He was born in Germany Feb. 1, 1815. They lived on a farm in Franklin Township, Harrison County. He died Apr. 25, 1878; Catherine died eleven years later, Feb. 20, 1889. Both are buried in St. Peter's cemetery. They had 5 children:

1. Elizabeth Seitz 1845-1898; married Philip C. Felker in 1864. They had 4 children:
   a. Katie 1865-1903; married Jacob C. Lottich
   b. George 1869-   ; married Annie Bickel, daughter of Johannes and Louise (Richert) Bickel
   c. Charley J. 1873-1888
   d. Lydia C. M. 1876-1912; married Edward H. Richert
2. Catherine 1848-1930; married Jacob Feig in 1866. They had 3 children:
   a. John 1868-1911; married Annie Hauck
   b. Charles 1872-1912
   c. Tillie 1875-   ; married Charles Cromwell
3. Saraha A. Seitz 1851-1885; married John Scharf in 1875. They had 4 children, 3 of whom died while young. Amelia, born 1880, married Ira Shewmaker.
4. John C. Seitz 1853-1908; married Catherine E. Bickel, daughter of Johannes and Louise (Richert) Bickel, in 1877. They had 6 children:
   a. Lydia 1878-   ; married John R. Kirkham
   b. Matilda Marie 1880-1922; married John B. Meyer
   c. Elizabeth 1883-1883

d. George 1884-1895
   e. Clara 1887-   ; married Cecil Stewart
   f. Clarence 1890-1936
5. Frederick Seitz 1856-1910; married Catherine Ackerman, daughter of Michael and Jacobenna Ackerman. She died Nov. 5, 1945. They had 7 children:
   a. Charles J. 1880-1900
   b. Laura 1882-   ; married Mose Proffitt
   c. John 1884-   ; married Clara Richert
   d. Elizabeth 1886-   ; married John Steele
   e. Mary 1888-   ; married William Schoen
   f. Margaret 1890-   ; married Charles Miers
   g. Jennie 1891-   ; married Tony A. Wolfe

The Hickman Family of Henry County
Eugene Studebaker Wierbach

The Reverend Joshua Hickman was born in Westmoreland County, Pennsylvania, April 10, 1766, the youngest son of Ezekiel and Elizabeth (Trammel) Hickman. When about thirteen years of age, he drove pack horses over the Allegheny Mountains to assist his father in equipping a company of men for service in the American Revolution. His father was later made lieutenant of his Company, which was a part of the Eighth Pennsylvania under the command of Colonel Daniel Brodhead. On January 13, 1785, when Joshua Hickman was nineteen years of age, he was married to Josinah Van Meter, daughter of Jacob and Catherine (De Moss) Van Meter (Van Metre), in Westmoreland County, Pennsylvania. This Jacob Van Meter was an early settler and landowner in this section of Pennsylvania and was descended from the Van Meter family which planted the first white colony in the Valley of Virginia. Joshua and Josinah Hickman settled on lands along the Cheat River lying partly in Pennsylvania and partly in what was later to become West Virginia. Here all of their children were born and many of them were married.[1]

From his Bible, we learn the names of Joshua Hickman's twelve children:[2]

Rebecca—b. April 8, 1787; d. May 29, 1866; m. Abel Williams (b. 1774, d. 1847).

---
[1] See "Marriage Bonds Filed in Monongalia, Virginia (Now West Virginia)," copied by Thomas Ray Dille, in *Daughters of the American Revolution Magazine*, LXII, ff.

[2] This Bible belongs to Mrs. Rose Hickman Estabrook of Springport, Indiana, and Mrs. Patricia Allen Gohring, Vice-Regent of Fort Industry Chapter, D. A. R., in Toledo, Ohio, both descendents of Joshua Hickman.

Lewis—b. June 9, 1789; d. in infancy.
Catharine—b. June 17, 1791; d. Feb. 22, 1849; m. Robert Perfect.
Jacob—b. Nov. 22, 1795; d. Feb. 27, 1869.
Mary Ann—b. Jan. 7, 1796; d. Nov. 8, 1853.
Elsy—b. May 16, 1798; d. Jan. 10, 1864; m. April 8, 1816, to James Dodd (b. Dec. 16, 1779; d. June 24, 1869).[3]
Ann—b. May 22, 1800; d. in infancy.
Sarah—b. Nov. 22, 1801; d. March 15, 1877; m. Jesse Ice.
Joshua—b. May 7, 1804; d. Jan. 12, 1885; m. Juilett (or Juliette) Moore (b. March 6, 1809).
Cynthia—b. June 9, 1806; d. June 10, 1853.
Ezekiel—b. Jan. 9, 1810; d. March 2, 1870.
William—b. Jan. 18, 1813; d. June 26, 1873; m. Clarissa Williams (b. 1817, d. 1881).

About the year 1826, the family moved to Indiana, locating in the northern part of Henry County.[4] Here Joshua Hickman served the community in the Regular Baptist Church, at the same time farming a large tract of land. Most of his children settled in the East Lebanon neighborhood, where they achieved prominence in law, medicine, and the arts. Joshua Hickman died on August 18, 1842, in Henry County. Three days before his death he made a will in which he made mention of all his children, leaving them land, money, stock, and farming equipment, and naming his youngest son, William, his executor. His wife died on June 3, 1857, in Henry County, and is buried beside her husband in East Lebanon Cemetery.

Births and deaths of the Hickman and Moore families:[5]
Joshua Hickman—b. April 10, 1766; d. Aug. 18, 1842.
Josinah (Van Metre) Hickman—b. Jan. 22, 1768; d. June 3, 1857.

Josiah Moore—b. Nov. 6, 1783; d. July 15, 1822.
Melinda Thomas—b. Jan. 22, 1786 [m. Josiah Moore]; d. Oct. 27, 1831.

---

[3] See the Dodd family Bible record printed below.
[4] The dates of the deaths of James and Elsy differ in the two records. Samuel Gordon Smyth, comp., *A Genealogy of the Duke-Shepherd-Van Metre Family* (Lancaster, Pa., 1909), 399-400; see also sketch of James T. Hickman, grandson of Joshua Hickman, in *Biographical Memoirs of Henry County, Indiana* (Logansport, Ind., 1902), 546-549. According to this sketch, the family moved to Henry County in 1830.
[5] This record was copied from the Bible belonging to Miss Byrd Hickman of Springport, Indiana. The copying was done by Eugene Studebaker Wierbach. Names are re-arranged, as they were copied without reference to family or sequence in the Bible record.

Juliette Moore[6]—b. March 6, 1809.
Anna Moore—b. Feb. 2, 1811.
Mary Moore—b. April 3, 1814.
James Thomas Moore—b. July 29, 1816.
Adeline Elizabeth Moore—b. Dec. 24, 1819.
Lydia Emma Moore—b. Dec. 24, 1822.

Joshua T. Hickman—b. May 7, 1804; m. Juliette Moore, April 17, 1827.

Josiah Moore Hickman[7]—b. Sept. 12, 1828.
William Trammel Hickman—b. Sept. 1830.
Josinah Van Metre Hickman—b. April 9, 1835.
James Thomas Hickman—b. June 28, 1837.
Lewis Joshua Hickman—b. Oct. 26, 1839.
Jacob Van Metre Hickman—b. April 11, 1842.
Charles Melette Hickman—b. July 19, 1845.

James T. Moore—m. Cynthia Ann Melette, June 18, 1839.

[6] Juliette Moore and the five persons whose names follow hers were evidently the children of Joshua and Melinda (Thomas) Moore.

[7] Son of Joshua T. and Juliette (Moore) Hickman, and grandson of Josiah and Josinah (Van Metre) Hickman. The six persons whose names follow that of Joshua Moore Hickman were evidently also the children of Joshua and Juliette (Moore) Hickman.

The Ancestry of John Hampden Holliday
Augustus R. Markle

In writing of any man, there is always much left out of the story, whether genealogy or biography is the object, for in a biography we necessarily must take ancestry into account, and in genealogy the mere parading across the page of a lot of names fails to bring into the picture the effect that ancestors had in producing the man. There is not room in this department of the *Magazine* to set out many of the features of his life nor to do more than name those forebears who had a part in determining the life and character of the man who became the first president of the Society of Indiana Pioneers, John Hampden Holliday.

Mr. Holliday was educated in the public schools of Indianapolis, and, after four years at the Northwestern Christian University, the predecessor of Butler College, he entered Hanover College where he was graduated in the Class of 1864. A little before his graduation, he enlisted in the One Hundred Thirty-seventh Indiana, a hundred-day regiment, and served for four months. He then re-enlisted in the Seventieth Indiana Infantry for three years, but was rejected by the medical examiner. After a short experience in the practice of law, he began work with the Indianapolis *Gazette* in 1866. In 1869, he founded a paper of his own, the Indianapolis *News*, the first issue appearing on December 7, 1869.

He retired from the *News* in 1892 and a year later helped organize the Union Trust Company, of which he became the first president. He resigned in 1899 to found the Indianapolis *Press* which had a short life, being sold a year and a half later to the *News*. Mr. Holliday then became president of the Union Trust Company again. In 1916, he became Chairman of the Board of Directors and was for many years connected with other financial and benevolent institutions of Indianapolis.

In 1875, Evaline M. Rieman of Baltimore became the wife of Mr. Holliday and to this union were born seven children. In 1916, Mr. and Mrs. Holliday presented to the City of Indianapolis their beautiful eighty-acre country place on White River between Crow's Nest and Broad Ripple, the city to have possession three years after the first of March following the death of the survivor of the couple. In 1920, Mr. Holliday announced the gift of $25,000 to the Emmerich Manual Training High School in memory of his son, John Hampden Holliday, Jr., who was a graduate of this High School in the Class of 1901. On December 23, 1917, the young man died while in army service at Washington, D.C.

The senior John Hampden Holliday was a charter member of the Indianapolis Literary Club; one of the founders of the Immigrants' Aid Association; long the chairman of the Indiana State Conference of Charities and Corrections; and for many years a ruling elder of the First Presbyterian Church and a trustee of the Presbyterian Synod of Indiana. For forty-six years, he served as a trustee of Hanover College, and, for a quarter of a century, as a trustee of McCormick Theological Seminary. He was one of the founders of the Indianapolis Charity Organization Society, now the Family Welfare Society. He was a thirty-third degree Mason and a member of Phi Gamma Delta. It was on October 20, 1921, at his country home near Crow's Nest on White River, that John Hampden Holliday died, at the age of seventy-five.

Born on May 31, 1846, in Indianapolis, to the Reverend William Adair Holliday and his wife Lucia Shaw Cruft, John H. Holliday was the product of two widely dissimilar stocks. His father, the son of Samuel Holliday, was born in Harrison County, Kentucky, a few years before the removal of the family to Indiana in 1816. His mother was born in Boston in 1805 and died in 1881.

The grandfather, Samuel Holliday, was born in 1779 to William Holliday and Martha Patton. Of the latter very little is known, but we know that William was born in Ireland in 1755 and died in Kentucky in 1812. His parents were Samuel Holliday, born in 1709, and Janet Adair. Samuel Holliday, the grandfather of John Hampden Holliday, married Elizabeth Martin (1781-1846). She was the daughter of Jacob Martin, a soldier in the Revolutionary War and his wife, Catherine Wilson.

In so far as a man is what his mother makes him, the New England ancestry of John Hampden Holliday had much to do with his life in later years, and it is of this side of his family that the most is known.

The mother of John H. Holliday was Lucia Shaw Cruft (1805-1881). Lucy was the daughter of John Cruft, who was born in Boston in 1769, and was married in 1799 to Lucia Crocker Shaw (1772-1812). John Cruft died in 1839. John was the son of Foster Cruft (1734-1800) who was married in 1757 to Ann Breck (1738-1827). Foster was the son of Edward Cruft (1690-1734) of Boston, who was married in 1715 to Abigail Foster. Ann Breck, wife of Foster Cruft and grandmother of John H. Holliday, was the daughter of John Breck (1705-1761) who was married in 1727 to Margaret Thomas. Margaret was the daughter of William Thomas and his wife Abigail, the year of her birth being 1708.

John, the father of Ann Breck, was the son of a John Breck (1680-1713) who was married in 1703 to Ann Patteshall (1678-1767). The father of the latter John Breck was also a John Breck (1650-1691) with a wife named Susanna. The father of this third John Breck was Edward Breck who died in Dorchester in 1662. He married Isabel Rigby.

Ann Patteshall (1678-1767), who married the second John Breck, was the daughter of Richard Patteshall (1636-1689) and Martha Woodee. Martha was born in 1669 to Isaac and Dorcas Woodee. The father of Richard was Edmund Patteshall, who died in 1675.

The grandmother of John H. Holliday and wife of John Cruft, Lucia Crocker Shaw, was the daughter of William Shaw, D. D. (1741-1816) of Marshfield, Massachusetts, who married Lucy Crocker (1744-1776) in 1766. The Reverend William Shaw was graduated from Harvard in 1762, and in 1815 received the degree of S. T. D. He was married a second time to Sarah Mather, and a third time, to Ann Checkley. The father of the Rev. William Shaw was also graduated from Harvard (class of 1729). He was born in 1708 and married Sarah Angier (1705-1768). The grandfather of the Rev. William Shaw was Joseph Shaw and his grandmother was Judith Whitmarsh (1669-1760), daughter of John and Sarah Whitmarsh. Joseph Shaw was the son of John Shaw of Weymouth, whose wife Elizabeth was the daughter of Nicholas and Elizabeth Phillips. This John Shaw of Weymouth was the son of Abraham Shaw, the immigrant from England, who married Bridget Best in 1616 and died in Dedham, Massachusetts, in 1638.

Sarah Angier, mother of the Rev. William Shaw, was the daughter of the Reverend Samuel Angier (1654-1719) who was graduated from Harvard in 1673. The Rev. Angier married Hannah Oakes in 1680. Samuel Angier was the son of Edmund Angier (1612-1692), who came to Cambridge from England and married Ruth Ames. Ruth was the daughter of the Rev. William Ames (1576-1633) and his wife Joanna Fletcher (1587-1644). Ames and his wife were immigrants to Cambridge, Massachusettes, from England. Edmund Angier's father was John Angier. Hannah Oakes, who married the Rev. Samuel Angier, was the daughter of the Reverend Urian Oakes (1631-1681), an early president of Harvard College. The father of Urian Oakes was Edward Oakes, who like his son, was born in England and became a resident of Cambridge, Massachusetts.

Lucy Crocker, who became the first wife of the Rev. William Shaw, was the daughter of the Rev. Joseph Crocker (1715-1772) of Eastham, Massachusetts, who married Reliance Allen (1715-1759) in 1739. Joseph was graduated from Harvard in 1734. He was the son of Thomas Crocker (1671-1728) who married Hannah Green of Boston in 1698. Thomas died in Barnstable in 1728, at the age of fifty-three. Thomas was the son of Josiah Crocker (1647-1698) who married Malatiah Hinckley, (1648-1714). Malatiah was the daughter of Governor Thomas Hinckley, born in England in 1619, and his wife Mary Richards of Cape Cod. The Governor died in 1706. The father of Josiah Crocker was William Crocker of Barnstable and his wife Alice. Josiah died in 1692.

Reliance Allen, who became the wife of the Rev. Joseph Crocker, was the daughter of the Rev. Benjamin Allen who was graduated from Yale in 1708. Benjamin married Elizabeth Crocker in 1712, and died in 1754. The father of the Rev. Benjamin Allen was James Allen of Martha's Vineyard (1623-1714) and his wife Elizabeth Perkins (1644-1722). Elizabeth Crocker who became the wife of the Rev. Benjamin Allen, was born in 1668 to Job Crocker (1644-1718) and his wife Hannah Taylor. Job was the son of William Crocker and his wife Alice.

The Holliday line from the earliest one listed in this brief family history runs as follows:

Samuel Holliday—b. Aug. 12, 1709 at Glen, Scotland; m. (2) Janet Adair; d. Rathfriland, County Down, Ireland.

William Holliday (son of Samuel and Jane Adair Holliday)—b. 1755 in Ireland; m. Martha Patton; d. 1812 in Kentucky.

Samuel Holliday (son of William and Martha Patton Holliday)—b. 1779; m. Elizabeth Martin (b. 1781; dau. Jacob and Catherine Wilson Martin; d. 1846).

William Adair Holliday (son of Samuel and Martha Patton Holliday)—b. about 1806 in Harrison County, Kentucky; came to Indiana in 1816; m. Lucia Shaw Cruft (b. 1805; dau. John and Lucia Crocker Shaw Cruft; d. 1881).

John Hampden Holliday (son of William Adair and Lucia Shaw Cruft Holliday)—b. May 31, 1846; m. Evaline M. Rieman of Baltimore in 1875; d. Oct. 1, 1921, in Indianapolis.

John Hampden Holliday, Jr., (son of John Hampden and Evaline M. Rieman Holliday)—b. about 1884; d. Dec. 23, 1917, in Washington, D.C.

---

[1] Additional biographical material on John H. Holliday may be found in the following: George Irving Reed, ed., *Encyclopedia of Biography of Indiana* (Chicago, 1895), I, 92-94; Will Cumback and T. B. Maynard, eds., *Men of Progress of Indiana* (Indianapolis, 1899), 474-477; Jacob Piatt Dunn, *Greater Indianapolis* (Chicago, 1910), II, 1006-1008; idem, *Indiana and Indianians* (Chicago,, 1919), III, 1225-1226; Kate Milner Rabb and William Hersehill, eds., *An Account of Indianapolis and Marion County* (Dayton, O., 1924), IV, 406-410; Indianapolis *News*, Oct. 21, 1921.

The Hollowell Family

LESTER D. PREWITT

There is a legend which relates that in the seventeenth century three Hallowell brothers came to America from England. Two of them settled in Pennsylvania, the other going farther south. The latter was a very loud and forceful preacher. The people insisted on writing his name *Hollowell* instead of *Hallowell*, and the descendants still spell the name with an *o* in the first syllable.

Thomas Hollowell, second of the name, son of John and Sarah Hollowell, of Norfolk County, Virginia, was born on December 4, 1739, and married Mary Peele (or Peelle), daughter of Robert and Elizabeth Peele. The cermony took place on December 7, 1760, in Quaker meeting in Northampton County, North Carolina. Thomas came to Orange County, Indiana, in 1812, and died prior to 1830.

John Hollowell, father of the second Thomas Hollowell, died in 1751 or 1752 in Norfolk County, Virginia; his will was proved April 16, 1752 (recorded in Will Book 1f, p. 246). The will of John Hollowell, husband of Sarah Rountreé, mentions a cousin Thomas, and a brother Thomas, and children (Rachel Copeland, Mary, Sarah, Rachel, John, and Thomas). In Will Book 5f of Norfolk County, Virginia, are recorded wills of two Thomas Hollowells—one of them (p. 208), dated June 16, 1693, probated September 15, 1693, mentions children (Thomas, John, William, Elizabeth, Katherine, and Luke). The other will (p. 22), dated March 15, 1686, probated May 17, 1687, mentions a wife Alice, and children: Edmond, Thomas, Henry, Joseph, Benjamin, John, Sarah, Elizabeth, Alice. Sarah, the wife of the first John Hollowell was the daughter of Moses and Sarah Rountree. Moses died in

Perquimans County, North Carolina, in 1755. His will, made on July 21, 1755, mentions his wife, Sarah, and children: Sarah, Hannah, Ledy, Ann. The will of his daughter Hannah, probated in 1759, mentions sisters Sarah and Ledy, and is witnessed by Joe and Abner Hollowell.[1]

Mary Peele, wife of the second Thomas Hollowell was born on February 2, 1742 (o.s.) and died on January 11, 1813. She was the daughter of Robert Peele (or Peelle) who was born on June 29, 1709, and died on July 13, 1782, in Northampton County, North Carolina.[2] Robert married Elizabeth Edgerton and they moved from Nansemond County, Virginia, to Northampton County, North Carolina in 1742. Elizabeth died April 26, 1749. Robert Peele, Jr., was a son of Robert and Judith Peele. Judith's will was probated in August, 1756, in Northampton County. A Robert Peele is listed as having contributed to the cause of American liberty during the Revolutionary War.[3]

The marriage of Thomas Hollowell and Mary Peele is recorded as follows: "1760, 12, 7. Thomas, of Perquimans Co., s. John and Sarah Colony of Va., Co. of Norfolk, m. Mary Peele, in Rick Square NH. [Northhampton County]."

In 1931 the family Bible of Thomas Hollowell was found in an attic at Paoli, Orange County, Indiana, and is now in the possession of Joseph A. Hall, a great-great-grandson. Nothing is recorded of John and Sarah Hollowell save that they lived in Norfolk County, Virginia, and were the parents of Thomas Hollowell who lived in North Carolina. The Bible records the death of the wife of Thomas as follows: "Mary Hollowell, wife of Thomas Hollowell, late of North Carolina, but now of Indiana Territory, departed this life the 11th day of the first month, of 1813, at about 8 or 9 o'clock at night, aged 70 years and 9 months lacking 2 days."

The record of the descendants of the Hollowell family was collected by John J. Hollowell of Farmer City, Illinois. He died on October 5, 1934. Prior to his death, he sent a copy of his material to Lester D. Prewitt, Forest City, Iowa, who has compiled the following outline adding some data collected by himself.

---

[1] Will Book, 1755, North Caroina (Office of Secretary of State), 37.

[2] North Carolina Will Book, No. 1, 253.

[3] Stephen B. Weeks, *Southern Quakers and Slavery* (*Johns Hopkins University Studies in History and Political Science*, Extra Volume XV, Baltimore, 1896), 190-191.

Children of Thomas and Mary Peele Hollowell:[4]

Abigale (Abigail)—b. Dec. 26, 1761; m. 1784 to John Spivey; children: Elizabeth (b. 1785), Exum (b. 1787), Mariam (b. 1790), Charity (b. 1794), Becca (b. 1797), Abba (b. 1800), Ephraim (b. 1802). John Spivey, the husband of Abigale Hollowell, died on October 10, 1805.

Sarah—b. Dec. 24, 1763; m. 1785 to Ralph Fletcher; children: Mary (b. 17877), Joshua (b. 1790), Achsah (b. 1793), Betty (b. 1796), Jesse (b. 1801), John (b. 1805).

John—b. Jan. 11, 1766; m. 1786, to Miriam Overman; children: Henry (b. 1787), Jesse (b. 1790), Mary (b. 1792), Sarah (b. 1794), Jonathan (b. 1796), Eli (b. 1798), Aaron (b. 1801), John (b. 1803). John Hollowell and his family moved from North Carolina to Indiana Territory, in April, 1807, and settled near the present town of Valeene, Orange County. He was probably the first white settler in that county. His brother Robert and family moved to the same vicinity a few years later.

Miriam—b. 1769; m. 1804, to John Hobson; no children listed in records.[5]

Robert—b. 1772; d. April 30, 1865; m. Oct. 23, 1794, to Elizabeth Cox, (dau. Thomas and Phebe Cox); five children.

William—b. 1775; m. 1797, to Phebe Cox; s. Robert (b. 1802; c. 1804). Phebe may have been a sister of Elizabeth Cox, since her name is the same as that of Elizabeth's mother. No further record of this line.

Thomas—b. 1777. No further record.

Joseph (Josse)[6]—b. Aug. 16, 1780; moved to Indiana in 1809; d. 1822 (about), Orange County; m. Elizabeth Woodward of North Carolina (Elizabeth—b. Jan. 16, 1778; d. July 1857; dau. Josua [Joshua] and Mary Woodward); five children. The father of Elizabeth Woodward Hollowell died in Wayne County, North Carolina, in 1789, and his will was probated in April of that year.

---

[4] Thomas Hollowell, who married Mary Peele, was a son of John and Sarah (Rountree) Hollowell.

[5] Hinshaw, *American Quaker Genealogy*, I, 308, gives the marriage date as April 15, 1804, at Contentney meetinghouse, Wayne County, North Carolina. This was a second marriage for John Hobson.

[6] The name *Josse* is formed from *Joseph*, and should not be confused with *Jesse* as was done by J. J. Hollowell in his records.

Children of Robert and Elizabeth (Cox) Hollowell:[7]

Smithson—b. 1775; m. Rachel Chenoweth. Smithson Hollowell lived on a farm near Hardinsburg, Washington County, Indiana. He was a faithful quaker, and twice each week made the seven-mile journey on horseback to the Lick Creek Quaker Meeting in Orange County. Children of Smithson and Rachel (Chenoweth) Hollowell were: Robert (m. Sarah McIntosh), John (m. Phoebe Colclasure), William (m. Emily Coulter), Thomas (m. Malinda Coulter), Maryanna (m. Martin Kinkade), Ellen (m. Harvey Walter), Martha (m. Leander Hardin).

Michal—b. 1777; m. William Lindley. Children of William and Michal (Hollowell) Lindley were: Edmund (b. 1817; d. 1833); Areanna (b. 1818; d. 1833, of cholera); Uriah (b. 1820; d. 1853), Alfred (b. 1822; d. 1891; m. Martha J. Maxwell), Elizabeth (b. 1824; d. 1860; m. Samuel Lindley), Asenath (b. 1825; d. 1911; m. 1849, to Elisha Parker), Hiram (b. 1827; d. 1893; m. (1) Laura White and (2) Elizabeth Woodward), Sarah (b. 1829; d. 1907; m. 1850, to Cader Newsom), Jonathan (b. 1832; d. 1926; m. (1) 1852, to Elmira Starbuck and (2) 1858, to Ann Fisher), William (b. 1838; d. 1928; m. (1) 1865, to Harriet Shaw and (2) to Margaret Ward), Walter (b. 1840; d. 1862), Milton (b. 1841; d. 1887), Laban (b. 1843; d. 1923; m. Anna Frazier), Hannah E. (b. 1845; d. 1855).

Nathan—b. 1779; d. 1865; m. Nancy Everett. Children of Nathan and Nancy (Everett) Hollowell; James (b. 1821; d. 1895; m. (1) 1841, to Celia Thomas and (2) 1859, to Mary Amanda Trueblood Lindley, widow of Jonathan Thomas Lindley and dau. William Penn and Anna Trueblood), Elizabeth (b. 1822; d. 1863; m. 1850, to Joseph Newsome), Robert (died unmarried), Joseph A. (b. 1824; d. 1897; m. 1844, to Deborah Dixon), Nathan (no data), Nancy (b. 1838; d. 1867; m. 1854, to John A. Lindley).

Peggy—b. 1800; m. Thomas Lindley. Children of Thomas and Peggy (Hollowell) Lindley were: Eli, Robert, Elizabeth, Charles, Nathan, William, Aba, and Sarah.

---

[7] Robert Hollowell, who married Elizabeth Cox, was a son of Thomas and Mary (Peele) Hollowell.

William—b. 1803; m. Mary Lindley. Children of William and Mary (Lindley) Hollowell were: Michal (m. Wood Boyd), Elizabeth (m. Jesse Boyd; thirteen children,[8] one of whom, Lindley Boyd, m. Sarah Jane Miller).

Polly (Mary)—b. 1806; m. Exum Morris; one dau. Margaret (b. 1826; d. 1912; m. John Hall, who was born in 1821 and died in 1907). Polly (Hollowell) Morris died soon after the birth of her daughter. After the death of his wife, Exum Morris moved to Parke County, Indiana, where he married a second time and reared a family. Children of John and Margaret (Morris) Hall were: Robert W. (b.— 1843; d. 1863), Exum (b. 1845; d. 1929; m. Sarah J. Trotter), Mary Ellen (b. 1846; d. 1853), Richard W. (b. 1849; d. 1900; m. Margaret Gardner), Anna J. (b. and d. 1851), Catherine (b. 1852; d. 1897; m. Bayless Palmer), Nancy M. (b. 1854; d. 1858), Joseph A. (b. 1857; m. 1879, to Mary Frances Apple), Laura Decker (no data), Morton W. (b. 1864; m. Louisa Teaford), Leulla (b. 1870; m. James A. Durrett).

Children of James and Cecelia (Thomas) Hollowell:[9]

Robert Thomas—b. 1842; d. 1867.

Amos K.—b. 1844; d. 1921; m. (1) Adeline Parker and (2) May I. Kramer.

Nathan—b. 1847; d. 1874.

James S.—b. 1849; m. Sara Engle.

Julda J.—b. 1853; d. 1898; m. Christian Stiefel.

Iram—b. 1856; d. 1858.

Children of James and Mary A. (Trueblood-Lindley) Hollowell:[10]

Elwood L.—b. 1860, d. 1898, m. 1890, to Hannah Esther Newby.

Edmond J.—b. 1863, d. 1888.

John J.—b. 1865; m. 1888, to Jeanette A. Gibbens.

Nancy—b. 1869; d. 1929; m. 1892 to Ora A. Morris.

---

[8] *History of Lawrence, Orange and Washington Counties, Indiana* (Chicago, 1884), 580.

[9] James Hollowell, who married Cecelia Thomas, was a son of Nathan and Nancy (Everett) Hollowell.

[10] This is the same James Hollowell (son of Nathan Hollowell), who first married Cecelia Thomas. His second wife was Mary A. (Trueblood) Lindley, widow of Thomas Lindley.

Children of Joseph and Elizabeth Hollowell Newsome:[11]
Mary Emma—b. 1852; d. 1932; m. 1906 Milton Hanson.
Nancy M.—b. 1854; d. 1865.
Lysias E.—b. 1858; m. Eliza J. Gaston.

Children of Joseph A. and Deborah (Dixon) Hollowell:[12]
Charles—b. 1846; d. 1928; m. Anna B. McCoy (d. 1931).
Silas D.—b. 1850; d. 1924; m. 1874 to Phioba Scaaf (d. 1930).
Rufus—b. 1851; d. 1909; m. Elvira Smith.
Nathan L.—b. 1853; d. 1918; m. Minnie Cooley.
Mary Elma—b. 1856; d. 1859.
Morris W.—b. 1858; d. 1932; m. 1901, to Kate Smith.
Walter—b. 1861; m. 1880, to Katherine Schaffer.
Martha E.—b. 1864; m. 1884, to Atwood H. Rowley.
Robert E.—b. 1868; m. 1892, to Ophelia Carter.

Children of John A. and Nancy (Hollowell) Lindley:[13]
Isabel Ann—b. 1856; m. John Kelamo.
Nathan A.—b. 1857; m. 1880, to Ida Florence Apple.
Martha E.—b. 1859; m. 1879, to Worth Atkinson.
Homer—b.1860; m. 1899, to Bessie Hanna.

Children of Josse Woodward and Martha (Cloud) Hollowell:[14]
Mary (May)—m. James W. Chritton; resides at Rocky Ford, Colorado.
Laura—b. ——; d. Dec. 14, 1932, Sioux City, Iowa; m. Feb. 18, 1885, to James H. Belt (b. Jan. 27, 1855; d. June 20, 1929); children: Laurence J. (b. March 31, 1887; m. Nov. 23, 1917, to Kathryn Newland), Laura L. (b. Sept. 9, 1893; d. Dec. 24, 1834, Sioux City, Iowa; unmarried).

---

[11] Elizabeth Hollowell, who married Joseph Newsome, was a daughter of Nathan Hollowell and sister of James Hollowell.

[12] Joseph A. Hollowell, who married Deborah Dixon, was a son of Nathan Hollowell, and brother of James and Elizabeth Hollowell.

[13] Nancy Hollowell, who married John A. Lindley, was a daughter of Nathan Hollowell, and sister of James, Elizabeth and Joseph A. Hollowell.

[14] Josse Woodward Hollowell, who married Martha Cloud, was a son of Joseph and Mary (Woodward) Hollowell, and a grandson of Thomas and Mary (Peele) Hollowell. Martha Cloud was a daughter of Joel and Rebecca (Thompson) Cloud. Martha was born in Orange County, Ind., on Jan. 24, 1824, and died on Sept. 14, 1880, in Iowa County, Iowa. She was buried beside her husband in Koszta Cemetery. The mother of Martha (Cloud) Hollowell, Rebecca (Thompson) Cloud, was born on Feb. 10, 1786, in N. C., and died on November 19, 1844. Joel Cloud (father of Martha and husband of Rebecca) was born on July 4, 1787, in N. C., and died on Sept. 26, 1834. His marriage to Rebecca Thompson occurred in 1811, in Orange County, N. C. The parents of Rebecca (Thompson) Cloud were Samuel and Elizabeth (De Bow) Thompson. Elizabeth when a widow received a pension on Samuel Thompson's Revolutionary War service. Widow's Pension File, L. S. C. No. 4605, in Pension Records, Washington, D. C. Samuel's will is recorded in Book 5, p. 42, in Iowa County, Iowa.

Children of Lawrence J. and Katherine (Newland) Belt were: James Lawrence (b. Aug. 26, 1921), Janet K. (b. Dec. 15, 1928).

Joel T.—b. 1842; d. before 1902; m. Alice Denslow.

Elizabeth—d. 1902, prior to the death of her father, James H. Belt.

Evelyn Jane—b. No. 27, 1847, Iowa City; d. July 14, 1802; buried in Hollowell lot at Koszta, Iowa; m. Dec. 2, 1866, Iowa City, to George W. Ringler (b. Aug. 15, 1845, Athens Co., Ohio; enlisted in Co. G, Thirteenth Regiment Iowa Infantry; d. Mar. 22, 1893; buried at Koszta, Iowa; son Reuben Jacob and Elizabeth Jane Black Ringler; grandson of Jesse and Catherine Boyer Ringler, and George and Fannie Carter Black). For marriage of Evelyn Jane Hollowell to George W. Ringler, see Marriage Record Book C, p. 89, Iowa City, Iowa.

Children of George W. and Evelyn Jane (Hollowell) Ringler:[15]

Nettie—b. April 15, 1868; c. May 12, 1868.

Charles—b. Nov. 13, 1869; d. Sept. 21, 1882.

June (Juniata)—b. Mar. 20, 1872, Iowa Co., Iowa; d. Dec. 8, 1925, Forest City, Iowa; buried in Maringo Cemetery; m. April 12, 1898, to William Roscoe Prewitt (b. July 11, 1868, Owen Co. Indiana, near Freedom; migrated to Iowa in 1876; resides at Forest City, Iowa); one son, Lester Dee (b. Aug. 24, 1899, Victor, Iowa; m. June 28, 1928, to Lela May Wolf, Iowa). For marriage record of June Ringler to William Roscoe Prewitt, see Marriage Record Book G, p. 76, Iowa City, Iowa.

Sanford—b. Jan. 20, 1876; m. Jan. 26, 1904, to Frances Brown, Kirksville, Missouri.

Wilford Peele—b. Sept. 14, 1777; d. Oct. 17, 1934; buried at Waverly, Iowa; m. Jan. 31, 1906, Bremer Co., Iowa, to Anna Donlon (dau. Michael and Anna Cummings Donlon); children: Hazelton, Edith, Donald.

Edith—b. July 29, 1880; m. Mar. 10, 1903; in Iowa Co., Iowa, to Orval G. Eben (b. Mar. 9, 1880 in Iowa Co.); one dau. Evelyn Charlotte (b. June 9, 1908, in Two Harbors, Minnesota; m. Oct. 2, 1934, to Morris B. Toreyson, at Duluth).

---

[15] Evelyn Jane Hollowell, who married George Washington Ringler, was a daughter of Josse Woodward and Martha (Cloud) Hollowell.

The Jacob Hoover Family
John M. Burkett

Jacob Hoover, the third son of Andrew (Andreas) and Margaret Fouts (Pfautz) Hoover (Hŭber) was born in 1754 and died in 1821. He married Elizabeth ———— in Randolph County, North Carolina. The second son, Andrew Hoover (1752-1834), married Elizabeth Waymire in Wayne County, Indiana, and the record of their ten children has been given in the Waymire pamphlet, published by Dr. William M. Reser of Lafayette, Indiana, in 1925. There have been many prominent persons among the descendants of this family, including the prominent antislavery leader, George W. Julian.

Children of Jacob and Elizabeth Hoover:

Jacob Hoover—b. 1777; d. 1856-59; m. (1) Catherine Yount (b. 1781; d. 1814); m. (2) in 1833, Mrs. Sophia (Plummer) Waymire (b. 1783; d. 1859); lived much of the time in Wayne County, Indiana.

Daniel Hoover—b. June 13, 1780; d. Aug. 24, 1814; m. (1) Rachel Waymire (b. April 9, 1779; d. January 14, 1806); m. (2) Jan. 8, 1807, Mary Sinks (b. April 20, 1777; d. 1830); dau. of George Sinks); lived on the Stillwater, near the National Road, Montgomery County, Ohio.

John Hoover—b. Dec. 24, 1783; d. Aug. 5, 1849; m. Elizabeth Jeffries; lived in Tippecanoe County, Indiana.

Elizabeth Hoover—b. ————; d. 1838; m. Austin Davenport (b. ————; d. 1837); lived in Boone County, Indiana.

David Hoover—b. Sept. 19, 1787; d. December 3, 1835; m. Rebecca Bonine; lived in Boone County, Indiana.

Joseph Hoover—b. Dec. 27, 1788; d. Sep. 29, 1851; m. Elizabeth Young (b. 1789); eleven children; owned mill of his grandfather's in North Carolina now known as Skeen's Mill.

Samuel Clark Hoover—b. Mar. 1, 1796; d. Jan. 8, 1876; m. Mrs. Sarah (Jeffries) Eller; clerk of court, Lafayette, Indiana.

Mary Hoover—b. 1785; m. Wood Arnold; lived in North Carolina.

Nancy Hoover—b. ————; d. May, 1826; lived in Marion County, Indiana; m. Chesley Ray (b. 1798; d. 1869).

Andrew Hoover—b. ——; d. 1839; m. Nancy ———; lived near Zionsville, Indiana.

Children of Jacob and Catherine (Yount) Hoover:[1]

Jacob Hoover—lived in Iowa.

William Hoover—b. 1803, d. ——; lived in Nevada, Iowa; unmarried.

Elizabeth Hoover—b. February 7, 1805; d. February 16, 1864; m. Enos Baldwin (1807-1860); buried in Courter Cemetery, Miami County, Indiana; six children.

Nancy Hoover—m. Jesse Morris.

John Hoover—b. November 18, 1808; d. 1872; m. Rachel Maudlin (1811-1894); lived in Cass County, Indiana; nine children.

Daniel Hoover—lived in Iowa (?).

Mary Hoover—b. 1812; m. Asa Baldwin (1812-1896); lived in Aroma, Hamilton County, Indiana; several children, including Eli, who lived at Anderson, Indiana.

Susan Hoover—b. May 1, 1813; m. Enos Bond (b. July 22, 1810; d. February 27, 1893); lived in Henry County, Indiana; nine children.

Eli Hoover—b. June 1, 1815; d. January 13, 1880; United Brethren preacher; m. (1) Sarah Beaver; four children; m. (2) Elizabeth Turnipseed; five children; lived in Bennetts, Miami County, Indiana. Many of this family moved to Halstead, Kansas.

Hannah Hoover—b. August 26, 1820; m. William Cook; seven children.

Catherine—b. October 12, 1821; d. April 10, 1876; m. Daniel Waymire (b. January 8, 1825; d. January 18, 1898); lived in Montgomery County, Ohio; five children.

Children of Daniel and Rachel (Waymire) Hoover:

Jacob Hoover—b. February 11, 1798; d. April 11, 1861; buried in Mount Hope Cemetery, Athens, Indiana; m. Sarah Curtner (?), b. 1802, d. ——; lived in Carroll and Fulton Counties, Indiana; 2 children.

Frederick Hoover—b. January 22, 1800; d. August 23, 1858; m. Sophia Curtner (b. 1800; d. January 22, 1875); buried in Argos Cemetery, Indiana; 7 children.

---

[1] This list of children and all the lists that follow to the "Children of Jacob and Sarah (Curtner) Hoover" are the grandchildren of Jacob and Elizabeth Hoover, and the great-grandchildren of Andrew and Margaret (Fouts) Hoover.

Daniel Hoover—b. September 2, 1801, d. April 25, 1863; m. Sarah Coble (b. September 11, 1801; d. January 4, 1862); minister, Christian Church, in Carroll County, Indiana; two children.

Elizabeth Hoover—b. February 11, 1804; d. March 8, 1820; m. Jesse Hutchins (1797-1863); lived in Wabash County, Indiana; nine children.

Mary Hoover—b. January 24, 1810; d. early; m. John Cox (1800-1855); lived in Cass County, Indiana; three children, including Andrew J. Cox and Mrs. Ezra (Matilda) Jones.

Sarah Hoover—b. August 9, 1811; d. January 10, 1871; m. Philip Woodhouse; lived in Cass County, Indiana; six children; descendants live near Twelve Mile, Cass County, Indiana.

Susannah Hoover—b. April 24, 1814; d. July 20, 1851; m. Isaac Newman; lived at Denver, Miami County, Indiana; six children.

Children of John and Elizabeth (Jeffries) Hoover:

Alexander Hoover—b. November 5, 1805; d. October 5, 1851; m. Malinda Gwinn (1815-1902); five children.

Henry Hoover—b. January 17, 1807; d. November 9, 1873; m. Sarah Curtis, daughter of James and Elizabeth (Byrket) Curtis; buried in Mount Hope Cemetery, Fulton County, Indiana; nine children.

Mary Hoover—b. January 21, 1809; d. December 11, 1891; m. Lewis Prill (1804-1876); buried Athens, Indiana; six children.

John Hoover—b. March 22, 1811; d. 1850 (?); m. Mary Arnold; lived in Tippecanoe County, Indiana; five children.

Elizabeth Hoover—b. June 26, 1816; d. January 20, 1884; m. Edward Friback; lived in Tippecanoe County, Indiana; one infant child.

Jacob Hoover—b. 1818; d. 1882; m. (1) Maria Ann Earl; six children; m. (2) Martha M. Weir; two children; lived in Tippecanoe County, Indiana.

Samuel Hoover—b. March 10, 1823; d. August 11, 1871; m. Sarah Koffel; lived in Iowa; five daughters and one son.

Levi Hoover—b. July 31, 1825; m. Lydia Nicewander; lived in Nebraska; three children.

David Hoover—b. December 22, 1827; m. Adanath Bell;

lived in Tippecanoe County, Indiana; five children.

Lemuel Hoover—b. September 3, 1830; m. Katherine Parvis; lived in California.

Children of Elizabeth (Hoover) and Austin Davenport:

Eliza Davenport—m. George Love; lived in Indianapolis.

Henry H. Davenport—b. 1821; m. Mary Laton; shoemaker, Boone County, Indiana; six children, two of whom served in Civil War; grandchildren live in Decatur, Illinois.

Mary Davenport—b. 1824; m. Andrew Hopkins; lived at Zionsville, Indiana; four sons, two of whom served in Civil War.

Milton S. Davenport—b. March 2, 1830; m. (1) Mary I. Gates; m. (2) Mrs. Julia Ann Debruiler; m. (3) Mrs. Mary J. (McCenziel) Law; Zionsville, Indiana; many children.

William Davenport—b. 1833; m. Mary Ann Ballinger; carpenter, Boone County, Indiana.

Children of David and Rebecca (Bonine) Hoover:

Jacob Hoover—b. May 27, 1808; m. Sarah Lowe; lived at Ottumwa, Coffey County, Kansas; eight children, of whom two sons, Martin B. and John J., served in the Civil War.

Isaac Hoover—b. August 1, 1810; d. 1866; m. Susan Lane; lived in Coffey County, Kansas; seven children, one residing in Indiana; Mrs. Rosalie Maines, living on College Avenue, Indianapolis, is a descendant.

Mary Hoover—b. May 27, 1812; d. 1903; m. Elijah Cross; lived at Zionsville, Indiana; ten children.

Children of Joseph and Elizabeth (Young) Hoover:

Henry Hoover—d. 1868, in Hamilton County, Texas; m. Mary Peery; six children.

Ephraim Hoover—b. 1813; m. Julianna ———; lived in Polk County, Iowa; nine children.

Joseph Hoover—b. October 10, 1816; d. December 22, 1837; m. Mary Nance; lived in Randolph County, North Carolina; eleven children.

Jacob Hoover—(no data)

Andrew Hoover—(no data)

Dolly Hoover—m. Joseph Pool; lived in Randolph County, North Carolina; thirteen children.

Polly Hoover—b. 1816; m. Larkin (?) Arnold; lived in North Carolina.

Eliza Hoover—b. 1815; m. William Rush; four children.

Sallie Hoover—m. William Prevo.
Tenie Hoover—m. Daniel Davis.
Margaret Hoover—m. Andrew Johnson.

Children of Samuel Clark and Sarah (Jeffries-Eller) Hoover:
Alexander F. Hoover—b. 1826; d. 1872; m. Mary Ellen Carpenter; three children, including Samuel Carpenter Hoover, Winthrop Avenue, Indianapolis.

Samuel Atwood Hoover—b. 1834; d. 1916; m. Jessie Sluss; two children, one of whom is Fred P. Hoover, of Bloomington, Indiana.

Children of Nancy (Hoover) and Chesley Ray:
Nettie Ray—b. October 6, 1818; m. Franklin Imbler (1818-1880); buried in Eagle Village Cemetery, Boone County, Indiana; three children.

John Ray—b. May 2, 1822; d. May 22, 1902; m. Jane Jennings; lived at Zionsville, Indiana; three children, including Chesley Ray, (b. September 29, 1845; d. October 27, 1915; m. Eliza Franklin; Civil War service; lived at Trader's Point, Indiana).

William Ray—b. 1824; d. 1900; m. Nancy ———; lived in Wisconsin.

Children of Andrew and Nancy Hoover:
William Wesley Hoover—b. 1826; d. 1907; m. Cassia Sloan, (b. 1833); grocer in Indianapolis; four children, including the late Elgin J., grocer on Schurman Avenue, Indianapolis.

Jacob Niles Hoover—b. 1831; m. Martha ———; lived at Russellville, Putnam County, Indiana; three children.

Children of Jacob[2] and Sarah (Curtner) Hoover:
Eli Hoover—born Sept. 20, 1820; d. Jan. 1, 1862; buried in Mount Hipe Cemetery; m. Mary Jane Lowe (b. June 1, 1826; d. Sept. 1, 1852) four children; m. (2) Sarah Moore (b. 1839).

Sarah Hoover—b. 1835; m. Richard McIntyre; no children.

Son of Elizabeth (Hoover)[3] and Jesse Hutchens:
Daniel Hutchens—b. Feb. 22, 1820; d. Jan. 27, 1896; m. Jemima Jones; nine children.

---

[2] This Jacob Hoover who married Sarah Curtner is a son of Daniel and Rachel (Waymire) Hoover, and the grandson of Jacob and Elizabeth Hoover.

[3] This Elizabeth Hoover who married Jesse Hutchens is a daughter of Daniel and Rachel Waymire Hoover, and a granddaughter of Jacob and Elizabeth Hoover.

The Jonas Hoover Family
John M. Burkett

The father of Jonas Hoover was Andrew Hoover (Andreas Húber) who was born on Jan. 29, 1827, at Ellerstadt in the Palatinate. Andrew died in 1794 in Randolph County, North Carolina. Arriving in the United States on Sept. 9, 1738, he married Margaret Fouts (Pfautz) in Lancaster County, Pennsylvania, in about the year 1745. Shortly thereafter, Andrew and his wife went to Maryland, locating between the present towns of New Windsor and Union Bridge in Carroll County. The land acquired here was on Pipe Creek. Two Fouts families settled nearby at nearly the same time. In about the year 1763, all three families sold their lands and migrated to North Carolina where they acquired land on the Uwharrie River. These lands were in that part of Rowan County which later became Randolph County.

Numerous descendants of Andrew Hoover came to the Northwest.[1] Among them were many who were descended from Jonas Hoover, his eldest son. A number of these settled in Indiana. Jonas Hoover[2] was born in 1748 (possibly in 1746), and died on June 15, 1828. He married Rachel Briles, the date of whose birth is not known. She died on Jan. 28, 1843, at Back Creek, in Randolph County, North Carolina.

Children of Jonas and Rachel (Briles) Hoover:

John Hoover—b. 1780; d. Feb. 16, 1851; m. (1) Millicent Winslow (d. Sept. 27, 1842); m. (2) Rachel Whisehunt (b., 1800, Randolph Co., N. C.)

Davied Hoover—b.——; d.——; m. Polly——; lived in N.C.; about seven children.

Elizabeth Hoover—b. 1776; d. 1850; m. Valentine Waymire (b. 1870; d.——); lived at Independence, Warren County, Ind.

---

[1] Andrew and Margaret (Fouts) Hoover had thirteen children: Jonas, Andrew, Jacob, Daniel, John, David, Peter, Henry, Elizabeth, Rachel, Susannah, Mary Catherine.

[2] This is not the Jonas Hoover whose family was treated in an article by Dr. William M. Reser (*Indiana Magazine of History*, March, 1937, XXXIII, 101-104). That Jonas Hoover was a son of Daniel Hoover, a grandson of Andrew Hoover, and nephew of the Jonas Hoover whose family is dealt with in the present article. The information now presented has been gathered from the notes of Dr. Reser and the writer who have done much research on the Hoover family. It is believed that this is the first time that data relative to the family of the elder Jonas Hoover have been published. For facts relative to Andrew Hoover, see Major Calvin Kephart, *National Genealogical Magazine*, 1929; Grace Julian Clarke, "Andrew Hoover comes to Indiana", *Indiana Magzine of History* (Dec., 1928), XXIV, 223-224.

Andrew Hoover—b. 1780; d. 1852; m. Catherine——in N. C.; no children.

Hannah Hoover—b. ——; d. ——; m. Samuel Hardister in 1806.

Nancy Hoover—b. 1785; d. ——; m. Moses Mills (d. near Fishers, Hamilton Co., Ind., 1840); four or five children, who left Hamilton Co. between 1850-1860.

Rachel Hoover—b. ——; d. ——; m. Miller Davis. (Two grandchildren, Winslow and James H. Davis, lived at Emporia, Kansas).

Mary Hoover—b. 1795; d. 1879; m. Daniel Warren (in War of 1812); lived near Carmel, Ind.

Children of John[3] and Millicent (Winslow) Hoover:

Jonas Hoover—b. Jan. 13, 1802; d. Jan. 16, 1896; m. Mary Newby (b. Jan. 18, 1803; d. July 15, 1878); migrated to Hamilton Co., Ind., 1832, and to Spring Creek Tp., Mahaska Co., Iowa, near Oskaloosa about 1842; six children.

Gulielma Marie Hoover—b. Nov. 22, 1806; d. Apr. 16, 1873; m. Stephen Hinshaw (b. July 3, 1803; d. Sept. 25, 1854); migrated to Hamilton Co., Ind., 1833; buried at Carmel, Indiana, Cemetery.

Rachel Hoover—b. May 23, 1809; m. Johnson Gibson (b. 1790; d. April, 1857); lived in Hamilton Co., Ind.; eight children. One child remained in Indiana, Sarah Gibson (m. Isaac N. Beeson). A grandchild of Isaac N. and Sarah (Gibson) Beeson, Mrs. Frank T. Sink is in business in Carmel, Ind. The children of Johnson and Rachel (Hoover) Gibson, other than Sarah, migrated to Kansas.

Elizabeth Hoover—b. Dec. 26, 1811; d. ——; m. Isham Partis. The family left Hamilton Co., Ind., for the West after 1850.

Millicent Hoover—b. Nov. 18, 1817; d. Feb. 25, 1848; m. Milton Burns; lived in N. C.

Caroline Hoover—b. Mar. 31, 1819; d. Feb. 16, 1852; buried at Carmel, Ind.; m. Farley Miller; four children.

John Hoover—b. Aug. 30, 1821; d. May 2, 1892; m. Elizabeth Whisenhunt; lived in N. C.; quakers or friends; ten children.

---

[3] John Hoover, eldest son of Jonas and Rachel (Briles) Hoover and grandson of Andrew and Margaret (Fouts) Hoover.

Eleazor Hoover—b. Dec. 12, 1823; d. 1903; m. Augustina Gibson; lived in Ind., Ia., and Mo.; one child.

Alfred Marsh Hoover—b. Dec. 21, 1826; m. ——; ten children; lived in Randolph Co., N. C.

Children of David[4] and Polly Hoover:

Adam Hoover—b. 1808; d. 1879; m. Catherine——; lived in Randolph Co., N. C.; eight children.

Andrew Hoover—b. 1811; d. 1888; m. Nancy Young; lived at Baker's Corner, Hamilton Co., Ind., and in Lyon Co., Kan.

Jacob Hoover—b. 1813; d. 1894; m. Elizabeth Jane Robbins (b. 1834; d. 1898); lived at Point Isabel, Ind.; two children.

Children of Valentine and Elizabeth[5] (Hoover) Waymire:

Absalom Waymire—b. 1795; d. ——; five children.

Frederick Waymire—m. Mary —— (b. 1799; d. 1843); lived in Warren Co., Ind.; six children.

Isaac Waymire—m. Rachel—— (b. 1805; d. ——; lived in Madison Co., Ia.; eight children.

Solomon Waymire—b. 1811; d. ——; m. Louisa Walters; lived in Nemaha Co., Neb.; nine children.

Alexander Waymire—b. 1816; d. 1895; m. ——; two children.

Samuel Waymire—(no data in regard to birth, death or marriage); eight children.

Jacob Waymire—b. 1822; d. 1897; soldier in Civil War, Forty-eighth Indiana; m. Elizabeth Lovejoy (b. 1822; d. 1896); U. B. preacher (last charge at Neodesha, Kan.); fifteen children.

Children of Daniel W. and Mary[6] (Hoover) Warren:

Ruth Warren—b. 1814; d. 1888; m. Ezekiel Clampitt; lived at Sheridan, Ind.; nine children.

William Stewart Warren—b. 1825; d. 1904; m. Ruth B. Carey (b. 1832; d. 1927); druggist at Carmel, Ind.; three children.

Rachel Warren—b. 1821; d. 1863; m. Thomas Mills; lived at Cicero, Ind.; ten children.

---

[4] David Hoover, second son of Jonas Hoover and brother of John Hoover.
[5] Elizabeth Hoover, daughter of Jonas Hoover and sister of John and David Hoover.
[6] Mary Hoover, daughter of Jonas Hoover and sister of John, David and Elizabeth.

Zina Warren—b. 1831; d. 1917; m. Isabella Thomas; three children (Mrs. Emma Puckett, of Carmel, Ind., is one of the three).

Mary Ann Warren—b. 1834; d. 1915; m. Edwin Harvey (b. 1833; d. 1917); lived at Carmel, Ind.; six children (Mrs. Lee R. Pfaff of Carmel, Ind. is one of the six).

Daniel W. Warren, Jr.—b. 1839; d. 1929; m. Julia Ann Mitchener; two children (Mrs. Martha J. Ward of Indidianapolis is one of them).

Angeline Warren—b. 1842; d. 1925; m. (1) John Gray; m. (2) Levi Jackson; lived at Sheridan, Ind.; six children by John Gray.

Susan Warren—b. 1828; d. 1910; m. William Lindley; one child.

Children of Stephen and Gulielma Marie[7] *(Hoover) Hinshaw*:

Millicent Hinshaw—b. Oct. 15, 1827; d. Mar 22, 1887; m. Ellis Willis Jessup (b. Nov. 15, 1824; d. Mar. 26, 1909); lived at Plainfield, Ind.; thirteen children. (Among the thirteen are: Dr. John T. Jessup, Elwood, Ind.; and Mrs. Frank W. Weer, Anderson, Ind. Further details can be furnished).

Andrew Hinshaw—b. Jan. 10, 1829; d. Nov. 9, 1911; m. Sarah Ann Hiatt; lived at Emporia, Kan.; eight children.

John S. Hinshaw—b. Mar. 3, 1830; d. Dec. 13, 1916; m. (1) Jemima Sanders; m. (2) Mary Jane Cruse; no children by first wife, but ten by second wife. (Among the ten are: Mrs. Martha A. Woodward, Lapel, Ind.; John C. Hinshaw, Carmel, Ind.; and Lemuel H. Hinshaw, Zionsville, Ind.)

Thomas Hinshaw—b. Feb. 26, 1832; d. Sept. 5, 1872; m. (1) Susannah O. Dimmitt; m. (2) Julietta Evans; m. (3) Lydia Davis; four children—one by first wife, two by second wife, and one by third wife. (Living now are: Franklin P. Hinshaw, Carmel, Ind.; and Perry Hinshaw, Indianapolis, Indiana.

Enos Hinshaw—b. June 12, 1834; d. Jan. 5, 1900; m. Martha R. Haines; seven children (Albert A. Hinshaw of Carmel, Ind., is one of the seven).

---

[7] Gulielma Marie Hoover was a daughter of John Hoover and a granddaughter of Jonas Hoover.

William Henry Hinshaw—b. Dec. 6, 1839; d. Aug. 3, 1909; served in Civil War; m. Anna M. Barnett; lived in Kansas; four children.

Rebecca Hinshaw—b. Sept. 6, 1841; d. ——; m. George Pruitt; buried at Westfield, Ind.; eight children.

Martha Hinshaw—b. Dec. 20, 1844; d. Jan. 22, 1901; m. (1) Smith Estes; m. (2) Stephen H. Rich; three children by second marriage.

Ira Hinshaw—b. Mar. 22, 1847; d.——; m. Gulielma Hiatt; lived in Kansas; three children.

Children of Adam[8] and Catherine (——) Hoover:

Rebecca Hoover—b. 1829; d. ——; m. Thomas Lambeth; lived in N. C.; three children.

David Y. Hoover—b. 1831; d. 1900; soldier in Civil War; Thirty-fourth Indiana; m. (1) Nettie Rush; m. (2) Sarah Harvey; m. (3) Rachel Victoria Hoover; lived at Fairmount, Ind.; three children by first marriage and four by third marriage; children live in Chicago.

William H. Hoover—b. 1832; d. 1894; m. Sarah Newby; lived in Randolph Co., Ind.; ten children (D. Sherman Hoover who lives in Washington, D. C., is one of the ten).

Alson Hoover—(no data in regard to birth, death, or marriage); lived in N. C.; three children.

Isaac Hoover—(no data in regard to birth, death, or marriage); lived in N. C.; two children.

Andrew L. Hoover—no data.

Alexander A. Hoover—b. ——; d. ——; m. Sarah Etta Hoover; lived at Caldwell, Idaho; no children.

Lucinda Hoover—b. ——; d. ——; m. Al Ridge; lived in N. C.; three children.

Children of Andrew[9] and Nancy (Young) Hoover:

Thomas Hoover—b. 1834; d. 1904; m. Katherine Briles; lived in Hamilton Co., Ind.; six children (Rachel Victoria Hoover, third wife of David Y. Hoover (see above) was one, as was Andrew S. Hoover of Fisherburg, Ind.)

Alexander Hoover—b. 1836; d. 1913; m. Rebecca J. Ridge; lived at Hortonville, Ind.; five children (William H. Hoover, Township assessor, Hortonville, is one of them).

---

[8] Adam Hoover, son of David Hoover and grandson of Jonas Hoover.
[9] Andrew Hoover, son of David Hoover, was a brother of Adam Hoover.

Margaret Hoover—b. ——; d. ——; m. Dolphus Finnel; lived at Emporia, Kan.; one child.

Susan Hoover—b. 1844; d. ——; m. Jacob C. Beals; lived in Hamilton Co., Ind.; seven children.

David Hoover—b. ——; killed in Civil War, Eighty-ninth Indiana.

Nancy Jane Hoover—b. 1848; d. ——; m. Henry Johnson; lived at Sheridan, Ind.; ten children.

The Hughes-O'Neill Family
IDA HELEN MCCARTY

The Hughes and O'Neill families intermarried in Ireland for many generations. The name O'Neill is illustrious in the annals of Ireland, Wales and Spain. The first Earl of Tyrene was created in 1542 at Greenwich. The Hughes family in early days was an off-shoot of the O'Neill clan.

Thomas Hughes married his first cousin, Bridget O'Neill. Both Thomas and Bridget were entitled to the Hughes Coat of Arms. They came to America to escape religious persecution in Ireland, and settled in Loudon County, Virginia, in the year 1739, bringing with them the brother of Thomas, Felime (or Felix) Hughes. They came from Inver, Ireland, which is in Donegal County, Ulster. There they left great estates and many relatives. The father of these sons was Felime (or Felix) Hughes, who remained in Ireland.

Children of Thomas and wife Bridget O'Neill were: Felix, John and Thomas. Felix, the eldest, was born in Inver, in 1723. He married Cintha Kaighn, an only daughter, and had four sons and two daughters. John (or John Hugh) married Mary Hunter of Loudon County, Virginia. The record of the line of Thomas may be found in *Memoirs of My Family*, by Thomas Hughes (Baltimore, 1880). Thomas and John are named in the Leesburg charter as incorporators of that town on the Patomac. Felix died in Green County, Pennsylvania, in 1805. The Hughes family had wealth and became large landowners, first in Virginia and later in Pennsylvania. They retained house servants whom they brought from Ireland.

Felix Hughes built and maintained a blockhouse at a place near Carmichaelstown in that part of Westmoreland County, Pennsylvania, that subsequently became Washington County. In a later division of Washington County the area containing the town became Green County. Reference is made to this blockhouse in a memorandum of Captain Isaac Craig's march from Carlyle to Fort Pitt. Captain Craig was in command of a detachment of Proctor's artillery and stores in 1780. The memorandum states that the said command reached the Felix Hughes place on June 21. A descendant, Thomas Hughes of Baltimore, speaking of his ancestors, Felix Hughes and son James, relates that the Hughes family settled east of Fort Duquesne, where Felix Hughes built and maintained the blockhouse already mentioned for the protection of families of the settlement from Indians.[1]

Felix and Cintha (Kaighn) Hughes had four sons and two daughters. The family migrated to Indiana. The sons were James, Thomas, Barnett and John. The name of one of the daughters was Elizabeth; that of the other is not known.[2] It was because of persecutions endured by the families in Ireland from English rulers and officers that the O'Neill and Hughes families were glad to aid in the struggle of the American colonies for independence. They were fighting Irish. Felix Hughes and three of his sons, James, Thomas and John, fought in the Revolutionary War. The father served as a private,[3] enlisting on August 7, 1777, in Captain Adam Foulke's Company of third-class militia, then in the service of the United States under the command of Jonathan B. Smith. Felix Hughes also served in Captain Jeremiah Fisher's Company, Philadelphia militia, commanded by Colonel William Bradford.

Children of Felix and Cintha (Kaighn) Hughes:

James, the eldest son, was born in 1750. He married Cassandra Dunn (Scotch parentage; b. Jefferson County, Pennsylvania) in 1772. He erected a stone mansion for his wife. The first white settlers, not far from Carmichaelstown were the Hughes, Swann and Heller families. James Hughes was one of the first school teachers in this part of Pennsylvania. He was also tutor for sons of wealthy families in that

---
[1] *Pennsylvania Archives*, Fifth Series, III, 968-69; S. B. Nelson, *History of Baltimore* (1898), 482; Thomas Hughes, *Memoirs of My Family* (Baltimore, 1880).
[2] These are the grandchildren of Thomas and Bridget (O'Neill) Hughes.
[3] *Pennsylvania Archives*, Sixth Series, I, 61, 494.

part of Pennsylvania. He owned several slaves and was a man of exceptional ability. He was the first Commissioner of Green County, Pennsylvania. The year 1796 was the most prosperous of his life, for in that year he inherited much land in Kentucky from his brother John (killed by Indians not far from Shelbyville, Kentucky), and also much land in Indiana which John had received for his Revolutionary service in "taking the Illinois." This land was part of that on which the present city of New Albany stands.

James Hughes enlisted in the third Pennsylvania Regiment, under Colonel Hazen, on November 13 or 15, 1776, and was transferred to the Commander in Chief's Guards.[4] He reënlisted on December 27, 1781. Dr. Carlos E. Godfrey, in his *History of the Commander in Chief's Guards* (Washington, D. C., 1904), gives the signatures of most of the men comprising the Guards. Among them is the signature of James Hughes, which checks with the signature on an original lease made by him to Andrew Rude, on the fifth day of March, 1792, for land in Cumberland Township, Washington County, Pennsylvania. Dr. Godfrey shows that James Hughes was transferred to the Chief's Guards on March 20, 1780. James Hughes, who had lived a useful life, died at the home of his son-in-law, Jacob Burley, near Waynesburgh, Pennsylvania, in 1807. He was buried in the O'Neill burying ground, in the vicinity of Carmichael, or Carmichaelstown, Green County, near the grave of his father, Felix Hughes. This is the burial place of many of the O'Neill and Hughes families, of those who came to America prior to 1739 and of many who came later.

Thomas Hughes, the second son, married Elizabeth Swann, of Loudon County, Virginia.

Barnett, the third son, removed to Kentucky and left many descendants.

John Hughes, the youngest son, went to Kentucky also, and was killed by Shawnee Indians in 1780. He never married.

Elizabeth, one of the two daughters, married William Hunter, a Revolutionary soldier. They removed to Kentucky. Information relative to the second daughter is lacking.

---

[4] *Ibid.*, Fifth Series, III, 779, 934.

James and Cassandra (Dunn) Hughes had nine children. Among them were: Thomas, Felix, or Pheline (b. 1774; m. Mary Donnelly; large family); Mary (b. Mar. 2, 1878; m. Jacob Burley, or Burleigh, near Waynesburgh, Green County, Pennsylvania).[5]

Children of Jacob and Mary (Hughes) Burley:[6]

Cassandra—m. Rezin B. Howard, at Cameron, Va. (now W. Va.).

James—m. (1) Mary Alexander; m. (2) a sister of Mary Alexander, at Moundsville, Virginia (now W. Va.): member of the Virginia Legislature and the Convention of 1860.

Cintha—m. Jefferson T. Martin (United States Marshall for the western district, and later member of the Legislature of W. Va. from Moundsville).

John—m. (1) ——— Clark; m. (2) Olle Cameron.

Tamer—m. Joseph Hicks, or Hix.

Sarah—b. 1805; d. 1847; m. William Jackson Howard (brother of Rezin B. Howard, who married her sister, Cassandra).

Elizabeth—d. early.

Joshua—m. Catherine Roseberry (his cousin) of Wheeling, Virginia (now W. Va.).

Mary—m. Bernard Connelly.

Thomas—m. ——— Cameron.

Martha—m. ——— Bellton.

Children of William Jackson and Sarah (Burley) Howard: Alfred Taylor, William Jackson, Jr., Joshua, Samuel, Maria, Ellen, Virginia, Eliza, Anne, Sarah, Margaret, Jane.[7] All of these children married and many of their descendants live in Ohio and Indiana.

William Jackson Howard, Sr., was the son of Samuel (b. 1770; son of Rezin and Esther Ashbrook Howard of Hamp-

---

[5] These are the grandchildren of Felix and Cintha (Kaighn) Hughes, the great-grandchildren of Thomas and Bridget (O'Neill) Hughes.

[6] These children of Jacob and Mary (Hughes) Burley were the grandchildren of James and Cassandra (Dunn) Hughes, the great-grandchildren of Felix and Cintha (Kaighn) Hughes, and the great-great-grandchildren of Thomas and Bridget (O'Neill) Hughes.

[7] These are the grandchildren of Jacob and Mary (Hughes) Burley, the great grandchildren of James and Cassandra (Dunn) Hughes, the great-great-grandchildren of Felix and Cintha (Kaighn) Hughes, and the great-great-great-grandchildren of Thomas and Bridget (O'Neill) Hughes. The author, Ida Helen McCarty, is the daughter of Marshall B. and Ida Helen (Douthett) McCarty.

shire, Virginia). Samuel came *via* covered wagon to the home of his son Robert George Howard in Indiana. He died there at the age of ninety-two, and is buried in the Masonic Cemetery, at Montpelier, Blackford County, Indiana. William Jackson Howard, Sr., moved to Athens County, Ohio, and there Sarah (Burley) Howard, his wife, died. She is buried in the Howard Cemetery ("Concord"), near Trimble, Ohio. Following her death, he married Sarah Alderman, a widow, and they came to Blackford County, Indiana. Adjoining their farm, between Pennville, Jay County, and Montpelier, was the farm of Robert George Howard, his younger brother. William Jackson Howard, Jr., married Sinai Carpenter of Noble County, Ohio. Their daughter, Alice Ida Howard, married William Alexander Douthett of Morgan County, Ohio. Their daughter, Ida Helen Douthett, married Marshall B. McCarty. They live in Pennville, Indiana, today.

The Kennerly Family
Katharine Cushman Hoke

Samuel and Ellen (or Ellin) Kennerly settled in Orange County, Virginia, in 1735, and later in Culpeper County, in what is now Rappahanock County, Virginia. Samuel Kennerly's will is dated October 22, 1749, and that of Ellen, his wife, is dated October 28, 1753, both done in Culpeper County.[1]

Their son, James Kennerly, married Elizabeth James, daughter of John James. They moved from Culpeper County after 1762, to Augusta County, Virginia, near Waynesboro, on the south fork of the Shenandoah River. A certified copy of the will of James Kennerly, dated June 23, 1797, may be found in the County Clerk's office, Augusta County, in the file case marked "Old Unrecorded Deeds."

James Kennerly, son of James and Elizabeth (James) Kennerly, was born on August 3, 1734, and died in 1827. He married Susannah Long, who was born on December 9, 1747. He seems to have preceded his father to Augusta County, Virginia. He was in Captain Robertson's Company

---

[1] This account is taken from the unpublished story, "The Cushmans of Sullivan County, Indiana, and Related Families, Kennerly, Sherman, Rundle," compiled by Katherine Cushman Hoke. A typewritten copy of the manuscript is on file in the Indiana State Library.

of Virginia Militia in 1777 and 1778, as shown by entries (pages 71, 81, 82, 100, 101, 102, 142, and 222) in the military record book of the proceedings of the court martial of that district, in the City Clerk's Office at Staunton, Virginia.

Children of James and Susannah (Long) Kennerly:[2]

Philip—b. Oct. 18, 1769; m. June 19, 1794, to Jane Carthy. They moved to Logan County, Kentucky, in 1807, where Philip died on Oct. 5, 1821. His wife died in 1837. They had six children.

John—b. Oct. 18, 1771; m. Aug. 13, 1796, to Catherine Harpine, daughter of his father's second wife. They moved to Logan County, Kentucky, where he died before 1829. The widow and children probably moved to Sullivan County, Indiana. Their daughter, Catherine Kennerly, married David Cushman on January 8, 1837, in Sullivan County, Indiana.[3]

James—b. March 23, 1774; m. (1) April 3, 1806, to Lucy ————. The ceremony was performed by his brother, the Reverend Philip Kennerly. They had one daughter who died young. James married second a Mrs. Rebecca Bowen (nee Withers) near Charleston, South Carolina. They moved to Tuscumbia, Alabama. Four children were born to them.

Joseph—b. Dec. 23, 1775; m. Mary Christian. They lived near Lynchburg, Virginia, and later moved to Patrick County, Virginia. They had no children.

Mary—b. Feb. 10, 1780; m. March 3, 1801, to John Ewell, of Albemarle County, Virginia. They moved to Tennessee in 1847.

Catherine—b. Aug. 2, 1782; m. May 19, 1803, to Mathew Robertson. They moved first to Kentucky, then to Washington County, Indiana. They had nine children.

James Kennerly, son of James and Elizabeth (James) Bennerly married (2) Mrs. Mary Harpine (*nee* Bear), widow of Thomas Harpine. Mary Bear was born on Jan. 11, 1760.

---

[2] These are the grandchildren of James and Elizabeth (James) Kennerly and the great-grandchildren of Samuel and Ellen Kennerly. The birth dates are from the family Bible now in possession of a descendant in Philadelphia. In the author's copy of this article, the maiden name of the wife of the third son (James) of James and Sussannah (Long) Kennerly is given as *Lucy Kennerly*.

[3] Catherine Kennerly was the grandmother of Katherine Cushman Hoke, author of this article.

Children of James and Mary (Bear-Harpine) Kennerly:[4]

Thomas—b. Jan. 22, 1790; a Methodist minister; m. Ann Carnagie, whose mother inherited Greenway Court, seat of Lord Fairfax, in Virginia; three children.

Susan—b. Jan. 1, 1792; m. (1) Jan. 17, 1809, to James Clemmons. Genevieve Yost, of Topeka, Kansas, is a descendant of Susan Kennerly by her marriage to James Clemmons (Clemens). Susan Kennerly's second husband was a man by the name of Weaver whose full name is not known.

Samuel—b. Jan. 31, 1794; a Methodist minister; m. Mrs. ———— Lafferty, of Leesburg, Virginia; lived on his father's old homestead; died there in 1870; seven children.

Jacob—b. April 5, 1796; a Methodist minister; m. Amanda Cravens; moved to Shelby County, Indiana; three children.

Elizabeth—b. Aug. 20, 1798; never married; d. during the Civil war.

Jane—b. Sept. 7, 1800; m. Sept. 28, 1820, to her cousin, Henry Bear; moved to Missouri.

Ann—b. Jan. 7, 1804; m. John Withers Bowen in South Carolina; moved to Alabama, later to Logan County, Kentucky, and still later to Arkansas; d. there in 1864; three children.

Children of John and Catherine (Harpine) Kennerly:[5]

————, a daughter; m. Seth Cushman, son of Seth and Nancy (Rundle) Cushman (b. 1806, in New York). They had no children. Seth, Jr. m. (2) Mary Wolverton (b. 1826, in Indiana). They had four children by this marriage.

Catherine—b. April 30, 1810, in Logan County, Kentucky; m. Jan. 8, 1837, to David Cushman, in Sullivan County, Indiana. He was born Jan. 17, 1812, at Onondaga, New York, came to Indiana about 1816, and died on March 10, 1876. Catherine died on Feb. 16, 1888, at Sullivan, Indiana, at the home of her daughter, Marie Buff. David Cushman and his wife Catherine (Kennerly) are both buried in the Mann Cemetery, in Turman Township, Sullivan County, Indiana. Catherine was a charter member of the Christian

---

[4] See Note 1

[5] These are the grandchildren of James and Mary (Bear-Harpine) Kennerly; the great-grandchildren of James and Elizabeth (James) Kennerly; and the great-great-grandchildren of Samuel and Ellen Kennerly. These children were not only the grandchildren of James and Mary Kennerly through their father, but the grandchildren of Mary (Bear-Harpine) Kennerly through their mother, who was a daughter of Mary (Bear) Harpine by her first marriage.

Church at Big Springs, near their home. Children: Thomas (b. Nov. 19, 1837); Arbaces (b. Sept. 27, 1839); Caroline (b. April 29, 1842); Maria (b. Dec. 31, 1847); Harriet (b. Aug. 8, 1844; d. March 3, 1845); John K. (b. Feb. 8, 1847; d. Feb. 16, 1847); Nancy Ann (b. July 23, 1850; d. March 1, 1851); Mary Catherine (b. Jan. 28, 1852; d. Nov. 6, 1871).

Harriet—d. 1873; aged 68 years; m. Parkeson Sherman (d. 1863; aged 56 years). Both are buried at Mt. Pleasant Cemetery, Terre Haute, Indiana. This record was found in the courthouse at Terre Haute, in file box 41. Children: Mary Catherine (b. Aug. 1, 1836; d. 1923; m. John Newton Drake); Albert Law (m. Jan. 5, 1876, to Mary Foxworthy); George Sherman (m. Emma Overholser).

Arbaces Cushman—second son of David and Catherine (Kennerly) Cushman, was born on Sept. 27, 1839, near Graysville, Sullivan County, Indiana, on the David Cushman farm. He enlisted in the Civil War on Sept. 27, 1861, as a private in Co. I, Second Regiment, Indiana Volunteer Cavalry. He was promoted to sergeant, and received an honorable discharge at Indianapolis on Oct. 4, 1864. He then entered Jefferson Medical College at Philadelphia from which he was graduated in 1869. On March 23, 1871, he married Mary Gray (b. December 15, 1845; dau. Joseph and Nancy Sherman Gray; d. Nov. 29, 1915). Arbaces Cushman died on April 8, 1909. Both he and his wife are buried in the Mann Cemetery, Turman Township, Sullivan County, Indiana.

Children of Arbaces and Mary (Gray) Cushman:[6]

Katharine—b. Dec. 31, 1871, at Graysville, Indiana. She attended Union Christian College and the Indiana State Normal School. On Apr. 14, 1896, at Jeffersontown, Kentucky, she married Fred Hoke (b. Aug. 9, 1870). He was the son of Andrew Jackson and Mary Frances (Snider) Hoke; three children.

Joseph—b. Aug. 23, 1873, d. Sept., 1874, at Graysville, Indiana.

Grace (twin sister of Joseph)—b. Aug. 23, 1873, d. Sept., 1876, at Graysville.

---

[6] These are the grandchildren of John and Catherine (Harpine) Kennerly, the great-grandchildren of James and Mary (Bear) Harpine Kennerly, the great-great-grandchildren of James and Elizabeth (James) Kennerly; and the great-great-great-grandchildren of Samuel and Ellen Kennerly.

Ethel—b. Aug. 25, 1876, at Graysville; attended Union Christian College, Merom, Indiana; m. on Nov. 17, 1899, in Sullivan County, Walter Turman (a dentist, of Marshall and Harrisburg, Illinois) ; two children.

Guy Arbaces—b. June 14, 1882, at Graysville; d. March 17, 1934; m. June 21, 1903, to Harriet Turman (dau. Return Jonathan and Anna Wible Turman); six children.

Children of Fred and Katherine (Cushman) Hoke:[7]

Cushman J.—b. Jan. 25, 1897, at Graysville, Ind.; graduate of DePauw University; attended Harvard University; m. Margaret Shoptaugh, March 26, 1899 (dau. Frank and Margaret Hillis Shoptaugh of Greencastle, Ind.)

Frank—b. March 26, 1899, at Graysville; graduate of Swarthmore College; m. Elizabeth Marmon (dau. Walter and Annie Hall Marmon), Oct. 18, 1924; one daughter.

Mary—b. Aug. 5, 1901, at Sullivan, Ind.; graduate of La Salle Seminary, Auburndale, Mass.; m. Perry W. Lesh (s. of Charles and Ora Wilkins Lesh), Sept. 3, 1921, at Indianapolis; two children.

Children of Walter and Ethel (Cushman) Turman:[8]

Katherine—b. May 3, 1900, at Marshall, Ill.; m. James Lyman Schill, Dec. 26, 1922; both graduates of Butler University; three children.

Joseph Austin—b. April 15, 1906, at Marshall, Ill.; m. Frances Paddock; three children.

Children of Guy Arbaces[9] *and Harriet (Turman) Cushman:*

Paula Mozell—b. Sept. 1, 1904, at Graysville; m. Lee Sills, Aug. 6, 1926.

Arbaces Edward—b. Mar. 6, 1908; m. Clarice Gibson of Danville, Ind., Aug. 17, 1932; one son.

Virginia Katherine—b. Feb. 23, 1910, in Texas; m. George Whitmore, July 23, 1928; three children.

Max Turman—b. Feb. 25, 1913; d. Aug. 12, 1914, at Graysville.

Maxine Lucile—b. Aug. 12, 1915, at Graysville.

John Pershing—b. Jan. 1, 1919.

---

[7] These are grandchildren of Arbaces and Mary (Gray) Cushman.
[8] These are also grandchildren of Arbaces and Mary (Gray) Cushman.

[9] Guy Arbaces Cushman was a brother of Ethel (Cushman) Turman and Katherine (Cushman) Hoke. His children were, or are, grandchildren of Arbaces and Mary (Gray) Cushman.

In the foregoing family history only the descendants of James Kennerly (m. Susannah Long) son of James and Elizabeth (James) Kennerly have been given. The elder James Kennerly and his wife (dau. of John James) had the following additional children: Reuben, William (served under George Matthews in the Revolutionary War), Benjamin, Thomas, Samuel, Mary, Elizabeth (m. ——— Poindexter), Kitty (m. ——— Craig).

Mary (sister of James Kennerly, Jr.) was born in 1736 and lived until 1834. She married George Strother (b. 1732; brother of Captain John Strother). Mary's second husband was Patrick Lockhart.[10] Of the three children of George and Mary (Kennerly) Strother, John and George died without issue, but Mary Strother, the daughter, married Col. George Hancock. A granddaughter of Colonel and Mrs. Hancock, Henrietta Preston, became the first wife of Albert Sidney Johnston, and, after her death he married her cousin, Elizabeth Griffin, another granddaughter of Colonel and Mrs. Hancock. A daughter of Colonel and Mary (Kennerly) Hancock, Julia Hancock, married William Clark, of the famed Lewis and Clark expedition and brother of George Rogers Clark. General William Preston of Kentucky was a grandson of Col. George and Margaret (Strother) Hancock.

[10] Mary (Kennerly) Lockhart is mentioned in her father's will as *Mary Lockhart*. Miss Annie Kennerly of Lewisburg, Ky., is the historian of the Kennerly Family. She is the great-granddaughter of James Kennerly, son of the elder James Kennerly, who was in turn the son of Samuel Kennerly who came to Virginia in 1735.

The Light Family

Lester D. Prewitt

Jacob Light is the first of this family that can be located. In 1790, he was living in South Carolina, the only person bearing the name *Light*. In 1818, he died in Anderson Parish, South Carolina. His wife died earlier. His estate roll (No. 393) in Anderson Parish, mentions his son Tyce (Mathias) who was born in South Carolina on June 7, 1769. He moved to Kentucky after 1802. Then, in 1807, he settled in Harrison County, Indiana, where he died about 1826 (estate box

No. 49). He was married in South Carolina to Mary Catherine Moore, who was born in that province on February 12, 1774, and died in Clay County, Indiana. She was the daughter of Hugh Moore. Her grave is in Franklin Township, Owen County, Indiana.

The children of Tyce (Mathias) and Mary Catherine (Moore) Light were: Abner, Hugh M., Isreal [sic], Robert, Isaiah, Fountain, Baird, Hester, and Anna. Robert, perhaps the youngest child, was born in 1810. Isreal, who came to Clay County, Indiana, in 1819, married Elizabeth Russell. No definite records have been found relative to Fountain, Isaiah, Hester (who married a Johnson), or Anna (who married a Wright).

Abner Light, son of Tyce (Mathias) and Mary Catherine Light, was born in South Carolina on February 6, 1795, and died on November 30, 1848. He married Elizabeth Burkett, who was born in North Carolina on September 13, 1796. She died on July 27, 1881.

Children of Abner and Elizabeth (Burkett) Light:

Washington Light—m. Sarah Maniers; three children (Rose, Anna, and Ella).

Tyce (Mathias) Light—m. Emily Jane Franklin on June 30, 1850; six children (Lou, Delia, Peggy, Jefferson, Lee, and Jane).

Isreal Light—b. in Owen County, Indiana, Dec. 3, 1824; m. (1) Elizabeth Vaughn, Jan. 15, 1852; two children (names not known); m. (2) Nancy Gooden, Apr. 23, 1857; children (Minerva, Mahala, Laura, Clara, Elizabeth, Alice, Anderson, Walter).

Mary Light—m. John Pickard; children (no data).

Pauline Light—m. John McAdoo; one son (Charles McAdoo).

Elizabeth Light—m. Owen D. Leach; children (no data).

John Light—m. Eliza Defoe; children (William, James M., John A., Samuel, Mary T., Millard Fillmore, Isabel, Charles, Ella E., Frank).

Lorenzo Dow Light—b. Feb. 28, 1827; d. Oct. 15, 1865; Union soldier (Corporal in Co. F., Ninety-seventh Regiment, Ind. Vol.; m. Barbara Kenayer, April 15, 1852 (Barbara—dau. George and Mary Harriet Kenayer; b. June 2, 1824; d. July 27, 1894).

Children of Lorenzo Dow and Barbara (Kenayer) Light:

Mary Maria Light—b. Jan. 3, 1853; d. July 18, 1935; unmarried.

Angeline Light—b. May 13, 1854; d. May 11, 1884; m. Lafayette Scott (d. Mar. 8, 1926).

Charles Wesley Light—b. Aug. 4, 1855; d. Oct. 1, 1856.

Jane Elizabeth Light—b. No. 2, 1857; d. July 27, 1933; m. John W. Watts (b. 1859; d. Jan. 6, 1935).

Sarah Isabel Light—b. Feb. 17, 1859; d. 1934; m. John P. Payne (b. 1856; d. 1936).

Zachariah Light—b. July 2, 1860; m. Elizabeth Burton (b. Feb. 4, 1861; d. Nov. 2, 1932).

Hugh M. Light, fourth son of Tyce and Mary Catherine Light, was born on December 26, 1801, in South Carolina. He settled on Eel River in Owen County, Indiana, in 1825, and transferred to Franklin Township in the same county later. He was a soldier in the Union army, first, in Company F, Ninety-sixth Indiana Volunteers, and later in Company B of the Thirtieth Regiment. He was first married to Barbara Harriet ————, and second, to Mrs. McConnell Dyer (Oct. 2, 1867). He died on March 19, 1885. There was one child by the second marriage, Ida, who died before her father.

Children of Hugh M. and Barbara Harriet Light:

Sanders, Eliza and Huldah Light—d. before 1884 (each of the three).

Albert Light—killed in battle at Stone River, Tennessee.

Blewford Light—m. Martha Jane Burton Jan. 27, 1853; d. at Kentland, Indiana.

Elizabeth Light—m. John Burton (b. in 1835; d. in 1920).

Fountain Light—b. June 2, 1842; d. in Owen County, Indiana; m. Sarah A. Kay, Oct. 18, 1863.

Baird (Bird) Light was born in Kentucky on August 13, 1805, and died in Owen County, Indiana, on February 6, 1867. He was buried in the Leach Cemetery east of Freedom, Indiana. On January 3, 1828, he married a widow, Catherine Lucas Lake, in Clay County, Indiana. The courthouse was destroyed by fire, but a record of the marriage is in the Reinstatement of Marriage Book (p. 67), and is mentioned in Charles Blanchard's *Counties of Clay and Owen, Indiana* (p. 67).

Children of Baird (Bird) and Catherine (Lucas) Light:

Tyce Light—b. Nov. 30, 1837; died in 1908; m. Sally Ann Packard.

Polly Light—m. Francis B. Martin.

Retta Ann Light—m. John E. Ooley.

Elizabeth Light—b. July 8, 1840, in Clay County, Ind.; d. Mar. 8, 1903, in Adair Co., Ia., m. De Wilton S. Prewitt on Aug. 5, 1866; children: William Roscoe, Leonard Wilson, Joseph Allen, Edna, George Ashley, Albert Wesley. Elizabeth Light and her husband were buried side by side in the cemetery at Fontanelle, Iowa.

THE LUCAS FAMILY

George Lucas moved from North Carolina to Clay County, Indiana, by way of Kentucky, in which county he entered land in Jackson Township on October 5, 1832, according to the Clay County Tract Book and Blanchard's *Counties of Clay and Owen* (pp. 287-288). Both he and his wife must have died before December 2, 1836, when his son Solomon Lucas and his daughter Catherine Lucas and her husband, Baird Light, joined in a deed to convey the land which he had entered in 1832 as shown by Clay County Deed Books, G, F, and I.

Children of George Lucas and wife:

Solomon Lucas—b. Sept. 24, 1816, in Kentucky; d. on July 12, 1883, in Harrison Township, Adair Co., Ia., to which he had migrated.

Catherine Lucas—m. Baird (Bird) Light on Jan. 3, 1828, in Clay County, Ind. Catherine Lucas married first a man named Lake. A daughter, Sally Ann Lake, married James Clark. Tradition says that Catherine Lucas married Lake in Kentucky and that he died while migrating to a new home. The young widow made a return journey to her father's home, partly on foot, carrying her baby. On the way, she obtained a ride on a load of peaches with a man who was driving to a town where she had friends. These friends took her back to her folks.

George Washington Lucas—m. Sarah ———.

Berry Lucas—m. Elizabeth ——— of Brown County, Ind.

Thomas Lucas—m. Jemima ———.

It is probable that a daughter of George Lucas married Oliver P. Cofer. It is also possible that a son died in Monroe County near Bloomington who had a son Thomas Lucas, a dentist.

THE MOORE FAMILY

Hugh Moore was born September 15, 1750, according to his pension application. He was married in South Carolina in 1772 or 1773 to Sarah French. Their daughter, Mary Catherine, was born in South Carolina on February 12, 1774, probably in Pendleton County. She was married to Tyce (Mathias) Light. She died in Clay County, Indiana. She was called "Polly" and had two brothers, John, born in 1778, and William, born in 1780.

Hugh Moore, father of Mary Catherine Moore, enlisted as a private in the Revolutionary War in the fall of 1776. He was from Pendleton County, South Carolina. In 1780 he was elected a lieutenant in Captain Parsons' Company, and served until November, 1782. On July 23, 1832, when granted a pension, he was living in Warren County, Kentucky. On September 19, 1838, his widow, while living in McCracken County, Kentucky, was granted a pension. They had fifteen children. The youngest, Marium, was born on May 15, 1805. She married Edward Stevens. Joseph, the second child, was born in May of 1776. Another of the sons was John A. Moore. Hugh Moore's pension number is W8473. In the Stub Entries to Indents Issued in Payment of Claims against South Carolina. Growing out of the Revolution (Book X, Part II, 162) is the record of a warrant (No. 3637) in payment for services of Hugh Moore as lieutenant in Roebuck's Regiment. Lieutenant Moore served in Captain John Nuckols' Company in February, 1771, during the Cherokee Indian uprising in Tryon County, North Carolina, as indicated in the *Records of North Carolina* (VIII, 517-518).

Hugh Moore was married to Sarah French who was born in March, 1754, in Jersey City, New Jersey. She died on January 2, 1854, in McCracken County, Kentucky. Her death certificate is on record in the Historical Building at Frankfort, Kentucky. She was a daughter of Joseph French who married Hannah Van Horne, granddaughter of William Olden. This marriage, the record of which is printed in the *Proceedings of the New Jersey Historical Society* (LIV, 198), occurred in New Jersey in 1749. The family moved from the Raritan River in New Jersey, to South Carolina in 1749, possibly to York County.

The Ross-Welles Family
WILLIAM ROSS TEEL

Our family Bible has a record of the marriage of Ephraim Ross to Annah Welles at Gilead Church, Hebron, Connecticut on April 20, 1786. These persons were my maternal great-grandfather and great-grandmother.

The Welles family has been traced back to Adam De Welles, Baron, who was born in Lincolnshire, England, about 1265. He was summoned to Parliament on February 6, 1299, and made a Baron; also he was appointed constable of Rockingham Castle and warden of its forests. He died in 1311.

As Baron he was allotted the Welles coat of arms, which was a lion rampant, sable with tail forked, and motto *Semper Paratus*, meaning "Always Prepared." We trace our Welles ancestry from him down to Thomas Welles I, who was born in Dudley, Worcestershire, England, January 10, 1694. Thomas Welles I, with his father, sailed from England to America in 1712, landing at Saybrook, Connecticut. There he was married on "ye 13th of May, 1716," to Elizabeth Merrill. In 1735 he moved to Gilead Parish, Hebron, Connecticut, purchased land, reared a large family, and died on February 4, 1760, aged 66 years. His wife, Elizabeth Welles, passed away at Hebron on December 2, 1770. Thomas and Elizabeth Merrill Welles had seven sons. One, Thomas II (our line), was born in Hebron on August 27, 1723, where he lived the rest of his days. In the old Church of England graveyard at Hebron, I copied this epitaph from his gravestone.

> In memory of Thomas Welles, who died
> September ye 1st 1805 aged 82 years and three days
> Full four score years I saw—
> But held this world in Vane—
> Resigned to natures law—
> Immortal life to gain.

Thomas Welles (II) was married at Hebron, Connecticut, in the Gilead Church on November 8, 1743, to Thankful Rowles, who bore him two children and died April 28, 1750. He later married Prudence Shipman on November 14, 1750.

The town of Hebron was incorporated in 1707, the site being purchased from Joseph Uncas, an Indian Sachem. Thomas Welles, the elder, was Captain of the town's first militia, and Captain John W. Welles, his brother, was one of a committee to divide the parish into school districts (Town Record, 60).

Bateman Welles, our ancestor, was the son of Thomas and Thankful Rowles Welles. He was born in Hebron and was evidently a man of substantial means for the time. He held many offices in the parish. He was married on February 12, 1769, to Annah Carter. There were seven children by this marriage. The first child, Annah Welles, born November 18, 1769, was our ancestor.

The first land entry in the name of Bateman Welles (Vol. 6, p. 272) is a deed to him of twenty and one-half acres from Mercy Post, dated February 8, 1776, and acknowledged before John Ashley, Jun., Justice of the Peace. He sold this parcel of land on November 4, 1793, to Shipman Welles (his son) for twenty pounds. In 1788 he bought sixty-two acres of Thomas Welles II (Vol. 8, p. 66), and sold this land for two hundred thirty pounds in 1793.

Annah Welles, my maternal great-grandmother, was married to Ephraim Ross at Gilead Church, Hebron, Connecticut, on April 20, 1786; she was at the time not quite twenty years old. By this union there were eleven children. The third child, Russell Ross, was my grandfather. He was born on April 16, 1791, at Cambridge, New York, a small town near the Vermont state line.

The Ross family was from Scotland, and Ephraim's father, Alexander Ross, served in the British Navy. He was stationed at Halifax, N. S.; his army record shows that he was appointed Second Lieutenant of the Twenty-third Company of Marines, Feb. 25, 1755, and became successively First Lieutenant and Captain of an independent foot-company which, however, was disbanded in 1768, when he was placed on half pay. The family always insisted that he was lost at sea. The tradition was that Ephraim Ross when a boy ran away from Halifax in the winter time and was picked up in a starving condition by Indians with whom he wintered, afterwards coming to New York. It is evident that after their marriage Ephraim and Annah (Welles) Ross moved to New York, as their son Russell was born in Cambridge, New York.

Land entries show that Ephraim Ross resided and owned property at Onondaga Court House, New York, a few miles south of Syracuse. The land was on the Onondaga Indian reservation, and the title was acquired by the United States some time near 1800. I have located exactly, by county deed records at Syracuse, the land on which the Ross family lived. The house, of course, disappeared long ago.

It may be interesting to tell why the family emigrated to Indiana. Just prior to the war with Great Britain in 1812, Ephraim Ross with the help of his brawny sons took a contract to build a brick schoolhouse for the commissioners at Onondaga Court House. This family were brick-makers and carpenters. When war was declared, the building was about half done; and Ephraim found that on account of the war, living, labor, and material so greatly advanced in price that if he were to finish the building, it would ruin him financially. He went to the commissioners, explained his predicament, and offered to give them the building half completed if they would release him from the contract. After a lengthy conference, he was told to proceed with the building, and that he should have a fair profit. He mortgaged or sold part of his holdings to pay for material and labor, thus finishing the building, whereupon the commissioners repudiated their verbal promise and held him to the contract. As a consequence, he lost practically everything he had.

The next four years must have been hard ones. The family was large, six boys and four girls, and some of the children were very young. The third son, John Ross, came to Indiana sometime after 1815 and located at Vincennes. The family decided to join him, gathered together their few belongings, and went to Pittsburgh in the late fall of 1818. The entire family with the exception of John Ross and possibly Russell took a keelboat down the Ohio river, and opposite Wheeling, West Virginia, the boat was frozen in the ice for most of the winter. They probably landed at "Yellow Banks," as Henderson, Kentucky, was then called, and traveled overland to Vincennes.

The family, with the exception of John, after a time went across the Wabash river to Crawford County, Illinois. They did not prosper there, as the soil was "crawfish ground," wet and marshy. The entire family had chills and ague. Terre Haute on the Fort Harrison prairies in Vigo County, Indiana, had been founded in 1816. Glowing reports of the place caused the Ross family to move there in 1821.

The children of Ephraim and Annah Welles Ross came with regularity, it appears: Bate (Bateman), 1789; Betsey, 1791; Russell, 1793; Polly Ann, 1795; Nancy, 1797; John, 1799; Harry, 1801; James, 1803; Sally Anne, 1807; Alexander, 1809; Emeline, 1812. It is noticeable that several of the names come from the Welles family—Bateman, Betsy, Russell, Polly Ann and Sally Anne.

Ephraim Ross spent the rest of his life at Terre Haute and died there on September 29, 1850, at the age of 93 years. His wife Annah passed away fifteen days later, also aged 93 years. Both are buried in an old cemetery at Terre Haute.

Quoting *The History of Terre Haute* by Blackford Condit: "The Ross family came here before 1824. Their names appear among trades and tradesmen as the first brickmakers of the town. The second Court House was made of brick, and it is a well authenticated fact that in an early day, the Ross Brothers made the brick of the town." Russell, Harry, and James, however, in due time engaged in merchandising. They had a store on the west side of the square where they sold calico at twenty-five cents a yard like their brother merchants.

Members of the Ross family were Presbyterians and were among the first to become members of the first Presbyterian Church to be organized in Terre Haute. Ephriam Ross and his son Alexander joined the Presbyterian Church on May 2, 1832. The Congregational Church was organized in Terre Haute on Dec. 30, 1834, by the Rev. Merrick A. Jewett, and among the members were Russell and Alexander Ross; so it appears that some of the Ross family withdrew from the Presbyterian Church and affiliated with the Congregational Church thereafter.

Russell Ross, my grandfather, married Elizabeth Almey (Aimey) in Vincennes on Jan. 29, 1823. She was said to be of French descent, and some of the family spelled the name "Aimee." She was born in Ovid, New York, a quaint, little, old town midway between Lake Cayuga and Lake Seneca, the prehistoric home of the two most westerly tribes of the original five nations, the Cayugas and the Senecas. It appears her family must have migrated to Vincennes, as she married Russell Ross there. In order to distinguish Elizabeth Almey Ross, who was called "Betsy," after her sister-in-law, Betsy Ross, she was known as Betsy Russell. After the death of Russell Ross on Oct. 23, 1841, Elizabeth, his widow, lived in a house on the east side of Fifth Street, north of Cherry Street in Terre Haute, with her son Rea Ross and her daughter Isabel Russell Ross, who later married Frank Gulick, a druggist. Elizabeth died on Jan. 28, 1858. The children of Russel and Elizabeth Almey Ross were:

> Emilie R. Ross—b. Mar. 7, 1825.
> Jesse Harvey Ross—b. Sept. 11, 1826; d. in infancy.
> Welles Ross—b. Apr. 9, 1829; d. in infancy.
> Henry Ross—b. Dec. 29, 1830; d. in infancy.
> Hellen Ross—b. Feb. 13, 1833; d. in infancy.
> Rea Ross—b. Feb. 24, 1834.
> Hellen Elizabeth Ross—b. Feb. 2, 1840; d. in infancy.
> Isabel Ross—b. Jan. 24, 1841.

Emilie R. Ross married Henry Helms Teel in Terre Haute on Dec. 27, 1842, when she was not quite eighteen years old. His father, John Teel, came to Indiana from Blount County, Tennessee, about 1820. At that time Indiana, having recently been admitted to the Union in 1816, had no roads fit for wagon travel. Indian trails used by early emigrants were "blazed" between points of travel through an unbroken wilderness. It is barely possible that the family came up to Knoxville, Tennessee, and embarked from there on flat boats, which were used in those days, for the long journey down the Tennessee River to the Ohio, which it joins at Paducah, Kentucky. The tradition is that the trip was made overland from Kentucky to a location in Owen County, Indiana, near Spencer. As horses were scarce and high in price, it is not likely that they could have transported their belongings and given each a mount, so the women rode and the men walked. Father's sister Adeline told me that she recalled having ridden horseback in front of her mother on this trip.

The Teel family, shortly after arrival, located at Cataract

Falls on Mill Creek, a fork of Eel River in Owen County. John Teel built the first grist-mill in that part of Indiana. In connection with grinding corn and wheat, he added a sawmill, using the same power. The land was being cleared, and lumber was in much demand for building the homes of the settlers, who were arriving rapidly at that time. For many years there lay in the bed of the Creek just below the Falls near where the mill was located a small mill-stone, or burr, from the ruins of the mill. It was my intention to have it taken to my home, but the ground was purchased by General Lew Wallace, who took the stone to his home in Crawfordsville where it remains today.

John Teel was a private in the East Tennessee Volunteers and probably served in the War of 1812. His company was commanded by Captain James Gillespie. The discharge, dated January 15, 1814, was as follows: "This is to certify that John Teel, a private in my company of East Tennessee Volunteers, has performed a tour of duty commencing on the Twenty-third day of September, 1813, and ending on the first of January, 1814, and his hereby discharged," signed, "James Gillespie, Capt. E. T. Volunteers." The following from *Memoirs of Andrew Jackson*, published by Putnam Waldo in 1819, would seem to indicate that this discharge was from service in the Creek-Seminole war:

Andrew Jackson was appointed Major General of Militia in 1796, and was acting in this capacity, when in 1812, Congress authorized raising a Volunteer Corp of 50,000 men to serve one year of enlistment. Late in 1813 occurred the Creek uprising and the massacre at Fort Minns, and the Tennessee militia men, veterans of the late war with Great Britain, were called into service by Governor Blount to serve one year within two years after enlistment. This army consisted of two Divisions, one of West Tennessee, commanded by Major General Andrew Jackson, the other East Tennessee commanded by Major General Cocke.

Levi Teel, an uncle of John Teel, served as a volunteer with General George Rogers Clark at the time of his expedition into the Northwest Territory and capture of Kaskaskia and Vincennes, and was awarded as a private one hundred eight acres of land in the Clark Grant in Indiana for this service.

John Teel's wife, Rebecca (Skidmore) Teel, passed away several years after the events just noted, and he married a second time. The new wife, it is claimed, was not kind to the children. At any rate, Henry Teel ran away when a lad and came to Terre Haute, where he lived in the family of Judge Amory Kinney. The judge educated him, and, as he was very studious, he acquired a good education for the time. He later became a school teacher. Following his marriage to Emily (Emilie) Ross, the young couple moved to Carlisle, Indiana, where Henry taught school. Later they lived in Terre Haute, where he taught school at the "Old Benny Hayes" schoolhouse on North Third Street for a time.

Henry Teel died in Sunset, Texas, in 1891, and his widow (Emily Ross Teel) died in Terre Haute on May 7, 1911, aged eighty-six years and two months. She was born near Terre Haute, east of where the County Infirmary is now located, and resided there almost her entire lifetime.

In the eighteen-twenties, Indians, probably Miamis, often came down the Wabash in canoes, and the squaws sold hazelnuts, moccasins, and beeded work to the villagers in Terre Haute. Emily Ross had very red hair, which is greatly admired by the squaws. They would stop at the log house, and her mother would let them take the child and place her on a blanket under the trees, so they could admire her hair and clothes. One time they gave her two beaded purses, beautifully made, lined with Bayeta cloth. I have them among my relics. Bayeta cloth was the material used. The scarlet uniforms of the British officers of those days were unraveled by squaws and the thread was rewoven in decorating moccasins and lining beaded bags.

The children of Henry and Emily Ross Teel were: Anna, Grace, Frank, and William Ross. Anna Teel married Horace G. Burt. There were two children by this marriage, Russell Ross Burt and Arthur Burt. Grace Teel married John A. Tenney of Madison, Wisconsin, and died at Juneau, Alaska, on Feb. 1, 1900. Frank Teel married Mary Craig. There were no children. William Ross Teel, the writer of this family history, married Katherine West at Terre Haute in 1894. Two children were born to this union, William Ross Teel, Jr., who died in infancy, and a daughter who still lives.

There are few members of the Ephraim Ross family in Terre Haute and Vigo County today. The family was once among the most prominent of the County. The only living members of the family besides myself and son that I know of are:

Mrs. James McCall, daughter of Julia Ross Perdue, lives in California. Mrs. McCall has three children, Dorothy, Alexander, and Mrs. William Halstead. Mrs. Halstead lives in Louisville, Ky.

Sadie Gulick, daughter of Isabelle Ross Gulick, lives in Pasadena, Cal.

Sue Ross Hendricks, daughter of Edward Ross, lives in Oak Park, Ill., and has two children, Victor and Ross Hendricks.

Harry Ross, son of Edward Ross, lives in Sullivan, Ind. He married Maude Reed, and they have two children, Verne and Reed.

Indiana Branch of Shipman Genealogy

Contributed by

Mrs. Sylvan L. Mouser*

I 1 Samuel Shipman, Sr., came to Clark County, Indiana, soon after the War of 1812 in which he served from New Jersey. He was descended from early American families chiefly of English descent. He was the only son of David Shipman who d. 10-12-1787, Morris Co., N.J., and of his wife Elizabeth (Betsey) Tingley, whose ancestry is given in Raymon M. Tingley, *The Tingley Family* (Rutland, Vermont, 1910), 30. She m. 2nd 7-4-1790, Benjamin Bonnell, III.) David Shipman was one of the children of Jabesh (Jabez) Shipman, Sr., a Revolutionary soldier who d. 1781, will probated 12-9-1781, Morris Co., N.J., and of his wife Phebe Rogers who d. 11-16-1792, intestate Morris Co., N.J., and whose ancestry will be published later showing lines established in D.A.R., and D.A.C. Samuel Shipman, Sr., was b.c. 1787, Morris Co., N.J.; r. Clark to Floyd Co., Ind., before 1820; m. Clark Co., Ind., 9-11-1818, Lavina Ann (Luan) Hatfield who came to Clark Co., Ind., from Va. with parents 1816, b.c. 1798, Va., d.c. 1863, New Albany, buried Fairview Cem., sister of John B. Hatfield; children: a, John L., b, Samuel, Jr., c, Mary A., d, William Kelber, e, said to be a daughter perhaps named Martha, who d. no heirs.

II. 1 John L. Shipman, s. of I, 1; b. 11-20-1825, New Albany, Ind.; d. 1-27-1870, New Albany, buried Fairview Cem.; pattern-maker for machinery for many of steamboats on Ohio and Mississippi, particularly for that of the well-known "Robert E. Lee" which won the race; m. 1-1-1850, New Albany, Lucinda Evelyn Graham, b. 5-27-1827, near New Albany, d. 4-25-1898, New Albany, buried Fairview; children: a, Samuel Charles, b, Anna Vesta, c, Durett F., d, Edward Walter, e, Charles, f, Cassius C., g, James David, h, Harry.

---

* Mrs. Sylvan L. Mouser née Evelyn Mae Shipman is a resident of Indianapolis, Indiana. All material given is from documentary proofs such as Bible records, cemetery records, state, and county records.

For all their descent see "Graham Genealogy," in *Indiana Magazine of History* (Bloomington, Indiana, 1905-   ), XXXIX (1943), 210-220. See also Bible records on microfilm in the William Henry Smith Memorial Library of the Indiana Historical Society, Indianapolis, Indiana. This is the author's direct line.

2   Samuel Shipman, Jr., s. of I, 1; b.c. 1827/8, New Albany, Ind.; r. Jeffersonville, Ind.; d.c. 1889, buried Walnut Hill Cem., Jeffersonville; m. before 1853, Clarrissa Lovell (or Lovelace?), d. 1906, Indianapolis; children: a, Anne, b, Emma, c, Will, d, Mary, e, Sally, f, George, g, Ella, h, Charles, i, Harry, j, Dan.

3   Mary A. Shipman, dau. of I, 1; b. New Albany, Ind., 1832; r. New Albany, Little Rock, Ark., Moravia, N.Y.; d. Moravia, buried there; m. 1st John W. Harmonson before 1850, New Albany, d. c. 1860, Little Rock; children: a, Florence Luella, b, Anna Elizabeth, c, William W., d, Minnie A.; m. 2nd 1862, Timothy T. Taylor, New Albany, Ind., d. c. 1864; no chilldren; m. 3rd Moravia, N.Y., Hiram Ercanbrack, b. 1816, d. 1897; no children.

4   William Kelber Shipman (called "Kelby"), s. of I, 1; b. 5-6-1841, New Albany, Ind.; r. Normanda, Goldsmith, Tipton, Rossville, Ind.; d. Rossville, 10-7-1913, Civil War veteran, gov't marker; m. 1862, Mary Jane Lutz, b. 4-7-1843, d. 9-12-1905, dau. of Jacob G. Lutz; children: a, Thomas, b, Carolina Eliza, c, Jacob Lorraine, d, Orville Evert, e, Ada May.

5   May have been 5th child, Martha, who d. no heirs.

III 1-8 Children of John L. Shipman and Lucinda Evelyn Graham, see "Graham Genealogy," in *Indiana Magazine of History*, XXXIX, 210-220.

9   Anna Shipman, dau. of II, 2; b. 1853; d. 7-16-1934; not married.

10 Emma Shipman, dau. of II, 2; m. Harry Brown; children: a, Harry, Jr., b, Mattie.

11 William Kelby Shipman, s. of II, 2; b. 2-14-1862, New Albany, r. Indianapolis; d. 2-10-1943, Indianapolis; m. Lida Katherine Spaulding, b. 11-4-1861, Jennings Co., Ind., d. 10-19-1943, Indianapolis; children: a, Ethel Amelia, b, Edward Glen, c, Maud, d, Stella.

12 Mary Shipman, dau. of II, 2; m. Homer Ball; children: a, Lula, b, Leila, c, Marcus, d, Granville.

13 Sally Shipman, dau. of II, 2; d. c. 1888, r. Indianapolis; m. Henry Adams; children: a, Clara.

14 George Shipman, s. of II, 2; r. Louisville, Ky.; d. there, buried Cave Hill Cem.; m. 1st Sally Brown; children: a, name unknown; m. 2nd Lillian Chandler, 1-8-1917, Indianapolis; no children.

15 Ella Shipman, dau. of II, 2; m. Joe Freund; children: a, Lee.

16 Charles Shipman, s. of II, 2; r. Fairland, Ind.; d. c. 1945; m. 1st Emma Luebtan about 1892; children, a, Kelby; m. 2nd

Flora Belle Miller Johnson, 12-8-1895, widow of Frank Johnson; children: b, Charles Vern.
17 Harry Shipman, s. of II, 2; d. young no childlren.
18 Dan Shipman, s. of II, 2; b. c. 1875, d. 1900, no chilldren.
19 Florence Luella Harmonson, dau. of II, 3; b. 1850, d. 1905 Moravia, N.Y.; m. 1st James E. Ogden, Sr., New Albany, Ind., b. 1848, d. 1928, buried New Albany, Ind.; divorced after 1869; children: a, James E. Ogden, Jr.; m. 2nd before 1873, Corydon L. Arnold, b. 1847, d. 1904 buried Moravia, N.Y.; chilldren: b. Nora E. Arnold.
20 Anna Elizabeth Harmonson, dau. of II, 3; b. c. 1852/4; r. Grand Rapids, Mich.; d. c. 1918; m. John Benedict, d. c. 1922; no children.
21 William W. Harmonson, s. of II, 3; b. 1856; r. Moravia, N.Y.; d. 1927, buried there; m. Rosette Holden, b. 1850, d. 1935; no children.
22 Minnie A. Harmonson, dau. of II, 3; b. c. 1858/9; r. Niagara Falls, N. Y.; d. 1925 buried there; m. 1st before 1885, Andy Eldredge; divorced; children: a, John Eldredge (who took name of Bills); m. 2nd Newton Bills, d. 1931; no children.
23 Thomas Shipman, s. of II, 4; b. 1866; r. Clinton Co., Ind.; m. and divorced Lida Pence; no chilldren.
24 Caroline Eliza Shipman, dau. of II, 4; b. 1869; r. Danville, Ill., and Covington, Ind.; m. Simon Jacobs, 6-10-1889; children: a, Don.
25 Jacob Lorraine Shipman, s. of II, 4; b. 7-26-1873; d. 7-25-1874.
26 Orville Everet Shipman, s. of II, 4; b. 3-4-1876; r. Rossville, Ind.; m. Margaret Jane Mohler of Delphi, Ind.; children: a, Goldie Elizabeth, b, Artus Elwood, c. Pauline, d, Paul.
27 Ada May Shipman, dau. of II, 4; b. 4-18-1881; d. 1-22-1908; unmarried.

IV 1 Harry Brown, Jr., s. of III, 10; r. College Corner; children: a, Walter.
2 Mattie Brown, dau. of III, 10; d. infancy.
3 Ethel Amelia Shipman, dau. of III, 11; b. 3-16-1895, Indianapolis; r. Beech Grove; m. 5-31-1917, Everett Hunt, b. 3-25-1895, Richmond, Ind., s. of Oliver Hunt (family history in hands of sister, Dorothy Hunt, Indianapolis); children: a, Marjorie, b, Loren.
4 Edward Glen Shipman, s. of III, 11; b. 11-26-1895, Indianapolis; r. Indianapolis; m. 7-5-1917, Indianapolis, Pearl Wilkins, b. 11-8-1899, dau. of Charles O. Wilkins and Laura E. Moore; children: a, Ethel May, b, Mary Katherine.
5 Maud Shipman, dau. of III, 11; r. Duluth, Minn.; m. c. 1920, Martin Haggardy, Sr., who d. at sister's home Chicago July 1946, buried Indianapolis; children: a, Martin, Jr.
6 Stella Shipman, dau. of III, 11; b. 5-28-1899; r. Indianapolis; m. 10-8-1917, Hugh M. Anderson; divorced May, 1944; no children.

7 Lula Ball, dau. of III, 12; d. Madison, Ind., buried there; m. ——?; children: a, Irene, b, ——?, c, ——?
8 Leila Ball, dau. of III, 12; r. Philadelphia, Pa.; m. Carl Bates, Sr.; children: a, Carl, Jr., b, Granville.
9 Clara Adams, dau. of III, 13; b. c. 1888; r. Indianapolis, and Oil Dale., Calif.; m. Walter Minnick; children: a, Helen, b, Dorothy, c, Arthur, d, Viola.
10 ——? child of III, 14; d. infancy.
11 Lee Freund, s. of III, 15; r. Louisville, Ky.; m. Anna ——?; children: a, LaVerne.
12 Kelby Shipman, s. of III, 16; d. infancy.
13 Charles Vern Shipman, s. of III, 16; b. 11-23-1897; r. Fairland, Ind.; m. 1-8-1918, Agnes McDonough; children: a, Joan Theressa.
14 James E. Ogden, Jr.; s. of III, 19; b. 1869; r. Homer, N.Y.; m. Katherine M. Ammerman, b. 1870, d. 1928, buried Moravia, N.Y.; no children.
15 Nora E. Arnold, dau. of III, 19; b. 1873; r. Moravia, N. Y.; m. Millwood Fitch; no children.
16 John Eldredge Bills, s. of III, 22; née Eldredge but took name of step-father Bills; b. c. 1885; r. N. Y., and Fla.; m. Alice —? of Niagara Falls, N.Y.; no children.
17 Don Jacobs, s. of III, 24; r. near Covington, Ind.
18 Goldie Elizabeth Shipman, dau. of III, 26; b. c. 1903; r. Frankfort, Ind.; m. Dr. O. N. Childress, D.D.S., 1927; no children.
19 Artus Elwood Shipman, s. of III, 26; b. 1906; r. Plainfield, Ind.; m. 1st Della Mae Miller; children: *a, Linda Sue; m. 2nd Martha B. Vice, sister of H. Paul and Geneva Vice; no children.
20 Pauline Shipman, dau. of III, 26; b. c. 1911; r. Rossville, Ind.; m. 1931 Maurice C. Peters; children: a, Patricia Louise, b, Terry Joe, c, Kenneth Lee.
21 Paul Shipman, s. of III, 26; b. c. 1914; r. Superior, Mont.

V 1 Marjorie Hunt, dau. of IV, 3; b. 12-4-1918, r. Beech Grove, Indianapolis; m. 3-16-1937, Leo Skillman; children: a, Sandra Lee, b, Deanna Joyce.
2 Loren Hunt, s. of IV, 3; b. 4-15-1933; r. Beech Grove.
3 Ethel May Shipman, dau. of IV, 4; b. 4-26-1918, Indianapolis; r. Indianapolis; m. 6-26-1936, Charles E. Burks, b. 11-4-1916; children: a, Billy, b. Patricia Ann.
4 Mary Katherine Shipman, dau. of IV, 4; b. 3-15-1921, Indianapolis; m. 3-27-1943, Leland P. Lux, b. 1-30-1916; no children.
5 Irene—?, dau. of IV, 7; m. Joe Alte.
6 Helen Minnick, dau. of IV, 9; m. Dr. ——? and divorced; r. Indianapolis.
7 Dorothy Minnick, dau. of IV, 9; m. and r. Oil Dale, Calif.
8 Arthur Minnick, s. of IV, 9; m. and r. California.
9 Viola Minnick, dau. of IV, 9; r. Indianapolis.

10 LaVerne Freund, dau. of IV, 11; b. c. 1915, nun in Order of Sisters of Ursuline, Louisville, Ky.
11 Joan Theressa Shipman, dau. of IV, 13; b. 10-8-1927, Indianapolis; r. Fairland, Ind.
12 Linda Sue Shipman, dau. of IV, 19; b. 1-19-1934; r. Plainfield, Ind.

VI 1 Sanda Lee Skillman, dau. of V, 1; b. 3-16-1939; r. Beech Grove.
2 Deanna Joyce Skillman, dau. of V, 1; b. 2-19-1942; r. Beech Grove.
3 Billy Burks, s. of V, 3; b. 9-17-1937; r. Indianapolis.
4 Patricia Ann Burks, dau. of V, 3; b. 9-1-1946; r. Indianapolis.
(For the rest of the Shipman descendants of the fourth, fifth, and sixth generations see "Graham Genealogy," *Indiana Magazine of History*, XXXIX, 210-220.)

The Steele Family

HARRY H. MARTINDALE

The first known ancestor in this family is John Steele, called the trader, of Hampshire, Virginia. The name of his wife is not known. He died in Montgomery County, Kentucky, in 1810, and is buried in the old Springfield Presbyterian Churchyard. His sons were John, Jacob, Samuel, Henry and Solomon.

John Steele, the eldest son, was born on January 25, 1761. He served as a private in the Revolutionary War in Captain Michael Stump's Company of Colonel Muhlenberg's Virginia Regiment. He was engaged in the defense of the town of Richmond from the British, and, while marching to that place, was in a skirmish at Silver Creek. He enlisted in April or May, 1781. He later served three months under Lieutenant Blue, and was with the Virginia troops at the siege of Yorktown. John Steele's pension claim is S.17706, and the last payment was made on April 1, 1836. Among his heirs were: William R. Steele, Lewis County, Missouri; Solomon Steele, Morgan County, Indiana; Samuel B. Steele, Callaway County, Missouri. These are thought to have been his sons. John Steele lived in Hampshire County, Virginia, and moved later to Montgomery (now Bath) County, Kentucky. He was erroneously placed on the list of Johnson County, Indiana, pensioners; he lived and died in Morgan County, Indiana.

Henry Steele, son of John, the trader, was born about 1771, and was first married to Mrs. Prudence Scott, a widow with two daughters. She was the daughter of Anthony Badgley of Hampshire (or Hardy) County, Virginia. Henry Steele and his family joined in the migration of some one hundred families which went under the leadership of the Reverend David Badgley, brother of his (Steele's) wife, Prudence, to the vicinity of Belleville, Illinois, in 1797. In three or four years, Henry Steele and family joined his brother John Steele in Montgomery County, Kentucky. About 1831, the two families came to Morgan County, Indiana. The children of Henry and Prudence Steele were: Jacob, Jesse, Beuniah, Hardin, Larkin, Henry, Elizabeth, and Katharine (m. Asa Maxey in 1814 in Kentucky). The children of Henry Steele by his second wife were Albert, Prudence, and John. Henry Steele died in Madison Township, Morgan County, Indiana, in 1844. Solomon Steele, son of John, the trader, lived and died in Fleming County, Kentucky. Jacob and Samuel, sons of John, the trader, stayed in Virginia.

The Stewart Family
By Susan W. Atkins

Two men, both by the name of James Stewart, were members of the company commanded by Captain William Harrod, which formed the nucleus of the regiment, serving under Col. George Rogers Clark, in 1779, with the base of supplies at the Falls of the Ohio on the island opposite Louisville. These men were from that part of Orange County, Virginia, where Shepherdstown is now located. They went to Redstone Fort, in Washington County, Pennsylvania, with the troops that served in the French and Indian War. These Stewarts may have been at an earlier date in Little Cove, Cumberland County, Pennsylvania. One of the oldest lists (1750) in East Pennsborough, Cumberland County gives: Widow Stewart, Middletown, 1781; James Stuart, John Stuart, William Stuart. In Cumberland County, Pennsylvania, in the early period, there lived, John Campbell Stewart and Arthur Stewart of Peters Township.

The Cumberland County (1768) original tax list, in Carlyle Court House, Commissioner's Office, shows the following:

 Moses Stuart .... 50 a
 James Stewart .... 50 a, Air Township
 Wm. Herrod .... 80 a (10 clear), 2 Horses, 2 Cows
 John Herrod .... 50 a (10 clear)

Wills recorded in Jefferson County, Ky., at Louisville, (Book L, pp. 244, May 11, 1812) include a will of Steven (Stewart, as mention is made of his son, James Harvey Stewart). A plantation on Pleasant Run, adjoining the lands of Thomas Downs, James Stewart, William Goodwin, and ——— Weather (to James Harvey Stewart). The residue to his three children, James H. Stewart, Priscilla Stewart, Cincha Stewart. Witnessed by James Stewart, William Goodwin.

Thomas Downs, James Stewart and William Goodwin, were the first settlers in the Silver Creek district of Clark County and were original members of Silver Creek Church. Thomas Downs was a first Justice of General Sessions of Clark County, Indiana Territory, formerly part of Virginia, appointed by William Henry Harrison as soon as he received his own appointment as Governor of the Territory.

Pioneers of the Surber Family
Maude Surber Swisher

Isaac Surber and his wife, Artemacy Mayfield Surber, were pioneers of Owen County, Indiana. The Surbers originally came from some province of Germany. The family lived there in prominence until after the Reformation in the sixteenth century. Then the family gave up titles and possessions during a struggle for existence while suffering from persecution and repression. Finally they fled to Holland and from that country migrated to America. The first of the Surbers to cross the Atlantic, sailed from Rotterdam on May 29, 1735, on the ship *Mercury*. At this time came Henry Surber, fifty years old, Hendryk, sixteen, and Varena, five. Others who came to America later were: Hans Surber, who left Rotterdam on the ship *Priscilla* on September 11, 1742, and Johannes, who left on the ship *Halifax* on September 22, 1752.

The writer's branch of the Surber family settled in Virginia, Captain Adam Surber and Colonel Jacob Surber being the first of this line. Both served in the Revolutionary War. After the War, members of the family migrated to Pulaski County, Kentucky. Isaac Surber was born in Virginia. He married Artemacy Mayfield in Kentucky in 1829. They came to Owen County, Indiana, settling on land near Gosport. Here they lived for the remainder of their lives, and here on their farm they reared their family.

The Mayfield family, that early settled in Virginia, came from England. The Mayfield Coat of Arms dates back to 1684. It may be described as a lion's head cut off and holding in the mouth a mayflower, golden or bright yellow. In the front crest are small perpendicular, but bright red, lines. The honor was bestowed because the Mayfields had helped to feed the people in a crisis. There are several old manor houses in England, located in Sussex, Derbyshire, and West Surrey that once belonged to Mayfield families.

Mayfield in Sussex is a very old town with the ancient row of timbered buildings, beautifully designed. The Archbishop's Palace, with the tradtion of the famed St. Dunstan (925 to 988 A.D.), clinging to it, is there. Dunstan, when Archbishop of Canterbury, crowned princes at Mayfield.[1] John Mayfield, Sr., who served as a soldier throughout the Revolutionary War, was born in Albemarle County, Virginia. He died in Pulaski County, Kentucky, in 1816. He was the father of Artemacy Mayfield Surber, whose mother was Clarinda Pleasants Mayfield (1749-1821). The marriage of Clarinda and John Mayfield took place in 1767.[2]

Isaac Surber was born in Wythe County, Virginia, in 1789, and died near Gosport in 1849. His wife, Artemacy Mayfield Surber, was born on October 9, 1804, in Pulaski County, Kentucky. The marriage occurred on November 3, 1829, in Pulaski County. They came to Owen County in 1830. Mrs. Surber outlived her husband by fourteen years, dying on February 9, 1863. Both are buried in the cemetery near Gosport, where a monument marks their graves.

---

[1] Reuben Newton Mayfield, "History of the Mayfield Family," *Compendium of American Genealogy: First Families of America*, edited by Frederick Adams Virkus, II, 122. See also references to Mayfield family *ibid.*, III, IV.

[2] The Pleasants were from Virginia where they intermarried with the Randolphs. Artemacy Mayfield Surber had a brother, John Mayfield, Jr. (1768-1813), who married Mary Wolfe (1790-1748).

Children of Isaac and Artemacy Surber:[3]

1. Elizabeth Surber—b. Jul. 12, 1830; m. Richard Mugg, Oct. 16, 1851; d. Mar. 27, 1883. Children of Richard and Elizabeth Surber Mugg (all born near Qunicy, Owen County, Indiana, were: Jeremiah, Joseph Thomas, Isaac Newton, John H., George McClellan, Riley Morton, Belle V., Benjamin Franklin, Charles Surber, Henry Mayfield.

2. Mary Surber—b. Oct. 5, 1832; m. Joel Ogles, Oct. 18, 1861; d. Jan. 15, 1891. Children of Joel and Mary Ogles: James I., Elmer E., Iviena, Ulysses Surber. All deceased.

3. Thomas Surber—b. Dec. 76, 1834; m. Nancy Montgomery, Nov. 9, 1863; d. Jan. 28, 1909. Children of Thomas and Nancy Surber: Charles, Frank, Oda, John, Curtis, Gurd, Samuel.

4. Thressa J. Surber—b. Feb. 15, 1837; m. W. M. Walters, Oct. 16, 1852; d. Sept. 7, 1865. Children of this family unknown.

5. Henrietta Surber—b. Feb. 15, 1837; m. (1) Frederick Stierwalt, Dec. 10, 1864, and (2) Rev. Runyon. Henrietta died March 28, 1928, leaving no children.

6. Sarah E. Surber—b. Nov. 30, 1841; m. Thomas Seay, Dec. 25, 1859; d. Sept. 14, 1867. Children of Thomas and Sarah Seay: Lillie, James.

7. Clarinda Surber—b. Feb. 22, 1844; m. William Riley Mugg, Dec. 10, 1864; d. Feb. 13, 1926. William Riley Mugg was a brother of Richard Mugg, who married Elizabeth, sister of Clarinda. Children of William R. and Clarinda Mugg were: Javis, Mandiza, Mary Maude.

8. Henry Clay Surber—b. Nov. 30, 1846; m. Mary Elizabeth Day Mallicoat, June 6, 1868; d. Sept. 14, 1885. Children of Henry Clay and Elizabeth D. M. Surber: Maude, Artemacy Gertrude, Claude Clay, Parker Albert. Maude (or Mary Maude) and Claude Clay Surber are yet living, the last in Indianapolis, Ind. (P.O. Box 706). Maude married James A. Swisher and lives at 411 N. Main Street, Paris, Ill. She compiled the records of this family and also placed a tablet in their memory in the Riverside Cemetery, Spencer, Indiana, where Henry Clay and Mary Surber, her parents, are buried. She is a member of the Daughters of the American Revolution through the service of John Mayfield, Sr. (Number 270639).

---

[3] These records were filed in the State Library (Genealogy Section) by Miss Ura Sanders of Gosport, Ind. Miss Sanders is a descendant of Isaac Mayfield (brother of John Mayfield, Sr.) who was also a Revolutionary soldier. Names and dates of births, marriages, and deaths, are given as far as known.

The Thiebaud Genealogy
Julie LeClerc Knox

The Thiebauds are among the finest old French-Swiss families in Switzerland County. The first member of that family to come to America was Frederick Louis. He was born in the Swiss Canton of Neuchatel on October 4, 1767, where he later married Harriet Prater. To this union eight children were born in Switzerland—Emily, Julia, Charles, Justine, Phillipine, Augustine, and Justi.

In 1812, they attempted to emigrate to America but after three months on the water their provisions gave out and they had to return. While at sea, Justi died and was buried in the ocean. Shortly after their return, another son was born and also named Justi. In 1817, they again embarked for America, presumably, from Havre de Grace on the "Maria Theresa," arriving in New York six months later. They traveled by land from New York to the Ohio River. An open keel barge transported them down the Ohio. During this journey down the river, Justine is said to have fallen overboard several times. After encountering many dangers and hardships, they landed about three miles west of Vevay, where they built a home. The first home was replaced about 1860 by what is still a fine old house, known as the Thiebaud homestead and now occupied by Mr. and Mrs. Robert Gaudin. The latter being a descendant of the Thiebauds.

I Frederick Louis b. October 4, 1767, d. December 24, 1846, m. Harriet Prater b. April 15, 1777, d. June 7, 1844.

  A Emily d. m. Alois Backman d.; B Julia d. m. David Emanuel Pernet d., who built the Black Horse Tavern at Mt. Sterling, Indiana; C Charles m. Elizabeth Weaver d., m. Caroline Bersot d.; m. Mary Anne Hood d.; m. Zelie Bersot d.; Charles d. 1872. Children of his various wives: Julius, Alfred, John Louis, James, and Bedford.

    1 Julius d. m. Kate Long d. Children: Ella, Josephine, and Jennie. (After death of Julius, Kate m. James Anderson and had one son, Ed, b. about 1877 and was drowned while yet young.)
      a Ella d. unm. January 31, 1886; b Josephine d. m. Mr. Weaver d. No issue; c Jennie m. J. P. Carter 1887. She died about 1941, some years after her husband. Their only child, Scott m. Belle Raglan about 1937. No issue.

    2 Alfred m. Eleanor Dufour, December 25, 1862. She was born July 27, 1836, and died December 7, 1900, many years after her husband. Children: Clarence, William, Eleanor, Thomas, Callie, and Belle.

a Clarence b. November 19, 1863, m. Mary Hill. No issue. He d. February 16, 1908; b Wm. b. February 20, 1865, m. June 28, 1888, Julia Eldred. He d. November 21, 1907. One child, Bird, b. March, 1899, m. Joseph King. N.f.r.

c Eleanor b. October 1, 1866, d. September 30, 1911, m. John Porter. No issue. d Thos. b. March 30, 1868, d. January 26, 1926, m. May Dillman. Children: Dillman and Mildred.

I^1 Dillman b. December 20, 1893, m. Grace Brown, 1914. N.f.r. I^2 Mildred b. July 22, 1897, m. Dr. John Keeling, December 16, 1917. Children: A^1 John D. b. May 2, 1919; A^2 James D. b. October 1, 1922; A^3 Carol Lu b. November 10, 1924; A^4 Mary Anne b. January 24, 1929. Thos.' second wife was Margaret Cook. Nf.r.

e Callie b. September 27, 1869, m. Chas. Cowell, May 10, 1888. She d. January 13, 1899. Children: Edwin B., Alfred B., and Lucille.

I^1 Edwin B. b. March 15, 1889, d. July 27, 1889; I^2 Alfred B. b. February 24, 1891, d. August 2, 1911; I^3 Lucille b. October 23, 1892, m. W. Clinton Duval. Children, adopted: John Robert and Katherine. N.f.r.

f Belle b. November 6, 1871, m. Carter Fowler, November 6, 1894, d. 1943. No issue.

3 John Louis b. 1826, m. Margaret J. McCallum, 1849. She d. 1861. Children: Chas. O., Orlena, and Hugh M.

a Chas. O. b. 1852, m. Emma Harrington, 1873, both d. One child, Henry d. in infancy and Gertrude Harrington b. February 1, 1878, m. Mr. McDuff and d. 1944. No issue.

b Orlena d. unm. yrs. ago. c Dr. Hugh M. d. 1935, m. 1910 Lura Tilley, b. May 13, 1874, d. October 11, 1937. No issue.

John Louis m. second wife, Rizpah Bowers, October, 1863. She died 1870. Children: Minnie Elizabeth.

a Minnie Elizabeth b. 1864, m. Andrew J. Porter, June 8, 1887. He d. 1946. Children: Clair, Lela May, and Elizabeth. I^1 Clair d. 1906 at high school age; I^2 Lela May m. Claude Jacquart. No issue. I^3 Elizabeth m. George Stewart, 1931. One child, George Jr. about 17.

John Louis m. third wife, Mary J. Johnston. No issue. Both d. for years.

4 James d. m. Carrie Oliver d. Children: Zellie, Oliver, and Earl.
a Zellie m. Mr. Day; b Oliver m. about 1897 N.f.r.; c Earl m. N. f. r.

5 Bedford m. Nan Harris. Both dead. Two sons. N.f.r.

D Justine b. May 29, 1809, d. 1888, m. Ulysses P. Schenck September 30, 1830. He was b. May 16, 1811, and d. November 16, 1884. Children: Emily, Harriet, Benjamin Franklin, Andrew Jackson, Ulysses P. Jr., Julia d. at 14, George d. of yellow fever, "down the river," unm., and several d. in infancy.

1 Emily, first wife of Dudley P. Craig, died soon after m. One child, Uly.
    a Uly m. Mollie Davis about 1889. Children: Chester, D. P., Paul, and Richard.
        I^1 Chester m. ————— d. 1946, several children, N.f.r. I^2 D. P. m. ————— d. 1940. Children ————— Gordon unm, Bettie m. John Graham, John N.f.r I^3 Paul m. No issue N.f.r. I^4 Richard m. ————— His daughter, Louise m. and a son unm. N.f.r.
Uly has been d. some years and also his father.

2 Harriet d. m. J. B. Tandy 1855. Children: Carroll Schenck and Justine.
    a Carroll Schenck b. May 30, 1856, m. Jeannette Carpenter, January, 1889. He d. October 20, 1926. Children: Jeannette, Harriet, Elizabeth, Julia, Mary, Justine ————— all born within eight years.
        I^1 Jeannette unm.; I^2 Harriet m. Chas. Meng. Children: Chas. Jr., Harriet, and Caroline.
            A^1 Chas. Jr.; A^2 Harriet m. Marshall Tharp about 1940. Children: John Carroll, Julia Caroline, and Harriet Ellen.
        I^3 Elizabeth unm.; I^4 Mary m. George Sutton. Three sons in college: H. H. Carroll Tandy, and John Lind. I^5 Julia unm.; I^6 Justine m. John Campbell. No issue.
    b Justine b. 1858, m. Chas. Cook October 19, 1882. Children: Geo., Justine, and Miriam.
        I^1 Geo. d. m. Grace Erway. Children: Geo. Jr. (d. in infancy), James, Justine Anne.
            A^1 James. unm.; A^2 Justine Anne m. Sam Milan. Three children: Geo., Wm., and Tandy.
        I^2 Justine m. Morris Miller. Children: Justine and Caroline.
            A^1 Justine m. Jas. Shaub; A^2 Caroline m. Jas. Figley. Two children. N.f.r.
        I^3 Miriam m. Clair Reed. Children: Carroll Schenck and Corinne.
Justine d. m. a second husband, J.S.T. Walker, d. No issue.

3 Benjamin Franklin m. Celestine McCullough b. March 14, 1840, d. December 23, 1885. He d. in the seventies. Children: Eugenia, Justine, and Corinne.
    a Eugenia m. 1887, Horace Eddy. Both d. Children: Ben. d. from effects of World War I, Josephine, and Corinne unm.;
    b Justine m. Maurice Zook. Both d. One son, Henry m. Had a son, John and a dau. N.f.r.
    c Corinne b. about 1872, d. December 18, 1936, m. Theodore Dahlmann b. in Germany. He d. 1916. One child, Celestine m. Mr. Elliott.

4 Andrew Jackson b. 1842, d. 1899, m. Lutitia Craig about 1891. She died July, 1928, after her second husband, Wm. Fry, had been d. several years. No issue by either husband.

5 Ulysses P. Jr., b. October 21, 1851, d. April 30, 1892, m. May 29, 1872, Flora Hall. She d. 1938. One child, Pearl d. 1930. She m. Dr. Oscar Wainscott about 1895. He d. a few years ago. One son, Schenck d. about 1944, leaving a wife and three young daughters.

E Phillipine d. m. Thomas Allen Haskell d. Children: Lucy Harriet, Caroline Julia, Henry Alfred, Phoebe, Charles Allen, David Emanuel, George W., Elizabeth, and John Louis who died at two, and Thomas J. Henry Alfred died at six.

1 Lucy Harriet d. m. Henry Peters d. One child, Julia.
    a Julia b. July 5, 1848, d. April 18, 1914, m. John P. Porter b. September 27, 1845, d. September 28, 1923. Children: Sara b. February 17, 1869, m. Kit Phillips. She is still living. John b. April 2, 1870, d. May 26, 1935, m. March 18, 1894, Celia Long b. January 31, 1870. She is still living. Child, Woodson b. September 3, 1895, m. October 16, 1923, Mrs. Leona Scudder. No issue.
Lucy Harriet's second husband was Benjamin Sebastian d. Children: Benj., Chas., Lucy, and Harry d. in infancy.
    b Benj. m. children: Ethel who m. Mr. Stokes, and Alma, Irene, and Dorothy unm.; c Chas. m. Kate ———— one son, Howard; d Lucy m. John Kelley. Children: Mabel m. Mr. Hodson; Ruth m. H. B. Nier, one child, H.B. Jr., and Nina unm.

2 Caroline Julia d. m. Larkin Lanham d. Children: Lucy m.; Harriet, Walter, Opha, Jane, Irene. N.f.r.

3 Phoebe d. m. Jonas McKay d. Children: Stella, Emma, Grant.
    a Stella b. August 5, 1859, d. August 4, 1910 unm.
    b Emma b. September 5, 1868, m. Noah Oliver d. She d. October 5, 1943. Children: Bazil d. at 21 December 6, 1918; Phoebe m. Frank Wilson. No issue. c Grant b. March 30, 1864, m. Stella Danner, October 23, 1888. He d. July 21, 1938. Children: Wilbur, George, Mary, and Josephine.
    I[1] Wilbur m. Lillie Moreillon, October 20, 1913. Children: George and Don.
        A[1] George m. Bettie ———— a baby, Don. A[2] Don d. in plane crash in World War II.
    I[2] George unm.; I[3] Mary m. Orin Lockwood, May 5, 1931. Children: Joan 17 and Mary Inis 7; I[4] Josephine m. Robert Gaudin May 30, 1938. Children: Grant about 9 and Robert 7.

4 Chas. Allen d. m. Melissa Peters d. N.f.r.

5 David Emanuel d. 1936, m. about 1870 Josephine Grey d. Children: Maude and Edward.
    a Maude m. Chas. Pate about 1891. Children: Chas. and Sybil, unm.
        I[1] Chas. m. ————. Children: a boy and a girl. N.f.r.

b Edward d. m. Mrs. Harriet Wilson d. March, 1948. No issue. She had several children by a previous marriage.
David Emanuel m. second wife, Indiana Henry, January 1, 1885, who was born February 21, 1848, and who d. about 1937. One child, Caroline Henry who m. Harry Wilson Haskell, stepson of her half brother, Edward, who took his stepfather's name. No issue.

6 George W. d. 1925, m. Susan McKay d. Children: Harley, Hosea, Afra, and Fred.
   a Harley m. ————. Several children. He is d. N.f.r.
   b Hosea d. 1928, m. Lizzie Hukill d. No issue. Hosea m. second wife, Mrs. Lorraine Coates, 1924. No issue. c Afra b. about 1875, m. about 1893, Rev. Geo. Anderson, native of Australia. Both d. Children: Mona and Eva.
   I¹ Mona m. ———— Anita ———— 1923. One daughter, Helen b. 1927; I² Eva m. Mr. McCallum. Have three sons, about college age. The McCallums were missionaries in China for some time but now in U.S.
   d Frederick b. August 16, 1877, m. Nell Coghill, March, 1902, d. December 29, 1935. Children: Nelson Wayne and Lucille.
   I¹ Nelson Wayne b. May 14, 1904, m. Jean Sullivan July, 1930. One child, Kay about 16; I² Lucille b. March, 1906, m. Harry Lamson, August 16, 1925. Children: Robert b. 1931, and John Michael about 1938.
George's second wife was Mrs. Ollie Oakley d. No issue.

7 Thomas J. d. m. Emma Banta d. Children: Hattie, Will, Mitchell, and Henry. N.f.r.

8 Elizabeth Haskell b. 1845, d. Thanksgiving Day, 1931, m. Wilk P. Hall, 1863. He was b. January 1, 1841, d. 1892. Children: Mary E., Sara W. and Adah.
   a Mary E. d. April 17, 1943, unm.; b Sara W. unm., c Adah m. Fritz Rabb and d. a widow 1937.

F Augustine d. m. Benoit Courvoisieur d. Their son, Frederick was Treas. of Switzerland County from 1866 to 1869, and P.M. from 1861 to 1862. N.f.r. Augustine's second husband was Joseph Dow d. N.f.r.

G Justi m. Mary Banta, June 6, 1839. (She was the dau. of Rev. Henry D. and Eleanor Van Os Dol Banta, one of thirteen children.) Children: Harriet Eleanor, Emily Jane, Frederick Louis, Henry D., Mary Anne, Charles, Benjamin Franklin, Rudolph Lamson, Morton Dow, Alice Augustine.

1 Harriet Eleanor b. April 16, 1840, m. Frederick Detraz, May 30, 1860. Children: Alice (lived only a day), Mary J., Marie Antionette, Henry B., Edgar A., Florence Lilian, Harriet Emily, Bertha Enola.
   a Mary J. b. December 20, 1862, m. Robt Scott, January 27, 1897. No issue; m. Eli Haskell, August 24, 1926, No

issue. Now a widow second time. b Marie Antionette b. April 25, 1865, m. Walter S. Conley, November 15, 1909. No issue; c Henry B. b. February 15, 1868, m. Mrs. Margaret Shaffer, September 6, 1932. No issue, d. February 15, 1946. d Edgar A. b. April 17, 1871, m. Mrs. Margaret Mains, July 22, 1922. No issue, d. April 3, 1945. e Florence L. b. December 4, 1874, m. Edgar V. McKay, March 1, 1900. Children: Mildred, Harriet, Detraz, Geneva Edwards, Edgar D., Lois Florence.

I^1 Mildred b. April 13, 1901, m. Leonard Wilson. No issue. I^2 Harriet Detraz b. May 7, 1904, m. Samuel Toll. Children: Samuel Jr., Gwen, and Phyllis. I^3 Geneva Edwards b. October 13, 1908, m. Frank Heacock. Children: Fred and James. I^4 Edgar D. b. April 26, 1913, m. Ruby Mossberger. Children: Linda and Kay. I^5 Lois Florence b. July 24, 1918, m. Rolland Rivard. Children: Edgar and baby son.

f Harriet Emily b. February 19, 1878, m. Cyrenius G. Haskell, April 2, 1902. Children: Fred B.; Harriet Emily's second husband was Chas. W. Hollingsworth, son, Sanford D. She d. March 28, 1945.

I^1 Fred B. m. Pauline Crane, August 4, 1926.

g Bertha Enola b. July 28, 1883, m. Geo. W. Reed, March 1, 1911. Children: Ruth L., Roger Henry, and Harriet Elizabeth. I^1 Ruth L. b. April 8, 1912, m. Clifford King July 18, 1931. Children: Clifford Randolph b. February 9, 1933, Clair Edward b. September 29, 1936, Frederick Lloyd b. July 31, 1944. I^2 Roger Henry b. January 14, 1915, m. Edith McKay June 5, 1937. Children: Paul Roger b. July 23, 1939, and Robert Wayne, January 9, 1941. I^3 Harriet Elizabeth b. October 21, 1919, m. Ralph Miller, November 8, 1947.

2 Emily Jane b. May 10, 1842, d. June 11, 1919, m. September 28, 1864, John S. Malcolmson b. December 29, 1842, d. April 24, 1914. Children: Perle, Della, Wm., Justi, Mary E., Francis B., and Edna G.

a Perle b. November 11, 1865, d. July 8, 1940, m. March 25, 1896, Stephen McKay b. October 13, 1867. No issue. b Della b. January 3, 1868, d. July 9, 1902, m. Arthur Smith, November 28, 1896. Arthur Smith b. September 6, 1868, d. September 30, 1945. A son, Stanley. c Wm. J. b. June 3, 1871, m. June 12, 1900, Cora Hart b. November 13, 1871, d. January 7, 1912. Children: Clair, Dale, John Hart.

I^1 Clair, Baptist minister m. Irene Lacy about 1931. One child, Wm. about 16. I^2 Dale m. Mildred Henderson. Adopted son, Don. I^3 John Hart m. Thelma Roehm, baby son, John about two years old.

d Justi T. b. February 24, 1876, d. September 3, 1924, m. March 4, 1908, Beryl Anderson b. June 25, 1882. No issue. e Mary E. b. March 28, 1878, d. September 3, 1897, unm. f Francis B. b. November 11, 1881, d. March 14, 1921, m.

October 19, 1910, Hattie Means b. May 3, 1888, d. January 10, 1938. No issue. g Edna G. b. August 24, 1885, unm.

3 Frederick Louis b. August 14, 1844, d. May 14, 1919, m. April 24, 1867, Sarah Malcolmson b. March 16, 1846, d. August 13, 1907. Children: Cora, Janette, Emory, Mary G., Louis C., William, Clifford.
  a Cora b. March 14, 1868, d. August, 1920, unm. b Janette b. December 9, 1871, unm. c Emory b. March, 1855, d. November, 1928, m. Louise Protsman. One child, Frederick m. ———— a son, Freedrick Louis b. 1946. d Mary G. b. August 6, 1878, d. December 25, 1944, m. April 7, 1903, Myrna Griffith b. August 28, 1876, d. September 10, 1945. Children: Helen, Frederick, Vernon, and Mary.

  I[1] Helen Josephine b. March 14, 1904, m. B. F. Darnall, December 21, 1929. No issue. I[2] Frederick b. December 17, 1906, m. Mrs. Bernice Drake Brandon, 1943. No issue. I[3] Vernon b. September 11, 1912, m. Sarah Swab, May 31, 1942. A child. Wm. Michael, about four years old. I[4] Mary b. July 24, 1913, m. F. F. Havey, October 26, 1935. Children: Judith about 13 and Timothy about 7.
  e Louis b. November 14, 1882, m. Golda Andrews, March 12, 1921. Golda b. 1888. No issue. f Wm. b. January, 1887, d. September, 1902, a school boy. g Clifford b. March, 1889, d. 1936, m. Amie Plank. Several children N.f.r.

4 Mary Anne m. Jas. Anderson. Children: Ora, Carl, Hazel, N.f.r.

5 Henry D. was drowned.

6 Charles V. b. July 5, 1851, d. August 5, 1905, m. September 26, 1877, Margaret Malcolmson, d. January 28, 1930, sister of Sarah and John who also m. Thiebauds. Children: Jessie and Lela.
  a Jessie m. Wm. Clapp, 1908. He d. 1913. No issue.
  b Lela m. Mr. Austin, 1920. A dau. Peggy, m. 1946. N.f.r.

7 Benjamin Franklin b. 1855, m. September 16, 1885, Alice A. Lamberson, d. Children: Lois and Thornton, twins and Marguerite and Lester N.f.r. Benjamin Franklin m. a second wife, Mrs. Clara Brindley, November 9, 1921. He d. April, 1925, and she d. July 15, 1940. No issue.

8 Rudolph Lamson d. about 1942, m. Angie Welch, d. November 25, 1880. Children: Curtis and Ledgreed. Rudolph Lamson's second wife was Rebecca L. Welch. One child, Morton Dow, d. 1948.

9 Alice Augustine m. Albert J. Shaw, April 1879. Both d. some years. Children: Grace, Earl, Justi, Hazel, and Gladys.
  a Grace m. October 30, 1901, John W. Knox, b. February 24, 1871, d. May 1, 1936. Children: Albert and Henry Kern.
  I[1] Albert b. 1902, m. Reba Cullum. No issue. I[2] Henry Kern b. 1906, m. Venita Montgomery. No issue.

b   Earl d. 1932. m. Dora Twineham 1911. Children: Chas. and Lucien.
  I¹ Chas. m. 1940 Wanda ————. Two little boys. I² Lucien unm. Seriously wounded in World War II.
c   Justi m. 1920, Carrie Craig d. One child, Elizabeth m. September 5, 1947, Ray T. McCord. Justi m. 1928, a second wife, Grace Golay. No issue.   d   Hazel m. 1914, Rodney Danner d. December, 1939. Children: Chas., Helen, Mary, and Robert.
  I¹ Chas. m. Doris Hardin, 1942. Child, Rodney about two. I² Helen m. December 23, 1939, Dr. John David Stepleton. A boy b. November 17, 1946. I³ Mary unm. Robert d. March, 1948, about 13.
e   Gladys m. Ethol Brown, 1919. Children: Norman b. 1921, and Lucy Alice b. 1933.

10   Morton Dow b. April 7, 1861, m. September 16, 1884, Lillie M. DeBarth d. Morton Dow's second wife was Mrs. Bessie Kaiser. No issue. An adopted dau., Mrs. Gertrude Gardner and a step son, R. S. Kaiser. Morton Dow d. 1946.

Information is gratefully acknowledged for information given to Mesdames Mollie Haskell, Bertha Reed, Stella McKay, Beryl Malcolmson, Rodney Danner, John Knox, Ethol Brown, Carroll Tandy and daughter Julia, Misses Sara W. Hall, Edna Malcolmson, Grace Griffith, Robert Coates, Mrs. Ray Morrison, Mrs. Nelson Haskell, and Mrs. Woodson Porter.

The John Vancleave Family

Edward S. Harvey

John Vancleave, son of Aaron Vancleave and Rachel Schencks, was born in Monmouth County, New Jersey, in 1739, and died in Jefferson County, Indiana, in May, 1812. John went from New Jersey to Rowan County, North Carolina, with his parents in 1751. From there he migrated to Kentucky with the colonists led by Richard Henderson in 1775, and came on to Indiana in 1811. His first marriage was to Mary Shepherd, but the time and place are unknown. At an unknown time, he married his second wife, Rachel Ryker (*nee* Demaree, widow of Gerardus Ryker), in Kentucky. Ryker was killed in the battle of Floyd's Defeat on September 15, 1781.

John Vancleave was at Fort Boonesboro during the Indian siege of that station, and he and his family were at Bryant's Station at the time it was attacked by more than five hundred Indians under Simon Girty and some British officers on August 16-19, 1782. It was during this attack that John Vancleave, Jr., who was then about fifteen years old, distinguished himself by shooting an Indian, who was standing on a high stump overlooking the Fort.

About a year previous to the attack on Bryant's Station, John Vancleave and his family were living at the station of his brother-in-law, Squire Boone, Jr., who married Jane Vancleave (widow of —— Cleft) in 1765 in North Carolina. The inhabitants of the Squire Boone Station, becoming alarmed about the Indians in the country, decided to remove to Fort Boonesboro for greater safety. They started on September 14, 1781. Squire Boone was suffering from a gunshot wound inflicted by an Indian bullet, and he, with his son Isaiah and a few others, remained behind to look after some stock. The party had proceeded about ten miles, and were in the neighborhood of Long Run, when they were attacked by the Indians.

Mary Vancleave, wife of John, was carrying one of her twin daughters (Nancy), and her oldest daughter, Rachel, was carrying the other twin (Sally). When attacked by the Indians, they were in the maze of a great forest. Mary was killed and Nancy was carried away. The other girls were taken prisoners, but Rachel still clung to Sally, who began to cry and fret. The Indians were almost ready to kill the child, when a party of horsemen from Boonesboro made a dash to the Indians and rescued the prisoners. The rest of the family, it seems, had fled for their lives pursued by the savages. Nancy, who was carried away by the Indians, was never seen again and her fate was never learned. This Indian attack has since been known as the "Battle of Boone's Defeat," although Squire Boone was not present at the time.

Two of the Vancleave boys, Aaron and Benjamin, were slender and fleet of foot, so they made their escape by following the horsemen. John Vancleave, Jr., a fleshy boy, could not run as fast as the others and was left behind. He made his escape by crawling into a hollow log and remaining there all night. The next morning he heard the scouts who were looking for the dead and came out of the log. He was rejoiced to find friends and went with them to the Fort.

When the two boys who escaped by running came to the river, the horsemen would not take them up with them, so they caught hold of the horses' tails and swam across. In that way they made their escape from the savages. After they had crossed the river, they hurried along as fast as they could, encumbered as they were by wet buckskin garments. Their pantaloons were watersoaked and heavy. Soon they began to drag under foot, and retard their progress. One of them rolled his pants up, and they were all right when they got dry, but the other boy cut his off at the bottom, as they gave down and began to drag under foot. When dry, they were too short and had to be thrown away.[1]

What was left of the family got together again at Boonesboro. Mary, the wife of John Vancleave, Sr., was found and buried beneath the branches of the forest trees, but the location of her grave is not known. John Vancleave, Sr., and his three brothers, Benjamin, Ralph, and William (Billy) settled on Bullskin Creek, a small stream in Shelby County, Kentucky, but their brother Aaron settled on Salt Creek, near Bearstown, and later in Washington, now Marion County, Kentucky.

Children of John and Mary (Shepherd) Vancleave:

Rachel Vancleave—b. Oct. 25, 1762; d. April 26, 1842; m. July 8, 1782, in Lincoln Co., Ky., to Peter Banta (b. May 17, 1760; d. May 12, 1829).

Leah Vancleave—m. Gerardus Ryker, son of Gerardus Ryker and Rachel Demaree.

John Vancleave—b. about 1767; m. Sept. 28, 1794, in Shelby Co., Ky., to his cousin, Eunice Vancleave, daughter of Benjamin. They came to Indiana, and their descendants are found in Indiana and some western states.

Aaron Vancleave—b. about 1769; d. Feb. 24, 1846; m. about 1791, to Elizabeth, daughter of Ralph Griffin. They moved to Montgomery County, Ind.

---

[1] These stories relating to the family of John Van Cleave are based on family traditions.

Benjamin Vancleave—b. about 1771; m. Jan. 1, 1801, in Shelby Co., Ky., to Sarah Kerns (daughter of Peter and Anna Jordan Kerns who came from Ireland); settled in 1814, in Orange County, Indiana, on land now owned and occupied by his great-grandson, Harley Vancleave.

Elizabeth Vancleave—m. March 4, 1794, in Shelby Co., Ky., to Aaron Vancleave, son of Benjamin. They were cousins, as shown in this record. Aaron and Elizabeth came to Montgomery County, Indiana, and have many descendants.

Nancy and Sally, twins—b. about 1781; further record of Sally has not been found; nothing known about Nancy after her capture by the Indians.

Children of John and Rachel (Ryker, nee Demaree) Vancleave:

Peter Vancleave—b. ——, d. ——, 1829, in Jefferson Co., Ind.; m. (1) Mar. 20, 1808, in Shelby Co., Ky., to Ann Kennedy; m. (2) July 25, 1816, in Jefferson Co., Ind., to Elizabeth Woodfill.

David Vancleave—m. Mar. 14, 1787; d. Nov. 18, 1825; m. Feb. 16, 1809, to Rachel Sweringen. They settled in 1822 in Decatur County, Ind. In 1836, they moved to Boone County, Ind., where they spent the remainder of their lives; buried in Hopewell cemetery, Boone County, Ind.[2]

---

[2] For an article by the author on "The Vancleave Family of Orange County," see *Indiana Magazine of History* (Sept., 1937), XXXIII, 366-367, and *ibid.* (Dec., 1937), XXXIII, 510-511, for an article, "The Benjamin Vancleave Family."

The Vandeveer Family

Mabel Van Dyke Baer[*]

John Vandeveer was typical of many of his North Carolina kinsmen and neighbors who left their native state to establish a new home north of the Ohio River. His children and their descendants in time spread into a number of southern Indiana counties, from whence some have gone out to serve their country in various capacities.

---

[*] Mrs. Baer, a resident of Washington, D.C., has done extensive research on the Vandeveers and is preparing a family genealogy for possible publication. The editors are indebted to Miss Dorothy Riker for editorial assistance.

The first of the family to come to America was probably Cornelis Jansz van der Veer (from Zeeland) who settled in New Netherland in 1659.[1] The progenitor of the Indiana branch of the family was John Vandeveer, who married Amelia Speer in Rowan County, North Carolina, in 1773.[2] During the Revolutionary War it is believed that he and his wife's brothers fought under General Francis Marion, the "Swamp Fox."[3] After the war he received a grant of one hundred acres of land in Surrey County, North Carolina, on the waters of Forbes Creek (the present Forbush Creek) which flows into the Yadkin River. He sold this land in 1797 to William Spillman, preparatory to moving to Kentucky. A George Vandevar received a grant of fifty acres on the same creek in 1793; he too moved to Kentucky and was described as a resident of Lincoln County in that state when he sold his North Carolina lands in 1799.[4]

John Vandeveer was on the tax list of Lincoln County, Kentucky, in 1803; he entered a tract of 166 acres on Wolf's Creek in Adair County about 1807; this he apparently lost to a prior claimant. By 1810 he and his children and related families had located in Henry County, Kentucky.[5] Four years later he purchased land in what is now Stampers Creek Township, Orange County (in Township 1 north, Range 2 east),

---

[1] William J. Hoffman, "Van Der Veer," *The American Genealogist*, XXII (July, 1945), 22-26; "The Dutch Ancestry of the Van Der Veer Family," *The New York Genealogical and Biographical Record*, LXXIX (April, 1948), 76-81; Lester D. Mapes, "Early Generations of the Vanderveer Family," *ibid.*, LXVIII (July, 1937), 202-216; Teunis G. Bergen, *Register . . . of the Early Settlers of Kings County, Long Island, N. Y. . . .* (New York, 1881), 323-325.

[2] Rowan County, N.C., Marriage Bonds, Part II, p. 441 (typed abstracts in Genealogy Division, Indiana State Library, Indianapolis).

[3] Letter from William T. Vandeveer, Taylorville, Ill., to author, November 22, 1921. General Marion's warfare was of the guerilla type and very few records regarding it were kept. John Vandeveer's Revolutionary War service has not been corroborated by any state or federal records.

[4] N.C., Department of State, Raleigh, Land Grants in Surry County; Surry County, N.C., Register of Deeds (filed in Courthouse, Dobson, N.C.).

[5] Adair County, Ky., Deed Records, Vol. E, p. 795 (filed in Courthouse, Columbia, Ky.); U.S., Bureau of the Census, *Third Census of the United States: 1810;* information from Kentucky State Historical Society, Frankfort, Ky., and from the National Archives, Washington, D.C.

where a number of North Carolinians and Kentuckians had already settled.[6] The land was within the bounds of Washington County until the formation of Orange County in 1816. John and Amelia (Speer) Vandeveer had a large family, all of whom came to Indiana. They were:

i. John, Jr., born 1783, married in 1804 in Adair County, Kentucky, Susannah French, daughter of James French of Cumberland County, Kentucky. (See below for their descendants.)

ii. Aaron, born February 7, 1785, died April 1857; married in Kentucky, Nancy French, sister of Susannah, and who died in 1871. They had six children born in Kentucky, four in Washington County, Indiana, and one in Sangamon County, Illinois. The family later lived in Christian County, Illinois, around Taylorville.

iii. George W., who married in Henry County, Kentucky, in 1812, Jane Eliza Speer. His second wife was Mrs. Nancy Kirkpatrick McWilliams, widow of Alexander McWilliams.

iv. Charles, who married in Lincoln County, Kentucky, in 1801, Hannah Jones.

v. Joel, born 1794, married Rachel Moore on October 4, 1815, in Washington County, Indiana. She was the daughter of the Revolutionary War soldier, William Moore, and his wife Rachel.

vi. Cynthia, born October 30, 1800, in Adair County, Kentucky; was married to Galvin Ralston, October 30, 1817, in Washington County, Indiana.

vii. Nancy, who was married to Jesse Elgin on January 28, 1819, in Washington County, Indiana.

viii. Polly, who was married to William Noblitt, son of John and Nancy Keys Noblitt of Virginia and Henry County, Kentucky. They lived a short time in Orange County, where he preached at the Rock Spring Church in 1826, then later moved to Martin County, and from there to Bartholomew County where he died in 1833.

ix. Amelia, born May 11, 1795, died March 2, 1860; married (1) in 1814, Abraham Noblitt, brother of William, and after 1840 (2) Mr. Hazelwood.

---

[6] Jeffersonville, Ind., Land Office Records (in National Archives, Washington, D.C.).

The father and three of the sons—John, Joel, and George—were listed as heads of households and living in South East Township, Orange County, in the 1820 Census. This township had been formed from Stampers Creek in 1817. The land that they had purchased lay along or near the trace or road that led from Louisville to Vincennes on the Wabash River. Wild buffaloes and Indians had passed this way in the early days; then the trace had been used by the first American soldiers and by the lonely mail carrier on horseback who had contracted to carry the mail between Louisville and Kaskaskia. It was one of the routes marked for improvement by the state legislature in 1820. Both Joel Vandeveer and his father served as overseers in improving the portion that passed their homes. Soon after this the trace was made a stage coach route. In the 1830's the state undertook to macadamize it, and again Joel Vandeveer was supervisor of the work from his house to Bosley's Springs. When state funds were exhausted, the further improvement and upkeep of the road was taken over by a private company and it became a toll road. Under such superintendents as John Frazier, 1844-1847, Michael Riley, 1848, and Joel Vandeveer, 1850, the toll collections were large enough to keep it in condition. Present Road 150 follows closely this same route.

There were other civic responsibilities, too, which the Vandeveers assumed in their new home. George and Charles Vandeveer served as constables for South East Township; Joel was a justice of the peace, township assessor, and trustee of school lands; and John (either Jr. or Sr.) served as overseer of the poor. Both John, Jr., and Charles were officers in the Indiana militia in 1816, the former as ensign and the latter as lieutenant. Soon after moving to Indiana, George opened a school in a log cabin which had a dirt floor and no windows; he later moved the school to a residence, where he continued to teach the children of the neighborhood until 1829. In 1846 he was school examiner for Orange County. Joel was elected to serve in the lower house of the General Assembly from 1833 to 1838, and again from 1844 to 1846. He was a Democrat in politics and attended the state convention of that party in 1840. During the 1830's he had a store, probably in his home, where he was licensed to sell "spirituous liquors and foreign groceries." To obtain this privilege he not only paid an annual fee of $5, but presented to the county commissioners a petition signed by twenty-four respectable freeholders, testifying that he was a man of good moral character.

The family had been affiliated with the Baptist Church in Kentucky, and on removing to Indiana the various members were active in the service of the church and in promoting its growth. The Stampers Creek Primitive Baptist Congregation was organized in 1818 and erected a church building four miles east of Paoli. Records are not available to show whether the Vandeveers were members of this congregation, but Rachel, wife of Joel Vandeveer, is buried in the cemetery adjoining the church. The Rock Spring Primitive Baptist Church group, which erected a meeting house near Valeene in South East Township, was organized in 1826 in the home of Charles Vandeveer. Charles, his brother Aaron, and brother-in-law William Noblitt were all licensed ministers in the Baptist Church.[7]

John Vandeveer, the father, died sometime before June 1, 1835. A deed executed on that date by George and his wife, Jane Eliza, mentioned Amelia Vandeveer as the widow of John, deceased.[8] John Vandeveer, Jr., purchased 160 acres adjoining his father's land in 1814; this he continued to hold until 1863. His wife's parents, James and Barbara French, also moved to Indiana and purchased land in the same area. John and his wife Susannah had a number of children. The names of seven are known:

    i. James, born March 10, 1810, in Cumberland County, Kentucky, married Caroline Brown on September 2, 1832, in Washington County, Indiana; (see below for their children):

    ii. Perry, born 1821; married Sarah Malina _____ and lived in Stampers Creek Township.

    iii. Harriet, married _____ Hockman.

    iv. Lewis W., born 1825, died July 31, 1863, and is buried in Rock Spring Cemetery, Orange County. Sarah J.

---

[7] Information regarding the activities of the family in Orange County was obtained from the Commissioners Records and from Goodspeed Bros. & Co. (pub.), *History of Lawrence, Orange, and Washington Counties, Indiana* (Chicago, 1884).

[8] Orange County, Ind., Deed Records, Vol. E, p. 323.

Vandeveer, who died March 12, 1906, and is buried in the same cemetery, is identified as "wife of L."

v. Bennett, born 1826; married Sarah C. Carlisle on May 7, 1859, in Orange County.

vi. Joel, born 1829; married Jemima Ann Monk; practiced medicine in Crawford County.

vii. Tandy, the youngest son, born 1833; married Martha Beckham; moved to Clay County, Illinois, and later to Taylorville, Illinois, where they died in 1883 and 1891, respectively.

James, the oldest son of John and Susannah Vandeveer, purchased land adjoining that of his father in 1834. He sold this four years later and lived for a time in Greenfield Township, Orange County, and later in Warrick and Pike counties, Indiana; after 1865 he moved to Clay County, Illinois, and lived near his brothers Bennett and Tandy. He died in 1869, and his wife Caroline in 1877; she is buried in Warrick County. James and Caroline Vandeveer had the following children, the first six of whom were born in Orange County and the last three in Warrick County:

i. Harriet, born 1836, married John F. Wire, Warrick County.

ii. John W., born September 11, 1837, died May 13, 1908; served in the Civil War as corporal and sergeant in the Ninety-First Regiment of Indiana Volunteers, Company B; married Elizabeth Ober Smith, born 1841 and died 1913. Both are buried in Selvin Cemetery, Pigeon Township, Warrick County.

iii. Stephen B., born 1840, died 1922, married Cordelia Mack; they were living in Clay County, Illinois, in 1870 and 1880; he served in the Civil War as private in the same company as his brother John W.

iv. Temperance, born 1842, married Louis Robinson in Warrick County.

v. Perry, born 1844, died 1914; married (1) Sarah M. Hanks; (2) Elen Monical, in Clay County, Illinois, 1874; (3) Martha A. Beard Slagley.

vi. Susanna A., born 1846, married Nathan Tomlinson about 1872.

vii. Joel, born 1848, was living with his widowed mother in 1870 in Clay County, Illinois.

viii. Josiah, born 1850, died 1912; married Florence _____ and was living in Gibson County in 1880.

ix. Louis Bennett, born 1856 in Boonville; died 1915; married Mary Ellen Gwaltney, daughter of Harris and Harriet (Barr) Gwaltney, born 1868 in Gibson County, died 1945. They are buried in Liberty Cemetery, Cynthiana, Indiana. Their children were: Welzie Wellington, William Harris, Curtis B., Stella, Nora, Ocie, Alva Lee, Harley A., and Clara Helen.

Welzie Wellington Vandeveer, the oldest son, was born near Haubstadt in 1887. After teaching school for three years he was employed by the Western Union Telegraph Company, the Goodrich Tire and Rubber Company, and the American Petroleum Products Company prior to 1925, when he founded his own company, Allied Oil, Inc. During his twenty-three years as president he built Allied Oil into a major business enterprise. After its merger with Ashland Oil and Refining Company in 1948, he turned his attention to a new enterprise, Vanson Production Corporation, which produces and distributes natural gas in the southwestern states. During World War II, as director of the Second Petroleum District of the United States, he was able to perform a valuable service in the government's program of oil conservation and distribution. In recent years he has served as a member of the National Petroleum Council, an advisory group which helped to overcome the acute oil shortage in Europe while the Suez Canal was closed.

The Woodburn Family*

The family of James Albert Woodburn is of Scotch-Irish ancestry on both sides of the family—Ulster Scots, who moved into northern Ireland in successive migrations from the time of Cromwell. On his mother's side, the Hemphills, Millens, Moffetts, and Chestnuts, came from County Antrim. The Woodburns came from County Derry, near Coleraine.

These Scotch-Irish came to America in several waves of migration from 1715 to 1775, though some came later. A few reached New England, some landed at Charleston, South Carolina, but the great bulk of them landed at Newcastle,

---

* It has been the privilege of the editor of Indiana Geneology, Martha Tucker Morris, to select the information in this article from *Woodburn History: Some Generations of a Family*, in order to present the genealogy of this family. A notice of the *Woodburn History* appeared in the June, 1937, issue of *Indiana Magazine of History*, 222-223. In the September issue of 1936, 231-247, there is an article, "James Woodburn: Hoosier Schoolmaster", by James Albert Woodburn.

Pennsylvania, and made their way gradually to the interior of Pennsylvania. From thence many migrated southward through the Shenandoah Valley of Virginia and settled in the Piedmont region of that state and the Carolinas. They were hardy frontiersman who later continued their migration toward the West. They served as a buffer between the colonial settlement and hostile Indians. Out of this stock came such leaders, as Stonewall Jackson, Andrew Jackson, John C. Calhoun, Sam Houston, James K. Polk, the Robertsons in North Carolina and the Breckinridges and the Blairs of Kentucky. The early Scotch-Irish were a sturdy stock, being, for the most part, small farmers and humble tillers of the soil. They usually disliked the British government, were Jeffersonian Republicans in politics and Presbyterians in faith. Such was the racial element to which the family belonged.

James Woodburn, the first known Woodburn ancestor, was born in County Derry, Ireland, in 1748; came to America in 1767; married a widow, Sarah (McGill) McMurray, in 1775; wandered about for a time without fixed habitation; had five children two of whom died in childhood; and finally settled among the Rockey Creek Irish in Chester County, South Carolina, where he died on August 21, 1812. Sarah McGill Woodburn was born in County Down, Ireland, in November of 1746. She was first married to William McMurray, and by him had five children by the time she was twenty-eight or twenty-nine years of age. Sarah died July 31, 1815, aged 69.

Children of James and Sarah (McGill) Woodburn:

Elizabeth Woodburn—born May 4, 1777; m. Thomas Craig, Sept. 29, 1801; lived in Alabama.

Margaret Woodburn—born Sept. 17, 1779; m. Matthew Johnson, Oct. 24, 1808.

Dorrance Woodburn—died May 26, 1784, aged 2 yrs., 4 mos., 3 wks., and 2 days.

Jean Woodburn—born June 4, 1784; died March, 1789, aged 4 yrs., 9 mos., 1 wk., 6 days.

Dorrance Woodburn[2]—born August 16, at Summerseat, Georgia; m. Rachel Johnston, Dec. 3, 1807.

Dorrance Beatty Woodburn, son of James, records his own birth as near Louisville, Georgia, August 16, 1786. He tells very little of his early life. It appears that he served two and a half years in the war of 1812, enlisting a little over three months after the declaration of war and being mustered out nearly three months after the negotiation of the peace. In the year 1823, or before, Dorrance B. Woodburn began to have qualms of conscience about his membership in the Associate Reformed Church. He was a diligent reader of the Bible, and to his mind human institutions ought to conform to Bible standards. The question of slavery and the relation of the church to that evil were now troubling his mind. It was probably in 1823, that he prepared a paper on "Slavery in South Carolina," addressed to Rev. Hugh McMillan, pastor of the Reformed Presbyterian Church, in Chester County.

The Reformed Presbyterians (Covenanters) admitted no slave-holders to their communion. Woodburn, chiefly on this account, now cast his lot with them. Rev. Hugh McMillan and his new church elder (Dorrance B. Woodburn) were active and bold enough in the anti-slavery cause to prepare and present a petition on slavery to the South Carolina Legislature. This old document, which is among the papers of Dorrance B. Woodburn, bears no date, but it could not have been written later than 1825 or 1826.

Dorrance B. Woodburn tells of his marriage on Dec. 3, 1807, in Chester District, South Carolina, to Rachel Johnston (born Nov. 4, 1788). He died near Bloomington, Indiana, on Oct. 21, 1856. His wife died earlier on May 7, 1848. He tells of the birth of his children, nine in number (all born in Chester District). The record, including the dates of death, is here given:

John Johnston Woodburn—born Sept. 29, 1808; died near Bloomington, Ind., October 30, 1874, aged 66.

Sarah McGill Woodburn—born Sept. 23, 1810; died 1891, aged 81.

Cynthia Woodburn—born Oct. 6, 1812; died Nov. 27, 1868, aged 56.

Eliza Ann Woodburn—born January 21, 1815; died Dec. 26, 1862, slightly less than 48.

James Woodburn—born Sept. 1, 1817; died Sept. 8, 1865, three days under 48.

William Woodburn—born March 21, 1820; died June 13, 1858, aged 38. (The fifth to die in a family of eleven, within ten years, William was the head of the household after his father's death in 1856. William Woodburn by his will, dated April 7, 1858, left all his property to his four sisters. Witnessed by T. A. Wylie, and W .S. Stormont.)

Margaret Woodburn—born Jan. 30, 1823; died Jan. 6, 1862; aged 39.

Matthew Walker Woodburn—born Jan. 21, 1825; died Jan. 17, 1855, slightly under 30.

Mary Lucinda Woodburn—born Nov. 6, 1828; died May 31, 1854, aged 26; m. to William Crowe, in fall of 1850; went to Princeton, Ind., with her husband; returned to Bloomington in 1852. (William Crowe, killed by automobile, July 28, 1923. One child, Louise Evelyn.)

From this large family that came to Indiana in 1830, there are few descendants. Six of the children of Dorrance B. Woodburn were never married: Sarah, Cynthia, Eliza, William, Margaret and Matthew. John Johnston Woodburn married Rosanna Harbison on July 18, 1837. She died on Aug. 25, 1867. They had one son, Thomas Craig Woodburn, who was born Nov. 3, 1839.

James Woodburn married Martha Jane Hemphill, daughter of James K. Hemphill, on April 16, 1846. The Hemphill family had moved to Indiana in 1832 from Chester District, South Carolina. Martha Jane, the oldest child, was born in Chester District on December 7, 1827.

Children of James and Martha Jane (Hemphill) Woodburn:

Laura Adelaide Woodburn—born Jan. 15, 1847; died in Benson, Minn., Oct. 1920, aged 73.

Walter Emmett Woodburn—born Feb. 7, 1849; died in Bloomington, May 6, 1906, aged 57.

Theophilus Wylie Woodburn—born Feb. 11, 1852; died in Benson, Minn., July 12, 1912, aged 60.

Ida Lizzie Woodburn—born Oct. 21, 1854; died in Monmouth, Ill., June 30, 1927, aged 72.

James Albert Woodburn—born Nov. 30, 1856.

Grace Helena Woodburn—born Oct. 23, 1864; died Feb. 27, 1922, aged 57.

The Vancleave Family of Orange County

Edward S. Harvey

Benjamin Vancleave was the son of John Vancleave and Mary Shepherd. He was born about 1771, as he is said to have been ten years of age at the time his mother and little sister were killed by Indians on September 14, 1781, at the Battle of Boone's Defeat. He was married in Shelby County, Kentucky, on January 1, 1801, to Sarah Kerns, daughter of Peter and Anna Jordan Kerns. Sarah Kerns had a sister, Marjory, who married John Vancleave, a cousin of Benjamin.

---

* The address of Edward S. Harvey is 418 East Washington Street, Lebanon, Indiana. Members of the Vancleave family may wish to write Mr. Harvey, as he has been compiling records of this family many years.

Peter Kerns and his family came from Ireland when Marjory was seven months old, and, in later years, they came with Marjory and her husband to Montgomery County, Indiana. They are buried on the old farm, a few miles south of Crawfordsville.

Benjamin Vancleave entered land in Stampers Creek Township, Orange County, Indiana, in 1813, where he settled with his family in 1814. A county history states that Benjamin Vancleave served on the first Grand Jury in Orange County, which met April 8, 1816, at the house of William Lindley.[1] From the same work, we find that sometime in the 'fifties Benjamin Vancleave was fatally injured at a barn-raising, near Millersburg, from a falling of some of the heavy timbers. Death occurred in a few days.[2] James Vancleave, who lived in Vernon Township, Washington County, Indiana, and whose parents were Benjamin and Sarah Carnes [Kerns] Vancleave, was born in Kentucky, in the year 1810. When four years old he came with his parents to Orange County, Indiana. *Marriage Records of the Vancleave Family*:

Aaron Vancleave—m. Nancy Galloway, June 5, 1827.
David Vancleave (son of Aaron, son of John)—m. Sarah Jane Vancleave (daughter of John, the son of John Vancleave), Aug. 16, 1831[3]
James Vancleave (son of Benjamin and Sarah Kerns Vancleave)[4] —m. Mary Lynn, Mar. 14, 1833.
Sarah Vancleave—m. Jackson McCoy, Apr. 13, 1837.
Elizabeth Jane Vancleave—m. George Rector, May 29, 1838.
Anna Vancleave—m. John P. Rector, Feb. 20, 1839.
Priscilla Vancleave—m. Aaron W. Remy, Aug. 30, 1839.
Benjamin Vancleave—m. Margaret Ann Galloway, June 14, 1844.
Ruth Vancleave—m. James Warren, Dec. 4, 1854.
Jas. A. Vancleave[5]—m. Elizabeth M. Allen, Mar. 7, 1865.
James L. Vancleave—m. Ruth Ann Spear, Apr. 22, 1865.
George Vancleave—m. Jane Kearby, Feb. 28, 1873.
Jacob K. Vancleave (son of James and Eliza Vancleave)—m. Armitta B. Hutchinson, Jan. 19, 1889.
Clorinda Vancleave—m. John T. Long, Apr. 29, 1889.
Flora B. Vancleave—m. Frank E. McLane, Oct. 15, 1889.
Mary Vancleave—m. James W. Bishop, Apr. 4, 1891.
Martha B. Vancleave—m. Wm. H. Martin, Nov. 11, 1891.
Edlward B. Vancleave—m. Dessie D. Lindley, Jan. 27, 1893.
Emma F. Vancleave—m. Fred O. Trinkle, Feb. 5, 1894.
Nannie E. Vancleave—m. James A. Martin, Jan. 5, 1984.

[1] *History of Lawrence, Orange and Washington Counties* (Chicago, 1844), 446.
[2] *Ibid.*, 408.
[3] David Vancleave and Sarah Jane Vancleave were first cousins, each being a grandchild of John Vancleave, Sr.
[4] The name *Kerns* is also found with the spelling *Carnes*.
[5] James A. and James L. Vancleave were probably cousins.

The Philburd Wright Family
EMSLEY WRIGHT JOHNSON

In his *Sketches,* Mr. Nowland wrote in 1876: "Among the early settlers of the Territory of Indiana was a large family of Wrights, who emigrated from Randolph County, North Carolina, and settled in Union County in 1813. From Union County a portion of them went to Wayne, and some to Washington County; later four of the sons came to Marion County."[1] Philburd Wright, one of the many persons of this name who came to Indiana, was born in Maryland in 1750. He became a pioneer of Indiana about 1813, taking up his residence in Union County near Brownsville, where he died in 1831, or 1833. It is believed that he served in the Revolutionary War, and later as justice of the peace in Randolph County, North Carolina, for about forty years. He married Elizabeth Reagen and to them were born the following children: Joshua, Caroline (Delilah), Sarah, Mary, Noah, Levi, Joel, Jesse, Elizabeth and Aaron.[2]

The family records of the three sons, Noah, Levi and Joel, are here presented:

Noah Wright was born in Randolph County, North Carolina on August 30, 1784. He moved to Indiana in 1808. He located first at Jeffersonville, where he manufactured brick for a year, and then farmed for a man named Holman for a time. He served one year on the frontier against the Indians, for which he was granted a land warrant for 160 acres. He did not receive the land, however, until forty years later, a short time before his death. Following Indian service, he returned to his home in North Carolina where he remained a year. He returned to Indiana in 1810 and settled in Washington County where he was employed in clearing land. He married on July 28, 1814, Susanna, daughter of Arthur and Mary Morgan Parr, natives of Rowan County, North Carolina.[3]

In 1831, Noah Wright came to Marion County, Indiana, where he purchased at different times a total of 640 acres

---

[1] John H. B. Nowland, *Sketches of Prominent Citizens of 1876* (Indianapolis, 1877), 149.

[2] This record was furnished by George T. Kepler of Cambridge City, Indiana, who received parts of it from Isaac N. Beard, his father-in-law, parts of it from Mary W. Sinks and parts of it from Melissa K. Justice. An additional son, Eli, is named in *Pictorial and Biographical Memoirs of Indianapolis and Marion County, Indiana* (Chicago, 1893), 243-44.

[3] "Memoir of Enoch Parr," *Indiana Magazine of History* (December, 1926), XXII, 371-453.

of land, and at that time also owned 420 acres in Hamilton County. He settled on a tract of 160 acres in Perry Township, Marion County, not an acre of which had been cleared, and there he lived until his death on July 11, 1863. He was an old-line Whig, later a Republican. He was a member of the first state legislature that convened in Indiana, and was sheriff of Washington County some five or six times. He was not a church member, but gave liberally to all denominations. His wife died on October 9, 1842. Seven children were born to them: Betsey A., David, Hiram, Isaac, Polly A., Susanna and Jasper N.[4]

Levi Wright was born in North Carolina on June 12, 1790, and was married to Sarah, daughter of William and Elizabeth or Betsey (Morgan) Wright[5] (born August 31, 1797, and died August 19, 1834). They moved to Indiana in 1810 and settled in Washington County, near Salem. Levi held prominent positions in the county and owned much land. He died in the old home near Salem.

Joel Wright was born in Randolph County, North Carolina, on February 5, 1795, and moved with his parents to Indiana Territory in 1813. In November, 1815, he located on the west fork of the Whitewater in what is now Wayne County. Then he moved to Marion County in December, 1821. He was married September 10, 1812, to Sarah Birely (born April 30, 1789). They had eight children: Alfred, Polly, Jinsey, Emsley, Phoebe, Elizabeth, Lucinda and Joel. All are deceased. Joel Wright died April 9, 1928.[6]

Children of Levi and Sarah (Wright) Wright:[7]

Mary (Polly) Wright—b. 1818; m. July 13, 1857, George Fultz; d. 1890; no children.

Henry Wright—b. 1820; m. Aug. 23, 1842, Rachel Goss; d. 1875; Children: George, of Emporia, Kansas; Charles of Genda Springs, Kansas, an attorney; Albert, of Kansas City,

---

[4] A sketch of Noah Wright is given in *Pictorial and Biographical Memoirs*, 243-44.

[5] A Revolutionary soldier, buried in the Wright Family Cemetery on the Harrison Deeny farm about three miles south of Salem, Indiana. A government marker was placed on the grave by the Christopher Harrison Chapter, D. A. R. of Salem. William was the son of Richard Wright, Sr., a private in the North Carolina militia, from Rowan County. Other children of Richard were Benjamin, Peter, Richard, Jr., John, Evins, Amos and Philburd. Philburd, born in 1768, was the first of the family to come to Washington County. Grant F. Wright, Route 4, Salem, Indiana, a descendant of Philburd Wright, has compiled a genealogy of this family.

[6] A sketch of Joel Wright is given in B. R. Sulgrove, *History of Indianapolis and Marion County, Indiana* (Philadelphia, 1884), 628. In this sketch his birth date is given as February 5, 1793, and May 12 is given as the date of his arrival in Indiana Territory. The name of his wife is given as Sarah Byerby.

[7] These are grandchildren of Philburd and Elizabeth (Reagan) Wright.

Missouri; Walter; Joel; Harvey, of Emporia, Kansas; Henry, of Guthrie, Oklahoma.

Jesse Wright—b. Sept. 30, 1821; m. March 25, 1852 to Matilda McAllister; d. June 4, 1856; children: Joel; Louisa (M. Timothy Callahan).

Lorinda Wright—b. 1822; m. May 8, 1844, to Sanford Carter; d. 1890; children: Elizabeth; Alice (m. John McCullough, lived in Livonia, Indiana); Cassius Morton (lived in Muncie, Indiana, and later in California); none living.

Louisa Wright—b. Oct. 6, 1827; m. David Colglazier, Mar. 26, 1851; d. Mar. 31, 1895; children: Levi, Isaac, Joel, Frances, Marion (d. in infancy), Rachel, William, Mary, Abraham, Walter, Sarah, Jacob, Catherine, John. Of these, Joel (b. Feb. 13, 1854; d. July 1, 1931) m. Adelia Cauble (dau. James and Eunice Hitchcock Cauble) Dec. 21, 1818. Nine children (three died young) were born of this union. This Joel Colglazier was an active member of the Washington County (Indiana) Historical Society and compiled many family records.

Joel Wright—b. Feb. 9, 1829; d. Sept. 19, 1851.

Marion Wright—b. Oct. 10, 1830; d. Dec. 30, 1852.

Levi Wright—b. 1833; m. Louisa Martin; d. in Indianapolis, date not known; children: Franklin, William, Eward, Aurt and Fred. Franklin became a doctor. He and his brothers William, Eward and Aurt live in Indianapolis. The address of Fred, also a doctor, is not known.

Emsley Wright[8] was born in Wayne County, Indiana, on February 18, 1820. When not quite two years old, he moved with his parents to Washington Township, Marion County, where he lived his entire life. He helped cut the virgin forests from the land where the statehouse now stands, and also worked on the construction of the canal through Marion County. He was a member of the Marion County Bar Association and for many years practiced law. He was also justice of the peace in Washington Township for eight years, and was president of the Broad Ripple Old Settlers Association. On January 27, 1848, he was married to Lucy Maria Strong who was born on June 10, 1828, and died on July 21, 1851, leaving two children, Mary and John. Mr. Wright was married a second time on December 20, 1855, to Clara

---

[8] Son of Joel and Sarah (Birely) Wright and grandson of Philburd and Elizabeth (Reagan) Wright.

K. Collins, who died on December 14, 1896. One son, George, was born to them, but died at the age of two and a half years. Emsley Wright died on January 11, 1897.

Mary Wright[9] was born near Augusta, in Marion County, Indiana, on November 23, 1848. On March 21, 1867, she married Joseph McClung Johnson, son of William K. and Virginia Johnson. Mrs. Johnson died on January 31, 1930. Joseph McClung Johnson was born on the Rockville Road (now Road 36) six miles west of Indianapolis, on April 1, 1843, and died on July 6, 1933.

Children of Joseph McClung and Mary (Wright) Johnson:
Cora Josephine Johnson[10] was born near Augusta, Indiana, on July 21, 1868. She never married and now lives with her brother, Elmsley Wright Johnson.

Emsley Wright Johnson[11] was born at Augusta, Indiana, on May 8, 1878, and was married (1) at Greenfield, Indiana, on August 8, 1906, to Katherine Griffin, of Greenfield. He was admitted to the Indianapolis Bar in 1903, since which time he has been in active law practice. Children: Mardenna and Emsley Wright, Jr. Mrs. Katherine (Griffin) Johnson died on January 29, 1918, and Emsley Wright Johnson married (2) Elizabeth Thompson on August 2, 1920. They live at 3447 Washington Boulevard, Indianapolis.

William Franklin Johnson was born in Whitestown, Indiana, on June 28, 1881. He was graduated from the Indiana University School of Medicine in 1906. In 1921, he married Gertrude Weirhaye. Their home is at 2102 Sugar Grove Avenue, Indianapolis.

---

[9] Granddaughter of Joel and Sarah (Birely) Wright, and great-granddaughter of Philburd and Elizabeth (Reagan) Wright.

[10] Granddaughter of Emsley and Lucy Maria (Strong) Wright, great-granddaughter of Joel and Sarah (Birely) Wright and great-great-granddaughter of Philburd and Elizabeth (Reagan) Wright.

[11] Author of this family history, son of Joseph McClung and Mary (Wright) Johnson, and brother of Cora Josephine Johnson (note 10).

INDEX

A

Abbott 3, 62
Abernathey 24, 26
Abernathy 28
Abraham 21
Abrams 13, 21
Ackerman 378
Acre 66, 72
Acrea 70
Adair 19, 382, 384
Adams . . 4, 6, 48, 141, 157, 158, 159, 162, 163, 171, 426
Adkerson 12
Adkinson 367
Agan 246
Agee 31
Akers 193, 199, 215
Akim 192
Akin 329, 333
Akine 233
Albers 3
Alden 55
Alderman 406
Alderson 51
Aldridge . . . 6, 8, 10, 24, 25, 26, 29
Alender 141
Alexander . . . 1, 4, 8, 23, 24, 26, 45, 47, 66, 71, 72, 89, 93, 96, 97, 101, 103, 111, 112, 113, 119, 124, 127, 141, 161, 405
Alexanders 108
Alison 1
All 211
Allburn 148
Allen 4, 7, 8, 16, 29, 30, 36, 66, 141, 149, 178, 209, 234, 384, 452
Allender 127
Allgood 36
Allhounce 1
Allison 6, 9, 46, 141
Almey 419
Alpha 63
Alsup 33
Alward 4, 8
Amans 76
Ames 383
Ammen 357, 359, 361
Ammerman 426
Anderson . . . 2, 4, 8, 17, 18, 34, 66, 71, 72, 141, 153, 170, 171, 173, 174, 175, 183, 205, 210, 212, 218, 221, 223, 224, 330, 335, 357, 360, 425, 432, 436, 437, 438
Andrew 38, 39, 40, 42
Andrews . . . 16, 21, 22, 327, 438
Angier 383
Apple 389, 390
Applegate 1, 65
Archer 66
Arman 16
Armstrong . . 6, 26, 27, 157, 170, 256, 309
Arnet 11, 30
Arnett 196, 209
Arnold 1, 9, 21, 46, 47, 48, 70, 86, 88, 95, 104, 111, 234, 392, 394, 395, 425
Arnott 171, 172
Arther 74
Arthur 20
Arwine 141
Ashby 9, 97, 119
Asher 1, 19
Ashley 9, 417
Askew 1
Atchison 11
Athon 36, 61, 63
Atkins 276
Atkinson . . 34, 37, 42, 234, 273, 274, 275, 365, 390
Austin 4, 24, 438
Ayers 6, 328
Aylor 350
Ayres 4, 9, 10, 18, 365

B

Babcock 19, 20, 25
Backman 432
Badders 194
Baden 25
Badger 268
Badgley 428
Bagwell 178
Bailey . . 10, 12, 15, 16, 31, 146, 189, 191, 192, 193, 194, 195, 199, 214, 224, 365, 366
Baily 28, 71, 212, 214
Baird 1, 172
Bakelshymer 33
Baker . . . 2, 4, 8, 10, 16, 30, 34, 45, 46, 48, 49, 145, 160, 161, 210, 268, 323, 360
Baldwin . . . 7, 13, 47, 48, 76, 78, 88, 91, 103, 110, 111, 119, 393
Bales 15, 166
Baley 234
Ball . . 1, 8, 12, 20, 25, 321, 326, 340, 342, 424, 426
Ballard 66
Ballenger 8
Ballinger 395
Banks 8
Banster 1
Banta . . . 127, 141, 334, 436, 441
Bardiaman 213
Barfell 1
Barfield 50
Barker 48, 274
Barkman 78
Barlow 288
Barnard 27, 30, 234
Barner 1, 9
Barnes 3, 4, 77, 251
Barnett . . . 66, 72, 234, 338, 341, 401
Barney 213
Barnhart 4, 5, 29
Barns 136
Barr 448
Barrett 72, 258
Barrick 268, 269
Barringer 61, 63
Bartholomew 112
Bartlett 355, 356
Bartley 152, 153
Bartlow 12
Barton 19, 94, 284, 350
Bass 103, 110
Basye 17, 66
Bates 1, 8, 21, 25, 27, 264, 426
Baughman 127, 141, 146
Baum 14
Bauman 287
Baxter 11
Bay 141
Bayman 11
Bayse 313
Beach 1
Beales 277
Beals 277, 402
Bear 407, 408
Beard . . 1, 6, 10, 192, 193, 214, 247
Beasley 214
Beasly 214
Beaty 364
Beauchamp 4, 6
Beaver 146, 393
Beavers 66
Beavins 66
Bebermeyer 335, 341
Beck . . 1, 4, 25, 26, 27, 28, 31
Beckes 125
Becket 29
Beckham 447
Beckner 357, 358
Bedel 77
Bedster 40
Beecher 223
Beeks 8, 251
Beel 8

Beeler 147
Beem 74
Beeson 277, 398
Belcher 45
Belding 167
Belek 38
Belfield 321
Belk 13
Bell 1, 2, 4, 6, 8, 14, 24, 47, 50, 51, 141, 175, 211, 212, 371, 394
Bellton 405
Belt 390, 391
Belton 329, 332, 337
Belyou 213
Benedict 425
Benefiel 3
Benefield . . . 186, 189, 190, 191, 197, 198
Bengaman 15
Benge 10
Benham 66
Benifield 195
Bennerly 407
Bennett . . . 21, 24, 28, 182, 195, 212, 223, 234, 280, 448
Bennifield 192, 193
Benny 20
Benton 4, 75, 76
Bergen 140, 141
Berry . . 1, 4, 8, 9, 11, 22, 23, 37
Bersot 432
Best 383
Bettens 230
Bettmann 334, 338
Betts 21
Bickel . . 372, 373, 375, 376, 377
Bickel Sr. 374
Biddle 27
Bidle 195
Bigelow 309
Bigger 30
Biggs 7, 25, 66
Bigler 341
Bilby 8
Bildeback 17
Bilderback 19
Billings 8, 24, 29
Bills 425, 426
Bilyew 196, 197
Birch 66
Birchfield 66, 72
Bird 4
Birdsong 267
Birely 454
Birkbeck 234
Biscoe 323
Bishop . . 1, 4, 17, 27, 79, 80, 81, 82, 84, 85, 164, 234, 275, 452
Black 14, 28, 150, 213
Blackburn 15, 38
Blackford 115
Blackiston 333, 337, 340
Blair 1, 5, 75
Blakely 331
Bland 30
Blanton 337, 340
Bleavins 67
Bledsoe 44
Blew 30
Bliss 311
Blood 3
Bloyd 47, 48
Blue 227
Blunk 70
Boas 33
Boats 191
Boehm 284
Boerner 230
Bogle 244
Boles 127, 192, 194, 195, 212
Bolin 8, 11, 13
Bolinger 214, 223, 224
Boltinhouse 19
Bond 39, 146, 276, 277, 278, 279, 280, 393
Bones 31
Bonine 50, 392, 395
Bonnell III 423
Bonner 173, 174

Bonnette	94	
Bonsack	359, 360	
Bonwill	8	
Booe	1, 4, 8	
Booker	51	
Boon	41, 153	
Boone	121, 125, 151, 154, 155, 363, 364, 376	
Boone Jr.	440	
Booth	71	
Boothe	72	
Borders	119, 191, 192, 193, 212	
Boren	93	
Boruff	249	
Boston	2, 178	
Bostwick	48	
Boswell	42, 160, 276	
Botts	191, 192, 193, 195, 197, 198, 199	
Bouchman	37	
Boulelain	94	
Bowen	15, 407, 408	
Bowers	24, 25, 433	
Bowlan	26	
Bowles	192, 193, 194	
Bowlin	67	
Bowls	67	
Bowlsby	23, 24, 31	
Bowman	281, 282, 283, 284, 285, 286, 287, 288	
Boyd	8, 10, 11, 14, 31, 279, 365, 389	
Boyden	44	
Boyer	61	
Boyers	29	
Bracken	365	
Brackenridge	48	
Bradburn	1, 4	
Braden	307, 308	
Bradford	35, 37	
Bradley	36, 255, 256	
Bradway	20, 24, 29	
Brady	67, 250	
Brag	4, 5	
Bragg	3, 8, 12, 26	
Bramin	47	
Brandenburg	156	
Brandenburgh	27	
Brandoin	94	
Brannum	6	
Branstetter	141	
Brant	48	
Brassie	44	
Brattain	50	
Bratten	29, 30	
Braven	35	
Braxton	37, 43, 45	
Bray	234	
Breaheave	191	
Breck	382	
Breeden	67	
Breeding	92	
Breedlove	192, 193	
Brent	362	
Brenton	86, 88, 89, 91, 92, 95, 97, 101, 102, 103, 104, 111, 112, 113, 117, 118, 119, 120, 121, 124, 125, 126	
Brewer	20, 42	
Briant	8	
Bridges	4, 23, 211	
Bridges Jr.	71	
Bridget	23, 30	
Bridgewater	40	
Bridwell	198	
Brierly	51	
Briggs	9	
Bright	74, 315	
Brightman	75	
Briles	397, 401	
Briley	67	
Brindley	438	
Briner	35	
Bringham	17	
Brinton	103	
Briscoe	47, 212	
Bristow	48	
Britts	360	
Broccas	16	
Brock	3, 50, 191
Brockus	16
Brodie	190, 192, 196, 197
Bromhall	27
Bronaugh	159
Bronson	349
Brookbank	212
Brooks	31, 318, 321
Brookshire	162
Broomhall	27
Brouen	35
Brown	1, 8, 9, 16, 17, 23, 24, 28, 29, 30, 51, 65, 67, 77, 145, 146, 168, 173, 174, 230, 234, 268, 279, 280, 290, 301, 334, 339, 345, 367, 376, 391, 424, 439, 446
Browning	198
Brownlee	9
Brubaker	359
Brummage	9
Brummet	127, 128
Brummit	141
Bruner	39
Bryan	250, 289, 290, 291, 292
Bryant	14, 49, 159
Buchan	348
Buchanan	245, 348
Buchannan	67
Buchanon	245
Buck	5, 9, 64, 65, 182
Buckallew	71
Buckelow	67
Buckhanan	41
Buckhannan	2
Buckhannon	1
Buckler	46
Buckner	234
Budd	11
Buenagle	288
Buff	408
Bulkley	5, 9, 10
Bull	71
Bullet	47
Bumgardner	335, 339
Bunch	195, 213, 214, 215
Bundy	51, 67, 293, 294, 295, 296, 297, 298, 299, 300, 301, 302, 303, 304, 306
Bunker	278
Burbage	24, 28
Burbridge	12
Burckhalter	25
Burgar	34
Burgess	10, 18, 25, 34
Burgher	50
Burk	16, 21, 24
Burkett	412
Burks	426, 427
Burley	405, 406
Burnett	67, 162
Burns	136, 254, 340, 398
Burr	9, 31, 77
Burress	21
Burroughs	22, 28, 200
Burrows	9, 31
Burt	21, 22, 25, 41, 370, 422
Burtin	1
Burtner	35
Burton	3, 5, 9, 413
Bush	14, 16, 17, 19, 145
Bushrod	320
Busick	43
Buskirk	217, 218
Busseron	94
Bussey	9
Butcher	17
Butler	9, 13, 49, 51, 74, 96, 103, 110, 111, 120
Butler Jr.	97, 117
Butlerton	264
Butt	71
Buzzard	158, 163
Bybee	67, 71, 72
Bylyew	196
Byram	9, 36, 39
Byrd	5, 359, 360
Byrket	394
Byrum	155

C

Cabe	314, 315, 316, 317	
Cable	153, 154	
Cagle	71	

Cahhal	195
Cahill	192, 194
Cain	7, 18, 51, 128, 141
Caise	191
Caldwell	1, 4, 5, 9, 13, 119, 307, 308
Callan	3
Callen	11, 12
Callis	371
Calton	352
Calvin	141
Camblin	21
Cameron	405
Cammack	38
Camp	48
Campbell	4, 5, 9, 17, 22, 27, 37, 40, 41, 43, 44, 49, 92, 93, 106, 109, 128, 141, 173, 292, 308, 309, 310, 322, 434
Canada	50
Canaday	23, 27, 51, 234
Canfield	61, 63
Capper	26, 28
Cardale	77
Carey	399
Carlin	3
Carlisle	447
Carman	67
Carmean	18
Carmichael	21, 258
Carnagie	408
Carney	12
Carpenter	1, 30, 40, 67, 288, 350, 396, 406, 434
Carr	21, 22, 37, 40, 41, 61
Carrack	13
Carrel	13
Carrell	67
Carrithers	190, 198, 210, 211
Carroll	9, 13, 72
Carson	27, 330, 334, 339, 341
Carson Jr.	338
Carter	35, 40, 44, 70, 74, 128, 190, 214, 321, 339, 367, 390, 417, 455
Carthy	407
Cartwright	20, 22, 26, 27, 28, 45
Carty	233
Carver	9
Carwile	25
Cary	5, 256
Casady	1
Case	39, 40, 67, 70, 95, 191, 193, 199, 200, 215, 228
Cash	107
Casiah	67
Cason	23, 25, 27, 30
Cass	197
Cassaday	22
Cassal	5
Cassell	220
Cassner	28
Castleman	350
Casto	27
Casy	235
Caterlin	5
Catt	94
Catterlin	1, 7
Caty	94
Cauble	455
Cazebier	47
Chalfant	64, 65
Chamberlain	17
Chamberlin	67
Chambers	1, 3, 9, 34, 37, 96, 101, 111, 115, 180, 181, 194, 210, 227
Chamlin	78
Chance	67, 71
Chancy	12
Chandler	41, 424
Chapman	1, 255
Chappell	89, 97, 99, 101, 103, 105, 106, 111
Charley	155, 156
Charlton	332
Chase	1, 25, 36
Chastain	44, 196, 197, 199
Checkley	383
Cheek	307
Chenault	22, 23, 24
Chenoweth	36, 388
Chesney	30
Chess	178

Chilcott 76
Childers 30
Childress 426
Chinn 1, 2
Chinoweth 47
Chipman 36
Choran 141
Chowning 191
Chrisman 282
Christian 64, 407
Christie 67, 230, 278
Chritton 390
Church 21, 67
Churchman 9
Clampitt 399
Clapp 58
Clark 15, 17, 18, 29, 36, 45, 63, 67, 139, 147, 210, 211, 325, 359, 360, 405, 411, 414
Clary 22, 29
Claspill 18
Claxton 34
Clayton 345
Clear 30
Clegg 174
Clements 35, 246
Clemmons 408
Clendenin 178
Clentine 251
Cleveland 39
Clevinger 28
Clifford 5
Clifton 38
Cline 30
Clinton 1, 5
Clipper 141
Cloud 39, 42, 390
Clugston 26
Clupper 141
Coale 67
Coalscott 9
Coate 233, 235
Coates 436
Cobb 45
Coble 61, 72, 394
Cochran 15, 141, 193
Cochrane 20
Cochren 174
Cochron 191
Cockerham 75, 78
Cockran 18
Coddington 22, 27
Coe 48
Cofer 415
Coffelt 67
Coffey 141
Coffin 11, 21, 278
Coffland 141
Coffman 28, 67, 214
Coghill 436
Cogshill 212
Colclasure 388
Cole 9, 181, 265, 308
Coleman . . 8, 9, 10, 12, 86, 110, 111, 119, 120, 291
Coleson 28
Colglazier 246, 455
Colle 319
Collier 350
Collins . . 58, 62, 63, 65, 78, 245, 456
Colvin 28
Combs 192, 193, 213
Comer 50, 67
Commons 233, 278
Compton 43
Comstock 78
Conaway 2, 9, 22, 23
Conder 40
Condict 48, 49
Conger 94
Congleton 76
Conkling 9
Conley 437
Conn 1, 22, 24
Connaway 9
Connelly 350, 405
Conner 1, 4, 6, 7, 9, 12, 13, 19, 333, 337
Conoway 362
Conrad 147, 156
Conrod 120
Converse 53, 56, 58, 59
Cook . . . 5, 9, 10, 11, 21, 23, 25, 29, 30, 36, 44, 50, 235, 301, 331, 336, 340, 341, 342, 393, 433, 434
Cooksey 67, 348
Cooley 5, 14, 74, 390
Cooly 67
Coombs 61, 243
Cooms 27, 28
Coon 6, 11, 136
Coonce 210
Cooney 196
Coonrod . . 86, 92, 93, 104, 111, 119, 125, 235
Cooper . . . 11, 34, 176, 235, 245, 264, 265
Cooprider 67, 72, 209
Coots 33
Coovert 7
Cope 146
Copeland 26, 37, 50, 163
Copelin 35, 36
Copland 76
Copsey 1
Corbin 2, 9, 11, 14, 20
Cordale 77
Corder 3
Corey 229
Corneleson 245
Cornelius 128, 139
Cornwall 1
Cornwell 42
Corwin 18
Cory 30, 31, 308
Cosby 21
Cosgrove 45
Coshaw 5, 9
Cotner 152, 153, 154
Cotton 212
Cottral 30
Cottrall 29
Cottrel 23
Cottrell 22, 24
Coulson 196, 268
Coulter 388
Covall 313
Covert 7
Cowell 433
Cowen 67
Cox . . 11, 17, 33, 38, 39, 43, 47, 48, 51, 67, 74, 75, 77, 195, 197, 213, 219, 233, 235, 387, 388, 394
Coy 6, 7
Crab 141
Craft 1
Crafton 67, 71
Craig 6, 74, 411, 422, 434, 439, 449
Cramer 128
Crandall 149
Crandel 28
Crandle 6, 10
Crane . . 25, 31, 74, 76, 141, 437
Craton 117
Cravens 244, 408
Crawford 1, 18, 26, 29, 175, 195, 197
Crayton 92
Creech 67
Creek 20, 21, 24, 25, 28
Crenshaw 78
Crislor 9
Crissman 30
Crist 22, 27, 67, 208
Critchefield 229
Croake 67
Crocker 384
Cromer 264
Cromwell 28, 31, 70, 71, 72, 377
Crose 15, 16
Cross 46, 395
Crossley 67
Crouch 1, 3, 19, 21, 24, 128
Crow 97, 235
Crowe 451
Crowfoot 12
Cruft 382
Crull 9
Crum 13, 21
Crume 1
Crummel 67
Crums 77
Crusan 24
Cruse 400
Crutchfield 36
Cruzan 31
Cruze 273, 274
Culbertson 12, 174, 175
Culley 141
Cullum 438
Cully 23, 30, 31
Culp 335, 339
Cumings 178
Cummin 120
Cummings 92, 391
Cummins 110, 210, 211
Cundiff 157, 160
Cunliff 162
Cunningham 4, 5, 6, 13, 21, 22, 30, 41, 193, 197, 198, 370
Cuppy . . . 14, 31, 209, 211, 212, 213, 214, 218, 223
Curl 274
Curran 64
Currey 233
Currie 173
Curry 36, 67, 185, 192, 215, 216
Curtis 8, 10, 273, 394
Curtner 393
Cushman 407, 408, 409, 410
Custer 9
Cutlar 5
Cutsinger 39
Cuzick 29, 30

D

Dagett 15
Daggy 337, 340
Dahlmann 434
Dailey 5, 9, 14
Dakey 3
Dale 1, 5, 12, 426
Dalgarn 71
Dalglish 174
Dallas 1, 141
Dalton 67, 71, 78
Dammann 377
Dampster 187, 221
Dance 9
Dangerfield 321
Daniel 5, 7, 9, 210, 211, 212
Daniels 296
Danner 1, 5, 9, 435, 439
Danning 267
Dare 26
Darnall 438
Darnell 9
Darr 176
Darroch 37
Darter 7, 9, 21
Dartes 5
Daugherty 360
Davenport 23, 340, 392, 395
Davey 26
David 145
Davidson 37, 158, 162, 324, 360
Davis . . 1, 9, 17, 22, 23, 24, 27, 29, 30, 34, 37, 45, 71, 128, 136, 141, 161, 163, 192, 193, 195, 197, 198, 199, 210, 213, 233, 235, 244, 331, 333, 349, 396, 398, 400, 434
Davison 160, 162
Davisson 50
Dawhitt 18
Dawson 1, 2, 5, 6, 9, 22, 50, 154, 236, 274
Day . . . 30, 47, 49, 75, 328, 329, 330, 355, 433
Dayhuff 38
De Moss 378
DeBarth 439
Deacons 27
Deakins 256
Deal 67, 70
Dean 150
Deardorf 23, 357, 358
Debolt 23
Deboy 24, 316
Debruiler 395
Decamp 6, 8
Decker 92, 119, 336, 389
Deever 29
Defendoll 95
Defoe 412

Defore 67	Duitt 62, 63	**F**
Degraaf 5	Dula 333, 338	
Degrauft 29	Duly 141	Faith 323
Dehart 19	Dumont 229, 306, 307, 308,	Fale 22
Dehaven 1, 9	309, 311, 312	Fansby 94
Deist 141	Dunbar 21, 25, 29	Fansler 288
Delabar 2	Duncan ... 23, 41, 48, 163, 349	Farel 4
Delapp 198	Dungan 2, 5, 6, 11, 12	Farlow 27, 36, 43, 50
Delard 34	Dunham 2, 9, 24	Farmer 15, 16, 26, 28
Delon 51	Dunn 9, 274, 403, 405	Farnsworth 18
Delts 272	Durbin 5	Farwell 311
Demar 62	Durham 33, 50, 63, 236	Fauntleroy .. 317, 318, 319, 320,
Demaree ... 141, 362, 439, 441,	Durman 8	321, 322, 323, 324
442	Durrett 389	Fautharp 14
Deming 331, 336	Dutton 67	Fearis 10
Demmett 17	Duval 433	Featherkile 42
Demoss 13	Dwiggins 23, 25, 27, 307	Feliden 10
Denison 1, 332	Dyar 67	Felix 275
Deniston 9, 11	Dye 27	Felker 375, 377
Denman 20	Dyer 71	Feltus 327
Dennington 30		Fender 22, 50
Denniston 23	**E**	Ferguson 10, 22, 23, 24, 27,
Denny ... 17, 33, 42, 62, 63, 67,		31, 45, 62, 63, 65, 190, 193,
71	Eacret 5	194, 219, 221, 227, 228, 313,
Denslow 391	Eades 70	316
Denton 259	Eagan 5, 7	Ferree 2, 5, 190, 191, 192,
Derringer 128, 141, 145, 146	Earl 394	194, 196, 197, 198
Derry 5	Early 6	Ferril 236
Detraz 310, 311, 436	Easly 6	Ferris 57
Devin 107	Easther 9	Ficklin 255
Deweese 348	Eben 391	Field 246
Dewey 21, 30, 62, 63	Eckara 67	Fields 37
Dick 148, 149	Eddy 9, 70, 434	Figley 434
Dicken 7, 11	Edgerton 386	Filpoat 2
Dickerson 2, 160, 163, 208,	Edmonds 8	Finch 2, 3, 4
337, 341	Edmondson 70, 371	Findley 75, 76
Dickey .. 2, 4, 5, 6, 9, 14, 158	Edwards 11	Finley 44, 183, 291
Dickings 67	Ehrhart 377	Finnel 402
Dickison 20	Eldre 157	Finney 10
Dicks 211, 233, 236, 367	Eldred 433	Fise 27
Dickson 9, 10, 356	Eldredge 425	Fish 5
Diest 141	Eldridge ... 203, 205, 206, 208,	Fisher 2, 20, 29, 388
Dietz 62, 63	210, 211	Fislar 167, 168
Dillard 337, 340	Elgin 444	Fitch 426
Dille 3	Eliot 212	Fite 64
Dillin 97, 99	Eller 392	Fitz Randolph 252
Dillins 108	Ellexson 41	Fitzgerald 47, 48
Dillman 182, 433	Elliot 38, 45, 105, 106	Fitzsimmons 159
Dillon 12, 236	Elliott .. 3, 4, 20, 24, 47, 49, 51,	Flack 24, 30
Dils 4	75, 78, 191, 434	Flanagan 67
Diltz 271	Ellis .. 9, 10, 13, 14, 16, 17, 19,	Fleener 136
Dimmitt 400	31, 39, 47, 49, 62, 67, 244	Fleshman 63, 156
Disher 12	Ellison 4	Fletcher 350, 387
Dishman 364	Ellwanger 373, 375	Flick 67
Ditto 274	Elrod 38	Flinn 176, 178
Divine 39	Elston 2, 23, 26, 178	Flinn Jr. 75
Dix 37, 236	Elwell 30	Flint 141
Dixon 7, 16, 33, 36, 38, 42,	Ely 15, 21, 67	Flowers 10, 370
44, 77, 274, 344, 390	Embree 5	Foglesong 267
Doak 35	Emely 12	Ford 6, 60, 62, 195, 196
Doan 9, 36, 38	Emery 214	Foreman 7, 375, 376
Dodd .. 166, 203, 210, 211, 248,	Emily 149	Foresythe 60, 63
379	Emmert 23, 24	Forgey 18
Dodds 199, 264	Emmons 22	Forman 351
Doerflier 258	Endsley 1	Forster 236
Dolsberry 141	Enfield 373	Fortener 67
Donelson 128	Engle .. 195, 199, 314, 315, 316,	Fosdick 20
Donlon 391	317, 389	Foshee 49
Dooley 163	Ennis 2	Fosher 24, 26
Dopson 74	Eoff 140, 141	Foster 3, 5, 21, 96, 382
Dorsey 49	Erton 40	Fou 38
Dosson 212	Ervin 10	Fouch 2
Doty 194	Erway 434	Foulk 60
Douden 141	Eskew 2, 7, 10, 14	Fountain 5, 14, 178
Douglass 74, 152, 153	Eskum 2	Fouse 15
Douthett 406	Essley 26	Foushee 321, 323
Douthit 2	Essly 31	Foust 15, 18
Dow 174, 439	Esteb 50	Fouts 50, 392, 397
Dowden 128, 141, 157	Estep 22	Foutz 25, 29, 31
Downey 290	Estes 401	Fowler 157, 433
Downing 71, 169	Etchison 30	Fox 182, 183, 211, 276, 310
Downning 67	Eugene 341	Foxworthy 159, 409
Downs 47, 62, 67, 429	Evans 5, 29, 38, 40, 86, 236,	Frakes 153, 208, 209, 213
Drake 1, 48, 67, 70, 71, 72,	365, 400	Frame 49, 360
222, 228, 409	Everett 388	Francis 5
Draper 9, 33, 78, 192, 236	Everson 254, 255	Frankebarger 359
Drexilius 351	Everts 25, 29	Franklin 14, 15, 19, 396
Druck 21	Ewalt 76	Fravel 286
Drummond 84, 85	Ewell 407	Frazee 10
Drury 29	Ewing 2, 10, 21, 25, 27, 30,	Frazier 7, 22, 44, 172, 388,
DuBois 94	31, 76, 92, 212	445
Dubois 23, 25, 26, 27	Eyestone 5	Frazure 7, 67
Dudley .. 75, 78, 192, 193, 215	Eystone 4	Fredd 344
Duffy 5, 335, 339, 340		Frederick 94, 110, 111
Dufour 229, 311, 432		

Freedly 70
Freel 15
Freeland 24
Freeman ... 2, 9, 10, 11, 25, 30, 35, 37, 39
Freit 39
French 332, 415, 444, 446
Freund 424, 427
Friback 394
Frisbee 50
Frisbie 47
Fritch 130, 146
Froggatt 280
Froment 210, 218
Frost 43
Frownfelter 135, 136, 144, 146, 147
Fruits 24
Fry 196, 434
Fryar 266
Fryberger 2
Fuel 2
Fulghum 280
Fullen 5
Fuller 2, 5, 20, 70
Fulton 34, 170, 171, 173
Fultz 454
Funk 152, 285, 338, 341
Funkhauser 286
Fuquay 49
Furgerson 268
Furguson 10
Fuson 209, 210

G

Gaby 21, 24, 29
Gage 30, 248
Gahn 145
Gailbreath 51
Gaither 152, 153
Galaspy 67
Galbreath 16
Galbreth 8
Galloway 452
Gambill 195
Gamble 328
Gambol 194
Gambril 30
Gamere 71
Gammon 39
Gard 2, 9, 10, 25, 31
Gardner 23, 159, 210, 212, 213, 369, 370, 389, 439
Garman 352, 357
Garner 50, 62, 362
Garrett 5, 9, 11, 278
Garrison 5, 10, 24
Garvey 221
Garwood 2
Gary 26, 29
Gaston 390
Gates 2, 10, 11, 16, 65, 149, 395
Gawdy 34
Geiger 102
Gentry 2, 25, 26, 48
Genung 329
Gerherd 141
Gerrel 67
Gherkin 44
Gibbens 389
Gibbs 40
Gibson 141, 327, 398, 399, 410
Gifford 5, 39, 46
Gilbert 31, 270
Gilbrech 71
Gilchrist 328
Gildea 70
Gilham 148
Gill 65, 146
Gillam 2, 5
Gillaspie 77
Gilleland 9, 23, 25, 26, 27
Gillespie 421
Gilliland 5, 24
Gillison 3
Gillot 328
Gillum 44
Gilman 325, 326
Gilmore 10
Gimble 373
Girty 440
Gish 357, 358, 359, 360

Gladish 97, 107, 110, 111
Glaesline 176
Glass 94
Gleason 5, 356
Gleitz 375, 377
Glen 174
Glenn 48
Glidden 128, 129
Glidewell 25
Glover 37, 210
Goble 27, 28, 29
Goddard 19
Godwin 67, 71, 349
Goe 5
Goett 275
Goff 2, 41
Goforth 77
Going 55, 56
Golay 230, 439
Goldsberry 16
Goldsmith 278
Good 31
Goodden 18
Gooden 129, 412
Gooding 10, 11, 13
Goodlander 9, 10
Goodloe 323
Goodrich 67
Goodwin 5, 6, 10, 429
Gorden 10
Gordon 9, 10, 141, 172, 174, 308
Gorman 2, 4, 141
Gornell 13
Gorrell 14
Goss 75, 78, 454
Gossett 9
Gott 23
Goudy 27, 29
Goutrey 78
Gowans 81
Gowens 67
Grabel 67
Grable 156
Grace 2, 341
Graham .. 23, 37, 48, 49, 81, 83, 175, 210, 264, 265, 327, 328, 329, 330, 331, 333, 334, 335, 337, 338, 341, 423, 434
Gran 1
Grant 210, 329
Grantham 76
Grave 51
Graves 67, 70, 360
Gray ... 2, 5, 15, 24, 28, 33, 47, 49, 101, 103, 112, 141, 172, 174, 175, 199, 321, 351, 400, 409
Graybill 359
Greeley 316
Green 2, 10, 16, 33, 39, 40, 67, 156, 237, 264, 370, 384
Greene 8, 51
Greenlee 250
Greeor 1
Greer 1, 4, 10, 369, 370
Gregg 332, 344
Gregory 34
Grenn 12
Greor 5
Grewell 2, 5
Grey 435
Griffen 321
Griffin .. 10, 320, 377, 411, 441, 456
Griffis 2
Griffith .. 5, 25, 60, 67, 74, 164, 211, 212, 213, 230, 438
Griffy 67
Griggs 28, 163
Grigs 28
Grigsby 190, 192
Grimel 2
Grimes 21, 31, 71
Grisard 230
Groendyke 6
Groenendyke 10
Groover 164
Grosclose 13
Grose 10
Grossclop 5
Grossclose 6
Grover 29
Groves 10, 153
Grunendike 10

Guard 10
Guest 152, 329, 331
Guilbert 348
Guilder 349
Guinn 16, 17
Guire 237
Gulick 423
Gunn 7, 10, 12
Gunnion 175
Gunthert 377
Gunton 42
Guntryman 208
Gutherie 176, 178
Guthery 176
Guthrey 178
Guthrie 176, 178, 179
Gwaltney 448
Gwinn 38, 141, 394

H

Hackleman ..4, 5, 7, 11, 14, 257
Hackworth 67
Haden 213, 214
Hadley 35, 37, 39, 40, 233, 342, 343, 345, 367
Hageman 276
Hagens 244
Hager 2, 332, 336
Haggardy Sr. 425
Haggart 141
Haines 150, 264, 400
Hainey 194
Haken 375
Halberstadt .. 347, 348, 349, 350
Halbert 3
Hale .. 2, 67, 160, 192, 194, 270, 326, 360
Hall ... 9, 25, 48, 64, 65, 68, 94, 157, 340, 342, 351, 389, 410, 435, 436
Hallett 1
Hallowell 385
Hamblen 129
Hamblin 141
Hamel 10
Hamer 10
Hamilton .. 1, 2, 4, 5, 6, 10, 11, 14, 22, 24, 28, 30, 31, 34, 75, 160, 161, 173, 214, 237
Hammack 212
Hammer 5, 8
Hammond 2, 60, 62, 63
Hamon 340, 341, 342
Hampton 162
Hanam 76
Hancock 27, 47, 168, 263, 264, 411
Hand 23
Handy 237
Hanes 28
Hankins 8, 10
Hanks 48, 108, 447
Hanly 351
Hanna 10, 23, 174, 210, 390
Hannah 174
Hannan 250
Hanners 77
Hanson 390
Hantwerk 71
Harbaugh 152
Harbin 94
Harbison 96, 97, 101, 102, 103, 110, 111, 112, 117, 451
Harbolt 223
Harden 5, 29, 136, 141
Hardenon 1
Hardesty 4, 5
Hardin 243, 244, 388, 439
Harding 2, 5, 30, 146
Hardister 398
Hardman 23, 25, 45, 64
Hardwick 157, 316
Hardy .. 4, 9, 10, 23, 188, 352, 353, 354, 355, 356
Harell 11
Hargrave 49
Hargrove 47, 48, 111
Harlan .. 1, 2, 5, 10, 11, 13, 21, 22, 23, 25, 26
Harlen 8, 10
Harlon 1
Harmon 42
Harmonson 424, 425
Harned 41, 48

Harp	71	
Harper	3, 11, 27, 28, 63	
Harpine	407, 408	
Harpold	275	
Harpole	48	
Harpool	68	
Harr	285	
Harram	16	
Harrel	9	
Harrell	5, 7, 14, 86, 89, 92, 105, 106, 109, 110, 111, 112, 113, 119, 122, 126, 183	
Harrick	93	
Harriman	30	
Harrington	433	
Harris	3, 6, 7, 8, 10, 23, 29, 60, 210, 211, 228, 269, 279	
Harrison	6, 8, 11, 103, 179, 237	
Harrold	5	
Harroll	25	
Harshbarger	357, 358, 360, 361	
Hart	5, 14, 35, 65, 191, 437	
Harter	2	
Hartley	60	
Hartman	62, 63	
Hartzel	26	
Harvey	25, 26, 39, 43, 51, 233, 252, 274, 346, 367, 368, 369, 400, 401	
Hasbrook	327	
Haskell	435, 436, 437	
Hasket	237	
Hasty	25	
Hatfield	11, 329, 423	
Hathaway	5	
Hauck	377	
Havens	5	
Hawes	31	
Hawk	5	
Hawkins	2, 5, 6, 7, 10, 50, 188, 190, 192, 193, 194, 195, 196, 256, 257, 297, 327	
Haworth	233, 237	
Hay	46, 60, 170	
Hayden	22, 26, 28, 160	
Haydon	350	
Hayes	4	
Haynes	15, 23, 27, 35	
Hays	2, 349	
Hayward	6, 10, 21	
Haywood	263	
Hayworth	21	
Hazelrigg	214	
Hazelton	21, 26	
Hazelwood	444	
Hazleton	24	
Heacock	437	
Heath	19	
Heaton	10, 14, 51	
Heavenridge	22, 26, 27, 30	
Heck	11	
Heckman	24	
Heddy	68	
Hedge	165	
Hedges	95, 163	
Heirs	6	
Heizer	2	
Heller	78	
Helm	2, 7, 12	
Helmick	25, 27	
Helms	129, 142, 182	
Helton	70	
Hemphill	451	
Hemsted	7	
Henby	299	
Henderson	2, 5, 7, 10, 13, 77, 86, 177, 179, 209, 237, 310, 437, 439	
Hendricks	2, 7, 9, 13, 28, 156, 164, 195, 199, 423	
Hendrix	2, 10, 164	
Henley	37, 42, 45, 51	
Henning	10	
Henry	5, 6, 13, 26, 129, 142, 436	
Hensel	371, 372, 374, 375, 377	
Herbster	161	
Herndon	348, 350	
Herrick	29	
Herrington	74	
Herrod	429	
Herron	28	
Hertsel	44	
Hesler	26	
Hess	62, 63	
Hessennauer	146	
Heston	18	
Hetzler	30	
Hiatt	36, 76, 142, 164, 280, 367, 400, 401	
Hibbs	10	
Hickman	15, 22, 28, 71, 166, 248, 378, 379, 380	
Hicks	14, 71, 77, 405	
Hiers	5, 6	
Hiett	76	
Higby	6	
Higdon	213, 214	
Higdon Jr.	214	
Higgins	12, 51	
Highbanks	103	
Highley	10	
Hilderbrand	23	
Hill	5, 10, 13, 23, 27, 42, 46, 138, 182, 187, 190, 191, 193, 195, 197, 198, 209, 210, 214, 217, 218, 223, 224, 225, 256, 320	
Hillis	10, 410	
Hilt	16	
Himes	360	
Hinckley	384	
Hinds	9, 60, 63, 255	
Hines	48, 183	
Hinman	48, 210	
Hinote	71, 72	
Hinshaw	398, 400, 401	
Hinton	6, 39	
Hippard	280	
Hislip	244	
Hite	282, 363	
Hittle	2	
Hix	44, 68	
Hobbs	6, 136	
Hobson	36, 45, 387	
Hoby	155	
Hockett	237	
Hockman	446	
Hodges	35, 210, 214, 216, 217, 222, 223, 302	
Hodgin	18	
Hodson	25	
Hoemler	36	
Hoff	15	
Hoffield	375	
Hoffman	284, 326	
Hogan	21	
Hogg	35	
Hoggatt	233, 237, 367	
Hogle	288	
Hoglen	337	
Hogue	25	
Hoke	409, 410	
Holaday	42, 233	
Holden	425	
Holladay	16, 238	
Holland	5, 6, 23, 25, 30, 75, 179	
Hollet	51	
Hollett	51	
Holliday	34, 37, 40, 380, 381	
Hollingsworth	21, 23, 27, 238, 279, 437	
Hollis	27	
Holloway	16, 21	
Hollowell	35, 37, 38, 245, 386, 387, 388, 389, 390	
Holly	259	
Holman	51, 77	
Holmes	19, 34, 41, 45, 75, 266	
Holoday	45	
Holoway	25	
Holson	68	
Holt	59, 60, 64, 68, 195	
Holz	339, 341	
Homer	155	
Honeycut	142	
Hood	19, 140, 261, 330	
Hooker	303	
Hoover	50, 74, 316, 392, 393, 394, 395, 396, 397, 398, 399, 401, 402	
Hope	112	
Hopewell	191, 193, 211	
Hopkins	172, 315, 395	
Hopper	21, 25	
Horn	83	
Hornaday	76, 92, 105, 107, 119, 274	
Horne	314	
Hornida	107	
Hornsted	3	
Horrell	2	
Horton	48, 71, 183	
Hosea	110	
Hoskins	196	
Hostutter	41	
Hottell	156	
Houck	194	
Hough	278	
Hougham	1, 6	
Houghham	2	
Houghland	6, 19	
Houghton	2	
Hougland	49	
Houpt	197	
Houser	153	
Houstain	195	
Houston	10, 60, 62, 63, 70, 190, 192, 195, 197, 198	
How	10	
Howard	10, 64, 65, 76, 182, 183, 261, 354, 356, 360, 405, 406	
Howe	35	
Howel	26	
Howell	4, 94, 344	
Howers	142	
Howk	62	
Howren	31	
Howser	155	
Hoyt	72	
Hubard	76, 177	
Hubbard	29	
Hubbell	2	
Hubble	3, 10, 14	
Huckaby	238	
Huckleberry	60, 63	
Huddleston	30	
Hudelson	255, 256	
Hudson	7, 12, 48, 68, 255	
Hudspeth	48	
Hues	70	
Huff	16, 21, 22, 74, 278, 328	
Huffman	1, 27, 283	
Hufman	68	
Huges	260	
Hughes	22, 145, 147, 179, 254, 402, 403, 404, 405	
Hughs	27, 60	
Hukill	436	
Hulbert	2, 12	
Hulin	142	
Hull	35, 279	
Huls	12	
Hummel	195, 198, 199	
Hunt	21, 22, 50, 51, 142, 233, 238, 245, 250, 259, 425, 426	
Hunter	18, 20, 22, 82, 152	
Hurd	142	
Hurdle	142	
Husband	47	
Hussey	278, 279	
Huston	6, 8, 17, 22, 23, 29, 42, 364	
Hutchens	50, 396	
Hutchins	36, 278, 394	
Hutchinson	23, 452	
Hutchison	39, 142	
Hyde	354, 356	

I

Ice	379
Igleheart	49
Iles	10
Imbler	396
Imel	6, 31
Imire	175
Ingalls	79
Ingals	83
Ingersull	16
Ingle	191, 192, 193
Ingram	197
Inman	153, 154
Inwood	335
Ireland	18
Irvin	6, 35, 174
Irvine	45, 175
Irwin	20
Irwine	10
Isaac	171

Isaacs 15	Kelley 47, 49, 74, 76, 129, 142, 339, 341, 435	**L**
Iseley 16	Kelley Jr. 76	LaFollette 360
Iseminger 74, 183	Kelly 23, 68, 149, 211, 233, 239	Lacefield 211
Iseninge 33		Lacock 219
Isgrigg 8, 9, 10	Kelsey 11, 14, 15	Lacy 239, 437
Isley 15	Kelso 3, 129, 136, 145, 243	Ladd 1, 6
Ivers 18	Keltner 29	Ladley 12
Ives 15, 325, 326, 327	Kenady 8	Lafferty 408
	Kenayer 412	Laforge 348
J	Kendal 6, 11	Lafuse 25, 27
Jack 5, 8	Kendall ... 9, 16, 158, 161, 165	Lafuze 22
Jackson ... 1, 9, 11, 64, 74, 172, 400	Kendrick 266	Lain 6
	Kennedy 15, 19, 129, 142, 273, 274, 328, 337, 442	Laing 173
Jacobs 2, 10, 74, 75, 425		Lair 10
Jacobsen 334, 338	Kennel 2	Lake 11, 12, 71, 413, 414
Jacquart 433	Kennerly 406, 407, 408, 411	Lakey 3, 7
Jager 230	Kenser 16	Lakin 6, 8
James 17, 46, 60, 406, 407, 411	Kentley 348	Lamb 18, 49, 89, 105, 122, 309, 311, 312, 313
	Kently 349	
Jamison 15, 175	Kephart 142, 145	Lambdin 37
Janney 14, 15, 16	Keran 343	Lamberson 438
Jarrald 96	Kercheval 228	Lambert 6, 163
Jay 21, 280	Kerkham 213	Lambeth 401
Jeffcoat 238	Kernodle 26, 29	Lamer 142
Jefferson 30	Kerns 362, 442, 451, 452	Lamson 2, 436
Jeffery 10	Kerr 16, 20	Lancaster 376
Jeffries 392, 394	Kessler 360	Lancing 35
Jeffry 5	Kester ... 205, 206, 208, 218, 219, 220, 221, 222, 227	Landers 68, 350
Jeger 157		Landes 23, 25, 29, 31
Jenkins 30, 152, 256	Ketcham 260	Landis .. 331, 335, 339, 340, 341
Jennings 22, 58, 396	Ketchell 76	Lane ... 6, 8, 93, 102, 109, 160, 395
Jenny 238	Keton 295	
Jerald 119	Key 15, 21	Langloy 16
Jerrald 103	Keys 444	Langston 21, 24, 26, 29
Jerrel 119	Kidd 6	Lanham 435
Jerrell 95	Kiernan 343	Lankford 72
Jessop 33, 50, 233	Killeon 68	Larance 297
Jessup 238, 400	Killion 68, 70	Larey 16
Jeter 45	Kimbrel 246	Large 18
Jewel 212	Kimery 71	Larimore 2, 6, 9, 11
Jewell 68, 213	Kinaston 13	Larkin 22
Jewlin 213	Kinder 14	Lartham 68
Jinks 4, 6	Kindle 11, 68, 78	Lassley 20
Job 28	Kindred 75, 177	Lassly 22
John 11, 50	King ... 9, 48, 61, 85, 263, 264, 265, 437	Laswell 211, 213
Johns 7, 12		Latham 70, 71
Johnson 2, 5, 9, 11, 12, 13, 18, 20, 28, 29, 30, 31, 34, 39, 40, 42, 48, 49, 61, 68, 75, 77, 96, 103, 111, 117, 129, 162, 172, 238, 256, 315, 344, 396, 402, 425, 449, 456	Kingery 27, 28, 29, 31	Lathers 11
	Kingry 21, 22, 23, 24, 26	Latta 172
	Kingsley 338	Laughery 63
	Kinkade 388	Law 6, 395
	Kinman ... 93, 95, 97, 114, 119, 122	Lawderback 11
Johnsons 108		Lawrence 47, 329
Johnston .. 15, 20, 29, 114, 279, 411, 433, 450	Kinnear 172	Laws 61, 62, 63
	Kinney 422	Lawson 11, 68
Jones ... 2, 6, 10, 11, 14, 15, 18, 24, 27, 30, 31, 33, 34, 35, 37, 38, 43, 46, 49, 50, 68, 70, 74, 77, 129, 165, 224, 239, 280, 322, 349, 368, 396	Kinser 15	Layton 6
	Kinsey 166	Laywood 239
	Kintzley 68	Le Clerc 230
	Kinworthy 18	Leach ... 65, 157, 158, 163, 165, 199, 412
	Kippers 2	
	Kirby 34	Leachman 159, 160, 161
Jordan .. 110, 125, 362, 442, 451	Kirckman 3	Leak ... 157, 158, 159, 160, 161, 162, 164
Jorden 18, 142	Kirk 39, 198	
Jose 288	Kirkham 213, 364, 376, 377	Lear 150
Judd 47	Kirkpatrick ... 6, 11, 21, 26, 28, 63, 173, 350, 444	Lebrook 21
Jukes 48		Ledbetter 162
Julian ... 2, 3, 289, 290, 291, 292	Kirkwood 5, 6, 175	Ledgerwood 170, 173
Julin 2	Kirtley 350, 351	Lee .. 11, 41, 46, 212, 254, 255, 327
Julyan 214	Kissinger 268	
Justice 11	Kitchen 3, 7, 220	Leech 94
	Klinack 3	Leedy 288
K	Kline 25	Leeper 27, 28
Kaighn 402	Klink 10	Leeright 47
Kain 129, 142	Klum 6, 7, 11	Lefforce 3
Kaiser 439	Knap 356	Leforce 11
Kaper 142	Knapper 19	Legg 7, 8, 11
Karnes 77	Knight 2	Lemmon 149
Karr 47	Knott 2, 6, 8, 10, 23, 24, 25, 30, 31, 164	Lemmons 30
Kaserman 145		Lemon 364
Kasserman 142	Knox 46, 438	Lemons 191
Kay 413	Knutt 22	Lemp 177
Keach 168	Koffel 394	Lenau 153
Kearby 41, 452	Kolb 6, 8, 10, 11, 12	Lenn 47
Keaton 297	Kraft 375	Lennen 24
Keefe 255	Kramer 389	Lennon 30
Keeling 433	Kreiling 268	Leonard ... 6, 11, 23, 35, 36, 40, 43, 45, 68, 92, 146, 151, 154
Keen 195, 197	Kress 76	
Keeney 24, 25	Krom 23	Lesh 410
Keever 31	Kulberson 12	Leslie 310
Keffer 24	Kuykendall 119	Lett 95
Keith 33	Kyger 22	Leviston 22, 23
Kelamo 390	Kyle 23	Lewark 11
Keller 75, 78, 142, 154, 256, 283, 288, 357		

Lewis 2, 10, 11, 12, 13, 21, 24, 29, 43, 46, 49, 50, 159, 160, 161, 239, 321	M'Grew 65, 66	McCall 423
Light 71, 411, 413, 414	MCampbell 61	McCallan 20
Ligthfoot 11	MCune 62	McCallum 433, 436
Lilley 21	Mabury 65	McCann 11
Limpus 13	MacJordan 276	McCarn 24, 27
Limpuss 5	Mace 68, 71, 72	McCartney 288
Lincoln 53	Mack 447	McCarty ... 2, 3, 12, 20, 51, 406
Linder 6	Macy 11, 22, 30	McCasland 172
Lindley .. 34, 37, 38, 39, 41, 43, 45, 239, 344, 388, 389, 390, 400, 452	Madden 23, 25, 367, 368	McCauly 22
	Maddox 228	McCay 4
	Maddux 371	McCenziel 395
	Magby 4, 210	McClain 46, 50
Lindsay 37, 40, 41, 83, 91, 109, 110, 117	Mager 21	McClanahan 193, 213
	Magner 46	McClane 46
Lindsey 27, 103, 119	Maguire 68	McClanihan 191
Lindy 94	Mahan 17, 41, 195, 211	McClannahan 186, 194, 196, 197, 198, 213, 218, 223, 224
Linley 70	Mahorney 360	
Linn 39, 72	Mailen 22	McClary 2, 47
Linney 239	Maines 395	McCleary 6
Lints 71	Mains 437	McClenahan 171
Linwell 11	Majors 29	McClintic 160
Lions 1	Malcolmson 437, 438	McClintick 161, 162
Lipes 163	Malin 308	McClure 119, 222
Lister 27	Mallery 55	McClurken 30
Liston 186, 189, 190, 192, 193, 197, 205, 208, 209, 213, 222	Mallicoat 431	McCollam 29
	Malone 190, 191	McColley 5
	Malott 99	McCollister 68
Lite 68	Mandeville 142	McComas 28
Littell 253	Maners 295	McComb 336
Little 50, 280	Manlove 5, 6, 11	McCombs 15, 51
Littlepage 49, 321	Manly 1	McConkey 6, 11
Littrel 2	Mann 31, 68, 174, 329, 331, 335, 340	McConnell 413
Littrell 21		McCord ... 29, 49, 336, 340, 342
Litz 182	Mansfield 11, 20, 21	McCormack 2, 4, 6
Liveley 260	Manvill 229	McCormic 61, 63
Livingston 129	Mapes 75	McCormick .. 11, 17, 19, 20, 55, 64
Lize 6	Maple 6, 11, 13	
Lloyd ... 203, 210, 211, 212, 213	Maquiston 23	McCoun 7
Loan 93, 108	March 50	McCoy ... 11, 22, 24, 53, 54, 55, 58, 59, 60, 61, 63, 74, 119, 206, 207, 390, 452
Lockhart 35, 411	Marchall 324	
Lockwood 13, 435	Marcum 199	
Lockyear 49	Mardock 239	McCracken 39, 45, 173
Lodenback 6	Margeson 11	McCrane 3
Loder 12	Maris 35, 37, 39, 130, 239	McCray 1, 2, 11
Logan 2, 15	Mark 11	McCreary 250
Lond 244	Marley 45	McCrory 6, 12
Lone 148	Marling 77	McCrosky 161, 214
Loney 25	Marlow 190, 195, 196, 197, 198, 199, 209, 213, 214, 215	McCrurey 11
Long 11, 13, 24, 31, 62, 70, 72, 129, 137, 142, 145, 146, 326, 406, 407, 411, 432, 452		McCulla 49
	Marmon 410	McCullough 24, 25, 28, 70, 71, 434, 455
	Marrich 93	
Loony 47	Marrick 104, 107, 108	McCune 61
Lord 325	Marsh 15	McCurdy 17
Lotspiech 338, 341	Marshall .. 33, 36, 77, 150, 233, 245, 246, 331	McDaniel 40, 210, 211
Lottich 375, 376, 377		McDavy 332
Loudenback 2, 3	Marshill 262	McDeed 16
Louderback 12	Martin 3, 4, 5, 6, 8, 10, 11, 12, 16, 28, 41, 61, 119, 130, 164, 208, 211, 212, 218, 219, 220, 382, 384, 405, 414, 452, 455	McDill 23, 26, 31, 172, 173
Lout 47		McDonald ... 45, 113, 130, 142, 332, 337, 341, 356
Love 4, 48		
Lovejoy 48, 399		McDonough 426
Lovelace 192, 193, 194, 199, 223	Martindale 51	McDowel 22, 28
	Marts 41, 212, 213, 214	McDuff 433
Loveland 330	Mary Pearre 294	McFarland 14
Lovell 424	Mash 75	McFerrin 12
Low 300	Maskale 10	McGarvey .. 186, 191, 195, 197, 198, 221
Lowder 239	Mason 3, 11, 23, 290	
Lowdermilk 70, 71	Masters 6	McGauhey 370
Lowe 6, 395, 396	Mather 383	McGee 223, 364
Lowell 47	Mathews 11, 177	McGeer 23
Lower 11	Mathis 177	McGeorge 16
Loy 47	Matthews 46, 171, 173, 174	McGill 449
Luark 11	Matthewson 48	McGlashan 142
Lucas 6, 9, 72, 414, 415	Mattox 245, 327	McGlothlin 5
Luce 48	Mauck 156	McGreer 23, 27
Luckett 152, 154	Maudlin 393	McGrew 64, 186, 189, 198, 212, 213, 214
Lucus 15	Mavity 44	
Luebtan 424	Maxwell .. 51, 68, 186, 189, 190, 191, 192, 193, 196, 197, 250, 388	McGuire 16, 18
Lush 341		McGuiston 31
Luster 119		McHaffie 27, 29
Luther 68, 72	May ... 130, 154, 155, 180, 245, 251	McIlhenny 130, 140, 142
Lutz 424		McIntire 33, 68, 70, 72, 154
Lux 426	Mayberry 2, 65	McIntosh 24, 30, 94, 388
Luzader 194, 196, 197	Mayer 22	McIntyre 396
Lybrook 30	Mayfield 364, 365, 430	McKay 251, 435, 436, 437
Lynch .. 28, 29, 30, 41, 42, 274	Maze 31	McKeand 175
Lynn 119, 153	McAdoo 412	McKee 174
Lyons 2, 3, 8, 11, 331	McAllister 455	McKeen 228
Lyser 78	McAter 24	McKever 24
Lyster 74	McBride 68, 199, 338, 341, 342	McKimmey 177
Lytle 256		McKimmy 191
	McCabe 38, 44	McKinley 72, 187, 191, 193, 196
M	McCaffie 30	
	McCague 173	McKinney 3, 208, 212, 213, 214
M'Garah 65	McCain 24, 95	McKinzie 150

McLane 45, 452
McLaughlin 1, 3
McLean 24, 29
McLoney 11
McMahan 21, 22, 28
McMains 157
McMakin 230
McManis 214
McManus 3
McMillan 174
McMillen 26
McMurray 449
McMurtry 48
McNabb 28, 34
McNamer 27, 30
McNeal 8
McNemar 24, 25
McNew 275
McPheeters 43
McQuoid 26
McRay 21
McVey . . . 27, 31, 34, 35, 37, 38
McWhinney 266
McWilliams 444
Mcclannahan 192, 195
Mcdonall 213, 214
Mcgarvey 193
Mckiney 214
Mckinley 68
Mckinney 211
Mead . . 6, 10, 19, 20, 25, 28, 30
Meade 93, 104
Meads 108
Means 310
Mears 11
Mease 47
Medcalf 11, 181
Medonall 213
Medonnall 214
Meek 28, 29
Meeker 3, 336, 340
Meigs 116
Melette 380
Mellett 166
Melone . . . 3, 36, 192, 193, 195, 197
Melser 26, 29
Melton 11, 68, 137
Menander 335
Menary 14
Mench 26
Mendenhall 230, 239, 278, 279, 280
Meng 434
Mercer 18
Merchant 30
Meredith 266
Meriam 43
Merida 130
Merret 47
Merrifield 6
Merriman 14, 137, 139, 146, 147
Merrydith 40
Mertens 144, 147
Messamore 27, 28
Messersmith 2, 5, 6, 9, 11
Messmore 29
Meyer 337, 340, 376, 377
Michael 20
Michel 1
Mickle 18
Midinger 286
Miekle 83
Miers 13, 68, 378
Mikesel 15
Mikesell 20
Milan 434
Milbourn 93, 101, 102, 108, 112, 142
Milburn 117, 120, 130
Miles 70, 156, 239, 356
Miley . . . 86, 92, 103, 108, 110, 111, 112, 113, 117, 118, 119, 125
Miley Jr. 92, 117
Mileys 108
Miller 1, 2, 3, 5, 6, 7, 9, 10, 11, 17, 19, 20, 22, 23, 25, 27, 28, 29, 30, 31, 48, 51, 61, 64, 65, 66, 72, 75, 130, 137, 142, 145, 153, 160, 170, 191, 193, 196, 199, 224, 264, 323, 327, 330, 333, 337, 343, 360, 375, 389, 398, 426, 434, 437

Millicye 15
Milligan 209
Millis 40
Mills . . 3, 11, 23, 27, 29, 31, 33, 70, 71, 211, 212, 239, 277, 278, 398, 399
Milne 272
Milner 10, 11, 12
Miner 23, 24, 29
Minnick 426
Minor 20, 22, 48
Mires 3
Mise 210
Miskill 11
Mitcheal 190, 191
Mitchel . . 28, 31, 192, 194, 321
Mitchell . . 37, 40, 182, 190, 268
Mitchener 400
Mixell 25
Mobley 142
Moesser 376, 377
Moffett 10, 21
Moffit 25
Moffitt 4, 17
Mohler 425
Molder 17
Monical 447
Monk 447
Monks 316
Monohan 17
Monroe 6, 10, 68, 78, 130, 142
Monson 361
Montgomery . . . 6, 12, 113, 157, 165, 246, 431, 438
Moon 157
Mooney 367
Moor 31
Moore . . . 1, 6, 8, 12, 40, 43, 68, 75, 77, 130, 142, 168, 169, 190, 192, 214, 248, 300, 302, 319, 376, 379, 380, 396, 412, 415, 425, 444
Moorman 42, 44
Moots 19
Mordue 275
Moreillon 435
Moreland 140, 142
Moreod 230
Morgan . . . 3, 11, 26, 28, 68, 77, 78, 210, 299, 454
Morphew 21
Morris 3, 4, 7, 8, 16, 34, 37, 42, 51, 72, 73, 175, 239, 261, 275, 389, 393
Morrison . . 29, 50, 84, 130, 146, 233, 239
Morrow 12, 61, 171, 364
Morton . . . 79, 83, 174, 175, 290
Mosely 3
Moser 35, 142, 195
Mosier . . . 130, 135, 142, 197, 199, 200
Mosir 196
Moss 25, 28, 31
Mostiller 68
Mote 233, 240
Mothershead 370
Mott 18
Moulder 43
Mount 11, 362
Mouser 336
Mow 26, 27
Mowery 6
Moyer 25, 26, 28, 29, 30, 40
Mugg 431
Mugler 148
Mullerin 371
Mullin 280
Mulvany 245
Mungal 83
Munger 11
Murdock 18, 320, 321
Murphey 9
Murphy . . . 18, 26, 68, 145, 337
Murray 19, 280
Murry 137, 162
Musgrave 240
Music 68
Muston 3
Myer 24
Myers 3, 12, 71, 142, 250, 359, 360

N

Nail 268
Nance 376, 395
Nantz 154, 210
Nash 3
Navity 35
Neal 145, 194, 198, 321
Neely 11, 130
Nees 30, 70, 71, 72
Neese 72
Neff 142
Neicely 27
Neidigh 137, 138, 139, 145
Neidlinger 142
Nelson 9, 12, 20, 23, 31, 72, 158
Nesbit 186, 189, 190, 191, 193, 194, 195, 196, 197, 198, 199
Ness 71
Nettleton 322
Neville 363
Nevins 209
Newby 33, 74, 75, 76, 302, 389, 398, 401
Newhouse 3, 7, 9, 12, 337, 341
Newkin 4
Newkirk 20, 180
Newland . . 3, 12, 22, 25, 33, 74, 390, 391
Newlin 38, 43, 44, 233, 240, 274, 367, 368
Newman 17, 153, 155, 333, 338, 376, 394
Newnum 29
Newsom 51, 388
Newsome 388, 390
Newton 331
Nicewander 394
Nicholas 3, 7
Nichols 6, 19, 37, 260
Nicholson 299
Nickels 27
Nier 435
Nixon 180, 302
Noble 1, 12, 30
Noblitt 42, 240, 444
Noe 77
Nofsinger 359, 360
Nogle 267
Noon 152
Norris 3, 10, 12, 22, 27, 28, 30, 44
North 20
Norton 3
Nuckles 68
Nugent 21, 30, 279
Null 137
Nutt 26
Nutter 22, 27

O

O'Banion 7
O'Neal 2, 6
O'Neill 402
Oakes 211, 383
Obeny 130
Obney 142
Odell 214
Odle 20
Ogborn 314
Ogburn 27
Ogden 27, 29, 425
Ogle 47
Ogles 431
Okes 212, 214
Oldham 6, 7, 12, 21
Olds 75
Olinger 9
Oliver . . 26, 130, 131, 138, 142, 433, 435
Olvy 28
Oneill 13
Ooley 414
Orr . . . 3, 4, 7, 11, 12, 13, 21, 23
Ortto 131
Orwin 3
Osbon 25, 26
Osborn 42, 70, 190, 367
Osburn 193, 195, 210, 211, 212, 215
Oscom 3

Osgood 62, 63
Osson 21
Oswalt 71
Otey 340
Ott 68
Ougham 4
Outsinger 35
Overholser 409
Overman 387
Owen 68, 323, 324
Owens .. 20, 24, 25, 61, 78, 213, 364, 365
Oxford 19

P

Pabody 305
Packard 414
Paddock 222, 227, 228, 410
Padrick 288
Page 12
Pagin 31
Paige 17
Pain 198, 199
Palmer 3, 45, 142, 336, 389
Pancake 96, 103, 110, 111, 112
Pane 68
Paradise 277
Parce 11
Parcut 19
Paris 50
Parish 71
Park 194, 198
Parker ... 12, 19, 47, 61, 62, 63, 70, 71, 77, 188, 206, 210, 215, 388, 389
Parkes 74, 212
Parkhurst 2, 3, 28
Parks 16, 93, 108, 120, 250, 311
Parlneyron 289
Parmerlee 131, 142
Parr 68, 453
Parrish 9, 11, 12
Parsley 131, 142
Parsons 159
Parten 9
Parter 8
Partis 398
Parvis 395
Pasko 47
Pate 435
Paten 31
Paton 9
Patrick 304
Patten 3, 7, 31
Pattern 23
Patterson ... 7, 8, 12, 13, 27, 28, 48, 131, 142, 164, 172, 174, 359
Patteshall 383
Patton 19, 40, 94, 188, 189, 191, 192, 193, 194, 196, 197, 217, 243, 316, 382, 384
Patty 17, 18
Paxton 23, 26, 28
Payne 15, 33, 70, 211, 213, 214, 228, 278, 413
Payton 6, 12
Pea 94, 101, 117, 119
Pearce 11, 38
Pearcy 62, 63, 260
Pearou 94
Pearson 3, 5
Peck 354
Peele 385, 386, 387
Peele Jr. 386
Peery 395
Peffley 360
Peirson 2
Pell 7, 154
Pelm 23
Pemberton 240
Pence 7
Pennebaker 155
Pennington 181
Penrod 47
Penrose 38
Pentecost 23
Penwell 3, 6, 7
Peoples 5, 8, 10, 12
Peppers 10, 12
Perdue 24, 61, 62, 423
Perfect 379

Perin 3, 5
Perisho 33
Perkins 2, 31, 35, 51, 384
Perkizer 194
Pernet 432
Pernund 3
Perrin 1, 3, 7, 9
Perrine 8
Perrott 37
Perry 23, 49, 168, 182, 183, 333
Personnett 12
Persons 18
Perverse 7
Pervo 240
Peters 29, 426, 435
Peterson 23, 349
Petra 357
Petre 28
Petty 7, 12
Peyton ... 26, 68, 70, 71, 111, 112, 212
Pfaff 400
Pfrimmer 148
Phebus 18
Phegley 71
Phelps 7
Phifer 78
Phigley 72
Phillipps 41
Phillips 48, 142, 213, 383
Phillis 2
Philpott 3, 7
Phipher 42
Phipps 70
Phips 68
Pickard 71, 72, 240, 412
Pickens 337
Pickering 301
Pickett 363
Picksley 4
Piersol 62
Pierson 45, 203, 205, 208
Pigg 164
Piggott 39, 44
Pike 50
Pinckly 70
Pindell 153
Piner 68
Pinkerton 12, 26, 172
Pinnich 274
Piper 350
Pirtel 195
Pirtle 194
Pitman 211, 212, 240
Pitts 68, 350
Pitzer 145
Pleasants 365
Plew ... 193, 194, 196, 197, 211, 212, 214
Plouchon 94
Plough 188, 190, 191, 211
Plummer 6, 7, 12, 392
Poak 7
Pogue 3
Poindexter 411
Poland 29, 31
Pollard 12
Pollock 172
Polson 246, 263, 264, 265
Pomernecke 109
Pomeroy 210, 211
Pond 12, 172
Ponell 169
Pool 3, 302, 303, 395
Poor 15
Porter 7, 10, 11, 12, 13, 44, 51, 433, 435
Post 417
Postgate 240
Poston 369, 370
Potter 17, 35, 270
Potts 38, 134
Pound ... 45, 189, 206, 208, 218, 219, 220, 221, 224
Pounds 222
Powel 3, 6, 196
Powell 9, 12, 25, 26, 28, 78
Powers 3, 20, 211, 251
Prater 68, 432
Prather 66, 77
Prathers 76
Preaus 323
Prentace 83
Prentiss 36

Presley 22
Preston 30, 411
Prevo 396
Prewitt 391, 414
Price 5, 7, 9, 14, 20, 31, 51, 61, 62, 63, 265, 314, 332, 333
Pride 89, 91, 95, 101, 102, 103, 110, 111, 112, 119
Prides 88
Prill 394
Prine 8
Pritchard 23, 26
Pritcher 68
Pritchet 22
Pritchett 165
Probus 26
Proffitt 378
Prosser 131, 132, 140, 142, 145
Prosses 39
Prostman 230
Protsman 229, 308, 438
Provolt 14, 15, 16, 17, 18, 19
Pruitt 257, 401
Puckett 400
Pugh 211
Pulliam 256
Pumphrey 7, 12
Purcell 187
Purdom 12
Putman 7, 9
Putnam 113

Q

Quail 143
Quick 29
Quinn 346

R

Rader 28
Ragan 31
Rager 335, 340
Raglan 432
Ragle 37
Railsback 21
Raines 187, 188, 190, 191, 192, 193, 194, 195, 196, 197, 198, 199, 221
Rainey .. 158, 159, 162, 165, 187
Rainland 3
Ralston 143, 175, 444
Rambo 21
Ramey 168
Ramsay 21
Ramsey 72, 146, 263
Ramsier 337
Randall 62, 63, 71
Ransford Jr. 222
Rapp 95
Rardin 21
Raridon 146
Rarrick 17, 18
Rasure 155
Rathburn 9
Ratherford 23
Ratliff 51
Rau 17
Ravenscraft 49
Rawley 68
Rawlings 264, 370
Ray .. 7, 27, 28, 29, 68, 392, 396
Rayburn 36
Raymond 35
Rea 7
Read 64, 65, 138
Reagen 453
Rease 64
Rector 364, 452
Reddick 26, 33
Redding 3
Reddish 28
Reece 12
Reed ... 3, 4, 5, 7, 9, 10, 12, 41, 46, 64, 68, 70, 72, 77, 138, 172, 211, 268, 423, 434, 437
Reeds 25
Reedy 94
Reese 7
Reeser 286, 287
Reeves 143, 158, 327
Reid 8, 12, 173, 313
Rementon 3
Remy 452
Rench 2, 3

Rentfro 24
Rephart 33
Replogle 20
Retherford 12
Reu 3
Reubison 38
Reynolds 3, 15, 16, 95, 161, 162, 233, 240, 301, 327, 367
Rheile 71
Rhoads 3, 364
Rhodes 36, 46
Ribble 38
Rice 30, 69
Rich 5, 11, 12, 25, 190, 192, 193, 194, 196, 198, 199, 215, 279
Richards 3, 5, 6, 7, 16, 384
Richardson 11, 146, 159
Richer 13
Richerson 69
Richert 374, 375, 376, 377, 378
Richey 16, 30
Rickenbaugh 24
Ricketts 333
Ricks 119
Riddle 357, 358
Ridenour 24, 29
Ridge 401
Rieman 381, 384
Rigby 383
Riggs 26, 158, 223, 233, 350
Right 3, 75
Rigney 269, 270
Riley 11, 35, 41, 177, 192, 209, 217, 275
Rinard 279
Rinearson 7
Rinerson 12
Ring 12, 22, 29, 31, 51, 190, 192
Ringler 391
Ringo 69, 72
Rinker 24, 25, 29, 31
Rintoul 171
Risden 9
Rish 268, 269
Risher 22
Risk 4, 7, 8, 9
Risley ... 91, 101, 102, 103, 110, 111, 124
Risleys 88
Rissler 152
Ritter 74, 136, 138
Rivard 437
Rizley 69, 70, 71, 72
Roads 35
Robb 25, 102
Robbins 36, 194, 326, 399
Roberts .. 13, 14, 17, 18, 19, 45, 48, 49, 69, 71, 168, 196, 262, 278
Robertson 75, 76, 173, 175, 188, 253, 254, 407
Robins 24, 143
Robinson 7, 12, 26, 31, 447
Robison 39
Rock 17
Roe 61
Roehm 437
Rogers .. 73, 180, 276, 277, 332
Rogerson 97, 99
Roisden 9
Roland 350
Roll 187, 244
Rollf 7
Ronald 2, 3
Ronnalds 5
Rooney 132
Rose 28, 29
Roseberry 405
Rosenbaum 177
Ross .. 10, 12, 43, 69, 183, 416, 417, 419, 422, 423
Rossell 7
Rountree 385
Rous 229
Routszong 30
Row 148
Rowe 148, 191
Rowland .. 12, 61, 63, 213, 215, 344, 346
Rowles 417
Rowley 390
Roysden 51

Roysdon 8, 9
Royse 263
Royster 9, 12, 13
Rozzel 228
Rubey 29
Rubottom 233, 241
Ruby 25, 27
Rucker 78, 168
Ruddell 64
Ruddick 33, 78
Ruddle 64, 69
Rude 138
Rumbley 3, 7, 12
Rumley 2
Runalds 69
Runcie 324
Rund 132, 143, 145
Rundel 211
Rundle 408
Rundols 241
Runicks 10
Runnels 69, 159
Runyon 25, 431
Rupe 29, 50
Rupp 372, 373, 376, 377
Rush 395, 401
Rusher 191, 193, 194, 197, 198, 199, 200, 210, 211, 212, 215
Russel 28
Russell 5, 7, 16, 61, 74, 187, 224, 412, 420
Rutherford 7, 27
Rutledge 158
Rutter 3
Ryan 64, 65, 66
Ryckman 92
Ryker 362, 439, 441, 442

S

Sailor 2
Sailors 3
Salyards 341, 342
Sample 5, 7, 12, 26, 30
Samuel 85
Sandefer 3
Sandeford 3
Sanders 6, 20, 29, 209, 295, 400
Sanderson 77
Sands 3
Sanford 42, 209, 213
Sankey 27
Sargent 15, 326
Satre 25
Saunders 13
Savage 4, 5, 13
Savarns 92
Sawyer 88, 354, 356
Saxon 6, 12
Sayer 325
Scaaf 390
Scamahorn 71, 110
Scamerhorn 69
Scarborough 297
Scarlet 69
Schaeffer 282
Schaffer 390
Scharf 376, 377
Schearmahon 88
Schenck 230, 433
Schencks 361
Schill 410
Schneider 375, 376
Schoen 378
Schoonover 16, 17, 243
Schrock 143, 145
Schuck 18
Scofield 4, 14
Scott 3, 4, 7, 10, 12, 20, 22, 23, 25, 26, 29, 30, 34, 43, 46, 48, 76, 163, 165, 174, 214, 287, 295, 326, 413, 428, 436
Scribner 36
Scripter 138
Scrotchfield 69
Sears 42, 43
Seaton 21
Seay 431
Sebastian 435
Seek 23
Seitz 372, 373, 375, 377
Selby ..92, 96, 97, 109, 110, 111
Self 42, 45

Sellebarger 357, 359
Sellers 63
Selsur 3
Selvey 3
Serring 21, 22, 29, 31
Server 147, 148
Severinghaus 333, 338
Severns 103
Seward 12, 21
Sewell 77
Seybold 40, 43
Shafer 20, 143
Shaffer 132, 143, 437
Shannon 21, 170, 172, 173, 174
Sharp 251, 314, 316, 369
Sharpe 61, 62
Shattock 241
Shaub 434
Shauls 12
Shaw .. 175, 191, 192, 193, 229, 383, 384, 438
Shaw Jr. 111
Shawhan 12
Shearly 12
Sheepler 1
Sheets 48
Shelburn 195, 217, 225
Shelburne .. 195, 198, 210, 212, 216, 218, 221, 224, 226
Shelby 12, 19, 22
Sheldon 36
Shelly 25, 26, 31
Shelman 143
Shepherd 16, 26, 282, 441
Shepler 13
Sheplor 3
Sheppard 316, 362
Sheriden 17
Sherman 138, 338, 409
Sherrill 356
Sherry 20
Sherwood 245, 246, 264
Shevalia 15
Shewmaker 377
Shewmon .... ·28
Shields ... 3, 10, 24, 25, 26, 28, 78
Shillingford 145
Shinkle 12
Shipley 4, 7
Shipman .. 265, 329, 332, 336, 337, 340, 417, 423, 424
Shipp 309
Shirley 3, 44
Shirts 3
Shively 272
Shnatterly 7
Shoemaker 26, 27, 51
Shoptaugh 410
Short 364, 365
Shortridge 12, 16, 26
Shotwell 248
Shriver 268
Shroyer 6, 29, 30
Shryer 64, 65, 66
Shuck 148, 377
Shull 69
Sibbit 12
Signer 211
Siler 139, 233, 241
Sills 410
Silvey 6, 7, 12
Simmer 352
Simmonds 2
Simmons 47, 222
Simms 12
Simon 16
Simons 297
Simpson 6, 7, 8, 26, 30, 43, 45, 212
Siner .. 192, 193, 198, 210, 213, 214, 215, 216, 217, 221, 223, 225
Sinks 392
Sisk 363
Sisson 145
Size 7
Skelcher 311
Skelton 48
Skidmore 421
Skillman 22, 426, 427
Skilman 24
Skinner .. 10, 31, 190, 192, 193, 194, 198, 214

Slack 71	Stebbins 1	
Slagley 447	Steed 69	**T**
Slater 365	Steel 13, 14, 173	
Slavin 69	Steele . . 139, 145, 146, 195, 378,	Tabour 74, 75
Slead 76	427, 428	Tagert 74
Sleeth 7	Stephens . . 7, 8, 10, 13, 74, 146	Tailor 241
Sloan 4, 396	Stephenson 4, 25, 48	Tait 175
Sluder 195, 197	Stepleton 439	Talbert 14, 17, 25
Sluss 396	Steratt 7	Talbott 42, 329
Smallwood 76	Sterritt 175	Talhunter 20
Smelling 6	Stevens . . . 7, 8, 11, 13, 133, 415	Talkington 20
Smelser 10	Stevenson 4, 21, 175, 241,	Talor 214
Smiley 10, 12, 24	256, 316, 330, 334	Tandy 434
Smith 1, 3, 5, 6, 7, 8, 9, 10,	Steward 21	Tannehill 267
11, 12, 13, 15, 21, 22, 23, 25,	Stewart . . 69, 93, 133, 143, 173,	Tanner 26, 78
26, 27, 28, 29, 36, 41, 46, 47,	378, 428, 433	Tarlton 47
48, 49, 50, 51, 69, 70, 74, 75,	Stibbens 11	Tate 13, 76, 365
89, 91, 92, 101, 103, 105,	Stibbins 19	Taylor . . 3, 4, 8, 17, 31, 43, 48,
106, 108, 113, 116, 117, 119,	Stice 192, 194	49, 69, 170, 174, 182, 199,
120, 121, 123, 124, 125, 126,	Sticker 264	213, 214, 217, 218, 223, 266,
132, 138, 139, 143, 145, 146,	Stiefel 389	271, 272, 325, 331, 370, 384,
147, 180, 194, 195, 197, 198,	Stierwalt 431	424
212, 213, 214, 251, 332, 336,	Stigler 71	Teaford 389
337, 340, 362, 369, 370, 371,	Stiles 23	Teats 230
390, 437, 447	Stimson 209	Tedford 3
Smithson 51	Stinson 24, 70, 143	Teel 420, 421, 422
Smock 140, 194, 209	Stith 30	Tegarden 45
Smutz 286	Stitt 8	Templeton 20, 25, 255
Smythe 322	Stober 359	Tenney 422
Snider . . 22, 25, 26, 27, 69, 133,	Stockdale 3, 7, 10	Test 280
143, 144, 145, 146, 409	Stockton 18, 20, 69	Teter 40
Snoddy 69	Stoddard 13, 14	Tevault 46, 47, 48
Snowden . . 22, 23, 24, 26, 30	Stokes 435	Teverbaugh 95, 111
Snyder 12, 145	Stone 7, 47, 49, 133	Tharp 7, 10, 13, 434
Soliday 29	Stonecipher 150	Thayer 349
Somers 13	Storie 175	Thiebaud 432
Sommers 199	Storm 17, 20, 33	Thieubaud 230
Sourwine 160	Stormont 450	Thing 325
Southard 19	Stott 5	Thirston 3
Soverns 120	Stout . . 4, 30, 45, 212, 254, 274	Thomas 1, 3, 4, 7, 8, 13, 14,
Sparkes 70	Stover . . 25, 26, 27, 29, 50, 250,	19, 22, 24, 28, 37, 47, 51, 69,
Sparks 2, 7, 9, 13, 70, 207,	282, 284, 285	71, 72, 143, 154, 222, 241,
208	Strader 69	274, 275, 379, 382, 388, 400
Spaulding 304, 424	Strattan 256	Thompson . . 2, 3, 4, 7, 9, 13,
Spear 45, 452	Stratton 316, 341, 342	14, 19, 20, 25, 38, 45, 69, 76,
Spears 360	Street 5, 13	157, 158, 160, 173, 175, 210,
Speer 443, 444	Streyper 220	213, 214, 225, 228, 241, 313,
Spencer . . 13, 133, 143, 241, 268	Strickland 157	322, 335, 340, 363, 369, 370,
Spergen 11	Strite 38	456
Spier 175	Strong 14, 24, 25, 455	Thomson 27
Spiers 175	Strother 411	Thorn 21, 174
Spillman 443	Strutt 61	Thornburg 316
Spitznogle 26	Stuart . . 4, 9, 63, 133, 139, 143	Thorne 337, 340
Spivey 387	Stubbins 362	Thornton 14, 15, 19, 21, 25,
Spivy 241	Stubbs 7	44, 241
Spooner 36, 38	Stucy 230	Thorp 70
Sprigg 25	Stump 139, 143	Throop 43
Spring 75	Sturdevant 69	Throyer 30
Springer 13, 22, 24	Sturgeon 173	Tiffany 4
Springeteen 308	Stutsman 31, 164	Tilley 70
Sprout 28, 31	Styles 21	Tilyer 7
Sprowl 61, 62	Suddith 244	Timmons 19
Spry 159	Suggett 256	Tincher 212, 214
Squires 27	Suit 15, 17	Tindall 377
Srawyer 6	Sullivan . . . 27, 28, 33, 125, 436	Tingley 423
St clair 216	Sullivant 23	Tinkle 287, 288
Stafford 2, 300	Summers 10, 22, 76	Tipton 199
Stagg 8, 24	Summey 20, 24, 25, 26	Tirey 6
Stair 357, 358	Sumpter 27	Tislow . . 86, 91, 92, 93, 95, 110,
Stalcup 41	Surber 429, 430, 431	111, 113, 114, 118, 119, 120
Staley 18	Sury 10	Tivebaugh 103
Stallcup 69	Sutherland 50, 180	Todd 230
Stamfield 33	Suttle 62	Tolbert 14
Stancil 206, 208	Sutton . . . 3, 4, 7, 10, 12, 13, 24,	Toler 23, 30
Standeford 39	63, 434	Tolliver 20
Standerford 75	Swab 438	Tolover 15
Standfield 75, 77, 78	Swafford 1	Tomlin 64, 65, 66
Stanfield 344	Swain 51	Tomlinson 447
Stanley 19, 27, 30, 31, 192,	Swann 23, 26, 27, 170, 172,	Toney 165
233, 241	174, 404	Tony 163
Stanly 22, 25, 51	Swartz 330, 334	Tool 195
Stansberry 15	Swayze 3	Toreyson 391
Stanton . . 21, 22, 24, 26, 27, 29,	Sweaney 78	Towell 36, 39, 44, 367, 368
297	Sweringen 442	Townsend 50
Stantz 21	Swift 2, 5, 13, 26, 143	Tracy 143
Staples 133, 143	Swine 78	Trail 7
Starbuck 23, 28, 51, 388	Swisher 431	Traill 359
Stark 7, 71, 190, 191, 207,	Switcher 8	Trammel 378
208, 210, 212	Swope 14	Tranum 69
Starns 28, 29	Sylvester 183	Travace 17
Starr 24, 28, 31	Symonds 297	Travis 13
Staten 29	Symons 50, 247, 270	Trayster 143
Staufer 285		Trekel 16
Stauffer 13		Trent 209
Stearman 230		Treuary 14

Tribbey 14
Tribble 70
Trimble 41, 45, 50
Trimbley 29
Trinkle 452
Trisbey 14
Trisler 182, 183
Trotter 322, 389
Trowbridge 13
Truax 274
Trublood 191
Trueblood 37, 193, 354, 388
Tucker 12, 15, 28, 251, 261
Tuel 75
Tullis 18, 19
Tumbeson 143
Tunstall 61
Turley 149
Turman 410
Turner ..3, 13, 70, 71, 133, 134,
  139, 143, 147, 173, 209, 301,
  321, 330
Turnipseed 393
Tutterow 145, 146
Tuttle 26, 143
Tweedy 7, 13
Twineham 439
Tyler 4, 42
Tyner ..1, 2, 4, 5, 6, 10, 13, 348
Tynes 5
Tyre 335

U

Uncas 417
Underhall 19
Underhill 17
Underwood 35, 45, 66, 278
Updegraft 7, 13
Utter 7

V

Vametre 17
Van Blair 22
Van Buskirk 7
Van Horne 315, 415
Van Kirk 48
Van Mater 9
Van Matre 8, 13
Van Metre 378
Van Vlair 12
Van Vleer 8
Van Vleet 8, 13
Vanada 47
Vanausdall 143
Vance 4, 274
Vancleave .. 269, 361, 362, 439,
  440, 442, 451, 452
Vancleave Sr. 441
Vandalsem 6
Vandegrift 4
Vanderen 255
Vandeveer 36, 38, 41, 442,
  444, 445, 446, 447
Vandolson 11
Vaneton 22, 24
Vangilder 4
Vanmater 8
Vanmatre 4
Vanmeter 1, 2, 4, 69, 71
Vannoy 28
Vanpelt 64, 65, 66
Vansicken 2
Vansickle 4
Vantrece 69
Vanvacter 30, 31
Vardaman 13
Vaughn 412
Vawter 305
Veach 26, 29, 166
Veasey 8
Veatch 2, 8
Venner 149
Verbryck 220
Vermilya 77
Very ... 329, 330, 331, 333, 335,
  336, 339
Vest 69, 274

Vestal 274
Veysey 13
Vibberts 338, 341
Vice 426
Vickrey 7, 8
Vieley 159, 163
Viliers 318
Vimcum 314
Voelker 376
Vogt 375, 376
Vondelo 275
Vontress 40

W

Waddle 23, 29, 30
Wade 15, 144, 145, 152
Wadham 318
Wadsworth 8
Waggener 64
Wagner 143, 364, 368
Wagoner 77, 191, 192, 193,
  194
Wainscott 435
Wakeman 284, 285, 286
Waldo 51
Wales 13, 23
Walker .. 1, 2, 4, 13, 14, 21, 22,
  24, 26, 28, 31, 36, 69, 70, 71,
  72, 75, 88, 101, 102, 103,
  111, 117, 119, 134, 143, 330,
  333, 334, 338, 341, 342, 434
Wall ... 192, 193, 194, 195, 198
Wallace 34, 41, 143, 171
Wallace Jr. 91
Wallas 134
Walling 7
Wallis 46, 143
Walls 190
Walpole 291, 292
Walter 61, 62, 63, 215, 388
Walters 191, 215, 399, 431
Waltman ... 127, 133, 135, 140,
  143
Walton 7, 277
Walyes 318
Wampler 145
Wandle 1
Ward .. 2, 4, 8, 14, 19, 21, 22,
  25, 26, 27, 29, 30, 31, 49,
  143, 194, 195, 197, 198, 199,
  230, 388, 400
Wardeman 4
Warden 36
Wardle 8
Warfield 62
Waring 321
Warner 173, 213, 214
Warnock 1
Warren .. 4, 398, 399, 400, 452
Washington 333
Wasson 26
Waterman 14
Waters 64, 65, 66
Wathen 64, 65, 66
Watkin 333, 338
Watson ... 42, 77, 78, 173, 212,
  242, 308
Watton 7, 13
Watts 24, 39, 413
Waugh 143
Way 50
Waymire .. 8, 15, 392, 393, 397,
  399
Weace 117
Weach 327, 328
Weales 230
Wease ... 92, 96, 103, 109, 110,
  111, 112
Weases 108
Weatherby 252
Weathers ..6, 64, 65, 69, 75, 77
Weaver .. 17, 24, 154, 214, 408,
  432
Webb .. 4, 8, 10, 13, 14, 39, 49
Webster 4, 8, 10, 69, 72
Weddel 77
Weddle 75, 76, 78, 143, 177
Wedgewood 355, 356
Weeks 30, 209

Weer 400
Weir 174, 394
Weirhaye 456
Welburn 70
Welch 174, 206, 438
Welden 28
Weldon 24
Weller 375
Welles 416, 417
Wells ... 14, 27, 34, 36, 46, 195,
  242, 276
Welsh 4
Wence 199
Wenzel 288
Wernert 375
West .. 15, 20, 26, 46, 222, 257,
  258, 279
Weston 353, 355, 356
Westover 4
Wetherall 328
Wetherman 191
Wetsel 28
Wheat 162, 163
Wheeler ..17, 20, 69, 70, 71, 77
Whelen 76
Wherett 2, 11
Wherrell 2
Wherrett 7
Wherritt 14
Whisehunt 397
Whisenhunt 302, 398
Whisman 21, 22
Whitaker 14, 139
White .. 4, 5, 7, 8, 9, 10, 14, 18,
  21, 24, 25, 39, 69, 76, 180,
  224, 288, 290, 315, 322, 368,
  388
Whitehead 50, 105, 119
Whitelock 8, 14
Whiteman 14, 28, 29, 31
Whitinger 29
Whitkinnack 75
Whitman 48
Whitmarsh 63, 383
Whitmore 410
Whitneck 27
Whitney 223, 308
Whitson 75
Whitted 364
Wible 269, 270, 362
Wick 4
Wickersham 28
Widener 69
Wilbur 335
Wilcox 8
Wilcoxson 150
Wilder 48
Wildman 268
Wile 6
Wiley 19, 69
Wilhoyte 62
Wilkerson 13
Wilkes 61, 69
Wilkie 175
Wilkins 41, 336, 425
Wilkinson 139, 319
Willard 242
Willey 8, 11, 14
Willhoyte 61
William 44, 323
Williams .. 2, 4, 5, 6, 8, 9, 10,
  11, 12, 13, 14, 19, 22, 23, 24,
  25, 26, 27, 30, 31, 39, 44, 49,
  50, 70, 74, 76, 119, 166, 177,
  242, 261, 287, 288, 308, 378,
  379
Williamson 30
Willis 4, 14, 21, 23, 24, 26,
  29, 30, 50, 51, 74, 195, 216
Willits 27, 51
Wills 218, 224
Wilson 40, 61
Wilson .. 2, 4, 5, 8, 11, 14, 19,
  22, 26, 28, 35, 37, 40, 42, 62,
  69, 71, 72, 74, 77, 94, 101,
  157, 159, 172, 197, 198, 209,
  233, 242, 279, 349, 382, 435,
  436, 437

Winans 208
Winchel 8, 30
Winchell 14
Winder 256
Winkler 46
Winshel 14
Winship 275
Winslow 397, 398
Winstandly 335
Wire 447
Wise 14, 43, 62, 157
Witham 4, 8
Withams 3
Withers .. 92, 93, 101, 111, 118, 407
Witherspoon 174, 331
Witt 23, 26, 27, 30
Wittenberg 71
Witter 25, 28
Witty 72
Wolf 268, 365
Wolfe .. 187, 194, 195, 197, 198, 364, 378
Wolverton 26, 65, 408
Wood .. 8, 10, 37, 254, 263, 362
Woodard 35
Woodburn 448, 450, 451
Woodcock 8
Woodfill 442
Woodhouse 394
Woodmansee 76, 77, 167
Woodruff 48
Woods 5, 8, 14, 22, 24, 30, 50, 140, 154
Woodsmall 211
Woodward 38, 51, 182, 194, 367, 387, 388, 400
Woody .. 42, 159, 233, 273, 274
Woodyard 4, 5
Woolen 369
Woolfolk 44
Wools 69
Woolverton 8, 13
Woorster 14

Wooster 3
Woothers 6
Work 61, 62
Worley 1
Worster 4, 5
Worth 14, 173
Wortman 26
Wray 180
Wright 4, 14, 16, 17, 19, 20, 21, 22, 24, 25, 26, 28, 29, 30, 39, 50, 65, 69, 72, 75, 76, 143, 149, 200, 242, 280, 453, 454
Wyatt 8, 28, 95
Wybrant 63
Wylie 15, 16, 19, 450
Wyman 197, 198

Y

Yager 350
Yager Jr. 351
Yaman 27, 28, 29
Yaryan 27, 28
Yergar 21
Yerley 321
Yetter 256
Yocom 72
Yoder 135, 143
York 210
Yost 408
Young 28, 29, 48, 51, 150, 183, 250, 275, 392, 395, 399, 401
Yount 17, 260, 392
Youse 1, 8, 22, 23, 24

Z

Zapp 333
Zenor 69, 70, 71, 148
Zimmerman 275
Zody 135, 143
Zollman 376